A Limited Edition
of

THE LIFE OF HERBERT HOOVER
The Humanitarian, 1914–1917

Presented by the Herbert Hoover
Presidential Library Association, Inc.

To:

Copy Number _____ *of 2,000*

THE LIFE OF
HERBERT HOOVER

★★

The Humanitarian
1914 - 1917

GEORGE H. NASH

W. W. NORTON & COMPANY
New York   London

Copyright © 1988 by Hoover Presidential Library Association, Inc.
All rights reserved.
Published simultaneously in Canada by Penguin Books Canada Ltd.,
2801 John Street,
Markham, Ontario L3R 1B4.
Printed in the United States of America.
The text of this book is composed in Janson, with
display type set in Trump. Composition and
manufacturing by the Maple-Vail Book Manufacturing Group.

Photographs are courtesy of the Herbert Hoover Presidential Library
and the Hoover Institution Archives.
First Edition

Library of Congress Cataloging-in-Publication Data
(Revised for vol. 2)
Nash, George H., 1945–
The life of Herbert Hoover.
Includes bibliographies and indexes.
Contents: v. 1. The engineer, 1874–1914—v. 2. The
humanitarian, 1914–1917.
1. Hoover, Herbert, 1874–1964.   2. Presidents—United States—
Biography.   I. Title.
E802.N37   1983   973.91'6'0924 [B]   82–14521

ISBN 0-393-02550-0

W. W. Norton & Company, Inc.
500 Fifth Avenue, New York, N. Y. 10110
W. W. Norton & Company Ltd.
37 Great Russell Street, London WC1B 3NU

1 2 3 4 5 6 7 8 9 0

T O
Thomas T. Thalken
and Robert S. Wood

Contents

Preface

THE book before you is the second volume of a comprehensive, multivolume biography of one of the most extraordinary and least known individuals in American history. My first volume, entitled *The Life of Herbert Hoover: The Engineer, 1874–1914*, was published in 1983. In the installment at hand, I begin to examine the second of his remarkable series of careers: that of an internationally acclaimed humanitarian who was responsible (it has been said) for saving more lives than any other person in history.

Hoover's philanthropic interests, of course, neither began nor ended in the time period covered herein. Nevertheless, between August 1914 and April 1917 humanitarian relief work in war-torn Europe—activity on a scale previously unknown and unimagined—was the dominant, defining motif of his life. This was the crusading mission that made his name a household word on three continents. This was the experience that made possible his eventual entry into American politics.

In the summer of 1914 Hoover was a prosperous, professionally esteemed, forty-year-old, international mining engineer living in London—and dreaming of a career of public service in the United States. The cataclysm that engulfed Europe that August changed his life. Within a few months, as the armies of several nations bogged down in the mire of trench warfare, Hoover founded and directed a volunteer, benevolent entity known as the Commission for Relief in Belgium, or CRB. As a neutral enterprise respected by the belligerent powers, it took responsibility for providing desperately needed food for more than 9,000,000 helpless Belgian and French citizens trapped between a German army of occupation and a British naval blockade. What appeared at first to be a short-term, emergency expedient instead developed into the greatest humanitarian undertaking that the world had ever seen. By the time it closed its operations in 1919, the Commission for Relief in Belgium had expended nearly $1,000,000,000—and had created a twentieth-century hero.

For Hoover the years 1914 to 1917 were a period of transition in which he finally forsook his private pursuits and began to traverse what he later called "the slippery road of public life." For a biographer the wealth of available documentary evidence on this decisive chapter in his odyssey provides an opportunity to study him at close range. To many scholars and other observers, the man who became our thirty-first president has long seemed elusive and puzzling. I hope that in the pages that follow, readers will come better to understand him.

The saga of Hoover and the CRB is important for another reason. Few people other than Hoover himself and certain of his contemporaries have ever written about this incredible venture in any depth. And not even they cared (or dared) to discuss all of its aspects with complete candor. For most Americans it remains an unknown or at best dimly remembered episode in a grim, appalling war "over there."

Yet Hoover's endeavor was (to borrow his own phrase) "an American epic" that in some ways was the prototype of much that was to follow in this war-ravaged century. In 1916 Lord Eustace Percy of the British Foreign Office described Hoover as "the advance guard and symbol of the sense of responsibility of the American people towards Europe." In more recent years the world has grown accustomed to American action to save lives and restore the fractured economies of far-off lands. Indeed, today such involvement is almost universally taken for granted. A famine in Ethiopia, a nuclear power plant failure in the Ukraine, a typhoon in Bangladesh: in the aftermath, American experts and assistance will be there. One reason for this expectation, one reason for its acceptance—although few today know it—is the institution created nearly seventy-five years ago by Herbert Hoover.

This volume, then, is in considerable part the forgotten story of a pioneering effort in global altruism. Let no one think, however, that humanitarian relief, because of its noble and generous purpose, is exempt from the "real world" of political intrigue, personal ambition, and diplomatic rivalry. Hoover's pathbreaking labors took place in the midst of a gruesome war that ultimately engaged the citizens of six continents. One must remember this context when one reads this account of the deeds that made him a "world-historical figure."

As those familiar with the first volume of my biography will know, in 1975

I was invited to undertake this project by the Herbert Hoover Presidential Library Association, a nonprofit, educational foundation located in Iowa. In describing our relationship, I can do no better than repeat here the words in my preface to Volume I: Under the terms of my contract with the Association, all decisions concerning the contents of the biography—including fact and interpretation, proportions and emphasis, inclusions and exclusions— are mine alone. No attempt has been made to control, circumscribe, or alter my research or my findings. The multivolume biography that I am writing was explicitly intended to be—and is—a work of free and independent scholarship.

And now it is my pleasure to acknowledge the many individuals who have facilitated my labors along the way. At the Herbert Hoover Presidential Library in West Branch, Iowa, Thomas Thalken, Robert Wood, John Fawcett, Mildred Mather, Dale Mayer, Dwight Miller, Cora Pedersen, Shirley Sondergard, and Patrick Wildenberg were unfailingly helpful and courteous. Indeed, the entire staff at the library has combined to create what has been for me a most congenial research environment. The same is true for the Hoover Institution on War, Revolution and Peace, a marvelous place in which to do scholarly work. There I am particularly grateful to W. Glenn Campbell, Charles Palm, and Elena Danielson, as well as their dedicated associates. At the Stanford University Archives—another magnet for this Hoover biographer—Roxanne Nilan, Judy Adams, Robin Chandler, Elisabeth Fischbach, and Linda Long were always cheerfully willing to answer my seemingly inexhaustible inquiries. So, too, when the occasion arose, was Margaret Kimball in the Special Collections Department of the Stanford University Libraries. At the Manuscript Division of the Library of Congress David Wigdor was a knowledgeable guide to his institution's treasures, as were Gerald Haines and Ronald Swerczek at the National Archives. In my hometown of South Hadley, Massachusetts, the Mount Holyoke College Library served from time to time as a virtual "branch office." In my adopted community of Iowa City, Iowa, the University of Iowa Library was a welcome mecca. I am happy to acknowledge the accommodating and hard-working staffs of these two institutions. While it is not possible to cite by name all of the people who have made my research and travel in the United States both rewarding and enjoyable, I continue to recall with special pleasure my visits to the libraries and archives cited in my Bibliographical Note.

As for assistance rendered abroad, I am pleased to record again (as I did in my first volume) my particular thanks to the late A. Chester Beatty; Mrs. W.R.B. Foster; L. A. Broder and Frances Vale of the Rio Tinto-Zinc Corporation, Ltd.; and D. S. Porter of the Bodleian Library at Oxford University. I am grateful also to Baron Beyens, Mme. Andrée Scufflaire of the Archives Générales du Royaume in Brussels, and Emile Vandewoude of the Cabinet du Roi (also in Brussels) for answering my queries about Belgian source materials and for kindly providing copies of certain documents.

On a different plane of interest, I continue to derive inspiration from the scholarly example and encouragement of two of my former mentors at Harvard University, Donald Fleming and Frank Freidel.

In preparing this volume I have once again benefited from the help of some excellent and conscientious typists. Crystal Wahl typed the entire first draft of my manuscript; Nadine Loescher prepared the entire final draft. Both performed superbly. It is a pleasure also to acknowledge the efficient help of Judy Kaeser in generating the unending stream of outgoing correspondence that accompanied my research.

In proofreading the galleys I have had the able and diligent assistance of Eleanor Cook and Jean Nash. At W. W. Norton & Company my editor, Donald Lamm, and his assistant, Amy Cherry, as well as their many colleagues, have skillfully shepherded my manuscript along the path to publication.

I am grateful to the following institutions for permission to quote from various documents cited in my footnotes: the Bancroft Library, University of California at Berkeley; Rare Book and Manuscript Library, Columbia University; the Columbia University Oral History Collection; the Herbert Hoover Foundation; the Herbert Hoover Presidential Library Association; the Huntington Library, San Marino, California; the Minnesota Historical Society; the Schlesinger Library, Radcliffe College; the Rockefeller Archive Center; the Stanford University Archives; the State Historical Society of Wisconsin; and the Yale University Library. Quotations from the Walter Hines Page diary appear by permission of the Houghton Library at Harvard University. I also have occasion to draw upon the Sir Herbert Samuel Papers and Andrew Bonar Law Papers in the custody of the House of Lords Record Office in London; quotations are reproduced by permission of the Clerk of the Records. Crown copyright material in the Public Record Office in Great Britain is reproduced by permission of the Controller of Her Majesty's Stationery Office.

Finally, I am pleased again to thank the Herbert Hoover Presidential Library Association for its unwavering support, encouragement, and appreciation of the requirements of a scholarly biography. As I wrote in the preface to my first volume, without the Association's continuing commitment no scholarly undertaking of this magnitude and duration would be feasible in these times.

More than a decade ago I moved from Massachusetts to Iowa, where I met two individuals whose interest in Herbert Hoover is unsurpassed and who have been unfailingly willing to share their insights and expertise. To them this volume is dedicated.

And—always—I think of my family, last but never least in my catalogue of heartfelt acknowledgments.

THE LIFE OF HERBERT HOOVER
The Humanitarian
1914–1917

1

The Earthquake

I

SITTING in his office in London's financial district on August 4, 1914, Herbert Hoover was a troubled man. On the surface it should have been otherwise. An orphaned child of Iowa pioneers, a distinguished alumnus of Stanford University, he stood at the pinnacle of his career—a mining engineer with a worldwide reputation and a growing fortune of at least a million dollars. Happily married, with two young sons, he was actively contemplating a new career of public service in the United States. Today was his son Herbert's eleventh birthday. In six more days he himself would turn forty. Shortly after that he was scheduled to depart for California and a month-long working vacation—another step in his long-planned return to the country of his birth and boyhood.[1]

Yet Hoover was not content. All around him portents of calamity were gathering. For more than a decade, London—the international capital of mining finance—had been his principal residence and base of operations while he had built a business empire that touched nearly every continent: zinc and gold mines in Australia, a fabulous silver-lead-zinc mine in Burma, copper mines and smelters in Russia, vast untapped mineral deposits in Siberia, reorganized oil companies in California, and more. A hundred thousand men worked for enterprises that he directed or in part controlled. Suddenly this whole edifice was in jeopardy. The "grand smash," the Great War, had come.

The previous week had been unbelievable. On Tuesday, July 28, the Austro-

3

Hungarian empire had declared war on Serbia. Since then the entangling web of European alliances had drawn taut, and, in an almost unstoppable chain reaction, a series of ultimatums, mobilizations, and declarations of hostilities had rolled across the continent. On the morning of August 4, German soldiers invaded neutral Belgium in a dash for France. That night England and Germany went to war.

As the armies of Europe prepared to march, the innocent and the neutral sought refuge. Hoover, in London, was comparatively fortunate: with a home in its comfortable Kensington section and an office at No. 1, London Wall Buildings, he was far from the immediate zone of combat. Other Americans abroad were not so secure. Scattered across the continent were at least 125,000 American travelers. It was the peak of the tourist season. Now, with frontiers closing, banks shutting down, telegraphic communication cut off, and transportation on land and sea disrupted, frightened American tourists rushed to London and—they hoped—passage home.

By Monday, August 3, more than 6,000 Americans had reached the British metropolis, only to find the banks closed and Atlantic steamship service nonexistent. That day more than 2,000 panicky travelers converged on the American embassy for assistance. Men cursed, women wept, in the crush. Many had lost their luggage during their frantic escape from the continent. Many could not locate hotel accommodations. Many especially women, schoolteachers, and art students—were penniless. Above all, the distraught Americans found themselves unable to convert their traveler's checks, money orders, and letters of credit into cash. No one in London, it seemed, wanted to accept such paper during the emergency. As a result a considerable number of Americans could not even purchase a meal.[2]

Monday afternoon the British government extended its traditional summer bank holiday for three more days.[3] Even as it did so, more than two thousand anxious American tourists assembled at the Waldorf Hotel. The meeting had been called the day before by Fred I. Kent, vice president of the Bankers Trust Company of New York. Traveling in Europe, Kent had arrived in London on the weekend and had foreseen the need for swift action. With help from several other prominent Americans present—notably a banker, Theodore Hetzler, and a diplomat, Oscar Straus—Kent implemented a plan. The mass meeting voted to establish an American Citizens' Committee, composed of four separate bureaus. One, chaired by Kent, would contact banks and hotels in order to revive the American travelers' instruments of credit. Another, headed by Straus, would call upon the American ambassador, Walter Hines Page. A third would confer with British steamship companies about possible passage back to the States. A fourth would attempt to trace lost luggage and resolve disputes between British hotel managers and their American guests.[4]

The next day—Tuesday, August 4—as all Britain quivered on the brink of war, Page cabled the secretary of state in Washington. In language drafted by Kent and Straus, the ambassador reported that the American Citizens' Committee had been formed with headquarters at the Savoy Hotel and that official action by the United States was now imperative. Page implored his government to send ships and gold to rescue his stranded countrymen. In fact, he noted (again at Kent's behest), if the government would announce that gold was on the way and that it would be delivered to Kent as an officer of Bankers Trust, Kent could borrow gold in England immediately and thus eliminate delay in helping his countrymen.[5]

A day later Page followed up with another urgent dispatch to the State Department: "Thousands of perfectly solvent Americans possess letters of credit but can not cash them. No banking transactions have taken place since the closing of banking hours" on August 1.[6] Clearly there was no time to lose.

Meanwhile, Kent and his colleagues were trying to unravel the financial snarl. Borrowing $20,000 in gold from two London banks against a shipment of Bankers Trust gold in mid-ocean, Kent opened an office at the Savoy and distributed amounts up to forty dollars to holders of American Bankers' Association traveler's checks. He also prepared to borrow additional gold as soon as a replacement supply was known to be on its way from New York.[7]

Even as he worked, however, the dimensions of the trauma were widening. From Dover, Folkestone, and other ports along the coast, trains were arriving without letup, each filled with bewildered and impecunious tourists. When the American Express Company finally reopened on August 4 for the first time since Saturday, 800 persons were in line. By the end of the day 6,000 individuals had received more than $200,000 in cash for their traveler's checks.[8]

The American embassy, the Savoy Hotel, and the office of American Express were not the only places where worried Yankees congregated on that fateful Tuesday. Down in the City (London's financial district) the new American consul general, Robert Skinner, was struggling with chaotic scenes similar to those at the embassy. As it happened, Skinner's office was only a block from Herbert Hoover's. During the afternoon the American engineer paid a visit to the consulate.

According to his wife Lou, Hoover did so in response to a telephone call from Skinner for assistance.[9] This was also Hoover's own recollection, long afterward, in his *Memoirs*.[10] Skinner, however, remembered the moment somewhat differently: in his account Hoover appeared at the consulate on his own initiative and volunteered his services, which the harried diplomat instantly accepted.[11] But whether Hoover volunteered or was invited, he stepped in at once and decisively. Gathering all the cash he could find in his office and from business associates, and telephoning his wife for £100 more at their home, he opened an office at the consulate that very afternoon. Here, with some assistants, he proceeded to loan small sums (at no interest and often without security) to more than three hundred Americans who had no other cash to live on.[12]

The next day, August 5, the mood of panic began to subside. At the consulate Hoover's informal relief effort continued. Two miles away, at the Savoy Hotel, hordes of tourists continued to register with the American Citizens' Committee, making a total of more than three thousand in two days.[13] Thanks to the efforts of the Citizens' Committee, the American Express Company, and others, at least some cash was becoming available and some London hotels were now willing to extend credit to Americans.[14]

Most welcome of all was the news from across the Atlantic. On August 5 the United States Congress appropriated $2,500,000 for relief of the stranded Americans. On the evening of the sixth the American cruiser *Tennessee* sailed from New York with a cargo of gold stashed in oaken casks.[15] Before the ship left, the State Department instructed Ambassador Page to draw upon American bankers abroad for $300,000.[16] Upon learning of this authorization, Kent and Hetzler obtained $300,000 worth of gold in London as an advance on the *Tennessee*'s supply.[17]

Despite these auspicious developments, the need for immediate succor was increasing. Not everyone reaching London possessed negotiable securities. At the Savoy Hotel, on August 5, a Milwaukee doctor appeared with a letter of credit for $2,500 and not a penny on his person. In another hotel stood a group of tourists with checks and letters of credit amounting to $18,000— and not even $10 in cash among them. By the sixth, Americans were known to be walking the streets hungry—with gold certificates in their pockets. Some of these tourists received help that day from Hoover in the form of small unsecured loans.[18]

By now the need to systematize the relief was apparent. Of the four subcommittees that comprised the American Citizens' Committee at the Savoy, none was exclusively designed to dispense financial aid to those in need. On August 5 and 6 Hoover and his wife took measures to fill this gap.

Visiting the Savoy on August 4, Lou Henry Hoover had noticed the large numbers of distraught women in the throng. The next morning she returned, convened the executive committee of the Society of American Women in London, and promptly organized a committee to assist unaccompanied American women and children in distress. Lou herself became chairman. In short order, and with the grateful approval of the Citizens' Committee, she set up quarters in the grand ballroom of the Savoy. A few minutes later the ballroom was opened for the day's business. Six hundred American tourists squeezed in.[19]

Lou's cool-headed efficiency was a precious commodity in the pandemonium prevailing at the Savoy. The all-male Citizens' Committee promptly added her to its membership—the only woman to be so selected. A few weeks later Lou told her parents that none of her female associates could think of a better person to lead them. Leaving her sons in the charge of a governess, she devoted herself full time to the challenge at hand.[20]

While the Resident American Women's Relief Committee was beginning to dispense money and reassurance to its female clients, Hoover was evolving a separate plan on his own. Here, before his very eyes, was a chance to fulfill his dream of being of service to his countrymen. Here was opportunity—if only he could grasp it. On Wednesday, August 5, he dispatched a private cable to one of his closest friends in the United States:

American Government will probably need appoint Special Commissioner in England to handle return of American Tourists. I would be glad undertake this work without payment. Have you any channel to suggest my appointment at Washington [?] American Ambassador [and] Consul General would no doubt support recommendation if made from independent quarters.[21]

The next day, without waiting for an answer, Hoover called together a group of about twenty prominent American businessmen in London. Most, perhaps all, were veteran members of the American Society in London, an organization of American citizens for whom the British capital was currently home. The meeting resolved to establish a "Committee of American Residents in London for Assistance of American Travellers," with Hoover as its chairman.[22] Many of the committee members were mining engineers and long-time associates of Hoover.[23] All were volunteers.[24]

The Residents' Committee immediately appealed for money from fellow Americans living in the city. To meet the varying needs of the displaced travelers, it quickly established two funds: one for loans to those whose credit was only temporarily frozen, and one, a benevolent account, for the outright distribution of charity.[25] Hoover subscribed liberally to both: £1,000 (about $5,000) to the loan fund and £200 (or about $1,000) to the benevolent fund.[26] In all likelihood no one contributed more substantially than he.[27]

The new committee moved rapidly on other fronts. Within twenty-four hours of its founding it had its own stationery and masthead.[28] Within forty-eight hours it established a branch adjacent to the Citizens' Committee's headquarters in the Savoy, as well as at three other locations.[29] On August 7 Hoover's group announced (in the words of one press report) that it had "assumed charge of the American relief work" and would henceforth "co-ordinate" the dispensing of assistance to traveling Americans[30] According to the dispatch, Hoover's organization was taking the place of the Kent–Hetzler–Straus committee.[31] Hoover and his colleagues even declared that they had organized under "official auspices," specifically the honorary chairmanship of Walter Hines Page,[32] although the ambassador had evidently not yet been consulted. Privately Hoover acknowledged to Page on the seventh that he was "taking your name in vain."[33] In the confusion of those August days the ambassador did not seem to object.

The Citizens' Committee spearheaded by Kent, however, was less respon-
sive. As early as August 8 Hoover complained to a colleague that the tourists'
committee at the Savoy was "dealing out money recklessly" and causing his
own group "a good deal of trouble" because of the lack of coordination.

> I have tried my best [said Hoover] to get them to leave the whole matter
> in our hands, telling them that we could deal with the situation systemat-
> ically through [the secretary of Hoover's committee], but they say they are
> not going to have our countrymen put to the necessity of going all over
> town to get a few shillings, and other clap-trap like that. I have no doubt
> that the matter will wear itself out in a few days, and we will get down to
> solid work.[34]

Certainly there was plenty of work to do. For the next two weeks the
American Citizens' Committee and the Committee of American Residents
collaborated to allay the crisis. While the activities of the two organizations
naturally overlapped, in practice there was a certain division of labor. The
Kent–Hetzler–Strauss group worked mainly with banks in New York and
London to open channels of cash and credit. Hoover's group took charge of
immediate relief.[35]

For tourists who had financial resources at home, Hoover's committee
organized a transatlantic cable transfer service, at a time when ordinary cable
communication was virtually unobtainable. By this means friends or relatives
in the States could transmit money to their loved ones in London. Eventually
nearly $100,000 was remitted from America in this way, with the tourists
paying only the cost of their original cabled plea for help.[36]

By August 8 an estimated 10,000 Americans had registered at the Savoy.
On the walls of its ballroom large black-lettered signs directed newcomers to
the various desks: registration, men's relief (Hoover's group), women's relief
(Mrs. Hoover's group), transportation, sailings, lost luggage.[37] Each day the
problem seemed to acquire new forms. Because as many as 25,000 pieces of
baggage had been left behind during their flight from the continent, many
arriving Americans lacked sufficient clothes to wear. It fell to Mrs. Hoover's
committee to collect and distribute secondhand clothing to the temporarily
needy and the destitute.[38] For the women and children who waited daily for
steamship accommodations home, Lou and her associates organized expedi-
tions to museums and art galleries.[39] Meanwhile, at the transportation committee's desk, volunteers aided by as many as thirty British travel agents at a
time arranged accommodations on the passenger ships that were at last beginning to sail.[40]

And still the refugees poured in. Around August 8 a subcommittee of
Hoover's Residents' Committee was formed to meet Americans reaching
London by rail. Wearing badges and American flag pins, the "incoming train

committee" greeted their compatriots on the platform, provided refreshments and medical assistance, loaned money to the needy, exchanged currency, and directed the weary arrivals to designated hotels and boarding houses around London. At times as many as 2,000 Americans stayed simultaneously at lodgings selected by Hoover's volunteers. In this way the distracted tourists, especially unaccompanied women, evaded speculators in steamship tickets, "white slave traders," and others eager to prey on the unwary. Sometimes, because of the wartime emergency, incoming trains did not arrive until far into the night; always representatives of the Residents' Committee would be there. Occasionally Hoover himself assisted.[41] At least once he missed his supper completely, staying at the station until midnight.[42]

Behind the scenes, however, all was not proceeding so satisfactorily. On August 9 Ambassador Page appointed a committee to disburse the $300,000 in gold advanced in London upon the security of the U.S.S. *Tennessee*'s cargo, still in mid-ocean. Page selected Fred I. Kent to chair this group; Herbert Hoover was not a member.[43] Nor did Hoover's residents' organization receive any of this sum; instead Kent evidently used it to reestablish the credit of tourists of means. Meanwhile Hoover's volunteer committee was operating entirely on its own resources—that is, on money that Hoover and others had subscribed. By mid-August it was loaning out thousands of pounds sterling daily, and its reserves were "practically exhausted."[44]

Such a disparity in resources might not have mattered except for the fact that, in Hoover's judgment, it was his committee that was doing the bulk of the work—and being treated superciliously besides. By August 14 the American engineer was thoroughly annoyed and ready (so he told a friend) to quit as soon as the U.S. government's relief commissioner aboard the *Tennessee* arrived in Europe. When he does, said Hoover, "I . . . propose to put it up to him that we handle the whole Government money through our Bureau, so far as English aid is concerned, or that we will withdraw our entire machinery and go. I simply cannot go on any longer with the Savoy bunch."

> . . . in all of our functions yesterday we provided in one form or another upwards of £2,000 for the stranded Americans, whereas the whole efforts of the Citizen's Committee amounted to £100, and that was paid out of Government funds. I have never been more humiliated in my life than I have been by this idea that a man in my business position, when I go to the desk and say that so and so has been investigated, is worthy of help and should be immediately paid so much money on such and such undertaking,—should be compelled to see the matter re-investigated and that two persons should be required to O.K. before my machinery becomes effective. This is not a situation that you and I can stand, in view of our position in the commercial world.[45]

As it happened, he did not have to endure such indignities much longer. On August 16 the *Tennessee* at last reached England, along with Assistant

Secretary of War Henry Breckinridge, twenty-four army officers, numerous clerks and other officials, and a stock of precious gold.[46] The next day Breckinridge journeyed up to the British capital, where he conferred with Hoover and Ambassador Page.[47] According to Breckinridge, shortly after he arrived in London Hoover sent an emissary proposing to absorb Breckinridge's mission into Hoover's own. The War Department official refused, stating that he had his own instructions and procedures and that his mission "could not share our responsibilities with anyone." Breckinridge became convinced that Hoover was a persistent fellow, "determined to handle any questions of relief flowing from America to the stricken of Europe. . . ."[48] Nevertheless, on the evening of August 17 he and Page formally invited the Residents' Committee to "take over the entire distribution of funds" in London. Such were Hoover's words in a report to his treasurer shortly afterward.[49]

Breckinridge's advent, in fact, provided the occasion for a fundamental restructuring of the relief apparatus. On August 19 the American Citizens' Committee decided to liquidate and transfer its duties to the Committee of American Residents. The Citizens' Committee, of course, had been organized by travelers who were themselves in London only temporarily. With the gradual return of transatlantic shipping service, many of its officers were preparing to sail home. The organized American community in London now assumed undivided management of the crisis.[50]

With the arrival of the *Tennessee* and the dissolution of the Citizens' Committee, Hoover's position was transformed. No longer was he an unfettered private actor; the embassy and the U.S. army were now watching him. On August 20 Ambassador page informed him that the government's disbursing committee would honor the vouchers and requisitions that the Residents' Committee had already spent.[51] At about the same time Page authorized Hoover's organization to draw upon and distribute the governmental funds that had just arrived on the *Tennessee*. This "subsidy" (as Hoover afterward called it) was, in his words, "most opportune."[52]

Despite the fact that by August 20 some 40,000 Americans had left London for home,[53] the size of Hoover's operation was undiminished. Each day thousands of travelers continued to visit the Savoy; each week thousands more arrived from the continent.[54] As a quasi-official relief agency, Hoover's committee was now obliged to institute elaborate accounting procedures for its use of the congressional appropriation, including hiring a firm of professional auditors.[55] At the peak of its activity the American Committee (as his group came informally to be called) comprised more than one hundred daily volunteers, not counting the various bankers, cashiers, auditors, steamship clerks, postal employees, and boy scout messengers also stationed at the hotel.[56]

Inevitably some friction arose. In all but humanitarian cases Hoover's committee insisted on financing the purchase of third class (steerage) steamship tickets only. His committee's resources were too limited, and the number of better berths available too few, to permit any other policy. Many

Americans accustomed to sailing first or second class were irate. But Hoover was not about to supply them money so that they could remain in London a month or two hoping for more commodious travel arrangements.[57]

Other complaints arose when travelers discovered that, contrary to their expectations, the American government was not going to provide them free transit home. Both Congress and Hoover, in fact, required repayment of loans from those who had sufficient resources. And Hoover refused to give money to those who could obtain it from America.[58] Determined to dispense charity only to the truly needy, the American Committee encountered much "aggressiveness and insolence" from irritated patrons, including charges that it was withholding money for its "own ends and pockets."[59]

Hoover's tolerance for such aspersions on his integrity was nil. When a dissatisfied professor of history at the University of Michigan heatedly accused the "Savoy Committee" of dishonesty and incompetence and threatened to take the case to the State Department, the engineer/executive responded with vigor. Pursuing his accuser by correspondence to Ann Arbor, Hoover defended himself in detail, even sending a copy of his rejoinder to the university's president and apparently to the board of regents as well. After a conference with the president, the overwrought professor apologized to Hoover and retracted all his charges.[60]

The professor's behavior was but a minor nuisance compared to what Hoover privately berated as "the rotten inefficiency of the whole of this Government Relief Expedition." While his volunteer committee had borne "the brunt of the whole business in London" at minimal expense, he fumed, the U.S. government had "sent a complete shipload of people over here at high salaries, kept them in fabulously expensive hotels, rented expensive quarters and engaged expensive staffs and then found that they were totally incapable of dealing with the situation. In practically every case they had to call in the local Residents, because of their lack of knowledge of local conditions."[61] Hoover was probably irked by the cumbersome paperwork that the government's military disbursing agents imposed upon his committee once it started handling public money: papers filled in duplicate, receipts, detailed financial estimates—2,284 vouchers in all.[62] He was especially irritated by Breckinridge, "a more complete idiot than whom I have yet to discover in a Public Office."

> He has occupied himself solely in Europe in travelling from one capital to another in special trains, calling on big potentates and explaining his great position in the United States, and he has practically ignored the whole of the relief work. As a result, we have been practically unable to get any co-ordination from any point on the Continent with London. . . .

The "whole thing," Hoover complained to a friend, was "one apalling travesty."[63]

The forty-year-old mining millionaire did not tolerate incompetents gladly. But such frustrations were mitigated by moments of levity. One day a well-dressed American woman indignantly declared a hunger strike at the Savoy Hotel rather than accept a mere steerage ticket home. She would starve herself to death, she said, unless the American Committee provided her a first class berth. All day long she was adamant, even in the sight of food at lunch time. But late in the day, when Hoover gave her a few shillings with which to buy her supper, the now famished protester relented—and was told she could obtain her steerage ticket tomorrow.[64] On another occasion an elderly lady refused to sail unless Hoover gave her a written guarantee that her ship would not be torpedoed. Hoover did so. "I knew," he told a friend later, "that there wasn't one chance in ten thousand that her ship would be harmed. If she came through all right she'd say I kept my word. If she was sunk she'd never have time to blame me!"[65]

In late August and September a new and more pathetic wave of Americans descended on London. Many were long-term residents in Europe who had lost their incomes in the terrible upheaval. Others were German-Americans who had been visiting relatives in central Europe, had exhausted their funds, and now had no means of returning to the United States. Some could not speak English; a considerable number were penniless. Hundreds arrived hungry and had to be fed on the railroad station platforms. The first ten days of September, in fact, comprised the most arduous phase of the American Committee's work. During the single week ending September 11, Hoover's organization paid out more than $100,000 to nearly 2,300 desperate individuals.[66]

By early October, however, the worst was over, and Hoover could begin to relax. During the preceding two months more than 100,000 American travelers had left Great Britain. Of these, 42,000 had registered in London with his American Committee, and many more had probably received some service from it. By October 9 his organization had given financial assistance to nearly 9,600 individuals, including the provision of 5,000 steamship tickets. At the railroad stations of London 2,600 arriving passengers had received cash on the spot, and more than 6,300 had gone to lodgings controlled by the American Committee. In all, Hoover and his friends had distributed more than $400,000 (mostly in loans), including about $150,000 in governmental appropriations.[67]

During these two strenuous months, Hoover had worked almost incessantly, day and night, without compensation, forsaking his business duties for what he called "getting the busted Yankee safely home."[68] Thanks to the sacrificial exertions of himself and his colleagues, and thanks to the free hotel space provided by the Savoy's management, the American Committee incurred little administrative expense.[69] The entire enterprise represented what was for Hoover a prophetic commingling of public and private spheres. Here was a team of citizen-volunteers, led by successful businessmen, operating under official patronage and distributing both its own and U.S. government funds.

Even Breckinridge acknowledged that a "paid organization" could not have accomplished what Hoover had done.[70]

Hoover was proud of his achievement—proud and curiously possessive. Both then and later he magnified his contribution to the founding of the tourist relief and minimized the parallel efforts of the Kent–Hetzler–Straus group. He asserted erroneously that his involvement in the crisis commenced on August 3 and that his activities thus coincided with (or even antedated) the creation of the American Citizens' Committee.[71] He stated that Ambassador Page had "pressed" him into managing the repatriation project, when in fact he had been eager for service and had even tried to have himself designated special commissioner by the Wilson administration.[72] In his *Memoirs* he even claimed that he attended the Citizens' Committee's first meeting on August 3, and at Ambassador Page's personal request besides. According to Hoover, after listening to "long profitless discussions" he finally intervened in the proceedings and offered to organize a residents' committee to bring "order" out of the chaos.[73] There is no evidence, however, that Hoover attended this meeting.[74] Nor, it seems, did Walter Hines Page invite him to do so. When Page dispatched a report to President Wilson on August 9, he described at length the work of Kent and the Citizens' Committee but failed to mention Hoover or his associates.[75] Contrary to Hoover's later recollections, his assistance to the stranded tourists began on August 4, not August 3, and his Committee of American Residents only took shape on August 6. He was not the first—or initially the most prominent—figure in the tourists' rescue.

But if Hoover later overstated his role in those first hectic days of August and claimed more centrality than his due, his actual contribution was substantial indeed. Thousands of Americans had reason to be grateful for his generosity, responsiveness, and dedication. He did not, after all, have to do it. And when the American Citizens' Committee disbanded in mid-August, the consolidated and multifaceted relief operation became his alone to direct, with the help of able associates like F. C. van Duzer and Clarence Graff. For several more grueling weeks Hoover was in command. His untiring and efficient service, and his handsome monetary contributions, won the admiration of Ambassador Page.[76] To him the ambassador wrote on August 20: ". . . I count ourselves exceedingly fortunate in having your Committee at our service. . . . We couldn't do the job without it."[77]

And having embarked on this "job," Hoover prepared to see it through. Early in the autumn his ad hoc organization formally changed its name to the American Committee, adopted a constitution and bylaws, and elected officers, including Hoover himself as chairman.[78] Its stated objective was simple: "to assist Americans and American interests in Europe."[79] Hoover believed that there were about 100,000 citizens of his country residing in Europe and that as long as the war lasted there would be cases of distress among them. We "cannot see our countrymen and countrywomen starve," he told the press. For the duration of the conflict, the new committee would have a duty to perform.[80]

I I

B Y early October Hoover was finally able to contemplate the world beyond the Savoy Hotel. Across the English Channel the "guns of August" had given way to the mud of autumn. Repulsed in September at the Battle of the Marne, German troops realized that a quick victory had eluded them. Their Kaiser's prediction was wrong: his troops would not be home before the leaves fell. From Switzerland to the Channel armed men were digging trenches and waiting for the advent of spring.

What should Hoover do now? Absorbed in the hurlyburly of a thousand daily tasks, he did not yet know that on August 4, 1914 his private career had effectively ended. On that day what seemed like an "earthquake" had shaken his settled world beyond recall.[81] No longer would mining engineering claim all his energies. In his own words many years later, he was "on the slippery road of public life."[82]

2

The Road to Public Service

L A T E in September Hoover and his wife prepared reports on the American Committee's accomplishments for Ambassador Page.[1] With relief work for the "busted Yankee" winding down, Lou and her two sons (Allan, 7, and Herbert, 11) sailed on the *Lusitania* for home on October 3. Lou planned to put the boys in school in California and then return to her husband in London.[2]

Hoover did not join his family on this voyage. For one thing, he told friends, he needed the money. Sending his wife and children back to America, he said, gave him greater "freedom of action" and curtailed his expenses substantially.[3] And with several mining company meetings scheduled in October, he confessed that he could use the fees granted for chairing them.[4] A millionaire on paper, with large stockholdings and investments, he was nonetheless short of ready cash.

Considerations of another sort also held him back. Early in September, a correspondent in New York asked him whether he would be interested in becoming president of the American Institute of Mining Engineers—the most prestigious honor in his profession. Hoover reluctantly declined to seek the prize. As the effective head of many London-based mining enterprises that were suddenly in disarray, he felt that "out of loyalty" to his associates he could not "expect to leave the situation now."[5] The "moral obligation . . . to stay at the helm now," he said, was "greater than ever before."[6]

As Hoover surveyed his business empire in the early autumn of 1914, a mood of pessimism swept over him. So many of his ventures were unconsummated, so much of his fortune unrealized. Out in Russia a £1,000,000 mining project was but one-third completed. In Burma the story was the same. In Australia the Zinc Corporation's facility at Broken Hill was completely shut down, its zinc concentrates cut off from smelters in Germany by the British naval blockade. Everywhere he looked, the "base metals" business, his "principal occupation for years," was "demoralised."[7] ". . . I am simply distracted in an endeavour to keep our machine going," he told a job-seeker on October 1.[8] A week later he confided that his business interests "at this end" had been "absolutely shot to pieces by the war."[9]

Yet if Hoover by October saw "little hope of making a living" in London during the European conflict,[10] he did not immediately give up trying. When cyanide for his mines became unavailable at a reasonable price in England in September, he decided to buy a shipment from—of all places—Germany. Living in London, he knew full well that British law forbade "any traffic with Germans from here." But the enterprising American engineer was not a man to be deterred by legal or bureaucratic barriers if a way around them could be found. Quickly he dispatched an agent to Switzerland to arrange with German representatives to ship cyanide down the Rhine to the neutral Dutch port of Rotterdam. Then he asked an American business associate in New York to become the ostensible purchaser. Hoover explained that the cyanide could be consigned to the American Express Company in Rotterdam and that his friend could either pay the money to American Express or perhaps remit directly to Germany. Since the United States was officially neutral in the current war, the British could not prevent the cash transfer. In this way Hoover's name could be kept out of the transaction. And once the cyanide was safely in Dutch territory, he could send it almost anywhere he pleased.

Hoover's scheme was a risky one, and he advised his American friend to exercise "a good deal of caution." Do not use the word *cyanide* when cabling to London, he warned. Use the code work *stock* instead, lest the British censors catch on. Hoover insisted that he was "not trying to facilitate anything for the King's enemies." In "actual fact," he asserted, "we are striving to keep the mines operating [in the British empire]." If that meant buying cyanide cheaply from the Germans, Hoover did not mind. Better that than buying it dear in Great Britain.[11]

Hoover's elaborate circumvention of British law apparently came to naught.[12] Such business adventures, in any case, were increasingly at the periphery of his life as the autumn of 1914 progressed. Across the English Channel, in the war zone of Belgium and northern France, a desperate drama was unfolding that would transform his life.

I I

IN 1914 the nation of Belgium was one of the success stories of Europe. With a population of nearly 8,000,000 in an area of about 11,400 square miles (scarcely one-quarter the size of Pennsylvania), it was the most densely populated and highly industrialized country in the world. Independent since 1830, and guaranteed in its neutrality by a European treaty of seventy-five years' standing, the little kingdom was both prosperous and civilized, world-renowned for its embroidered laces, its manufactures, and its art. In the summer of 1914 it possessed but one disadvantage: geography. It lay between Germany and France.

If the Kaiser's legions were to win the war quickly, they must outflank France's fortified Maginot Line and race through Belgium toward Paris. Despite valiant resistance led by King Albert, the little Belgium army could not stop the German tide. During August the capital city of Brussels and most of the country fell to the hated invader. With the capture of Antwerp on October 9, virtually all of Belgium, except for a tiny patch of coast, was in German hands.

The cost of the invasion had been staggering. Hundreds of Belgian villages had been destroyed, and more than a million terror-stricken refugees had fled their homes. All across the country factories were closed, commerce was paralyzed, postal and telegraphic communication were in abeyance. Horses and automobiles had disappeared—commandeered by the contending armies—while railway lines and canals lay damaged or ruined. In many parts of the land transportation of any kind was nonexistent.

Most ominous of all was the effect of the invasion on the food supply. During the first weeks of the fighting most of Belgium's stocks of food had been ravaged or requisitioned, and most of its 1914 harvest had been lost—a consequence of military action and of a lack of manpower to gather it. But this was only part of the problem. Before the war the little nation had produced, at most, only one-fourth of the cereal grains needed to feed her predominantly bread-consuming population. Three-fourths of her staple food, in other words, had come from abroad, in return for her exports of manufactured goods. Now, however, no exports were leaving—and no food at all was coming in. The hapless and demoralized citizenry was caught between a German army of occupation and a British naval blockade.[13]

By the beginning of September the first intimations of an impending emergency were discernible. In Brussels, where one-tenth of the entire country lived, food was becoming dangerously scarce, and the cost of it was soaring. More and more poor people were unable to buy. Writing home from Brussels on September 1, the first secretary of the American legation, Hugh Gibson, depicted a grim and worsening scene: "All the big factories are closed. Most of the shops have their shutters up and the streets are filled with idle people. Importations of foodstuffs even from the outlying districts have stopped dead." The diplomat predicted that the already considerable distress in the Belgian capital would become "enormous" "when the cold weather comes on."[14]

To cope with the mounting destitution, a number of Belgium's most eminent business leaders created in early September a private charitable organization known as the Comité Central de Secours et d'Alimentation. Its purpose was simple: to raise money with which to purchase and distribute food to the needy and unemployed in the Brussels district. The president of the committee, the industrialist Ernest Solvay, was the wealthiest man in the country. The chairman of its executive committee, Emile Francqui, was a leading director of the nation's principal bank. Two American businessmen in Brussels, Dannie Heineman and William Hulse, participated in the founding conferences; Heineman in particular had been a catalyst for action. Anxious to buttress its status with the German army of occupation, the Comité Central secured the formal patronage of the American minister to Belgium, Brand Whitlock, and his Spanish counterpart, the Marquis of Villalobar.

For the next several days the Comité Central implemented and coordinated relief efforts among the dozens of communes that encompassed Brussels' 800,000 people. If individual communes wanted subsidies from the committee, it announced, they must establish local volunteer relief agencies, set up efficient distribution centers, and offer uniform rations of seven ounces of bread and a pint of soup per day. Only the verifiably poor were to receive their food free, said the committee; all others must pay. And only actual provisions—not gifts of money—must go to the impoverished.[15]

Although the Comité Central dispatched Heineman and others to obtain fresh supplies wherever they could inside the country, the movement's organizers recognized at once that they must—somehow—procure additional food from the outside world. Perversely utopian though this might sound, as guns thundered and armies clashed along the Marne, the alternative was famine and starvation. And so on September 20, after nearly three weeks of anxious negotiations involving the Belgians, the German army, and various American intermediaries, the Comité Central at last was able to dispatch an agent named Millard Shaler to Holland and the United Kingdom. An American mining engineer and resident of Brussels, Shaler took with him a credit for £20,000 (or about $100,000) and instructions to purchase foodstuffs on behalf of the Comité. He also carried the written assurance of the German governor-general that the German authorities would not seize any provisions imported for the victualing of the Belgian civil population.[16] Without this document the entire mission would have been hopeless.

Arriving in England on September 26, Shaler quickly purchased 1,500 tons of cereals.[17] That was the easy part. His problem now was to secure an export permit from the British government, which had already prohibited the removal of any foodstuffs from its territory. To induce the British to grant an exception, Shaler contacted the Belgian legation in London. Working closely with the American diplomat Hugh Gibson, who arrived from Brussels on September 30, the engineer persuaded the Belgian minister to ask the British Foreign Office for the permit on October 1. A few days later the British government's Board of Trade replied affirmatively. Gibson, in the meantime, returned to Brussels.[18]

At this point a misunderstanding occurred that was to shape the entire outcome of the relief mission and, indeed, the course of world history. In authorizing issuance of the permit, the president of the Board of Trade instructed his deputy to inform the Belgian legation that all food parcels should be marked to show their American provenance (Shaler, the purchaser, being an American citizen). The British did not want the food shipment to be confiscated by their German enemy en route. The deputy therefore suggested to a Belgian legation official that "perhaps the safest way" to reduce this risk would be to "obtain the consent of the American Ambassador in London [Walter Hines Page] to act as Consignor" of the goods and to ship them to the Amercian minister in Brussels.[19] Since America had declared its neutrality in the European war, the intervention of her diplomats might safeguard the exported cargo.

What the British advanced as a mere procedural suggestion,[20] the Belgians construed as a demand. On October 6 the Belgian minister in London notified Ambassador Page that the British would permit Shaler's supplies to leave the country *on condition* that they be dispatched by the American embassy in London to the American legation in Brussels. Would the United States of America accept this responsibility? It was an extraordinary, probably unprecedented, request in the history of warfare: that a neutral government, far from the scene of battle, oversee the provision of foodstuffs to the capital of a belligerent country under enemy occupation. Uncertain whether to proceed, Page cabled Washington for instructions. If the State Department permitted him to become involved, he said, "it would be well to obtain a definite assurance from the German Government of their approval of this humanitarian project. . . ."[21] The next day the State Department ordered the American ambassador in Berlin to take up the matter with the German government.[22]

While the wheels of diplomacy turned slowly, conditions in Brussels were deteriorating. By the end of September 120,000 rations were being dispensed daily in the canteens of Belgium's capital city.[23] Arriving in London on the night of the thirtieth, Hugh Gibson reported the next day that food supplies in Brussels were "practically exhausted."[24] Meanwhile, in England itself, Belgium's misery was taking visible form in a horde of refugees—nearly 100,000 by mid-October—who had managed to make their way to Britain's shores.[25]

It was about this time (October 6) that Herbert Hoover first turned his attention to the Belgian tragedy. As chairman of the two-month-old American Committee, he had become an immediate authority on displaced persons and humanitarian relief. Early in October a British committee interested in the Belgian refugees approached his organization for assistance.[26] At approximately this same time, his intimate friend Edgar Rickard, publisher of the *Mining Magazine*, introduced him to an old friend, Millard Shaler.[27]

Spurred by the British committee's appeal for help and by Shaler's account of Belgium's plight, Hoover took an immediate interest. It did not take him long to develop definite opinions. "My own impression," he told an acquaintance on October 8, "is that American effort" in the field of European war relief "should be devoted entirely to" the situation inside Belgium. "The French, German, Austrian, English, and Russian peoples are quite well able to take care of their own," he said. It was Belgium that had been "the most innocent sufferer and the most acutely tried." To this same person he reported "that there is not a food supply in Brussels for more than two weeks and that something energetic must be undertaken at an early date or the situation there is going to become absolutely deplorable."[28] It was obvious from his words that more than a single shipment of food would be required to dispel the specter of starvation.

Shaler's visit and the British committee's plea could not have been more felicitously timed. With Lou and the boys on the high seas, his mining interests at a standstill, and the American tourist crisis largely resolved, the forty-year-old engineer-turning-philanthropist was free to consider the new challenge. On October 10 he called upon Ambassador Page at the American embassy. According to Page's later recollection, Hoover disclosed that "he was thinking of trying to help the Belgians to get food and asked whether, if he and his friends undertook that work and needed some diplomatic assistance, they could rely on [the ambassador's] help." Page, who considered Hoover's recent handling of the tourist problem a "remarkable" feat, assented with alacrity and enthusiasm.[29]

Having obtained this semi-official sanction, Hoover set out to convert a benevolent impulse into a plan. During the next week he consulted Rickard, John Beaver White, Millard Hunsiker, and other prominent American residents of London. Most, like himself, were mining engineers and members of the American Committee.[30] Leading members of this committee, in fact, were to comprise the nucleus of the new undertaking.

Within forty-eight hours of his interview with Page, Hoover was back at the embassy with a proposal. Meeting again on October 12, the two men agreed that a committee of Americans should be formed to "centralize and direct" American relief efforts for the Belgians.[31] It was a crucial decision. Two days later, in an interview with the *New York Herald*, Hoover urged all "American relief workers" engaged in charitable activities for Belgium to "combine into one commission" that would "embrace all the American committees already established in Belgium and in London." Hoover did not indicate where such a commission should be headquartered or who should take charge of its work. But taking note of the proliferating fund drives in America for Belgian relief, he declared that the actual expenditure of such money should be controlled by "persons familiar with existing conditions in Belgium." Otherwise there would inevitably be "overlapping and a great waste of energy and money."[32]

One factor complicating Hoover's campaign was the much-publicized influx of Belgian refugees into Great Britain. From the first, the chairman of the American Committee considered this to be a secondary problem. He told Page that the War Refugees Committee (the British organization that had asked him for assistance) could handle the refugees on its own and that fund raising in America for the refugees should be diverted to "the more critical area": Belgium itself.[33] In his press interview on October 14 he even bluntly suggested that the refugees be returned to their homeland. Settling them indefinitely in England, he asserted, would "only lead to demoralization" and "a worse situation" later on. "[T]here is no ultimate solution of the problem," he opined, "except by repatriation to their own villages and homes," very few of which (he claimed) had in fact been destroyed by the war. Such a task, he added, "could only be undertaken by an American organization" having Allied and German cooperation.[34]

All such schemes, of course, were contingent upon securing governmental approval, and as the days of October dragged by without word from Washington, Hoover's frustration mounted. It was now three weeks since Shaler had left Brussels, and still he did not know when his supplies would be on their way. What was happening? Page's cable to the State Department had gone out on October 6; six days later he had received no definitive reply.[35] Without Washington's approval, Page would not act as consignor of Shaler's cargo. Without Page's involvement the British presumably would not let the cargo sail. At this point, convinced that the U.S. government was responsible for the delay, Hoover reacted in a characteristic fashion: he exploded with a salvo in the press.

The chairman of the American Committee was no stranger to the ways of the media. During his prewar mining career he had learned well the uses of controlled publicity and the pleasures of exerting his influence through the press. Between 1912 and 1914, as an agent of San Francisco's Panama-Pacific International Exposition, he had attempted to pressure the British government into exhibiting at this world's fair. During this long campaign he had revealed himself to be an adroit manipulator of the levers of publicity.[36] Hoover, moreover, had many friends in the London press corps, including a strategically placed fellow Stanford alumnus, Ben S. Allen, at the Associated Press office. Fascinated by the power of newspapers and their potential for launching a public career, Hoover had long dreamed of buying one himself.[37]

Millard Shaler, too, was cognizant of the value of publicity. On October 6 and 10, at his instigation, the London correspondent of the *New York Tribune*, Philip Patchin, cabled urgent dispatches to America. Patchin explained that the food situation in Brussels was becoming desperate, that relief depended on American intervention, and that London was "awaiting with impatience" a reply to Page's message of October 6.[38] Patchin's reports were no doubt intended to exert pressure on the State Department to break the diplomatic logjam. But their tone was muted indeed compared to the blast that Hoover himself issued to American newspapers on the evening of October 12.

Hoover's document took the form of a statement by Millard Shaler. (Hoover's own name was not mentioned at all.) In it the envoy of the Comité Central depicted a city on the verge of starvation and violent upheaval—and a waiting stock of provisions "held up by lack of authorization from Washington." Pointing out that the State Department had been "unable to furnish a definite answer" to Page for nearly a week, Shaler demanded that his government cut the "diplomatic red tape."

> It has been reported that Washington awaits answer from Germany, to whom the matter was referred. Either the State Department should take action on its own initiative or should insist on Germany giving a speedy and definite answer. . . . The American government owes it from reasons of pure humanity to insist that Germany take favorable action or to make shipments through American diplomats, whether Germany agrees or not. I am certain Germany will agree if pressed. . . .[39]

There was no ambiguity in these words.

Hoover's combative press release ("Says U.S. Red Tape Starves Brussels," ran the headline in the *New York Tribune*) had no discernible impact on its intended target: the U.S. government.[40] More days passed—and only official silence emanated from Washington. While the diplomats dithered (or so he thought), Hoover perfected his plans. By October 17 he had conferred again with Ambassador Page. That evening, through a press dispatch probably filed by Ben S. Allen, the aspiring humanitarian disclosed the result:

> There has been initiated here [London] and referred to the Government at Washington a comprehensive scheme for the organization of an American committee with the purpose of taking over the entire task of furnishing food and other supplies to the civil population of Belgium, so far as American relief measures are concerned, under the official supervision of the American Government.

The dispatch revealed that Ambassador Page and Minister Whitlock would head the proposed commitee and that Hoover would be "one of the leading members." Furthermore, the new committee would not only ship supplies to Brussels but would also "concentrate and systematize the expenditure of the Belgian relief funds now being gathered in America." The advantages of such an American government-sponsored organization, the report contended, were manifest: it could overcome the fears of the European belligerents about possible misuse of the food, and it could avoid the dismal uncertainty haunting Shaler's unofficial mission. Meanwhile time was passing, Shaler was still waiting, and Brussels was in misery.[41]

Allen's story (if indeed it was he who transmitted it) may well have been ghostwritten. "Comprehensive scheme," "entire task": such phrases had a bold, Hooverian ring. The dispatch was significant in another respect: it suggested publicly for the first time that the sphere of the contemplated charitable effort was to be not just Brussels but the nation of Belgium itself. For some days, in fact, Hoover had been receiving clues that more than Belgium's capital was in need of succor. By mid-October emissaries from the Belgian cities of Charleroi and Liège had reached London and Hoover with the same distressed and pitiful appeal: Food. We must have food. Send us food.[42]

Still, Hoover could do nothing until diplomatic sanction had been obtained. Then, on October 17, a message came at last from the American ambassador in Berlin: "The German Government approves of the plan to supply the population of Belgium with food." The cable reached the State Department on Sunday afternoon, October 18.[43] The next day Acting Secretary of State Robert Lansing authorized Page, in London, to proceed in accordance with his cable of October 6: to serve, that is, as the consignor of food to Belgium by way of the American legation in Brussels.[44]

A full month had now elapsed since Millard Shaler had set out on his somber journey. Not an ounce of flour had come into Belgium during that time. In Brussels people were living on black bread alone.[45] From provincial cities and communes anxious burgomasters and civic leaders were besieging the Comité Central for help and begging Brand Whitlock and the Marquis of Villalobar to obtain permission for imports from abroad. No longer was it just a matter of feeding the destitute; everyone, rich and poor, faced an identical fate. And with the sickening specter of famine came another fear: of a last-ditch uprising by the starving, a rebellion doomed to bloody suppression by a ruthless German army of occupation.[46]

It was in these bleak circumstances that the Comité Central de Secours et d'Alimentation met in Brussels on October 15 and resolved to extend its operations to the entire country. The time had come, Ernest Solvay announced, to create "a kind of government" for the administration of relief. But such a step, although essential, would avail little unless there were actual food to distribute. For some days one of the committee's members, the American Dannie Heineman, had been conferring on just this subject with the German military, Brand Whitlock, and the Marquis of Villalobar. Heineman realized that the crisis had now transcended Shaler's attempt to procure a mere 1,500 tons of foodstuffs for the poor of Brussels. Instead, thousands, even hundreds of thousands, of tons must now be imported for the entire nation. To the Comité Central, Heineman reported that its diplomat-patrons had consented to seek British permission for such an augmented program, provided that the Germans gave the requisite guarantees. Heineman believed that the Germans would cooperate. The Comité Central therefore voted to seek the financial assistance of the Belgian government-in-exile and to send a delegation to London.[47]

The next day, October 16, the American legation was one of the busiest places in Brussels. That morning Solvay, Emile Francqui, and Emmanuel Janssen, representing the Comité Central, formally appealed to Whitlock to intervene with the German authorities. The Belgians arrived to find Whitlock already in consultation with Baron von der Lancken, "minister of foreign affairs" for the German governor-general. Von der Lancken was willing to make the necessary promises; he had, in fact, already asked Whitlock the day before to assist in an expanded revictualing scheme. (In previous days he had also made it plain that the Germans, while sympathetic, had no obligation under international law to feed the indigenous Belgian population and that Germany, in any case, lacked sufficient food to feed her own people and the Belgians, too.) With German cooperation assured, only the confirmatory documents remained to be drafted. Late in the day, in response to a written request from Whitlock, the German governor-general of Belgium, Field-Marshal von der Goltz, sent a written and formal reply: all provisions imported into Belgium by the committee under Whitlock's patronage would be exempt from requisition by the German army.[48]

During the day's conferences at the American legation, all parties had agreed that Whitlock's deputy, Hugh Gibson, should now return to London to obtain, if he could, the assent of the British government.[49] At 4:30 a.m. on October 17, Gibson left Brussels in the company of two representatives of the Comité Central, Baron Léon Lambert and Emile Francqui. Gibson was to report to Walter Hines Page; the two Belgians were to contact their minister to London and attempt to obtain Belgian relief funds raised abroad and controlled by their exiled government.[50]

As the three emissaries made their way to the Dutch frontier in the pre-dawn darkness, a cable from Brand Whitlock was en route to President Woodrow Wilson. "In two weeks," said Whitlock tersely, "the civil population of Belgium, already in misery, will face starvation."[51] In a separate dispatch to the State Department he explained why:

> In normal times Belgium produces only one sixth of the foodstuffs she consumes; within two weeks there will be no more food in Belgium; winter is coming on and there are thousands who are without home and without hope; it is necessary to extend the relief work to the whole of Belgium.

Whitlock told how both the local Belgian authorities and the German military had asked him and his Spanish colleague to sponsor an organization that would "revictual all of Belgium," how the Germans had promised to respect food imported for this purpose, and how all that was needed now was the British government's approval to send in the food.[52] This, Whitlock told Page, was "the one element lacking." With "all communications broken" between Belgium and the outside world, he said, "immediate action must be taken."[53]

To Gibson's Belgian traveling companions their mission of mercy seemed well-nigh hopeless.[54] In London Shaler's quest for a shipload of foodstuffs remained stalled, yet here they were heading for England on an errand that made his seem trivial. Arriving in the British capital late on October 18,[55] the envoys no doubt soon learned that the German government in Berlin had just approved an American-sponsored relief program, thereby presumably clearing the way for the export of foodstuffs from Great Britain. They were probably more surprised to discover that for more than a week a man named Hoover had been developing a plan to revictual Belgium from the outside and that his "comprehensive scheme" was nearly ready for implementation.[56]

I I I

T H E next day Hoover, Shaler, Lambert, Francqui, and Gibson conferred with Walter Hines Page at the American embassy in London.[57] They were joined by the Spanish ambassador to Great Britain, Señor Alfonso Merry del Val; as in Brussels, the neutral Spanish were taking an interest in the incipient humanitarian mission. The meeting inaugurated what became known as the "October conferences": four days of decisions and consultations culminating in the most remarkable charitable undertaking in history.

There was extra drama in that meeting on the nineteenth, for two of the participants, Hoover and Francqui, had previously met—and they were not friends. Thirteen years before, in northern China, they had represented rival European financial interests struggling to gain control of the coal-rich Kaiping mines. There they had evidently clashed, and, it was rumored, had become implacable foes.[58] When in 1905 the former Chinese manager of the mines alleged in court that Hoover and the Europeans had grossly violated the rights of Chinese shareholders, Hoover, on the witness stand, had strenuously demurred: the breaches of contract, he insisted, had begun not with himself but with Francqui.[59] Now, by an irony of war, the two had come again face to face.

What a study in character they made, these two resourceful individuals on whom the burdens of executing the relief program would largely fall. Francqui, fifty-one, was short, of dark complexion, and portly: "too well-fed" in appearance, Brand Whitlock remarked dryly, to be an ideal exhibit "of a starving *Belgium*." Balding over his forehead, with a black mustache, black hair, and large, brown eyes, Francqui was a man without illusions: reserved, relentless, and domineering, yet witty, worldly, and shrewd. As a brilliant young military officer he had helped King Léopold II conquer the Congo and had become, in China, a devoted instrument of his monarch's imperial ambitions. Now, at middle age, he was a financier, on his way to becoming one of the richest men in Europe.[60]

Eleven years younger than Francqui, and looking younger still, Hoover, at first glance, seemed less assertive. Few would have guessed that he had mining interests on six continents, had survived the Boxer Rebellion, and had already circled the world five times. Of medium height, thin, and clean-shaven, he had a curious habit, when conversing, of averting his gaze, thrusting his hands into his pockets, and nervously jingling the change. But Hoover's features also reflected a sturdy and combative temperament. Meeting him for the first time a few weeks later, Whitlock, with his novelist's eye, noted Hoover's sensitive and youthful appearance. But he noticed also that the engineer's face "wore a weary expression, as of one who dispensed too much nervous force and was always tired." And he observed above all the "broad, firm jaw" that betokened "a strong willed man of force and action."[61] Francqui had already noticed the same thing; Francqui labeled Hoover *une mâchoire* (a jaw).[62]

Each man—Hoover and Francqui—had experienced pain and emotional deprivation at an early age. Francqui had lost his mother when he was scarcely a year old and his father before he was eighteen. Hoover had lost both his parents before he was ten. At the age of thirteen Hoover had left school to work for an uncle's land company. At the age of fourteen and a half Francqui had joined the Belgian army. Each had acquired early the discipline of self-reliance and a burning ambition to succeed. Bold, decisive, and tenacious, accustomed to getting their way, could they forget their old animosities and work together now?

If the later account of a Hoover associate is accurate, the initial signs were not reassuring. Upon his arrival in London, Francqui learned from Shaler that an American-led relief effort was set to be launched and that Herbert Hoover was spearheading it. "What!" Francqui is said to have exclaimed. "That man Hoover who was in China? He is a crude vulgar sort of individual."[63] Nevertheless, the Belgian banker and his colleagues appeared at the American embassy on October 19.

No contemporary record of this critical encounter exists. Years later Dannie Heineman (who was not present) asserted that Francqui initially refused to accept Hoover's leadership of the proposed neutral commission because of his differences with Hoover in China.[64] Hoover, in his *Memoirs*, claimed just the opposite: that Francqui himself suddenly turned to him during the meeting and virtually implored him to take charge. "You alone," Hoover recalled Francqui as saying, are the man for this job.[65]

Hoover's recollection may have been colored by a tinge of retroactive melodrama.[66] But whatever the feelings between the former antagonists, the conference of October 19 approved in principle the fundamental outlines of the relief and agreed further that Hoover would direct operations outside Belgium. According to Hoover, Ambassador Page personally anointed him for this task.[67] And if Hoover's later recollection is accurate, he reacted characteristically: he told Francqui and Page that he accepted, provided that he have "absolute command." Such an undertaking, he remarked, could not be run by a "knitting bee."[68]

The next day, October 20, Hoover cabled Brand Whitlock in Brussels. The conferees of the nineteenth, he reported, proposed to establish a permanent, "purely American relief committee for Belgium" comprising Whitlock, Page, and "leading Americans in Brussels and London." The committee would systematically facilitate the shipment of supplies into Belgium under American government protection, and it would control the expenditure of charitable funds being raised in America for the Belgian cause. Hoover asked Whitlock for his comments.[69]

During the day Hoover prepared a lengthy memorandum on the problems of the undertaking for Ambassador Page. It was a model of lucidity. In rapid order the experienced executive summarized the actions that were imperative. German guarantees against seizure, for example, must be expanded. British permits for export must include the use of British ships. The numerous relief committees inside Belgium must be consolidated "on national lines . . . under strong centralized control." An American committee "will be set up" with headquarters in London. The two organizations—American and Belgian—must "interlock." And since "it is impossible to handle the situation except with the strongest centralization and effective monopoly," the two organizations "will refuse to recognize any element except themselves alone." There would be, in other words, no rivals.

Another pressing problem was financial. Working capital must be obtained, exchange operations initiated, and approval won from the belligerent governments. And while voluntary contributions were welcome, Hoover told Page flatly that public charity, "no matter how great," would be "irregular and of uncertain quantity." It was "absolutely necessary," he declared, to obtain subsidies from the Allied governments.

Hoover's blueprint for action contained one other crucial element. He was well aware that certain groups among the Allies opposed the very essence of his relief scheme. If, therefore, the "gateway into Belgium" were to be kept open, and if remaining food inside the country were to be protected from German requisition, it would be necessary to ignite a powerful, worldwide sentiment in defense of the rights of the Belgian people. Hoover consequently notified Page that "one of the first duties" of the relief apparatus would be "to create such public opinion . . . through the Press."[70]

Meanwhile the Yankee engineer was taking practical measures. On October 20 he and Shaler ordered the purchase in Page's name of 10,000 bushels of wheat, rice, beans, and peas—several times what the Comité Central had originally authorized.[71] By October 22 the two men had provisionally chartered four vessels to carry a quarter of a million dollars' worth of foodstuffs to Rotterdam.[72] For their part Francqui and Baron Lambert quickly secured £100,000 from the Belgian Relief Fund controlled by the Belgian government-in-exile in Le Havre, France.[73] This was an auspicious beginning, but one painfully incommensurate with the need. Already Francqui estimated that Belgium would require £200,000 in food every month.[74]

All these activities were dependent, of course, on obtaining the approval of the British government. But the Board of Trade's export permit of October 5 had applied to food destined for a single city, not a vast, open-ended relief undertaking for an entire country. To be certain of British cooperation, therefore, a new round of negotiations was necessary. This time Page need not wait for instructions. On October 20 Acting Secretary of State Lansing authorized him to do everything possible to win British assent to the expanded operation.[75] That same day Page, the Spanish ambassador, and the Belgians visited the British foreign secretary, Sir Edward Grey.[76]

At first the British government seemed willing. Both Grey and Prime Minister Asquith were favorably disposed;[77] Grey in fact told Francqui and Lambert that England approved the plan and would heartily cooperate.[78] Later in the day the Foreign Office duly notified Page that His Majesty's Government would not interfere with the shipment of food supplies from neutral ports in neutral ships into Belgium via Rotterdam—provided that the Germans kept hands off.[79] The next day the news for the friends of Belgium was better still: the British government (evidently Grey) promised to subsidize the relief to the extent of £150,000 a month.[80] Within twenty-four hours this news made its way into the American press, probably via Hoover and Allen.[81]

And then, as Hugh Gibson put it, "the roof fell in."[82] Sir Edward had spoken too soon. On October 21 it developed that a sizable fraction of Asquith's Cabinet vehemently opposed shipping any food whatever into Belgium. The duty of feeding the civil population rested with the German occupying army, they insisted. Moreover, how could one be certain that the Germans would leave such provisions alone? And even if they did, would not these imports simply free the enemy to requisition additional native-grown foodstuffs? Lord Kitchener at the War Office, Lloyd George at the Exchequer, Winston Churchill at the Admiralty, Reginald McKenna at the Home Office: all objected to the unprecedented scheme. Faced with a Cabinet rebellion of serious proportions, Asquith deferred a decision until he and his ministers could meet.[83]

The next day, October 22, the divided British Cabinet convened and decided "not to interfere" with the proposed relief undertaking.[84] Indeed, it offered to contribute £100,000 for the purchase of food in Holland for shipment into Belgium and another £50,000 for support of Belgian refugees on Dutch soil. But the Cabinet, significantly, was silent about a regular relief subsidy; Grey's £150,000-a-month commitment had vanished. And the ministry unequivocally refused to allow the export of any foodstuffs from England itself. England, too, was at war and needed its own food.[85]

The Asquith government's decision was a mixed result for Hoover and his associates. The British would let them proceed, and that was something, but how, without a subsidy, could they hope to finance their project for long? More worrisome still, what was now to become of the 10,000 tons of cereals that they had just purchased? Had the government rescinded its export permit of October 5? Belgium required food immediately; it might be weeks before an alternate flow of supplies could arrive from across the seas. Privately Gibson complained that the British were "crawfishing" on their earlier promise.[86]

Undaunted, Hoover refused to surrender. He had ordered the food, he needed it now, and he meant, come what may, to get it. Finally, after another week of pressure and vexatious delays, including the intervention of Ambassador Page at the Foreign Office and a personal visit by Hoover himself to the Board of Trade, the British government reluctantly permitted the foodstuffs already purchased in England to leave. But, it said, no more.[87]

Hoover had gotten his way, and if his associate Edgar Rickard is correct, he had taken a long chance in doing so. According to Rickard, Hoover first purchased the supplies, chartered the ships, loaded them, and only then— "when the hatches were closed"—asked the British for permission to make the first shipment! As Rickard told the story in later years, the senior British official whom Hoover called upon expressed regret that he could not assist him: the food was unobtainable, the railways were clogged, shipping was unavailable, the Channel was closed, war was on. Hoover listened, unimpressed. "I have attended to all this," he replied. "All I need now is clearance papers and . . . you are the only man who can grant them." The British official was staggered. "Young man," he exclaimed, "there have been men sent to the Tower [of London] for less than you have done." Still, he gave Hoover his papers and congratulated him.[88]

Rickard's anecdote was not entirely accurate. Hoover, in fact, duly filed his application for a Board of Trade permit through the Belgian legation, on the very day (or day before) he and Shaler ordered their 10,000 tons.[89] Nor, at least at first, did he actually load a vessel prior to obtaining clearance.[90] But as the days of late October passed by without result, Hoover's frustration intensified, until, on the twenty-sixth, he went to the Board of Trade and applied for the permits himself.[91] Not long afterward he privately recorded how he triumphed:

> Immediately this [relief] Commission was set up, they went into the market and purchased $250,000 worth of food, chartered ships, placed the food on board, quitely stated to the English Cabinet that the Belgian people are starfing, and said: "Are you going to allow this to go to the Belgians or not?" and having carefully advertised the purchases and the preparations for shipment and the date when the steamers could sail, there could only be one answer from the English officials.[92]

The chief of the accelerating relief mission was not a man to be constrained by bureaucratic inertia. He was in fact proud of his ability to brush aside such obstacles. "If one wants to get through the barriers of red-tape provided by universal officialdom throughout the world for the hampering of business," he wrote after this episode, "the best thing to do is to secure an Engineer."[93] Said Rickard with obvious admiration: "Hoover's way is to do things first and to ask permission later."[94]

Nor was he a man to stand idle while others pondered his fate. Around noon on Thursday, October 22, 1914, even before learning whether the British Cabinet would sanction his plans, Hoover convened a meeting in his office at No. 1, London Wall Buildings, in London, and formally launched his relief organization. Seven men joined him that day: Hugh Gibson, Clarence Graff, Millard Hunsiker, J. F. Lucey, Edgar Rickard, Millard Shaler, and John Beaver White. All were Americans; five were key members of his committee for the aid of American travelers at the start of the war. Four—Hoover, Rickard, Shaler, and White—were mining engineers. All except Gibson were businessmen.

To his assembled associates Hoover explained that Ambassador Page had asked him to create an organization "to carry into execution" the engagements recently made by Page and Whitlock. With brisk efficiency the meeting did just that. The organization would be called the American Commission for Relief in Belgium. The American ambassadors to Great Britain, Belgium, and Holland would be honorary chairmen; Hoover himself would be chairman; and Dannie Heineman, in Brussels, would be vice-chairman. Swiftly the meeting allocated responsibility for the multifarious tasks ahead. White, for instance, would handle the purchase and transport of foodstuffs in England; Rickard would take charge of publicity; Lucey would head an office in Rotterdam. Hoover further reported that arrangements were in readiness for "complete co-operation" with the Comité Central and that the nascent commission had access to £120,000, all from Belgian sources.[95]

Years later Hoover mentioned another decision taken that afternoon. During the proceedings, he recalled, John Beaver White observed: "We are about to handle millions of dollars. Some day some swine will rise up and say we either made a profit out of this business or that we stole the money." Hoover promptly retained the services of the distinguished accounting firm of Deloitte, Plender, Griffiths & Co.; the firm took no remuneration for its work.[96]

That same day (October 22) the Spanish ambassadors in London and Brussels became honorary chairmen of Hoover's embryonic organization, thereby strengthening its neutral and international character. In recognition of their diplomatic patronage (and sensitivities), the word *American* was dropped from the commission's name. (Nearly all the personnel, however, would be American.) In the days and months ahead the body was to be called by various names in various languages. But mostly it was to be known by its initials, CRB, an acronym soon to be famous.[97]

In many ways the organization that Hoover and his compatriots founded on October 22 was a peculiar one. Unincorporated, devoid of clearcut legal status, the infant enterprise nevertheless proposed to engage in worldwide commercial transactions and spend sums of unknown magnitude. Although sponsored by various ambassadors, it lacked the formal support of the United

States government. Despite Hoover's earlier hopes, the CRB at its inception was only a group of volunteers—in President Woodrow Wilson's words, "not governmental at all."[98] Apparently fearful of entangling itself in the European conflict, the Wilson administration declined to give the project official status. Nominally, at least, Page and Whitlock were acting merely as private citizens.

Hoover had little time to contemplate such anomalies. Shortly after the founding meeting in his office, he summarized its decisions in a letter to Ambassador Page. He asked the diplomat to approve an appeal to all Americans involved in charity for Belgium to cooperate with the commission. "As far as I can see," he added, "we are the only channel through which such relief can be introduced into Belgium, and the Comité Central is the only practical organisation through which it can be distributed."[99] A few hours later Hoover issued a statement to the American press in which he emphasized the role that his countrymen must play: if Belgium were to avoid "absolute famine," a "stream of food supplies" must come from the United States.[100]

Meanwhile Hoover endeavored to facilitate his access to the senior levels of the British bureaucracy. He asked Page to provide him some kind of certificate of introduction "with plenty of red seals." He suggested that the British government delegate someone who could "unravel the miles of red tape that to-day tangle our feet"[101]—especially at the infuriating Board of Trade. "The present circuit," he complained, was "perfectly awful."

> The Belgian Legation applies to the British Foreign Office for a permit. This no doubt goes through thirty or more hands and finally filters through to the Board of Trade where it passes through another thirty-two hands. It seems to me that it would only take a minute for the English Government to designate the man who signs the document in the end and to instruct him that he is to be approachable by one of us in person and without three million fences.[102]

On the evening of October 22 Hoover had a final meeting with Francqui and Lambert at the American embassy.[103] The next morning the two Belgians set out for Brussels; a few days after their return, the Comité Central became the Comité National.[104] If Francqui had initially been hesitant about Hoover's leadership, he was apparently mollified now. He told Brand Whitlock after his return that Hoover was just the man for the job.[105]

As Hoover retired on the night of the twenty-second to his home in the Kensington section of London, he probably did not discern the incredible magnitude of what lay ahead. Like most of those around him, he later wrote, he assumed that the war would end by next summer; then, presumably, Belgium's need would cease.[106] Nor, perhaps, did he fully comprehend how utterly unprecedented his enterprise was, and was destined to be. More likely he spent much of that night as he had the previous three: awake in his bedroom, pacing, pacing, concentrating on the here-and-now.[107] In Belgium over half a million people were receiving food from relief committees. In Charleroi there was nothing to eat but potato soup.[108]

Years later, in his *Memoirs* and elsewhere, Hoover tended both to magnify and to minimize his role in these events that transformed his life. He asserted that it was he who introduced Millard Shaler to Page around the beginning of October, that it was he who ghostwrote Page's cable to the State Department on October 6, that it was he who made the crucial suggestion that food be consigned to Brand Whitlock in Brussels as a way of securing British permission to export. Having catalyzed action in these ways, Hoover recalled, and having arranged for some publicity through a friend at the Associated Press, he had "no thought of further responsibility in the matter" until, to his surprise, Ambassador Page asked him on October 18 to come to a meeting with Emile Francqui. At this conference, so Hoover later recalled, Francqui and Page dramatically pleaded with him to assume leadership of the relief project, only to hear him reply that he must have a day to consider, a day to consult his mining associates and determine whether his financial circumstances would permit him to take this step. The next morning (October 20), wrote Hoover long afterward, he concluded that "duty called me to accept." In one of his reminiscences he even claimed that he spent "a prayerful night" with his wife on the subject, when, in fact, she was six thousand miles away in California![109]

Hoover's later memories were remarkably revealing of his self-image: a disinterested man of action to whom others instinctively turned, a doer who made things happen—but who always had to be asked. A man available for service—but out of duty, never desire.

These recollections of Hoover's were, of course, inaccurate. He did not introduce Shaler to Page in early October; Shaler never met Page before the sixteenth.[110] The suggestion that Brand Whitlock personally receive the food shipments came not from Hoover but from a British official at the Board of Trade. Nor, it seems, did Hoover draft Page's cable of October 6; his first known contact with the ambassador about the Belgian crisis occurred only on the tenth.[111]

But if Hoover eventually overstated his initial involvement in the relief drama, he conspicuously understated his activity in the week or so before the "October conferences." His later recollections did not mention his ghostwriting of Shaler's press release of October 12, his own press interview of October 14, his meetings with his associates and Page between October 10 and 16—all during the period that he later said he gave "no thought" to Belgian problems.[112] Nor did he recall the newspaper dispatch of October 17 announcing that he would be "one of the leading members" of an American-led relief agency. All these signs that Hoover actually *sought* the job of Belgian relief administrator, he later forgot or suppressed. Whatever Page or Francqui said to him in their conference on October 19, he could hardly have been surprised by an invitation to take command. In all likelihood, he expected it and knew what his answer would be.

For years, in fact, Hoover had been searching for just such an opportunity: an entreé into the "big game" of public service.[113] Perhaps he could not bring himself to admit that he had ever volunteered for such a trust. For a man imbued in youth with a "Quaker conscience," such a disclosure would only tarnish the prize.

Hoover's later self-portrayal, then, as the man who really got matters moving and then stood loftily aside until drafted into service was faulty. Still, he *was* taking a momentous step into the unknown, and he would not have been human had he not felt twinges of misgiving. The greatest war in history was raging; his wife and children were in another country; his mining affairs were in disarray. How could he attend to his business interests, his family obligations, and Belgian charity, too? Perhaps, during those long, frenetic days of mid-October, he sensed that there would be no turning back, that the pursuit of wealth would never again direct his energies. As it happened, one of his oldest college friends, Will Irwin, was staying with him in his London home at the time. On the morning of October 22, after another night of concentration and anxiety, Hoover walked down to breakfast, looked at Irwin, and said, "Let the fortune go to hell."[111]

I V

H o o v e r did not instantly renounce his private career or resign his mining directorates. Several years, in fact, were to pass before he cut loose entirely from his former career.[115] But from October 22, 1914 on, his thoughts increasingly were elsewhere. When Hoover made a commitment, he never went in halfway.

Perhaps it was not so unusual a transition. He was, after all, an engineer, a businessman, an accomplished administrator of resources and of men. A man of force and action. *Une mâchoire.* Perhaps his talents were precisely those that his new task would require. Across the Atlantic, his long-time business associate Lindon Bates thought so. Reading in the New York press in mid-October about Hoover's efforts to organize a relief commission, Bates cabled over to his friend: "It's a fine idea; you were always a born consolidator, and would consolidate the solar system if there was a chance to make a needed fundamental change in this wicked world."[116]

In the battle-scarred land of Belgium he would have his chance.

3

Who's Hoover?

WITHIN hours of the final "October conferences" the Commission for Relief in Belgium began to function. At its head were ten "provisional officers" (as Hoover called them). All were Americans; at least seven were engineers. For a London headquarters the chairman secured rent-free office space at No. 3, London Wall Buildings, just two doors away from his own office as a mining engineer.[1] But it was not mining that preoccupied him now.

In selecting his principal colleagues Hoover insisted on certain definite requirements. He wanted no "decorative personalities," no "titled nonentities."[2] He had seen enough such drones on mining company boards. Instead, he declared, "all officers of the Commission should be gentlemen of wide commercial experience and of the type willing to devote their entire time, at their own expense" to its service. They must possess "the spirit of self-sacrifice in full measure." Hoover did not want part-time dilettantes who had other "dominating interests"; conducting a business on such a basis, he said, was "utterly impossible." Nor did he want to divert precious charitable funds to administrative overhead. It was not "dignified," he told a Spanish diplomat, for the commission to be "dependent for incidental expenses upon those who are furnishing the funds for the purchase of food supplies." "Every penny" raised for food relief should be spent on just that: providing "actual food" to the Belgians.[3]

Hoover did not extend his principle to everyone in his organization. To those in "subordinate capacities" salaries were paid.[4] But for those at the top, it was otherwise. For the duration of the war neither Hoover nor his senior associates (with few exceptions) received any compensation for their services or even reimbursement for their expenses.[5]

The CRB's organizational efforts in London occurred against a background of mounting apprehension. By October 26, according to Hoover, more than a million Belgians were on the breadline, with but one to three weeks of supplies left in the entire nation.[6] Each day brought new evidence of impending catastrophe. Liège, Namur, Charleroi: "absolutely without flour"; Brussels: "we can scarcely finish the week."[7] All localities north of Limburg: no flour, sugar, salt, rice, peas, or beans.[8] The province of Hainault: workshops closed, 800,000 citizens too poor to buy their own food, the people as a whole "on the point of starvation."[9] Writing to Hoover from Holland on October 29, J. F. Lucey acknowledged, "We . . . have all underestimated the desperate condition of the Belgian people." Unless massive shipments of flour arrived quickly, Lucey feared that many Belgians would resort to violence and a futile insurrection.[10]

From Emile Francqui in Brussels came further disquieting news. As late as October 26 Hoover believed that he would need to ship "upwards of twenty thousand tons" of foodstuffs into Belgium each month.[11] That day Francqui cabled a new estimate: not 20,000 tons but at least 80,000 tons would be needed. The minimum monthly needs of the Belgian people, he said, would include 60,000 tons of wheat, 15,000 tons of maize, and 3,000 tons of rice and dried peas.[12]

Francqui's calculations were reasonable and in fact conservative.[13] Before the war Belgium had imported about 250,000 tons of these particular foodstuffs per month. Now the financier and his colleagues were requesting less than a third of this quantity. It amounted to a national ration of ten ounces per person per day.[14]

Even so, the financial implications of Francqui's message were staggering. At the time of his departure from London, the Belgian banker had envisaged that the necessary monthly import program would cost a million dollars.[15] Now he and Hoover knew better. By the end of October Hoover realized that his embryonic relief operation would have to raise four to five million dollars every month.[16] In one week the dimensions of his task had quadrupled.

If Hoover had any lingering uncertainties about the scale of the challenge ahead, he surely lost them now. This problem, he told an acquaintance on the twenty-ninth, "has developed into enormous proportions,"[17] and no early end was in sight. On November 4 he predicted that "feeding the population of Belgium is bound to extend over seven or eight months"[18]—in other words, until the next Belgian harvest.

To provide the food and resources with which to carry on, Hoover turned at once to the United States. On October 26 he dispatched an urgent cable to his wife in California. He asked her to seek the assistance of various prominent San Francisco businessmen, including several of his fellow trustees of Stanford University. If these men could assemble a shipload of gift food from California for the Belgians, he said, his organization would pay for the insurance and transportation. Alert to the power of local self-esteem, he pointed out that "our Commission is largely Californian and that we should have support of our own state."[19]

During the next several days the CRB chairman issued a number of similar pleas, including cables to the governors of thirty-one states.[20] To each his request was the same: organize agencies in your jurisdiction to collect food (or money to buy food) for Belgium. Hoover cleverly infused his messages with appeals to state pride. To the governor of Wisconsin he wrote: "It would be a matter of great gratification if the people in your state could furnish one or more shiploads of foodstuffs to be known as the Wisconsin ships."[21] To the governor of Kansas he wrote of "Kansas ships," and so on, state by state.[22] Hoover's cables were precise, emphatic, and unabashed. When, for instance, he wanted cooperation from a Chicago businessman, he wasted no words:

> There are one million persons at present on bread line in Belgium and what we need is absolute food, not clothing. It is our feeling that the grain market of Chicago should present us, in the name of Chicago, with one or more cargoes, these to be composed of wheat, beans, peas, and as much bacon as possible. . . . We should like to be able to announce to world that Chicago is contributing the first cargo. Would like immediate reply as to whether you can personally interest yourself in this effort.[23]

To stimulate the flow of charity from the world's leading neutral nation and grain exporter, Hoover launched a vigorous publicity campaign. On October 31 he released a dramatic personal appeal from King Albert of Belgium for American support of the CRB during the coming winter of privation. Hoover had just obtained the message via Hugh Gibson, who had visited the monarch at the front. While there Gibson obtained a similar document addressed to the women of America by Belgium's queen.[24]

To Albert's appeal Hoover attached a starkly worded message of his own. Seven million people were still in Belgium, he announced, and every one of them was in need. Writing in blunt, declarative sentences, he outlined the problem. "This is not a question of charity or relief to the chronic poor, it is a question of feeding an entire population." "The Belgians are helping themselves, but they can do little. The British and French are under such strain that they also can do little. Americans must feed Belgium this winter. There never . . . was a famine emergency so great."[25]

Hoover's longstanding interest in the press—and his prewar friendships with prominent journalists—now paid extraordinary dividends. Shortly before the CRB was founded he had become acquainted with Melville Stone, general manager of the Associated Press. With Stone's permission (probably granted at Hoover's urging) Ben S. Allen of the AP's London office turned his full attention to the CRB and immediately gave it unprecedented coverage.[26] For the next two and a half years he sent dispatches about it almost daily to the American press.[27] In the AP's London bureau Hoover recognized an invaluable ally—a virtual propaganda arm of his commission.[28]

Allen was not the only talented journalist (and Stanford man) to join the relief crusade. Hoover had known Will Irwin since their undergraduate days together twenty years before. An experienced journalist who was covering the war that autumn for the *Saturday Evening Post*, Irwin, in Hoover's estimation, was the "best press agent in [the] world."[29] Within three weeks of the CRB's founding he was on his way back to New York as its volunteer "publicity Manager in America."[30]

By mid-November the Commission for Relief in Belgium had inaugurated what Hoover proudly labeled "an enormous propaganda" in the United States.[31] "The Associated Press informs us," he told a diplomat, "that there has been nothing like it in years."[32] At the CRB's London office William Goode (an able journalist who had worked with Hoover before the war to promote British participation in the Panama-Pacific International Exposition) was churning out publicity regularly.[33] In New York Irwin was unleashing a torrent of press releases, pamphlets, and handbooks to newspapers and volunteer fundraisers.[34] Soon influential journals like the *Literary Digest, Independent*, and *Outlook* were printing laudatory accounts of the commission's work.[35] And when in November the CRB's New York office was opened, the Associated Press duly instructed its New York bureau to give the office "special attention."[36]

Almost daily, it seemed, the "press-agenting" of the relief (as Irwin called it) took new forms.[37] In one brilliant scheme, he and Goode recruited a galaxy of eminent British literary figures to explain the need to succor the helpless Belgians. For the next several months the "Famous Authors Service," as it was called, supplied syndicated articles by writers like Thomas Hardy and George Bernard Shaw to the principal newspapers of the United States.[38]

Not only poets and novelists but newspapermen in the field were called upon to serve Hoover's cause. Early in November he asked Edgar A. Mowrer of the *Chicago Daily News* to visit Belgium and investigate famine conditions with a view to generating publicity. Hoover explained that "publicity of this character" was "the very foundation of the support which we are receiving from the United States."[39] When Mowrer was ready to publish, the CRB asked Melville Stone to have the AP circulate his story widely.[40] Another cooperative American war correspondent was Frederick Palmer, whom Hoover had known since 1899. Returning to London from a trip to Berlin in November, Palmer, at his friend's request, prepared a statement on German attitudes toward the relief. Germany was embittered, he reported, and would never feed the Belgian population; rescue could only come from "outsiders."

His comments were printed at once in the American press and sent by Hoover to the British foreign secretary.[41]

And always the cry came for more. Do you have "detailed personal or horror stuff"? Irwin asked the London office at one point. How about obtaining an interview with King Albert or appeals signed by Belgian refugees?[42] Hoover himself asked Brand Whitlock for assistance in preparing a motion picture documentary showing the trek of foodstuffs from the seaports of America to the "waiting lines of Belgian victims."[43] So insatiable were the publicity men's appetites that, as Hoover remarked somewhat wryly, "we have to feed them with material every night."[44]

The immediate purpose of this immense publicity effort, of course, was to touch the heartstrings and pocketbooks of the American people. But Hoover had another motive as well. He knew that the British military strenuously opposed sending food into enemy-occupied territory. If his mission were to succeed, it must establish legitimacy and prestige. And this meant fashioning what he called "the club of public opinion"[45]—above all, *American* public opinion—as a weapon against the warring European powers. The purpose of his initial burst of newspaper "propaganda," he later acknowledged, was "to bring vividly before the world the right of the Belgians to import foodstuffs."[46]

And this in turn meant establishing the rights of the CRB. Time and again in these early days Hoover proclaimed the indispensability of his relief organization-in-the-making. He asserted that it was an "official body," appointed "officially" by the American and Spanish ambassadors, although President Wilson had made it plain that the American diplomat/patrons were acting in a private capacity only.[47] He asserted that his was "the only vehicle for transmission [of] relief into Belgium" and (through the Comité National) "the only efficient agency for the distribution of food within that country."[48]

In all of this Ambassador Page gave him strong support. The German army, declared Page to the State Department, had promised not to confiscate supplies shipped in by Hoover's commission. "So far as I know this assurance has not been given to any one else who may send food." Americans wishing to assist Belgium, said Page, should confer and cooperate with Hoover.[49]

The CRB chairman appreciated keenly the power of the instrument that he was forging. When formulating his appeal of October 31, he wrote and rewrote the document until he had it just right.[50] He knew the psychological and fund-raising value of a "strong punch of cable" dispatched from the "scene of action."[51] He knew, too, the importance of keeping his publicity under control. When in December certain members of his commission gave indiscreet interviews to the British press, his reaction was swift and determined. "These unauthorised statements," he charged, "have caused the utmost possible embarrassment to the Commission and even threatened to defeat its entire work." He therefore requested every member of the CRB to sign a pledge to make no statements about its work to anyone (including the press) while in its employ—and for six months thereafter. And he vowed to "discharge . . . every single soul" who did not sign the pledge immediately.[52]

There was one aspect of public relations, however, which Hoover did not enjoy: the publicity that he could not control, the publicity that was focused on himself. "Who's Hoover?" journalists were beginning to ask. Who was this Yankee dynamo who was organizing the greatest humanitarian effort that the world had ever seen? Soon inquisitive newspaper reporters were knocking at his door in search of photographs and personal stories. Hoover was uncooperative. What mattered, he insisted, was the institution, not the "glorified office boys" who ran it. To emphasize personalities, he claimed, would demean the cause. Hoover's associates thought otherwise. When he sent in the October 31 press release with the request that his own name be omitted, Ben S. Allen inserted it anyway, to his friend's annoyance and reproof.[53] Repeatedly Hoover refused to be photographed—an attitude that at one point provoked a heated argument with a colleague.[54] On another occasion William Goode unashamedly stole a photograph from the piano in Hoover's home and gave it to the press. It was a long time before he gained Hoover's "grumpy forgiveness."[55]

Yet if Hoover shunned intrusive personal publicity, he was assiduously attentive to the press coverage that he did receive—and quick to complain when any of it displeased him. Sometimes his sensitivity was acute. In January 1915 the *New York Tribune* published a highly complimentary profile of the CRB based on data supplied by the commission's New York office. The article reported that Hoover was considered by his profession to be "the greatest mining engineer alive," and it noted innocently that he had once been associated with the firm of Bewick, Moreing & Co., "an important London house."[56] Hoover had left this firm in 1908 and was not on good terms with his expartners. When, therefore, he saw the article, it was not the encomiums that he noticed but the reference to his erstwhile associates. "Tell your publicity department," he cabled New York, "that I do not think very darned much of their Tribune article January tenth. I see no occasion to advertise Bewick Moreing at my expense."[57]

Publicity alone, of course, could not feed Belgium, and even as Hoover's press campaign proceeded, other tasks crowded in. In Rotterdam Captain J. F. Lucey—engineer, army veteran, oil industry executive, Californian—was speedily organizing a network of docks, depots, and barges that would hasten the flow of arriving food by canal into Belgium.[58] In Brussels Shaler, Heineman, and the Comité National were struggling to create an apparatus that would distribute imported sustenance from the largest urban center to the tiniest rural commune.

The obstacles that faced them were immense.[59] Still, gradually, a workable organization took shape. Like the CRB in London, the Comité National de Secours et d'Alimentation was essentially directed by businessmen-volunteers: bankers, industrialists, *hommes de grandes affaires*. The periodic meetings of its executive committee took place in the nation's principal bank, the Société Générale de Belgique. In short order the CN developed an interlocking web of committees that could dispense and account for the food that was to come. At the top of the pyramid was an executive committee chaired by Emile Francqui; here all important policy was made. At the next level were eleven provincial committees—one for each province plus Brussels. Below these, regional committees in major popular centers. And finally, the communal committees, whose members ran into the thousands. Although private and stringently nonpolitical in origin, the Comité National soon acquired governmental characteristics—determining the size of relief rations, fixing the maximum price to be charged, consolidating recordkeeping, receiving and allocating funds. All rations, it decreed, were to be uniform; no one should suffer discrimination. To assure national unity and integrity of administration, representatives of the three great political parties—Catholic, Liberal, and Socialist—served together on most committees.[60]

Not all the barriers to success were on the continent. Back in London Hoover's first relief cargoes became mired in further delays. It turned out that no ship could be loaded on the Thames River after 7 p.m. and that none could set sail after dark. A severe shortage of workmen on the docks further retarded loading. Not until October 30 did the first shipment of foodstuffs leave Britain for Rotterdam. Not until November 4 did it reach Brussels via the canals.[61]

Slowly, fitfully, other food-laden vessels made their way to Holland. On November 16 came the S.S. *Tremorvah* from Nova Scotia—the first ship of gift food to arrive. On November 21 the S.S. *Massapequa*, chartered and stocked by the Rockefeller Foundation. When the latter vessel, containing the first donated food from the United States, reached the Rotterdam docks, five hundred stevedores jumped aboard and worked at a record pace to unload it. Men fought to take part in the operation; large crowds assembled and cheered. Within forty-eight hours the entire cargo—more than 3,500 tons of beans, bacon, flour, and rice—was ready for shipment into Belgium.[62]

But even as the first cargoes reached their destination, another problem was assuming awesome proportions. Hoover anticipated that of the four or five million dollars' worth of foodstuffs to be imported monthly, perhaps half this amount could be recovered from sales of food rations by the Comité National to those Belgians who could afford to pay.[63] But how could he actually acquire these sums from the Comité National? The Germans had forbidden the export of Belgian currency to countries at war with the Fatherland.[64] Furthermore, how could he cover the cost of feeding the growing numbers of Belgians who were destitute? Would charity suffice? And who would pay for purchase of the food in the first place?

From every point of view Hoover's resources seemed pitifully incommensurate with his needs. By October 29 he had garnered a mere £120,000 and had spent four-fifths of it already.[65] In addition, he had received a promise of £100,000 from the British government, a pledge it seemed reluctant to keep.[66]

To make ends meet, the CRB's chairman pushed ahead on various fronts. One was the worldwide charity appeal that he was orchestrating with such vigor in the press. A second was his reliance on voluntarism. Time and again during these early days he emphasized that he and his colleagues were "energetic and business people" who were devoting their full time without pay and at their own expense to Belgian relief.[67] The fact that this was humanitarian work made Hoover's task infinitely easier. During November two noted British shipping firms agreed to manage the CRB's ocean transport without remuneration.[68] In America nearly all railroad companies eventually carried relief food free of charge, while the city of New York furnished piers at no cost.[69] In Holland the government allowed Hoover free use of the state-owned telegraph lines.[70] As a result of these and innumerable other free services rendered by governments, business, and the CRB's own dedicated personnel, the commission was able to operate with a phenomenally low administrative overhead.[71]

Charitable appeals and gratuitous service were not the only expedients at Hoover's command. On October 29, with no funds at hand and none in sight (except the Asquith government's promised £100,000), he quietly purchased a shipload of food in New York for $225,000.[72] Hoover knew well that he had no money to pay for this cargo when it arrived and that if the British pledge did not materialize in the meantime he would be "very considerably embarrassed." But, characteristically, he took the risk. The best "weapon" to use against the English, he confided to a friend, would be to say (when the time came) that he had already bought the food and that "the whole thing will fall" unless they kept their promise.[73] Only days before he had used a similar tactic at the Board of Trade.[74] As it happened, the British government eventually produced the £100,000. Even so, Hoover had to acknowledge to his patron ambassadors in early November that his organization was "considerably over-spent."[75]

This willingness to take chances and hope for the best was typical of Hoover's behavior that autumn. Act first, explain later. Sometime afterward, when asked to divulge what had carried him through the chaos of those early months, he replied in a flash: "The fait accompli."[76]

But even boldness was not enough. Such desperate expedients only underscored what Hoover had foreseen from the beginning: that charity alone would never suffice. Certainly no one could count on eliciting an adequate stream of private contributions for seven or eight more months.[77] The conclusion, he informed the ambassadors on November 3, was inescapable: ". . . if the situation is to be handled properly and systematically we have got to have a substratum of Government subvention."[78]

Hoover's first target was the Belgian government-in-exile. Acting through

Chevalier Edmond Carton de Wiart, who became its London liaison to the CRB, Hoover boldly requested a subsidy of £100,000 a month to cover his transportation expenses. He also asked the Belgian government to direct its minister to the United States to place his considerable relief funds at Hoover's disposal.[79] As usual when the American executive wanted something, he pulled the strings from every direction. He cabled Lucey in Rotterdam that Francqui and his associates "should bring all pressure to bear on Belgian government. . . ."[80] Two days later he asked Francqui directly to "exert all of the machinery within your power" to have the Belgian minister in Washington instructed as Hoover wished.[81] Never at a loss for an argument, he told Carton de Wiart that there was no "more beneficent work" that the Belgian government could do for its civil population behind German lines than to guarantee the CRB its desired allowance.[82]

Such a sum, however, was only one quarter of what Hoover desired. For the remainder he turned his sights on the British and French governments. The prospects for success were not encouraging; as early as October 26 the British declined to promise anything beyond the £100,000 already authorized (but not yet delivered).[83] Nevertheless, on October 29 Hoover met with the American and Spanish ambassadors to Great Britain and laid plans to appeal anyway for a subsidy.[84]

On November 5 Hoover and some of his colleagues, accompanied by the patron-ambassadors, called upon Foreign Secretary Grey. Armed with a memorandum and a thick dossier of supporting documents, Hoover explained that only "a substantial substratum of government guarantee"—at least £400,000–500,000 a month—could possibly solve his swelling financial problems. Private charity and philanthropy were insufficient. The burgeoning cost of transportation was much on Hoover's mind during this interview, as it had been for several days. If only he could announce to the world that the CRB would pay for all transportation of food into Belgium, he was convinced the he could thereby stimulate a tremendous outpouring of food donations. To this end Hoover proposed that the British and French governments each contribute £150,000 per month for this purpose. As always, he was in a hurry. He told Grey that he would like to notify North America that very night that the CRB now had the means to pay for the "entire transportation" of relief commodities. Grey promised to consult his Cabinet colleagues.[85]

The next day the first breakthrough came—and from an unexpected quarter. In German-occupied Brussels Emile Francqui succeeded in negotiating a loan of £600,000 (or about $3,000,000) guaranteed by a consortium of Belgian bankers and financiers, some of whom had been associated with Hoover before the war in the Kaiping coal mining enterprise in China.[86]

Upon receipt of this sum Hoover informed Francqui that he had decided to apply it to the "sole purpose of providing free transportation of food-stuffs" into Belgium. Although the loan contained no such stipulation, Hoover added that he was announcing to the world that the sum *had* been advanced by the Belgian lenders "for this particular purpose." "To have mentioned this sum of money to the world otherwise," he said, "would tend to dry up the rills of charity," whereas announcing it as a transportation subsidy would "serve to stimulate them even more."[87]

At about this same time the Belgian government-in-exile agreed to provide the CN—and through it the CRB—£1,000,000 in working capital (although it did not make the transfer immediately). This sum Hoover proposed to use to supplement any failure of charity and thereby maintain an uninterrupted flow of food.[88] But unlike the "transportation" fund, he did not disclose to the press this new source of revenue. "Do not mention our large resources," he warned his New York agent, for it would destroy his charitable campaign.[89]

Although Hoover estimated that the £600,000 loan from Brussels would cover his transportation costs for three months,[90] he did not—and dared not—relax. Keeping up his pressure on the Foreign Office, he wrote to Grey's deputy, Lord Eustace Percy, on November 20. "We are getting absolutely 'up against it,' " he reported; we must obtain a regular governmental subsidy.[91] Five days later he addressed another plea to Grey. Charity alone, he said, was "most irregular and unreliable," and his current funds were "wholly and absolutely inadequate" to his needs.[92]

The British, however, were not to be stampeded. Replying to Hoover's far from diffident pleadings, Percy advised him not to "fix his hopes too high."[93] As the days of late November slipped by, an ominous silence appeared to envelop the Foreign Office.

Meanwhile the details of relief administration kept proliferating. By mid-December the CRB's London headquarters had a staff of forty persons, who, in one observer's words, would consider themselves "terribly overworked if they were working on a salary."[94] Arriving for duty at nine in the morning (an hour earlier than British custom), some did not leave until ten o'clock at night. Taking lunch in his office to save time, Hoover himself rarely returned home before seven in the evening; sometimes not before nine.[95]

But if the hours were long, the commission's offices were a paragon of efficiency. A leading London mining journal complimented the CRB on its "energetic and business-like" methods. It "is not run on the ordinary philanthropic lines as understood here," said the journal with satisfaction. "It fortunately has business men at the helm and the whole of the money placed at its disposal goes to the poor people it is intended for. . . . In other words, to put it bluntly, there is no plunder in this business."[96]

One other thing was also certain: whatever the Allied governments might ultimately decide about subsidies, as the winter of 1914–15 came on there was no "relief" in sight for Herbert Hoover.

I I

By late November 1914, less than a month after his initial public appeal, the first results of Hoover's "enormous propaganda" were manifest. Across the United States, the British empire, Italy, Spain, and elsewhere, concerned citizens were organizing to give assistance to the cause. Eventually over four thousand such committees came into existence around the world.[97] To an American philanthropist Hoover disclosed with pleasure that since he had instigated his publicity drive, some of the existing committees had nearly doubled their receipts.[98] In his adopted state of California his wife Lou herself conducted a lecture tour and garnered enough money to buy a shipload of gift food—one of the first from the United States.[99]

Even as Hoover's campaign gained momentum, other American efforts were proceeding—some of them dating back to the summer. In August William C. Edgar, editor of the *Northwestern Miller*, had initiated a drive among Midwestern grain millers; the eventual result was a shipload of free flour consigned to the CRB.[100] In September the *Christian Herald* had established a fund for European war widows and orphans; this, too, after consultation with Hoover, was applied to the relief of Belgium.[101] On October 21—the day before the formal founding of Hoover's commission—the Rockefeller Foundation resolved to interest itself in the plight of Belgian noncombattants. Less than two weeks later, the foundation announced plans to dispatch a shipload of gift food to Belgium via the American consul in Rotterdam.[102]

Throughout this period the Belgian minister to the United States, Emanuel Havenith, had energetically sponsored a number of relief movements, the most important of which was the Belgian Relief Committee in New York. Although the nominal president of this group was a Belgian priest named J. F. Stillemans, its effective head was the chairman of its executive committee, Robert de Forest, a well-known New York philanthropist. By the end of October the Belgian Relief Committee had amassed more than $250,000 in charitable contributions.[103]

This vigorous outpouring of assistance was a heartening measure of American sympathy for a brave little nation ground by the millstones of war. But for the "born consolidator" at the head of the CRB, it posed an immediate problem. If the charitable resources of the United States were to be mobilized effectively, coordination of effort would be imperative. Otherwise, confusion and competition could ensue. It soon became evident, however, that not all of the existing American relief organizations were prepared to yield preeminence to a newcomer.

To organize the American end of his relief enterprise Hoover turned first to Thomas Fortune Ryan, a wealthy New Yorker with large mining interests in the Belgian Congo. While visiting London in late September, Ryan had been contacted by Millard Shaler and had promised to donate $200,000 to the Belgian relief cause.[104] He had then returned to New York, where, it was reported on October 21, he would shortly be "looking after" the American operations of the projected relief commission.[105]

Through Shaler, then, on October 22, Hoover formally invited Ryan by cable to join the CRB, establish its New York office, and purchase cargoes for shipment from America.[106] When Ryan did not immediately respond, Hoover asked another New Yorker, Lindon W. Bates, to assist. An internationally known civil engineer, he was one of Hoover's closest friends.[107] Bates speedily assented, as did his wife, who agreed to set up an organization of American women to support the CRB.[108]

On October 26 Ryan cabled his acceptance of membership on the nascent relief commission; Hoover thereupon renewed his request that the millionaire financier head its committee in New York.[109] It quickly developed that Ryan had other plans. Aligning himself with de Forest, he informed Hoover on October 30 that the "best results" would issue from cooperating with the Belgian Relief Committee and concentrating all fund raising and food collecting in its hands. Creation of a separate Hoover-controlled body, he asserted, would cause "confusion and perhaps friction."[110]

Without waiting for Hoover's response Ryan and de Forest's brother constituted themselves a "Supply Committee" to collect American monetary contributions for Belgian relief, convert them into foodstuffs, and arrange for their shipment to Europe.[111] Announcing their plans in the press on November 3, Ryan and his associates (with the Belgian minister's concurrence) urged all Americans to funnel their contributions to them.[112]

Ryan's cabled messages of October 30 were followed by a patronizing letter from Robert de Forest. Among other things, de Forest was president of the Charities Organization Society and vice-chairman of the American Red Cross. Noting pointedly that his Belgian Relief Committee antedated Hoover's by many weeks, de Forest declared his readiness for "complete cooperation on this side of the water" with what he chose to call the "London American Committee." To this end he requested Hoover to "simply concentrate everything" with the Supply Committee and his own Belgian Relief Committee. If this is done, he said with an air of self-assurance, "we will, I think, keep everything in line."[113]

Hoover was considerably annoyed. Ryan "has totally failed to rise to the situation," he complained.[114] Instead of providing the $200,000 that he had promised, the business magnate had demanded that the CRB itself put up half the money for a $300,000 cargo to be purchased jointly in New York with de Forest's group.[115] Hoover reluctantly acceded, but he emphatically did not consider this "an act of appropriate broadmindedness in a situation of this kind."[116]

Nor was he pleased by Ryan's and de Forest's bid for primacy in the United States. Accordingly, on November 2 he cabled Ryan that he would be glad to cooperate with the de Forest committee in "all matters involving New York and vicinity." (He told Bates the same day that he intended to use the de Forest committee "for local purpose only.") He further informed Ryan that to avoid "local jealousies" in America all relief appeals would emanate from London—in other words, from himself.[117] As for the Supply Committee scheme, Hoover acquiesced but asked de Forest to make Bates a member.[118] Meanwhile he informed Bates privately that he expected to establish a "stronger organ" than Ryan's and planned to use Bates's membership on it as a "stepping stone to push you in some important position later."[119]

Ryan lost little time in replying. *All* money used for buying and shipping relief commodities, he rejoined, should be concentrated in his Supply Committee. Otherwise "economical results" would be lost.[120] It was clear that Hoover was getting nowhere.

Rebuffed in his attempt to localize the New Yorkers' sphere of influence, Hoover turned to his principal supporter. On November 4 he informed Ambassador Page that he was "getting into a frightful muddle in the States." He claimed that the Ryan–de Forest attempt to consolidate "all Belgian matters . . . into their hands" was "producing a most disagreeable reflex" in western parts of the United States. Hoover bluntly suggested that "if we are going to organise up the foodstuffs coming from all quarters of the Globe and the moneys for its distribution we have got to have some kind of official recognition that puts us above outside criticism and petty interference." "Nothing infuriates us," he continued, "like the suggestion that has been thrown out that we are a self-appointed body pushing our way into a situation that other people are better able to look after." Indeed, said Hoover, he and his colleagues would be "delighted to retire . . . tomorrow" if a "more efficient organisation" could be established in their place. But, he said, the CRB's leaders insisted that "if they are going to do a job they are going to do it themselves." And while ready to cooperate with "well-meaning" people, they were "not going to be bossed from any quarter when such interference absolutely destroys their effectiveness."

Hoover therefore demanded that the United States government issue a statement granting "recognition" to the Commission for Relief in Belgium. The Wilson administration should tell the American people that the CRB had been set up by Page under U.S. government protection, that the commission was "absolutely neutral," that it was the "only vehical" that the government would support for shipment of food into Belgium, and that all transportation matters "should be taken up directly with us and nobody else." Furthermore, said Hoover, it was "essential" that the British government also recognize the CRB and desirable that the German government officially countenance it as well. What it came down to, in his view, was this: ". . . in order to accomplish our work we have got to build up our prestige. . . ."[121]

In a separate letter to Carton de Wiart, Hoover asserted that de Forest's committee was "non persona grata" in much of America and that "sectional feeling" made a single national collection agency "impossible." According to Hoover, it was "absolutely necessary" that the Belgian government officially instruct its representatives abroad to cooperate with his agency as the "only institution" through which all relief work outside Belgium should be "centralised."[122] The very next day he asked Sir Edward Grey to recognize the CRB as "the only body properly founded for this work."[123]

Hoover was now convinced—or so he professed—that the Belgian Relief Committee's "attempts to monopolise [the] whole situation in America" would "lead to disaster."[124] But even as he strove to foil the Ryan–de Forest axis by securing a diplomatically sanctioned monopoly of his own, another, more formidable actor appeared on the scene. On November 1 the prestigious Rockefeller Foundation announced that it was launching a massive campaign to aid the suffering noncombatants of the war. Within a few days, it disclosed, a distinguished commission would sail for Europe to investigate needs and devise an appropriate program. Although the foundation did not confine its sphere of interest to any one country, the plight of Belgium figured uppermost in its press release. Quoting cables by Hoover and Page describing Belgium's need, the foundation announced the chartering of a ship to carry 4,000 tons of food supplies to the Belgian people.[125]

Instantly Hoover scented trouble and made a transparent effort to forfend it. In a cable to John D. Rockefeller, Jr., he immediately welcomed this "magnificent announcement"—and asked the foundation to pay the CRB's "incidental expenses." Such a contribution, he suggested, would amount to less than $5,000 a month, and it would enable the commission to state publicly that all donations were "clear of organization expenses." The entry of the Rockefeller behemoth onto the landscape, however, caused Hoover considerable uneasiness, and his cable showed it. He emphasized to the American philanthropist that the CRB had been given "international standing," including "assurance of support" from the British, Belgian, and French governments. (Just what support, he did not say.) Above all, he invited the Rockefeller Foundation to nominate a person to serve on the CRB "to represent your interests thereon" and ensure "efficient cooperation."[126] On the surface it was a generous gesture. But the effect would be to obtain the foundation's imprimatur for his commission—and before the Rockefeller investigative team reached Europe.

This was, in fact, precisely Hoover's objective. That same day (November 2), he induced Ambassador Page to cable a friend at the Rockefeller Foundation. Page asserted that the foundation's announcement that morning had unwittingly had a "discouraging effect" on the CRB's fund raising in London. Some donors, he reported, argued that there was no further need to give money. Some wondered whether the dispatch of Rockefeller investigators discredited the CRB. Therefore, said Page, he was asking the foundation *at the CRB's request* to notify the press that it was "working through the Commission" on Belgian matters. The effect of such an announcement, of course, would be to confer further legitimacy on Hoover's group and remove any hint that the foundation might be preparing to supplant it. Probably reflecting Hoover's fear of such a possibility, Page asserted flatly (and otherwise gratuitously) that the CRB was "the only channel that can distribute food in Belgium."[127]

Hoover's attempt to co-opt the Rockefeller Foundation failed. On November 5 the foundation joined instead with the Belgian Relief Committee, Ryan, and Havenith in effecting a fait accompli of their own. Under their plan, de Forest's committee in New York would henceforth centralize all American contributions for Belgian relief, while the foundation would furnish all ocean transportation for such goods. The Ryan–de Forest Supply Committee was superseded. Ignoring Hoover's cabled request of November 2 to join *his* organization, and instead bypassing him entirely, de Forest and the Rockefeller Foundation (represented by Starr Murphy), cabled directly to Ambassador Page:

> We are depending upon your arrangements for distribution. We are announcing above arrangements through Press. Shall keep you constantly informed and trust you will co-operate to prevent competitive solicitation and purchases. Any American committees organized at your instance should be instructed to remit money to New York Belgian Relief Committee and to contribute only in accordance with our public announcements, otherwise we may bid against ourselves.[128]

Three days later the Rockefeller Foundation released the details to the American press, again without consulting Herbert Hoover. Appealing jointly with de Forest and Havenith for the channeling of all American money and food to the Belgian Relief Committee, the foundation announced the opening of a terminal in New York harbor. All shipments consigned to the Belgian Relief Committee, it added, would be transported across the Atlantic free of charge (at least until December 31). As for distribution of this food inside Belgium, this, said the foundation, was being handled by "the American Committee in London, of which Ambassador Page is Chairman. . . ."[129]

At first glance the foundation's announcement might have seemed to be welcome news to Hoover. For days he had been lobbying strenuously with the Belgian and British governments for large transportation subsidies. Now the Rockefeller Foundation was generously offering to convey every relief cargo from America at its own expense.

To a suspicious Hoover, however, the foundation's decision betrayed a less laudable motive. Early November 6 the Murphy–de Forest cable arrived at the American embassy; Page promptly asked Hoover what reply was necessary.[130] As it happened, later that day an unforeseen cable left Brussels for London: Emile Francqui's announcement of the £600,000 loan to the CRB from the Belgian bankers.[131] Francqui's communication reached Hoover no later than November 7. It was a godsend. Seizing his opportunity, he decided at once to apply this sum solely to transportation expenses.[132] Armed with this unexpected weapon, he was ready to combat what he perceived as the Rockefeller–de Forest drive for hegemony in the United States.

Hoover's counterattack began on November 7. At his request Ambassador

Page dutifully dispatched a blunt cable to the Rockefeller Foundation, a cable in all likelihood ghostwritten by Hoover personally. Said Page to Murphy:

> The Commission for Belgian Relief requests me to say that your telegraph puts the Commission in embarrassment. They have received a European subsidy to cover entire cost transport not only from any interior point in the United States to Belgium but also from many other parts of the world. . . . If you arrange for transportation you will denude them of the sum you spend which they are able to command for the sole purpose of transportation.

Page insisted that the CRB was the "only organization" which would be recognized by the belligerents and the "only organization" which could "coordinate this work from all quarters of the globe." Shipping arrangements, he added, must be made in London. The Rockefeller Foundation should use its funds to purchase food only, and leave transportation matters to the CRB. The ambassador reiterated Hoover's willingness to appoint a Rockefeller representative to his commission. Indeed, the CRB, said he, would use any of its surplus money to buy food in America through the foundation "if you will cooperate." But he also added this: "It is vital to prevent overlapping that you should publicly announce that you are working in close cooperation with the Commission. . . ." In short, Hoover was willing to work with the Rockefeller Foundation if it coordinated its actions with *him*—and not the other way around.[133]

Having enlisted the pliable ambassador, Hoover stepped up the pressure from other directions. In a cable of his own to de Forest on November 7 he complained that the Rockefeller–de Forest initiative was "doing utmost damage [to] our arrangements."[134] That same day Millard Shaler, who was again in London, cabled separately to Ryan that the foundation was "seriously jeopardising [the] whole effort here." Only the CRB, said Shaler, could introduce and distribute food in Belgium. Moreover, it now possessed a "large subsidy for [the] sole purpose" of paying for the conveyance of foodstuffs. Shaler claimed (without explanation) that the Rockefeller plan would "destroy" much of this subsidy. It was therefore "absolutely necessary," he argued, that the foundation immediately announce that it would purchase and collect food *only*, leaving shipping to the CRB.[135] Shaler's blunt, insisting phrasing had a distinctly Hooverian sound.

For the next several days Hoover repeatedly used the Belgian bankers' loan to buttress his American position. On November 8 he informed the press that the CRB now had a fund enabling it to pay for any transportation charges throughout the world—an offer far more encompassing than Rockefeller's.[136] On November 12 he announced receipt of the $3,000,000 check.[137] Although neither of these press releases explicitly stated that the CRB *had* to use the loan money for transportation, Hoover's personal communications were unequivocal. To Havenith, de Forest, and the patron-ambassadors themselves, his assertion was unfailingly the same: the loan from Brussels was advanced for the "sole purpose" of funding transportation.[138] Furthermore, it must be expanded by "actual members" of the CRB "under control from here"—that is, London.[139]

In a private letter to Lindon Bates on November 13, Hoover explained the alleged background of the Belgian loan:

> You can take it as an absolute fact that the Rockefeller Foundation and De Forest have tried to get us out of this job. I put the situation frankly up to our Belgian Colleagues in Brussels, told them that these gentlemen in New York would be glad to take the job in charge and that we would be glad to retire from it, and they unanimously agreed that they, being business men of important order and having great responsibilities in this matter, could not consent to handing over what they considered the most essential link of the whole scheme into the hands of professional charity workers, and they agreed that if we would continue and would establish our own organisation they would see us through financially and would insist that we were the sole funnel through which everything must be done in Belgium. To back up their assurances they immediately put up $3,000,000 and placed it unreservedly to my credit here in London to be used for the sole purpose of the shipping and transportation side of our organisation.[140]

Two days later he added that the Belgian bankers were providing his financial backing on "personal ground[s]"—support that they "refuse [to] give to any institution," support that they insisted was "absolutely conditional [on] my remaining [in] full control [of] their funds."[141]

Hoover's private explanations to Bates of the Belgian loan negotiations were detailed, emphatic, and highly convenient to himself. But were they true? There is no evidence that Hoover had any contact—certainly no personal contact—with the Brussels bankers in the days before the loan was proffered; the actual negotiating had been done by Francqui. The loan in fact was approved on November 6, before the bankers could even have heard about the Rockefeller Foundation–de Forest cable of November 5, and probably before Hoover himself learned of it.[142] Nor is there any evidence that the bankers made their loan conditional upon Hoover's administration of the money. The terms of the transaction, as reported by Francqui to Hoover on November 7, contained only two stipulations—neither of which had anything to do with Hoover personally.[143] More importantly still, as Hoover's own correspondence with Francqui revealed, the $3,000,000 loan was *not* restricted to transportation at all.[144] Upon receipt of the check on November 12, Hoover informed Francqui that he and his colleagues had *decided* to apply the fund for this purpose and to announce that it had been given with this proviso, lest (he said) the loan discourage charitable giving.[145] There was no obligation, however, for him to use the loan in this fashion. On November 14—the day *after* his long apologia to Bates—Hoover wrote to Francqui: "It will greatly further our efforts and back up our campaign if you gentlemen [in Brussels] will also take the strong attitude that this money has been provided only for transportation purposes."[146] In other words, seven days after he first invoked the "sole purpose" argument, Hoover asked the Belgians to concur with this "stipulation" that he on his own initiative had invented and then attributed to them!

There is no better measure of Hoover's anxiety about developments in America during early November than his misrepresentation of the terms of the Belgian loan. Convinced (as he told Francqui) that the Rockefeller–de Forest combine was seeking to "over-tower all other effort" in the United States,[147] he fought back with every argument available, including the supposedly ironclad terms of his banking friends in Brussels. But why? Why was it so essential that he and he alone control the transportation of foodstuffs to Rotterdam? Such a consolidation no doubt made administrative sense. But clearly more than a desire for efficiency was agitating the CRB's chairman.

To Lindon Bates and various others Hoover offered this answer: a New York-based Belgian relief movement would "dry up" charitable giving in the American West.[148] There is "one critical fact evident from every quarter," he asserted to Bates, and this was that the "West and Middle West will not be dominated by or filter through" the Belgian Relief Committee or Rockefeller Foundation.[149] That was what de Forest wanted to do, Hoover told Brand Whitlock: "dominate the whole United States." The West and Midwest, he said, would have none of it.[150] Hoover presented no evidence for his claim (except a message apparently sent by William C. Edgar of the *Northwestern Miller*), and one suspects that his real concern went deeper. For if the Rockefeller Foundation and de Forest did become dominant in America, they could emerge as a rival.

This, then, was why control of the transportation was so crucial. Hoover did not mind if the Belgian Relief Committee and its ally confined themselves to purchasing and collecting food, as innumerable organizations were already doing across America. He in fact approved and encouraged such decentralized grass-roots efforts. But if any single agency in the United States should establish itself as the focal point for reception and transportation of food supplies, it would automatically (as Bates put it) become "paramount."[151] And this both men were determined to prevent—particularly since, according to Bates, de Forest's committee was inefficient, had "preempted [the] position," and had made people unaware of Hoover's "officially preeminent status."[152]

But Hoover's apprehension went deeper still. "Having a dreadful time with jealous organisations New York," he cabled to his wife on November 9.[153] Increasingly he became convinced that the Rockefeller Foundation and de Forest were scheming not only to control the *American* relief scene but (as he told Bates) "to get us out of this job" entirely.[154] To be sure, in their press release of November 8, the foundation and de Forest had explicitly stated that actual distribution of relief supplies was in the hands of the "American Committee in London."[155] Nevertheless, six days later Hoover accused the foundation of having "totally ignored our existence" in its "repeated press propaganda."[156] Hoover insisted that "if this problem is to be handled with any results it has got to be handled by one single organisation at this end," and he warned that if the Rockefeller Foundation or other American relief groups were permitted to "independently import foodstuffs into Belgium," there would "simply be chaos of the first order."[157] It was "absolutely fundamental," he declared to Whitlock, "that the control of all shipping should pass through our hands here in order that the stuff may arrive under our control in Belgium, and we, on Mr. Page's assurance, are taking the perhaps hoggish attitude that no cargo will be allowed into Belgium except through us."[158]

Hoover's suspicion that the Rockefeller Foundation planned to establish an independent relief channel into Belgium (and supplant his own) no doubt explained his repeated and otherwise irrelevant insistence that his was the only conduit into that country. This concern was almost certainly groundless. The foundation had in fact announced that it would transport American food to "the European port most accessible to Belgium"—in other words, the neutral city of Rotterdam.[159] From there, presumably, the CRB would take over. But Hoover's fears were not allayed by de Forest's condescending cables, or by the foundation's failure to respond promptly to his cable of November 2 and Page's of November 7, both offering cooperation (albeit on Hoover's terms). Nor could he be reassured by the departure for Europe on November 11 of a three-member team of Rockefeller Foundation investigators known as the War Relief Commission.[160] For him it betokened a plot by the aristocrats of the relief world to shunt him and his fellow volunteers aside.[161]

All of this, of course, revealed just how badly he wanted to head the Belgian relief.

The CRB chairman did not confine himself to private letters of complaint to friends and sympathetic ambassadors. On November 10 the *New York Times* carried a curious dispatch from London. The article reported "apprehension" that the "failure" of American relief agencies to "co-ordinate their work" with Hoover's group would result in "confusion" and "lack of efficiency." Specifically, the article cited the "danger" that various organizations in the United States would commit the "grave mistake" of trying to "direct the relief work" from there and create more than one agency for conveyance of food into Belgium. The article noted that the CRB had already secured a relief channel and had "official recognition" besides, including contributions from the British government. (In fact, the CRB had received only one such contribution—on the very day the *Times* story was filed.) Citing the Rockefeller Foundation by name, the report averred that "complications" would occur if the foundation tried now to "run its own system of supplying food" to Belgium.[162]

Now it was the foundation's turn to be angry. The *New York Times* article reached its offices the day after Page's cable announcing Hoover's transportation subsidy and his "embarrassment" at the Rockefeller actions. Later that day (November 10) Starr Murphy of the foundation sent Page a blistering reply:

> Utterly unable to understand statements in cables from your Committee and in London cables published in New York papers to the effect that Foundation is failing to act through your Committee. Have made no shipments and do not intend to make any shipments except through your Committee. Our published statements here have invariably made that clear and we have stated that yours is the only channel. Cannot understand how Hoover Committee could misunderstand our position or have allowed such impression to get into the Press. Effect on public most unfortunate. Your cables requested us to buy food and ship in neutral ships. We have [done so]. You have never asked us to discontinue or stated before to-day that your Committee was in position to provide transportation.

Murphy declared that if Page had the money to subsidize transportation, including the foundation's ships, the foundation would gladly "have you assume this burden." And in a stinging conclusion he asked: "Have you perfected any organisation for assembling material in this country, transporting to seaboard, chartering ships, and forwarding to Belgium, if so, apparently nobody here has heard of it."[163]

Murphy's cable reached London on November 11. The next day Hoover in reply emphatically denied that either he or any member of the CRB had made a statement to the press "indicating slightest misunderstanding with Rockefeller Foundation."[164] It is unlikely that Murphy believed him.[165]

Perhaps goaded by the foundation's rejoinder, Hoover promptly expressed his "keenest desire" to cooperate and renewed his ten-day-old offer to do so (on his conditions)—an offer still not directly acknowledged in New York.[166] But it was not apparent that such collaboration would have to occur in a new context. Claiming afterward that he could wait no longer for the foundation's response, Hoover on November 11 decided to "cut the Gordian Knot of these warring factions in America and get to it with our own organization."[167] That day he asked Lindon Bates to open a branch office of the CRB in New York to handle all "shipping and transportation questions" in the United States.

Hoover emphasized to his friend that he was not proposing to compete with any organizations already engaged in soliciting money for relief. He had "no desire whatever," he said, "to manage their business or take their credit." His only purpose was to offer such agencies "our machinery" for the free transport of their collected goods. As for the Rockefeller Foundation and the Belgian Relief Committee: "If these organisations wish to cooperate closely with us we shall be delighted. They cannot enter Belgium without us."[168]

Having thus thrown down the gauntlet to his competitors, Hoover promptly renewed his terms of cooperation. He offered the foundation the right to name a member of the CRB in London and New York; he offered de Forest a representative on its New York branch only.[169] But, he told Bates, any such appointees "must be in minority."[170] And to Bates he left no doubt as to who was to be in charge:

> . . . I wish to get it firmly in your head that the Ambassadors here consider that they are merely helpers to the Commission. The New York attitude that we are a sort of Office Boys collected together to carry out the Ambassadors' orders is somewhat mistaken as the repeated statement we receive from these gentlemen is that they are here to do our service and the whole responsibility of this business is up to us.[171]

Despite his professed willingness to collaborate with the Rockefeller Foundation and de Forest, and despite his statement to the press that his organization was cooperating "in a most cordial manner" with American relief agencies,[172] Hoover privately remained adamant and bitter. "You can take the following as an absolute fact," he told Bates,

> and that is, that I have been given the personal responsibility not only of this three million dollars [the Belgian bankers' loan] but also of another million which has been subscribed in cash and my colleagues and I have been appointed by the Belgian Government to receive and expend a further sum of five million dollars which they will supply to us in monthly instalments, this latter fund to be used for the purchase of food stuffs so as to ensure an even supply in case charity fails so that we now have a total of nine million dollars absolutely under our control and we do not propose to be dictated to by any little hole in the corner organisation in New York like De Forest's Committee which might secure five or six hundred dollars. We have done our level best to come to some co-operative basis with them, we have cabled them repeatedly, they make their announcements without consulting us as to co-ordinating policy and attempt to dictate to us right and left. . . . There is no place in the World where there is such unlimited snobbery as New York and because we happen to be common or garden people they do not seem to think we deserve even the treatment that is ordinarily meted out to servants.[173]

Writing to Brand Whitlock, he declared: ". . . I am afraid we shall need, in Western terms, a 'show down' at a pretty early date as to who is going to run the business."[174]

Hoover now moved decisively to solidify his American beachhead. He instructed his California friends to disregard the Rockefeller Foundation's offer to charter their relief ship and told them to adhere to their previous arrangements instead.[175] He requested Bates to ask the Belgian minister in Washington to purchase a cargo to be shipped via the CRB (and not the "New York bunch").[176] He sent the Rockefeller Foundation a cable asserting that the Belgian bankers' loan was "absolutely conditional" on his controlling it completely.[177] He let it be known that *his* transportation fund (unlike the foundation's) covered transportation expenses within the United States.[178] He offered to reimburse the foundation's costs for the three ships it had already chartered but insisted that shipping must be centralized in London, where it could be "infinitely better managed" than from New York. It was "folly," he cabled the foundation, for the two of them to compete in either food purchasing or transportation; it would only raise prices. The two functions must be separated, with "single control non competition and continuous regular flow foodstuffs."[179]

On November 19, the CRB's New York office at last opened under the direction of the commission's new vice-chairman, Lindon Bates. This office, he announced, would handle transportation only—and had the money to pay for it all. Bates informed the secretary of state that the CRB was "prepared to accept the full responsibility of transport."[180]

Meanwhile Hoover was maneuvering to detach Emanuel Havenith from his alliance with the relief groups in New York. As usual, he went at it relentlessly. At the end of October, through Carton de Wiart in London, he asked the Belgian government-in-exile to instruct Havenwith to transfer to the CRB all relief funds that he had collected in the United States since the outbreak of the war.[181] Not a man to rely upon a single form of persuasion when more than one was available, Hoover promptly asked J. F. Lucey to approach Francqui for support. As if this were not enough, the CRB chairman himself then asked Francqui to pressure his government. Havenith and his associates, said Hoover, must not only convert their resources into food and ship it to him. They must also communicate directly with his commission "as being the central body through which all matters must be handled."[182]

A few days later the Belgian foreign minister directed Havenith to come to an understanding with Hoover concerning the acquisition and transport of goods. But the Belgians, too, were showing signs of resistance. Instead of telling Havenith to surrender his accounts to the CRB, the foreign minister urged him to try to concentrate all relief funds in America in his *own* hands.[183] Unaware of (or perhaps indifferent to) this twist, Hoover immediately asked Havenith to "hold the funds at your disposal subject to our recommendation as to their application."[184]

It soon transpired that Havenith was not inclined to board the Hoover express. Instead of collaborating with the CRB, the minister allied himself with Ryan and de Forest and, a few days later, with the Rockefeller Foundation as well.[185] According to de Forest, Havenith had agreed to give his relief money to *him*.[186]

Hoover was furious. It is "absolutely necessary," he told Carton de Wiart, that the Belgian government instruct its diplomats abroad to communicate with the CRB and accept its advice about the disposal of their relief funds. It was "vital" for purposes of coordination that the CRB "have a direct say" over such money.[187] In a cable to J. F. Lucey for relay into Brussels. Hoover accused Havenith of favoring de Forest's "local New York Committee." The "only solution" to all these "jealousies" among various relief bodies in America, he said, was an immediate command to Havenith to place all the funds under his influence at our disposal and "accept absolute directions from us."[188]

Absolute, absolutely: how often these word sprang from Hoover's pen during these tense days. Blunt, demanding, and self-assured, he rarely seemed unsure about anything. But then, as he was discovering daily, the world of philanthropy was no place for the meek.

By mid-November the consequences of Havenith's untrammeled activism were becoming manifest. In fifteen states and numerous cities he and various Belgian consuls had established relief committees of their own under the patronage of the national Belgian Relief Fund, of which Havenith was president. In some cases these committees (complete with "territorial monopolies" granted by Havenith) postdated the governors' committees established in response to Hoover's appeal of November 2.[189] To further complicate matters, by mid-November Havenith was barely on speaking terms with de Forest, who, having secured Havenith's imprimatur for New York State, was busily creating new committees elsewhere without consulting him.[190]

Apparently intent upon creating a relief empire of his own, Havenith was in no mood to take orders from what he evidently saw as a johnny-come-lately in London. On November 16, the Belgian minister informed Bates that he had received no instructions from his government to cooperate with the CRB and that until his prior instructions were altered he could not and would not cooperate.[191] Apprised of this by cable, Hoover immediately contacted the Belgian minister of the interior, Paul Berryer, who was visiting London. This time the Belgian government fell in line. On October 18 Berryer cabled an unequivocal message to his legation in Washington. The Commission for Relief in Belgium was the "executive agent" of the Comité National, he said. Havenith should centralize transportation as much as possible in the hands of the CN and CRB. Every American group, he added, "especially Rockefeller," should purchase food with their funds and leave transport to Hoover.[192] Not surprisingly, Hoover ghostwrote this cablegram.[193]

A few days later Lindon Bates informed Hoover happily that Havenith's committees "will undoubtedly come into our system."[194] But the Belgian diplomat was not to be captured so easily, and suddenly a new reason arose for securing his blessing at once. Although Hoover had publicly announced that the CRB would cover all transportation costs for relief shipments from anywhere, he was simultaneously lobbying American railroad companies to grant him *free* carriage of foodstuffs in the United States.[195] Unfortunately, some companies had already granted this privilege to Havenith's committees and were unwilling to transfer the favor without his consent. And this the Belgian minister seemed in no hurry whatever to give.

With these critical negotiations stalled, Bates on November 23 demanded that Havenith receive "peremptory orders" to "recognize us."[196] Two days later—and probably not by coincidence—the Belgian minister of the interior instructed Havenith from London to give "most active co-operation" to the CRB and its American branch, especially to facilitate free rail service.[197] In a separate message to one of Havenith's colleagues Hoover asserted: "Our plan [of] getting free rail transport America depends on Havenith's cooperating immediately and entirely" with Bates.[198] A few days later, again no doubt at Hoover's instigation, Brand Whitlock cabled an appeal from Brussels for all American relief money to be consolidated in Hoover's hands. Any attempts to work "independently," he warned, would endanger "the whole enterprise."[199]

In the face of this Hoover-orchestrated barrage, the Belgian minister in Washington capitulated. "I am requesting railroads give you free transportation," he wired Bates on the twenty-sixth.[200] With this terse telegram Hoover's supremacy was confirmed. But Havenith and certain Belgians on de Forest's committee did not take kindly to this denouement, and their relations with the commission remained frosty. Hoover, for his part, became convinced that some of these Belgians were trying to impress their exiled government with their success at raising relief money in America.[201] In any case, by the end of November virtually every railroad in the United States had agreed to carry Belgian relief donations to the seaboard free of charge.[202]

The Rockefeller Foundation, de Forest, and Havenith were not the only parties in the United States who evinced an interest in Belgium in the autumn of 1914—and not the only ones who threatened Hoover's ascendancy. On October 23 Ambassador Page suggested to an American charity official that a single national relief committee for Belgium be established in America and headquartered in New York. Such a course, he argued, would eliminate duplication of effort.[203] About ten days later, apparently on his own initiative, Page asked President Wilson to appoint such a "central wholly American committee," through which "all organizations" might convey food to Hoover.[204] Wilson promptly asked his confidant, Colonel Edward M. House, to make the appropriate arrangements.[205]

But who would comprise such a committee? Sometime in late October the CRB's chairman in Brussels, Dannie Heineman, cabled a prominent New York banker, S. R. Bertron, and asked him to head Belgian relief activities in the United States. Heineman's invitation was unauthorized by Hoover, and Bates, upon learning of it, warned his friend to "watch Heineman . . .

and remember Benedict Arnold."[206] But now the genie was out of the bottle. After consulting Colonel House, Bertron petitioned President Wilson to initiate a comprehensive "National Subscription" by way of a public letter of appeal. Bertron suggested himself as the possible addressee of the letter.[207]

House's effort to integrate the existing fractious relief bodies into a single fund-raising organization soon foundered. "You have no idea," he wrote to Page, "of the jealousies that are engendered by any attempt to curtail authority and concentrate it in the hands of an effective few."[208] Nobody, it seemed, wanted a single national committee. Some feared that the appointment of such a group by the President would be a breach of America's neutrality in the war.[209] De Forest contended that such a move was too late and that all that was needed now was a small "Concentration and Supply Committee" in New York.[210] When Page's letter of October 23 calling for a central committee was printed in the New York Times on November 11, de Forest's group immediately announced that its Belgian relief work was already coordinated and that contributions should be sent directly to it.[211] Bertron, on the other hand, urged the president simply to name a one-man "centre of information," preferably in New York. It did not take much perspicuity to guess the identity of his candidate.[212]

Despite these storm signals, presidential intervention seemed imminent. On the morning of November 12 the Washington Post reported that Woodrow Wilson had decided the previous evening to appoint a "central committee" to "take charge of" all Belgian relief work in the United States and cooperate with "the international committee abroad."[213] In the nation's capital it was rumored that Hugh C. Wallace, a banker and Democratic Party activist, was the President's choice to chair the committee.[214] On the fourteenth, in fact, Wilson personally drafted (but did not issue) a press release appointing Wallace as the 'common agent" of the various relief parties.[215]

Watching these developments from afar, Hoover was deeply disturbed. The idea of establishing a national committee, he told William C. Edgar, was "a perfect nightmare." The only requirements for a cooperative effort, he insisted, were "a single transportation agency" in London and "local autonomy" in the United States.[216] Such an arrangement, he told a Rockefeller Foundation official—along with "the stimulation which we can give by direct appeal from the scene of action and the publicity" that the London headquarters could generate—would yield "a larger supply of foodstuffs than any other form of effort. . . ."[217]

Very possibly at Hoover's inspiration, Edgar telegraphed President Wilson on November 12. The central committee scheme, he declared, was utterly unnecessary and undesirable. The status quo was quite satisfactory, all relief agencies were working in "utmost harmony" under Hoover's direction, no "professional philanthropist" or "scientific charity expert" was necessary. "We need no direction save that of Mr. Hoover. . . ."[218] Meanwhile, on another front, the CRB's New York press agent, Will Irwin, was lobbying Colonel

House against the proposal. His argument: the American West would never send its goods to Europe through "a New York 'charity trust' bunch."[219]

In the end House's labors came to nothing; the President of the United States decided not to involve the government officially.[220] But scarcely had this squall subsided when a report reached London that the Wilson administration was under pressure to send a commission to Europe to take charge of Belgian relief work there! At once Hoover's chief patron protested to the President and secretary of state. Such a move, declared Ambassador Page, would be a "fatal mistake." It would disastrously interfere with "an exceptionally efficient group of trustworthy and devoted men" and would "throw the whole work into chaos." It would "openly discredit my judgment without cause." Page reported that the Allied governments were "wholly satisfied with Hoover's integrity, efficiency, and devotion," and that any change of personnel would "wholly upset" the existing diplomatic arrangements.[221]

The ambassador's abrupt, categorical language had a curiously Hooverian flavor. Had Hoover in fact ghostwritten this cable, too, for the obliging ambassador to dispatch? If so, it was probably not the first time—or the last.

The State Department immediately notified Page that the President was unaware of any movement to replace the CRB with an American government commission.[222] But the embattled engineer-turned-humanitarian could scarcely be blamed for suspecting the worst. Just a few days before, Secretary of State Bryan had notified Page that the department had received inquiries about Hoover. "We take it for granted," Bryan added somewhat ominously, "that you have examined" his "record and standing."[223] From Washington also came word that the secretary of the interior had asked a noted California mining attorney, Curtis Lindley, to prepare a report on Hoover for the President. From Lindley himself (an old friend) Hoover discovered that certain American army officers whom he had offended during his relief work for American travelers back in the summer had now initiated (in Hoover's words) a "campaign at Washington . . . directed against me."[224]

Hoover seethed with anger. This "seems to me the final limit in the business," he exclaimed, and he yearned for a chance to rebut whatever "mischief these fellows can think of."[225] To Lindley he poured out his feelings of righteous resentment:

> It is really difficult for me to take the matter seriously for I want nothing from the President or anyone else in this World except my good name amongst all men. As to my social standing, I have broken bread with lawyers, engineers, Earls, Viscounts, plain Knights, Chevaliers, Prime Ministers and Ex-Prime Ministers, Members of Parliament, United States Senators, Congressmen, Editors of Newspapers, miners, porters and sundry other persons. I regret that I have never organised these efforts into that Social Status which of course can only be evolved by close attention to the feminine side, shoots, hunts, balls, dinners and so forth. As you

know, on the contrary, I have preferred a modest existence and with my off-time devoted to literary work. I have but few things to parade to the World and the best of these was to be chosen by my countrymen here in London, where I have lived these many years, to represent them in this general World emergency. As to my financial status, I can manage to rub along on the professional income of about $100,000 per annum which I have assembled annually for some years and my colleagues in business even encourage me to draw a considerable part of it while I am at work for the Belgians, a testimony of their affection and a guarantee that I will pay my bills.

The source of the trouble, he went on, was the "wholly and absolutely useless" War Department contingent that had wasted at least $200,000 of government money during its "pretentious expedition" to save the "stranded Yankee" tourists in Europe during the summer. Hoover had been privately caustic in his criticisms of the army men's conduct. As a result, he admitted, he could hardly expect "favourable personal comment" from them now.[226]

But if Hoover was understandably vexed, he could only have been gratified by the backing that he now received from his friends. "You can tell inquirers," said Page to the secretary of state, "that Hoover is one of the most efficient and trustworthy and devoted men I have ever known and of the best financial rating."[227] Ben S. Allen cabled that in "character social and financial eminence . . . there is none in London in his class."[228] Clarence Graff, treasurer of the American Committee during the summer and a founder of the CRB, declared: "He is one of the finest characters I have ever known and in all this work is actuated solely by motives of pure philanthropy. His organizing ability approaches genius. . . ."[229] In America Lindley told the secretary of the interior that probably no mining engineer in the world had "larger experience and higher connections" than Hoover and that no American living abroad had "a higher financial, mining or social status."[230] The secretary himself stated that Hoover was "probably the greatest mining engineer that the world holds today."[231]

With encomiums like these sizzling into Washington, it was not likely that Hoover would be displaced. This incident, also, quickly passed.[232] But such episodes were not apt to strengthen his faith in human nature. Apparently the army officers had accused him of mishandling funds during his American tourist relief labors. Explaining afterward to Lindley the elaborate precautions that he had in fact taken at that time (including the hiring of a reputable accounting firm), Hoover remarked: "We have followed the same procedure in the work of this Belgian Relief Committee, and we are handling over $7,000,000 per month, and I expect some kind friend will ultimately bob up and charge us with having stolen a portion of it, as that seems to be the modern fate of all who are interested in humane work."[233]

No, Hoover would not be ousted, nor would he be "consolidated up" (to use his phrase) with anyone. But could he come to terms with the Rockefeller Foundation? In the week after he authorized Bates to set up an American branch of the CRB, both the foundation and de Forest showed signs of conciliation.[234] Insisting that the foundation wished to cooperate with Hoover, Starr Murphy pointed out that it had not known about his transportation plans before November 5 and hence had made its own arrangement with the Belgian Relief Committee. But if the CRB was now prepared to handle transportation effectively, the foundation had no wish to interfere. In fact, Murphy was willing to discontinue its shipping services as soon as the CRB was ready.[235]

Hoover was delighted. Claiming once again that it was "impossible" to "divert our special funds" to other purposes than transportation, the CRB chairman welcomed the coming accommodation.[236]

Privately the Rockefeller Foundation wondered whether Bates was a wise selection to supervise Hoover's operation in America—a sentiment shared by Ambassador Page. Although regarded as a brilliant engineer, Bates had been much less successful as a businessman, causing some of his prewar associates to lose substantial sums of money.[237] Hoover himself had spent much of the past two years rescuing his friend from several disastrous oil ventures.[238] Nevertheless, Bates was Hoover's man in America, and with him others must deal. On November 20 he, de Forest, and the Rockefeller Foundation finally reached a "modus vivendi": de Forest's committee would become the recognized Belgian relief collection agency for New York and the surrounding region only.[239]

In London the news was even better. That day the Rockefeller Foundation's War Relief Commission, headed by Dr. Wickliffe Rose, arrived in England. The next morning the three commissioners met Hoover and Page at the American embassy. For a time the conference went awkwardly, with an "aggrieved" Hoover complaining that the foundation had not "dignified him by answering or acknowledging a single communication." But after Rose admitted that the foundation had failed to respond adequately, the atmosphere improved. By the end of the nearly four-hour meeting the commissioners had been favorably impressed. Hoover "is evidently strong-headed," they noted, "and completely dominates his office but is willing to discuss."[240]

They soon were convinced of much more. He is "an engineer of large experience and of very unusual ability," Rose wrote to Murphy in New York.[241] "He is a man of most generous impulses" who, out of his own pocket, was supporting several young American mining engineers who had lost their jobs because of the war.[242] Ambassador Page told the commissioners that before making Hoover chairman of the CRB he had carefully investigated his credit and standing in London. The results had been "extremely favorable." The British government, he added, had made a similar investigation, with a similarly satisfactory outcome.[243]

If the War Relief Commission had any doubts about the integrity and efficiency of the CRB, they were quickly dispelled. "The London Committee is thoroughly established," Rose reported to New York. "It is doing the work well . . . and I see no necessity for any other even if it were possible."[244] Within three days of the commission's arrival Hoover told friends that it was "thoroughly in line with us" and that "a plan of thorough co-operation" was "practically settled."[245] According to Hoover, Rose and his colleagues had already recommended to their superiors that the Rockefeller Foundation subsidize the CRB to the extent of £100,000 a month if the CRB could raise £200,000 elsewhere. Hoover speedily used this offer as wedge in his unremitting effort to pry a subvention out of the British government.[246]

Back in New York at the end of November, the press announced the "coordination" of all Belgian relief efforts in the United States. As already arranged, the CRB would control transportation, while the Rockefeller–de Forest interests would gather supplies.[247] Within a few weeks, as Bates's organization was perfected, the Rockefeller Foundation closed its New York depot and withdrew from the transport business completely.[248] The foundation did not, however, abandon its solicitude for the hungry nation across the seas. By the end of December it had purchased nearly $1,000,000 in food supplies for the CRB's use—an enormous boon at a time when shipments were irregular and barely sufficient to meet the need.[249]

With the securing of the Rockefeller Foundation's seal of approval, the principal challenge—real or imagined—thus far to Hoover's preeminence in Belgian relief work disappeared. But what a wearing struggle it had been. To Lindon Bates's wife he declared in early December:

> The amount of small jealousy that exists around amongst the Belgians themselves and amongst Relief Committees and professional charity workers throughout the world, and the malice which they can all of them display at times is beyond belief. Were it not for the haunting picture in one's mind of all the long line of people standing outside the relief stations in Belgium, I would have thrown over the position long since.[250]

I I I

SUDDENLY, shortly before Christmas, another potentially menacing threat arose. In the United States the just-retired ambassador to France, Myron T. Herrick, announced plans to establish two "American Relief Clearing Houses" for assistance to the destitute noncombattants of Europe. As Herrick explained his conception, the U.S. Chamber of Commerce would appoint the organization's central committee, which would then supervise the collection of all funds in America and their distribution to the needy in Europe. Among other things, Herrick said, the clearinghouses would do "detailed work" in Belgium and France and would audit the accounts of various relief agencies lest any "confusion" or duplication occur that would "dim the honour and glory of the work." On December 16 the former ambassador discussed his intentions with President Wilson.[251]

Hoover immediately sensed danger. A former Republican governor of Ohio, Herrick was being touted as a presidential candidate in 1916, and more than one observer suspected that his "clearinghouse" scheme was an engine for his ambition. With his political allies and Chamber of Commerce friends (who could provide a ready-made national organization), and with the support of charity leaders like de Forest (who endorsed the plan), Herrick could be a powerful force indeed. When in mid-December Will Irwin (at Hoover's request) called on the politician-diplomat,Herrick and his associates suggested that the CRB amalgamate with *their* organization—as a subsidiary branch, of course. Irwin concluded that a politically motivated patronage machine was in the making.[252]

Fearful that Herrick might become a magnet for "our previously disturbing factors" (like de Forest), Hoover responded with a deft combination of carrot and stick. As with the Rockefeller Foundation in November, he first tried to lure his potential adversary into his orbit. To this end he asked Bates to invite Herrick to become an honorary chairman of the CRB, from which perch he could (in Hoover's honeyed words) "give the Commission the benefit of his advice and good judgment which we will all value most highly."[253] (Hoover did not really want to do this, he confided to Bates, unless it was necessary to quell Herrick's "agitation.")[254] To Herrick himself Hoover dispatched a long cablegram asserting that the CRB was the "only channel" for revictualing Belgium, that it was thoroughly organized and efficient, and that Herrick's attempted interposition of his clearinghouse threatened to cause the CRB "considerable embarrassment." This commission, Hoover warned, "must stand absolutely by itself."[255] Probably at Hoover's request the faithful Ambassador Page dispatched a cable to Herrick & Co. directing them (in Hoover's words) "to absolutely keep their hands and dogs off or there will be trouble."[256]

In the end "trouble" was averted. Herrick's American Relief Clearing House was established in Paris but with a sphere of interest that apparently excluded Belgium.[257] By mid-January Hoover considered that the threat was past.[258] The CRB, in Bates's word, was "impregnable."[259]

The weeks ahead were not devoid of sporadic aftershocks from the struggles of the autumn. Bates continued to fret about Havenith and de Forest; Colonel House, for one, came to feel that Bates was partly responsible for the continuing friction.[260] But the battle for leadership was now largely over, and Hoover was quietly triumphant. "I hear that Ryan is full of venom against me," he wrote to Bates in January, "because he says I schemed to become a member of this Commission and then did not continue him in the work."

The fact of the case is, that he failed to reply to every communication of mine with one exception, that he joined with de Forest—exactly the thing I did not want and then turned round an independent fund to make bargains with me instead of acting as the New York agent of the Committee. Furthermore, he ignored my repeated requests to ask you . . . to join with him and so forth and so forth. . . . I do not care what he thinks, and I am glad to be disassociated from him and all of his ilk and I could not have asked for the whole business to have turned out in a better manner than it has done which is chiefly due to your diplomatic capabilities at that end. I imagine that all the notoriety seeking charity world gets greener with envy every day, as this is now the greatest charity that the world has ever seen. . . .[261]

When Bates reported trouble in February with William C. Edgar, Hoover advised him not to worry: we can"hypnotise" Edgar if he travels to Europe, "and having taken his [cargo of] flour we can let him safely go back with a lot of thanks documents from the Belgians." As for the Belgian Relief Committee, Hoover was tough and unrepentant:

I do not wonder at all that the De Forest line contingent are sore, as they thought they could treat us like school-children, and have found that here has grown up the one organisation which is pointed to with satisfaction by all of the belligerent Powers, and with pride by all good-feeling Americans. They might have enjoyed considerable participation in it if they had played the game with us, but they themselves, by their own acts, put themselves out of court, and I am not at all sorry.

You can always bear in mind that the people who are going to control this Commission are the people who control the money and the people who control the international agreements, and that we have both of these things in our grip.[262]

The CRB chairman was right. By the early winter of 1915 fewer and fewer people needed to ask: "Who's Hoover?" Many powerful Americans and Belgians had coveted a piece of the Belgian relief pie; a forty-year-old mining engineer had outmaneuvered them all. Do not fear, he told a friend, "that there is any soul on earth who can jar me from this position."[263] The supreme command of "the most extensive relief enterprise ever undertaken"[264] was in one capable set of hands: his.

4

A Piratical, Benevolent State

I

LAUNCHING publicity, stimulating worldwide charity, pursuing governmental subsidies, creating a transportation monopoly, fending off interlopers and rivals: these were not the only problems that absorbed Hoover's energies during the frantic autumn of 1914. If only life had been so simple. . . .

It had not taken Hoover long to set up a functioning organization in London, nor Captain Lucey to do the same in Rotterdam.[1] But in Belgium, behind enemy lines, Yankee efficiency did not prevail so swiftly. Time and again Lucey protested at the absence of detailed instructions from Brussels. How should he apportion the cargoes that were beginning to arrive at Rotterdam? To which Belgian destinations should he send them, and by which canals? When would the Brussels office tell him what he needed to know?[2]

Emile Francqui pleaded with Hoover to understand the obstacles against which he and his associates struggled. No telephones, no domestic telegraph service, no use of the railways; no right to leave one's own community without a pass from the hated German army.

In a word, my dear Hoover, those living in one town in Belgium are as isolated from the inhabitants of another town, even if that town be only 20 Km. distant, as someone inhabiting the centre of Africa is from Europe. . . . Here, I repeat, there are nothing but continual and unforeseen troubles, inertia of every description, a chaos of difficulties paralysing everything.[3]

Under the terms of the October arrangements with the British and German governments, all food imported from Rotterdam was to be consigned to Brand Whitlock personally. Using his power of attorney, Whitlock delegated the power to receive these shipments to the three American consuls in Belgium and to various CRB representatives as they arrived.[4] In addition, Whitlock had the assistance of Dannie Heineman and William Hulse. Fortunately for the infant commission, Heineman spoke German fluently and was popular with the occupying authorities.[5]

As the first shipments of food began to cross into Belgium from Holland, the multiplying burdens of relief work threatened to overwhelm the Americans in Brussels. Negotiating continually with the Germans over passes and sundry permissions, and absorbed in almost daily conferences with the Comité National, neither Whitlock, Heineman, nor their colleagues had much time for organizational details.[6] On one occasion barges of food arriving in Brussels could not be unloaded because the skippers had no bills of lading. When the skippers called at the American legation for help, Whitlock himself had to go out in search of Heineman, only to discover that he was absent from his office. Finally the harassed diplomat visited Francqui and discussed procedures for releasing the barges. By the time the snarl had been resolved, at least half a day had been lost.[7]

Such confusion obviously could not persist. On November 23 Whitlock urgently requested the CRB to send over eight or ten young French-speaking Americans to assist in the work of the Brussels office. The commission's operation in Belgium, said Francqui to Hoover separately, could not be "absolutely efficient" until it had at least one "delegate" attached to each provincial committee of the Comité National.[8] Hoover, too, had reached the same conclusion. Early in November he had begun to recruit a "corps" of "young college men speaking French [and] used to roughing it" who could, he told Francqui, serve as "guardians" at various points in Belgium and facilitate communications throughout the country.[9] Privately he was convinced that Americans were more efficient executives than Belgians—a sentiment that Whitlock shared.[10]

The need for personnel to handle administrative chores was not the only reason for augmenting the CRB's staff inside Belgium. As independent neutrals, Americans would be freer to traverse the country than would the native population. Moreover, as foreigners exempt from coercion, Americans could negotiate unhesitatingly with local German commanders—something that Belgians naturally feared and loathed to do.[11] Above all, as representatives of an international humanitarian agency supported (albeit "unofficially") by the diplomats of two neutral governments, the CRB's resident representatives could help to protect the imported food from German seizure or interference—could ensure, in other words, that the Germans kept their promises.

But who, on such short notice, could be enlisted for such a delicate mission? As it happened, at this very moment a considerable number of American graduate students—including nearly one hundred Rhodes scholars—were enrolled at Oxford University.[12] With the aid of one of their members, Perrin Galpin, Hoover quickly recruited more than forty enthusiastic volunteers for service during the coming six-week Christmas recess; they were to be paid out-of-pocket expenses only.[13] On December 4 the first contingent left London—all having been duly exhorted to be neutral in every word and deed. By Christmas more than twenty-five "Yanks at Oxford" were working for the CRB throughout Belgium—acting (as one of them later put it) as "a sort of unofficial diplomatic corps representing the interests of the Commission."[14] During December also Hoover arranged to send twenty automobiles into Belgium for his staff and received permission to import the requisite gasoline.[15] The German military permitted the young Americans to travel freely.[16]

At the end of November Hoover himself made his first foray into Belgium.[17] It was an eerie journey. Preparing to board a neutral vessel at the English coast for the trip across the Channel to Rotterdam, he stood in line for three hours before being ordered to disrobe completely for a search. Arriving finally at the Dutch–Belgian frontier, he was stripped and searched again, this time by a German soldier, although he already held a German visa. As he passed through the stark barbed-wire fence that marked the border, he felt a peculiar sensation that he was entering "a land of imprisonment."[18]

Accompanied by the Rockefeller Foundation's three-member War Relief Commission, Hoover arrived in Brussels on Sunday afternoon, November 29, and plunged at once into conferences at the American legation.[19] For the next three days he thrashed out problems of organization and finance with Whitlock, Heineman, Shaler, Francqui, and others, while the Rockefeller representatives investigated, questioned, examined, and cross-examined—and grew more supportive and impressed.[20] Observing Hoover for the first time, Whitlock found him to be just as Francqui had described him: "the type of American business man, a face somewhat brutal, *fruste* [rough, unpolished], very direct, positive, able, speaks little but everything he tells counts."[21]

Hoover remained in Brussels until December 2.[22] Before his departure the Comité National convened a formal meeting at the headquarters of the Société Générale. There, in the resplendent conference room adorned by marble busts of King Albert and Queen Elizabeth and by portraits of monarchs past, Hoover found himself and his country eulogized by Ernest Solvay. His voice quavering with emotion, the great Belgian industrialist thanked the generous and practical people across the sea who were responding so nobly to the plight of his little nation. Rising in tribute also, Francqui acclaimed Hoover as "a man of great heart" and "great activity" who had succeeded in just a few weeks in assuring Belgium enough food to last three months. Thanks to

Hoover's tireless devotion, said Francqui, the people could "face the future without excessive anxiety."[23]

It was probably not the fulsome Gallic tributes that lingered in Hoover's mind as he returned through the lines to London. For now he knew—more than words and statistics could ever tell him—what relief in Belgium meant. The country, he later wrote, seemed to be in a state of "suspended animation." No one smiled. No children played. At every street corner in Brussels stood a helmeted, hobnail-booted soldier of the conquering German army. In Antwerp, near which he passed on his journey in, burned-out buildings and houses stood "gaunt and naked" against the sky. In Louvain he saw remnants of a magnificent university library that had been willfully and ruthlessly destroyed.[24]

But most haunting of all were the faces: of men and women without work, of mothers with babies in their arms waiting in line for a ration. In Brussels alone, by early December, 218,000 adults—more than one-third of the city's population—were receiving their food without payment at 137 canteens. Here, clutching the ration cards issued by their communal authorities, the destitute queued up for their daily dispensation of coffee, soup, and bread, prepared for them ahead of time at fourteen vast municipal kitchens.[25] Visiting one such canteen on the cold, gray morning of December 1, Hoover and Whitlock watched as hundreds of the poor—some in wooden shoes—stood uncomplainingly in the rain, shivering, grasping bowls and pitchers and the precious little cards that would guarantee them a meal. Upon receiving his or her allotment, each would pause, bow, and utter a single word: *"Merci."* Tears welling in his eyes, Whitlock had to look away. Hoover, too, averted his gaze and silently stared into the distance.[26]

The stoicism of the impoverished and the dedicated efficiency of the relief workers could not, however, erase one fact that weighed on Hoover's mind as he drove toward the Dutch frontier. Despite the first arrivals of food from abroad, despite Francqui's brave words about the future, the situation inside Belgium was grave. In Brussels only five days' supply of flour was left; in Liège and certain other cities, barely half that amount.[27] Worse still, because of the six-to-eight-week interval between the chartering of faraway relief ships and the delivery of their cargoes at Rotterdam, the flow of food into Belgium in December would be minimal. After Christmas the CRB's shipments would become regular and adequate. But during the two or three weeks *before* Christmas there would be a frightening "hiatus."[28]

Where could he turn to supply the looming deficiency? Not a government in Europe allowed the export of food from its borders, yet help from America would not arrive in time. With a sense of urgency bordering on desperation, Hoover stopped at the Hague on his trip back to Rotterdam and appealed to the Dutch foreign minister for an emergency loan of 10,000 tons of flour, to be replaced by the CRB from its incoming cargoes later on. Four days later the Dutch government assented.[29] But it was not enough.

On December 3 Hoover returned to London, where he was met by his wife Lou, who had just arrived from the United States.[30] For the next half-year they were seldom parted. Young Herbert and Allan, however, were not with her. They had remained in California—Allan with his grandparents, Herbert with family friends—to attend school.[31] Hoover could not know it, but he would not see his boys for another eleven months.

Even as he waited for an answer from the Dutch government, the CRB chairman sought assistance elsewhere. Before making his quick trip to the continent, he had attempted to borrow from the British government 20,000 tons of Canadian flour currently being stored in England. His application had been flatly rejected. Now, with the specter of starvation looming more starkly than ever, he resolved to try again. The morning after returning to London, he went with a British friend to see Charles Masterman, a member of the British Cabinet. Sympathetic to Hoover's cause, Masterman immediately arranged for him to call upon a fellow Cabinet minister, Sir Herbert Samuel. Entirely in accord with his American supplicant, Samuel set up an appointment with Prime Minister Asquith. That very afternoon Hoover entered Asquith's office.

The conversation did not begin auspiciously. According to Hoover, the prime minister was quite unsympathetic to the CRB's cause. It was not the legal or moral obligation of the British to feed the Belgians, he declared, but that of the German invaders. Indeed, it was contrary to British interests that Germany should be thus relieved of her responsibility—and a "monstrous idea" that the British should send in food "simply to fill the vacuum created by German requisitions." But Hoover had come too far to yield to a prime minister's objections. Instead (as he recalled afterward in a memorandum) he unleashed a barrage of his own:

> With some abruptness, I pointed out that the civil population had been brought to this pass through the action of the British [blockade]; that if the British claim that they were fighting the war on behalf of Belgium were true, they would be unable to substantiate this claim in history if they allowed, or prevented others from saving, the Belgian population from decimation by starvation or through slaughter arising out of starvation riots; that although the British Government refuse to give us assistance, they do not dare to put an end to our shipment of foodstuffs from America into Belgium if they wished to hold one atom of American public esteem; that disregarding right or wrong obligations of the Germans (which obligation I told them the Germans entirely denied) that I was convinced that the Germans would not feed the Belgians, and that they must certainly starve unless the activities of this Commission continued. . . .

As for the Canadian flour, Hoover told Asquith "that I was not asking the British Government to give one penny, I was simply asking permission to purchase 20,000 tons of flour for which we would pay, or we would borrow it and undertake to replace it as fast as the ships could arrive from Canada; that I knew the 20,000 tons of flour was in the warehouses, that it was not intended to use it [in England] until April, and that there was ample time to replace it in full before that time provided the British Fleet maintained control of the sea."

Taken aback by Hoover's aggressiveness, Asquith remarked that it was not customary for him to be addressed in this tone. At once Hoover (so he recorded) "expressed regret and apologised on the ground that my emotion for the results which must ensue from a negative reply on his part, was sufficient to justify any tone which I had used." It did not sound like the most penitent of confessions.[32]

Hoover's encounter with Asquith may have been even more dramatic than this. Less than three weeks later he gave Brand Whitlock another account of his interview, an account that Whitlock promptly recorded in his diary. According to this version, before meeting the prime minister Hoover wrote a letter to Will Irwin in New York exposing the growing British opposition to the relief on military grounds and concluding: "Hold this until I send a cablegram releasing it, then blow the gaff, and let the work of revictualing go up in a loud report that shall resound over the world to England's detriment." Taking a copy of this letter into his interview with Asquith, Hoover remarked that England had "America's sympathy only because America feels pity for the suffering Belgians." Then, producing the letter to Irwin, Hoover said, "I will send a telegram at once, and tomorrow morning the last vestige of pity for England in America will disappear. Do you want me to do it?" Asquith replied that he was not used to being talked to in this way but eventually added: "You told me you were no diplomat, but I think you are an excellent one, only your methods are not diplomatic."[33]

Whitlock's account may have been embellished—perhaps by Whitlock himself, with his novelist's love of a good story, or perhaps by Hoover, a talented raconteur. (No copy of Hoover's alleged letter to Irwin has been located.) Nevertheless, by his own admission Hoover had told Asquith that the British did not dare to interdict the flow of American foodstuffs into Belgium if they wished to retain "one atom of American public esteem." He had not hesitated to brandish his ultimate weapon: "the club of public opinion."

And it worked. Although Asquith continued to oppose the flour shipment in principle, he informed Hoover that he would acquiesce if the president of the Board of Trade gave his consent; the president was the Cabinet minister responsible for Great Britain's food supply.[34] Conferring immediately afterward with Samuel and Masterman, Hoover was told not to become discouraged but "to make my case stronger in every influential quarter which I could command."[35] Perhaps in consequence, that very day he issued a lengthy report on his trip to Belgium to the American press. "It is difficult to state the position of the civil population of Belgium without becoming hysterical," he declared. Seven million people were "surrounded by a ring of steel and utterly unable by any conceivable effort of their own to save themselves."[36]

On Monday, December 7, at Samuel's request, Hoover appeared before the British Cabinet's committee on food supplies. Among those present were the president of the Board of Trade and the home secretary. The chairman of the CRB was given ten minutes to make his case. A masterful expositor in such small-group situations, Hoover invoked three arguments. He claimed that the relief was actually militarily beneficial to Britain, since it encouraged the Belgians in their passive resistance to their conqueror. He asserted that, having gone to war for Belgium, England had a humanitarian duty to prevent "what might be the greatest tragedy of the War." Perhaps most persuasively of all, he stated that if the CRB were obliged to admit publicly that it had received no British support, he "feared for the effect it would produce" on American attitudes "toward this War." A few minutes later the Cabinet committee agreed to loan the Canadian flour.[37]

So the Belgians would not starve, at least not before Christmas. But while Hoover was relieved (as he told a friend) from "the deepest gloom,"[38] he could feel no genuine elation. The British posture toward his relief project was hardening. Hoover had sensed the change immediately upon his return from Brussels.[39] To the British Cabinet the responsibility for Belgium's misery lay squarely with the Germans. After all, they had invaded the country and had taken over its government. It was consequently their obligation to feed the civil population.[40] By permitting foodstuffs to pass into enemy-occupied territory, the British, in their view, were not only subverting their own naval blockade but lifting a burden on their adversary besides.[41] Why, the British wondered, should they allow fresh food into Belgium while the German army was confiscating native foodstuffs and had given no promise that it would cease?[42] Were not the British in effect providing their foes with foodstuffs by succoring 7,000,000 people whom Germany would otherwise have had to feed out of her own diminishing supplies? At the War Office Lord Kitchener (according to Hoover) even suggested that if the Belgians were allowed to starve it might help the Allies, since the Belgians would rise in revolt and force the Germans to divert troops from the front.[43]

Alarmed by this mounting antipathy, Hoover did his best to appease it. He denied repeatedly that the Germans were obstructing the relief or obtaining any of the imported foodstuffs.[44] "Not one mouthful has gone down a German throat yet," he said in mid-December.[45] "Not one loaf of bread or one spoonful of salt that we have introduced has been taken by the military."[46] (About the *native* foodstuffs, however, he was publicly silent.) Hoover also contended that the provisioning of Belgium actually benefited the Allied armies. Bear in mind, he told a British friend, that the civil population of Belgium

is engaged upon a strike, refusing the operation of Railways, arsenals, mines and factories, that the provision of foodstuffs by the Commission enables them to continue this strike and that this incommodates the Germans to the extent of maintaining troops in the country and the loss of a large quantity of material which they could otherwise obtain.

In fact, added Hoover (ever resourceful in argument and still anxious to get a subsidy from the Allied governments), "the £1,000,000 per month which this Commission costs would be the cheapest military operation that Great Britain has yet made."[47]

Again and again the CRB's leader asserted that, whatever the British might say or think about international law and obligation, Germany herself would never feed the Belgians. German public opinion, he reported, was too embittered at the Belgians for thwarting their plan for a quick military victory, and for continuing to resist now, ever to undertake to feed them, particularly when Germany's own food supply (and national existence) might thus be jeopardized. In German eyes the Belgians' continuing passive resistance helped the Allies; hence the Allies should support the Belgian population. Furthermore, said Hoover, the Germans insisted that it was not *their* fault that Belgium faced calamity; it was the fault of the Allied naval blockade. Before the war Belgium had regularly imported most of its food from abroad. As far as the Germans were concerned, it was perfectly free to do so again—if the British fleet would permit it. It was not *our* armed forces, said the Germans, that prevented Belgium from obtaining its necessities from overseas.[48]

In forcefully conveying the German viewpoint to the British, Hoover made it clear that he was not acting as an advocate.[49] And in his public pronouncements he was careful to summarize both belligerents' points of view.[50] But the trouble, he told an American audience in mid-December, was that by the time the argument about moral responsibility for feeding Belgium had been settled, the Belgians themselves would have starved. While Europeans argued endlessly about right and wrong, he said, "seven millions of humanity" were "already in the hoppers ready to pass between these two gigantic millstones." That, for Hoover, was sufficient reason for Americans to act.[51]

As usual, the CRB chairman argued his case with ingenuity. He issued a powerfully written humanitarian appeal to British and American newspapers.[52] He offered a comprehensive defense of the CRB before the American Luncheon Club in London on December 18; Ambassador Page introduced him. Except for speeches at mining company meetings and talks before the student body at Stanford University, it was probably the first public address of his life, and it was copiously reported in the press.[53] Privately, he warned a prominent British earl that the "English people cannot afford to have the question of responsibility in case of failure on the part of this Commission through lack of resources, put up to the judgment of the neutral world."[54]

But Hoover knew that he could not rely on humanitarian appeals alone. If the hardheaded objections of the British military were to be overcome, he must win more cooperation from the Germans. On December 5, therefore—

one day after his interview with the British prime minister—he asked the American ambassador to Berlin, James Gerard, to persuade the Germans to leave the remaining native Belgian food sources alone. After all, Hoover said, "it must be vital to the Germans that we should continue this work, and if they could only view the matter from an enlightened position, I feel sure that the good feeling of the German people would cause them to order a complete cessation of local requisitions."[55]

But Hoover did not stop there. About a week before, he had cabled Gerard to ask the German government for nothing less than a monthly subsidy of 5,000,000 marks—an amount equal to one-quarter of his need. Not only would such a grant quell criticism of Germany's attitude toward the Belgian poor, he argued; it would compel Great Britain and France to follow suit.[56] Then his financial woes would be over.

In his letter to Gerard on December 5 Hoover renewed his request. Once again he invoked the carrot (and stick) of American public opinion. If the Germans would announce (he said) that they would contribute their share to saving the poor people of Belgium, much American antipathy toward them would dissipate.

All of the destruction in Belgium and the levying of food-supplies for the support of troops can be defended as a war measure, but to allow these people to starve while under their material control will raise a storm in the neutral world fifty times the volume of that which has already been created by any local destruction. It is my belief that the belligerent nation which refuses to participate in the succor of these people will yet have to carry the brand of Cain as their murderers. On the other hand, any kindness held out to them in this time of dire necessity will bring with itself credit which in after history will wipe out nine-tenths of the charges of ruthlessness in war.[57]

The Germans' reply to this mix of warnings and blandishments did not come for nearly a month. Meanwhile British dismay at the Belgian relief began to take disturbing forms—or so it appeared to Hoover. By mid-December the CRB had chartered a fleet of more than thirty vessels to transport its cargoes to Rotterdam. Unfortunately, the British government insisted that all of them be of neutral registry—a requirement that was becoming increasingly onerous.[58]

On November 5, therefore, Hoover asked Sir Edward Grey for permission to use British vessels in his work. The foreign secretary made no commitment but surmised that his government's decision would hinge on whether the Germans promised not to molest such ships.[59] On November 23, following Hoover's inquiry through diplomatic channels, the German government duly agreed to the British condition but suggested that these nonneutral craft carry appropriate documentation of their purpose.[60]

And so began another facet of the commission's ever more complicated labors. Every relief ship sailing from America had to receive an American customs certificate describing its cargo and destination, a permit issued by the German ambassador in Washington, a safe conduct pass from a German consul at the port of embarkation, and a pass from a British consul as well.[61] In addition, the vessels were required to fly large white flags with red letters reading "Commission Belgium Relief Rotterdam" and long banners with similar markings attached to the vessels' sides.[62] In this way the CRB's fleet might hope to run the gauntlet of warships and submarines that lurked in the Atlantic, the English Channel, and the North Sea.

Barely had Hoover effected these arrangements when an unexpected cataclysm struck. On December 2 the British Admiralty issued a circular urging British shipowners not to carry food cargoes to Holland. Such voyages, it warned, were not covered by the government's insurance scheme.[63] Convinced that this pronouncement was a deliberate assault on his relief work by that "sanctuary of British militarists" (as he later called the Admiralty), Hoover emphatically protested.[64] Clarifying its policy, the Admiralty quickly announced that its circular was not intended to apply to ships in the CRB's employ. Nevertheless, it refused to extend government insurance coverage to any such British-registered vessels.[65]

Inadvertent or otherwise, the effect of the Admiralty's circular was devastating. At every British port, transportation charges and private insurance premiums for sailings to Rotterdam instantly skyrocketed. Already strapped for funds, the CRB now faced an unforeseen expense of £30,000–40,000 per month. Even at the new exorbitant rates few vessels were available for service; fear had overwhelmed self-interest among the panicky shipowners. As a result, at the very moment in December when Belgium's food reserves were at their nadir, it was practically impossible for the commission to secure cross-Channel shipping.[66]

Hoover swiftly moved to overturn the Admiralty's ruling; as always he found ways to bring pressure to bear. On December 8 he asked the Belgian government-in-exile to approach the British government with a proposal. Hoover wanted the Belgians to promise to indemnify the British for any loss of British-owned ships on CRB business between England and Rotterdam—provided that the British government extend its insurance plan to such vessels.[67] But Hoover was not content to let the wheels of diplomacy turn at their own deliberate pace. Just two days later he notified a British Cabinet minister that the Belgians *had agreed* to make this guarantee. He thereupon asked the British to do the rest.[68]

Hoover's report was no doubt of interest to the Cabinet official. But was it, at this point, correct? It is not clear that the Belgian government had yet assented to the overture that Hoover had just imputed to it. If not, he was very possibly perpetrating a bluff.[69] If the British government now acquiesced in the offer on the assumption that the Belgians had actually made it, it would be difficult for the Belgians to disavow their "commitment" when they discovered that the British had already accepted it! As for Hoover, if challenged he could always plead misunderstanding or forgivable overzealousness in a righteous and struggling cause.

In any case, on December 19 the harried British government yielded and accorded Hoover the insurance arrangement he sought; £30,000 a month,he said, was thereby saved.[70] The Admiralty had been forced to retreat. A few days later the German government promised not to molest British-owned CRB vessels on their return voyages from Rotterdam.[71] The shipping crisis of December was over.

On the matter of finances, however, the British were far less accommodating. By December 1 Hoover still had received no answer to his pleas of November 5 and 25 for a substantial monthly subsidy. As the days of December passed, it became increasingly evident that His Majesty's Government was not at all disposed to oblige him—and certainly not while the Germans continued to seize native supplies inside Belgium.[72] When the Cabinet met on December 4 it did not explicitly reject Hoover's request. But a friendly minister told him afterward that if he pressed for a formal response now it would surely be negative. Hoover prudently dropped his petition—for the moment—and waited for the Germans to respond to his similar appeal through Ambassador Gerard.[73]

In the meantime the CRB chairman worked feverishly to obtain financial support elsewhere. By early December the Comité National had accumulated a steadily increasing fund of money from the sale of food rations to those Belgians who could still afford to pay (at this point, 80% of the population). Unfortunately for Hoover, under the circumstances of the war none of this money was transferable to the world outside. How, he wondered, could he liquefy these unexportable assets? In late November and early December the CRB, CN, and the Belgian government-in-exile worked out a simple but ingenious exchange scheme. Under its terms the Belgian government would furnish the CRB a monthly subsidy in London. In return the Comité National would take an equivalent amount from its food sale receipts inside Belgium and distribute this sum as salaries and pensions to government employees, retired civil servants, soldiers' wives, the elderly, and others to whom the exiled government owed money. In this way Hoover would obtain cash in London for food purchases, the Belgian government would fulfill its obligations, and at least some Belgian citizens would thereby be kept off the "soup" lines.[74] Through the American legation in Brussels Hoover quickly ascertained that the German administration in Belgium had no objection to the plan.[75]

But where was the enfeebled Belgian government to find the money with which to pay Hoover in London? Exiled at Le Havre, deprived of its national tax base, it was almost totally dependent on loans from its allies. Furthermore, in early December Hoover discovered that the British government had refused to lend the Belgians money for relief purposes.[76] Nevertheless, early in January the Belgian government somehow scraped up a first monthly installment of £1,000,000 for the London account of the Commission for Relief in Belgium.[77] Some of this money may have come from the British *sub rosa*.[78] But whatever the source, Hoover knew that this latest expedient could not succeed for long unless he opened the gates to the British and French treasuries. And *that* depended, more than ever, on the Germans.[79]

While Hoover waited for word from Berlin, the burdens of managing the CRB continued unremittingly. "You will scarcely realise the volume of labour which is entailed upon this office here" in London, he told Brand Whitlock. This "is one of the largest enterprises in this city."[80] But as Hoover was learning daily, the relief "business" was rarely routine. In the last days of 1914 still another problem rose to vex him.

In the three weeks since his trip to Brussels at the end of November, the CRB's internal difficulties on the continent had deepened. In Rotterdam J. F. Lucey had not only shipped food into parts of Belgium without consulting the Brussels office but had even telegraphed the German governor-general directly at one point, ignoring Whitlock entirely.[81] On another occasion, when he had learned of a shortage of salt in a certain Belgian province, Lucey had promptly smuggled two tons of salt across the Dutch border, despite Dutch law to the contrary.[82] Perhaps most seriously of all, when he had heard about the impending shortfall in food shipments into Belgium in mid-December, and the consequent threat of famine and violence, Lucey, again without consulting anyone, had borrowed the needed flour from the German army. Hoover had managed to assuage British sensitivity about this act of unorthodoxy, but when Ambassador Page had heard about it, he had told Hoover, "You will be the death of me yet."[83]

Hoover admired men of initiative and was not afraid to take chances himself, but Lucey's unconventional management style disconcerted even him. When Whitlock pleaded with the CRB chairman to do something about the Rotterdam office,[84] Hoover had to admit that Lucey, although a man of great executive ability, was "a bull-in-a-china-shop . . . [who] seems to have overstepped every boundary I endeavoured to trace around him with regard to non-interference in Belgium."[85] On December 14 Hoover informed Whitlock that he hoped to visit Belgium shortly to develop "a more systematic organisation of our whole problem there."[86]

For the harried Whitlock it could hardly be too soon. For in Brussels, too, the situation was deteriorating. At the time of his visit to Belgium Hoover had brought in an American named Jarvis Bell to "take charge" of the CRB's Brussels headquarters. It was hoped that he could thereby relieve Dannie Heineman of some of the administrative detail. Instead, Bell and Heineman had quarreled bitterly over control of the office, with Bell (according to Whitlock) attempting to oust Heineman completely, and Heineman "loth to recognize any authority other than his own." To Whitlock it seemed that

Heineman, as one of the principal founders of the relief movement inside Belgium, should not be abruptly dumped from an enterprise that in significant measure was his creation. Furthermore, with his ability to get along with the Germans, he was too valuable an asset to lose.[87]

By mid-December Bell and Heineman were irreconcilable antagonists, and Whitlock was driven to request that Bell be recalled. "By some sad fate," the American minister remarked, "everyone who comes in here feels that he must assume command of the entire situation, oust everybody from all authority, and establish as it were, a government of occupation, possibly the result of a conspicuous example before them."[88] It was not the last occasion he would have to express such sentiments.

The confusion and friction at the Belgian head office soon generated predictable consequences. Arriving in Brussels for their assignments, the first Rhodes scholars received few instructions other than a general admonition to be neutral. But what, precisely, were they supposed to *do* in the provinces? No one at headquarters seemed to know. Were they to be transport managers, inspectors, diplomatic troubleshooters? Where did their responsibilities end and those of the Comité National begin? Scattering into the field, the graduate students eagerly set about supervising communal food distribution, inspecting canals, organizing committees, and doing whatever seemed necessary to facilitate the flow of nourishment to the Belgians. But uncoordinated energy was no substitute for unity and clarity of purpose.[89]

Worse yet, the American legation staff in Brussels quickly concluded that with some distinguished exceptions the recruitment of Rhodes scholars had been a mistake. Less than two weeks after the first contingent's arrival, Whitlock asked Hoover to stop sending over "such young and inexperienced men." Too many, he said, lacked maturity and discretion. "They . . . have not yet passed the stage where they know better than anyone else just how things should be done."[90] One volunteer told Whitlock that God had called him to go to Belgium; Whitlock decided "to obtain, through Hoover's intercession, a call for him to go back."[91] We cannot risk filling the country, he stated, with "a lot of impulsive, ignorant young doctors of Philosophy."[92]

Whitlock's deputy, Hugh Gibson, was even more exasperated. These volunteers are driving us "nearly frantic," he exclaimed. "We already have too many 'leaders of men' who are ready to assume the entire charge, not only of the distribution of food, but of our international relations as well." Most of the Rhodes scholars, he fumed, "are half-baked kids who ought not to be allowed to leave school."[93]

Nor were American diplomats the only ones to be disturbed. According to Gibson, the German army was "distinctly annoyed at the type of man we are sending in and their behaviour here."[94] Nor were the Belgians, some of whom tended to regard the CRB as a mere purchasing agent of the Comité National, overjoyed by these energetic young foreigners intervening in all directions and scooting hither and yon in their automobiles.[95]

It was not without justification, then, that one American volunteer later described the Belgian branch of the CRB in December 1914 as "an organization without any."[96] By mid-month Hoover knew that he had to act fast.

On December 20, accompanied by his wife, the commission's chairman left London for Brussels.[97] In a way it was a trip like those of his prewar mining days, when he had spent Christmases in places like Australia, China, and even the high seas. But this time his holiday spirit was muted. On Christmas Eve the Hoovers attended dinner at the American legation in Brussels; not even the mistletoe made the season seem real.[98] In one of the government office buildings the German had placed Christmas trees at every window. Hoover commented dryly that they should have been decorated with bayonets.[99]

The CRB's chief officer lost no time in imposing order on his branch office. Whitlock was delighted and relieved. "I admire this man Hoover," he wrote, "who has a genius for organization and for getting things done, and beneath all, with his great intelligence, he has a wonderful human heart."[100] In a letter afterward to a friend in America, Hoover confided what he had done:

> We have had great trials over [on] this side through the conduct and attitude of the Belgian Committee and part of our Commission who were in control in Brussels. Things got on to such a footing, that it was brought home to me, that unless an immediate revolution took place we might afford one of the greatest scandals of the War and be in a position that would damn the balance of our lives. After many sleepless nights, I went to Belgium and found everybody dead against me. I stayed there a little over two weeks, and as a result, I first brought Whitlock to my side within twenty minutes—I had the Belgians my way in 24 hours and in a week the Americans in control were either bashed into line or were eating out of my hand.[101]

In short order Hoover moved the CRB's Brussels headquarters out of Heineman's office and into separate facilities at 66, rue des Colonies. The master executive also "insisted" (he said) on nominating a Belgian of his personal acquaintance to "the executive administration of the Comité National." This Belgian, Chevalier Emmanuel de Wouters d'Oplinter, became the liaison between the CN and the CRB. Hoover had known de Wouters since 1901, when they had managed the Kaiping coal mines in China for several months before the arrival of Francqui.[102] As in London and New York, so, too, in Brussels: wherever possible Hoover was staffing his organization with old friends whom he could trust and perhaps dominate.

In addition, Hoover prepared a lengthy statement of the functions of the CRB inside Belgium. Among other things, he stipulated that its delegates be attached to every provincial committee of the Comité National and that CRB men (not Belgians) have "absolute charge" of imported food until it was ready for distribution at the communal level. Only then would the foodstuffs cease to be commission property; only in this way could the patron-ambassadors' responsibility for safeguarding the imports be fulfilled.[103]

Despite this broad definition of authority, Hoover did not intend that his few dozen agents inside Belgium should actually handle food shipments or monetary receipts. Instead, in his words, they would act as "controlling and inspecting managers of 100 grocery stores per man"—as inspectors, really, "to see that the Belgians did the job properly and honestly."[104] Hoover also dispatched representatives of the CRB's accounting firm to audit the books of the Comité National. In short, he told a friend, "I have . . . generally revamped the situation until it is under our control, and if we go wrong it is our fault."[105]

The CRB chairman had no intention of permitting any such outcome. Perhaps in deference to Brand Whitlock's wishes, Jarvis Bell was soon on his way out of Belgium.[106] The problem of Dannie Heineman, however, was more delicate. A skillful intercessor with the Germans, he had been invaluable as a kind of unofficial diplomat during the early stages of the relief—and continued to be for some weeks to come. But Hoover had been warned by Lindon Bates not to trust Heineman and was determined to shunt him aside. In an exhausting negotiation he succeeded in getting Heineman to yield. (Few could best Hoover in a head-to-head confrontation.) He remarked afterward that it was "the greatest psychological battle" that he had "ever fought and won."[107] And he told Bates with satisfaction a bit later than Heineman and Hulse had finally realized "who they were dealing with" and had "psychologically entirely dropped out of the business already and . . . will entirely do so otherwise before we have finished."[108]

But then the unexpected happened. Heineman suggested that J. F. Lucey take charge of the Brussels office until Hoover's designated replacement arrived from America. But just when Hoover thought that he had it all arranged, Lucey, eager to return home, refused to take the assignment. An agitated Hoover was at wit's end until Brand Whitlock stepped in and persuaded Lucey to change his mind. It was an early instance of Whitlock's principal contribution to the relief project: smoothing the ruffled feathers of the prima donnas around him.[109]

But not even Whitlock could keep Hoover from crossing swords with the formidable Marquis de Villalobar. Of all the contentious personalities with whom the CRB chairman had to deal, the Spanish minister to Belgium was the most extraordinary. He had been born with a misshapen head, no hair, mere stumps for legs, and one hand that resembled a goat's hoof. Skillfully concealing his deformities with a wig, artificial legs, and gloves over his arms, the strong-willed Spanish aristocrat had successfully pursued a career as a diplomat. Well-educated and indeed gifted in mind, he was also endowed with ample vanity as well as a legendary temper.[110] He soon found occasion to use it.

The Commission for Relief in Belgium had been founded, of course, under joint American and Spanish auspices, and Villalobar was one of its patrons. But in much of the international press it was commonly referred to as the *American* Commission for Relief in Belgium—a misnomer that Hoover did little to discourage. To him the Spanish presence was essentially ornamental. He told the Rockefeller Foundation's War Relief Commission that the Spanish took "no active part in the management" of the CRB and that "the whole active managing members" were Americans.[111] It was a state of affairs that could easily engender diplomatic friction.

With the Marquis de Villalobar it did. Two days before Christmas this "mad, touchy Spaniard" (as Whitlock called him) descended on the American legation "in a towering rage." For more than half an hour he pounded his fist on the table and denounced a letter that he had just received on CRB stationery. The letterhead did not have his name in the proper location, he complained; the CRB was slighting him. "I am the one who started all this," he stormed, demanding a meeting with Hoover and Francqui. The ever conciliatory Whitlock arranged it but felt jarred and exhausted by "all these clashing and petty spirits, all these human stupidities."

The next day Villalobar met Hoover at the legation. At first the meeting went satisfactorily, with Hoover displaying an excellent combination of firmness and tact. Finally everyone agreed upon a revised letterhead that met the imperious Spaniard's desires. But then, when all was settled, Hoover abruptly told Villalobar that Spain had done nothing for the relief work and was not entitled to any representation on it! The diplomat remained silent—this time—but the episode portended troubles to come.[112]

One more task awaited Hoover's skills and will before he returned to London. Like Whitlock and Gibson, he soon concluded that the "idealistic uncommercial College man" was unqualified for "the driving work of this Commission." While the young Rhodes scholars had courage, zeal, and an admirable spirit of self-sacrifice, as a group they lacked commercial experience and aptitude.[113] And that, for the work ahead, was essential. Hoover was consequently obliged, as he put it, "to remove some 10 or 12 idealists from a sphere of labour where they felt they had the chance of their lifetime to do some good."[114]

In the years ahead the CRB's staff inside Belgium continued to consist mainly of young college-educated men, including a number of Rhodes scholars. Most of those who served became Hoover partisans for life. But the directors in Brussels were almost all middle-aged businessmen, and the recruitment of younger volunteers became more selective.[115]

Lucey's interim appointment to head the Brussels office proved an immediate success. Whitlock thanked Hoover for selecting this "remarkable man"— "a sort of field marshal" who was "pure gold all the way through."[116] But when Lucey left for America a few weeks later, Hoover was greatly relieved. The trouble, he told Lindon Bates, was that in patting [Lucey] on the back and giving him great publicity and having people cultivate up his tremendous enthusiasm, I developed in him a considerable swelled head, and he got quite out of control before he left here. He was convinced that he knew a lot more about running this job than I did. . . .

The diplomatic aspects of the relief work, continued Hoover, required "a masterly handling." Unfortunately,

Lucey has not the most childish conception of what the psychological currents are that we have to forfend, and as he got to a state of mind that he would not accept orders from me and attempted to monkey with the diplomatic buzz saw himself, I found repairing damage which he had created occupied a large part of my time.

Lucey, he added, was "a perfect jewel" as a man and a businessman, "but, as matters stand, it has got to be recognised by everybody associated with this work, that I am the boss, and that any attempts to minimize the importance of my leadership would do the work infinite harm when it comes to the delicate situations which I am compelled to meet daily."[117]

At the beginning of January 1915 Hoover returned to London.[118] One more rickety plank in the CRB edifice was nailed down; in Brussels as in New York and London, his leadership was now unchallenged. As he journeyed back across the Dutch frontier toward the Channel, there was still another accomplishment to savor: on December 26 the German Foreign Office had promised that the German army in Belgium would not requisition any further indigenous food while the CRB itself was sending in supplies "and for a reasonable time after the last delivery."[119] Two days later Governor-General von Bissing confirmed the pledge and authorized the CRB to establish any controls it wished over its relief distribution system.[120]

Controversy would soon erupt over the precise terms of this German guarantee. But for the moment Hoover found reason for hope. Perhaps now he could finally induce the British and French to grant him the subsidies he desperately required.

I I

B y the beginning of January 1915 20% of the population of Belgium was entirely destitute, unable to pay for a loaf of bread per day.[121] As the Allied blockade of its ports tightened, as industries deprived of imported raw materials laid off employees (and put others on reduced weeks), and as miners, railway workers, and others refused to work for the Germans, the demands upon Hoover's organization burgeoned. Clearly more and more Belgians would have to depend on charity as the war went on.[122] And Hoover, for one, anticipated no end to the conflict for several months.[123]

The concomitant financial burden was increasing as well. Thanks in part to the hoarding policies of embattled European governments and the cutting off of Russian exports through the Black Sea, the price of available foodstuffs in North America was soaring.[124] Already the commission's monthly imports cost 25% more than Hoover had estimated in early November.[125]

To keep his shipments flowing without interruption and avert the grim "hiatus" that had nearly occurred in December, the CRB's leader was obliged to authorize purchases two months in advance of delivery. In early January he did not have enough cash to do so. Nevertheless, he went ahead and ordered $4,500,000 worth of food in excess of the CRB's known or anticipated assets. To cover this amount he and several associates had to pledge their personal fortunes as security; evidently as part of this transaction he himself signed a note of indebtedness for $600,000.[126]

All this was a "gamble," Hoover acknowledged, but he hoped that by the time the cargoes actually arrived the CRB would be able to find the money for the payment.[127] "There is nothing stingy about him," said one of the members of the Rockefeller Foundation's War Relief Commission; "on the contrary his tendency is to go ahead faster than those about him are willing to follow. . . ."[128] The commissioner added that Hoover's deed was "probably more magnanimous than wise."[129]

The CRB chairman's act may not have been quite as risky as it seemed. On January 9 the Belgian government's finance minister formally promised to absorb the loss if food prices should fall and the relief organization lose money in its handling of the government's subsidy. The CN and CRB, he said, were simply "attorneys for the State," with no responsibility "beyond the execution of their commission."[130] A few days later Hoover told a friend that he had "a qualified guarantee from the Belgian Government against personal loss to any of the members, but of course this is dependent on the survival of the Government."[131] In addition, he had persuaded that government to take over "the whole of my machinery and its liabilities" as soon as peace was declared. But these agreements were contingent upon the restoration of Belgian independence and its exiled government after the war—an outcome that was scarcely certain at the beginning of 1915.[132] If this did not happen, Hoover could yet be left without recourse.

In the meantime he could only struggle against the specters at hand and hope for the best. "I can now see food supplies for these people until about the middle of March," he told a friend on January 10, "but what are we going to do after that date I have not now the remotest idea. . . . This business is a sort of hot penny which I cannot drop. . . ."[133]

To square the circle Hoover resorted to various ingenious expedients. With the Belgian government he arranged a four-month extension of the exchange plan under which he received funds in London equivalent to the amount distributed to pensioners and others out of Comité National receipts inside

Belgium. In mid-January he calculated that this would earn him about £700,000 per month.[134] It would also keep in circulation the huge sums of money accumulating in Brussels from the food sales. At the same time he asked the British to permit the creation of a separate exchange program under which private individuals and institutions abroad could funnel money to persons inside Belgium via the commission.[135]

And all the while, Hoover kept up his "agitation" with the British.[136] On January 6 he told Lord Percy at the Foreign Office that under present financial arrangements the CRB could not go on beyond mid-February. He indicated also that the Comité National's leaders were furious at the Allies' lack of support of the Belgians' great campaign of passive resistance—a worrisome bit of news (if true) for the British. He disclosed that the American ambassador in Berlin expected to induce the Germans to put up £250,000 a month for the CRB—leading Percy to wonder whether the Germans just might do so to gain American favor. Whether Hoover really anticipated such a German move is doubtful. But it certainly was in his interest to dangle this possibility before the British.[137] With each passing week he was becoming more adroit at playing off one belligerent power against another.

The next day Hoover's friend Frederick Palmer released a statement in London to the American press. Just back from Belgium (where he had spent much of the Christmas holiday with the Hoovers), the journalist declared: "Two-thirds of the population is idle. They get no work. . . . There is no doubt that the Belgians are getting the food intended for them. Not a mouthful is going to the Germans. . . . If the relief should cease there would be riots. The people would throw themselves on the German bayonets. . . ."[138] It was a compelling and timely statement, which Hoover could not have written better himself. Perhaps he did write it himself.

And still the statistics grew grimmer. By January 19, when the CRB issued its first comprehensive printed report, its working capital, in Hoover's words, was "wholly inadequate." Each month the organization must spend £1,250,000 for food and transportation. About half of this sum could be recovered from the sale of rations to the still-prosperous inside Belgium. But the distribution of free food to the destitute now absorbed a monthly total of £660,000, only a fraction of which was covered by charitable giving from abroad and by other devices.[139] And "the era of gift-food from America," he told a Rockefeller Foundation representative, was "practically over."[140] As a result Hoover now faced a monthly operating deficit of £400,000–500,000. If he did not find other revenue sources soon, he confessed, "the clock must ultimately run down. . . ."[141] Confidentially he informed Lindon Bates that through various loans and exchange mechanisms he had been promised £1,200,000 in February and might obtain the same amount in March. But "[h]ow long I can go on building up this financial air-castle I do not know."[142]

To further complicate matters, in early January the German government announced that it was imposing an indemnity on the provinces of Belgium of 40,000,000 francs per month.[143] Having abjured the seizure of foodstuffs, the occupying power seemed determined to extract an advantage in another form. The effect across the Channel was immediate. On January 12 the British Cabinet resolved to contribute to the Belgian relief—*if* the Germans abandoned their food levies *and* their financial exactions.[144] Evidently the British did not expect the Germans to relent, for the next day Sir Edward Grey told Hoover that he "need not hope for support" from His Majesty's Government. As long as the Germans maintained their exploitative scheme, he said, the British would not finance the CRB at all.[145]

But perhaps the door was not irreversibly nailed shut. The foreign secretary agreed with Hoover that if the Germans could be persuaded to give up their indemnity, he, at least, would consider his government obliged to support the relief commission financially. Grasping at this opportunity, Hoover at once asked Ambassador Gerard in Berlin to approach the Germans. Ever resourceful, the canny engineer-humanitarian suggested that the Germans stipulate that they would cease their monetary exactions only if the British agreed to finance the CRB![146]

While Hoover waited for Berlin's reply, he continued to lobby for British acceptance of his private financial exchange scheme. On January 21 he had a meeting on this subject with Chancellor of the Exchequer Lloyd George and other senior British officials. If the American executive expected this interview to be perfunctory, he was in for an unpleasant surprise. As soon as he completed his presentation, Lloyd George announced that he was entirely opposed to the Belgian relief enterprise, benevolent though it was, and had vetoed the proposed exchange plan. For indirectly, if not directly, it was aiding the enemy of his country. The introduction of food and money into Belgium, he declared, only provided more resources with which to endure German requisitions and financial levies. Above all (as Hoover later recorded the chancellor's argument), "in relieving the Germans from the necessity of feeding the civil population we were directly prolonging the war, which was bound to be one of wholly economic character and that economic pressure was the principal method by which the Allies would ultimately win." The blockaded nation of Belgium, he said, was like a besieged city. By provisioning its civil population the CRB was "prolonging the resistance of the garrison." The chancellor of the exchequer was convinced that in the last resort the Germans themselves would feed the people of Belgium.

A routine appointment now turned into a battle for survival. But just as Hoover had been unafraid of Prime Minister Asquith in December, so now, a few weeks later, he seemed equally unintimidated by Lloyd George. At once the Yankee humanitarian launched an all-out rebuttal. The Germans, he said, had seized no imported CRB food and had now promised to seize no native food either—a pledge they were so far scrupulously keeping. (Actually there were already numerous instances of violations, but Hoover may not yet have known this.[147]) The exchange scheme would introduce no new money into the country but would merely revolve the money already there. Hoover recited (without endorsing) the German claims that it was the British blockade which had created Belgium's ordeal and that Germany did not have a sufficient surplus to feed the French and Belgians behind its lines. Already, he said, some rioting had occurred in Belgium; already some civilians in German-occupied France were dying of starvation—but the Germans had not altered their policy. In short, he was positive that the Germans would never feed the distressed civilians of Belgium.

The enemy's attitude is monstrous, Lloyd George exclaimed. Be that as it may, Hoover rejoined, the British government had entered this war for the avowed purpose of vindicating the existence and neutrality of small nations and of preserving "the continuance of democracy as against autocracy." It would be "an empty victory," he added, "if one of the most democratic of the world's races should be extinguished in the process. . . ." Hoover appealed to the English people to disregard the "dubious" military advantages to the Germans and assure that the Belgians survived. Show magnanimity to these people, he pleaded—a magnanimity that would "outlast all the bitterness of this war."

Suddenly Lloyd George turned to his colleagues and said abruptly· "I am convinced. You have my permission." The commercial exchange plan was approved. Turning to Hoover before leaving, he remarked (in Hoover's later paraphrase) that "the world would yet be indebted to the American people for the most magnanimous action which neutrality had yet given way to."[148]

In the judgment of the CRB's earliest historian, Hoover's successful encounter with Lloyd George was "the most signal triumph of his diplomatic career."[149] The chancellor of the exchequer himself was afterward quoted as saying that Hoover's presentation was virtually the clearest exposition he had ever heard on any subject. For fifteen minutes, he said, Hoover had spoken flawlessly—not a word too many or too few—gesturing with one hand and with the other jingling the change in his pocket.[150] It is possible that the wily chancellor was less impressed by the cogency of Hoover's arguments than by a recognition of the value of American good will. The United States, after all, was rapidly becoming the indispensable source of money, food, and arms for the Allies, and the American people were known to be very exercised about little Belgium. Still, Hoover had done far more than gain approval of his commercial exchange scheme; he had won a powerful convert to his cause. Until then Lloyd George had been an ally of Kitchener, Winston Churchill, and other Cabinet opponents of the relief on military grounds. Henceforth he was to be an able and influential supporter.[151]

The meeting of January 21, 1915 was a turning point in Hoover's struggle against the British, but it did not in itself secure the permanent fixed subsidy that he sought. It now became apparent that if the logjam were ever to be broken he would have to intervene in Berlin. This was, to say the least, unorthodox; there was already a patron-ambassador in the German capital.

But as the interview with Lloyd George and the shakeup of the CRB's Brussels office had shown, the best results seemed to occur when Hoover, "the boss," took command. His powers of exposition, mental agility, and forcefulness of mien and expression had helped him to dominate mining company boards before the war. Now he was finding that these same attributes had their impact upon diplomats. "Somehow I feel like doing what that man asked me to do," said the Argentine minister to London after a session with Hoover.[152] The CRB's chairman was discovering that the most effective advocate of the relief work was himself.

On January 26, therefore, Hoover set out from London for Germany. His objective was clear: no more levies of any kind in Belgium by the Germans, in exchange for the financing of his relief work by the Allies. But before he left the English seaside town of Folkestone for the trip across the Channel to Holland, a characteristic tactic occurred to him: why not put pressure on Berlin ahead of time by unleashing "a storm of public opinion" in the American press? Abruptly changing his plans, he hastened back to London to "create public feeling" in his tried and successful manner.[153]

On January 27 he cabled Secretary of State Bryan in Washington, described his impending mission, and asked him to approach the German ambassador, Count Bernstorff. Only six days earlier the CRB's chief executive officer had told Lloyd George that the relief was of only "dubious" military value to the Germans. Now he told Bryan (for the benefit of Bernstorff) that the CRB's operations actually gave the Germans a "vast" military advantage that "far outweighs the value" of their forced indemnity. As usual, he bluntly wielded his favorite—indeed, his only—weapon: "The Germans cannot afford to have these issues tried in the court of American public opinion, and they can well afford, not only from a point of view of military advantage but also of American public opinion, and above all of humanity, to have this question settled" on Hoover's terms.[154]

Meanwhile he labored over a comprehensive document for the American newspapers. Seeking British collusion in pressuring the Germans, he consulted Lord Percy about the wisdom of issuing a press statement and even asked Percy to examine his draft. Unfortunately, Percy revised it into a form that Hoover considered completely anti-German and hence unpublishable. In the end he reverted to his original version.[155] On January 30 he released it through his usual conduit: Ben S. Allen of the Associated Press.

"The Commission takes the gloomiest possible view of the ultimate future," he began. "The problem is rapidly growing beyond the reach of private philanthropy." After explaining the imperative of governmental subvention and the attitudes of each belligerent, he proposed his *via media*. Most Belgians will die, he declared, unless the belligerents "come to an arrangement." "Our only court of appeal," he concluded, "is American public opinion."[156]

Having thus instigated (he hoped) a furor in the American press, Hoover promptly left for Berlin—determined, he later wrote, "to besiege the German Government at the top directly and on all fronts."[157] Arriving on February 1, he was joined by Hugh Gibson and Dannie Heineman from Brussels.[158] For the next ten days he conferred with a succession of senior German officials, including the finance minister, the foreign minister, and Chancellor Bethmann Hollweg himself.

The visiting American found wartime Berlin to be a far different city from London. Every official, even the civilians, wore uniforms; the military—and the military mind—were dominant. Only once on his visit did he hear a German laugh. These were "the Spartans of Europe," he felt; "massed regimentation was their bent." For the first time since ancient Greece an entire nation was organizing itself for "total war." He knew now that the stalemated conflict would not "be over in the spring."[159]

Despite the unpromising atmosphere Hoover pressed ahead with his proposal. Time and again he insisted that his relief work was actually "of the greatest military importance to the Germans, for a starving population on the lines of communication would be the greatest menace." Time and again he stressed that the German levies had had a "disastrous" effect on American public opinion and that as long as Germany continued to behave in this manner, it was "absolutely hopeless" for her to expect American sympathy. No German act would do more to win over the American people, he opined, than ending monthly impositions on the helpless Belgians.[160]

The government of the Kaiser was unmoved. While professing gratitude for the CRB's work and willingness to support it in other respects, Bethmann Hollweg and his colleagues categorically refused to lift their forced indemnity. It was utterly impossible, they said. German public opinion would not allow it; indemnities for the support of an occupying army were legal under international law; the imperial government was not going to let the British boast that they had forced their enemy to relent.

Instead, the Germans countered with a variety of complicated financial alternatives, none of which appealed to Hoover. (They were "wholly and absolutely impossible," he said with customary force.) But in the end, when it had become clear that his original proposal was dead, he began to develop with the head of the Reichsbank and others a plan for raising $50,000,000 for the relief by means of a loan to be floated in America, guaranteed by the Germans, and repaid by the Belgians after the war. The security for this loan would consist of food sale receipts to be held by a special "relief bank" inside Belgium. The Germans would promise not to interfere. A bit later the Germans even offered to advance the $50,000,000 themselves in New York, although ultimately Belgian banks would have to repay it.

Hoover, of course, had no power to impose a $50,000,000 debt on the Belgian nation, and he soon told the Germans that the Belgians, notably Francqui, should be consulted. But he knew that in the last extremity he might have to implement some such measure. Whatever its defects, it would help to keep the Belgians alive.[161]

The "relief bank" proposal was still pending when Hoover returned to London, via Brussels, in mid-February.[162] In one respect his mission had failed: the Germans had *not* yielded to the British demand for abolition of the forced indemnities. The "club of public opinion" had proved insufficient. At one point Bethmann Hollweg even remarked that American opinion seemed of little value, since Hoover's countrymen were already selling arms to the Allies and would probably continue to do so, thereby prolonging the war.[163]

But the Germans were not, perhaps, completely indifferent to Hoover's entreaties. They had, after all, seemed quite anxious to devise a satisfactory financial arrangement. Moreover, Hoover had bluntly informed them that the CRB "hung on a slender thread of sentiment" in England and that a mere "breath" could blow it away. If so, he warned, Germany would then have ten million starving Frenchmen and Belgians to contend with.[164] For whatever reason—humanitarian, diplomatic, or military—the Germans were not prepared to see the commission collapse.

On February 15 Hoover reported the disappointing results of his journey to Lord Percy, who set to work on preparing a reply.[165] But Hoover surmised that the British might still be loath to "thrust us into the arms of the Germans for our financing"[166] and thereby let the enemy score a diplomatic victory among the neutrals. His hunch proved correct. On February 17 Lloyd George called him to his office. The Cabinet would meet the next day, he disclosed, and would consider the question of the relief. While Kitchener and Churchill were strenuously opposed to its continuation, the chancellor of the exchequer declared that he himself was now unreservedly supportive. He therefore asked Hoover to prepare a strongly worded memorandum for use at this critical meeting.[167]

Within three hours Hoover returned to the exchequer with his document. Every argument that he could muster was there. Within thirty days, he said, "decimation" of the Belgians would begin unless foodstuffs came in from abroad. The Germans would never supply such goods, he asserted; that expedient was "hopeless." Switching arguments again, Hoover minimized the relief's military advantage to the Germans and played up instead the value of the Belgians' passive resistance to the Allies. He noted, too, that Britain had gone to war for the "sole purpose" of defending the integrity of Belgium, whose people must now "starve or be slaughtered" unless support were given. Of all the reasons he adduced, the one that hit home the most was probably this: that if his relief work should "fail to receive the sympathy and support of the English people, it would have a most serious bearing on the whole attitude of public sentiment in the United States."[168]

The next day, February 18, 1915, brought word of victory at last. After the Cabinet meeting at noon Lloyd George informed Hoover that His Majesty's Government had decided to recommend to its French ally a joint subvention of £1,000,000 per month. This subsidy would take the form not of direct grants to the CRB but of nominal loans to the exiled Belgian government for "Mr. Hoover's fund." The arrangement would last until summer. You have taken a load off our hearts, Hoover said. "You have made a good fight," Lloyd George replied, "and deserve to win out."[169]

It is impossible to know what combination of motives prompted the British government to accede so suddenly to Hoover's desires.[170] From the CRB's point of view, of course, it did not matter. But on February 4 the German government had announced that as of February 18 all waters surrounding Great Britain and Ireland would be included in a "war zone" in which German submarines would roam; any British merchant ships found therein would be destroyed.[171] The economic dimension of the war was taking an ominous turn. More dependent than ever on food and munitions from the United States, the British may not have wished to give offense over the relief. Back in the autumn the Tory leader Arthur Balfour had remarked to an American journalist, "How fortunate it was for the sake of our relations with America, that we had the outrage on Belgium."[172] How fortunate it was for Hoover now that the British still needed America.

Nevertheless, it had been a close call. Lloyd George knew that he had no authority to give money outright to the Belgians. He could either seek parliamentary approval of such a gift or disguise the transaction as a loan. Unwilling to risk a public debate in the House of Commons, he chose the latter course. Hoover, for his part, was now free to eschew the unpalatable alternative of a cumbersome German-sponsored "relief bank."[173]

Meanwhile Lord Percy had been drafting a Foreign Office statement about the Germans and had sent it to Hoover for comment. What form, however, should this declaration now take? Having first tied a subsidy for the CRB to the Germans' lifting of their Belgian indemnity, the British had now backed down and granted the money anyway. Would they care to admit their defeat publicly? But more importantly, on his trip to Germany Hoover had made a critical discovery, as he related confidentially to his New York associates: The "state of mind of the various warring people in Europe," he reported, had now reached the level of "frenzy."

> . . . the German state of mind is such that if the German people thought for one moment that the English were anxious that the Belgians should be fed, they would at once stop food coming into Belgium, and endeavour to use the cry "the Belgians must starve with us" as a weapon to force the hand of the Allies. . . .

The German attitude toward occupied northern France, Hoover found, was ever harsher.

> . . . if the Germans felt that it would be any pressure on the Allies, they would have no hesitation in making hostages out of these ten million people. I, therefore, came back with the firm conviction that it was for us to

maintain by all means the conviction in the German mind that the English and the Allies generally were extremely discontented with our feeding of the Belgians; were against it on military grounds, and that we were only able to keep the Channel open through the British Fleet with the greatest possible difficulty, and that the British people were refusing to help the Belgians.[174]

In collaboration, therefore, with the British Foreign Office, Hoover prepared a carefully worded exchange of letters between himself and Sir Edward Grey—letters that would give the Germans the erroneous impression that the British were not assisting the CRB at all. On February 24, 1915 Grey's letter and Hoover's reply were published.[175] Citing the Germans' adamant refusal to abandon their Belgian indemnity, the foreign secretary declared that the proposed arrangement between the British government and the CRB had "broken down." No direct British subvention of the CRB's charitable work was possible, he said, until the Germans altered their policy.[176] In response, Hoover expressed his profound regret at this blow to his hopes "of finding some accommodation between the belligerents" for the financing of his charitable department. Nevertheless, he averred, the commission would persevere—appealing, as always, "to the mercy of the people in every land."[177] Nothing was said in either letter about the massive *indirect* subvention that the British government had just promised the CRB through the medium of the Belgian government-in-exile!

The Grey–Hoover exchange was an early illustration of a technique that the CRB chairman employed effectively in the years ahead and, indeed, for the rest of his life: the carefully crafted but seemingly spontaneous public document, designed to create an appearance that was sometimes quite divergent from reality. "The only way to misread a document," Judge Learned Hand is said to have remarked, "is to read it literally." With Hoover it was often so. The interior history of his prearranged pronouncements could be more revealing than the surface meaning of his words.

It is not known whether the Germans were deceived by Hoover's elaborate ploy. But the release of the two letters had an unintended side effect in the United States. In recent weeks friction between the CRB and Robert de Forest's Belgian Relief Committee had again developed in New York. In early February a Belgian diplomat named de Sadeleer who was a member of this committee had forwarded to his government anonymous charges of graft and inefficiency in the commission's New York office. Among other things, Lindon Bates was said to be receiving a princely salary of $500 a week.[178]

When these allegations reached Hoover in London, he erupted in anger and disgust. Calling the derogatory charges "absolute lies," he demanded that they be officially investigated and denied. If de Sadeleer did not cooperate at once, Hoover threatened to raise the issue personally with King Albert on a visit planned for early March.[179] The Belgian government also deplored the allegations but asked Hoover to ignore them as "ridiculous" and "beneath contempt."[180] But the CRB chairman was in no mood to let the matter drop. He and his colleagues had sacrificed their business interests, jeopardized their "private fortunes," and even risked their lives for the Belgian cause, he said, and they were "not going to be charged with dishonesty by any damned soul that lives."[181]

Hoover and Bates quickly traced the trouble to a New York-based Belgian merchant named Lionel Hagenaers, who had been handling shipping for the Belgian Relief Committee. In Hoover's eyes it was obvious that a resentful Hagenaers was "anxious to force his way into our business."[182] Privately he charged that the Belgians on de Forest's committee seemed eager to impress the Belgian government "with the success they met with in bleeding money out of the Americans—hence the extreme zealousness on their part to be considered something entirely apart" from the general American relief movement.[183] He accused the de Forest group of failing to practice "team work," particularly by refusing to confine its efforts to "the locality immediately adjacent to New York" and to recognize "the fact that the controlling of this entire enterprise by necessity rests" with the Commission for Relief in Belgium.[184]

While Hoover was attempting to repel the de Sadeleer–Hagenaers–de Forest combine, the Grey–Hoover letters appeared in the American press, unwittingly providing his embittered American rivals a chance to recapture their lost prominence. Seizing on what it mistakenly perceived as a setback to the CRB, the Belgian Relief Committee announced in New York on February 24 that Great Britain's refusal to grant a monthly subsidy (it failed to notice the word *direct*) had made it critically imperative to obtain additional revenue in the United States. The committee therefore renewed its own appeal for contributions. In a subtle slap at Hoover, it declared that it was basing its program on reports received from Brand Whitlock, Henry van Dyke (American minister to the Netherlands), and the Comité National—which, it noted pointedly, was actually distributing the food sent into Belgium. The committee declared that it would proceed on course unless advised otherwise by these sources. It conspicuously failed to mention Herbert Hoover.[185]

Lindon Bates was furious at the Belgian Relief Committee's "presumptuous" and "unauthorized" press release.[186] Hoover, too, was incensed. In his opinion de Forest's group was led by "glory hunting Belgian pinheads and professional charity workers" whose unfettered behavior was "subversive to the whole organisation" and threatened to discredit the CRB in America—a development that could jeopardize its standing abroad and cause "most infinite damage to the whole work."[187] To him the purport of de Forest's announcement was plain: that, with the CRB supposedly rebuffed by the British, we, the Belgian Relief Committee, would now save the Belgians, by working directly with the Comité National, Whitlock, and van Dyke.[188] But Hoover advised Bates not to worry. I am "preparing a blow that will smash whole business to complete atoms," he cabled.[189] "We will train a machine gun on our troublesome friends this week. . . ."[190]

The CRB chairman now masterminded a counterattack. As it happened, President Wilson's confidant, Colonel House, was visiting London at the time, and with him Hoover discussed his New York troubles.[191] Finding him sympathetic, Hoover prompted Ben S. Allen to ask House for a statement for the Associated Press. The colonel obliged with warm words of commendation and noted that the CRB was "the sole agency through which food can reach Belgium." Herbert Hoover, he added, "has made an international reputation and merits it." House's words speedily appeared in the *New York Times*.[192] To head off an end run by the de Forest committee via Holland, Hoover boldly requested Minister van Dyke to forward to him any messages that van Dyke received from the CRB's New York enemies.[193]

But the *coup de grâce* was still to come. According to Hoover, the status of the CRB had been "more definitely defined" and the conditions of its existence "more precisely set up" in recent weeks. Using these developments as a pretext (his real reason was to outmaneuver de Forest), he asked Walter Hines Page on February 27 to address him "a sort of mandate as to what all these limitations summarise." Overlooking no detail, Hoover presented Page with a draft.[194]

The next day the British government announced a drastic tightening of its naval blockade in reprisal for the German "war zone" decree of early February.[195] That same day, the complaisant ambassador sent Hoover a letter reciting four "regulations" that were, he alleged, "made necessary" by the "present maritime conditions" and by the CRB's "diplomatic arrangements." He requested Hoover to share this information with all contributors to the relief effort in Belgium. Within hours Hoover released the letter to the press.

In incisive (and probably Hooverian) prose Page dutifully listed the "regulations." First: "All foodstuffs must be the absolute property of the Commission for Relief in Belgium. . . ." Second: They "must become the property of the Commission at the point of departure on the high seas"; only in this way, he claimed, could deliveries inside Belgium be secured. Third: All food "must be transported in ships under the control of the Commission because these are the only ships whose safety the belligerent governments guarantee." Fourth: "The distribution in Belgium must be carried out absolutely under the control of the Commission because supplies cannot reach the people through any other channel and because the guarantees hold only with reference to food that belongs to the Commission." Said Page in closing, "[N]o food can be transmitted otherwise" than in compliance with these requirements.[196]

With the issuance of Page's letter, the last lingering challenge to Hoover outside Belgium ended—and with it the first phase of the great relief struggle. "There is only one gate into Belgium," he declared on March 3, "and that is held open by this Commission. There is only one road leading to that gate from the United States and that road starts from the Commission's office at 71 Broadway, New York."[197] The American engineer-turned-humanitarian had reason to feel content. On every front—shipping, personnel management, diplomacy, finance, and public relations—he had shown singular resourcefulness and drive. Such a man could be forgiven if at times he seemed to think that only he was indispensable, that only he could rescue Belgium from catastrophe. More likely than not, he was right.

I I I

B Y the end of February 1915 the Commission for Relief in Belgium had become what Hoover from the first had wanted it to be: an institution. In a little over four months he had built up an organization handling "the largest problem ever undertaken by way of relief."[198] Tens of thousands of people on several continents had become involved: volunteer fund-raisers in America, Australia, Canada, Great Britain, Italy, and Spain; engineers, farmers, bankers, accountants, shippers, and grain merchants in the United States; owners and crews of several dozen cargo ships crossing and now recrossing the oceans; diplomats and government officials in at least seven countries; stevedores and lightermen operating six hundred tugs and barges along canals from Holland into Belgium; inside Belgium itself, approximately 40,000 volunteers manning an elaborate apparatus of food distribution at scores of regional warehouses and more than 2,500 communes.[199] And in London, at the nerve center, coordinating, controlling, and planning, was a small group of Americans led by a great engineer.

Hoover himself appeared to sense the epic qualities of his endeavor, as his letter to a Belgian priest in early March attested:

To beg, borrow and buy nearly $1,800,000 worth of food every week; to ship it over seas from America, Australia, the Argentine and India; to traverse three belligerent lines; to transport it through a country with a wholly demoralised transportation service; to distribute it equitably to over 7,000,000 people; to see that it reaches the civilians only and that it is adapted to every condition from babyhood to old age and to do this with a machinery operated by the self-denial of volunteer effort, is a labour only rendered possible by the most steadfast teamwork on the part of all. . . . We are under daily zealous surveillance of all the governments involved; . . . we maintain an investigation department of our own; we have put into force every method and check for efficiency and neutrality of conduct which our advisors and ourselves could invent; the accounts of our many branches are audited and published every fortnight. . . . This organisation has gained for the American people, not only by the generous American gifts but also by the integrity and efficiency of its administration, a bright spot in the esteem of Europe and we have the right to demand the absolute confidence and support of our fellow countrymen.[200]

Certainly the CRB had the esteem of those it was delivering from starvation. By the end of February its Brussels office was receiving two thousand letters of thanks a week.[201] In schools, shops, and private dwellings, grateful Belgians displayed homemade American flags; to J. F. Lucey the country looked "like the Fourth of July."[202] The CRB's barges, warehouses, and automobiles also displayed the Stars and Stripes (as a form of diplomatic immunity); when the young American volunteers drove by on their errands, peasants saluted.[203] On George Washington's birthday throngs of Belgian citizens walked the streets of Brussels—all wearing red, white, and blue.[204] According to Lucey, the Belgians were amazed that one country could be so "kind" to another.[205]

"A piratical state organized for benevolence": that, said one British government official, was the Commission for Relief in Belgium.[206] And indeed, the relief organization did possess some of the attributes of a government. It had its own flag; it negotiated "treaties" with the warring European powers; its leaders parleyed regularly with diplomats and government ministers. Inside Belgium, it fixed the price of its food rations at a level somewhat above cost, thereby extracting from the well-to-do a tax to defray its charitable expenses. It even had a "pirate" leader in Hoover, who enjoyed informal diplomatic immunity, traveled virtually wherever he wished, and possessed a document from the Germans that said: "This man is not to be stopped anywhere under any circumstances." In fact, Hoover may have been the only person permitted by the British government to cross the English Channel without having his luggage and documents examined.[207] (After the unpleasantness of his first trip, there were no more undignified searches at border points.)

Attaining this status had not been easy. To make the commission "serve its purpose," Hoover confided to Bates in March, they had had to "fight inch by inch to build up its prestige"—"the key to large sums of money."

> . . . it was by fighting these positions step by step; winning them every time; gaining prestige with every battle, that we have ultimately got to this position where we are able to practically intimidate people into giving their support. In other words, our position is sufficiently large in the world's eyes at the present moment, that if we denounce any one of the belligerent Governments for inhumanity it has a sufficient amount of force to cause them to pause on almost any transaction.[208]

But if the CRB was now an institution, it was one shaped, inspired, and governed by a single individual. "[O]ne does not work for Hoover without working under his orders," a Belgian associate later remarked.[209] Before long, admiring co-workers were calling this man the Chief.[210]

Why, some wondered, was he doing it—sacrificing career, security, and family life for an ever more extended period of time? What motives and aspirations impelled him through his unending heavy labors? On his February stop in Brussels a German official crudely raised this point. "Now we are all very human," he said, "and I want to ask you a man to man question. What do you Americans get out of this business? Why are you doing it?" Struggling to control his temper, Hoover tried to explain that his was "a humane effort" but finally gave up—unable, he told his questioner, to be "emphatic enough to leave any impress" on him.[211] Hearing of the conversation afterward, Brand Whitlock remarked with disgust that the Germans seemed utterly unable to understand disinterested humanitarian sentiments.[212]

Hoover's humanitarian concern was genuine, as was his haunting apprehension that, if he should fail, millions of innocents might die. But other motives also molded his conduct. Having embarked, he told an American club in London, on a task "entrusted largely to the American business man," he and his colleagues believed "that it was up to us to demonstrate that business could be applied to philanthropy in our hands with an efficiency and an integrity which should be a creditable mark on our national history."[213]

And not just American business but America itself. We "are making a stupendous effort to justify our countrymen, not only in efficiency and skill, but in broad dealing and humanity," he wrote to Ambassador Gerard in December.[214] Addressing the first brigade of Rhodes scholars to depart for Belgium, Hoover emphasized this theme:

> When this war is over the thing that will stand out will not be the number of dead and wounded, but the record of those efforts which went to save life. Therefore you should remember that in this duty you have not only a service to render to these people, but that you have a duty to this Commission, and above all that you have a duty to your own country. . . .[215]

This awareness of the unique and privileged part he was playing in an international drama of unprecedented magnitude seemed never to be far from Hoover's thoughts. He told a colleague that theirs was "probably the greatest work that will ever come within the scope of our life time" and that even though they would suffer substantial pecuniary losses, "it is something to have left behind and of more use than money."[216] The CRB chairman insisted that neither he nor his associates had any desire for credit or publicity,[217] and in these early months there was no evidence that he envisaged a still larger role for himself on the world's stage. But that he *was* on stage he already recognized acutely. And as he told Lindon Bates in early 1915, if he could continue the commission on its present course with enough financial support, "we are going to make it a monument in American history."[218]

Pervading Hoover's daily letters and memoranda was the dynamism of a man in the prime of life, a man who loved accomplishment and took pleasure in the exercise of power. This, too, drove him on: the sense that he was using his abilities to the fullest in a cause both practical and just. For all his anxieties and vexations, his prewar restlessness was gone. He was, in truth, enjoying himself.

He was winning admiration ,as well. Despite the British government's ambivalence about the raison d'être of his relief commission, the Foreign Office certified the organization to its French ally as "both trustworthy and businesslike."[219] Colonel House commended Hoover to President Wilson as one who "seems to be doing a great work in an unselfish and efficient manner."[220] But probably the most enthusiastic tribute came from the man who more than any other had supported the CRB and its chief in these critical, formative months. On January 12, 1915, in the course of a letter to Woodrow Wilson, Ambassador Walter Hines Page observed:

> Life is worth more, too, for knowing Hoover. But for him Belgium would now be starved, however generously people may have given food. He's gathering together and transporting and getting distributed $5,000,000 worth a month, with a perfect organization of volunteers, chiefly American. He has a fleet of 35 ships, flying the Commission's flag—the only flag that all belligerents have entered into an agreement to respect and to defend. He came to me the other day and said, "You must know the Commission is $600,000 in debt. But don't be uneasy. I've given my personal note for it." (he's worth more than that.) . . . He's a simple, modest energetic little man who began his career in California and will end it in Heaven; and he doesn't want anybody's thanks.[221]

Herbert Hoover, ca. 1917.

Herbert Hoover as chairman of the Commission for Relief in Belgium, ca. 1917.

*Lou Henry Hoover at a Belgian relief fund-raising bazaar in Palo Alto, California,
1915.*

Herbert Hoover (seated, center) and his CRB colleagues in London, August 1916.

Walter Hines Page.   *Brand Whitlock.*

Emile Francqui.

Vernon Kellogg.

Hugh Gibson.

General Moritz Ferdinand von Bissing,
Governor-General of Belgium (1914–
1917).

FoodShip

for BELGIUM

© 1915. R. WILLIAMS

HELP FILL THE
INDIANA SHIP
WITH
WHEAT, FLOUR AND EVAPORATED MILK
FOR THE NON-COMBATANTS IN BELGIUM

All foodstuffs purchased in this State will be shipped to Belgium **FREE OF ALL CHARGES.**

Will you do your share toward feeding more than a MILLION AND A HALF DESTITUTE BELGIANS?

MAKE CONTRIBUTIONS TO YOUR LOCAL COMMITTEE
OR THE
INDIANA COMMITTEE
OF
THE COMMISSION FOR RELIEF IN BELGIUM
753-5 LEMCKE ANNEX, INDIANAPOLIS, IND.

HENRY LANE WILSON, Chairman   STOUGHTON A. FLETCHER, Treasurer

Belgian relief poster (U.S.A.), 1915. (Photograph copyright © 1986 by the Board of Trustees of the Leland Stanford Junior University. All rights reserved. Commission for Relief in Belgium. Collection of Hoover Institution Archives)

5

The Undiplomatic Diplomat

I

On February 22, 1915 the Commission for Relief in Belgium was four months old. Thanks to Hoover's successful campaign for a regular subsidy from the French and British governments, his infant "institution" had a modicum of security at last.

Throughout the winter of 1914–15, however, a new catastrophe threatened. From the Swiss border westward to the North Sea stretched a 400-mile maze of trenches, machine guns, and barbed wire: home (if one could call it that) to millions of armed men. Behind the German side of the lines lay not only virtually all of Belgium but a strip of northern France nearly the size of Massachusetts. In this industrialized region between the war zone and the Belgian frontier lived more than 2,000,000 hapless people.

When the CRB was established back in October, no one had made provision for the populace of this German-occupied territory. For one thing, the battle lines in that sector had not yet stabilized. But it was not long before intimations of adversity reached Hoover's ears. Dependent, like the Belgians, on imports for much of their sustenance, yet isolated by German armies from the outside world, by early winter the citizens of several northern French cities were running perilously short of food.[1] From Lille, Tourcoing, and Valenciennes alone came word of 250,000 people on the verge of starvation.[2]

Between November and January the CRB and Comité National extended their operations to two French border districts that fell within the jurisdiction of the German government in Belgium, thereby rescuing about 130,000 Frenchmen from famine.[3] But there was only so much at this point that Hoover himself could do. Strained to the limit financially, unsure as yet of any governmental subvention, he had neither the resources nor the authority to set up a comprehensive relief program on French soil. When emissaries from Lille and Valenciennes appealed to him in Brussels in late December, the CRB chairman expressed his willingness to help. But he added that he could accomplish nothing unless the French government provided the necessary political and financial backing.[4]

The disappointed delegates returned to their occupied communities and asked the German army for permission to travel to Paris to lobby the French government for relief.[5] To *Paris*, not imperial Berlin. Like Hoover, they were convinced that the invading army would not assist them.

Meanwhile, upon returning to London in early January, Hoover did his best to publicize the developing tragedy. Ten thousand French peasants in the Meuse River valley, he told the press, were "absolutely without food," and many had already died of starvation.[6] (To the British Foreign Office he put the number of dead at two thousand.)[7] That very week, with German permission, CRB volunteers rushed thirty tons of flour to the distressed region.[8] Clearly, however, more systematic efforts were imperative.

At the same time that he was stoking the furnace of publicity, Hoover notified Ambassador Gerard in Berlin that he was "not adverse to taking on the extra burden" of feeding the French. However, as in Belgium, he expected cooperation from the various governments. Since the services of his commission were voluntary, he remarked, the "least recompense" that the French could render would be "a substantial subscription to our funds for Belgian work."[9] So far Paris had done nothing.

Hoover's steps in behalf of northern France brought little immediate result. Shortly after his return to London he appealed to the French ambassador for assistance. Four, five, six weeks went by—and no response came.[10]

Late in January, while still enmeshed in his battle for financial survival, Hoover was approached by a former American consular official in behalf of the city of Lille. The local merchants had provided him money, he said, to purchase 10,000 tons of grain a month for relief. He thereupon offered Hoover a deal: if the CRB would import the grain and sell it to the people of Lille at a price far above cost, he, Hoover, and Hoover's colleagues could divide the profit. Outraged and insulted, Hoover threw the man out of his office. ". . . I have not the nervous energy to associate or mix with men of this character in any business matter, however minute it may be," he fumed.[11] The gentlemen of the CRB, he told a friend, "are here for humanitarian reasons. We are giving our time and paying our own expenses and do not propose to take advantage of the fact that we have a food monopoly to damn our immortal souls. . . ."[12] If the French government wants its people fed, he declared, "it may make us a formal request and we will take the matter in hand," in accordance with "the best ideals of the American people" (provided, of course, that the French furnished the money). But he was certainly not going to feed France as a "commercial transaction" or enter into "a corrupt relationship" with his American caller.[13]

At the end of January Hoover left London for Berlin—determined not only to lift the punitive German levies on the Belgians but also to discuss the issue of northern France. He knew well that before he could convince Paris to help him, he must obtain pledges from Berlin not to interfere. In a press release designed to put pressure on the Germans, he cited the ordeal of 3,000,000 Frenchmen languishing behind the German lines—a figure almost a million too high.[14] But Hoover, with his keen sense of publicity, surely realized that 7,000,000 Belgians plus 3,000,000 French equalled 10,000,000 human beings in all—a figure with much more propaganda value than 9,150,000. And so, not for the first or last time, he rounded out his numbers for psychological effect.

In Berlin the CRB chairman found German officialdom ready to permit full-scale relief operations in the region and ready also to give the necessary guarantees.[15] But what, now, about their enemies? The president of the French republic, for one, was said to be adamantly opposed to any such undertaking.[16] Another tug-of-war with the Allies was in prospect.

Back in London in mid-February, Hoover turned to a visiting American who had just offered his services to the CRB. A close friend of Theodore Roosevelt and a prominent Bull Moose Progressive, Gifford Pinchot had studied in France as a youth and was fluent in the French language—no small asset. Wasting no time, Hoover appointed him to the commission and dispatched him on a mission to Paris. If Pinchot could persuade the French to support the CRB, Hoover intended to place him in charge of its operations in occupied French territory.[17]

Pinchot carried with him a bluntly worded personal letter from Hoover to President Raymond Poincaré. The "situation in northern France," the CRB chairman reported, was "acute to the last degree." "Actual starvation" was "in progress"; already French women and children were rummaging for food in German army garbage dumps. Already, too, the CRB was feeding 400,000 French people behind the lines—a burden it could not continue to bear without "financial assistance." In fact, Hoover announced, he had been compelled to issue orders to terminate the delivery of foodstuffs across the Belgian frontier into France in less than two weeks. "It is no use dividing the food between the Belgians and the French in order that all may die," he said. "We have no right to take money provided to feed the Belgians and give it to the French."

Hoover therefore pleaded for funding from the French government—which still had not responded to his appeal of more than a month before. The invading Germans, he insisted, would not save the starving French; the Germans said they did not have enough food for themselves. Furthermore, they were not going to deplete their own stocks and "prejudice their own people" by feeding the enemy. Hoover again disclaimed any eagerness to add to his onerous burdens. But if the French government supplied the money, he promised, "we will feed these people." And, he reminded Poincaré, "there is no other engine through which this service can be performed at the present time. . . ."[18]

Hoover's salvo never reached its destination. Upon arriving in Paris, Pinchot tried in vain to see the French president and foreign minister.[19] Hoover, in London, was irate. Is the French government ready to save its own people from starvation or not? he demanded to know. We must get a definite answer. Cabling to Pinchot on February 25, he wheeled out his heaviest artillery:

> If French government are not prepared to give us positive reply, I propose make statement to press of the world that we have up to now fed the people along the border, that our resources do not permit us to continue, that we have applied to French government for aid, that we do not believe this is a proper appeal to the world's charity, that the responsibility for the death of these people rests on the French nation itself, and I propose to do this simply to free this Commission from responsibility as to what will follow on withdrawal of our present supplies.[20]

It soon became apparent why the French government did not care to confer with Hoover's representative. Like the British, the French were extremely reluctant to concede a role in principle for the independent relief commission. But more importantly, at this very moment the Allies were enforcing a rigorous embargo on food shipments into Germany. If the French government now permitted food purchased with its own money to pass through its own blockade in order to feed its suffering citizens behind enemy lines, the German government could demand that *it* be allowed to import food for *its* suffering citizens. Furthermore, any official recognition of the CRB, in the French government's view, would be tantamount to acquiescence in the "inhuman" German conduct in northern France. So averse were the French even to acknowledging the commission's existence that they declined at one point to discuss it in writing with the British government.[21]

On the other hand, President Poincaré and his Cabinet colleagues were under growing pressure at home to feed their beleaguered compatriots, and they were evidently loath to refuse publicly to do so. When Pinchot arrived, therefore, Poincaré and Foreign Minister Théophile Delcassé resorted to a simple expedient. Unwilling to give a definite answer to Hoover's appeal, they simply avoided meeting the carrier of his message.[22]

Finally, on February 26, after five days of total frustration, Pinchot obtained a mere five-minute interview—not with the president or foreign minister, but with the French minister of finance, Alexandre Ribot. Speaking "unofficially," Ribot declared in confidence that his government would not openly feed its people behind German lines. Nor would it formally approve expenditures of the Belgian government for the CRB. But, he added, money *would* be provided to the Belgian government-in-exile and "no inconvenient questions" would be asked.[23] In other words, like their British ally, the French would not *directly* assist Hoover's work in northern France but instead would quietly—very quietly—supply money for this purpose through the Belgians.

In early March Pinchot traveled to Le Havre, where he obtained the Belgian government-in-exile's assent to the indirect subsidy plan—provided, however, that Germany agreed not to requisition the imported food and provided further that at least five American CRB men should inspect the distribution on the spot.[24] On March 9 Hoover asked Ambassador Gerard to secure Berlin's acceptance of these terms. At this point the CRB's leader seemed confident of success—or so he intimated to Gerard. He informed the ambassador that he now had sufficient funds to feed the people of northern France if the Germans acquiesced in these conditions.[25]

This money, however, was not yet in hand, and as late February yielded to March, signs multiplied that the French government's commitment to Pinchot was tenuous. Alternative proposals kept cropping up. Might not relief money be raised by a charitable drive in France itself? Might not food be shipped from Marseilles by rail to Switzerland and then across Germany into northern France (instead of through the naval blockade into Rotterdam)? More disconcertingly still, on March 10 Hoover discovered that two Swiss army officers had already inspected occupied French territory and had announced that *they* would take charge of its relief with the consent of the French government.[26] The next day he learned that Paris was actively considering a plan to evacuate the entire population of the invaded territory across German lines—thereby eliminating any need for a relief commission at all.[27]

Hoover's opinion of these ideas was categorical. A public subscription campaign in France, he told Pinchot, would not "even touch the fringe of [the] problem."[28] It would merely "relax the pressure on the French Government to deal with it in a broad and efficient manner."[29] The proposal to evacuate over 2,000,000 French civilians out of German-held territory, he declared, was "perfectly ghastly."[30] As for the Swiss plan to ship supplies north by rail from Marseilles, it was "wholly impracticable," too expensive, and too slow. "There is in fact only one way to handle this problem," he insisted, "and that is through this Commission."[31]

The French government soon discarded the Swiss alternative as too costly and cumbersome.[32] But Hoover was taking no chances. Around the beginning of March he asked Louis Chevrillon, a prominent French mining engineer whom he had known before the war, to lobby the French government in the CRB's behalf. Chevrillon promptly "lit fires" (in Hoover's words) under the reluctant French authorities; in this he was joined by business and political leaders from the famine-threatened districts.[33] By March 9 he could report that the government's options had narrowed to two (reliance on the CRB or a mass evacuation) but that word of its decision was still a few days off.[34]

Accustomed to getting things done in a hurry, Hoover was becoming increasingly agitated. Reports from the field indicated that conditions in France were far worse than those in Belgium.[35] To feed 2,000,000 Frenchmen a tolerable ration, he would have to import 13,000 tons of wheat, 1,200 tons of beans, 500 tons of bacon, and 1,200 tons of rice per month at a cost of £300,000. But how? We must have money for this, he cabled Pinchot on March 15. We must have money "at once."[36] To the Belgian government-in-exile he addressed a similar plea.[37]

Privately Hoover now regarded the extension of his work to French territory as "inevitable." But publicly he maintained his pose of intransigence. "I have refused to go further, and have even threatened to stop," he told a friend, "unless I have a formal agreement from the French Government covering the question of finance" through July. Nor did the Germans escape his drumfire. Unless they solemnly gave the CRB "adequate respect and protection," he warned, "we will not do anything. . . ."[38] And still the days passed.

Finally he could stand it no longer. On March 20 he left London for France—determined to cut through the fog of diplomatic ambiguity.[39] That same day (and probably after conferring with him) the British Foreign Office instructed its ambassador in Paris to urge the French government to "come to some definite decision" about its relations with the CRB. The Foreign Office gently stated the obvious: that if the commission was to feed 2,000,000 Frenchmen, it must have French government money to do so.[40]

Stopping first at Le Havre, Hoover consulted with the leaders of the Belgian government-in-exile. The meeting was not productive. Two weeks before, the Belgians had promised Pinchot to finance the relief of northern France (on the assumption that the French government would pay the bill). Now, however, Hoover discovered that the French and Belgians had apparently never formalized this understanding.[41] Accompanied by Emile Francqui and another member of the Comité National, Hoover hastened to Paris and a showdown with the elusive French. He would not be kept waiting for long.

On March 22 Hoover and his colleagues met Théophile Delcassé. Suddenly the clouds disappeared. The foreign minister expressed great surprise. What! Had not the Belgian government told the CRB? The French Cabinet had already come to a "satisfactory understanding" concerning relief work in its occupied territory!

Later that day, the components of this plan were set forth in an informal memorandum, signed only, apparently, by Francqui. The document stated that the French government would have "no official relations" with the CRB or the Comité National but would be "grateful" to them for assistance in the German-occupied districts. As for finance, the exiled Belgian government was now authorized to withdraw from its account at the Bank of France and turn over to the CRB "all sums necessary" for the relief of the needy in northern France. All money thus withdrawn would be replaced—although by whom the document did not explicitly say.[42]

The next day the decisive memorandum was sent to Le Havre. Four days later, back at his office in London, Hoover received a check from the Belgian government for 25,000,000 francs (equal to $5,000,000) for the French portion of the relief.[43] More would come henceforth on a monthly basis.

Two days before he obtained this initial deposit, Hoover announced to the press that negotiations for feeding 2,500,000 French civilians had at last succeeded. Faithful to the subterfuge that governed his mode of funding, he declared: "The French Government was unable to come to the assistance of these unfortunate people, so the commission arranged a series of banking credits on behalf of the various communal authorities which are cut off from the rest of the country by the German Army."[44] He did not disclose that the source of these "banking credits" was the government in Paris itself.

For the next two weeks Hoover and his colleagues labored to extend their organization and make the necessary arrangements with the Germans. Rail and canal service must be established, warehouses and milling facilities set up, local and regional committees formed, prices fixed, bakeries regulated, ration cards distributed, and financial mechanisms created in more than 2,100 separate communes covering 8,100 square miles.[45] All this in a region where military operations took precedence, where industrial activity had halted, where French males of draft age had either joined their own army or been virtually imprisoned by the enemy, where civilians could not travel outside their own community, and where a hostile army ruled. Even as the diplomatic negotiations continued, the CRB expanded its distribution of vital supplies. During March, according to Hoover, more than half a million French civilians were fed, while in early April the first shipments of flour reached Lille and Valenciennes at last.[46]

Finally, on April 13, Hoover's director in Brussels signed three "treaties" with the German high command on the western front. The German army authorized the CRB to feed occupied France and pledged to leave the commission's food supplies alone. In addition, the Germans permitted the stationing of a dozen commission delegates of American nationality in the region in order to supervise the distribution and verify the German guarantees. But because these Americans would be living in militarily sensitive areas, they would have to be accompanied at all times by German officers, and all their communications would be censored. Each delegate, the agreement stipulated, was expected to behave as "an honorable citizen of a neutral state."[47]

Hoover decided to install a CRB "ambassador" at the German army's Great Headquarters in Charleville, just a few miles behind the front lines.[48] The man who was to have been his chief representative in northern France, however, never got there. At the end of March, Gifford Pinchot attempted to cross from Holland into Belgium on commission business. Laden with correspondence and dispatches (including items foolishly supplied by American minister van Dyke), he aroused the suspicion of German border agents, who requested that he and his baggage be searched. When Pinchot refused, he was promptly detained in Antwerp while the governor-general of Belgium considered what to do. To further complicate matters, on his way through Holland Pinchot had committed the indiscretion of visiting his sister and brother-in-law, the British minister to the Hague. For the German military, always on the lookout for British spies, this was evidence enough. Asserting that Pinchot was pro-Ally (which was true) and had made anti-German remarks, Governor-General von Bissing expelled him from the country. His service to the CRB was over.[49]

Hoover was chagrined that he had selected for his enterprise anyone whom the Germans could have found "any semblance of a cause" for rejecting.[50] But Pinchot's departure, though embarrassing, was not fatal. Eventually Hoover selected as a successor an old friend and Stanford University professor, Vernon Kellogg. With graduate training from the University of Leipzig, fluency in German, and a singular gift of tact, Kellogg was to be one of his greatest assets.[51]

The CRB's work in its new sphere would not be devoid of tension. Unlike their counterparts in Belgium, Hoover's men in northern France were not free to roam at will or converse uninhibitedly with their native associates. At every moment, even in their personal living quarters, a German officer was present. Bereft of privacy, unable to utter their innermost thoughts (except at weekend conferences in Brussels), many CRB representatives in northern France suffered nervous breakdowns. Few could stand the strain of the assignment for more than six months.[52]

But for the moment, in the spring of 1915, these and other stresses lay mercifully in the future. What mattered for the present was that another wearisome struggle had been won. Once again Hoover and his associates had overcome the resistance of a belligerent government. Like the British Cabinet before them, and like the CRB's jealous rivals in America, the French now knew that whatever this man Hoover wanted, he meant by all means to get.

I I

IN the early months of the war, most of Hoover's battles had been waged against the Allies. Some indeed must have wondered whether in his zeal to save the Belgians, vindicate American ideals, and administer—even monopolize—the relief work, his diplomacy had been truly symmetrical in application. In response to his constant pleadings and bludgeonings, the Allies had reluctantly permitted the shipment of food into enemy-held territory—and largely at their own expense besides. Yet what, during this same period, had the Germans done? What concessions had Hoover extracted from them? On his only visit to Berlin, and despite his "club of public opinion," the Germans had resolutely refused to lift their punitive levies on the Belgian nation. Repeatedly they had vowed that they would not and could not feed the millions of enemy civilians under their control, and Hoover had taken them at their word. While the Germans had made various promises, and had readily allowed the CRB to organize, their cooperation thus far had cost them nothing.

But if Hoover initially aimed his fire primarily at the Allies, he was not to do so for long. As the spring of 1915 broke over Europe, it became the Germans' turn to feel the force of his formidable will.

On his way back from Germany to London in early February, the CRB chairman stopped briefly in Brussels. His trip was not without incident; for a time prior to his departure, the German authorities held up authorization for his wife to accompany him. The episode did nothing to enhance his esteem for Teutonic bureaucracy.[53]

The problem of passports, in fact, was much on Hoover's mind during his journey. Despite assurances by the German Foreign Office that his men inside Belgium would receive all necessary passes to travel throughout the country, in early winter the German passport bureau in Brussels turned alarmingly obstructive. Delays in granting travel permits became ever more irksome; routine applications went unprocessed for up to weeks at a time.[54] As if in counterpoint with their foe across the English Channel, the Germans seemed to be having second thoughts.

The reason for this turnabout was simple. Scooting about the countryside in automobiles to the cheers and salutes of the populace, acclaimed as agents of benevolence whom the invader could not control, the men of the CRB boosted the Belgians' morale and steeled their determination never to submit to their oppressor. This development increasingly rankled the German army. Who were these ubiquitous young Yankees with American flags aflutter on their motorcars? How trustworthy were they? Might they not be spies? Why should they be permitted to wander freely behind our lines in wartime, in a country that we have conquered and now govern? At one point the governor-general himself apparently asked aloud who was running Belgium anyway: his army or the CRB delegates? Under the circumstances, German determination to curb these foreigners grew.[55]

To Hoover this intention was intolerable. The very purpose of the CRB inside Belgium was to supervise the distribution of food and establish that the Germans were not cheating. For these tasks freedom of travel was indispensable. To the German army, of course, the presence of such alien inspectors seemed unnecessary and nearly insulting. After all, the governor-general had decreed that the CRB's food would be left alone—orders were orders— and that was that. If any soldier committed an infraction, the military authorities would handle the case. To Hoover—and behind him, the British Cabinet—the word of a German general was not sufficient.[56]

The seemingly minor issue of passports, then, was critical to the continuance of the CRB, and on the evening of February 11, 1915 Hoover took the matter to the governor-general of occupied Belgium, Baron Moritz Ferdinand von Bissing. Forty years old, aggressively American, and with no knowledge of the German language (he had failed the subject in college), Hoover confronted a seventy-one-year-old Prussian army officer who looked (in Brand Whitlock's words) "like an aged drill-sargent." Slight of build and of no more than medium height, with a "cannon ball of a head" and a black mustache extending across his firm jaws, von Bissing was dressed in full uniform, including helmet, high boots, and a sword.[57] Hoover found him "arrogant" and "pompous"; Hugh Gibson gibed that he was the only German general who could strut sitting down.[58]

Through an interpreter Hoover tried to make his case for liberality in the issuance of passports. The governor-general replied ominously that the CRB had "too much liberty already," that its men were "running to and fro all over the country," and that Hoover must rearrange his relief work so as to reduce—not expand—the need for passes. When Hoover stated that his men had to oversee the distribution of 90,000,000 kilos of food per month, von Bissing rejoined that the Belgians themselves could distribute the food and that the CRB merely needed a man at each provincial warehouse. Unable to get the governor-general to budge, Hoover dropped the subject—for the moment.[59]

At this point a less assertive individual might have given up. Not Hoover. The next morning, "boiling with rage" (in Whitlock's words),[60] he drafted a letter to von Bissing. The "primary reason" for the existence of the CRB, he declared, was to create machinery that could assure the British that the imported food reached the Belgian people only. Without the freedom of movement to conduct "our daily work of supervision, inspection, and accounts," he could not take responsibility for making such assurances. Hoover staunchly defended the integrity of his American volunteers; there was no reason to think that such "gentlemen" would engage in espionage. And then, for the first of many times, he invoked his ultimate threat: unless the CRB could establish "friendly relations and trust" with the German authorities, it would be "compelled to withdraw" from its work, and all food shipments from the outside world into Belgium would "necessarily cease."[61]

Still angry at von Bissing, Hoover met later in the day with his deputy, Baron Oscar von der Lancken, head of the "political department" of the German government in Belgium. The "whole structure" of the relief was in jeopardy, Hoover asserted. He could not hold his staff together if they were subjected to further restraint. They would "not stand the iron heel like the Belgians." To still another German official Hoover complained of being treated "like spies instead of gentlemen." Von der Lancken promised to reopen the question with the governor-general.[62]

Having done his best to bestir the German bureaucracy, Hoover returned immediately to London. A week later old von Bissing replied. While professing support of the commission's humanitarian efforts, the German general noted that he would act only in accordance with the "irrefutable" principle that he alone would control the administration of "the country entrusted to me." The Prussian baron thereupon demanded that the number of CRB personnel inside Belgium be reduced to twenty-five (barely half their current number) and that their rapid turnover be stopped.[63]

The governor-general's letter was more than a rebuff; it was a challenge. Who indeed *was* going to control the relief: the Germans or the neutral commission? On March 6 Hoover reacted characteristically. That day he wrote to Brand Whitlock that the British government had been giving him a "severe drilling." How many people do you have in Belgium? they had asked. When Hoover had replied, "About fifty," they had thought the number too low. The CRB chairman expressed alarm at the turn that events were taking. The British "military party," so skeptical of the commission to begin with, was "gaining ascendancy daily." If it knew, said Hoover, that his Belgian staff was now to be cut to a mere twenty-five members, its reaction might be "positively disastrous."[64]

With the British lion roaring (or so he claimed to Whitlock), Hoover turned next to Berlin. On March 9 he asked Ambassador Gerard to intervene with the German government. As usual, he made his case emphatically. The attitude of von Bissing and his henchmen, he said, had left him "entirely discouraged." If the CRB were to maintain "proper executive control" over its work and make its assurances credible, it was "absolutely necessary" that he have the right to station "at least fifty people" inside Belgium.[65]

It did not take long for word of Hoover's maneuver to travel from Berlin down to Brussels. And when it did, the governor-general was enraged. Appointed directly by the Kaiser, and "especially jealous of his prerogatives," he welcomed intrusions from no one—not even the chancellor himself. Not only was the "touchy" von Bissing offended (said von der Lancken to Whitlock), the Germans were not going to recognize the CRB officially at all—only the Comité National and its diplomat-patrons.[66] But Hoover, for his part, was unrepentant. He had gone to Berlin, he argued, to allay a "perfect storm" of pressure from the British. People do not realize, he asserted, "by what a delicate balance this whole business continues."[67]

It is not clear that Hoover's position in London was nearly as precarious as he represented. More likely than not he was playing the game of *using* British "pressure" as a battering ram to achieve his objectives. It was frequently convenient, in fact, for him to claim that those terrible British militarists made him do things that he desired to do already. It was essential, too, to keep the Germans believing that "perfidious Albion" was breathing down his neck. But in this case, his interests and those of His Majesty's Government were probably congruent.

Under pressure from his superiors in Berlin, the elderly von Bissing backed down. On March 21 he announced that the CRB could employ about ten more persons inside Belgium after mid-April if necessary. The governor-general covered his retreat with various complaints and denials. It was all a matter of misunderstanding, he contended. Why, Dannie Heineman himself (who had been acting as an intermediary) had agreed that the staff reduction was just! Von Bissing insisted that he had not tried to restrict the commission's control system. Indeed, he asserted, no American supervision of German guarantees was even necessary since he had given his solemn word! And in a final sally, he flatly rejected Hoover's demand to be the sole arbiter of the number of Americans admitted into Belgium. That figure, the German stated, would be fixed according to need, "to be investigated by me as well."[68]

Hoover did not particularly mind the governor-general's somewhat petulant letter. The "main points," he told Whitlock, had been conceded; the rest was a mere "rattling of the sword."[69] But von Bissing never forgave Hoover for going over his head to Berlin. The troubles between them had just begun.[70]

The CRB chairman's joust with the German baron was soon overshadowed by other events. On February 4, 1915 the German government announced that as of February 18 all waters surrounding the British Isles were to be part of a new "war zone," in which German submarines would destroy enemy merchant ships on sight. Although neutral vessels would not be deliberately attacked, the Germans warned that mistakes might occur. Three days before the decree took effect, the imperial government advised Hoover's commission to avoid the war zone entirely and instead take a designated route north of Scotland and down a narrow sea-lane to the Dutch coast.[71] Several days later, the German consul in Rotterdam refused to issue safe conduct passes for commission craft returning from Holland to British ports, despite previous assurances that properly marked CRB vessels could cross the English Channel in daylight without harm.[72]

The CRB's shipping business, in Hoover's words, now came to an abrupt "dead end." For nearly three weeks in February and early March he was unable to obtain a single charter.[73] With the French government still obstructing him on the feeding of its occupied provinces, with von Bissing on the warpath over passes, Hoover now had to do battle on still another front. Never, it seemed, did his problems come toward him in single file.

Quickly he asked the Germans to reconsider. He pointed out that the British government required all CRB vessels to stop at the port of Falmouth for inspection and instructions. He declared that it was "utterly impossible" to deliver "one pound of foodstuffs" to Holland via the north-of-Scotland route; shipping under those restraints was unobtainable. He demanded that the German government instruct its submarines to respect his shipping between England and Holland. Every Belgian relief ship, he noted, carried banners that were "visible for miles." If the Germans could not take this step, then continuance of his mission was "absolutely hopeless."[74]

Fortunately for Hoover, and for the millions whose hopes rested on his shoulders, there were sympathetic ears in Berlin. On March 5 Foreign Minister von Jagow announced that the ships of the commission, if properly marked, could proceed unharmed across the Channel.[75] Once again the relief vessels started to move.[76] But now a new concern agitated the German navy:

the CRB's food ships from North America were calling first at British ports. Might not these vessels, it wondered, be carrying contraband? Might not the duplicitous British be using CRB markings as a disguise to protect ships filled with materials of war? Late in March the Germans accused three specific ships of having brought munitions to England while flying the CRB's flag.[77] If true, it could be the death knell for the commission.

Hoover promptly disputed the charges. Two of the ships, he reported, were actually British Admiralty colliers that had come from Canada. Their cargoes evidently did include war material as well as some Belgian relief supplies that they had been persuaded to take on in Halifax. The nonrelief part of their cargo had indeed been discharged at an English port. But neither of these ships had belonged to the CRB, had borne its flag and banners, or been subject to commission control. As for the third ship (which was under contract), it, said Hoover, had carried nothing but foodstuffs and "a certain amount of Red Cross material for the Germans themselves." None of its cargo had been placed upon English soil. "I will voluntarily go to crucifiction," he declared, "if the Germans or anyone else on earth can show that we have transported one solitary ounce of war material other than Red Cross supplies, under our flag."[78]

The escalating war of nerves soon ceased to be verbal. On March 21 a German airplane attacked several vessels including the CRB's *Elfand* in the North Sea. Fortunately no damage occurred.[79] But less than three weeks later, in the broad morning daylight of April 10, the CRB ship *Harpalyce* was torpedoed without warning by a German submarine in the English Channel. The vessel carried a German safe conduct pass and displayed a one-hundred-foot-long identifying banner visible for five miles. Seventeen crew members, including the captain, were lost.[80]

Hoover was outraged:

Here is a ship [he told Ambassador Page] engaged in this work, not only destroyed in contravention of every sacred assurance of Government undertaking and of humanity but the assurances that we have universally given to shipowners and insurers that if they would engage in this traffic they would be free from attack, is blown to the winds; every contract we have made for ships and insurance based on this agreement is shattered, the work brought to a standstill, and the lives of 10,000,000 people imperilled.

I simply find myself totally unable to express in sober language a proper characterisation of this action. It is absolutely in its complete barbarism without parallel in the last century. I count myself as not being given to hysterics over the abnormal events of modern warfare but if this action can be reconciled with any military necessity, or, to put it on its lowest plane, of any military advantage, then we can but abandon any hope that civilis-

ation has yet accomplished anything but enlarged ruthlessness in destruction of human life.

If the Commission for Relief in Belgium is "worthy of the American people,"
he said,

> it is now time for the American Government to come forward and say
> what they are going to do about this. . . . If there is any sacredness in
> undertakings between the German and American Governments and if
> America counts our work for anything it has now come a time for our
> President to demand in common humanity, consideration for us and the
> people who serve us.[81]

Hoover's indignation was intensified by his feeling of moral responsibility
toward men on the seas in his service. We assure sailors (he told a friend)

> that if they go to sea with our documents and our markings that they are
> going to be free from attack. We put these men under bond that they will
> not endeavour to protect themselves. They preceed blindly and without
> precautions on the faith of these assurances and their death [is] nothing
> short of assasination. There is nothing in international liability, military
> necessity, or, on its lowest plain, in military advantage, in sinking one of
> these ships, it is simply murder gone mad. Were it not that any false step
> on our part might jeopardise the lives of nine millions of people, I would
> bounce forward with a statement that would be as black a mark as has ever
> been put up against any nation yet.[82]

The destruction of the *Harpalyce* plunged the work of the CRB into "perfect turmoil."[83] On April 16 the German legation at the Hague announced
that it would no longer issue safe conduct passes to commission ships returning to British ports—despite the fact that these vessels usually needed to stop
in England to obtain fuel for their next voyage.[84] The next day, in apparent
retaliation, the British Admiralty forbade the CRB's fleet to venture into or
out of Rotterdam. Within less than a week the transportation of food to Belgium had come, in Hoover's words, to "a complete stop."[85] In Brussels Brand
Whitlock compared the revictualing to fitting a stovepipe: "as soon as we get
one side adjusted the other side comes off—and the pipe is hot."[86]

With ship captains in England and Holland now unable to move their food
cargoes (and holding the commission accountable for demurrage costs), with
the very existence of the relief enterprise in the balance, Hoover reached for
every weapon available. He drafted a cable to Washington (for Walter Hines
Page to sign) asking President Wilson in the name of humanity to intercede
through Ambassador Gerard in Berlin.[87] To Gerard himself Hoover ghost-

wrote a separate cable (which Page duly signed) asking for a renewed German commitment on passes.[88] The Commission for Relief in Belgium, said Page, was "totally unable" to induce ships to sail to Rotterdam unless it could provide a safe conduct for their return, and he warned that the *Harpalyce* incident was strengthening the hand of those British politicians who opposed the relief on military grounds. The German government, said Page, had better accede to the commission's "moderate requests" if it wanted the work to continue. He also suggested that the Germans take "appropriate action" to preserve their "good name" after the *Harpalyce* tragedy.[89]

Hoover also fired off a barrage to Brand Whitlock. "If the Germans are endeavouring to break down this Commission," he wrote, "they are going about it in the proper manner." Their attitude toward the shipping question was "diabolical." "It appears to me," he added, "that the Germans in Berlin have no realisation of the value of this enterprise to them from a military point of view. . . ." If Governor-General von Bissing appreciated this fact he would advise Berlin to "leave our ships alone and give us all the safe-conduct passes we ask for."[90]

It is hard to know whether Hoover really believed what he had just said to Whitlock: that the Belgian relief gave a military advantage to the Germans. But he knew that this was the kind of argument that might impress a Prussian general, and he obviously hoped that Whitlock would use it with von Bissing. Hoover was becoming expert at tailoring his arguments to his audiences, and in this communication he may only have been reciting (as he often did in such cables) the particular "line" that he wished his correspondent to take.

In the midst of the uproar the German Foreign Office retreated. On April 18 von Jagow informed Gerard that German submarine commanders had been ordered to leave properly marked CRB vessels alone. The Foreign Ministry had also instructed its legation in Holland to furnish safe conduct passes to commission ships for their voyages back to England, provided that they carried no return cargo and were obliged by contract to return to English ports.[91] The lifeline across the Channel was restored.

But the Germans' response to the *Harpalyce* incident was much less satisfactory. Early in May they acknowledged sinking a vessel in the Channel on April 10 but insisted that it had displayed no CRB markings. (Hoover had eyewitnesses and photographs to the contrary.)[92] In the end, since the ship had been insured, its owners received compensation for their lost property.[93]

Barely had the *Harpalyce* affair subsided when new trouble emanated from Brussels. On April 12 a German-language newspaper in New York published an interview with Governor-General von Bissing, an interview implying (in Hoover's words) that the CRB was "a lot of commercial pirates operating under the cloak of charity." When Hoover learned of this later in the month, he was furious. "Every German official in Belgium," he told Ambassador Gerard, must know perfectly well that there are now 1,500,000 people being fed gratis from the public canteens and that these canteens are being supported by this Commission. Also General von Bissing is perfectly well aware that whereas we do sell foodstuffs to those who can still pay, at a small margin of profit, this margin of profit goes to assist in the support of the canteens and to make up some part of the deficiency which must be otherwise supplied entirely by public charity. . . . If we are to maintain this machinery in existence after [the next harvest] it is going to be necessary . . . that General von Bissing shall remove the stigma which he has placed over this body of idealists.[94]

Hoover promptly sent his Brussels office a cable threatening (in Brand Whitlock's words) "to stop the whole enterprise" unless von Bissing repudiated the interview. Whitlock transmitted the cable to the Germans, who refused to show it to von Bissing because of its perceived reflections upon his character! Instead, the Germans asked Whitlock to remove Hoover's offending language and submit a more diplomatic note. Whitlock agreed to do so, and the matter was evidently resolved.[95]

But tension between the Germans and the Americans was growing. On May 8 two CRB delegates were arrested in the province of Luxemburg; the next day the pair was released.[96] In London Hoover was beginning to believe that "there is nothing that an American can do which in German eyes is not founded on sinister motives no matter how much the Germans themselves may benefit from it."[97]

The von Bissing interview and other petty harassments were soon subsumed by a far greater crisis. On May 7, 1915 the British passenger ship *Lusitania* was sunk by a German submarine off the Irish coast. Nearly 1,200 people, including 128 Americans, lost their lives.

For several tense days a diplomatic break between Germany and the United States seemed probable, and with it the forced withdrawal of American relief personnel from inside Belgium. Hoover therefore took preliminary steps to replace his volunteers in Belgium with neutral Dutchmen if necessary. He also accelerated food shipments so that the Belgians would be "well stocked up" in case of a "shock."[98] Privately he was confident that his humanitarian enterprise would continue in any event—the Germans were quite anxious that it should—and that, except for the introduction of Dutch volunteers into German-held areas, the vast relief mechanism could function unchanged, if less efficiently.[99] Still, the thought of installing Dutch or Spanish workers for Americans on Belgian soil, he confided to a friend, filled him with "profound depression."[100]

As it happened, the *Lusitania* affair passed—but not Hoover's troubles with the Germans. Like the larger inferno around him, the "relief war" had more than one front. Even as German U-boats were putting the CRB's fate in doubt, the CRB chairman was discovering something else: the occupiers of

Belgium might be good at keeping their promises, but they were equally assiduous at creating loopholes.

Toward the end of December 1914 the German undersecretary of state for foreign affairs, Arthur Zimmermann, had orally promised Ambassador Gerard that the German army would not seize any further native food supplies in Belgium as long as the CRB was importing food. But when, a few days later, it came time to reduce this pledge to writing, Zimmermann had suddenly inserted a reservation: the Germans would refrain from requisitioning only the native food and forage that the CRB *would specifically have to replace.* On January 21 Governor-General von Bissing had confirmed this. Since the CRB was then importing only about a half-dozen kinds of foodstuff, this meant that the Germans were free to scize *every other* kind of indigenous food that they liked.[101]

As if to leave no doubt about his intentions, on March 12 von Bissing refused to broaden his pledge. Only native-grown items, he said, that the CRB itself was also importing were exempt from seizure by his forces. Other items—like potatoes, hay, and oats—were not. More seriously still, the governor-general disclosed that his government's promises were not indefinite in duration (as Zimmermann had implied) but merely covered native food already in the country in mid-January. In other words, they did *not* apply to the next harvest.[102]

Immediately a new emergency loomed. Hoover's monthly Allied subsidy was scheduled to last until June—just prior to the summer's new crop. The Belgian people would need this harvest; it could supply perhaps one-third of their requirements. But if the Great War were still raging, would their German masters let them have it? If not, would the Allies acquiesce? Or would their subvention—and the entire relief program—come to a terrible halt?

On April 6 Hoover got his answer: Lord Eustace Percy of the British Foreign Office informed him bluntly that the Germans must "scrupulously respect" the coming harvest or the British would reconsider their "whole attitude." In the British view, the Germans had promised in December to seize no more foodstuffs in Belgium—period. Any attempt now to qualify their pledge was unacceptable. The enemy, said Percy, must not "divert to their own use one ounce of the food" that would otherwise go to the Belgian people. Furthermore, the Commission for Relief in Belgium must continue adequately to monitor the German guarantees and must receive German cooperation while doing so. His government had compromised on many points, Percy declared, but it would not compromise on this.[103]

It now fell to the overworked Hoover to initiate yet another series of negotiations. Even before receiving Percy's letter, he asked Ambassador Gerard to consider interceding with the Kaiser. At this point the CRB chairman was reluctant to approach the German Foreign Office. Such a tactic only enraged von Bissing, and the civil authorities in Berlin had no control over the old general anyway.[104] But Gerard was unable to make any headway either. By

May 1 all Hoover's efforts had stalled.[105]

On that day he decided upon a daring maneuver. On his own initiative he asked Lord Percy to write him a letter warning that unless the Germans guaranteed not to seize the coming harvest, the work of the CRB would have to end on August 15. Hoover told Percy that he wanted a "lever" against the Germans. The British diplomat agreed to supply it.[106]

Later that day, even before receiving Percy's prearranged communication, Hoover composed a letter of his own to Berlin. He told Ambassador Gerard that he had just received an "intimation" from the Allies that if the Germans did not agree to respect the Belgian harvest the Allies would insist that the CRB cease operations and "absolutely dissolve" as of mid-August. If, however, the Germans consented to this stipulation, he was confident that he could secure the necessary finance to sustain his enterprise. But, he asserted, "the whole future" of his work now rested on Germany's willingness to make the necessary promise. Hoover did not tell Gerard that he himself had solicited this "intimation."[107]

Gerard promptly conveyed this alarming "news" to the German government, as Hoover, of course, wanted him to do.[108] Meanwhile, on May 4, Percy duly sent Hoover the "threat" that he had requested. Time is running out, the British official warned. It was "self-evident" that unless the Germans unequivocally guaranteed the forthcoming harvest against seizure, the work of the CRB would "in all probability have to stop when the harvest matures. . . ."[109]

The British government was not as committed to its ultimatum as its admonitory words suggested. Percy in fact deliberately wrote his letter in unofficial form, thereby freeing his superiors to pursue other courses if they chose. But the Hoover-inspired communication was not entirely fictitious in content. None other than Sir Edward Grey privately admitted that he was "incline[d]" to the view that unless the Germans came to satisfactory terms the CRB would have to terminate its mission.[110] Hoover might be bluffing to intimidate the Germans, but the danger was real that the British might yet give credence to his bluff.

Hoover's remarkable collaboration with the Foreign Office underscored a deepening trend in the spring of 1915: as his difficulties with the Germans multiplied, his cooperation with the British grew more intimate. Whatever His Majesty's Government might think of the relief project in principle, its confidence in Hoover personally was rising. When the governor-general of Australia, among others, questioned Hoover's reliability because of some allegedly disreputable mining connections, the Foreign Office vigorously came to his defense: in his administration of the Belgian relief, it said, he had "shown himself capable, straightforward and disinterested. He has always invited and facilitated the fullest investigation. . . ."[111]

Perhaps the most extraordinary testimonial to Hoover's growing stature in British eyes came late that spring from the head of the War Office, Lord

Kitchener, one of the most vehement opponents of the CRB. According to Hoover, Kitchener sent for him one day and asked him whether he would renounce his American citizenship and become a British subject. Why? Hoover asked. Because, came the reply, the British wanted him to do a "great service" for their government. Hoover responded that he would be glad to perform any service for the British within his power. But aside from his feelings of patriotic sentiment he was afraid to become British. "I should soon lose my Yankee energy," he said.

Afterward Hoover recounted this conversation to Walter Hines Page. You have thrown away a peerage, the ambassador remarked. "Good God!" Hoover grunted in disgust—and said no more.[112] The last thing he wanted was to be a member of the House of Lords.

What, precisely, had Kitchener been driving at? During the month of May the Asquith government was rocked by news of a scandalous shortage of shells for its army on the western front. During the ensuing uproar the prime minister was obliged to establish a coalition ministry, including a new Cabinet-level department to supervise munitions production. Hoover later told Brand Whitlock that Kitchener had proposed to make Hoover minister of munitions if he would change his citizenship.[113] But to Ambassador Page, Hoover reported only that the British government had suggested an unspecified "great service." Page learned elsewhere that it evidently wanted Hoover to become a principal assistant to the new minister of munitions, Lloyd George.[114] But whatever the exact character of the "service" that was offered to Hoover (and which he may have exaggerated to impress Whitlock), there could be no better measure of his ability than that Kitchener had sent for him at all.

Meanwhile Hoover's campaign to safeguard the 1915 harvest encountered an unexpected obstacle—a consequence of a too-successful ploy. When Emile Francqui of the Comité National heard the "news" that Hoover might close down operations on August 15, he registered a speedy objection. British approval of the relief in October 1914, he argued, had been granted on one condition only: that the Germans would respect *imported* goods. Francqui, of course, did not want the Germans to seize the forthcoming harvest. But even if they did, he asserted, this was not a valid pretext for the British to quash the entire relief effort. The importations should continue regardless.[115]

Now is was Lord Percy's turn to complain. The Comité National, he told Hoover stiffly on May 26, ought to recognize that the British were trying to protect the Belgians' own harvest for them and should not complain about the British action. The "whole value of our attitude as a means of putting pressure on the Germans," he added, "will be compromised if the Comité National regard us as hard-hearted tyrants instead of backing our attitude up with what influence they have in Belgium. . . ."[116]

And if Hoover still regarded Percy's "threat" of May 4 as a mere "lever," the British thought differently now. "There is . . . no 'bluff' about our actions,"

Percy advised Hoover. We are "in deadly earnest about stopping the whole arrangement" if the Germans do not come to terms.[117] There is no evidence that *this* letter was "inspired."

In his communication of May 4, Percy had given Hoover a deadline of the end of the month. But the sinking of the *Lusitania* upset Hoover's timetable, and it was not before June 7 that he crossed the Channel for a fateful confrontation.[118] As usual, before leaving he tried to exert pressure upon the Germans. He wrote ahead to Brand Whitlock that the British were "fairly in earnest" about their ultimatum.[119] He asked Lindon Bates to tell an influential German friend in America that the Allied governments had given "absolute orders" to the CRB to import no food for Belgium beyond August 15 unless Germany gave the necessary pledges.[120] Presumably Bates's acquaintance would communicate this "fact" to Berlin. And in a lengthy letter to his chief representative inside Belgium—a letter clearly written for German consumption—Hoover recited the practical benefits of his relief work to the occupation forces: starvation and "great disturbances" had been averted, the local currency sustained, the "wheels of commerce" revived, "the path of [the German] civil government greatly smoothed out." He emphasized, too, the "constant running fight" that he was supposedly still waging with the British military, as well as the tremendous personal and professional losses that he and his colleagues were incurring. We are making "great sacrifices," he declared, "and we do feel that we should receive the support of the intelligent and able men who control the German Government of Belgium." (This was hardly what he thought of von Bissing & Company, but he was not averse to using flattery when he had to.)[121] With these familiar arguments he prepared to lay siege in Brussels—and, if necessary, Berlin.[122]

Privately Hoover felt "very despondent" (in Lord Percy's words) about his chances of success. In the midst of the still-boiling *Lusitania* crisis he could hardly rely on the U.S. government to exert any influence on the Germans.[123] Percy, too, was apprehensive. He feared that unless the British gave in and let the Germans confiscate most of the Belgian harvest, the British would face the "unpleasant alternative" of "leaving Belgium to starve"—with a resultant international outcry not against the Germans but themselves.[124] Percy was also aware that tens of thousands of idle and defiant Belgians were using Hoover's relief food to stay alive. Faced with starvation after a CRB withdrawal, they might well be obliged to work for the Germans on military projects in order to obtain their daily bread.[125] For all their tough talk, then, about being "in deadly earnest," the British had less leverage than it seemed.

On the evening of June 9 Hoover arrived in Brussels and plunged into a maelstrom of negotiations.[126] From the start he was furious at the Germans— furious at what Whitlock, in his diary, called their unending "insult, suspicion, contempt, [and] hatred" directed toward the Commission for Relief in Belgium.[127] At one point von der Lancken clumsily excluded Hoover from a general meeting of relief patrons and officials; the baron claimed that he preferred to see Hoover privately. When Hoover learned of this snub he affected unconcern. He knew, he said, that he was *persona non grata* with the Germans.[128] But the CRB chairman was not a man to be slighted without resenting it.

Nor was he one to tolerate disloyalty in his ranks. Within two days of his arrival, "the usual antipathy of Villalobar and Hoover for each other" (as Whitlock called it) surfaced spectacularly when Hoover heard that the Spanish minister had been disparaging the CRB behind the scenes. Infuriated at Villalobar for poisoning the Germans' minds against the commission, Hoover notified Brand Whitlock that he and his associates were ready to quit the relief work entirely.[129] His ominous words had their desired effect. Upon learning of Hoover's remarks, Villalobar at once praised the commission to Whitlock as "an excellent organization" that must be fought for and saved. The Spanish aristocrat even professed to "think well of Hoover whatever he may think of me." The gullible Whitlock was delighted by his words.[130] The chairman of the CRB knew better.

Villalobar was not the only Spanish diplomat with whom the Yankee executive had clashed. Back in March he had lost his temper at a meeting with the Spanish consul-general in London. Hoover had promptly apologized and had asked the official to remember that "the load of a debt of £1,400,000, for which I stand personally liable, is sufficient to drive one quite out of his temper once in a while."[131] And indeed the strain was unending. But more than overwork and the volatile chemistry of personality accounted for Hoover's difficulties. In his *Memoirs* he remarked laconically that Villalobar "did not much like Americans."[132] Nor did Hoover himself seem to care much for the Spanish. Despite his professions of regret to the Spanish consul-general in London, within two weeks Hoover kicked him upstairs. "He is not only no good, but butts in occasionally and makes trouble," the Chief confided to a friend. "We therefore decided to have some honorary vice-chairmen and promote him to that job." Hoover did not mind a few harmless Spanish names on the commission's masthead—as long as the "actual executive staff" was American.[133] But for Old World hauteur and hypocrisy he did little to conceal his disdain.

German arrogance and Spanish meddling were not the only drains on his scanty reserves of patience during this visit. According to Hugh Gibson (who was Whitlock's chief deputy at the legation), Hoover arrived in Brussels "filled with irritation" at Whitlock's perceived laziness and unassertive demeanor toward the Germans. In the ensuing days, said Gibson, Hoover "was treated to one bad experience after another and his irritation changed to disgust and rage." The result, Gibson confessed, was "a hellish week for me for I have had to be the buffer. . . ."[134] Harassed on every side, Hoover was coming to regard Whitlock as a diplomatic dilettante who was spending far more time on his literary interests than engaging in the "rough stuff" of Hoover-style diplomacy.[135]

Like Hoover a Californian, and like Hoover a man of driving energy, Gibson sympathized with the CRB chairman. "It is a shame to have him do all the hard work, get no credit and no support from people who shd overwhelm him with it," he wrote on June 25, "but I don't see that his rage is going to do any good."[136] Still, the young diplomat noticed more to this man than his abrasiveness and quickness to anger. Hoover might offend British prime ministers, German generals, and Spanish diplomats by his blunt and at times bullying manner, but to those who worked under him it was a different story. "I should like to see H.C.H. run for President," Gibson wrote to his mother that June: "He has all the qualities required—rare common sense and judgment—wonderful executive ability—and high idealism of a practical sort. The only trouble is nobody ever heard of him."[137]

Despite the growing personal strains in Brussels, Hoover quickly achieved some success. On June 16 the Germans agreed in principle to reserve the 1915 crop to the Belgian people.[138] But principle was one thing, precise understandings another. And as Hoover already realized, the Germans were adept at evasions. It soon turned out that their promise of nonrequisition applied only to native wheat and rye, and not to potatoes, hay, or other indigenous crops to which they obviously intended to help themselves. Another complication also emerged: Just how would the food that Belgian farmers harvested be gathered and distributed to the rest of the population? It seemed that General von Bissing had some very definite ideas.[139]

And so ensued a week of discussion and anxiety. While Whitlock, Villalobar, and Francqui took the lead in conferring at length with von der Lancken, Hoover remained discreetly in the background, preparing memoranda for their use.[140] On June 17 the two sides reached a formal accord. Von Bissing would reserve the complete wheat and rye harvest for the Belgian civil population; in return the CRB and Comité National promised to import all necessary foodstuffs for another twelve months, until the harvest of 1916. As for the exact manner of distributing the native crop, the general would decide that later.[141]

It was now necessary to gain the approval of Berlin.[142] But as the next several days passed with no word of confirmation from the German capital, Hoover grew restive and gloomy. By June 22 he could contain his frustration no longer.[143]

That day he wrote a memorandum for Whitlock to convey to von der Lancken—a memorandum designed to jolt the Germans in a hurry. Hoover claimed that only a settlement of the harvest question was preventing the CRB from signing a contract to use German-owned cargo ships that were currently interned in neutral ports. Each day's delay, he asserted, was costing the commission £5,000. He claimed that only with "a great deal of difficulty" was he restraining the British government from issuing a public statement that would embarrass the Germans on the harvest issue, and he professed his "keen desire" that the Germans make an announcement of a settlement first. Indeed, he said, it would be "most disagreeable to us" if the British now made it appear that the Germans had yielded under British pressure! Finally, and not for the last time, he hinted at resignation and withdrawal. "It is perfectly immaterial to the CRB," he said loftily, "whether or not these negotiations reach a successful consummation, except as to their interest in the people of Belgium." If the German government did not want the CRB to continue, he said, "it would be only too glad to retire from the entire situation. . . ."[144]

Hoover's seemingly frank memorandum was partially, perhaps totally, a bluff. There is no evidence that he was on the verge of acquiring German ships interned in neutral waters; those negotiations had been dragging on for months.[145] Nor is it at all certain that the British were really hankering to issue a pronouncement in the press. To be sure, Hoover had received a cable to this effect from London just a few days before, but it is at least conceivable that he secretly instigated this cable in order to put more pressure on the Germans.[146] Nor is it likely that the CRB's guiding executive would have serenely "retired" from the relief if the Germans had decided to terminate it. Passivity in the face of challenge was not a part of his temperament.

It is not known whether Hoover's message had any effect on its recipient. But just two days later, on June 24, von der Lancken assured Whitlock that Governor-General von Bissing would confirm in writing the agreement of June 17. That very afternoon Hoover returned to London.[147] Ten days later the general formally signed his letter of assent.[148]

The scene of battle now shifted across the Channel. Clearly Hoover had brought back much less than the British had demanded. Only two native crops had been brought under the commission's protection. Moreover, the Germans in return had attached a condition of their own: that the CRB continue its imports at current levels, without interference, until the summer of 1916. Would the British and the French agree to that?

Back in London on June 28, Hoover promptly announced his accord with von Bissing to the American press. He did not disclose that it was contingent upon the Allies' permitting him to carry on for another year.[149] Perhaps he regarded this as a formality. Or perhaps he was again playing fait accompli. It would be hard for the Allies to object to the agreement once he had proclaimed it as operative in the press of the world's leading neutral power.

That same day, June 28, Hoover opened his campaign to secure the British guarantees.[150] At this point a new squall broke on the continent. For several months Governor-General von Bissing had evinced increasing displeasure with the operations of the Comité National. From an ad hoc committee established in Brussels the previous summer, it had burgeoned into a veritable state within a state, extending to every village in the country. To the German authorities the ever-expanding functions of this far-flung apparatus carried alarming potential for espionage and incitement of popular resistance to the invader. As the Comité tightened its control over its local affiliates, its political designs seemed all too apparent. The Germans were even more disturbed when, in April, the Comité instituted a special program of relief benefits for the unemployed. At this point more than 600,000 Belgians were jobless, and the Germans had been hoping to recruit them (on penalty of hunger and destitution) to work for their masters. But now, thanks to the Comité National's welfare programs, the unemployed could sustain themselves without working and thus frustrate the scheme of their oppressor.[151]

In the spring of 1915 Germans decided to restrain this autonomous giant and, above all, its department of *secours*.[152] Several weeks of "investigations" and discussions followed, with Francqui and Hoover each insisting that distribution of relief food and money must rest solely with the Comité National.[153] The Germans apparently did not mind the general process of revictualing (*alimentation*).[154] But the subsidization of the destitute, and especially of the destitute unemployed, was something else, for through it, in their view, the Comité National was financing a rebellion.[155] Meanwhile, across the country, many mines and factories remained silent—the consequence of both the British blockade and Belgian determination. Brand Whitlock called it a "general strike."[156]

Then, on June 26, with the harvest question apparently settled, Governor-General von Bissing made his move. In a letter to Whitlock and Villalobar, he announced a set of regulations restricting the Comité National and interposing German authority between it and its local committees. Henceforth, he decreed, his "civil" administrators were to keep themselves fully apprised of the Comité's activities. To this end they were to attend all meetings of the CN's provincial and regional committees. Henceforth, too, the German "civil" authorities were to censor all correspondence of these committees. No longer were these bodies to be permitted to give instructions to communes, make inquiries of them, receive data from them, or send them questionnaires without first consulting the relevant German administrator. Von Bissing further forbade the CN to supply any sanctions whatsoever (such as the threat to withhold food) against anyone—individually or communally—in an effort to enforce its instructions. As for unemployment relief, the German authorities, said he, would now see to it that such relief did not "hinder the resumption of work by the laboring population." In particular, from now on no worker could receive relief who "refuse[d] remunerative labor."[157]

Von Bissing's draconian announcement caused consternation inside Belgium.[158] Hoover, in London, was also worried. In a letter to Ambassador Page he tacitly conceded that the Germans had a point. Philosophically, Hoover considered the CN's *secours chômage* (unemployment relief) to be "socially wrongly founded": it distributed money "as a right to the unemployed" instead of "actual food as an emergency support pending employment."[159] ". . . I cannot see anything but social harm," he told the Belgian finance minister, "in giving workmen payment as a right for idleness."[160] (To forestall the Germans, the CN soon switched from monetary payments to 90% payment-in-kind.)[161] He knew very well that the effect of this policy was to underwrite a strike by railwaymen and other workers. He knew, too, that the Belgian army had smuggled money into Belgium to pay the strikers and that the Belgian government had tried to use the CRB for the same objective: a ploy it had vigorously resisted.[162] Now, as he had anticipated, the Germans were finally cracking down.

Nevertheless, Hoover could scarcely acquiesce in the new measures. It was a *sine qua non* of his agreements with the Allies that the Germans must not interfere with the distribution mechanism. Moreover, if the Comité National lost its power to withhold supplies from recalcitrant consumers and middlemen (such as bakers), how could it govern Belgian food consumption efficiently and equitably? To Hoover it was obvious that the Germans intended to use his food imports to compel the Belgian citizenry to work for the occupying army. The CRB could not let itself be manipulated for such an unneutral and illegal purpose.[163]

Privately Hoover now feared the worst. The "most miserable form of failure seems to confront us," he told friends: a breakdown of the commission not on "any broad international issues" but on "detailed internal trouble"— "points of minor issue between the belligerent Powers."[164] But if the CRB chairman was characteristically pessimistic, he also detected a way out. The British government had not yet ratified the results of his harvest negotiations. On June 30, therefore, and again (in all likelihood) on ensuing days, he asked the British to make their acceptance *conditional* on several *new* requirements, which he himself composed. Among them: that the Germans leave care for the destitute alone and that any German regulation of the CN and CRB must first receive *British* approval![165]

The British were happy to oblige. On July 7 a member of the British Cabinet, Lord Crewe, addressed a letter to Walter Hines Page. In brisk and at times Hooverian prose, he officially declared that his government accepted the harvest accords—subject to certain conditions. After denouncing the Germans' earlier seizures of native foods, Crewe recited his stipulations, in language that followed Hoover's almost verbatim. Among other things, the CRB and Comité National must administer aid to the destitute "as heretofore." Any German agreements with, or regulations of, the two relief agencies on any subject must receive *British* assent before consummation. If the Germans tried to use the CRB–CN relief "machinery" to force the Belgians to work for them, the British government's own arrangements with the CRB would "cease."[166]

As soon as Hoover received Crewe's letter, he cabled to his headquarters in Brussels. Postpone negotiations with the Germans until further notice, he ordered; the British have imposed new conditions.[167] Hoover did not reveal that it was he who had helped to devise them.

Meanwhile, on the very day of Crewe's ultimatum, Whitlock and his associates in Brussels had independently reached a compromise with the Germans. Backing away from their stubborn determination to rein in the Comité National, the German authorities now agreed not to attend its provincial and regional level meetings (the Belgians would never stand for that). Instead, local German officials would confer with Belgian committee heads *before* and *after* such meetings and in this way be apprised of their decisions.[168]

Less than twenty-four hours later, Hoover's cabled bombshell arrived in Brussels. When Whitlock heard that new British demands were on the way, he was thunderstruck, "utterly discouraged," and "sick at heart." At first the American minister railed at the British.[169] But when the text of Crewe's note finally reached him on July 15, a different explanation suggested itself. So "brutal in tone" was this message (thought Whitlock), so "stiff in its demands for recognition" of the CRB, that he was convinced that Hoover had written or inspired it. The American minister also noticed that the communication completely ignored himself and his fellow patron Villalobar and instead made it appear that only the CN and CRB had conducted the negotiations. Whitlock professed to be indifferent to this omission. Not Villalobar, however, who erupted in a blaze of indignation. It took his American colleague half an hour to calm him down.[170]

At this point the pacific Whitlock resorted to a stratagem of his own. As it happened, the Germans had already orally conceded the substance of the British demands before Crewe's letter got to Brussels. Instead, therefore, of sending Crewe's "impolite" and "ugly" note on to von der Lancken (and thus upsetting the diplomatic applecart all over again) Whitlock and Francqui *rewrote* it in softer, more diplomatic language and submitted this revised version to the baron.[171]

The tactic succeeded. On July 19 von der Lancken informed Whitlock that the Germans accepted all the British conditions. Written confirmation, he said, would be forthcoming in a day or two. Confessing that he felt "ninety-five years older" than before the negotiations started, Whitlock conveyed the happy news to London.[172]

Meanwhile, apparently disturbed by the absence of any definitive results in Brussels, Hoover himself left London for Belgium on July 17.[173] In all likelihood he carried with him a copy of still another letter from the British government: this one from Foreign Secretary Grey to Ambassador Page. In plain and possibly prearranged language Grey enumerated nine "definite conditions" for the continuation of Hoover's work—nine requirements that were an "absolute minimum." Among them: the Germans must not interfere in any way with the CRB's and CN's distribution of food to the Belgian people.[174] Hoover reached Brussels on the evening of the nineteenth. The next morning he learned from Whitlock that the Germans had already settled.[175]

Or had they? For the next several days the promised confirmatory letter from von Bissing failed to materialize—to Hoover's mounting displeasure. With every day the still-unsecured harvest was ripening. Ignoring Whitlock and his conciliatory ways, Hoover telephoned von der Lancken himself and demanded that the Germans reply promptly to Whitlock's revision of Lord Crewe's letter. Von der Lancken was annoyed. Under the terms of the relief work, his communications were supposed to be with the CRB's diplomatic patrons, not with this impertinent engineer.[176]

Von der Lancken's irritation soon turned to fury. A few days earlier, the American embassy in London had sent a copy of Lord Crewe's letter of July 7 on to Ambassador Gerard, who had submitted it in its undiluted form to the German government. On July 25 a copy reached Brussels—untempered by Brand Whitlock's *politesse*.

Von der Lancken was most definitely not amused. Hoover inspired that note by Crewe! he charged. Not only that, the Germans had intercepted a letter to the CRB's Brussels director stating that the British Foreign Office would do whatever Hoover desired! Meeting the diplomatic patrons on July 26, the German official (Whitlock's words) "raged on for half an hour"—red-faced, "mad as a bull." Whitlock tried to placate him. Hoover was "perhaps not always courteous," he admitted. Hoover approached problems directly, like a cowboy.

Finally, Villalobar and Whitlock hit upon an argument that apparently mollified the baron. The British note that had gone to Berlin, they explained, was irrelevant; *they* had not written it. *Their* letter to von der Lancken had been polite, and he had already accepted it in substance! Whitlock also warned the German that if he and his associates, who always insisted on dealing with the "eminent patrons," carried on like this much longer, they would have "patrons but no food coming in." Hoover, said Whitlock, was "the foreman of the work" and performed the truly important tasks.[177]

Three days later the Germans yielded at last. In a formal letter to Whitlock in behalf of the governor-general, von der Lancken pledged that the CRB and Comité National would enjoy "all liberty of action necessary" to fulfill their mission and that any changes in German regulations would be communicated through Whitlock to the British government. Moreover, the occupying authorities promised never to use the CN to coerce Belgians into working for the German army in contravention of international law. The previous understandings about the harvest were confirmed.[178]

Shortly afterward Hoover asserted that it was pressure from Berlin that had forced von Bissing to capitulate.[179] Certainly the arrival of Lord Crewe's unexpurgated note in Brussels had brought the diplomatic pot to a boil. Whitlock, of course, believed that his well-mannered diplomacy had brought the Germans around.[180] Whichever was correct, by the end of July the two great battles had been won. The Belgian harvest of bread grains had been protected and the independence of the two relief agencies reaffirmed. The German drive to get control of the *secours* had been foiled, and Great Britain and France were free to extend their financing of the CRB.[181]

Hoover was now obliged to turn his attention to northern France. Here the writ of von Bissing's administration did not run, and to secure this harvest Hoover had to negotiate directly with the German field army. In late July, therefore, he visited the Great Headquarters in Charleville and conferred with a representative of the General Staff. At every moment of his visit, both day and night, he had a military "escort."[182]

Unlike their brethren in Belgium, the German forces in occupied France had some claim to its harvest, since German soldiers had furnished seeds to some peasants and had helped to cultivate the land. The administrative difficulties were tremendous, but within a few weeks the commission and the Germans reached a settlement that the British grudgingly accepted. The German army would requisition the entire French harvest but out of it would deliver a specified portion of flour and potatoes to the commission at cost. Hoover's organization would have to import the rest. After several more weeks of parleys and correspondence the CRB chairman extracted an increased subsidy from the Allies for his efforts in northern France. But so unwilling still was the French government to recognize the commission officially that Hoover, in his correspondence, had to identify his source of revenue as unnamed French "institutions."[183]

To control the collection and distribution of the Belgian crop of wheat and rye, von Bissing in early August created a German-controlled Central Harvest Commission *("centrale")*, on which the CRB and Comité National were represented. First, the German army would seize all the bread grains in the country, thus preventing peasants from selling their crops to speculators and driving up the price of bread. Then the *"centrale"* would purchase this supply from the peasants and resell it to the Comité National at cost. All other transactions were outlawed. In short, between the native food sources and the Hoover–Francqui distribution agencies, von Bissing interposed a single governmental middleman.[184] The relief of Belgium was becoming more and more complex.[185]

The agreements of the summer of 1915 by no means resolved all of Hoover's difficulties. Indigenous fodder crops (oats and hay) were unprotected, and the governor-general quickly commandeered most of them for the German army. Outraged at this action, the British government forbade the CRB to import any oats and hay—and only allowed Hoover to import maize if it was used for human consumption exclusively.[186] Cattle, too, were not covered. Even as Hoover negotiated with the Germans in June, they rounded up Belgian cattle and horses and drove them through the streets of Brussels.[187] Plenty of problems lay ahead.

The CRB's victory, then, was not total, but it was—in Hoover's words to Lord Percy—"the absolute maximum" he was able to obtain, and it was large enough to permit the enterprise to continue.[188] The Germans' concessions on the harvest eventually yielded Hoover more than 200,000 tons of native wheat—only 20% of the total needed annually for the bread ration, but a crucial quantity nevertheless.[189] In the long, arduous struggle he had left behind him a train of angry egos, but for the most part had gotten his way.

And more than 9,000,000 trapped people were still alive.

6

Acrimony and
Accomplishment

I

MANY years after the Great War a veteran of the CRB defined its mission inside Belgium succinctly: "The raison d'être . . . was to supply the British with sufficient assurance that the Germans were not taking the food, so that they would permit it to go through the blockade."[1] Such a task, of course, inevitably led to tension with the Germans. They, after all, had conquered the country and were bound to resent a little group of youthful Americans (whose own country was selling arms and food to the Allies) scurrying about Belgium in search of evidence that the Germans might be cheating on their pledges.

But also implicit in the CRB's responsibility was tension of a different sort. For Hoover's men had to verify not only that the Germans were not *taking* the imported food but that native Belgians were not *giving* or *selling* it to them: that the food, in fact, was being distributed fairly and exclusively to its intended recipients. To fulfill this obligation the CRB considered itself obliged to inspect the procedures of the Comité National. Friction between the two relief bodies was thus almost inescapable, and with men of force like Hoover and Francqui at the top, the chances for discord increased further.

The initial response of the Belgian populace to the CRB was overwhelming. Arriving American delegates were lionized; some were given residence in luxurious chateaux.[2] American holidays became days of "manifestations" by Belgians forbidden to celebrate their own.[3] After sacks of American relief flour were emptied, Belgian women embroidered them by the hundreds with patriotic symbols and messages of thanks and returned them as gifts to the United States.[4] Schoolchildren by the thousands sent notes to their American benefactors.[5]

This popular spirit of gratitude never vanished. But as the initial shock of war abated, and as the work of relief became routine, differences between the commission and the Comité National emerged. From the outset some of the CN's leaders tended to regard the revictualing of their nation as essentially a Belgian enterprise, and the CRB as a kind of useful adjunct—a simple external purchasing agency that acquired the food which Belgians themselves paid for and distributed. To the Comité's ruling spirits their elaborate network of 40,000 volunteers, including the leading bankers and businessmen of the country, was far more crucial to success than the average of only thirty-five men who comprised the CRB's presence inside their country. Although the Comité's directors welcomed the diplomatic support and boon to morale that the CRB provided, they were not disposed to subordinate themselves to a few "striplings from across the seas" who knew little about business or Belgium.[6]

From the beginning Hoover believed that the Comité National should manage the "detailed execution" of the relief work,[7] but his own perception of the two agencies' relationship was quite different. It was his task—imposed on him by the British—to validate the German guarantees of nonrequisition, and this, to him and them, required an energetic staff on the scene. The British insisted on it, he said.[8] They were "not prepared to accept the Comité National or any other organization than this as the responsible controllers."[9] Only a neutral entity entirely immune from German pressure would suffice. The CRB, he declared, was under a constant "search light" from a hostile British military, and to fend off their attacks it must fulfill its obligations meticulously. The Comité National, he wrote, has "got to give us their support on such things as we require" as we "fight this battle with the outside world."[10]

Not all the pressure came from Great Britain. As the responsible trustee for enormous sums of food and money from many countries, Hoover felt a "positive obligation" to determine that the gifts in his care reached their destination and were parceled out without favor or waste. "There is no question," he told Brand Whitlock, "that we shall sooner or later be investigated from top to bottom, and it would be no defence to say that we handed over our functions to the Comité National." The engineer-executive also felt a deep responsibility to the American businessmen whom he had asked to serve without pay as his associates: "It would be a crime for which I should never forgive myself as long as I live, if, as the result of failure on my part to provide such organisation and such safeguards as are required, the reputation of these men should be called into question."[11]

All he was insisting upon, Hoover wrote at one point, was that a sufficient number of Americans be "spread over Belgium" to enable him to determine that the Comité National was fulfilling the British requirements and his own, and, if not, to report "weakness" to the leaders of the Comité for remedial action.[12]

When challenged, however, the CRB chairman became markedly more assertive. In late February 1915, when the rival Stillemans–de Forest committee in New York attempted to bypass the CRB and establish its own channel of relief into Belgium, Hoover inspired Ambassador Page to assert in writing that the "distribution in Belgium must be carried out absolutely under the control" of the CRB. Note this fact, Hoover instructed his New York office: "Distribution in Belgium is now absolutely carried on by this commission." The Comité National is "only advisory."[13] In a separate letter he referred to the Comité as "simply an advisory body" on food distribution in Belgium and even stated that it was "largely composed" of members of the CRB![14] In a technical sense Hoover was correct: under the current regulations, CRB delegates did indeed have "absolute charge" of imported food "until its distribution to the communes."[15] But the Comité National's role in the relief effort was much more dynamic than the word *advisory* connoted.

Two weeks later, when rumblings of dissent from Belgium reached him, Hoover again spoke plainly, if less expansively:

> I may be over-agitated [about the need for a strong CRB presence inside Belgium], but it does appear to me . . . that there is an inclination on the part of those in Belgium to take the attitude that this Commission are the exterior agents and local servants of the Belgian National Committee, and that it has practically no other function nor responsibility. I have not the slightest desire to trespass on their amour-propre or to interfere with their actual executive work, but there is a line that has got be be drawn here, and we are going to draw it, out of interest to every man concerned in this business.[16]

Hoover's broad interpretation of his responsibilities met resistance within his own ranks. His Brussels director from February to April, an engineer named A. N. Connett, argued that the young CRB delegates should be advisers and inspectors only, not administrators, and that key decisions should be made by the Comité National. Moreover, he claimed, the number of American representatives should be few—in fact, no more than two per province.[17] To Hoover, engaged in a critical struggle with General von Bissing over the CRB's numbers and freedom of travel, it was "absolutely essential" to have "at least" two men per province.[18]

Connett's independence did not meet with favor in London. Early in March Ambassador Page himself notified him by a letter (which Hoover transmitted) that there should be many CRB men in Belgium and that they should "maintain executive control" over relief activities.[19] At first Connett prepared to call in his delegates and implement this order from above. "However," he later wrote, "after a night's sleep and a frank talk with Mr. Francqui, I changed my mind. We both are confident that the Ambassador's letter was inspired in London Wall Buildings [Hoover's office] and not in Grosvenor Gardens."[20]

Confronted by this insubordination, Hoover insisted that Page's letter "emanates from direct official pressure" of the British government.[21] But Connett was unimpressed and unmoved. Having penetrated Hoover's disguise (or so he thought), he changed nothing—to Hoover's growing disgust. In mid-March Hoover confessed to a friend that Connett "has allowed Hinemann and Francqui to get the better of him in Brussels. . . . I shall have to go over and fight the old battle over again when [Connett's successor] arrives. I yearn a great deal for [J. F.] Lucey and his combative moments."[22]

Connett soon left the CRB's Brussels office, as in fact he had been intending to do. Hoover replaced him with another engineer, Oscar T. Crosby, and expressed the hope that he would "stiffen up the administration" inside Belgium. Clearly stricter supervision of the communes was becoming necessary. Reports of adulteration of food, of issuance of incomplete rations, of inadequate storage, and other abuses were increasing.[23] Alas for Hoover, Crosby, too, adopted a minimalist view of the CRB delegates' duties, and the problem remained unresolved.[24]

With the demarcation of authority between the two relief bodies uncertain, and with each inclined to enlarge its sphere of influence, it was not long before difficulties erupted. One issue concerned recordkeeping. From an early date Hoover insisted on compiling elaborate data on food distribution down to the communal level and on auditing the Comité National's own accounts. Every "bag of foodstuff" must be kept track of, he said; ". . . we have got to be able constantly to prove our case."[25] The CRB chairman soon showed that he meant business. When the CN's initial reports reached him in March, he frankly condemned them as "not acceptable," thereby evidently rankling the CN's leadership.[26]

Another source of friction was the CRB's display of the American flag atop all relief depots and warehouses in Belgium, as well as on its imported automobiles.[27] Intended as a form of diplomatic protection for the food supply, the practice soon offended not only the Germans but certain prominent Belgians as well, who resented this constant advertisement of the American role.[28] During April, therefore, upon instructions from Brand Whitlock, the commission ordered the American flag flown only over the principal warehouse in each province. At all other storage facilities, the Comité National's flag was to wave. The commission also requested that certain food stores known colloquially as *magasins américains* no longer be designated by that name. The Comité National was only too eager to comply—so much so that it ordered its subcommittees to stop using the word *American* anywhere. More boldly still, it ordered the removal from its local depots and stores of all signs bearing the name of the CRB itself.[29]

By early June the CN's leaders were "very irritated" at Hoover's commission and increasingly disposed to assert their independence.[30] Relations were not helped by their sharp divergence over the fate of the forthcoming harvest: while Hoover was endeavoring to put pressure on the Germans, Francqui was demanding that the British allow food imports to continue *regardless* of what the Germans did. Fearful that Hoover's undiplomatic diplomacy had alienated Governor-General von Bissing, Francqui urged the CRB chairman to leave the negotiation of "internal" Belgian questions to Crosby and Whitlock. They could deal successfully with the German authorities, he said. Hoover could handle "external business."[31]

By June Hoover was equally irritated at the Comité National and complained at length to Brand Whitlock:

> I am not contending that the Belgian people are not grateful; they are in fact overwhelmingly grateful to America and to yourself personally and this is as we should all desire.
> Our real difficulty lies in the lack of esteem and consideration which the C.R.B. possesses as an *institution* in itself. It has always been my belief, that a great work cannot be done by individuals but only by *institutions* and the association with a successful institution is sufficient gratification for any individual. Curiously enough, abroad the C.R.B. is a household word and the reflection of this is the daily facilitation of our work. . . . Yet here, in Belgium, we seem to have no position as an institution. The daily treatment of our men—the grudging civility—by the Germans is sufficient evidence of this. My observation leads me to believe, this is as much as anything else due to the reflection of Belgian attitude. Possibly, as you say, internal politics lead them to minimize the institution and also the attitude of our Spanish colleague [Villalobar] has something to do with it.

Hoover insisted that the "prestige" of the CRB must be "built up and constantly safeguarded." If the commission "held as high a position in Belgium as it has abroad," he claimed, "our daily labour would be frought with much less difficulty and humiliation." The CRB chairman asserted that he sought no personal praise. But the *institution*, he said, must be "properly mentioned and considered on every possible occasion."[32]

The "dominating vital importance" (as Hoover put it) of the CRB was, of course, precisely what the Comité National refused to acknowledge. As June yielded to July, Francqui and his colleagues took an increasingly independent posture, even to the point of making important decisions without consulting Hoover. The CN's determination to squeeze out the CRB was abetted by Villalobar and the Germans, each of whom had their own reasons for clipping the Americans' wings.[33]

By mid-July Hoover could tolerate this no longer. Returning to Brussels for the second time in a month, he resolved to force a showdown. He first "informed" Whitlock that he wished to terminate the CRB altogether. Now, he said, was a good time to retire, provided that some alternative import mechanism could be devised.[34] Privately, Hoover had not the slightest intention of retiring. Just five days before, he had cabled a friend in America that there was "no hope" of his returning to California until the war was over. "To do so," he said, would leave in "absolute chaos" an "enormous enterprise on which millions of people are dependent."[35] But if he could convince the Comité National that he really did mean to withdraw, and could maneuver it into begging him to stay on, he might oblige it to alter its attitude. In short, once again he was bluffing.

On July 20, 1915 Hoover met the CN's leaders. No doubt to their astonishment, he suggested that the time had come to consider the withdrawal of the CRB from relief work inside Belgium. The people of Belgium, he argued, and in particular the Comité National, now had sufficient freedom of movement, German guarantees, financial resources, and organizational stability as to require "no help from any other nationality." In short, the administrative assistance of Americans was no longer necessary.

Faced with Hoover's seemingly genuine offer, the Comité National hastily retreated and asked his commission to stay on. They needed the CRB, the Belgians pleaded; they could not get along without its diplomatic, psychological, and even administrative support. As an independent, humanitarian body, it must "continue to act as the guardian of the Belgian people." If American assistance were withdrawn, the "cohesive character" of the internal relief network would disintegrate. All this the Belgians asserted (according to Hoover's account of the meeting).

Hoover immediately relented and at once drew up a "treaty" defining the two agencies' "administrative relations." Among other things, it stipulated that administration of *alimentation* and *secours* would be a "joint undertaking" and that CRB personnel would be members of the CN's executive committee and of all its lesser committees as well.[36] Once again Hoover had gambled his way to victory—and had gotten what perhaps he wanted most: a document acknowledging his indispensability.

Emile Francqui promptly held a dinner in Hoover's honor; no doubt the compliments flowed freely with the wine.[37] During the rest of the summer the two men worked together on plans for the coming year.[38] Still, as Hoover was soon to learn, the "treaty" of July 20 had not resolved "the conflict of authority."[39] It had brought not peace but a truce.

I I

"THE only trouble is nobody ever heard of him." By the summer of 1915 Hugh Gibson's lament was losing its validity. Throughout the English-speaking world the Commission for Relief in Belgium—and, inevitably, its chairman—were receiving increasing acclaim. Press clippings from the newspapers of England and America filled volumes of scrapbooks at the CRB's offices.[40] Journals of opinion applauded its labors.[41]

Not all this publicity was spontaneous. In April, at Hoover's suggestion, his associate William Goode launched the National Committee for Relief in Belgium, a fund-raising agency for the United Kingdom. Supported by the royal family and other influential Britons, Goode's organization generated considerable public attention and more than £2,500,000 in voluntary contributions over the next two years.[42] Meanwhile, in the United States, the CRB's energetic New York headquarters distributed weekly news sheets to 2,630 newspapers and magazines and maintained a staff liaison to the press.[43]

Hoover himself contributed to the flow of publicity in late summer by issuing a comprehensive printed report on his commission's first eight months of work. It was an impressive document, more than forty pages long, and it was quoted at length in leading American newspapers.[44] From President Wilson (to whom Hoover sent a copy) came hearty praise for "a work wonderfully done."[45] The *Economist* (edited by Hoover's good friend Francis W. Hirst) hailed it as "a classic in the literature of relief." "Never before," Hirst added, "has a task of such magnitude been grappled with . . . ; never in any of the lesser enterprises of the same character has such organising ability been shown and such success achieved."[46]

Hoover fervently believed that his management of public relations had been the key to his success thus far. It was his cultivation of "public opinion," he told Francqui in June, that had kept the food streaming into Belgium. It was the threat of rousing the "undoubted indignation" of the CRB's "vast clientele" that had often been his "only successful weapon" against the Allies and the Germans.[47] It was publicity that had stimulated the tremendous early outpouring of American support, enabling his mission to acquire "moral prestige" in the eyes of the belligerent powers.[48]

Yet even as Hoover manipulated the levers of American popular sentiment, his old ambivalence toward overtly *personal* publicity reasserted itself. Several times in 1915 he insisted that the CRB's press campaigns must be conducted "with dignity or not at all." And dignity, he made it clear, did not include "circus 'stunts' " or "personal puffs."[49] Any publicity, he asserted, and especially any of a personal character, "produces to me the most acute mental distress and it induces a creeping of the flesh for hours after even a bare scanning of it."[50] When in mid-winter Will Irwin placed two such articles about him in the New York press, Hoover was mortified:

That I feel intensely humiliated by both these documents does not express it, and I feel that all I have striven for for years in the estimation of my countrymen is practically undermined by lowering me to the level there represented; that it either comes to this, or that I have totally failed to rise to the level which I had assumed by way of intellectual, cultural, and financial attainments. To be a [mining] promoter and a humorist, and things of that kind have not been within my life's ambitions.[51]

Ambition, dignity, humiliation, cultural attainment, the estimation of his countrymen: these words revealed that despite his public persona of disinterested altruistic efficiency, Hoover was extremely self-conscious about what he was doing—and acutely anxious to succeed. Like many other orphans who grow up determined to make good, he seemed both to crave and shrink from recognition.[52] How he coveted public esteem yet hated the visibility that came with it. When in July his friend William Edgar eulogized him in the *Bellman* as an American hero,[53] Hoover responded swiftly:

Stuck here [in a Paris hotel] waiting for a train I'm mighty vividly reminded of you by finding a copy of the Bellman with your rotten article in it. If you keep that game up I shall be unable to move about the world in quietness and decency. In London these days I have given up riding in Busses because all the old ladies tap me on the back with the handles of their umbrellas and demand to know, "Young man why are you not in Karkai"? [khaki] (or however you spell it) Next time it will be "Oh you are the Relief man arent you"?

Hoover thereupon gave Edgar a lengthy "inside" account of CRB affairs but warned at the end that it was "for your sole information and not for your damned Bellman."[54]

Hoover's good-humored irascibility on this occasion suggested that perhaps he was not as discomfited by public attention as he professed to be. Still, the CRB chairman resisted efforts to cheapen and personalize the relief, even as his own position of prominence steadily magnified.[55]

In the late summer of 1915 Hoover's attitude toward publicity helped to precipitate the most dangerous internal trauma that the commission ever faced. For some time he had been having difficulties with his New York office, headed by his trusted friend Lindon Bates. From the outset Bates had quarreled with the leaders of the rival Belgian Relief Committee. While Hoover had taken Bates's side in these disputes, several outsiders—including Ambassador Page, Colonel House, and the Rockefeller Foundation—had considered Bates an unfortunate selection for his job.[56] Evidently tactless and inclined to dominate all with whom he worked, the noted civil engineer resisted attempts to coordinate his office with the London headquarters. According to Hoover, he also began to issue the kind of "personal publicity" so offensive to the CRB chairman's sense of dignity.[57] By May some of Hoover's colleagues were so exasperated that they urged a drastic reorganization of the New York office, but Hoover, loyal to his old friend, did nothing.[58]

Then, on May 7, 1915, Bates's son Lindon, Jr., a rising New York political figure en route to Europe as a CRB volunteer, drowned at sea when the

Germans torpedoed the *Lusitania*. The younger Bates died heroically—giving his life belt to a woman passenger just moments before the great ship went down.[59] For a time his distraught parents clung to the hope that their thirty-two-year-old son might yet be rescued alive. Hoover, too, found it difficult to face the dismal truth; to his anguished friends he composed a cabled message:

> Although hope hourly diminishes my heart protests that you cannot be called upon for this sacrifice in this service of humanity. In these many years of intimacy of ideals and aspirations he has grown to be my own. I can say no more. Hoover.[60]

A few weeks later young Bates's body was discovered off the Irish coast.[61]

From the king of Belgium, Theodore Roosevelt, and others, messages of condolence poured in—and were printed in the New York press.[62] In the aftermath of this tragedy, Hoover later asserted, the elder Bates's mind began to manifest some "curious obsessions." Grief-stricken and already suffering from "great nervous strain," he developed an even deeper appetite for "personal publicity," as well as a virtual compulsion to claim that Americans—catalyzed above all by himself—were the principal financial supporters of the Belgian relief (a contention that was not in fact true).[63]

In late August the problem came suddenly to a head when the *Saturday Evening Post* published a long account of the work of the CRB's New York branch. Edited in advance (at least in part) in the New York office itself, the article lauded the commission as "the greatest private enterprise ever undertaken in this country." According to the *Post*, the CRB's rapid transformation into "one of the most efficient business machines of the world" was "due primarily to the genius of Lindon W. Bates." The article even claimed that most of the commission's work was actually done in New York (not Europe) and that "its enormous executive burden" was "borne almost entirely by Mr. Bates and Mr. Hoover." In effect the piece placed Bates on a pedestal equal to, if not higher than, his chief.[64]

Hoover's response was instant. This article, he informed Bates, contained "46 absolute untruths and 36 half-truths of a character which is entirely misleading." Its general thrust was to claim that "the New York branch of the Commission is the whole thing"—an impression quite untrue. The turnover of charitable funds in London, for instance, was currently ten times that in New York, while the "administrative labour" of the organization was as great at each of its twelve branches in Belgium and northern France as in the office in New York. Furthermore, said Hoover, the article conveyed the misleading impression that the American people were actually keeping Belgium alive, when in fact they had contributed only a small fraction of the total benevolent gifts and foodstuffs shipped into that country. The circulation of such "nonsense," Hoover declared, could only offend readers of the article in Canada, Great Britain, and elsewhere. Moreover, such personal publicity would give "all wise and important people" the idea that the CRB was an "advertising bureau" for its members and that it was advancing its "individual interests" first. All commission publicity must be truthful and advantageous to the Belgian people, he said firmly. Anything else was "below the dignity and purpose of this whole effort." The CRB, he warned, "has not been founded to advertise its Chairman, Members, or employees. . . ."[65]

Hoover urged Bates to abolish the New York office's weekly news sheets for the press and to concentrate instead on sending material to the commission's local committees. The era of daily press releases was "entirely over"; reliance on "strong decentralized committee organization" was now a more effective fund-raising technique. "Announcements of importance must be made in London," he declared. Only the London office was in a position to assess the sensitive "political phases" of any public statement.[66] And, he added separately, the publicity man who advertises that he advertises commits an "infantile mistake."[67]

Hoover also informed Bates that he was sending over one of the commission's founders, John Beaver White, to discuss publicity questions and arrange "a definite basis of co-operation" for the coming year.[68] (Hoover hoped that White, as second in command to Bates, could keep the New York branch "on proper lines.")[69] In addition, the CRB chairman invited Bates to visit Belgium and inspect its operations (something no one in the New York office had yet done). "You cannot gain any appreciation of what it means to drive this machine, London, Rotterdam and twelve separate organizations in Belgium," he told Bates, "unless you have seen it."[70] Privately Hoover felt that the New York office had a parochial view of the organization. He told William C. Edgar that Bates's branch had never really been "attuned to the Commission as a whole."[71] Only New York, he said later, had never had a volunteer office; it thus lacked the "spirit" of the rest of the CRB.[72] Still distressed by the *Saturday Evening Post* article, Hoover sent Edgar a copy of his pungent letter to Bates. Edgar's *Bellman* immediately published a scathing denunciation of the *Post*'s exaggerations, gross misstatements, and "injudicious exploitation of Mr. Bates."[73]

If Hoover thought that he could quickly extinguish his New York troubles, he was soon and severely disappointed. Stung by his rebuke, Bates apparently became convinced that Hoover was seeking to oust him from the commission and (in Hoover's words) "humiliate him before the World."[74] In the next few weeks friction between London and New York mounted, with Bates denying that he had any advance inkling of the *Post* article's tenor and insisting that it had been "most helpful" to the CRB.[75] Despite Hoover's pleas, Bates declined to go to Europe; perhaps he suspected that Hoover would stage an office coup in his absence.[76] When Bates at one point interfered in European matters beyond his domain, Hoover replied bluntly: "Right or wrong all matters general policy must be left to my judgment."[77]

Finally, on September 22, Hoover cabled a command: "For political reasons do not wish one more word publicity or public appeals to emanate from your office. Applies here as well and includes your news sheet."[78] Bates agreed to the suspension—"temporaily"—but retorted that he now expected Hoover to release nothing about American matters from *his* office without first consulting New York.[79]

By the end of the month, according to Hoover's associate Edgar Rickard, the New York office's publicity sheets were causing "serious trouble" inside Belgium and were even threatening to "jeopardise [the] entire existence" of the relief commission. (Rickard gave no evidence for this assertion.) No doubt speaking for Hoover, Rickard wondered aloud whether Bates's "personal loss" had affected his judgment and had led to his current "belligerent defiance."[80] Meanwhile, to the acute embarrassment of many in the CRB, Bates announced to the press that he planned to erect a 115-foot reproduction of Pompey's Pillar in Egypt atop a mountain in upstate New York as a memorial to his departed son. The pillar would be surrounded by searchlights and would be visible for miles both day and night.[81]

By mid-October Hoover realized that he was getting nowhere. Angry at Bates's insubordination,[82] he confessed to friends that he was in "a devil of a mess again with New York" and that he must travel there quickly to resolve it. The crisis, he realized, had become one of "acute personal order" between himself and one of his closest friends.[83]

Before sailing, the CRB chairman addressed a seven-page explanation of his public relations policy to his wayward branch office in New York. Asserting that objectionable publicity had brought the "whole existence" of the relief work "almost to the breaking point," Hoover reminded his confreres that the commission "in my ideal, is an *institution;* that as an *institution* it will have a small corner in history and it will be sufficient reward for any man's labour that he was associated with it and to be known as one whose self-sacrificing voluntary efforts helped to make it." Any advertisement of the CRB as such, he said, "gives a Barnum & Bailey aspect to this work which is undignified, and is beneath the ideals which have dominated the whole work." As for personal publicity, Hoover acknowledged that his own name had appeared in the press more than anyone else's. But this, he said, had been inevitable (since he was chairman), and he had tried to minimize it all he could—refusing "times out of number" to cooperate with journalists eager to prepare "personal 'write-ups' " about himself. He pointed out further that the German authorities read the CRB's American press coverage and that New York could not possibly comprehend European conditions and the possible political implications of its publicity at any given time. Therefore, he concluded,

you may take it that for the future there is to be no publicity of any kind from the Commission for Relief in Belgium, except that which I have personally edited with due consideration of its political and human bearing.

As I have the responsibility of maintaining the position and character of this working organisation with the various belligerent governments I have simply got to control the statements for which I necessarily have the responsibility, and I cannot permit such statements unless I have personally canvassed them myself. If anyone in the Commission believes that this is an attempt to stifle individuality, my only wish is that he should seek for fields where his publicity necessities can be exploited without reflecting on this work or jeopardising the lives of millions of people. There is no man, including myself, who cannot be replaced in this work—or it would be a sign of bad organisation.[84]

Two days later Hoover personally cabled Bates that the commission's patron-ambassadors had commanded the cessation of all publicity, direct or indirect, pending Hoover's "reorganization of this organ."[85]

On October 16, 1915 the CRB's commander-in-chief left England for the United States.[86] He was on the high seas on October 22 when the "institution" which he had forged celebrated the first anniversary of its founding. He could only be heartened by a cabled congratulatory message from his fellow commission directors in Europe. The unblemished "integrity, efficiency, and high purpose" of the CRB, they said, was due to Hoover's "unusual personality and unselfish devotion." The directors emphatically demanded a revamping of the New York office and an end to its current disruptiveness. The commission, they insisted, "must be coordinated, governed, and presided over by one mind. The refusal of [the] New York office to accept this basis of organisation imperils the entire work and the millions dependent upon it."[87]

On October 24 Hoover reached New York City and took up quarters at the Belmont Hotel;[88] it was his first visit to the United States since March 1914.[89] Although the reasons for his journey were worrisome, there was at least one silver lining. Nearly five months earlier his wife Lou had gone back from London to California; now she brought their boys east by train to see their father for the first time in a year.[90]

The next day Hoover conferred with Bates, John Beaver White, and the commission's New York treasurer, Alexander Hemphill, chairman of the board of the Guaranty Trust Company. It quickly transpired that the crisis was worse than he had dreamed. While Hoover was still in London, and without consulting anyone, Bates had secretly gone to the State Department, Justice Department, and Senator Henry Cabot Lodge of Massachusetts with a massive dossier accusing Hoover of unneutral and even criminal misconduct.[91]

Specifically, Bates charged that as head of the CRB Hoover had repeatedly violated the Logan Act of 1793, which prohibited American citizens from engaging in unauthorized negotiations with foreign governments on matters in "dispute or controversy" between the United States and those governments. Quoting numerous excerpts from Hoover's confidential correspondence to his New York office, Bates showed that Hoover had negotiated on all sorts of sensitive issues with Allied and German officials, including blockade policy, contraband, the use of interned ships, and similar subjects far removed (so Bates claimed) from the charitable work of Belgian relief. The CRB, said Bates, was now a virtual government, issuing ultimatums and "dealing with the foreign powers as one sovereign to another." Certainly, he argued, the State Department and its representatives abroad had never intended to authorize Hoover so to act. He also suggested that American diplomats like Walter Hines Page did not really know all that Hoover was up to.

But Bates went much further than this. The entire nature of the commission, he contended, had been transformed. No longer was it "a purely food-giving charity"; now it was an "organ" and "agent" of the Allied governments, increasingly dependent on their concealed subventions. No longer was it "a representative American body" with an "American character." Instead it was turning into a "London-centralized corporation" entirely dominated by its chairman. Leaving no grievance unmentioned, Bates accused Hoover of concentrating "absolute dictatorial power" in his hands, of failing to consult the New York office, of reducing it to passivity on policy questions, and of suppressing its publicity.

The engineer-turned-antagonist was especially critical of a scheme that Hoover had been evolving since mid-summer. Confronted with economic paralysis and deepening destitution inside Belgium, and with a consequent staggering drain on his slim resources, Hoover had proposed to create an "Industrial Section" of his struggling relief commission. This body would purchase noncontraband raw materials abroad and import them into occupied Belgium, whose factories would then convert them into noncontraband manufactured goods. These would then be exported under CRB protection for sale to the world outside. All this would be done with the belligerents' approval. The Allies would permit this exception to their blockade, while the Germans would pledge not to requisition the raw materials or finished products. In this ingenious manner, hundreds of thousands of idle Belgians could resume productive employment, receive wages, and thereby stay off the relief rolls. In addition, the profits from the transactions could be turned over to the CRB for the purchase of additional relief food.[92]

To an alarmed Bates, Hoover's novel proposal threatened to transform the CRB into a "commercial venture" and "nation-building enterprise . . . fraught with dangerous aspects" and potentially "serious complications" for American neutrality. It would "deeply involve America in European affairs" and establish a possibly "dangerous precedent" for "non-charitable intervention in a belligerent country." For the head of the CRB's New York office there was only one escape route from this quagmire. To the Department of State he suggested that the time had come for the United States government to withdraw its support of the CRB unless the commission was restored to its alleged former status as a charity and unless Hoover's "claim to absolute power" was abandoned.[93]

Reading a copy of this dossier in Bates's own presence on October 25, Hoover was amused and then appalled. While his friend asserted that he had gone to the State Department out of patriotic duty, Hoover was certain that the document had been prepared for "sensational publication" with the object of embarrassing him. The CRB chairman bitterly denounced his associate for using extracts from their private correspondence and for failing to consult any of his New York colleagues about his deed. Noting Bates's tenseness during this conversation, Hoover concluded that his friend's mind had become "deranged."[94]

The CRB's leader immediately consulted various prominent men in New York, including Hemphill, former Secretary of Commerce Oscar Straus, and President Wilson's confidant Colonel House, who advised him often during the following days.[95] To House, Hoover seemed unable to understand how he could have been so mistaken in his judgment of Bates.[96] To Hemphill it was apparent that Hoover's "peremptory stoppage" of the New York office's publicity machine had jolted Bates into filing his "exposé" with the State Department.[97] Hoover himself conceded that his demand some weeks earlier that Bates stop interfering in the CRB's negotiations with foreign governments had perhaps been "too abrupt."[98] Now it seemed that Bates was getting his revenge.

It was immediately obvious to Hoover that Bates's retention in a prominent executive capacity was impossible. On the other hand, a summary dismissal of his New York director was also out of the question. Anxious to present "an unbroken front to the World," Hoover wished to avoid any hostile publicity that might endanger his commission's prestige. Furthermore, convinced that he was dealing with a case of mental illness, he desired to handle the matter sympathetically and avoid any "humiliation" of his old friend. For the next several days he searched for a formula that could meet these competing objectives.[99]

Meanwhile there was the U.S. government to satisfy. On October 28, Hoover took a train to Washington, where he met the next morning, at his request, with two senior officials of the State Department.[100] At the outset one of them asked him wryly whether he was "prepared to spend a thousand years in jail."[101] To his astonishment he found the department thoroughly disturbed, particularly by the CRB's "Industrial Section" scheme and by the possibility that the commission might be setting precedents embarrassing to the U.S. government in its campaign for the vindication of neutral rights in wartime. So alarmed, in fact, was the department that on October 16 it had ordered Walter Hines Page and Brand Whitlock to resign immediately as patrons of the CRB if its Industrial Section came into being.[102]

Senator Lodge was also perturbed. Not only had Hoover clearly violated the Logan Act, he told the State Department; the CRB's financing also raised "grave" and awkward questions about the Allied blockade policy and America's relationship to it. Sending charity from American citizens was one thing, said Lodge; distributing money supplied by belligerent governments was another.[103]

Hoover was incredulous. Could all of this really be happening? Before his trip to Washington, he had found it almost impossible to take Bates's charges seriously. After all, he told Hemphill, "all our relations" had been conducted "in full knowledge" of the patron-ambassadors of America, Spain, and Holland, as well as of the belligerent governments themselves.[104] But now, at the request of the State Department, he found himself obliged to respond in writing to Bates's dossier. And if the later recollection of the CRB's official historian is correct, a federal court in Baltimore was on the verge of indicting him under the Logan Act.[105]

In three separate letters to the department the CRB chairman presented his defense. He stressed the humanitarian purpose of his work and the "extraordinary esteem and privilege" that he and his associates enjoyed in every country in which they served. He claimed that all the commission's arrangements, including its financial subsidies, were known to every belligerent and that the Germans fully approved them. He denied that the CRB had established harmful precedents any more than had the Red Cross or other humanitarian agencies, or that it had in any way acted "to defeat any proper objects of the American government in foreign relations." The CRB had not been guilty of a single "atom of moral turpitude." In short:

> If the intervention of our nationals to create a bridge over an impasse which daily threatens the lives of suffering people, and if their success in the preservation of this mass of humanity in any way jeopardizes our national repute, it seems to us that *all* the world has gone mad.

As for the proposed "Industrial Section" or *Comité Industriel* (as it was now called), Hoover explained its humanitarian objectives in detail and rebutted Bates's "preposterous" accusations. With the possibility growing, he said, that the overburdened Allies might cancel their relief subsidy any day, the "only hope of preventing starvation" was to generate "a minimum of exports which may be exchanged for food. We have no idea of rehabilitating Belgian industry beyond this point." In answer to Bates's claim that he was trying to create a "mercantile-charitable trust," Hoover insisted that the "absolute and sole object" of the Comité Industriel was "to stimulate employment and exports merely from a *relief* point of view, and it operates without profit to itself." How could such a project, approved and supervised by the belligerents themselves, interfere with American diplomacy or trade "in the slightest degree"?

Hoover recognized that his industrial revitalization plan was a daring one and, indeed, that the CRB was "a unique departure in diplomacy." But he pleaded for the department to remember that the current war was "the greatest crisis the world has yet seen," imperiling "huge masses of helpless civilians," and he urged that "bridges to aid the civil population should be constructed." To do this the continuing support of American diplomatic personnel was indispensable. If the State Department withdrew its diplomatic patrons now, he warned, the CRB might well collapse. The embattled humanitarian closed with a heartfelt appeal:

> Even in these days of fierce contentions and hatreds, which are at times directed even to our own countrymen, no criticism has been leveled at the Commission for Relief in Belgium. From the nature of things, our people are much engaged in commerce with some of the belligerents and our country is subjected to much adverse criticism. But out of all this fishing for profit in this pool of blood, the one refutation that our people are without humanity and ideals is the Commission for Relief in Belgium and the other philanthropic efforts of the American people.[106]

While in Washington Hoover met for the first time Secretary of the Interior Franklin K. Lane, who had defended him staunchly a year before against charges by American critics. Lane promised his all-out support.[107] More and more of the American government was becoming embroiled in the Bates affair.

According to Hoover, the State Department quickly concluded that Bates's allegations were groundless and that he had probably designed his dossier more for publicity purposes than to elicit a governmental response.[108] But then, on October 29, Bates struck again. In a new communication to the State Department he called attention to a confidential letter that Hoover had sent through Bates's office to Colonel House in mid-August, a letter that Bates had already quoted in his dossier. In this letter to House, Hoover had enclosed a copy of memorandum that he had prepared, he said, "at the request of a cabinet friend of mine here" (London). (Much of this document, too, was excerpted in Bates's dossier.) In this memorandum Hoover described German attitudes toward the war (he had just returned from the German military headquarters in northern France) and urged the British to abandon their embargo on food shipments into Germany. By lifting their *food* blockade (which he said had failed anyway), Hoover argued, the British could dampen the "fire of hate" in Germany and create conditions for peace talks in the autumn.[109]

To the agitated Bates this was the most convincing evidence yet that Hoover had indeed violated the Logan Act and had wandered far from his responsibility to succor the Belgians. Warning the State Department that the existence of Hoover's secret memorandum was now known to a New York newspaper, Bates declared:

This memorandum, avowedly prepared at the request of a British Cabinet friend, sent to the confidential advisor of the President . . . by one who has been at the same time the guest of the German General staff and a confidant of British Ministers, is manifestly contrary to the pledges under which the Commission members are given access into Belgium. It constitutes a continuing jeopardy to Americans there, to the Commission and those it has been trying to serve. It seems highly improper that the Commission here and abroad be used in the fashion indicated.[110]

In yet another letter to the State Department, Hoover took issue with these dangerous allegations:

As to [Bates's] statement that the memorandum enclosed was prepared for a *British* cabinet friend, [this] is nonsense, as, so far as I know, I do not enjoy acquaintance to the degree of friendship with any of these gentlemen. However, it was prepared for a cabinet friend in a neutral government. This gentleman, like myself, and every other well thinking neutral, was anxious to consider and advance any arguments to either of the belligerents which would tend to ameliorate the pressure upon civilians on both sides during this war.[111]

Hoover's rejoinder was highly implausible. Contrary to his assertion to the State Department, by mid-1915 he was well acquainted with several members of the British Cabinet, including the foreign secretary, Sir Edward Grey. (Before the war Grey had actually borrowed Hoover's car on one occasion for a Sunday afternoon drive.)[112] Hoover also had frequent and friendly dealings with Lord Eustace Percy, his principal contact at the Foreign Office, and at least occasional meetings with numerous Cabinet officials like Lord Crewe, whose famous harvest ultimatum of July 7 he had at least partially ghostwritten. Moreover, while ambassadors from neutral countries certainly lived in London, neutral *Cabinet* officials did not. Interestingly, too, Hoover did not name the neutral figure in London to whom he had supposedly sent his memorandum. In fact, at the very time he wrote the memo, Hoover was actively attempting to persuade the British government to lift its embargo on food.[113] In all likelihood the document that he supplied to Colonel House was a part of this campaign and was indeed prepared for a sympathetic British Cabinet official. It is a measure of Hoover's anxiety two months later that instead of openly admitting this fact he instead resorted to a dubious and unconvincing denial.

The State Department apparently accepted Hoover's explanations. In any case, on the night of October 30 he returned to New York—convinced (he later wrote) that all he had left to fear was "sensational publicity." The next morning he conferred with his friend Will Irwin and the editor of the New

York *World,* no doubt on ways to keep the story from damaging the CRB in the press.[114]

For the next few days Hoover attempted to negotiate an agreement with Bates that would remove him from effective control, save his face, and avert a public explosion. To his distraught friend Hoover wrote that he hoped that there would be "no break in your association with a work to which you have shewn such devotion."[115] But as the days passed with no definitive settlement, Hoover confessed that his patience was approaching "practical exhaustion." How much longer, he wondered, could he continue to consider Bates's "personal feeling and position"? After all, Hoover could not stay on in New York indefinitely.[116]

The CRB chairman was particularly upset by Bates's failure to pledge to maintain the confidentiality of the commission's internal correspondence. "Such things as he has done in the last ten days," Hoover told a friend, "are absolutely intolerable to the continued existence of any organisation on earth." While the CRB's formal arrangements were "fully known" to all belligerents, and its procedures "freely open" to its neutral patrons, its confidential correspondence (according to Hoover) naturally contained comments that, if revealed publicly, could seriously embarrass its work. No one who considered himself a gentleman, he said, had "any right whatever to make any reserves as to the absolutely confidential nature of this correspondence."[117]

At one point, according to Hoover, Bates did promise to keep confidential all of Hoover's correspondence to him on relief matters and to keep their dispute (and the correspondence) out of the press. That was Hoover's version; Bates denied it. Distraught, "deranged," or otherwise, he was not going to let Hoover maneuver him into suppressing the relevant evidence. "When the interests of the country are at stake upon a matter as important as the affairs of this Commission," he rejoined, "there can be no confidences. The Commission affairs must be above board and open to the light of day."[118]

On November 2 Hoover informed his London office that the situation was "very delicate" and that he had a "streak of insanity to deal with."[119] Over Bates's objections he was now trying to induce several prominent individuals to join the executive committee of his New York office. But some were reluctant to do so while the contention festered, unresolved.[120]

Meanwhile Hoover mobilized his supporters in Europe. On October 31 or thereabouts his British associate William Goode (who was in New York at the time) dispatched an urgent cable to Ambassador Page. Although Hoover later remarked that the State Department by this time had agreed that there was nothing to Bates's charges,[121] Goode himself portrayed a more somber picture. According to him, there was a movement afoot in Washington to induce Hoover to resign as head of the CRB. The State Department, Goode added, did not appreciate "how implicitly British and other Governments rely on Hoover's personality and how impossible it would be to carry on this whole work if he threw it up." He asked Page to inform the U.S. government of "necessity Hoover remaining at helm."[122]

It is highly unlikely that Goode sent his message without Hoover's knowledge. It is even possible that Hoover helped him to write it.[123] In any case, the ever helpful ambassador asked no questions and at once cabled the secretary of state:

> The Commission for the relief of Belgium is Hoover and absolutely depends on Hoover who has personally made agreements with the Governments concerned and has carried these delicate negotiations through only because of his high character and standing and unusual ability. If he is driven to resign the Commission will instantly fall to pieces. The governmental sources of money will dry up and the work will have to be abandoned. I believe that no other man in sight could have done this task and I know that no other can now carry it on.[124]

It was for loyalty like this that Hoover, years later, acclaimed Page as "the soul of intellectual integrity" and "one of the blossoms of American life which justify our civilization."[125]

At this point the unexpected happened—another fruit of Hoover's friendship in high places. Through the apparent intercession of Secretary of the Interior Lane, President Wilson invited the CRB chairman to meet him at the White House on November 3.[126] The night before, Hoover dined in New York with Colonel House, who counseled him on how to approach the chief executive.[127] Later that evening Hoover and John Beaver White took the overnight train down to Washington.[128]

The next morning the two men called on the President; their interview could not have gone better. Warmly commending the commission, Wilson explained that its troubles had come to his notice but that the State Department had found no grounds for Bates's charges.[129] The President was greatly impressed by Hoover. "He is a real man," said Wilson afterward to his future second wife. He is "one of the very ablest men we have sent over there"—"a great international figure. Such men stir me deeply and make me in love with duty!"[130]

During the meeting Wilson offered to make a public statement in the commission's behalf. Seizing the opportunity, Hoover asked him to do so immediately. The commission chairman also asked Wilson to use his influence to persuade several New York business leaders to join an enlarged executive committee of the CRB in that city. The man in the Oval Office assented.[131]

Later that day the President of the United States issued a glowing statement to the press. He declared that his administration was "highly pleased" with the Commission for Relief in Belgium. It had done its work "to the entire satisfaction" of the belligerents, he said. It had been the source of no "international complications" whatever but instead of "international good will and disinterested service."[132] Hoover knew now that any attack by Bates would have much less adverse effect. That day also the President wrote personal letters to seven men named by Hoover (including Hemphill, White, and Oscar Straus), urging them all to join an expanded New York committee that would cooperate with Hoover in administering the CRB's work in the United States. He gave the letters to Hoover to deliver.[133]

That same afternoon the CRB's chairman left Washington by rail for the north. Barely stopping in New York City, he took the midnight train to Boston to confer the next day with Henry Cabot Lodge. In a brief and amicable meeting Hoover dispelled the Republican senator's lingering concerns. While Lodge still believed that Hoover had violated the Logan Act, the senator now judged these violations to be only "technical." On the questions of Allied subsidies and the effect of the CRB's "Industrial Section" on blockade policy, Lodge declared himself satisfied, although "the importation and exportation of goods in belligerent territory" was "a very delicate business" in which the U.S. *government* should not engage. With this caveat, Lodge praised the CRB's work as "one of the finest things ever done by a neutral in war."[134] According to Hoover, Lodge promptly wrote a letter "sitting upon Mr. Bates" and warning him to leave the relief project alone.[135]

Hoover now hastened back to New York.[136] Woodrow Wilson's letter to the New York businessmen had been successful; from most of the addressees acceptances promptly came.[137] Hoover "has a no more ardent admirer than myself," Hemphill told the President.[138] Hoover's direction of the CRB was "masterful," said Straus.[139] Although Melville Stone, the general manager of the Associated Press, was obliged for various reasons to decline Wilson's invitation, he, too, regarded Hoover as "a marvel of efficiency, integrity and modesty." Bates, said Stone, was a "marplot . . . consumed with a desire for publicity."[140]

On November 5 Hoover convened a meeting of the business leaders to whom Wilson had written.[141] Although the President in his letters had asked them simply to join an "enlarged" executive committee in New York, Hoover now announced that he had asked Wilson to help him create a *new* committee.[142] On Hoover's recommendation the gentlemen present decided to constitute themselves as the "New York Committee of the Commission for Relief in Belgium" and to supplant at once the *existing* executive committee, on which Bates and two of his loyalists still sat. In this way the old, Bates-dominated arrangement was neatly superseded. The new committee at once selected John Beaver White as the director of the commission in New York.[143]

But what now of Lindon W. Bates? Hoover still believed that Bates had to be eliminated from any position of power.[144] Yet for all the vexation that his old friend had caused him, and despite his conviction that Bates's behavior could only result from "extreme maliciousness" or "a disordered mind,"[145] Hoover remained reluctant to force him off the CRB entirely. On November 4 he told Bates that he still hoped his friend could be associated with the great work until the end. And then, in frank but gentle tones, he wrote:

There is one personal word which I would like to say and that is that I am convinced that after months of overwork in a cause that appeals to every sympathetic temperament, you were last May already at a point near nervous collapse when that great blow fell upon you. Since then you have not been your oldself, and I am sure that if you will for a time disassociate your mind absolutely from these complex problems you will adopt entirely other views and methods.[146]

Perhaps at Hoover's request, that same day Hemphill invited Bates to become a member of the reconstituted board.[147]

Two days later the New York committee held its second meeting, with Bates present by invitation.[148] Apparently chastened by President Wilson's public endorsement of the commission, and convinced (so he said) that he must be "a sacrifice,"[149] the rebel came quickly to terms. Under pressure from the assembled committee members (except Hoover, who left the room), he formally withdrew his charges and asked the State Department to return his dossier, on the grounds that his concerns had been "fully satisfied by the authorities at Washington." Responding to Hemphill's invitation, Bates expressed his readiness to serve on the new committee "without office" and promised to engage in no "critical publicity." After much discussion, the committee voted to defer a decision and to consult absent colleagues about it. But informally the members present apparently promised Bates an official invitation from the President of the United States himself.[150]

At this point, the new committee was clearly willing to add Bates to its membership—a move in which Hoover concurred, if only to preserve a facade of unity.[151] Whatever Bates's transgressions, he was a well-known resident of New York City with the ability (if he chose) to incite what Hoover's wife called a "newspaper scandal."[152] But at once complications arose. Immediately after the meeting Hoover and two of his colleagues asked Colonel House to persuade President Wilson to invite Bates to the White House, ask him to join the new committee, but order him to behave! House energetically demurred. Bates was "subdued" and "apologetic," he said. Such an action would only inflate his ego all over again and appear to exonerate his misdeeds. The New York committee should leave Woodrow Wilson out of this and appoint Bates itself if it desired. Hoover and his friends acquiesced.[153]

But if President Wilson would not appoint Bates, who would? Believing that this was not a question for the New York committee alone, Hoover stated that the CRB's directors abroad should be consulted and did so by cable on November 7.[154] From his London office came a swift reply: Bates should be eliminated completely. He "has forfeited all claim for consideration," said Edgar Rickard and four others. Bates's "retention in the circumstances would be equivalent to whitewashing" and would expose the commission to "further acts of disloyalty and treachery."[155] Ambassador Page concurred; so did the Comité National.[156]

The New York committee now decided to postpone action until Hoover could return to Europe and confer with his colleagues there.[157] Back in London on November 20, the CRB chairman requested New York to take no action until the commission's patron-ambassadors examined the case.[158] Meanwhile Bates, having heard nothing from either the New York committee or President Wilson for nearly two weeks, considered himself betrayed. In a letter to Hemphill on November 19 he revoked his letter of two weeks before in which he had withdrawn his charges and had promised not to instigate adverse publicity.[159] Once more he contacted the State Department, this time accusing Hoover of "callous absence of consideration" for many who had served him well in the past year.[160]

With Bates again on the warpath, the New York committee grew more anxious to purchase his silence. On November 22 it urged Hoover to let it seek a nominal appointment for Bates from the President, if only to keep a "united front" and avert the need for possibly harmful public explanations. The committee, in fact, felt an obligation to make this request—a commitment it understood that Hoover had approved.[161]

Hoover, in London, was now trapped. Whatever his private feelings, he felt "bound in good faith" (by the November 6 gentlemen's agreement with Bates) to join in the New York committee's recommendation to the President.[162] But the rest of the CRB did not. In scorching terms every commission director in Europe—supported by Page and the Comité National—demanded that Bates be excluded completely from the New York committee and that their cable be exhibited to President Wilson. Bates's "actions constitute in fact a vindictive and malicious attempt to destroy what he cannot dominate," they said. His disloyal behavior could not possibly be condoned.[163]

Before the New York committee could act, Bates himself cut the knot. On November 24 he informed Hemphill that he considered his association with the CRB to be over. He thereupon released the New York committee from its "honorable verbal agreements" of November 6.[164] Two weeks later the committee informed the press that Lindon W. Bates had retired.[165]

Hoover was undoubtedly relieved. ". . . I have never in my life met with an instance of this character," he told associates in early November.[166] For years Bates and his wife had been among his most devoted friends. It was because (said Mrs. Hoover) of what the Bateses had once been, and because of their "strenuous efforts" for the CRB, and because of "the terrible shock of the Lusitania" that Hoover had "treated the problem absolutely differently than he would have done with almost any other man, under almost any other circumstances."[167]

But if the personal trauma was painful, the institutional legacy was positive. As a result of President Wilson's intervention, the "moral prestige" of the CRB was greater than ever. From Wilson, the State Department, and Colonel House on down, every outside participant in the drama had immediately or eventually sided with Hoover.[168] Within the CRB itself, every director and manager (except for two or three of Bates's friends in the New York office) had supported the Chief without reserve.[169] And as a result of the crisis he now had a New York executive committee that comprised some distinguished men of affairs, including (at an early date) Henry L. Stimson, his future secretary of state.[170]

As for Bates, the distinguished civil engineer never reconciled with the man he had once called his "most intimate friend and business associate for many years."[171] Instead, he became a source of derogatory allegations for some of Hoover's bitterest political enemies and even expressed willingness to testify against Hoover in congressional hearings.[172] In 1924, at age sixty-five, he died.[173]

I I I

ON November 9, 1915 Hoover sailed from New York for London; his wife and two sons accompanied him.[174] An entire year had now passed in the life of his relief commission, and what a year it had been. A year of ceaseless labor and endless trouble from directions both predictable and unexpected, a year of delicate diplomacy and feisty personal encounters. British and French Cabinet ministers, German generals, Spanish diplomats, Belgian bankers, American charity officials: all had felt the force of Hoover's personality.

Not all of his negotiations had been successful. His imaginative proposal to revive Belgian industry through controlled imports and exports never came to fruition; the British and the Germans could not agree on how to dispose of any profits.[175] His attempt to build a stable relief fleet for the duration of the war by chartering German cargo ships interned in neutral ports also failed. While the Germans and British eventually approved the idea (subject to many restrictions), the French government vetoed it. This was "dealing with the enemy," it said, and the Germans would benefit. To an angry Hoover the myopic French action was one of the worst examples of "war stupidity" he ever encountered. As a result he was forced to use increasingly scarce *Allied* shipping—to the Allies' own detriment.[176] But on the vital points he prevailed.

By late 1915 the enterprise to which the forty-one-year-old American had devoted himself without stint had grown to extraordinary proportions. It is "a great economic engine," he told Bates in September, "resting on government support and financial credits, [and] it is going to expand steadily in that direction. It is no longer a charity beggar of the old type and it takes on the dignity of a government."[177] During its first year the commission shipped nearly 1,000,000 tons of foodstuffs into Rotterdam from food sources as distant as Argentina and Australia, in 186 full and 308 partial cargoes. The value of the imports was nearly $69,000,000.[178]

The Commission for Relief in Belgium is "the biggest commissary undertaking the world has ever seen," wrote an admirer in the *New Republic*.[179] In northern France and Belgium its distribution apparatus extended over 19,000 square miles. From 240 regional warehouses the foodstuffs went out to more than 4,700 separate communes, each with its own food store administered by a local committee.[180]

In addition to providing a standard bread ration *(alimentation)* to the entire population, the relief organization gave additional assistance *(secours)* to the destitute. As the months passed, the administration of this benevolence became ever more complex. Each commune had its own canteen for the needy, an outlet entirely separate from the food stores maintained for general provisioning. Besides superintending the daily distribution of *secours ordinaire* at breadlines and soup kitchens, the Comité National provided funds for the aid of laceworkers, refugees, artists, destitute young mothers, pharmacists, displaced persons, widows, orphans, families of absent soldiers, the unemployed, and others. For many of these groups special committees and welfare agencies came into being and administered the subsidies.[181]

Of greatest interest to Hoover were the programs for aid to the children. Early in 1915 the relief organization created a special committee to deal with this sector of the populace. Under its guidance and stimulus, the Belgians developed a comprehensive *"soupe scolaire"* program for school-age youths; it ultimately fed hot meals daily to hundreds of thousands of youngsters between the ages of three and sixteen. (For those under three, separate canteens were established.)[182] Some months later Hoover described the operation of a typical school canteen. His pride was almost palpable:

On the closing of school at 4 o'clock, the small boys and girls form in line and march to the nearest canteen. . . . In one end of the room the 200 little girls take their places at long tables; an equal number of boys jubilantly make a rush for their places at the other end. Each table is decked with an American flag. The flags of the Allies cover the walls of the room. In one corner two industrious, good-natured cooks are stirring immense cauldrons of soup and rice, each holding 400 quarts, or enough for two shifts of children of 400 each. Young lady volunteers (there are thousands of them engaged in every sort of charitable work in Belgium), gowned in white, at a given signal, when the children are all ready, start busily serving the soup. There is no limit placed on the quantity—one, two, or three bowls, according to the appetite of the partaker, as this in many cases is the only "square meal" the children have during the day. Then follows the rice, and exceptionally on this one day, there is brown sugar to go with it. From the welcome shout that goes up, it is evident that sugar in Belgium, as elsewhere, is a much appreciated rarity. At the end of half an hour, 400 little girls and boys troop out and go to their own homes, where in many cases the kitchen larder is practically empty.[183]

With each week, it seemed, the perplexities of relief administration multiplied. It was necessary, for instance, for Hoover and the CN to take over flour mills and regulate millers and bakers, including their prices and margins of profit. It was necessary to establish milling ratios—the percentage of wheat that should be ground into flour.[184] The higher the percentage, the darker the flour and the bread. Soon some Belgians complained that the dark *"pain du ravitaillement"* was ruining their digestion. The determination of a satisfactory compromise bedeviled Hoover for months.[185]

Throughout all this activity Hoover's accountants and those of the Comité National compiled an endless stream of audited data. It was "the apotheosis of business applied to philanthropy," proclaimed Ben S. Allen.[186] Of all the statistics that were garnered and promulgated, three in particular seemed to give Hoover pleasure. First, he was administering his fantastic enterprise at an overhead of well under 1%.[187] Second, he and his associates were distributing bread in Belgium at a price lower than in London (yet were still making a profit applicable to the benevolent fund).[188] Third, thanks to their pioneering child-feeding operations, the infant mortality rate in Belgium and northern France was actually declining—and to its lowest point in history.[189]

Still, as the second year of the relief started, the need seemed on the verge of outpacing him. The number of destitute in Belgium, he reported in August, had reached 2,750,000, more than one-third the population.[190] And as the price of foodstuffs crept upward around the world, so, too, did the cost of revictualing and the consequent strain on the Allies' fixed subsidies.

But the longer the CRB persevered, the greater grew public admiration for its achievement. "It is not good will which distinguishes this Commission," said the *New Republic* in July. "There has been plenty of that all through history. It is the fact that scientific organization has been made the servant of good will."[191] The CRB, said Lord Curzon in October, was "a miracle of scientific organisation."[192]

But to those who knew it best the CRB was more than a "miracle," more than a "scientific" triumph. For it bore the singular imprint of one remarkable man. As Walter Hines Page and William Goode had said—and few would have disagreed—Hoover was the commission, and the commission was Hoover.[193]

7

Between Scylla
and Charybdis

I

IN mid-November 1915 Hoover and his family reached London. Their ocean journey had been a comfortable one, although (as Lou remarked to a friend) her husband had grumbled because the voyage was so slow.[1] As always, there were problems to solve and tasks to perform—like the gigantic clothing campaign that he had just launched in the United States. Since the outbreak of the war millions of destitute Belgian citizens had been unable to acquire any new clothes. Now a harsh winter was approaching, and Hoover feared that ill-clad Belgians could die of overexposure. He pleaded for the American public to contribute $5,000,000 in new clothes or materials from which Belgians could fashion their own garments.[2]

Within two weeks of his return to London, the CRB chairman was on his way to Brussels for at least the eighth time since the war began.[3] On November 30 he and his staff in Belgium enjoyed a nostalgic Thanksgiving dinner of imported "turkey" and sweet potatoes; that same day the Marquis de Villalobar held a luncheon in his honor.[4] For some time Hugh Gibson had been urging the temperamental Spaniard to change his antagonistic attitude toward Hoover. For the moment he seemed to acquiesce. A few days later Gibson himself arranged a "love feast" for Hoover, Villalobar, Francqui, and various other relief leaders in order to "smooth over some of the scars of battle." Hoover was bored—he hated such affairs—but he "played his part well," said Gibson, and the dinner, at least outwardly, was a success.[5]

Hoover had not come to Brussels, however, to engage in time-wasting rituals of "brotherly love."[6] As usual, troubles were piling up. Once again the German "civil" government was maneuvering to get control of the charitable department of the Comité National. All across the country reports were multiplying of German violations of the guarantees—minor infractions in themselves but disturbing ones nevertheless. In Brussels the CRB's new assistant director was encountering petty bureaucratic delays in answering his urgent correspondence. When he protested, the Germans accused him of insulting them. Most mysteriously of all, in early November Baron von der Lancken asked the commission to expel three of its representatives from the country. The charges against them were serious, he said, but he refused to divulge their nature.[7]

Confronted by these manifestations of unfriendliness, Hoover immediately counterattacked. He asked Hugh Gibson to "inform" von der Lancken that the CRB was seriously contemplating withdrawing from Belgium and terminating the entire relief effort. *That* would make the Germans take notice! Gibson speedily obliged, warning German officials that the situation was grave. The CRB volunteers inside Belgium had suffered harassment, "affronts," and "outrages" for months, he reported, and could submit to such indignities no longer.[8]

Hoover probably had no intention of aborting his humanitarian mission. But in the "big game" of diplomacy a bluff, if plausible, can be an effective weapon. Having invoked it against the powerful von der Lancken, Hoover now wielded it deftly behind his back. At once the CRB chairman instructed his representative in northern France to announce that the CRB would probably have to pull out of Belgium and that, if it did, the German army would have to feed 2,000,000 Frenchmen on its own. Hoover knew well that the German army leaders near the front wished his relief enterprise to continue. (The last thing they wanted was a desperate, starving population just behind their lines.) He knew, too, that some of them even wanted him to extend his operations to German-occupied Poland—a prospect that he was already exploring. But now, playing his hand to the hilt, he passed the word that with his Belgian work on the brink of collapse he could not possibly consider expanding his efforts elsewhere.[9] He told von der Lancken personally that he would "absolutely refuse" to discuss the Polish question until the CRB's circumstances in Belgium improved.[10]

Hoover's high pressure paid off. Within days, the German army's senior liaison officers to the CRB in northern France were aboard a train bound for Brussels. The situation in Belgium was becoming intolerable, Hoover told them. An "absolute pack of [German] bureaucratic underlings," riven by departmental jealousies, was subjecting the CRB to "tyranny," "incompetence," and "intolerable destructive inquisition." Quickly intervening in the matter (as Hoover hoped they would), the officers persuaded Governor-General von Bissing to create a special government bureau to work full time with the CRB and Comité National. The new department would include English-speaking officers sympathetic to the relief undertaking.[11]

Once more Hoover had gambled and gotten his way. Hugh Gibson chortled that Baron von der Lancken was "beginning to realise that Herb of our London House is a regular fellow and is the ticket for soup from his point of view."[12] On one issue, however, the German diplomat stubbornly refused to budge: the three CRB men whom he had declared unacceptable must go. According to his sources, the trio had transmitted militarily sensitive information from northern France to the CRB's bureau chief in Rotterdam (and thence to the Allied governments) prior to the German army offensive in September. In short, the three Americans were spies.[13]

To Hoover these charges were absurd. Two of the three men, he pointed out, had not even come to Europe until after the German offensive![14] The other had been in Rotterdam, not behind German lines, at the time.[15] But if the accusations were demonstrably baseless, whence had they emanated in the first place? Reluctantly von der Lancken named his source: a young German-American named Erdlets in the CRB's Rotterdam office.[16]

Hoover, in his own words, was "dumbfounded."[17] Only weeks before, Lindon Bates had turned against him. Had another trusted associate now done likewise? Racing over to Rotterdam from Brussels, the CRB chairman confronted Erdlets, who emphatically denied under oath that he had supplied any information to the Germans. Taking Erdlets's deposition back to Brussels, Hoover presented it to a startled von der Lancken, who agreed to withdraw his charges and close the case. The American "spies" were exonerated.[18]

Although Hoover's document sufficed for the German military, he shortly discovered that it was worthless. Erdlets was a former mining associate who had suffered financial and personal reverses during the war and had threatened to commit suicide because of them. Taking pity on his friend, Hoover had given him a salaried position with the CRB in Rotterdam and had even paid for his ailing wife to return to America.

Alas for Hoover, his benevolence had gone unrequited. Once in Rotterdam, Erdlets had plotted to oust his superior, C. A. Young. Exposed and rebuffed in his intrigues, the disgruntled employee had contacted German intelligence agents in Holland. To these he had repeated a melange of anti-German remarks that he had heard around the office—all nicely embellished with tales of British espionage operations in which Young was supposedly participating.

Sometimes the "revelations" had a comic tinge. At one point, when Major Wallace Winchell of the Salvation Army had visited Rotterdam en route to Brussels, Young had jocularly asked whether he was the head of the Salvation Army's intelligence service. Erdlets had duly reported the joke to his literal-minded German friends. Shortly thereafter Major Winchell had been forbidden to enter Belgium.[19]

Shocked by this evidence of Erdlets's misbehavior, Hoover nevertheless hesitated. If he fired his unfaithful friend immediately, the Germans might infer that he had coerced Erdlets into his denials. The CRB chairman therefore decided to let the undeserving employee remain in Rotterdam for a decent interval and then remove him. It was to be a painful mistake.[20]

For the moment, however, the Commission for Relief in Belgium had survived what Hoover acknowledged to have been a "severe crisis."[21] During its aftermath he felt obliged to send several conspicuously anti-German colleagues out of Belgium—at a considerable cost in efficiency.[22] But the affair did have one positive consequence: the new German liaison bureau, known as the Vermittlungsstelle, succeeded in reducing friction between the commission and the German authorities.[23]

In early December Hoover returned to London, where he spent the holidays with his family at his home on Hornton Street, Kensington. There, on Christmas Eve, he entertained members of the CRB's staff.[24] But the Christmas season was scarcely a joyful one. He could not yet know it, but the bizarre "spy" episode had inaugurated what was to be the unhappy pattern of the coming year: endless obstruction and adversity, first from one direction, then another.

I I

By late 1915 the CRB's distribution network inside Belgium had been in place for a year. Despite the strenuous efforts of Hoover's American volunteers and Emile Francqui's Comité National to perfect it, as the months passed disturbing practices began to develop, including a thriving black market in imported foodstuffs. In agricultural areas where other food was available, many Belgians sold their relief rations to traders who quickly resold them at a profit to needy Belgians in the cities. Some of this food, unsupervised by the CRB or CN, found its way into the hands of German purchasing agents, who thereupon shipped it to the Fatherland or the western front—thereby belying Hoover's claim that "not one ounce" of CRB food benefited the Germans.[25]

Another and more vexing problem concerned the foodstuffs raised inside Belgium itself. As a result of the agreements with Governor-General von Bissing in July, numerous indigenous food sources, including cattle, pigs, and fodder, had gone unprotected from German seizure. Late in the year, the occupying army took advantage of its self-created loophole. Operating through Belgian intermediaries and German trading firms, it began to purchase considerable quantities of meat and live animals from Belgian farmers. Thus even as the CRB was importing certain foods into Belgium from abroad, the Germans were simultaneously sending *other* food out of the country.[26]

It was not long before the British intelligence service discovered what was happening. His Majesty's Government did not fail to notice that whereas the

CRB imported an average of only 750 tons of bacon and lard per month in early 1915, it brought in an average of 5,000 tons per month by November—an odd and suspicious development.[27] On December 13 the British decided to retaliate. Under pressure from the Admiralty, the Foreign Office ordered Hoover to suspend all shipments of bacon and lard until further notice.[28] Three days later it expanded its list of forbidden imports.[29] Writing in behalf of his government, Lord Eustace Percy declared that the crackdown implied "no loss of confidence" in Hoover or his commission. But he made it plain that the British could no longer countenance relief measures that appeared simply to replace native products bought or seized by the enemy.[30]

Hoover responded with vigor. His vastly augmented pork and lard importations, he insisted, were not the result of German malfeasance but of increased need. The price of pork inside Belgium was skyrocketing, and fewer and fewer people could afford to buy it—forcing the CRB to increase its imports of this commodity for the destitute. Furthermore, as native supplies of butter diminished, more and more Belgians, he said, were switching to lard—adding further to the growing demand for this product. Hoover acknowledged that the number of live pigs inside Belgium had declined drastically during 1915. This was not, however, primarily because of German army purchases (although these did occur) but mainly because Belgian farmers, lacking bread as well as fodder, had been compelled to kill and consume their own livestock. In short, if the Germans were acquiring some native food (and Hoover did not deny it), it was, in his portrayal, an incidental effect of economic pressure.[31]

To Lord Percy and others, Hoover insisted that his distribution practices were sound:

> . . . we maintain a system of about 125 district warehouses, under our direct control, throughout Belgium. The food-stuffs are shipped under seal and our own flag to these warehouses and from these centres the commodities are drawn weekly by the Communal Committees and placed in the communal warehouses. At the communal warehouse the bacon and lard are distributed daily or weekly, on production of a ration ticket entitling the holder to his ration. These tickets are issued by a separate committee whose business it is to make sure as to the civilian character of the holder and to determine whether the tickets shall be given free to the destitute, partially paid for by those who have some resources, or paid for in full by those who have means. As a check on this system, we maintain a series of inspectors and we require a monthly return from the Communal warehouses as to the foodstuffs which they issue. These are all aggregated and agreed with the emissions from our Regional warehouses and the whole are agreed with our Rotterdam shipments.[32]

In fact, said Hoover, it was possible to "trace the course of any parcel of foodstuff from New York to the actual Belgian who consumes it."[33] Once again he asserted that "not one atom" of imported fats reached the German army. And once again he argued that "every ounce" of his shipments was needed.[34]

Hoover's defense of his policy was plausible but not completely persuasive. The CRB might be able to trace every parcel of imported food to an actual Belgian consumer, but it could not prove that the Belgian actually consumed it.[35] More seriously, from the British point of view the critical problem lay not with imported foodstuffs (which were reasonably protected) but with *indigenous* food sources (which were not). And whatever the economic circumstances of the peasants or the urban poor, the undeniable fact was that the Germans *were* obtaining food inside Belgium—at the very time that millions of Belgians were scraping by on rations largely paid for by the Allied governments.

Nevertheless, Hoover's elaborate rebuttal proved effective. On December 22 he testified before a special subcommittee of the British government's War Trade Advisory Committee. The next day the British temporarily lifted their ban on pork shipments while they considered what broader policy to formulate.[36]

On December 31 the British decision came, in the form of a stern letter from Sir Edward Grey. Citing the Germans' increasing purchases of native food supplies (particularly cattle and pigs), their continuing levy of 40,000,000 francs per month on the Belgian people, and the CRB's growing volume of imports, Grey declared that the situation had become intolerable. The foreign secretary thereupon demanded that *all* export of *all* food sources of *all* kinds (including livestock) from Belgium must be "absolutely prohibited" by Governor-General von Bissing. Moreover, all such articles must be denied to the German army of occupation. If the Germans would not agree, then, said Grey, his government would reconsider its entire attitude toward the relief commission. The British could not stand idly by, he said, while the commission's work degenerated into "a method of replacement instead of one of relief, and an encouragement to the Germans to deplete the resources" of little Belgium.[37]

Grey's ultimatum was an unwelcome surprise to Herbert Hoover. On top of all his other burdens he was now required somehow to extract sweeping new concessions from the Germans, at a time when Germany's own food supplies were dwindling.[38] More troubling still, Grey's note reflected a sudden hardening of British sentiment—a disturbing portent for the year ahead. Even the sympathetic Lord Percy believed that a "crisis" in the relief was at hand.[39] And if moderate men like Grey and Percy felt this way, one could imagine the attitude of the British hardliners.

Almost daily now British displeasure with the CRB was surfacing. In mid-December the ever-hostile Admiralty attempted to cancel government insurance for British ships sailing to Rotterdam for the CRB.[40] Although Sir Edward Grey successfully resisted this move,[41] Admiralty opposition did not abate.

Why couldn't the CRB use neutral vessels only? the British asked. Impossible, Hoover replied. Neutral shipping was too scarce; "unless this whole thing is to break down, we must have the right to charter British ships."[42] Nevertheless, during December the CRB was unable to hire a single British vessel for three weeks. Hoover suspected that Admiralty interference was the cause.[43]

Meanwhile the CRB for some time had been distributing tin containers of condensed milk to mothers of children in Belgium and northern France. Suddenly, in late December, the British ordered it to return these tins to Holland after use. The British feared that the Germans—desperately short of such tins themselves—would seize them and send them to Scandinavia to be filled with preserved meat.[44]

Hoover immediately protested. To collect all these empty containers, at least in northern France, and send them back on German canal craft was, he said, "simply hopeless." Besides, the tins were not reusable anyway.[45] Impressed by his objections, the British temporarily permitted him to continue; 120 tons of condensed milk went on their way.[46] But when, a little later, the French government accused the Germans of using the tins for hand grenades, the CRB was obliged to establish a laborious retrieval system—one more consequence of the increasingly desperate war.[47]

The storms of late December were but premonitory squalls. In the early weeks of 1916 trouble beset Hoover on nearly every front. In Belgium the German authorities were loath to accede to the new British demands.[48] In Britain itself a rising wave of antirelief agitation, coupled with a growing shortage of shipping and the blatant requisitioning of relief vessels by the Admiralty, was jeopardizing the CRB's ability to transport its precious supplies. By mid-January Hoover had been unable to charter a single British ship for weeks. For the first time since his work began, an interruption in deliveries to Belgium loomed.[49] Gloomily he confided to Ambassador Page that the breakdown of the relief seemed "not far off."[50]

From America, too, the news was disturbing. Despite the strenuous efforts of himself and his associates in the United States, the CRB's clothing drive had fallen far short of expectations. Hoover was bitterly disappointed— "entirely discouraged" and even "somewhat disgusted" by the attitude of his countrymen. The citizens of the belligerent European countries, he noted, had been more generous.[51] The CRB's leader blamed his campaign's failure on "the general lassitude of the American people" about European relief and on the machinations of Lindon Bates:

There can be no question that through Bates the misery in Belgium and Northern France will be measurably increased during the winter and if there is any division of Hell into compartments appropriate to people's crimes, the people who have committed plain, ordinary, wilful murder will be entertained in Palace Hotels compared to the apartments that will be assigned to people who have committed such acts as this.[52]

To further complicate matters, in mid-January the members of the CRB's New York advisory committee began to fear that they might be held personally responsible for the mounting financial commitments of the relief commission, including its multimillion-dollar food purchases in America.[53] Hoover did his best to reassure his nervous colleagues. In mid-February he even instructed his attorney to draft a document to be signed by Hoover personally, pledging his entire fortune against any liability that might befall the New York committee.[54]

Hoover's gesture was less daring than it seemed, since the Belgian government had already promised to assume any losses that his commission might sustain.[55] Nevertheless, no one anywhere could accuse him of less than total commitment to the cause. His colleague Vernon Kellogg, for instance, was serving in Belgium while on leave from Stanford University. Unknown to Kellogg, Hoover sent Stanford several thousand dollars with which it paid Kellogg what he assumed to be his sabbatical salary. Otherwise Kellogg, who was not well-to-do, would have been without income.[56] According to Brand Whitlock, Hoover was personally covering the expenses of the CRB's representatives inside Belgium—to the extent of $35,000 per year.[57] Typically, however, the CRB chairman concealed his generous deeds. He knew, for example, that Professor Kellogg would be crushed if he discovered that his chief was secretly subsidizing him.[58]

For Hoover personally the multiplying crises could not have come at a less opportune time. During December his body began to exhibit what his wife called "wheezing in the machinery," including severe headaches and a stiff throat. By New Year's Day he was seriously ill, with a painful abscess in one ear. The result was that for the next ten days or more he was confined to his bed in London.[59] You have burned your candle at both ends and in the middle, too, the doctors told him. One opined that he would be lucky if he did not have to abandon his work entirely for three months. Hoover scoffed at such medical talk: ". . . I am infinitely better acquainted with my own mechanism than they are," he told a friend.[60] Nevertheless, despite his intention to cross the Channel in mid-January, he was compelled to remain at home for most of the month and was forbidden by his doctor to travel to Belgium.[61]

It was, perhaps, just as well. In the dark days of January 1916 he was needed more in London than in Brussels.[62] From London he could direct his unrelenting campaign to obtain the relief fleet that he desperately needed.

In early February he achieved a breakthrough: under prodding from the relief commission the Belgian government-in-exile formally requisitioned all ships flying the Belgian flag anywhere in the world and ordered them into the exclusive service of the CRB. By this stroke Hoover obtained about twenty vessels, or about one-third of the tonnage he required.[63] On other fronts, however, success eluded him. The British government flatly refused to seize and transfer twenty-five Belgian-owned ships sailing under British registry.[64] In fact, the Admiralty even snatched away several ships already under charter to the relief enterprise.[65] And despite his unremitting efforts, *German*-owned vessels languishing in neutral ports remained out of reach.[66]

Still, Hoover did not give up easily. As soon as the British turned him down, he attempted to force them to retreat. As he indicated to a friend, his tactics were not subtle:

> . . . I have informed the French government formally, that shipping under the Belgian flag will be unable to entirely supply the Belgian people, and that reluctantly we have been compelled to take the decision that we cannot ask the Belgian people to starve in favor of the French, and that the responsibility for the people in Northern France is primarily that of the French Government and that unless they can furnish shipping we have to decline to continue. This attitude has produced a perfect storm in Paris. . . .[67]

Hoover hoped to "direct the hurricane" of French alarm squarely against the British; in this way he might procure those twenty-five vessels after all.[68] But when His Majesty's Government refused to yield, the CRB's chieftain was himself obliged to retreat. His threat to withdraw from northern France went unfulfilled; somehow he found additional shipping on the world market.[69]

It was not surprising, as the days of January swirled by, that Hoover wondered for a moment whether all his efforts were worth it. The commission "is getting hammered from all sides," he told Hugh Gibson. "Altogether, I am free to confess that this business has gone on too long and that our accumulated wickedness in attempting to feed 9,000,000 of people is now coming home to roost, and I find staring [at] me in my dreams a large poster entitled 'Go back to the lead mines', in which occupation one obtains a modicum of human gratitude and a large liberty from hammers of all sizes, from tackhammers up to pile-drivers."[70]

But Hoover had little time for moods of withdrawal. On January 21, 1916, in the midst of all his other anxieties, the British Foreign Office informed him of a devastating discovery: elements of the relief organization inside Belgium had sold thousands of tons of imported rice to German agents, who in turn had shipped it through Holland into Germany. The Foreign Office demanded a full accounting and a return by the Germans of an equivalent amount of rice. Unless this were done within thirty days, said the British, they would reconsider the question of *all* relief imports, since it would then be obvious that neither German pledges nor Hoover's own apparatus could be relied upon.[71]

The Foreign Office's letter represented the most dangerous threat yet to the CRB. This was not *native* Belgian food that the British were talking about but the neutral commission's own imports, all supposedly safeguarded to the very last ounce. If British confidence in Hoover's control system were not soon restored, the provisioning of Belgium would cease.

Hoover was humiliated and outraged. "To have this case put up to us," he told a colleague,

> and to have received this letter from the English Foreign Office at this juncture in our delicate situation has made me so angry that I almost choke. It amounts to a practical betrayal of ourselves by the Belgian Local Committees, and has been the worst blow against our personal integrity which we have had since the beginning. . . .

Here I am, he said, insisting daily to the British government that all my imports "go absolutely to the civil population." Now his assurances stood contradicted, and his British supporters stood defenseless. If this rice leakage should become public knowledge, he warned, "popular clamour" in England would quickly force an end to the relief. Indeed, he wondered whether he was even "justified in going on with the business if the Belgians themselves are going to betray the trust which we must necessarily repose in them as to detailed distribution."[72]

In short order, Hoover addressed a stinging letter to the Comité National— a letter that he hoped Emile Francqui could use to "pound the table" and bring the recalcitrant Belgians into line. (It was not Francqui and his Brussels colleagues who were at fault, said Hoover; it was the CN's provincial committees that did not adhere to instructions.)[73] Declaring that he had "absolute proof" that local Belgian relief committees were selling foodstuffs "right and left," and that a "considerable tonnage" had been sold to the Germans, he bluntly called the Belgians to account:

> The blame primarily lies on the Belgian people, and it does seem to me that if the Belgians themselves are not willing to cooperate with us in maintaining the integrity of our assurances and guarantees, the whole question of provisioning the people falls immediately to the ground, and it is utterly impossible that we should continue this work. I cannot state too emphatically that these Committees have jeopardised the whole food supply to the Belgian people and that if we fail to overcome this blow the responsibility for the debacle is absolutely upon their heads.

Hoover demanded that the guilty Belgian local committees confess their illicit transactions. It was no use making denials, he said. The British government had the evidence.[74]

The case of the missing rice underscored Hoover's growing conviction that the Comité National had to be reorganized.[75] Even before the Foreign Office delivered its bombshell, Hoover was aware that "irregularities in the distribution" of his imports were occurring and that the "corrupt practices" of certain Belgians must be quelled.[76] In early January he even proposed that the Comité National be required to cut off the food supply to any community where such violations occurred in the future.[77] (The Germans had already forbidden such reprisals.)[78]

Hoover's angry outburst to the Belgians produced results. On February 3 the Comité National reprimanded its provincial committees for neglecting to establish adequate inspection and control services. Citing the actual sale of relief goods by communal committees to private businessmen, it threatened to cut off relief supplies to provinces that did not reform.[79] Despite this crackdown, Emile Francqui was not at all pleased with Hoover's letter. While conceding that small leakages had occurred, the Belgian contended that their importance had been exaggerated and that his control system was reducing abuses to a minimum. Hoover, he charged, had been unjustly harsh on the Belgian people.[80]

Nevertheless, by early February Hoover and his American colleagues believed that stricter supervision *was* imperative—and that their own involvement in it must increase.[81] The CRB's control, said Hoover's deputy in Brussels, "must be extended directly to the people. . . ."[82] Despite the Comité National's creation of improved provincial inspection services in late 1915, food control at the local level remained ineffective. Frequently communal committees disregarded regulations laid down in Brussels. To the independent-minded communal leaders, long accustomed to local autonomy, such edicts from above often seemed intrusive and insulting.[83] The result, as Hoover later admitted to Lord Percy, was an "enormous amount" of inadequate bookkeeping, "nonenforcement of the ration system," political favoritism in the dispensation of *secours*, open reselling of imported stocks—and ultimately leakages to Germany.[84]

While Hoover labored to reorganize the relief apparatus inside Belgium, he strained to hold the British at bay. Late in January the anti-CRB agitation emanating (in part) from the Admiralty threatened to erupt into Parliament and the press. Only by intense behind-the-scenes maneuvering, including sessions with several leading MP's, was Hoover able to prevent a dangerous parliamentary debate over the German food purchases.[85] His great aim, he confided later, was "to keep the powers that be from going into the Press with their belligerent literature. . . ."[86]

Privately Hoover acknowledged on February 8 that the leakages of imported foodstuffs had now been shown to be much larger than he had previously believed.[87] Nevertheless, that very same day, in a letter to the Foreign Office, he minimized the illicit trafficking in rice. Relying upon reports from his staff and an exhaustive study of bills of lading, Hoover asserted that of the 1,200,000 tons of food which had passed through the port of Antwerp since the previous September, only 400 tons—a negligible amount—had leaked. The problem, he now claimed, had been tremendously exaggerated.[88]

Meanwhile, through his diplomat-patrons in Brussels, Hoover attempted to get the Germans to yield to the British and prohibit all exports out of occupied Belgium.[89] Despite Brand Whitlock's assurances to London that German agreement was near,[90] by the beginning of February no definitive results had been achieved.

Hearing that the German authorities in Belgium had referred the matter up to Berlin, Hoover wrote to Ambassador Gerard for help. In anxious terms the CRB chairman reviewed the deteriorating political climate in England: the growing "snowball of public opinion" against the relief work, the "rising tide" of parliamentary sentiment for tightening the naval blockade. And in contrast to what he was telling the British, Hoover now reported that the Germans *were* abstracting food from Belgium in far from negligible amounts. ". . . [I]f the British public had the remotest idea that the Germans were taking 2,000 head of cattle out of Belgium per week," he wrote, "we should not last 20 minutes."

Just weeks before, Hoover had insisted to the British that his massive pork imports of late 1915 were largely unrelated to German procurement of Belgian cattle. Now, to Gerard, he admitted that they were:

> The number of cattle in Belgium has apparently decreased 60% or 70% since the war began. The result of this has been that the population are much under supplied with fats, butter, milk, etc. We therefore started issuing a ration of about 50 grammes of Bacon and Lard per diem to the most destitute members of the community 7 months ago and have been forced to gradually extend the social area of this ration until we were importing over k[il]os. 10,000,000 of Bacon and Lard per month and suddenly these imports, which were, in truth, abnormal enough, dawned upon the British Admiralty. . . .[91]

It is often hard to know, for this period in Hoover's work, just when and to whom he was telling the truth. To the British he repeatedly downplayed the extent of food leakages and German cheating. To Ambassador Gerard, however, and to the Belgians as well, he made the German violations appear massive—no doubt to strengthen his case for drastic countermeasures. Shrewd and calculating, the CRB chairman was adept at maximizing or minimizing the problem at hand—depending upon his audience and his needs.

With the pot boiling in London and now Berlin, Hoover departed for Paris on February 9—his first cross-Channel excursion since his illness.[92] He wished to persuade the French to pressure the British to seize private vessels and turn them over to the CRB. He hoped, too, to enlist greater French support for his enterprise generally. For nearly a week he consulted with senior French officials, including members of the General Staff and President Poincaré himself, who expressed his admiration for Hoover's efficient labors.[93] In the end the CRB chairman did not obtain the particular ships he sought. But thanks in considerable measure to his forceful advocacy, the official French attitude toward the relief improved markedly. From this point forward the government in Paris proved a willing ally in his struggle to extract concessions from the British.[94]

Hoover's quick trip to Paris also brought success in another area. For some weeks a number of French politicians and businessmen from German-occupied northern French territory had been attempting to import additional foodstuffs via Germany and Switzerland—independently of the Commission for Relief in Belgium. To Hoover such schemes were totally unacceptable. If separate (and perhaps competing) relief organs were created behind enemy lines they could only complicate his already difficult problem of control. The CRB chief therefore objected strenuously. As he put it later to a British friend, "there is positively no hope for this business unless there is monopoly."[95] Under pressure from the CRB (and possibly from their own government), the local French relief leaders backed down.[96] The commission's exclusive "franchise" remained intact.

On February 16 Hoover returned to London—and yet another caldron of trouble. Back in December he had asked for British permission to increase his monthly imports to Belgium and northern France.[97] Now, two months later, he learned to his horror that the British planned to reduce his quota severely.

To Lord Percy at the Foreign Office Hoover exploded with indignation. The British calculations of necessary imports, he said, were "scandalous." In the case of northern France, they reduced the ration to "an absolutely unendurable basis." "No one with any human bowels has the right to force a ration on these people so enormously below the subsistence point. . . ." He therefore refused to take any responsibility for imposing such a hardship on nearly 10,000,000 people. If, he said, the French and Belgian governments

> determine that their populations should be reduced to the state of misery that is here projected, it, at least, relieves us of moral responsibility and leaves us to reconsider our position as to whether we care to continue as an implement of such pressure . . . . if further reductions are to be made, which to our certain knowledge mean the absolute deterioration in health of these populations, it cannot be expected that we shall continue this work.[98]

Hoover's protest (and implicit threat to resign) were unavailing. For the British, too, were seething—at the Germans. By mid-February His Majesty's Government still had not received a reply to its demand of December 31 for an end to German food seizures inside Belgium. Instead, according to the Foreign Office, the Germans were continuing to requisition food throughout the country. Losing patience, Sir Edward Grey on February 23 demanded an immediate answer from the enemy. Until then, he warned, the CRB's imports would be drastically curtailed.[99]

The foreign secretary was not feigning his displeasure. That same day the Foreign Office issued a new list of permissible shipments. For Belgium: instead of the 126,400 tons per month that Hoover had requested, it allowed only 68,100 tons—12,000 per month less than in 1915. For France: instead of the 48,600 tons he desired, it authorized 30,040 tons—or roughly 5,000 tons per month less than before.[100]

The British decision was immediately overtaken by events of a more promising sort inside Belgium. In the last week of February the CRB and Comité National agreed to amalgamate their supervisory organizations into a single Department of Inspection and Control under the joint and equal direction of their representatives. The new bureau, headquartered in Brussels, would oversee the provincial inspection services, conduct meticulous surveys, and employ teams of investigators to ferret out abuses. At the provincial level also, the existing inspection services were fused. From now on, Belgian heads-of-household who received relief rations would be required to promise in writing not to resell their allotments. If they violated this pledge, or if other serious infractions occurred, their cases would be referred to the Belgian courts (which were still functioning with German permission). In effect, the CRB and Comité National—both private organizations without formal legal standing—had just decreed that resale of their food supplies was a punishable offense. As long as Belgian public opinion and the courts sustained them, their word was law.[101]

The precise meaning of the new control arrangement, however, was less clearcut than it seemed. Shortly before the new bureau was created, Hoover informed Lord Percy that the "entire inspection staff in Belgium" was being shifted from *joint* control by the CRB and CN to "sole control" by the commission.[102] A few weeks later he reiterated that the reorganized bureau was "entirely under American direction."[103] The actual documents, however, stated otherwise. Why? Some months later Hoover implied to the British that the new bureau was only nominally a "joint" one, structured that way "in order not to offend Belgian susceptibilities."[104] It is doubtful that the Comité National had the same understanding.

Whatever the proper interpretation of the new accord, it clearly entailed an extension of the CRB's influence inside Belgium, and it did not come about without cost. Francqui, for one, objected vehemently. The Comité National, he declared, was quite capable of controlling food distribution itself; there was no need for the CRB to interfere.[105] Other members of his executive committee also resisted.[106] But after much discussion, the Belgians and Americans came to an agreement—or so, in Brussels, it seemed.[107]

Suddenly the theater of controversy shifted to London. On February 21 Francqui and Baron Léon Lambert of the Comité National arrived in the British capital from Belgium. The Marquis de Villalobar accompanied them. The ostensible purpose of their journey was to deliver the long-awaited German reply to the British demands about native foodstuffs. On the surface the news was good. In a letter in behalf of von Bissing, Baron von der Lancken agreed to prohibit the export of all foodstuffs from occupied Belgium. But the Germans' offer was conditional: they would do this if the British stopped seizing CRB ships *and* if the British promised to let the Belgians import as much food as the Comité National deemed necessary. The Comité National—not the Commission for Relief in Belgium.[108]

Such, then, was the German counterproposal. Why, however, was it necessary for three men to transmit its contents personally to the United Kingdom? It quickly transpired that Francqui and his companions had other axes to grind. Instead of presenting their message to the British government in the usual manner—through the Spanish and American ambassadors in London (both friends of the CRB)—Villalobar and Francqui insisted on approaching the British Foreign Office directly. They conspicuously did not invite Hoover to join them. To Hoover the import of their action was transparent: Francqui and his colleagues in Brussels wished to bypass the CRB and establish direct relations with the British government. Ever attentive to the diplomatic fine print, Hoover noticed that the German reply—which the Comité National endorsed—seemed designed to "sidetrack" his organization and shift responsibility for the guarantees onto the Comité. To the CRB chairman the handwriting on the wall was only too legible: Francqui and the Belgians, abetted by Villalobar, were willing to play ball with the Germans—and squeeze the Americans out.

Distressed by these perceptions and by what he considered a deliberate "campaign to minimise" his organization, Hoover resorted to his *ultima ratio*. Less than twenty-four hours after the trio from Brussels reached London, he informed Ambassador Page that the time had come to dissolve the CRB and place the relief entirely in Belgian hands.[109]

At this point Page advised his fellow American to resign[110]—precisely the advice that Hoover did *not* want to hear. The CRB chairman had no desire to sacrifice himself alone. According to Page, Hoover could not "come to giving up the work unless absolutely compelled to."[111] Perhaps he feared that if he did withdraw, the commission might continue without him.

Instead, with the concurrence of his American colleagues in London, he adopted a cleverer tactic. Writing to Page on February 24, he suggested that the *entire* CRB withdraw and transfer its responsibilities to the Comité National. After all, he pointed out, the chaotic conditions of late 1914 had long since vanished. Belgium was stabilized now, Belgians were free to move about, the relief apparatus was functioning efficiently, and the financial underpinnings were in place. Surely, he claimed, the revictualling of Belgium could now proceed under exclusively Belgian control.[112]

It is very doubtful that Hoover believed his own arguments or expected the Allies to accept them. Barely two weeks before, the French government, for the first time, had given him its enthusiastic support. It was hardly likely to reverse itself now and entrust the victualling of its conquered territory to Belgians who had never even been there. As for the British, the CRB chairman knew full well that in the wake of the recent leakages of pork and rice, the Foreign Office had little faith in the Comité National's competence or its ability to resist German pressure. Furthermore, only three days before Hoover submitted his offer to withdraw, Sir Edward Grey himself informed Page that if the Americans were ousted from the task of distribution inside Belgium, the "feeling here would be strongly opposed to continuing the system of Belgian Relief."[113] Hoover was almost certainly aware of this before he prepared his letter. He already knew, therefore, that the British were extremely unlikely to accede to the schemes of the visitors from Brussels. No doubt this made it easier for him to make his self-abnegating "offer."

Meanwhile the Marquis de Villalobar (who by now, according to Brand Whitlock, hated Hoover)[114] was busily proceeding with his own designs. It seems that Baron von der Lancken had approached the Spanish diplomat with a grandiose proposal to end the war. Under this plan the German army would voluntarily withdraw from Belgium, and the warring powers would convene a peace conference in Brussels—through the mediation, Villalobar hoped, of the king of Spain. In such an event Villalobar himself would presumably occupy the limelight. According to Francqui, the Spanish minister to Belgium was eager to convey this peace feeler to London—and, not coincidentally, to promote his personal ambition to become the Spanish ambassador to Great Britain.[115]

But if Villalobar was motivated by visions of self-aggrandizement, he was also a willing ally of his travel companions. Dining with Prime Minister and Mrs. Asquith, he stressed the CN's political value to the Allies—a claim that quickly got back to Hoover via Asquith's wife.[116] In a visit to the Belgian legation Villalobar even declared that the Americans were no longer needed inside Belgium. Instead, he asked the Belgian government-in-exile to help him place the Comité National in complete charge.[117]

To Hoover himself on the twenty-fourth, the Spanish diplomat was a bit more circumspect. The purpose of his mission, he disclosed, was to impress upon the Allies the immense political services that the Comité National was rendering to their cause. It had become a "government within a government," sustaining Belgian morale, encouraging popular resistance to the enemy, and keeping the unemployed from having to work for the German army. The Allies, he said, did not fully understand the Comité's significance. The CRB, of course (he added), was only concerned with relief. Although Villalobar did not quite say so, the implication of his remarks was plain: the Comité National, not the CRB, was the truly indispensable body.[118]

Hoover was—or professed to be—amazed. If this is your view, he replied, the CRB would have to "reconsider" its "whole position." Convinced (or so he said) that the Spaniard's statements were "dangerous for the whole future of the relief," he asked him to consider whether the Comité's political ambitions might not generate a disastrous conflict with the German authorities.[119]

Hoover was not amused by Villalobar's effort to drive a wedge between the Belgian government and the CRB. He was no less furious at Baron Lambert, who had been telling people in London that the CRB men in Belgium were a group of high-living college boys having a good time.[120] As it happened, he did not have to worry about Villalobar for long. Informed by Page of the CRB's professed willingness to retire, Sir Edward Grey responded at once that it was out of the question. The relief of Belgium, he declared, would continue under commission control or not at all.[121] In a letter to Villalobar a few days later, Grey pointedly referred to Hoover as "the only person directly and personally responsible for the manner in which the whole work, both inside and outside Belgium, is carried on." And in a barely veiled rebuke to the Spanish diplomat, Grey remarked that neither "diplomatic representatives of neutral powers" (meaning Villalobar) nor Belgian citizens under foreign domination (meaning Francqui) could be held responsible for the conduct of the relief. Instead, Grey hoped that "all parties concerned in this matter" would do everything possible to "lighten" the "heavy burden" of the agency that *was* responsible: the "great neutral" Commission for Relief in Belgium.[122]

Repulsed by the Foreign Office and by Hoover's unexpected maneuver, the visitors from Brussels raced for cover. In an anxious letter to Ambassador Page, Emile Francqui pleaded for Hoover to stay on. Without Hoover's "most active cooperation," he said, the continued relief of the Belgians would be "absolutely impossible." Certainly he, Francqui, could not conceivably bear the burden of administration alone.[123] Villalobar, too, expressed concern and insisted at length that he bore no animosity toward Hoover.[124] When Baron Lambert called at the commission's office, Hoover told him bluntly that he and his associates were "depreciating" the CRB in order to satisfy their "idle vanity." In doing so, he warned, they were destroying Allied confidence in the very foundations of the relief project. According to Hoover, the baron was reduced to tears.[125]

By the end of February the Villalobar–Francqui–Lambert "conspiracy" (as Page called it) was dead, and the CRB had survived what Hugh Gibson called its "greatest crisis."[126] On March 1 Hoover informed Brand Whitlock that because of the Allied governments' attitude, he was "reluctantly compelled to abandon the hope" of liquidating his commission.[127]

The CRB chairman was not about to rely unaided, however, on the good will of the British Foreign Office. At this juncture a representative of the Rockefeller Foundation named Frederic C. Walcott was in London after touring Belgium and northern France. On February 28 Hoover requested Walcott to write him a letter evaluating the commission's inspection and control system.[128] Walcott immediately responded with a press release extolling the CRB's "remarkable efficiency" and its leader's "genius for organisation." The Germans were stealing no supplies, he claimed. If imports were stopped now,

Belgium would face "wholesale starvation" within a month.[129]

On March 13 Sir Edward Grey formally requested Hoover to reconsider his offer to withdraw. The British government, said Grey, would permit the relief to go on only if the "entire responsibility for it both inside and outside Belgium" was borne by private neutral citizens who had complete freedom of travel. Only the CRB met these criteria. Either it would continue to direct the relief "as heretofore" or the entire enterprise would cease.[130]

Hoover immediately reaffirmed his willingness to stay on. But, as always, he sought to extract as many concessions as he could. He now asked the British to recognize that "absolute perfection" in his work was impossible and that occasional minor leakages would occur. And, he asserted, it was "absolutely hopeless" to proceed unless he obtained the cooperation of all British government agencies (including, though he did not say so, the Admiralty). Hoover stated that he was going ahead on the "clear understanding" that he would henceforth enjoy this cooperation.[131]

It was not until mid-May that the British foreign secretary confirmed Hoover's "understanding."[132] By then Hoover had felt anew the antagonism of his enemies at the Admiralty.

Meanwhile, inside Belgium, the new inspection and control service began to operate under the energetic direction (on the CRB side) of a young Princeton graduate named Joseph C. Green. By late spring the machinery comprised more than two hundred inspectors, detectives, attorneys, and other agents, all of them ultimately responsible to Brussels. The implementation of this system at first aroused considerable resentment.[133] According to Green, the "petty local spirit of the Belgians could not brook without protest such a centralised organisation."[134] In the province of Brabant, defiance and outright noncompliance continued for months until Hoover personally intervened. Even after the new system was in place, the bureau was unable to stop the flow of native food products into German hands. Along the Belgian–German border extensive smuggling operations sprang up. But for supplies brought in from outside, the new control system was more effective. By imposing careful accounting practices, systematic inspection, and other methods (including the prosecution of hundreds of offenders in the courts), the CRB and CN during 1916 largely succeeded in suppressing illicit traffic in imported food.[135]

On another front, too, the news, for a change, was positive. In mid-April, after weeks of further negotiations in Brussels, Governor-General von Bissing at last banned all German army requisitions and purchases of native foodstuffs. He also forbade the shipment of virtually all indigenous food products out of the country. In return he requested only two concessions: that occasional unauthorized purchases of food by individual German soldiers be tolerated, and that exports of native commodities in obvious excess of native needs be allowed. The government of Great Britain acquiesced.[136] Whether the Germans would actually enforce their decrees, of course, remained to be seen. But at least for the moment a modus vivendi had been reached.

Even before this favorable outcome was assured, Hoover had begun to press the British to restore the cuts in his import quota that they had imposed only weeks before. To further his objective, he journeyed to Brussels in late March for a personal inspection of conditions in the field.[137] The endless crises, quarrels, and intrigues were again having an effect upon his health. Brand Whitlock, for one, found him "very tired" and "worn out by his work."[138] At one point, pacing back and forth in Whitlock's office, Hoover remarked wearily: "Well, the principal fact is that at eleven o'clock on the morning of March 24, 1916, the revictualing of Belgium still goes on."[139]

Four days later the CRB chairman traveled to northern France. He told Whitlock beforehand that he wished to obtain a "moving story to take back to England with him."[140] But even he was not prepared for what he saw. In the city of Valenciennes every meat shop was closed, including one that had been reduced to selling dog meat, and the shelves of every grocery store were "absolutely bare."[141] Throughout the region milk, butter, and potatoes were "absolutely exhausted"; only the CRB's shipments stood between the populace and starvation. Yet as a result (said Hoover) of the British government's reduction of his imports, the daily ration had been reduced to a level that "will not support life." In Lille sickness and the mortality rate were rising. At Roubaix the announcement of the lowered rations had caused riots; in reprisal the Germans had seized men for forced labor.[142]

Appalled by his findings,[143] Hoover returned quickly to London and pleaded for the right to send in more supplies. "I feel my utter inability to draw for you an adequate picture of the unutterable depression and despair of these people," he told Lord Percy. Here was the CRB, struggling "to alleviate this mass of misery," yet being forced to "appear as an instrument of torture" since it had to "refuse the pleadings" of the people for more food.[144] Hoover also requested an increased quota for Belgium (where the number of destitute had now reached 5,000,000) and did his best to minimize the abuses and fraud that had plagued him during the past winter. There "has been no leakage in our imports worth mentioning," he now asserted. And thanks to the new American-run control system, such leakage was "absolutely impossible." Hoover conceded that smuggling of food into Belgium from Holland was flourishing but insisted that most of the traded commodities were Dutch, not his own. As for exports of native food into Germany, the Germans, he said, had already prohibited it and were sincerely enforcing their pledge.[145]

Hoover's passionate beseechings were successful. Only six days after he submitted his request, the British government granted him everything he sought for northern France: an increase of 7,100 tons per month.[146] A few weeks later, after the Germans issued their new decrees against nonrequisition, the British authorized a similar increase for Belgium.[147] For the embattled CRB chairman—and more importantly, for 9,000,000-plus civilians—it was a crucial victory.

Hoover's winter of discontent, however, was not over. For many months the CRB had been "hectored and harassed" (as he put it) by a hostile British Admiralty, convinced as ever that the relief of Belgium was benefiting the enemy.[148] During the winter the Admiralty's determination to destroy the CRB seemed to grow. And as it did, its campaign against Hoover became personal. In January a Captain Hall of British naval intelligence pressed Hoover to supply him with data on German military operations in Belgium and northern France. Citing his neutrality, Hoover firmly refused. Not long afterward, what Hoover called "criminal investigation agents," apparently representing the Admiralty, began to interview his mining associates in London in an evident attempt to dig up "dirt" about his past. The investigators also evinced interest in his "national leanings." Inquiring about this at the Foreign Office, Hoover was advised that "great opposition" was building against the commission but that the storm would "blow over."[149]

Upon returning from Belgium in early April, he found instead that the storm had only intensified. Pressured by what Lord Percy called "a multitude of minor scamperers in the rabbit warren of war administration," including a "chair-borne admiral" in British naval intelligence, the Foreign Office had felt obliged to set up an investigation of the CRB by Sir Sidney Rowlatt, a distinguished British judge.[150] By the end of March Rowlatt had received evidence from British sources alleging that Hoover was untrustworthy, that he had sinister business connections with German mining interests, and that his imported foodstuffs had gotten into German hands.[151]

With Hoover's standing as head of the relief now imperiled, the Foreign Office asked him to submit to questioning by Justice Rowlatt. The CRB chairman's first instinct was to refuse. My "naturally combative disposition," as he later put it, "impelled me to other courses. . . ." But on reflection, and fearful that his actions might only "add further misery" to the Belgian people, he agreed to cooperate with the inquiry.[152] On April 7 he conferred with the judge.[153]

The interview proved to be an unsettling one. The judge raised questions about Hoover's prewar business career, notably his involvement in a Chinese mining dispute that had culminated in a London trial in 1905—the trial at which he had testified against Francqui. (Hoover's controversial behavior in this case was to interest his enemies and cause him vexation for years.)[154] Disturbed by the judge's line of questioning, Hoover offered to release his longtime personal solicitor in London from attorney-client confidentiality so that he could testify about Hoover's past. ". . . I have not a jot to hide in this world," said Hoover, and "I should be glad for [my solicitor] to give you information on anything."[155] Rowlatt, however, felt it "impossible to arraign a man's whole life" and therefore declined the offer.[156]

But Hoover was not about to let matters go at that. On April 12 he vented his frustration in a letter to Ambassador Page. The Yankee humanitarian acknowledged that anyone in his position of international responsibility must be "prepared to submit" to independent investigation. But there was a tremendous difference, he asserted, between open, competent scrutiny of his *work* and a "personal inquisition wherein I am summoned to answer anonymous attacks upon my private character." This "whole proceeding," he complained, was "one of deep humiliation." It verged upon "a presumption of guilt and necessity to prove innocence," without even "the ordinary rights of justice and the facilities of evidence." Portraying himself as a suffering servant who had sacrificed vital business interests "to serve the Allies in ameliorating the misery of the war," Hoover hoped that Rowlatt would report favorably. But if not, then "the authors of this outrage" (meaning his accusers) should be brought forward "to meet me that the thing may be gone into to the very bottom."[157]

Hoover had a well-developed capacity for the expression of righteous indignation. But mixed in with his impulse to do battle was a streak of tenderness and even sentimentality. It now transpired that it was this trait which had helped to create his present embarrassment. For at about this time he discovered that one of the "sources" for the Admiralty's allegations was none other than his former employee, Erdlets. Hoover had recalled Erdlets from Rotterdam in January, had reprimanded him, and had given him seven days to return to America. Convinced that Erdlets was suffering mental problems, Hoover had generously offered to help him find a job again in the mining field, where, he hoped, the youth might recover his equilibrium. Hoover had even written letters of recommendation for Erdlets to mining friends in New York. Instead, however, of showing gratitude for his friend's exceptional kindness, Erdlets had contacted the British Admiralty during his week in London and had poured out "a mass of lies" about the CRB, including the charge that Hoover had "corrupt dealings" with the Germans.[158] For the second time in six months the Chief had been betrayed by a friend.

Erdlets was now in New York City, working with a prominent pro-German businessman. Hoover asked his CRB bureau head in New York to spend "a little of my private money to put a watch on Erdlets and see what he is up to."[159]

As it happened, Hoover received no further trouble from his ex-employee. Nor did he receive any difficulties from Justice Rowlatt. Instead, on April 13, in a meticulous report based on data from many sources, the British judge exonerated the relief commission and (as Lord Percy put it) "demolish[ed] the mare's nest" perceived by the Admiralty. Rowlatt concluded that there was no evidence that the CRB's imported foodstuffs were being diverted from their proper recipients or that any significant leakages were occurring. Throughout the war, he said, it had acted responsibly and in good faith in attempting to prevent misapplication of its supplies. (Rowlatt did not address the problem of native foodstuffs; this was beyond the purview of his inquiry.) As for Hoover's supposed German connections, it was true that Hoover's mining companies had sold products to German companies before the war.

But there was no evidence that he was "pushing any prospective business with Germany" while directing his humanitarian mission. As for Hoover's conduct in China in the years 1899–1901, Rowlatt reported that he had too little evidence to evaluate it. But its relevance to the question of Hoover's integrity as CRB chairman seemed to the judge "in the last degree remote."[160]

In the words of a Foreign Office official, Rowlatt's report was "a complete vindication" of Herbert Hoover and the Commission for Relief in Belgium.[161] When, a few weeks later, a member of the War Trade Advisory Committee objected to increasing relief shipments into Belgium, Lord Robert Cecil of the Foreign Office, citing Rowlatt's report, politely told him to lay off. Hoover and the CRB, he said, were completely reliable.[162] But the "vicious attack by British militarists" (as Hoover called it) left a permanent residue of bitterness—and an ineradicable mistrust of the military mind.[163]

The British government, along with various English friends of the relief enterprise, now hastened to bury the controversy and assuage Hoover's wounded sensibilities.[164] On May 5 the British-based support group known as the National Committee for Relief in Belgium held its annual meeting at Mansion House in London. Hoover attended, addressed the convocation, and was cheered. So, too, was Prime Minister Asquith, who heaped praise on the CRB:

> A noble friend and colleague of mine, Lord Curzon, has described Mr. Hoover's work as: "A miracle of scientific organisation." (Cheers). That, I believe, is not an over-statement. . . .
>
> I am desired to express on behalf of the Government our deep gratitude to Mr. Hoover and to those American citizens who have so nobly given up their time and their occupations without recompense, and to a large extent without recognition, to this work of purchasing, shipping and distributing the supplies which alone enable the population of Belgium to keep body and soul together (cheers). It is one of the finest achievements in the history of humane and philanthropic organisation (cheers).[165]

A few days later Sir Edward Grey finally replied to Hoover's letter of March 18 requesting the cooperation of all British government departments with his enterprise. Yes, Grey assured him, all parts of His Majesty's Government would now cooperate with "this humanitarian work . . . in the closest possible way." The CRB had its "complete confidence."[166]

Hoover was free at last—until the next crisis.

I I I

WITH the coming of spring, 1916, there was no end to the anxieties and "pin pricks" (as Hoover called them) that constantly bedeviled the CRB.[167] Despite the decrees and solemn assurances of von Bissing, German purchases of native-grown Belgian foods (and open export of them to Germany) continued on a flagrant scale, with but few efforts by the authorities to stop it.[168] As always, the Germans cited loopholes in their pledges—claiming, for instance, that the fats they took from abattoirs were only "waste" and that the vegetables they requisitioned were surplus, hence legitimately subject to seizure. In France, meanwhile, and at times in Belgium, too, relations between Hoover's men and the Germans became tense, particularly in early spring, when it appeared that the sinking of the *Sussex* by a German U-boat might precipitate war with the United States. On this occasion Germany yielded to President Wilson and gave up its unrestricted submarine attacks. But behind the German lines in Belgium, CRB officials were subjected to searches, interrogations, and—for the first time—censorship of all their correspondence.[169]

Not all Hoover's difficulties emanated from the Germans. In Paris, to his extreme annoyance, the French government continued to support efforts by other relief organizations to import food into northern France from Switzerland.[170] In England his efforts to pry loose the Belgian-owned vessels flying the British flag made no headway whatever.[171]

Each week, it seemed, brought some new chapter in what Hugh Gibson called "the endless crises of the CRB."[172] In late April the German army deported tens of thousands of Frenchmen for forced labor far from their homes; vigorous protests by the commission helped to halt this outrage.[173] In April and May came the grim uncertainty of the *Sussex* affair; for days Hoover feared it might mean the "extinction" of his undertaking.[174] In June, in the wake of German seizures of Belgian textile materials, the British government forbade the CRB to ship into Belgium anything more than its current stocks of clothing.[175] During the summer and fall the CRB struggled to keep the German army in Belgium from seizing the 2,000-plus horses needed for food deliveries. In the end, after months of protests and negotiations, the Germans let the commission retain only horses unfit for military service—and required, with Prussian thoroughness, that each such horse be branded with the marking *CRB*.[176]

As the spring of 1916 melded into summer, still another problem confronted Hoover. All of his laboriously negotiated harvest agreements applied only to the crops of 1915. Now, with a new harvest coming on, he was obliged to renegotiate his contracts.

In the case of the occupied zone of Belgium, the task proved agreeably routine. On July 8 Governor-General von Bissing essentially renewed the arrangements of the previous year giving control of all cereal crops to the Comité National.[177] In the case of northern France, however, it was a different story. There, in 1915, the Germans had insisted on taking approximately two-thirds of the harvest for themselves, at the same time reserving to the native population a supply equal to 100 grams of flour and 200 grams of potatoes per person per day. Now, a year later, the British and French began to argue that this was not enough—that the Germans should henceforth renounce the *entire* native harvest, just as they were required to do in Belgium.[178]

Hoover was disturbed by the hardening Allied attitude. Aware of mounting antipathy inside Germany to his relief work, he realized that the time was hardly ripe for conveying new Allied demands to their adversary. He recognized, too, that the Germans had a legitimate claim on at least some of the products of occupied French soil. In many places they had cultivated the fields themselves or had provided seeds and labor to the peasantry.[179]

Nevertheless, the Allies were determined to wring further concessions if they could. On July 7 Lord Robert Cecil of the British Foreign Office demanded that the entire harvest of northern France be turned over to the civilian populace. This, he said ominously, was an "absolute condition of the continuance" of the CRB.[180] Privately the French government was willing to settle for less and authorized Hoover to do so if necessary.[181] But publicly, at least, the Allies stuck by their ultimatum, and Hoover, caught in the middle, was left to his own resources.

The CRB chairman at once had Ambassador Gerard approach the German government, which duly arranged for a conference with the General Staff.[182] On July 27, therefore, Hoover arrived in Brussels en route to Berlin. Linking up with Vernon Kellogg, who had been negotiating down at Charleville, he departed on August 3 for the German capital.[103]

Once more the specter of possible failure weighed upon him. To a young CRB volunteer it seemed that Hoover was on the verge of a nervous breakdown.[184] To Brand Whitlock, so different in temperament, it seemed that he never relaxed.[185] His task was not made any easier when the British Foreign Office chose this moment to issue a tough pronouncement through the press: all food in German-occupied France and Belgium must be reserved to the civil population alone and controlled by American neutrals, or the Allies would exact "reparations" by arms and by world opinion.[186]

For Hoover the British government's move could hardly have been more ill-timed. Inside Germany complaints were rising that the inhabitants of Belgium and northern France were actually eating better than the Germans themselves.[187] Hardliners such as Count von Reventlow were demanding that their government seize the crops of the occupied countries and expel the CRB completely.[188] Why, they cried, should Belgians evade the effects of the Allied blockade while citizens of the Fatherland had to suffer? Even worse, while on the train to Berlin Hoover learned that the German government was about to examine the whole question of relief for the occupied territories. Senior military and civilian officials had been invited to participate.[189] According to the press, the future of the CRB was "not particularly bright."[190]

On the morning of August 4 Hoover and Kellogg arrived in Berlin to discover that the great conference on the fate of the commission was about to begin. The two Americans were not invited. Instead, they were asked to have tea later in the day with Quartermaster-General von Sauberzweig and two liaison officers from the Great Headquarters in northern France.[191]

At four o'clock Hoover, Kellogg, and the Germans duly gathered for tea; the quartermaster-general drank whiskey and soda. Here the Americans learned the grim result of the day's proceedings: the relief work had come under violent attack and was very likely to be terminated. The German officials had been particularly enraged by Great Britain's latest ultimatum. Several had demanded that their government categorically reject it, abolish the relief then and there, and blame the British blockade if the Belgians starved. Hoover and Kellogg at once dissociated themselves from the British statement and tried to plead their humanitarian case. But in this turbulent hour the persuasiveness of their arguments was uncertain.

Then the unexpected happened. Quartermaster-General von Sauberzweig, who had been consuming one glass of whiskey after another, began to speak. He revealed that his own son had just been horribly blinded for life in a gas attack on the western front. He confessed that it was he who had ordered the execution of Edith Cavell, an English nurse living in Brussels, in late 1915 for espionage and for smuggling Allied soldiers through German lines. Although Cavell was undeniably guilty, her severe punishment had aroused international revulsion. Now von Sauberzweig, feeling the pangs of conscience and of alcohol, referred to himself ironically as "the murderer" and remarked that the neutral nations considered him "the most infamous of men."[192]

As the general continued his doleful monologue, Hoover spotted an opportunity. Perhaps he could turn the German's remorse to advantage. The CRB chairman later described what transpired next:

The General obviously did not like the kind of publicity he had received in the neutral world. The Relief was apparently about to blow up. I said to Dr. Kellogg that I wished to make a further statement to the General about the whole relief matter and asked him to translate fully. I said that the conclusion of the German authorities would mean death for millions of people, mostly children; that as he was responsible officer he would be portrayed to the world as a monster infinitely bigger and blacker than the picture they drew of him after the Cavell incident. I elaborated the theme to cover the whole German army. And as my temperature rose I emphasized this theme so strongly that Kellogg hesitated to translate my language and said so. But Major von Kessler injected that he would translate. And he did it with no reservations. It appeared that he had been fighting our battle all day and was himself in no good humor. The General made no immediate reply. Then suddenly he remarked that there might be something in what I said. Whether it was the threat, the whisky, or his grief, or the human appeal that moved him, I do not know. He directed von Kessler to inform Minister [of the Interior] Lewald that he thought the negotiation ought to continue. He would be obliged if the Minister would take the matter in hand and settle it.

We broke up at once and with von Kessler went to the Ministry. Lewald seemed relieved to hear von Kessler's authorization.[193]

Once again Hoover's bluntness and resourcefulness in argument had brought him victory. Evidently as a result of von Sauberzweig's action, the high conference of German officialdom did not abolish the relief of Belgium. Instead, Hoover was allowed to carry on and the "Reventlow gang" (as Kellogg called it) was repulsed.[194] Better still, the Germans agreed in principle to reserve a greater proportion of the northern French crops to the local population than in 1915. Not all the crops, to be sure, but more. Hoover and Kellogg promptly hurried out of Berlin before the Germans could change their minds.[195]

Three weeks later Kellogg and Major von Kessler of the General Staff confirmed this agreement in writing. The German army promised to reserve to the occupied French population enough food to permit a doubling of the daily ration of potatoes and flour for the coming year. In return the CRB promised, among other things, to try to increase its imports and obtain a greater Allied subsidy for its work in the affected region.[196] This was not all that the Allies had demanded, but it was enough.[197]

The Germans, however, imposed one condition: the Allies must not gloat about the result in the newspapers.[198] The Germans did not want it to appear that they had yielded to the British ultimatum. Kellogg, in fact, feared that if the British did try to make that claim, the Germans would repudiate the agreement in toto![199] Hoover therefore promptly asked the French and British to "suppress any exultation" and not to "rub it in."[200]

Back in London, Hoover told Lord Percy about his incredible interview with von Sauberzweig. And from the experience the head of the CRB drew a lesson: that what these "big, fat, retaliatory Germans" feared most of all was the "brand of Cain" stamped upon them by public opinion. The episode may have strengthened his belief in the efficacy of what Percy called "moral reprobation as an instrument of foreign policy."[201] Certainly it seemed that when the chips were down few on either side were prepared to ignore public sentiment entirely.

Hoover's summer of travail was not quite over. The Allies' subsidies and sanction for his work in northern France were due to expire on September 1.[202] Moreover, he had just pledged to the Germans to extract more support from the Allies for the coming year. In mid-August, therefore, he turned his attention to the other side of the diplomatic seesaw.

The CRB chairman was determined not only to augment his subsidy but also to eliminate an irritation that had been annoying him for months: the French government's encouragement of alternate food shipments into enemy-held territory from Switzerland. To a French colleague he asserted that this action had "jeopardized" the "whole position" of the commission. How could he maintain before the Germans that only his organization could handle the revictualling if the French turned around and set up other channels of distribution? It was not "fair to us," he exclaimed, "to ask us to continue in this work without our being considered the absolute pivot on which the whole ravitaillement hangs. . . ." Hoover professed "no desire for a monopoly," at least in the acquisition of outside food for shipment. But "unless we can control these streams, it seems absolutely hopeless to expect us to protect the people from the military authorities." He thereupon threatened to withdraw from northern France unless the French government agreed to open no channel of food into the region without the CRB's prior approval.[203]

On August 24 Hoover left London for a series of conferences in Paris with Allied officials. Here he learned that the French government had just given 30,000,000 francs to an independent committee to purchase foodstuffs in Holland. If the CRB fell short of supplies, the French foreign minister said, he proposed that this committee be allowed to operate in northern France under Dutch auspices. Hoover immediately protested. These Dutch and Swiss schemes, he argued, "completely undermined" the CRB's ability to protect the people and augured "an era of intrigue and rivalry" in which he and his associates would not join. If the French wanted some other nationality to assume the relief burden in their lost territory, he would be "only too delighted" to step aside. But whoever took charge, he contended, must have "a complete monopoly in order to deal competently with the German authorities." Lord Eustace Percy, who was present, backed him up.[204]

For two more days Hoover discussed, argued, and lobbied with Allied leaders, explaining his need for an increased subsidy for northern France (from 20,000,000 francs to 35,000,000 francs per month). He insisted that the CRB alone must negotiate with the Germans and must control the transport of all commodities gathered in the world outside. Furthermore, no foreign agent of these committees should be allowed to enter northern France. (Such a development could play into the hands of the Germans.) On August 28 the French government agreed in entirety to his requests. Once again threats and persistence had paid off; his subsidy—and his monopoly—were secure.[205]

And so, as the leaves began to turn across Western Europe, the commander-in-chief of the CRB "army" could look back on a summer of accomplishment. In both Belgium and northern France the structure of relief was in place for another twelve months. Agreements in principle, of course, were one thing; implementation of them quite another. As it turned out, the wheat and potato harvest of 1916 in northern France fell far below estimates; for this reason, among others, the Germans refused to deliver anything like the rations they had promised.[206] Still, the French people were grateful for what they did receive and for the organization that had made it possible. "What would have become of us without the American Commission?" one of their leaders asked in November.[207] What indeed?

8

Opportunities Denied

I

Hoover did not do much looking back, however, as 1916 wore on. There wasn't time. Even as he struggled to cope with feeding 9,000,000 Belgians and Frenchmen, requests for his humanitarian services arose in other, more distant theaters of the Great War.

It was on his trip to Germany in February 1915 that he first became significantly involved with the ordeal of another war-ravaged region. While in Berlin he conferred with the Rockefeller Foundation's War Relief Commission, which had just returned from German-occupied Poland on the eastern front. With the precedent of Belgium before it, the commission was discussing a Polish relief plan with the German authorities. Hoover himself was in Berlin to demand (among other things) improved treatment for his personnel inside Belgium. Discerning a chance to form a united front, he quickly proposed that the CRB and the Rockefeller representatives announce jointly that the Rockefeller Foundation would refuse to enter Poland unless the Germans granted "uniformly liberal treatment" to relief workers in Belgium and Poland *both*. As always, Hoover was looking for every instrument that could advance his objectives. Instead, to his annoyance, the foundation's representatives pursued an independent course, culminating in the creation of the International Commission for Relief in Poland in the spring.[1]

The Rockefeller group soon paid a price for its aloofness. By late May the infant commission had been unable to purchase food for its work in a single

European country.[2] In desperation a Rockefeller Foundation representative asked Hoover to pressure the British to let the CRB sell some of *its* supplies to the Rockefeller group for export to Poland. The agent also asked the CRB to "guarantee" the Rockefeller undertaking before the Allied governments.

Hoover was thoroughly angry. He would *not* "guarantee" the Rockefeller Foundation, he replied, nor would he "move one inch to be of further service to the German people" until his troubles with the Germans in Belgium were resolved. The CRB would not "for one minute" consider shipping food to Poland unless the German government itself made the request. And if it did so, the commission would act only if the Germans pledged not to requisition native foodstuffs inside *Belgium*. As for the Rockefeller Foundation, Hoover declared tartly that its request to him "amounted to a confession of failure" and came "rather late in the day." If the CRB was now to "relieve the Foundation of the extremely difficult position that they had got themselves into through wholly incompetent handling of their problem, and failure to take action that was effective, we should require a pretty distinct understanding" about "our future relations."[3]

It is unlikely that the foundation's emissary appreciated the CRB chairman's tongue-lashing. So far as is known, the Rockefeller mission to Poland had no further contacts with Hoover's organization. Instead, the German government announced in May that it had enough food supplies to sustain the population of occupied Poland until the next harvest. In other words, there was no need for outside intervention. With that news, the Rockefeller effort to revictual Poland collapsed.[4]

During the summer and fall of 1915, however, conditions on the eastern front unexpectedly deteriorated. As the German army smashed across Poland (capturing Warsaw on August 1), the retreating Russians adopted a "scorched earth" policy. Four thousand villages were burned. Two million Poles lost their homes. The harvest of 1915 was devastated.[5]

By late October the consequences of the calamity became apparent. At this point the German General Staff and the principal charity organization in Warsaw sent out an appeal—not to the Rockefeller Foundation but to the man who was already becoming the international symbol of humanitarianism on a scale undreamed of in human history: the forty-one-year-old Herbert Hoover. Send someone to visit the war-scarred area, they asked. Send someone to determine whether the Commission for Relief in Belgium might intervene.[6] Hoover authorized Vernon Kellogg to investigate.[7]

In mid-November Kellogg returned to Brussels with a somber message. Food supplies in German-occupied Poland, he reported, were scarce and becoming scarcer. In some areas people were living in hovels and subsisting on potatoes alone. Of 7,500,000 affected people, the great bulk were at least partly dependent on charity (or about to be). In the industrial cities hundreds of thousands of factory workers were idle. Faced with such an emergency, the resources of private charity were nearing exhaustion. The Poles, said

Kellogg, asked only for the kind of assistance that the CRB was already rendering in Belgium and northern France.[8]

In a separate document the archbishop of Warsaw and other distinguished Poles petitioned the commission to extend its operations to their beleaguered land.[9] For his part, Hoover, on a trip to Brussels in early December, discussed the question informally with an officer on the German General Staff. Hoover knew that before the Allies could ever approve such a scheme he would need various guarantees from the Germans. The staff officer assured him that Germany would cooperate fully and (among other things) reserve all foodstuffs in Poland to the native population.[10]

Even so, the task, as Hoover told his colleagues, was "surrounded by a thousand difficulties." To meet the Poles' necessities he would require at least $5,000,000 per month—far more than charity alone could provide. He would need to set up "economic cycles" of exchange and payment, to obtain shipping from America to Stockholm and then across the Baltic Sea to Danzig, and to obtain Allied creation of another gap in their blockade. And of course he would need to wrest promises from reluctant belligerents.[11] "I am trying to do something for Poland," he told a friend in mid-December,

> but I have learned a thing or two about the relief business, and I am not going to attack this thing until or unless we can get the various belligerent Governments to agree on a few fundamentals which have given us such unceasing trouble in Belgium, because we did not have the foresight to perceive what would be the outcome of this war a year in advance.[12]

Privately Hoover confessed to feeling "profound depression" about the Polish relief proposal. The chance of winning assent for it seemed "very remote." But of one thing he was certain by mid-December: that if this project "is to be done, it can only be done by" his commission. It was therefore, he said, the "duty" of himself and his associates to try.[13] On December 22, 1915, in a letter to Foreign Secretary Grey, he formally offered the CRB's services for the revictualing of Poland.[14]

Hoover's letter could hardly have been submitted at a less opportune moment. Weeks, in fact, were to pass before he received a reply. These were the weeks of the CRB's most dangerous shipping shortage to date, of British demands for an end to German food seizures in Belgium, of rising Admiralty antipathy to Hoover and his work, and of growing popular clamor in Britain for a tighter—not looser—blockade. With the demise of his Belgian operation a distinct possibility, Hoover considered the prospects for Poland to be virtually nil.[15]

Still, one must try—and hope. According to a London mining journal in early January, Hoover himself was contemplating a trip to Poland.[16] (A month earlier, when he was in Brussels, Lou Henry Hoover told a friend that her husband might soon be going on an extended tour of Poland and other countries.)[17] But if the CRB chairman had such intentions, the abscess in his ear put an end to them. Instead, in mid-January, he sent one of his lieutenants along with a Rockefeller Foundation representative on a new journey to Poland.[18] The two came back with a bleak confirmation of Kellogg's findings.[19]

Meanwhile, down in the Balkans, where the Great War had started more than a year before, still another tragedy was unfolding. In the autumn of 1915 the nation of Serbia was overrun by the armies of Germany, Austria-Hungary, and Bulgaria. Hundreds of thousands of civilians fled the onslaught; perhaps one out of every two perished.[20] By December Hoover, in London, was receiving entreaties from the Serbian minister, the German General Staff, and the American Relief Clearing House in Paris to investigate conditions in this newest zone of tribulation.[21]

The CRB chairman, however, was not convinced that haste was necessary.[22] The real problem, he told one correspondent, was the Serbian refugees (who were already receiving assistance from the British), not the civilian population now living behind enemy lines.[23] This population, he said, was overwhelmingly rural, and he was quite "satisfied that no European peasant who has possession of his harvest fails to provide himself with a complete year's food-supply, and, in times of invasion, that he does not fail to hide it most efficiently."[24] While he conceded that the plight of Serbia would eventually become perilous, he was convinced from experience that "the first appearance of a situation of this kind is worse than the reality" and that as order was reestablished "invisible supplies" would "come to the surface," just as they had in northern France in the winter of 1914–15.[25]

Moreover, Hoover was not about to be stampeded without first securing the governmental guarantees and subsidies that were indispensable to success. It was "infinitely better," he told one relief official, that the civilian population "should suffer for a little while in order that the situation may be sufficiently black to induce governments to take such measures. It is hopeless to feed populations in this number by charity as all the charity available to Servia would not feed the population for three weeks." All in all, he asserted, it was the "wildest folly to jump into a situation of this kind half-cocked and without proper international understandings."[26]

Both Hoover and the British Foreign Office continued to suspect that Serbia's actual need was limited and that the country could in fact be made self-supporting.[27] Nevertheless, in a meeting with the Serbian minister to Great Britain on December 26, he did agree to dispatch a CRB investigator to the scene.[28] Until a report was forthcoming, he declared early in the new year, it was "absolutely useless" to proceed.[29]

In the meantime the question of creating a nongovernmental relief mechanism for Serbia began to surface. Taking up the issue with H. O. Beatty of the American Relief Clearing House, Hoover made it clear that if a neutral relief agency were to be formed, he or his agents should administer it. It is "no use having the usual charity cranks with such organisation," he declared. Instead, we must have "commonsense, solid, business people, used to dealing with large affairs. . . ." He promptly recommended J. F. Lucey, his former relief director in Rotterdam, for the position.[30] (Lucey in fact had just volunteered for it privately, and Hoover had privately agreed.)[31]

Hoover thereupon offered the American Relief Clearing House's director a seat on the board of such a CRB-dominated organization. Hoover conceded that an entirely independent agency could be created. But this, he continued, would have "great disadvantages" since such a body would lack the prestige of his already-functioning commission. Besides, Belgium was "the only school from which we could draw men of proper experience" for work in Serbia. In short, if a relief mission to the Balkans were to be organized, Hoover intended that the CRB should control it.[32]

This now-familiar insistence on monopoly was not aimed exclusively at Beatty, who in fact replied that there was "no organisation so capable as your own for this work" and that Hoover should be left "free and untrammeled to carry it out" as he pleased.[33] The CRB's chairman also meant to exclude the Swiss, who were providing support for a private Serbian relief effort based in Geneva.[34] On January 24 he told Beatty that if the two of them should launch a committee to aid the Serbs, the Allied governments would be pleased if it had no "Swiss association." They wanted it (he said) to be "cleanly American." No doubt thinking of his troubles with the intriguing Marquis de Villalobar, Hoover remarked that the "inclusion of other neutrals" in his Belgian work had caused "embarrassments" which need not be transferred to a new front.[35]

Even as the CRB's chief executive endeavored to lay the groundwork for a relief enterprise in Serbia that would be "purely American"[36] and immune from Old World intrigues, his entire initiative was bogging down. In Berlin during late January, his representatives were unable to obtain passes for an inspection tour of the afflicted region. While the Germans privately intimated that conditions inside Serbia were grave, it seemed that they had ceded control of the area to their Austro-Hungarian and Bulgarian allies, who showed no signs of desiring Hoover's help.[37] Nor, apparently, did the British or the French.

During the next several weeks the Swiss committee in Geneva succeeded in shipping a trainload of food supplies into Serbia, where it was distributed without obstruction—evidence enough, the committee's president asserted, that the Austrians would cooperate.[38] For Hoover, experienced in the methods of the occupying power in Belgium, such a one-time success proved nothing and was in any case beside the point, since private charity could not possibly fulfill the need. The imperative was to establish a foundation for systematic assistance.[39]

Then, in mid-April, the exiled premier of Serbia personally asked Hoover in London what he would do. The CRB chairman replied firmly that he would do nothing unless the Allies or the Foreign Office requested his aid in writing, unless the Allies disclosed how much they would subsidize the project, and unless they explained what guarantees they would demand of the enemy. Only then, said the American engineer, would he go to the Austro-Hungarians and the Bulgarians. That can be arranged easily, said the Serbian official; he would act immediately upon it. Ten more days elapsed; the premier was not heard from. Instead, to Hoover's disgust, the Serbian leader contacted the Rockefeller Foundation and asked *it* to organize the relief of Serbia. "Frankly," confessed Hoover to a friend on April 26, "I am sick of this business and intend to sit entirely quiet on the above outlined position."[40]

As all this was occurring, the issue of Poland was also meandering through the diplomatic obstacle course. On February 5, 1916, after more than six weeks of silence, Sir Edward Grey finally replied to Hoover's letter. Noting that the Germans and Austrians were systematically confiscating and even exporting native Polish foodstuffs for their own use, the foreign secretary rejected Hoover's proposal—so long as these practices continued. But if, he said, the Germans and Austrians stopped their food seizures and made certain other concessions, a Hoover-led relief program for Poland might be possible.[41]

Hoover was somewhat encouraged by Grey's response—at least, he said, "the door is not completely shut"[42]—and at once sought the necessary guarantees from Berlin.[43] The CRB chairman believed that "the more humane section of the English Government" really wished to assist Poland and that a generous "counter offer" now from the Germans would put the Germans "right in public opinion" and lead to a breakthrough.[44] As usual, he was attempting to play one side off against the other.

A few days later the German government in Warsaw duly promised that if the CRB undertook to assist Poland, the native Polish food supply would not be exported. Instead, all except "surplus" potatoes would be reserved exclusively for the native population—and the German "constabulary."[45] It remained to be seen whether this would be enough to mollify the British.

To expedite the negotiations and gain British acceptance, Hoover and Frederic Walcott of the Rockefeller Foundation now prepared a limited Polish relief proposal that placed much of the burden on the Germans. Under its terms the CRB would import 40,000 tons of certain foods per month for approximately 4,000,000 Poles living in various cities. (This, Hoover believed, was the sector most in need.) In return, the German government would furnish these cities certain other foods and, in addition, would revictual the remainder of the occupied population (11,000,000 people). Moreover, the Germans would facilitate the financing and supply all the shipping. The undertaking would cease on October 1 with the arrival of a new and presumably sufficient harvest.[46]

On February 21 Ambassador Page submitted the Hoover–Walcott memorandum to the Foreign Office.[47] Walcott, who had recently returned from the continent, reported that the Germans would accept these terms.[48] If the British did also, he and Hoover planned to travel to Poland immediately.[49] Hoover himself was far from sanguine. "I always approach this practically hopeless subject," he told a friend, "with feelings of depression."[50]

Still, as long as there was "an atom of hope," as he put it, Hoover vowed to fight on.[51] And fighting, for him, was no defensive matter. In late February he launched a characteristic lobbying assault on the British. He conferred with influential persons inside and outside government—"fully fifty" different individuals by February 24.[52] He asked Walcott to write a series of articles on Poland for *The Times*.[53] He asked the State Department to put pressure on the British ambassador to the United States; the department obliged.[54]

Most ambitiously of all, he asked Colonel Edward House (who was visiting London at the time) to persuade President Wilson to intercede with the Allies. It was the Allied naval blockade, said Hoover, that was threatening "to cause the death of millions of absolutely innocent people." Wilson's personal intervention, he said, was the "only hope" he could see "by which the lives of 3 to 5,000,000 people can be preserved." Never bashful in such matters, Hoover instructed House on just how to tackle the British:

> I have the feeling that if President Wilson would make it clear to the Allied Governments that the American Government was greatly concerned that by the application of their implement of blockade they were producing human disaster beyond all comparison, that unless they provide exceptions to this blockade in favour of these populations that the attitude of the American Government toward the Allied Governments would materially change: I have the feeling that we will win the point we need. . . .[55]

All in all, it was a classic Hoover campaign: endless "jawboning," behind-the-scenes stimulation of public opinion, and the manufacture of pressure from all directions. How often in the past he had used similar tactics to engineer mining stock flotations! Now he was attempting to "float" an enterprise to rescue several million lives.

Hoover's "public opinion" strategy, however, could only succeed if its target *cared* about public opinion—and, in particular, the opinion of America. During the late winter of 1916 it became apparent that *British* public opinion had other preoccupations. In both the British populace and Cabinet, demands were growing for imposition of a total blockade, without exceptions, even for the civil populations of conquered allies.[56] From the standpoint of the British navy, one breach in its embargo was bad enough, without creating one or two more. Indeed, on a trip to Paris Emile Francqui discovered evidence that Hoover's Poland-Serbia initiative had provoked the backlash.[57]

According to Hoover, the Foreign Office, although privately sympathetic to his plan, was "absolutely timorous" about bucking the popular tide.[58] The

British government was also incensed by the ongoing German requisitions in Belgium—hardly the best endorsement of German *bona fides* in Poland.[59] And the CRB itself was under relentless assault by the Admiralty.

Still, Hoover was undeterred. On February 22 he asked Lord Northcliffe for support of his Polish undertaking. The powerful press baron refused and declared that he would oppose the plan in his newspapers. But Hoover, a friend reported, was just as "pugnatious" as Northcliffe and "brought him around to a somewhat more moderate view."[60]

All this "agitation" (to use Hoover's word) cost him the further enmity of the "blockade wing" of the British government.[61] But it may have had one useful consequence. Both he and Walcott suspected that their campaign for Poland may have saved the *Belgian* relief from destruction by its British enemies.[62] Hoover might not be allowed to expand his operations, but at least he could keep what he had.

Despite his persistent and zealous efforts, the Polish relief controversy dragged on into March, then April, then May. It was not until May 10 that the Foreign Office, after consulting with its Russian ally, replied to the Hoover–Walcott memorandum of February 21. The British announced their acceptance of the proposal but attached some tough new conditions. The relief project and its constraints, they now said, must encompass *all* of Poland, including the sector occupied by German's Austrian ally. The German "constabulary" must not receive any native foodstuffs. And from now on Germany and Austria-Hungary must themselves adequately supply and feed Serbia, Albania, and Montenegro under neutral supervision.[63] The diplomatic duel was escalating.

By now five wearisome months had elapsed since Hoover's first approach to the British government. Five months, and still no compromise in sight. On all sides it seemed agreed that Hoover should take charge of the Polish aid mission if it were organized.[64] But could it even *be* organized before it was due to expire (October 1)? By May 27 Hoover was again depressed, convinced that the case was "hopeless."[65]

Three days later Ambassador Gerard relayed Germany's response to the British. The Germans were willing to purchase and ship the proposed imports from overseas into Poland, and even to contribute some of their own food supply to the Polish cities. But they were *not* willing to extend the enterprise to Austrian Poland or to take responsibility for Serbia, Albania, and Montenegro. They did not control those countries, they claimed, and could not force Austria-Hungary to comply. And as for the German "constabulary" (150,000 strong) inside Poland, the Germans insisted that it must be fed on local food.[66]

The British government was unmoved. Germany certainly could control the Austrians if she wanted to, the Foreign Office retorted. Poland, it insisted, must be considered a single unit as a matter of principle; His Majesty's Government would not countenance enemy schemes to divide Poland politically for postwar purposes.[67]

The result was deadlock and defeat.[68] Not even the belated intervention of the U.S. government could change the outcome. On July 8 the State Department asked the European belligerents "in the name and interests of humanity" to permit the relief of Poland.[69] Two weeks later President Woodrow Wilson personally appealed at last to the heads of state of the five principal warring powers to cooperate in alleviating Poland's plight.[70] His letter achieved no success; the differences among the belligerents proved unbridgeable.[71]

By mid-summer Hoover's original proposal was obsolete. Not only was a new harvest coming on; the Germans proceeded to announce that no relief would even be necessary in Poland after October 1. Any suffering in the meantime, they asserted, would be Britain's fault.[72] Apparently the Germans planned to help themselves to the ripening Polish harvest. Hoover thought so.[73] So, it appears, did the British.

Perhaps to forestall this very thing, on July 26 the British issued a "final proposal": they would cooperate in an expanded American-sponsored relief undertaking only if the Germans and Austrians refrained from taking any native crops or foodstuffs in Belgium, France, Poland, Serbia, Albania, and Montenegro.[74] This was the ultimatum that so infuriated the German army leaders and very nearly provoked them to extinguish the CRB altogether. Had it not been for Hoover's tea-and-whiskey party with General von Sauberzweig, the worst result of all might have happened.[75]

And so the long campaign to enlarge the CRB's mission of mercy collapsed. Perhaps at this stage of the Great War no other outcome was even possible. By publicizing their ultimatum, in fact, the British may have been counting on the Germans to reject it. But aside from saving the commission from its Allied critics in early 1916, Hoover's agitation for Polish relief had one enduring effect: by publicizing the wartime ordeal of the Polish people to the citizens of America and the Allies, he helped to hasten the day when Polish aspirations for independence would find fulfillment.[76]

As for Serbia, its only recourse was the neutral neighboring country of Romania. But in mid-1916 Romania declared war on the Central Powers, thereby eliminating itself as a source of supplies for enemy-held territory. Nor by this time did the need seem so compelling. Early in the summer the Austro-Hungarian government asserted that it had enough food to feed occupied Serbia unaided—an announcement that, however accurate or inaccurate, effectively destroyed the rationale for outside intervention.[77] Fortunately for the Serbs, their native-grown harvest of 1916 was excellent.[78]

I I

B Y the autumn of 1916 the Commission for Relief in Belgium had been in existence for nearly two years. On the luncheon room wall in its London office someone placed a placard: "This cannot go on forever."[79] Yet some-how, despite the opposition of powerful Allied and German leaders, the flow of food continued, and hungry people were fed.

Why did the belligerents tolerate this unprecedented and at times irksome intrusion into the theater of war? Why did they put up with the endless importunings of this abrasive foreigner named Hoover? For the Germans the answer is obvious: when all was said and done, Hoover's organization relieved them of the burden of caring for more than 9,000,000 people. Without the CRB, the German army would either have had to import scarce food from other sources, divert troops to suppress food riots, or let millions suffer and perhaps starve. None of these alternatives was a palatable one.

For the British the answer is more complex. If Hoover's work indirectly benefited the German army (by making its burden of occupation easier), it also conferred certain advantages on the Allies. The importation of food and the distribution of it under neutral supervision made it possible for hundreds of thousands of unemployed Belgians to engage in passive resistance. With-out the sustenance provided by Hoover and the Comité National, many Bel-gians would have had to collaborate with the Germans on military tasks (such as road construction) in return for a daily ration. The British Foreign Office was acutely aware of this possibility.[80] It was also, in mid-1916, under con-siderable pressure from the French government to let the relief of northern France continue, lest the morale of the French army suffer. Even if the Brit-ish had wanted to terminate the relief, they would have found it difficult indeed to resist the pleadings of their French and Belgian allies.[81]

By 1916, in fact, the British were face to face with a dilemma. Repeatedly they had threatened to terminate the relief in order to force the recalcitrant Germans into line. Yet His Majesty's Government now realized that if it actually did so, it could drive the exiled Belgian government into making a separate peace—a goal that the Germans were energetically pursuing. In a memorandum to the British Cabinet, Lord Cecil confessed that for this rea-son the British threat to cut off food shipments to Belgium was "a weapon too dangerous for us to use."[82]

There was still another reason for the survival of Hoover's commission. Particularly during the early months of the war, the Allied governments (and to some extent the Germans as well) were anxious to court the United States and benefit from American neutrality. And from the outset—as they well knew—American public opinion identified with the plight of the Belgians. If the CRB's work was of some military advantage to the Germans, it was of immense *political* advantage to the Allies. The very existence of the CRB was a standing rebuke to the Germans in American eyes, a constant reminder of the unprovoked invasion of August 1914.

It was this factor above all which testified to the wisdom of Hoover's strat-egy for dealing with the warring powers. From the outset he perceived that his success depended on mobilizing American public opinion to a point where neither the Allies nor the Germans would dare to offend it. By the time British popular sentiment began to turn against the relief—by the time, that is, that the demands for total war began to overpower the appeal of liberal humanitarianism—by then the CRB was well entrenched, Hoover an American hero, and the political cost to the Allies of stopping the relief too great. Brand Whitlock put it succinctly. "It pays to advertise!" he said.[83]

But even "advertising" was not all-powerful as the war continued. Advertising, after all, did not bring about the revictualing of Poland and Serbia, whose sufferings were much worse than those of Belgium. Indeed, it is unlikely that the CRB itself could have been established in the year 1916. Only in the autumn of 1914—when the war still seemed likely to be short and when nineteenth-century humanitarian sentiments still moved the British government—only then could Hoover's great undertaking have been launched. Once it was formed, his administrative acumen and skill at public relations helped to forge an institution too respected, and too American in character, to be abolished by governments dependent on America for money, arms, and food.

So despite all its trials, the Commission for Relief in Belgium went on. During its second year of operation it delivered more than 1,300,000 tons of supplies at Rotterdam for shipment into its sphere of operations.[84] A fleet of more than fifty vessels made 725 voyages to bring this cargo to its destination.[85] Allied subsidies for the twelve months exceeded $100,000,000.[86]

And always, at the heart of this enterprise, was one commanding figure. "Mr. Hoover is a perfect wonder," declared Frederic C. Walcott, "one of the most remarkable men I have ever met. . . ."[87] He is "a perfect genius for organization."[88] Dean David Barrows of the University of California, another CRB associate, agreed. Speaking to an audience of Stanford students in September 1916, he said: "The situation in Belgium to-day is so extraordinary that if Hoover lost heart or died, in a few days the Belgians who are dependent on him would feel the pinch."[89] This was perhaps an exaggeration. But few who knew Herbert Hoover would have thought it far from the mark.

9

The Suffering
Servant

I

On the morning of September 23, 1916 Herbert Hoover sailed from Holland on a neutral Dutch steamer bound for the British coast. He was on his way back from Belgium to London—a journey he had made at least a dozen times since the war began. Each time he had risked without incident the submarine-infested waters of the English Channel and the North Sea. This occasion, however, was nearly to be his last.

Shortly after his vessel, the *Prins Hendrik*, left port, six dark objects appeared on the high seas. They were torpedo boats, and they were German. Forcing the Dutch ship to land on the Belgian coast, the Germans proceeded to seize sixty-seven passengers, including several Allied mail carriers and escaped prisoners of war.

The *Prins Hendrik*'s ordeal was not yet over. Scarcely had it been permitted to resume its voyage when the Germans stopped it again for a further search. Hoover, curious, watched the drama from the deck. It was now broad daylight over the Channel.

Suddenly a French airplane buzzed overhead. Spotting the enemy's torpedo boats, the pilot unleashed a heavy bomb; it exploded only twenty yards from the *Prins Hendrik*. At once shrapnel sprayed across the deck, wounding the passenger standing next to Hoover and puncturing the ship's hull in twenty-three places. Somehow Hoover himself escaped injury—except, he noted wryly, for a crick in his neck caused by watching the French pilot take aim.[1]

The *Prins Hendrik* made its way to England without further trouble. But Hoover's brush with death became the subject of newspaper headlines on two continents.[2] What would have become of the relief commission if the French bomb had landed closer still? Many must have shuddered and wondered.

The CRB chairman himself had little time for such speculation. Autumn 1916 was upon him: a season of deepening gloom. Inside Belgium 6,000,000 people—nearly double the number of a year before—were now dependent on ration cards for food beyond their daily allotment of bread. Native food sources, particularly potatoes, were becoming scarcer; tuberculosis and other signs of diminished vitality were spreading.[3] According to one estimate, 1,500,000 school-age children were beginning to show the effects of malnutrition.[4]

On a trip to Brussels in September Hoover personally witnessed the growing misery. One day he visited a relief station where more than a thousand children were standing in line for a meal. Suddenly a Belgian relief worker dragged a child out of the queue. The little one screamed and resisted, to no avail. Why are you doing this? Hoover asked. Because, the worker replied, that child is of normal weight. Only underweight children showing signs of starvation may be fed today. There is not enough food to go around.[5]

As conditions inside Belgium deteriorated, so, too, did the CRB's finances. Despite the fact that the price of bread was cheaper in Brussels than in London, despite the fact that Hoover and his principal colleagues were working for nothing, despite all the savings that Yankee efficiency and humanitarian sentiment could achieve, by mid-1916 the commission's expenditures inside Belgium were exceeding its income by more than $2,000,000 per month.[6] Hoover might cut costs in his own organization, but he could not control world food prices, and outside Belgium the cost of food was rising. Inside Belgium, meanwhile, as the effects of economic paralysis spread, fewer and fewer could afford to pay for what they received. By October the Anglo-French subsidy to the CRB of £1,000,000 per month, initiated in early 1915, was plainly and painfully inadequate.[7]

Hoover refused to be deterred by these financial impediments. To meet the worsening threat of malnutrition, he and his associates launched a program of supplementary rations for Belgian children in the form of special meals served daily in the schools.[8] This alone would cost an additional million dollars a month. To secure this sum he turned to familiar territory and tactics. Unleashing a volley of publicity, he appealed to the American people for assistance.[9] According to one of his lieutenants, more than 1,250,000 Belgian children were "slowly starving to death."[10]

As usual, Hoover's methods were resourceful. During October he dispatched an associate to Rome to obtain the blessing of the Pope. At first success was doubtful; many Irish-American clergy considered the CRB to be pro-British and opposed any intervention by the Holy See. But on October

28 Pope Benedict XV emphatically endorsed Hoover's work and asked the Catholic children of America to aid their brothers and sisters inside Belgium. The papal message was released in the United States in early December, just in time for Christmas fund raising. It was one of Hoover's greatest public relations coups.[11]

The American public proved receptive to his campaign. Especially gratifying was the response of his fellow mining engineers, who organized a "syndicate" to sell "shares" in a "corporation" called "Belgian Kiddies, Ltd." By this device, duly advertised in the mining press, the engineers quickly raised $120,000.[12]

Hoover heaped thanks on his fellow professionals. The work of the CRB, he said, was "to the largest degree due to American engineers," who had combined a "unique capacity for pioneer organisation," "commercial adaptability," and physical stamina with a measure of "courage, devotion, and idealism . . . to be found in such a degree in no other profession."[13] But, as always, he knew that private fund raising was not enough.[14] Public appeals could arouse sympathy and thus exert pressure on the belligerent powers, but the vast bulk of the commission's income was derived from the Allied governments. It was this source that would have to bail him out now.

On October 7, 1916 Hoover beseeched the Allies to double their subsidy for the CRB's Belgian work.[15] Near the end of the month he achieved partial success: an increase of 50% from £1,000,000 to £1,500,000 per month.[16] It was enough to keep his head above water.

The commission's troubles, however, rarely came in orderly succession. For many months the German authorities had been seething with frustration at the spread of unemployment inside Belgium. While the German Fatherland was straining under ever more acute labor shortages, forcing women and even children into the fields, hundreds of thousands of *Belgian* workers were living in conspicuous idleness, sustained by the daily rations of the commission and the Comité National.[17]

Determined to exploit this supply of untapped labor, the Germans had tried repeatedly to gain control of the relief distribution apparatus, only to be thwarted by Hoover and his Belgian allies.[18] From time to time also, the Germans had attempted to bribe Belgian workers with offers of high wages, again without success. In April 1916 the occupying army had even deported more than 20,000 French civilians from the vicinity of Lille for forced labor in the countryside. The brutality of the operation had shocked the world, and the project had soon been abandoned, thanks largely to the intervention of the CRB.[19]

But as the war grew more desperate and the Allied blockade more constrictive, the anomaly of Belgian unemployment overwhelmed the inhibitions of the German military. In the fall of 1916 its patience ran out. Seizing tens of thousands of Belgian workmen, it shipped them to the Fatherland for compulsory labor. No German act since the summer of 1914 so aroused Belgian hatred and horror. In village after village terror reigned as men were taken from their families and loaded on railway cars. When Belgian burgomasters refused to hand over lists of the unemployed in their villages, German press-gangs seized employed and unemployed alike. In some instances deportees received only bread and water along the way; the CRB was forbidden to feed them full rations.[20]

The Germans rationalized their policy with humanitarian arguments. They pointed out that unemployment inside Belgium had reached 650,000—more than half the industrial workforce—with what they alleged were increasingly demoralizing results (such as drunkenness). The provision of paid work inside Germany, they claimed, would be beneficial to those who had lost their jobs because of the British blockade.[21] Few Belgians or outsiders were deceived by these protestations. As a beleaguered Germany mobilized its remaining manpower for the demands of total war, the imperial army command decreed that conquered peoples must do the same.[22] Military necessity, not solicitude for the idle, was its motive.

As the press-gangs accelerated their roundups, Hoover attempted to intercede. "I fear it is the beginning of the end," he wrote to Brand Whitlock on November 8. The CRB chairman urged his American colleague to make a thunderous protest at once. "It may result in nothing," he admitted, "but it will have put the American stamp on it in indelible terms, and if we do nothing else for Belgium we will go down in a blaze of indignation at this, its worst of any trials since the first agony."[23]

Despite his own anguish at the deportations, Whitlock was unwilling to "go out" (as he put it) in "a blaze of glory." Hoover, he recorded in his diary, was "wrought up to a great pitch of excitement" and wanted him to make a "ringing" protest. But this, said Whitlock, was no time for "hysterics."[24] It was not the first occasion that the two men, so different in temperament, disagreed on how to deal with the Germans.

Yet if Hoover was indignant, and eager for others to take a stand, he was careful not to jeopardize his own position. The CRB's first duty, he believed, was to the millions of Belgians left behind, not the thousands who were being deported. When, in October, he was asked to prepare a dossier for the State Department on the Germans' earlier outrages at Lille, he willingly complied but requested that his statement be kept confidential. If it ever leaked out, he warned, it "would mean our total obliteration from the North of France."[25] In late November he asked President Wilson to denounce the Germans' violation of what he called "the most elementary principles of human liberty." But he asked also that the commission's name not be mentioned.[26] As Hoover saw it, the only hope of reversing German actions lay in the "pressure [of] public opinion and protest by neutral governments."[27] Anxious to salvage the relief if he could, he avoided public comment on the deportations—except to deny that members of the CRB or Comité National were being seized.[28]

It was not in the commission's interest, he told colleagues, "to offer any opinions in our own name."[29]

On November 29 the United States government joined the international chorus of condemnation. If the massive deportations continued, it declared, they could be "fatal" to Hoover's work.[30] A few days later the Allied governments vehemently condemned the Germans' "slave raids" and warned that the entire relief operation was in danger of collapse.[31] Still the roundups continued, including, by mid-December, hundreds of Belgian employees of the relief.[32] All the assurances that only the unemployed were being taken, that only nonmilitary work was being performed, that no one was being mistreated—all these assertions, Hoover told the State Department, were "absolutely untrue."[33]

Nevertheless, by mid-December it was clear that the CRB, in Hoover's words, had "weathered" the deportation "storm."[34] However provocative the Germans' misdeeds, the Allies declined to wield their ultimate weapon.[35] Not even "the most antagonistic circles" in the British government, said Hoover, cared for "the prospect of starving a great mass of women and children" in reprisal.[36]

I I

F o r two years now Hoover had battled with German, British, French, and even American critics of his ongoing mission of mercy. In the autumn of 1916 all these vexations were overshadowed by disturbance from yet another source: the leadership of the Comité National.

Hoover's latest troubles with his Belgian counterparts had begun, in fact, several months before. Early in March Emile Francqui, Baron Lambert, and the Marquis de Villalobar had returned to Brussels from England—foiled in their plot to oust the CRB from its position of prominence inside Belgium. It soon became apparent that Francqui and certain of his colleagues had abandoned neither their attitude nor their objective. Repulsed in their frontal assault in London, they had quickly contrived other ways to cut Hoover and his organization down to size.

By early May, Hoover's chief deputy in Brussels, William B. Poland, detected rising hostility toward the CRB among various prominent Belgians—an attitude he attributed to Villalobar's "machinations," Francqui's desire to monopolize the credit for the relief, and Whitlock's "marked . . . lack of support" for the CRB.[37] One of the first manifestations of this antagonism occurred at the Comité National's general meeting on May 4. According to Poland, the air was filled with encomiums of the CN and Villalobar, while the achievements of Hoover, Brand Whitlock, and the CRB were scarcely mentioned.[38] That same day the Comité National's executive committee (headed by Francqui) boldly ordered the CRB's flag removed from all local relief warehouses. Henceforth, it decreed, only its own flag could be flown. Furthermore, no longer were these warehouses to be identified on signs as *magasins américains*; from now on they were to bear the name of the Comité National only. The CN claimed Brand Whitlock's approval for these decisions.[39]

Whitlock's behavior, in fact, had displeased Hoover and his associates for some months. While officially supportive of the relief and appreciative of Hoover's contribution, Whitlock was irked by what he considered the zealotry and tactlessness of the CRB "boys" (as he disdainfully referred to them in his diary).[40] Nor was he much impressed by Poland, whom he accused of "utter lack of diplomacy and savoir-faire."[41] It did not help matters that Whitlock was an ardent devotee of Woodrow Wilson, while most of the youthful CRB volunteers admired Wilson's archrival, Theodore Roosevelt.[42] But fundamentally the problem was one of temperament. A conciliator by nature and a diplomat by appointment, Whitlock had little stomach for the often aggressive tactics of Hoover and his friends. To Hoover, on the other hand, Whitlock was a weak and "sensitive dreamer" who "recoiled from every emergency" and preferred writing his diaries and novels to fighting for the rights of the CRB.[43]

There was, indeed, considerable validity to Hoover's perception. "How I would like to shirk the whole business!" Whitlock confessed at one point in his diary.[44] While the American diplomat (like Hoover) loathed the Germans, his pacific disposition irritated his more assertive compatriot. Whitlock the artist, the diplomat, hated confrontations and "scenes." Hoover, the man in a hurry, did not care whose toes he stepped on.

Hoover's estimate of Whitlock derived in part from Hugh Gibson, who had served as first secretary of the American legation in Brussels since 1914. From the outset of the relief effort Hoover and his fellow Californian had collaborated closely. By 1916 they were intimate friends. Like Hoover, Gibson was energetic, resourceful, efficient, and quick to flare up at any slights to his dignity. Like Hoover, too, he despised the Germans—and they knew it. Thirty-two years old in 1915, Gibson was an example of the younger men-on-the-make with whom Hoover had associated himself in his mining days and with whom he was surrounding himself now. Gibson unabashedly looked up to Hoover—and was probably shrewd enough to realize that he would go farther if he did. By the end of 1915, perhaps as yet unconsciously, he had hitched his diplomatic wagon to Hoover's rising star.

During 1915, meanwhile, Gibson's relations with Whitlock and the Germans deteriorated. To Whitlock it seemed that Gibson was "truculent and impetuous," "touchy on all points of honor," inclined toward Rooseveltian "swashbuckling," and ever eager to "rattle the sabre in the scabbard."[45] To Gibson, Whitlock seemed indolent, more interested in golf and country rides than in his official duties, and all too willing to foist the hard work onto his assistant.[46] By 1916, after a series of clashes and controversies, German patience with Gibson was exhausted. In early February they declared him *persona non grata*. Whitlock, who considered him "not wholly blameless," acquiesced in his expulsion without protest.[47]

Gibson was bitter, convinced that a jealous Whitlock had schemed to get rid of him.[48] Hoover quickly sided with his friend and took the same view of Whitlock's motivation.[49] But the CRB chairman did more. In collaboration with Ambassador Page, he quickly obtained an appointment for Gibson at the American embassy in London.[50] There the displaced young diplomat assisted the CRB in the months ahead—even ghostwriting drafts of some of Hoover's "blasts" at his enemies.[51]

But Gibson's departure from Brussels continued to rankle. As soon as he arrived in London he and Hoover teamed up on a scheme of their own: eviction of Whitlock from *his* post inside Belgium. On February 20 the two men called upon President Wilson's confidant, Colonel House, who was visiting London on a peace mission. Gibson told House that Whitlock had "outlived his usefulness" in Belgium because of ill health and conditions he could not control and should instead be appointed ambassador to Russia. Hoover, too, asserted that Whitlock lacked the "physical condition" to stand up to the "machinations" of Villalobar and the Germans.[52]

Hoover and Gibson may well have believed that Whitlock's health was impairing his effectiveness. Certainly Whitlock's diaries were replete with references to his illnesses, frayed nerves, and general weariness. During the Edith Cavell episode in October 1915, for instance, he had actually been bedridden, obliging Gibson to carry the burden for the American legation. But it is doubtful that simple concern about Whitlock's health was motivating Hoover and Gibson now, as House himself suspected. "I have a feeling," he recorded in his diary, "that Hoover thinks Whitlock has received more credit than he deserves. . . . I think [Hoover] is exceedingly jealous of the work he has done for Belgium, and whether he has done it all and Whitlock nothing, as he and Page suggest, is something I cannot tell."[53] It appeared to House that an effort was underway to oust Whitlock from Belgium and "put Hoover and his men in full control there."[54]

Nevertheless, the colonel disclosed to Hoover that he had already urged the State Department to appoint Gibson minister to Brussels if (as seemed likely) Whitlock accepted another diplomatic assignment. Hoover was delighted.[55] Seizing his opportunity, he speedily wrote House a letter enthusiastically recommending Gibson as Whitlock's successor. But if, Hoover added, the Germans should object (as he knew they might), he suggested as a second choice that David Barrows, dean of the University of California, be appointed first secretary of the legation and then chargé d'affaires upon Whitlock's departure. Barrows had just begun to work in Belgium for the CRB and was, according to Hoover, a man of "ambassadorial timbre."[56] He was also a friend who had publicly acclaimed Hoover as the indispensable linchpin of the relief.[57] Thus if House and the State Department listened to

Hoover's advice, either Gibson or Barrows—both Hoover loyalists—would replace Whitlock, and Hoover would have in Brussels a man like Ambassador Page in London: a man he could rely upon and dominate.

Meanwhile, after talking with Hoover (but before receiving his letter), House again asked the State Department to send Gibson back to Brussels if Whitlock left. The colonel reported that according to Hoover the relief work would be "seriously injured" unless Gibson returned to Belgium, first as chargé d'affaires and later as minister. Whatever House's suspicions of Hoover's motives, he was willingly cooperating in the Hooverian plan.[58]

The Hoover–Gibson coup attempt soon foundered. Whitlock, it turned out, had already declined to take the diplomatic post (Russia) that the State Department had offered him, partly because he did not care to have Gibson succeed him. If Gibson had been put in charge in Brussels, said Whitlock privately, "he would have lasted . . . no more than two weeks."[59] A month later, in response to an inquiry from Washington, Whitlock warned that Gibson's return would "create embarrassments."[60] And so Gibson stayed in London.

At this point Whitlock knew nothing about the maneuvers that had gone on behind his back. But before long Emile Francqui, among others, tipped him off, to Hoover's manifest alarm.[61] On March 31, 1916, on a trip to Brussels, an agitated Hoover denied to Whitlock that he and Gibson had plotted to dislodge him and install Gibson in his place. Instead, Hoover attributed the rumor to the malevolent Villalobar and Lambert. Gullible as usual, Whitlock dismissed the story as a "silly tale."[62] It was only a year and a half later, from Colonel House and a prominent Belgian, that he finally learned the facts: that Hoover and Gibson had indeed conspired against him and that Hoover had asked the British to pressure the Belgian government-in-exile into demanding Whitlock's recall.[63] From that point on, and for the rest of his life, Brand Whitlock detested Herbert Hoover.[64]

But if Whitlock in Hoover's eyes was a frail reed whom he could neither lean upon nor control, it was not the American minister to Brussels who was the prime source of friction as 1916 progressed. It was the Comité National. By early spring, according to Poland, "well-defined anti-C.R.B. propaganda" was emanating from "certain quarters" in Belgium to the effect that Hoover's men were well-paid agents, not volunteers, and that America was profiting handsomely from its food shipments into Belgium.[65] These deprecating rumors struck at the heart of the commission's aura of humanitarian idealism and formed an unpleasant backdrop to the Comité National's removal of CRB flags and posters from relief warehouses.

It was not long before friction produced heat. Up to this point Hoover's commission had had little to do with the internal management of the Comité National's department of benevolence, or *secours*. But in the spring of 1916 the CRB decided to exert closer supervision over this facet of the relief enterprise, particularly the distribution of clothing. Hoover accordingly assigned a young American, Milton Brown, to be his delegate to the Comité National's clothing dep tment. Brown was instructed to compile periodic reports on all clothing produced, stockpiled, and distributed in Belgium and northern France.

Hoover's action incensed the Comité National's chief of *secours*, Emmanuel Janssen, who promptly refused to give Brown any data whatever on native clothing supplies. It was one thing, apparently, for the CRB to gather statistics on goods that it actually imported. But why should it have any jurisdiction over what the Belgians manufactured for themselves? To Janssen it probably seemed insulting for a youthful American to come in and look over the shoulder, as it were, of the business elite that was managing the Comité National. For a strong-willed man like Janssen (who according to Brand Whitlock was anti-American),[66] the arrival of Brown no doubt looked like another case of Yankee meddling and aggrandizement.

To Hoover and his colleagues, however, the affair had a different cast. The CRB had just completed a massive clothing drive in America. How could it properly apportion this material, and keep track of its use, unless it had comprehensive data on the supplies and necessities of the Belgian people? *Secours* to the destitute might be largely administered by Belgians, but it depended upon contributions from abroad, and for the stewardship of these contributions Hoover considered the CRB independently responsible. To further complicate matters, only weeks before, the British government had abruptly stopped all CRB imports of clothing after learning that the German army was seizing native wool and woolen products inside Belgium. Hoover knew that the British would not relent unless he—not the Belgians—established a check upon the indigenous clothing operation. Hence his appointment of Milton Brown.

The result of this clash of perspectives was an acrimonious row in May between Hoover and Janssen. Only after vehement arguments and the soothing intervention of Whitlock was a deal struck. Brown would gain unlimited access to all clothing data but would have no "administrative functions" or control over Belgian staff. Janssen, in return, promised to cooperate fully and professed his "great esteem" for that "eminent man," Herbert Hoover. Shortly afterward the British government reluctantly permitted the CRB to ship into Belgium the clothing stocks it had on hand—but none further—on condition that the CRB guarantee "a strict system of control." The CRB, be it noted, not Janssen or Francqui.[67]

As if quarrels with the Comité National were not enough, in the spring and summer of 1916 Hoover became embroiled in an argument with the Belgian government-in-exile. On April 17 he submitted to Belgian minister of finance van de Vyvere an audited account for more than $65,000,000 that the CRB had spent through the end of 1915—money that had been funneled to it from the Allies via the Belgian government. Hoover asked van de Vyvere to issue a formal "quittance of [the CRB's] responsibility" for the expenditure of this sum.[68] Instead, van de Vyvere appointed two Belgians to examine the commission's accounts and promised to "officially confirm the regularity" of Hoover's work as soon as he received their report. But the minister added that he would grant no *final* "discharge" until his exiled government returned to Belgium and verified all the accounting data.[69] More pointedly still, he declared that his government considered the CRB and CN to be its "mandatories" not only for all funds it sent to them but for all *other* funds that the CRB expended, including charitable donations raised in the United States.[70]

Hoover was furious. In a memorandum for Ambassador Page's signature, the CRB chairman bluntly denied that his organization, as a totally neutral entity, was the "mandatory" of any government whatsoever. Nor, he added, did it have any "legal liability" toward the Belgian government-in-exile. As for charitable contributions obtained from the general public, these, said Hoover, were an "absolute gift" to the CRB, a gift that it was free to dispose of in Belgium at its "sole discretion." No one else, he asserted, could distribute this money unless such agencies were "under the untrammelled control" of his commission.[71]

But Hoover was not content to hide behind the protective shield of Page. A few days later he addressed to van de Vyvere a stinging, point-by-point rejoinder. The CRB, he declared, as a body of self-sacrificing volunteers, was not inclined to continue unless it had "complete confidence, complete liberty of action and complete freedom from all liability whatsoever." It would be quite impossible to hold such a group of men together, he asserted, if they were to be "subjected to a financial responsibility extending perhaps over years"—until, in other words, van de Vyvere and his colleagues returned to Belgium (whenever—if ever—that might be). The CRB, Hoover said bluntly, "accepts no financial responsibility to the Belgian government whatever." It accepted only "moral responsibility" (including legal liability for misappropriation of funds). But inasmuch as it had now presented carefully audited accounts to the Belgian government, the CRB demanded "immediate discharge" even from this.

As for the Belgian government's notion that the commission was its "mandatory," Hoover declared this to be "entirely incompatible" with his organization's neutrality and international commitments. And as for charitable funds raised independently from nongovernmental sources, the CRB, said he, was their "exclusive trustee" and would dispose of them, and account for them, without "intervention" from anyone.

Hoover then reminded van de Vyvere of the Belgian government's promise in early 1915 to indemnify him and his fellow commission directors for any personal loss sustained at the coming of peace. He now offered to release the Belgian government from this guarantee (if the Allied subsidies continued). But if, he added pointedly, the Belgian government did not "unreservedly" accept his position on every issue between them, it should let his organization do what he had offered to do in February 1916: namely, resign, withdraw, and let the Belgians carry on by themselves.[72]

Hoover, of course, knew very well that his offer was unlikely to be accepted. Whatever the exiled government might desire, he knew that the British would never countenance his replacement by a group of Belgians. Francqui and Baron Lambert could testify to that. This knowledge was Hoover's ace in the hole. He could therefore loftily offer to resign in the confidence that he would never be required to do so.

Van de Vyvere apparently did not call Hoover's bluff. Instead, their disagreement now expanded to embrace another, more politically sensitive, issue: the disposition of the relief organization's assets at the termination of the war. By mid-1916 it was apparent that when the conflict finally ended, the CRB and Comité National would be able to liquidate their holdings (such as food in transit) with a substantial cash surplus. Two delicate questions now arose: how was this profit being generated, and to whom should it ultimately belong? To the Belgian government-in-exile, the profits were earned by the manipulation of currency exchange and by use of the loans that it had received from the Allies and in turn transmitted to Hoover. The surplus was therefore government money. To Hoover, however, the profits were the result of the unpaid services of thousands of volunteers all over the world, including shipping firms that had forgone commissions and railways that had not charged for transporting relief supplies. The CRB and CN, therefore, should alone determine the profits' allocation.[73] With the equivalent of millions of dollars in funds at stake, the stage was set for trouble.

And so began a three-cornered struggle that drew Hoover into the vortex of Belgian politics. On one side was the Belgian government-in-exile at Le Havre, France—Catholic, clerical, and fearful of the postwar ambitions of Emile Francqui and his associates. On the other side was Francqui and the banker-dominated leadership of the Comité National—liberal (in the European sense), staunchly anticlerical, touched with Freemasonry, and possessed of a potential "political machine" that reached into every Belgian hamlet. According to Brand Whitlock, "the [Le] Havre gang" wished "to prevent the Comité National gang from having all the credit," while Francqui yearned to oust the Catholic government after the war and sought control over relief profits as an instrument to that end.[74] In the middle stood Hoover—willing, even eager, to leave behind "an institution to commemorate the Relief."[75]

The question of disposal of profits soon ceased to be academic. Sometime in 1915 Francqui had conceived the idea of creating an institution for the support of higher education in Belgium. The executive head of the Comité National was evidently inspired by the CRB's use of Rhodes scholars and by the example of the Rockefeller Foundation, whose representatives had toured his country during the early months of the war.[76] In any case, in the spring of 1916 he secretly convened in Brussels a committee of representatives of the principal Belgian universities. During the next two and a half months the group developed a plan for a great University Foundation, to be endowed with leftover relief money after the war. Among other things, the foundation would provide loans to impecunious Belgian university students and subsidize postdoctoral scientific research.[77]

To realize his dream, however, Francqui had to overcome the resistance of his government-in-exile, and notably the Catholic conservative van de Vyvere, who suspected him of aspiring to be a dictator.[78] The CN's master administrator also had to gain undisputed title to the relief profits. During the spring and summer of 1916 he devoted himself energetically to these objectives.[79] We must not let the Belgian government "put us in a state of tutelage," he told Hoover.[80] At one point Francqui even warned his government that if his and Hoover's postwar "projects" were "thwarted in any way whatever," the two men would simply distribute the accumulated money "to all the passers by in Brussels rather than be obliged to entrust the spending of it to third persons."[81]

Meanwhile Hoover, who was evidently sympathetic to Francqui's general aim,[82] had come forward with a proposal of his own. He suggested to Francqui that the CRB's expected end-of-the-war surplus be used to establish a scholarship exchange program for Belgian and American university students.[83] Such a proposal must have seemed innocent enough to the CRB chairman, whose interest in education was strong and whose own life had been transformed by the opportunity to study at Stanford. But in a land where education was a bitterly sectarian issue, danger flags soon waved. Soon the Catholic-dominated government-in-exile laid claim to *all* of Hoover's funds.[84]

Anxious to reach a settlement with van de Vyvere, Hoover apparently dropped the exchange idea for the time being. Instead, in midsummer, he urged that the prospective surplus be employed to create a Belgian foundation for "the stimulation of scientific and industrial research"—in essence, the plan already formulated by Francqui's committee. "Such foundations," Hoover added, had been "the greatest factor in the remarkable advancement of American higher education and research during the last 30 years." To assuage the sensitivities of various politicians, he emphasized that such an institution would be nonsectarian, nonpolitical, and noncompetitive with existing teaching facilities. He insisted, too, that he and his American colleagues were not attempting to impose any scheme upon the Belgians or to intrude into their internal affairs.[85]

Like Francqui, Hoover seemed anxious to achieve an understanding of this issue as soon as possible. Probably they feared what the government-in-exile might otherwise do when it returned. To this end Hoover submitted a memorandum to van de Vyvere in mid-July—a memorandum that, if approved, would authorize the CRB and CN to expend any profits they derived from "volunteer service" as they saw fit, for "the benefit of the Belgian people."[86] But when Hoover in his followup letter appeared to concede that certain of the relief effort's profits might yet be turned over to the Belgian government, he received a swift rebuke from Francqui. Warning Hoover that the Comité National admitted no such claim, Francqui declared that if the relief were ended tomorrow, the CRB's assets (with one exception) would belong not to the government-in-exile but to the Comité National, and the Comité National alone.[87] From van de Vyvere, on the other hand, came only a disconcerting silence.[88]

Caught in the crossfire of political rivalries, Hoover consulted Brand Whitlock. Let the quarreling Belgians "fight it out among themselves,'" the diplomat counseled, and then yield the profits to whatever institution they agree upon.[89] Perhaps in this spirit, Hoover offered in September to "account to" the Belgian government after the war for any profits that his commission might then possess. He did not, however, specifically promise to surrender these profits, nor did he renounce his theory of their origin. Perhaps for that reason he apparently received no answer to his offer.[90]

Shortly thereafter, Hoover unabashedly submitted some accounts that reflected his views on the profits question. This time the Belgian finance minister bestirred himself with alacrity. These profits, the official averred, were "governmental moneys."[91] And there, after more than half a year of contention, the matter rested, unresolved. The disposition of surplus money and the establishment of the University Foundation would have to await the end of the war.

Meanwhile the question of accounting was generating tension between Hoover and Francqui. Back in 1915, when the Germans had tried to acquire control over *secours* money as a lever on the Belgian unemployed, Francqui and Hoover had resorted to a statistical subterfuge. To protect the CN's considerable profits from its sales of foodstuffs, the CRB had agreed to carry this surplus (as well as benevolent funds sent for indigent Belgians from abroad) on its own account books in London. On May 6, 1916 Francqui reminded his American colleague of this arrangement.[92] Replying on May 27, Hoover now proposed to alter the relief effort's recordkeeping by henceforth distinguishing between the value of the CRB's voluntary services and the value of profits derived from the Comité National's food sales. The former sum would put a dollar figure on the CRB's gratuitous contributions to the Belgian people. The latter amount would represent the relief effort's "tax" on the native population.[93]

Hoover's announced reason for this revision was to provide "some tangible form of appreciation" to the businesses, banks, railways, and individuals around the world who had given such an "enormous sum of voluntary service."[94] After all, it was precisely such services that had enabled him to keep his costs down, including the cost of food sold to well-to-do Belgians. But the CRB chairman probably had another objective as well. Throughout the spring of 1916 he seemed anxious to differentiate his organization's achievements from those of the Comité National.[95] Not coincidentally, this was the season of his burgeoning dispute with the Belgian government-in-exile. Hoover's proposal, then, to revise his accounting methods may not have been as ingenuous as it looked. In all likelihood he was seeking not just to show "appreciation" for the volunteer labor of his commission and its supporters but to establish an uncontested claim to the profits from this labor after the war.

Whatever the CRB chairman's motive, Emile Francqui immediately smelled a rat. Apparently suspecting Hoover of trying to reap credit from the relief work, the Belgian banker objected strenuously to drawing any distinction between the CRB's and CN's services to his people. The two bodies were "one and the same undertaking," he argued. Each was simply "the prolongation" of the other. There should be no differentiation between money collected inside Belgian and outside; the receipts of the two organizations belonged to them jointly. Clearly provoked by Hoover's action, Francqui revived his old contention that the CRB had no independent authority or role to play inside his country. The Comité National was paramount on Belgian soil, he declared, and within these boundaries he alone was in charge of the joint relief organization.[96] At about this same time he began to spread the story that it was he and his colleagues, not the CRB men, who had really initiated the Belgian relief in 1914.[97]

Francqui's memorandum evoked a quick rejoinder from Hoover. I am not seeking credit for the relief, he protested. ". . . I do not really care whether Belgian relief is ever heard of once we can get the job done."[98] What mattered now was not questions of individual or organizational preeminence but the accomplishment of a mission:

> It simply comes down to the fact that there were two organisations, one in Brussels and one in London, composed of men willing to devote their time and effort to this work, who naturally came together and at once undertook to build up organisations which have so far carried on the task with success. . . . The only hope for the success of such an enterprise is to build up institutions which embrace in their membership many thousands of devoted and influential people. . . . This we have done by the creation of thousands of subordinate committees in Belgium and thousands of subordinate committees in America, England and elsewhere. All these thousands of people are aggregated around us, feeling themselves part of the institution of high purpose and conduct, and thereby we gain not only their service but an enormous influence which fortifies us from destruction by any ill wind. So far as the C.R.B. or C.N. personnel, work or influence are concerned, they could not have been gained or held a day as simply Herbert Hoover or Emile Francqui but only as an institution.

The "whole ambition of the Americans," Hoover insisted, was "to carry on their part of the task efficiently and it matters not who shall go down to posterity as having taken the first steps in Belgian relief." As for apportioning praise among the various American volunteers, he simply recorded his "impression" that someday "it will be necessary to make a directory to embrace the names of all the gentlemen who have performed the task of 'saving Belgium' and I shall be proud enough to get amongst the letter Hs inside the Directory."[99]

It is doubtful that Francqui was persuaded by Hoover's professions of self-effacement. The CRB chairman, in any event, was not about to rely on homilies about mutual cooperation. In late June the British government inquired about the CRB's degree of independence inside Belgium. It is not clear whether this was a coincidence or a communication inspired by the CRB chairman. In either case, Hoover at once grasped this opportunity to transmit Francqui's feisty memorandum to the Foreign Office. The tone of Hoover's covering letter was moderate. The Belgian people, he told Lord Percy, have

> built up, under most terrible difficulties, a strong institution in the shape of the Comité National, [and] have a natural desire that it should be steadily and systematically held to the forefront as a rallying point of Belgian sentiment and solidarity, and that its brilliance should not be diminished by a parallel and too prominent a foreign institution.

He pointed out that the Comité National had grown in "influence and strength" since the war began, that life in Belgium had become more settled, and that some of the CRB's early functions were no longer so essential. He asserted that he and his American colleagues wished "simply to serve the Belgians" and to do so without friction. He therefore asked the British government for permission to "entirely" subordinate the CRB's apparatus inside Belgium to the Comité National—in other words, to accept Francqui's memorandum! "I am anxious to agree with Mr. Francqui" on the desirability of this change, Hoover wrote. My associates and I "do not care an atom what position we occupy in the scheme so long as the Belgian people are fed."[100]

At first glance Hoover's letter to Lord Percy was extraordinary. Nothing in his personality or his conduct of the relief thus far suggested that he was anxious to subordinate his commission to anyone. Yet here he was, magnanimously offering to curb the CRB's powers and let Francqui attain the victory he had been thwarted from achieving only months before. Why? Was Hoover really giving up? Was he at last tiring of the bickering and intrigue?

Like so many of his earlier threats and "offers," Hoover's letter to Percy, in all likelihood, had no such meaning. Surely the CRB chairman realized that the British Foreign Office, after all *it* had said and done in recent months, was not about to call upon Belgians to police the relief work by themselves. Knowing this, the CRB's chief executive could offer to subordinate himself freely, generously, and without risk. Such a letter had an advantage of which the document-conscious American was very probably aware: it created an appealing appearance of self-sacrifice that might prove useful in future controversies. Frequently, in fact, in his public acts and gestures, Hoover adopted a posture of almost Olympian idealism—the pose of a suffering servant who did not "care an atom" about worldly power and prestige. Such an exalted persona, of course, was at variance with his private memoranda and correspondence, in which such very human qualities as pride, anger, ambition, and concern for his place in history found frequent and pungent expression.

No, Hoover had not given up the fight against the aggrandizing acts of the Belgians; he was simply retreating strategically to his unyielding final line of defense. On July 15 his tactic bore fruit. On that day Lord Percy informed him that the British government most definitely would *not* rely on the Comité National to conduct the relief work unaided inside Belgium. Instead, said Percy, the "whole foundation" for the enterprise must remain what in British eyes it had been from the start: a "distinctively neutral" endeavor in which Hoover's commission (not the CN) must have sole and "undivided responsibility" for the importation and distribution of food. The British diplomat insisted that the CRB must retain an "entirely independent" presence inside Belgium and that it must monitor not only German adherence to the guarantees but also the "justice and equality" of actual food distribution by the Belgians. If any opposition arose to the activities of the joint Department of Inspection and Control, he declared, the CRB must notify the British government. Furthermore, all warehouses must be administered and controlled by the CRB, and all food must remain commission property until delivered to individual consumers.

Percy professed the Allies' "entire confidence" in the "efficiency" and "good will" of the Comité National. But he pointed out that the Belgians, as subjects of an occupying army, were in no position to provide the assurances that an independent neutral organization could supply. While conceding to the Belgians a paramount role in "the detailed labour of distribution," Percy made it plain that in British eyes the senior partner in the relief project was the Commission for Relief in Belgium.[101]

Percy's emphatic letter must have been music to Hoover's ears. On point after point it precisely paralleled his own conception of the relief undertaking and of his organization's position within it. Indeed, in places the British official's communication had a noticeably Hooverian sound. More likely than not, this was not a coincidence.

At any rate Hoover now had the document he wanted: an official British rebuttal to Francqui. Even better, he obtained a suggestion from Percy that the letter be circulated to the Comité National and its subsidiaries.[102] Armed with this weapon, the CRB's chairman traveled to Brussels in late July.

Yet no sooner did Hoover reach Belgium than he hesitated to press his advantage. He told Brand Whitlock that "certain Belgians" considered the commission to be acting like a "task master" and that he wished, if at all possible, to avoid the "least appearance" of such a posture. He therefore decided not to deliver Lord Percy's letter for the time being and instead to "make another try" at cooperation. It was not that all was well inside Belgium. The head of the CN's *secours* department, for one, did not exude what

Hoover considered proper "good will" toward his American associates. Still, the CRB's chairman informed Whitlock that he hoped "by patience" to "worry through . . . to the end somehow."[103]

Hoover's reluctance to stage a showdown was uncharacteristic. Patience and forbearance, after all, had not exactly been hallmarks of his administration up till now. Why this sudden about-face? Perhaps he felt that the Belgians had a point and that a noisy quarrel could only cause harm. Perhaps he did not care to engage in further polemics with Francqui while he was simultaneously trying to come to terms over future disposition of relief profits. Then, too, in late July Francqui was recuperating from heart trouble—a circumstance not conducive to confrontation.[104] Perhaps Hoover did not think the relief would last much longer in any event; he told Brand Whitlock that the war might end in October.[105] If peace were indeed so imminent, it might not be worth the effort to alter the relationship between the two relief bodies at this late date. Whatever his reasoning, Hoover decided in midsummer not to confront the festering conflict head on.[106]

Within weeks, however, it was obvious that his policy of "worrying through" was failing. At the crux of the difficulty was the joint Department of Inspection and Control, headed—on the CRB's side—by a twenty-nine-year-old Princeton graduate, Joseph C. Green. Emile Francqui had never reconciled himself to the bureau's existence or to the prominence of the Americans within it. At first he had tried to cajole Green with heavy-handed, back-slapping comradery, unctuous references to him as *mon cher ami*, and endless invitations to dinner. Then, one day, he attempted to give Green a direct order. When the young American politely declined to carry it out, the portly Belgian erupted in rage, pounding the table, shaking his double chin, and literally tearing out his hair. After that, Francqui ignored Green entirely and (according to Green) maligned him assiduously behind his back.[107]

Nevertheless, by late summer Green and his Belgian counterpart, van Gend, had succeeded in establishing an aggressive inspection service throughout Belgium.[108] As a result of their efforts, hundreds of cases of illicit trafficking in imported foods were prosecuted in the Belgian courts,[109] and a more systematic supervision of the relief was implemented down to the grass-roots level. Not all Belgians were happy with the bureau's new efficiency and determination, but at least to Green it seemed that a satisfactory outcome had been attained.[110]

And then the hurricane struck.

I I I

I N early August Hoover left Belgium for London. The very next day Francqui launched a campaign to bring the joint department under his exclusive control. From now on, he decreed, the bureau could send out no letters unless he himself had countersigned them. The result was immediate delay in correspondence. In one case, Francqui simply tore up a letter he disliked and ordered Green, through van Gend, to send no more of that kind again. Francqui next ordered that the department's correspondence bear a stamp instructing recipients to send their replies not (as heretofore) to its office in the CRB building but to the separately housed inspection department of the Comité National. In this way Green would become totally dependent on whatever information the CN's chief deigned to pass along.

Francqui also ordered the department's surveillance officers in the field to address their reports to van Gend's office rather than Green's. Similarly, until midsummer Belgian *procureurs du roi* had submitted their reports on court cases involving food regulations directly to the young American. Now, in August, Francqui ordered that all such documents go only to *his* office. Even worse, Green discovered that in many such instances Francqui simply suppressed entire cases, while at other times he "edited" documents extensively before passing them on. On one occasion Francqui loudly berated a Belgian court official for giving information to the CRB. Pounding his fist on the table, the CN's leader shouted, "Ne donnez rien aux américains; ce n'est pas leur affaire" ("Don't give anything to the Americans; it is none of their business").[111]

Francqui's increasingly blatant anti-Americanism angered Green, who later accused the CN president of possessing no "finer feelings" whatsoever. Francqui thinks money is "all-powerful," Green charged. "He is utterly incapable of believing that any man can do anything except for his own personal advantage . . . in the financial sense." He has "absolutely no conception" of the meaning of words like patriotism and self-sacrifice.[112] Hoover, too, was incensed. On a trip back to Brussels in September he poured out his frustration to Brand Whitlock, who shared his disgust at Francqui's "pettiness" and "double-dealing."[113] But nothing changed.

In October Francqui became bolder still. In a series of exchanges with Hoover's latest chief deputy in Brussels, Vernon Kellogg, the Belgian formally proposed a radical revision of the work of inspection and control. The present system, he contended, was "a complete mess." The Department of Inspection and Control had "substituted itself" for the "responsible management of the departments of the Comité National" and had even issued orders contradicting those of the CN's division chiefs. The result, he alleged, was confusion and laxity of administration in the provinces and communes. Francqui attributed the problem to the fusion of the CRB and CN control services in February 1916—an act he now called a "mistake." He therefore urged that the work of the Department of Inspection and Control be divided. The CRB would monitor and enforce German compliance with the terms of the relief. The Comité National would oversee the actual distribution of food to the Belgian people. In other words, Hoover's organization would be confined to checking up on the Germans; Francqui's organization would have exclusive suzerainty over his countrymen.[114]

Kellogg immediately demurred. He emphasized that the neutral commission was required under its international commitments not only to protect imported food from German seizure but to verify the "equitable distribution" of this same food to the Belgian consumers. While the CRB did not presume to dictate actual methods of distribution, it must, he said, have "some intimate share" in the "inspection and control" of this process. Francqui's proposal, he pointed out, would essentially return the system to the pre-February 1916 status quo, a condition unacceptable then and now to the CRB. In his letters to Francqui, Kellogg did not quite say so, but his meaning was clear: the American-led commission was in Belgium not only to watch the Germans but to watch the Belgians as well.[115]

At Kellogg's request Francqui agreed to defer the issue until Hoover returned to Brussels later in the month. But the Belgian warned that the Comité National would eventually act in the matter "in perfect freedom" and would preserve its "principle of independence" with "jealous care." And he warned further that Hoover, in London, should not act impulsively and "dictate—as he said to me he sometimes does—instructions to Lord Percy or the Foreign Office." The oppressed people of Belgium, said Francqui, "deserve to be treated with some delicacy." It would be "regrettable," he added bluntly, if they had to "endure the yoke" of a "useless," "dangerous," and "odious" "intervention."[116]

Francqui professed not to mind if the CRB assisted the Comité National in its tasks. But independent supervision of food distribution was something else:

> Do not forget, my dear Mr. Kellogg, that the C.N., which is a national institution, sprung from the will of the Belgian people, is alone responsible towards the Belgian people and their government for the repartition of the food. . . .
>
> Your claim to control, *for others*, the Belgians who are all devoting themselves gratuitously for their country would come as a surprise to the leaders of the C.N. and should even be legitimately refused by them. . . .

Francqui insisted that his organization had always distributed food "equitably and without the least hitch" and that the character, disinterestedness, and organization of the CN were the "surest guarantees" of equitable conduct. In short, there was no need for an independent and demeaning check upon his committee.[117]

In one respect Francqui had a point: the Commission for Relief in Belgium had certainly evolved far beyond its original purpose of assuring that the Germans adhered to their guarantees. But the Belgian financier-turned-benefactor did not appear to recognize that there had been a reason for this expansion of the CRB's role. Rampant black marketeering, outright food sales to the Germans, and other acts by the Belgians themselves had led to the creation of the joint Department of Inspection and Control in the first place. Self-regulation under the Comité National had not sufficed—not for the British government, whose support was all-important. After the exposés of early 1916, an embarrassed Hoover was determined that never again would his organization be an unwitting legitimator of the practices (or malpractices) of certain Belgians. Francqui, however, apparently considered the joint bureau to be a reflection on his leadership, and the CRB as a competitor for his countrymen's esteem. He may also have had another motive. Hoover, Green, and other Americans were coming to suspect him of using the relief as a form of political patronage.

Viewing these developments from London, Hoover grew increasingly alarmed. A pattern was emerging, a pattern suggesting that Francqui's defeat in London in February had neither chastened nor enlightened him. First, in the spring, had come the anti-American rumors and insinuations, the disparagement of the CRB's motives, and the removal of its flags and placards from Belgian relief warehouses. Then, in August, had come the bureaucratic warfare against Green and the systematic effort to hamstring the joint Department of Inspection and Control. Now, in October, Francqui was audaciously labeling the CRB's inspection-control work a "yoke of intervention" and openly demanding a reversion to the unsatisfactory arrangements of the past. Disturbed and fed up, Hoover decided to act.

He did so with characteristic drive and cleverness. On October 16 he asked his ever-faithful ally in London, Ambassador Page, for a precise statement of the responsibilities of the CRB as the relief effort commenced its third year.[118] But Hoover was too skilled a bureaucratic warrior to let matters go at that. A few weeks earlier, during a conversation in Brussels, Brand Whitlock had remarked to him that if the situation inside Belgium deteriorated, he, Whitlock, could ask the British government to define the relationship between the Comité National and the CRB.[119] Now, in London, Hoover told Ambassador Page that Whitlock *had requested* such a formal British statement (which Whitlock had not, in fact, done).[120] Under the impression, then, that *Whitlock* desired British intervention, Page, on October 18, formally asked the British foreign secretary to delineate the commission's duties inside Belgium.[121]

Hoover's maneuver was an effective one. He undoubtedly knew that if he alone appealed to the British, the result would carry little weight with the Belgians. But if he could make it appear that *Brand Whitlock* sought British assistance, the CRB's position would be strengthened. Whitlock, at last, would be fully enlisted on the commission's side and pulled away from (in Hoover's eyes) his detached and dithering passivity. Moreover, by imputing to Whitlock the objective that he himself was pursuing, Hoover could obtain what he wanted and not have to take as much criticism for it inside Belgium. Whitlock, of course, was not yet aware of what Hoover had done.

Even as Ambassador Page prepared to approach the British Foreign Office, new trouble was brewing on the continent. On the morning of October 18, Hoover learned that agents of Francqui had just seized the files of the head office of the Department of Inspection and Control, forcing it "by violence" to cease effective operations. Furthermore, Francqui had ordered the Belgian staff of the bureau no longer to report to Green and had told the *procureur-général* himself not to cooperate with CRB men in prosecuting infractions of the food regulations. Hoover at once composed letters to Percy and to Page. This development, he said angrily, was the "final act" of a "systematic campaign" conducted for nine months by "a small group of Belgians to relegate the American participation in relief in Belgium to a purely ornamental position. . . ." It was a "final humiliation" to the entire American staff inside the country—idealistic men who had performed "humane service" at "great personal sacrifice." If we surrender to this outrage, he declared, it would be "an act of dishonesty towards the Allied Governments and the people who have entrusted us with the large sums of money and amounts of foodstuffs which we administer." The only "error" that the CRB had committed, he said, was that it had been too conciliatory, too deferential to the Belgians. Out of kindness to the Belgians it had watered down the Allies' demands for American control "to a point where they have now been repudiated."[122]

Page successfully counseled Hoover not to submit his letter to Lord Percy. The ambassador feared that such a startling missive might cause the British to choke off food imports altogether until the entire relief structure was reorganized. It could also jeopardize the increased Allied subsidies that Hoover was then on the verge of obtaining. But the ambassador, too, was disenchanted with events across the Channel. In a letter that same day to Whitlock, Page threatened to withdraw his support for Francqui as head of the Comité National if any more such incidents occurred. The time has come, said Page to Whitlock, for the two of us to "take a stand" against the CN in order to protect the CRB from such treatment. Hoover, said Page, "deserves our personal shelter" and must not be expected to "take personally on his back the entire brunt of these matters." Evidently vexed (like Hoover) at Whitlock's perceived aloofness from the fray, Page bluntly demanded that his diplomatic colleague "settle these relations once and for all" during Hoover's upcoming visit to Belgium.[123]

Two days later the British foreign secretary, Lord Grey (formerly Sir Edward Grey), replied to Page's request for clarification of the CRB's status. It was a thunderous endorsement of Hoover's position. The "whole foundation and condition" for the relief work, Grey declared, was this: the CRB—and the CRB alone—must have "undivided responsibility" not only for importing food but for controlling its distribution and allocating the money raised from distributing it. The "whole work," he insisted, must be "absolutely controlled by an independent neutral body." Only the CRB could possess the necessary "freedom of movement" and "independence from political and personal pressure" to administer the relief program effectively in German-occupied territory. Only a "distinctively neutral" relief operation could command enthusiastic neutral support abroad. Hoover's commission, said Grey, must therefore be "entirely independent" inside Belgium, and the Comité National must act as its "agent." The Department of Inspection and Control must supervise "the whole relief organisation" and must do so "independently."

As for imports, all must remain the "absolute property" of the commission from the point of origin to the final consumer, and every warehouse inside Belgium must be its property and designated as such. In no other way, Grey claimed, could the food be adequately protected. Similarly for relief money: here, too, the CRB was to be in control and the CN to act as its "agents." On "no other conditions" than these, said Grey, could Great Britain permit the relief of Belgium to continue.[124]

Grey's letter bristled with uncompromising language—words like absolute, absolutely, independent—and its tone was apodictic. Had Hoover himself helped to draft the document? More than one person soon suspected that he had. But whatever its authorship, the larger, more important point could not be denied: on this fundamental issue of policy the Americans and the British Foreign Office were in complete accord. To Emile Francqui the Commission for Relief in Belgium, with its three dozen or so volunteers inside his country, was a mere appendage to *his* organization, 40,000 strong. But to Hoover and the Allied governments, the truth was the other way around. Without the CRB, there could be no relief of Belgium.

As if his letter to Page were not enough, Gray immediately followed up with a "confidential" note to the ambassador that same day. The foreign secretary declared that his government's "whole confidence" in the efficiency of the relief work inside Belgium rested on knowledge of the "detailed working" of the Department of Inspection and Control. Without this, he asserted, he would be "wholly unable" to advocate any increase in imports and subsidies for the commission. Indeed, without this knowledge his faith in the absence of leakages to the Germans would be "wholly destroyed" and he would be placed "in the gravest position" in the British Cabinet. Even *current* food imports might cease. In short, an effective inspection/control service was the sine qua non of British support. The message, at least nominally, was Grey's, but the diction was that of Hoover.[125]

It is impossible to tell whether Grey was truly in earnest about the specter that he "confidentially" raised. Certainly the threat of lost subsidies and suspended food shipments could be a powerful missile to launch at Francqui. Certainly the British were doing everything to create the appearance—perhaps even the reality—of extreme dissatisfaction with conditions inside Belgium. That very same day, October 20, Lord Percy chastised Hoover for the "jejune" report he had just transmitted from the Department of Inspection and Control—a document rendered sketchy by Francqui's campaign of sabotage. Percy warned that various British officials were getting the impression that the Comité National was going easy on the Germans and deliberately keeping the British "in the dark."[126] Percy's letter may or may not have been solicited. In either case, it became another part of Hoover's arsenal.

Fortified by Lord Grey's resounding endorsement, the CRB's chairman prepared to journey over to Belgium. But before he departed, his faithful friend Page tried again to whip Brand Whitlock into line. In a letter probably drafted, at least in part, by Hoover himself, Page warned that the entire relief effort hung by a "very delicate thread." Large sectors of the Allied populations were against it, he said, and it survived only because it was assumed to be under independent neutral control and sustained by American public opinion. If the word spread among the Allies that Americans were *not* in "the forefront and control" inside Belgium, "the whole thing would break down." And if the Belgians did anything to "controvert" the Allies' original understanding of the enterprise, it would be—if known—"the death knell of the entire relief."

Page asserted that the British had been alarmed for months by reports of the CN's "subjection" of the Americans. Only Hoover's forbearance and minimizing of these incidents, he said, had forestalled a crisis. But now the Comité National had gone too far. By removing the CRB's name from relief buildings, by deliberately ignoring the CRB in its reports, by negotiating with the Germans independently and portraying the commission as a mere "importing body," it had created conditions under which the United States government's support was "wholly impossible." In a sentence reminiscent of one that Hoover himself wrote a few months earlier, Page declared: "The Comité National is not the pivot on which the relief revolves in Belgium."

Why should American involvement in Belgium be so "offensive to the *amour propre* of the Belgians"? the ambassador asked. It was "unfair" that the American role should be portrayed as a "minor" contribution. If Hoover and his associates should decide for personal reasons to withdraw, Page said he would be obliged to tell the State Department that no group of Americans could hope to succeed in their place. Hoover, he claimed, had "entirely" abandoned his professional work and income as a mining engineer and had made "a greater financial sacrifice" than any other person of any nationality (a slap, perhaps, at the wealthy banker Francqui). If, said Page, Hoover should now be made to suffer "deliberate interference" inside Belgium, it would be "too much" to ask him—or his patron-ambassador—to continue. You and I, said Page to Whitlock, "cannot be put in a false position by countenancing the growth in Belgium" of an organization at variance with that prescribed by the Allied governments.[127]

Page's militant letter and the salvo from Lord Grey reached Whitlock in Brussels a few days later. The American diplomat instantly perceived the barrage for what it was: "Hoover's heavy artillery shelling the trenches before he brings up his infantry . . . for a final battle with Francqui."[128] As usual,

Whitlock took a standoffish view of the quarrel. Only a month before, he had denounced Francqui's duplicity. Now, in his diary, he accused Hoover of causing much of the trouble by his tactlessness and "tone of severity." The Americans did not appreciate the Belgians' "embarrassment" about receiving charity and should not exacerbate matters by hinting that there was a "lack of appreciation" for their work. Hoover, wrote Whitlock, "would drive everybody with a bull whip; he is a strong man with a good heart, but lacks diplomacy in his dealings with Francqui. . . . A plague on both your houses!"[129]

Hoover, of course, had long since concluded that Francqui needed more than "diplomacy." On October 26 the CRB chairman left London for Brussels—convinced that it was "absolutely necessary to face the Comité National issue once and for all." The "attitude of the Francqui group," he told a friend, was "the most discouraging thing about the whole Relief." Hoover revealed that when he had approached Ambassador Page to obtain a definition of the CRB's relationship to the Comité National, he had tried to involve the Belgian government-in-exile in the process. Instead, that government had "shirked the whole position."[130] Apparently, for reasons of domestic politics, it did not care to quarrel with Francqui.

Hoover arrived in Brussels on October 29—only to find that Whitlock had not yet delivered Lord Grey's letter to the Comité National.[131] Whitlock was profoundly embarrassed. He had not (he confessed in his diary) solicited this letter at all. Yet here it was before him, complete with the claim that he had. Now, thanks to this misimpression, he was being thrust into a quarrel of which he was "sick to death."[132] Furthermore, the letter, in his opinion, was "too direct and brutal"—not the kind of document to mollify heated passions.[133]

Despite Hoover's eagerness for a showdown, he did not immediately visit Francqui. Instead, he avoided the Belgian for nearly five days—no doubt waiting for the dilatory Whitlock to forward the blast from Lord Grey. In the meantime, on October 31, the CRB's chairman endeavored again by letter to convince his Belgian antagonist of American good will:

> . . . I wish my dear Francqui that you could get one fixed view in your mind. That is: this group of 150 American volunteers today give their full time to the service of the Belgian people; are not in this work for adventure . . . they are not working for the Belgian, British, French, German, Spanish or American Governments, they are not working for the Comité National or the well-to-do people in Belgium; they are in the service of the destitute in Belgium, and this alone.

"All the protective measures," he continued, all the " diplomatic worry, shipping, purchase, finance, accounts, inspection, technical details of all sorts of a business now involving 25,000,000 francs per month, from our view are all simply cogs of a machine which in the end serves" the destitute millions of Belgium.[134]

Hoover's letter proved useless. By the beginning of November Joseph C. Green was reporting the Department of Inspection and Control to be in "almost complete disorganization," with its American director—himself—entirely cut off from his inspectors.[135] Even worse, Francqui now intimated that he and the Belgian government-in-exile had made a deal: the government had recognized the Comité National as its representative inside Belgium; in return, Francqui had promised not to challenge the government for national leadership after the war. Entrenched more than ever at the pinnacle of Belgian society, Francqui was now demanding that the Comité National be treated with the respect due a sovereign government.[136]

In part the developing conflict was inevitable. As Hoover had remarked to Lord Percy in June, many Belgians naturally wished to exalt the CN as "a rallying point" of national "sentiment and solidarity" and resented the seemingly competitive presence of the CRB.[137] Francqui, in particular, repeatedly boasted of his organization's success in sustaining national unity in the face of German attempts to divide and manipulate his countrymen.[138] But intertwined with this difference of perspective was the clash of two commanding personalities. Francqui (said Brand Whitlock in November) was "quite blown with pride" and was taking on "the powers and rank of a dictator."[139] And Hoover, though he had once professed not to "care an atom" about the CRB's place in the scheme of relief, was now insisting upon recognition of the CRB's supremacy inside Belgium. To Whitlock it must have seemed that his own observation nearly five months before was still valid: "The differences between [Hoover] and Francqui seem irreconcilable, because both are strong men, and each would rule."[140]

Certainly the personal antagonism between the two men was deep by late 1916. Privately Hoover referred to Francqui as a "financial pirate"[141]—an apparent allusion to Francqui's earlier career in the Congo and China as an agent of Belgium's imperialist monarch, Léopold II.[142] Probably echoing Hoover's viewpoint, Green depicted Francqui as the head of a "corrupt financial ring" in Brussels, a man whose unsavory reputation was "known in the financial circles of three continents."[143]

Francqui, for his part, reciprocated. Banging his fists on a tea table at Brand Whitlock's residence on November 3, he railed at the Americans' manners (probably meaning Hoover's) and even referred to the CRB volunteers as "the American invasion." "We have one master," Francqui exclaimed; "we don't want two." The Belgium financier then threatened to "expose" Hoover. "You know, Monsieur," he said to Whitlock, "I have written a book of more than six hundred pages—a history of the revictualing. All the details are there. . . . Does Hoover wish to risk being shown in his true colors in a book which will remain the standard history, which will be read all over the world?"[144]

It was not until November 3 that Whitlock gave Francqui a copy of Lord Grey's letter of October 20. His face dark with fury, the Belgian read the document and exploded: "It is Hoover who wrote that. I know his style." Hitting the paper with his hand, he added, "That is the limit!"[145]

The prospects for peace between the CRB and CN, then, were not encouraging as the two chiefs began their discussions. By now their dispute had gone beyond the single issue of inspection and control. It now affected the entire network of subsidies that the CN was supplying to private charitable organizations within the borders of the occupied nation. Back in August Hoover and Francqui had concluded that general appeals abroad for Belgian relief were no longer effective. What was needed now was more focused fundraising for carefully earmarked purposes. Thus a citizens' committee in America, for example, might raise money for a specified Belgian town or a particular needy group such as orphans. Such money would be then funneled through the CRB to these preselected recipients. During the autumn of 1916 Hoover duly implemented a worldwide campaign along these lines. As a device to stimulate giving, he promised donors to obtain receipts for their gifts from the donees. But when, a few weeks later, he attempted to remit some of this money directly to its designated beneficiaries, Francqui and Janssen angrily refused to let him. Rather than acquiesce in what they evidently perceived as a Hooverian act of aggrandizement, they even returned at least one American donation.[146] The allotment of grants to charities, they believed, was their own business. To Hoover their antagonism betrayed a desire not only to suppress evidence of American generosity but also to use charitable money for political advantage—an immoral purpose in which he could not allow the CRB to be implicated.

Hoover promptly warned Francqui that the international fund drive in progress must either be conducted as previously agreed upon or the "propaganda" in its behalf abandoned entirely.[147] Go ahead and abandon it, Francqui retorted; Belgium no longer needs foreign charity anyway! Thanks to new resources provided (he said) by his government-in-exile, the Comité National could carry on its *secours* program unaided.[148] Faced with this astonishing assertion of self-sufficiency, Hoover agreed to terminate his charitable "propaganda," provided that the CN publicly request its cessation.[149]

On another front progress was similarly slow in coming. Backed to the hilt by Lord Grey, Hoover insisted that legal title to the relief operation's foodstuffs and money must rest with neutrals. Only in this way, he asserted, could its property be fully protected. To Francqui such a step was quite unnecessary; all such goods and moneys were amply protected already. But if, he added, some "anxious minds" thought otherwise, then title to relief property ought to be vested in the legations of the three neutral patron-governments: the United States, Holland, and Spain.

No, replied Hoover; the Commission for Relief in Belgium (not the legations) had long since been designated as the official importer. Furthermore, both the British and American governments insisted upon this arrangement. The CRB, said Hoover, was the legal owner of imported goods. Therefore, every mill, warehouse, soup kitchen, and relief document (including ration cards) should be marked with the name of the CRB as well as that of the CN.

Very well, said Francqui, we shall affix inscriptions to our relief buildings *in German* declaring that the contents therein belong to the CRB! In this way German soldiers will be warned not to touch them. (In this way, too, the fact of CRB ownership would be concealed from all Belgians who did not read German.) Similarly, said Francqui, we will put a notation of CRB ownership on accounting books and related documents.

But why, the Belgian financier wondered, should we put the commission's name on ration cards? Even Lord Grey did not demand that. Grey had only requested that the CRB guarantee the imports up to the moment of distribution to the consumer. Since the CRB's ownership of the food ceased at that point, it was "useless" to print a statement of ownership on the cards themselves. Hoover, however, saw it differently. The CRB's and CN's names *should* be carried on the cards, he claimed, because the cards were a "contract with the owner of the food."[150]

And there it was. To such a level had the quarrel now degenerated. Emile Francqui did not want the name of the CRB printed on Belgian ration cards; Herbert Hoover did. Though each man clothed his desires in the language of legality, it was obvious that each coveted recognition for his organization's accomplishments inside Belgium. There seemed but one difference between them: Hoover was willing to share it; Francqui apparently was not.

Credit—"that detestable thing called credit!" Brand Whitlock lamented in his diary on November 7. Vanity, jealousy, and the desire for credit, he said, were destroying the relief of Belgium.[151] As if Francqui were not enough of a burden, the Marquis de Villalobar (said Whitlock) was "toiling like [a] patient spider" to "exalt himself" while pretending to be the American diplomat's friend.[152] How Whitlock longed "to get away from it all"—away from "this hell . . . now made diabolic by the machinations of enemies in the livery of friends."[153] Francqui, Janssen, and Villalobar "have taken the heart out of me," he confessed, "and I can no longer work with any pride or enthusiasm."[154] It was the way a weary Hoover felt when he yearned to go back to his lead mines.

At the outset of his visit, Hoover had hoped to assemble "the important men in Belgium," lay the issue before them, and instigate a revolt from within the Comité National against what Whitlock called "Francqui's dictatorship."[155] The CRB chairman's plan, however, soon collapsed. Few Belgians would stand up publicly against the brilliant and domineering banker. As Green observed, Francqui *was* the Comité National, and his intimidated associates knew it. "Some of them hate him, most of them fear him, and all of them agree that he is the one man who can hold the National Committee together, and keep Catholics and Liberals and Socialists from scratching each other's eyes out."[156]

So it was Francqui, then, with whom Hoover was obliged to deal. For more than a week in November he did so—talking, arguing, corresponding, and struggling to come to terms. To Hoover such negotiations were almost a form of physical combat. Unable to sleep for two consecutive nights, he emerged from one grueling session looking (in Whitlock's words) "worn and haggard."[157] It was exasperating. "I have tried honestly and earnestly to arrive at a solution which forfends a humiliation of America in this organism," he exclaimed to Whitlock at one point, "and every word written and spoken [has been] in a tender feeling to the Belgian people and their representatives and their real interests."[158] Francqui, no doubt, thought differently. And the verbal duel went on.

At the same time that he was seeking a modus vivendi with Francqui, the CRB chairman's supporters were keeping the pressure on in London. The leader of the Comité National evidently believed that the Allies' newly augmented subsidy would free him from dependence on the CRB for charitable funds and would liberate him at last from these pushy and intrusive Americans. The British, however, had other ideas. On November 7 Lord Grey announced that the increased Allied subvention was *conditional*. Profits from food sales inside Belgium, he stipulated, could only be distributed to agencies that the *CRB* determined to be protected from German interference. These German guarantees, he said, must be given to the CRB and "not merely" to the Comité National. From now on the commission must share in the "management and control" of every single domestic Belgian organization receiving money from relief revenues.[159] Once again, thanks to the British, the commission's sphere of influence was expanding.

Meanwhile Hoover was being forced to shore up a weak point in his armor: the suspicious origin of Lord Grey's letter of October 20. The CRB chairman denied to Francqui that he had ghostwritten this letter or even inspired it.[160] Evidently his denials were not persuasive, for on November 10 he reported to Whitlock that "reckless statements" were circulating in Brussels about the letter's origins—statements that evidently placed the responsibility for that hardline communication squarely on Hoover's shoulders.

Anxious to dispel these embarrassing rumors, the CRB's chief executive wrote Whitlock a three-page letter offering his version of the circumstances leading up to Grey's message. According to Hoover, Whitlock had told him in September that the best solution to the growing tension with the Comité National would be for Whitlock to ask the Allies through Ambassador Page for a precise definition of the commission's role inside Belgium. According to Hoover, Whitlock had promised to make this request immediately in writing to Page. A few weeks later, however, when the crisis with Francqui had worsened, Hoover had approached Page, only to find that no such letter from Whitlock had arrived. Because (said Hoover) there had been a delay in mail deliveries from Brussels, Page had cabled Whitlock saying that he knew of Whitlock's wishes. Page had then added that unless he heard to the contrary he would contact the Allied governments as Whitlock desired. No message was forthcoming from Whitlock. In the meantime, according to Hoover, Vernon Kellogg had asked Whitlock directly whether he had written yet to Page. No, Whitlock had replied, but I will cable to him at once. At this point Page's cable had arrived, announcing that he would act unless Whitlock stopped him. Hearing nothing from Brussels, Page had then gone to the British government, and Foreign Secretary Grey had acted.[161]

Hoover thus placed responsibility for the chain of events leading to Grey's letter solely on Whitlock and absolved himself of any catalytic role whatever. He also appeared to explain why, if Whitlock had really wanted Grey to intervene, there was no document to that effect bearing his signature. It is not known what Whitlock thought of Hoover's explanation. Certainly it directly contradicted the diplomat's denial, in his diary, that he had ever solicited such a communication from Page. All Whitlock had done (so he wrote) was to suggest to Hoover in September that *if* matters reached a crisis he (Whitlock) could *then* ask the British to intercede. Whitlock's diary said nothing about promising to contact Page immediately.[162]

What, then, had happened? Had Hoover misunderstood Whitlock in September? Or had the American minister to Brussels made the promise and then, in his timorous manner, reneged? Or had Hoover, without authority, pushed ahead, portraying his desire for a showdown as Whitlock's own, only to deny responsibility for this action now? Certainly there had been similar episodes in Hoover's past of aggressive, even impulsive behavior followed by elaborate efforts at self-justification.[163] Had he, as so often in the last two years, resorted to the fait accompli? In all likelihood the answer was affirmative.

Despite his denials to Francqui, then, it is very probable that the CRB chairman had indeed instigated Lord Grey's letter. Under the circumstances, of course, he could scarcely admit that he had done so.

By November 10 it appeared that Hoover and Francqui had narrowed if not entirely resolved their differences. Willing to compromise if he could, Hoover agreed to separate supervision of German guarantees from oversight of food distribution—if this change applied only to Brussels and if the provincial inspection/control bureaus were left unchanged. Francqui, for his part, appeared to accept Hoover's views on the handling of specially earmarked charitable donations and promised to label all relief goods as CRB property. The Belgian leader, however, refused to permit a commission representative to be formally attached to the CN's department of *secours*. On this and certain other issues Hoover "agreed to disagree."[164]

For a brief moment it seemed that the two titans had reached, in Brand Whitlock's words, a "truce."[165] But then, on November 11, the tenuous compromise was shattered. In a long letter to Hoover, Francqui announced his delight that the two men were again "in perfect agreement." Inasmuch as this was so, he declared, Lord Grey's letter of October 20 could now be discarded. Its proposals were unworkable, it did not comprehend the current situation inside Belgium, it did not understand the history of the relief, it contained "flagrant inaccuracies." Even worse, Francqui now claimed that Hoover knew this and concurred with him. You yourself (he wrote Hoover) understood even before Grey's letter arrived that the Foreign Office's ideas were infeasible. "I admit indeed," Francqui added, "that far from defending the propositions of the Foreign Office, you have not hesitated to declare to us that they seemed to you impracticable."

Having thus disposed of Lord Grey's obnoxious letter, Francqui now refused point-blank to recognize that relief supplies and funds were CRB property. There were "irrefutable reasons" for rejecting this British demand, he asserted—reasons which "we have all" (meaning Hoover, too) "unanimously recognized." Fundamentally those reasons were political: the Comité National had put its name on buildings all over the country as a way of sustaining national sentiment and morale. Francqui now agreed (although he said it was unnecessary) to insert "Commission for Relief in Belgium" on certain relief documents and on posters wherever imported food was found. But, he added firmly, the Comité National's name would also be maintained "everywhere" in order to preserve its governing principles and to sustain the feeling of "national unity" that it had engendered at such great cost.

Francqui again asserted that Belgium no longer needed outside charity or "propaganda." Nevertheless, he asked Hoover to retain his worldwide net-work of volunteer committees. Why? Because, said Francqui, as "you have pointed out to us," such committees helped to keep the British government in line:

. . . as you have told us, it is thanks to the well-conducted press campaigns which you can organise in America by means of these committees that you succeed in having exercised by American public opinion upon the British Government a pressure which prevents our common work from being interfered with.

Francqui expressed confidence that Hoover would now be able to make the British Foreign Office understand its "error" and persuade it to "admit" that the new Francqui–Hoover arrangement was the only feasible one. After all, he said, this solution was "based on practical common sense," it answered "a political necessity," and, "above all," it was "in reality" Hoover's idea. In Hoover's effort to mollify the British, Francqui added grandly, "you will find the greatest support with the Belgian Government."

Francqui closed in tones of unctuous condescension:

. . . I beg you, whenever you foresee that some fact is likely to create a disagreement of principle between us, to come and see me immediately and not again wait five days as has been the case this time. In the interval, indiscretions are committed, rumours are circulated and there is an accumulation of bad temper. Come and speak to me quite openly, and without that somewhat aggressive air which I have never seen in you before, as to one who has but one desire: to help you overcome all difficulties. You have seen that in spite of these many occasions for friction, my goodwill has been complete, and that it has been efficacious seeing that we have come to an agreement.[166]

Francqui soon told Brand Whitlock that his letter to Hoover had been "an act of friendship."[167] If this was friendship, Hoover needed no enemies. Francqui's patronizing tone was no doubt offensive enough. Far more embarrassing—and dangerous—was his defiant criticism of the British government and his claim that Hoover privately agreed with him. If Hoover should now show this letter to the Foreign Office, he might have a difficult time explaining himself—as the wily Francqui surely knew. To Whitlock the Belgian's letter was "an old trick in special pleading": ascribing to Hoover admissions that he had never made.[168] To Hoover himself it undoubtedly looked like a sly and tawdry attempt to drive a wedge between himself and his British sponsors.

But the clever Belgium had been clever once too often. Instead of graciously terminating the dispute, he had only aggravated and prolonged it. Shortly after receiving Francqui's communication of November 11, Hoover left Brussels in fury—vowing, he told Whitlock, to "transfer the whole fight to London" and "lay a train of powder to blow up Francqui."[169]

Before doing so, the chairman of the CRB addressed one final letter to his Belgian counterpart—a letter designed, in part, to neutralize Francqui's attempt at "paper history."[170] Hoover asserted that Francqui had "misunderstood" his remarks about Lord Grey's letter of October 20. Yes, said Hoover, I did say that Lord Grey's terms were impracticable, "but with the context that the terms were impracticable without the co-operation of the Belgians, and that with this co-operation you and I could settle an administration so as to obtain the real objective of the British Government." Hoover also claimed that Francqui had misquoted him about the usefulness of CRB propaganda as pressure on the British government. "That the British Government needs pressure to induce it to kindness to the Belgian people," said Hoover, "is a proposition so preposterous as to disprove itself. What I did tell you was of the importance of the propaganda in maintaining the British public opinion in supporting the Government and in the weight of the neutral opinion upon the Governments who hold doors to Belgium." To Francqui, no doubt, such a distinction seemed sophistical. But Hoover's intended audience, at this point, was less Francqui than Lord Grey.

In blunt prose the American humanitarian recapitulated the issue between himself and Francqui:

> I tried to assure you time and again that there was no interest or intent in either ourselves or the Foreign Office trying to dominate our Belgian colleagues, but on the other hand, that what we wanted was through collaboration to carry out the basic principles laid down by the British Government: i.e., neutral protection of the relief and the people through neutral ownership and through the right of neutral participation in administration, to maintain an entire neutral color. This is the entire issue. It is not a question between you and me; it is a question between the Belgians and the British Government. I deny absolutely being the inspiration of the above theory of the relief. It is the British Government's theory, and the American Government's theory and it has existed since the first imports were permitted into Belgium, and it has been very widely departed from during the past few months.

Hoover denied, too, that he had "any personal preferences in the matter." Unfortunately, "one great difficulty" in the past three weeks had been that Francqui had construed his suggestions "as the imposition of my own personality, representing some strange personal interest or intrigue of mine rather than the acceptance of such proposals, on the plane of joint interest to the Belgian people." Hoover insisted that he sought no "return or compensation" for performing what he considered "a duty in justice and not in charity" to the Belgian people. Any such pecuniary gain, he said, would lower the "self-esteem" of himself and his colleagues.

Hoover warned Francqui that he was making a fundamental mistake in depriving himself of the CRB's "neutral ramifying support." The morale of the Belgian people, he said, was more stimulated by evidence of external support than by encouragement of pride in their internal self-help activities. He warned, too, that "the incidents of the last few months" could only disturb the British government and undermine Allied patronage. All that was needed to satisfy the British and the commission alike, he said, was "a frank joint administration" such as had been in existence in various provinces of Belgium until recently.

At any rate, the time for argument was over. ". . . I propose to leave the entire matter to others to settle," he informed Francqui. Let the British and Belgian governments, along with the American and Spanish patron-ambassadors in London, determine "the real principles underlying this organisation."[171]

Weary and depressed, Hoover returned to London on November 16.[172] Two maddening, grueling weeks had elapsed, and nothing had changed. In Brussels Green reported that the central office of the Department of Inspection and Control was "completely demoralized."[173] Hoover's own mood seemed to match. After spending the evening with him on the sixteenth, Hugh Gibson wondered "how long human endurance can stand up under the strain that man has been subjected to all these months."[174]

American flour en route to Belgium.

A CRB ship bound for Belgium.

Commission for Relief in Belgium headquarters in Brussels.

A CRB warehouse in Belgium.

Central clothing supply station in Brussels.

Preparing food for the relief stations.

Waiting for one's daily food in Belgium.

Food for the Belgian children.

Food in a Belgian classroom.

Belgian gratitude for the CRB's work.

Belgian school children thank America.

War bread, 1915.

The Hoover family, January 1917 (left to right; Allan Hoover, Herbert Hoover, Lou Henry Hoover, Herbert Hoover, Jr.).

10

Victory at Last

I

B Y now the rift between the CRB and the Comité National had developed into a diplomatic entanglement of ominous dimensions. So far no word of the affair had leaked to the unsuspecting public. But if it did, the effect could be incalculable. The danger was growing that the international relief apparatus which had kept more than 9,000,000 people alive would blow apart from dissension at the top.

Hoover was discouraged when he reached London, but as Hugh Gibson noted, the CRB chairman was not a quitter; he "never says DIE."[1] The very next day he began to marshal his forces for a showdown.[2] As always, his principal ally was Walter Hines Page. In a ten-page letter to Lord Grey on November 20—a letter probably drafted, at least partly, by Hoover himself—the ambassador declared that the CRB's effectiveness and "prestige" in the eyes of both the German government and world opinion depended on its maintaining an active and independent presence inside Belgium. The Comité National's deliberate minimizing of the commission's role in administration, he asserted, was impairing its execution of its duties. The "root of the whole difficulty," he contended, was the CN's refusal to "welcome the frank and loyal cooperation" of the CRB in the supervision of relief inside Belgium. Page claimed that Francqui was deliberately taking the CN into "the realm of political activity." *This*, he said, was the reason it was trying to "submerge and minimize" the Americans' participation. The ambassador warned that he could not "countenance" this improper mingling of politics and philan-thropy.[3]

In a separate dispatch to the State Department Page was less diplomatic. Unless "radical change" occurred, he declared, he would advise Hoover to withdraw all Americans from the relief of Belgium. They should not con-tinue "in a situation which is not compatible with a dignified American par-ticipation and the carrying out of guarantees for whose performance they stand responsible to all of the belligerent governments and to the charitable world in general."[4]

While Page was raising the prospect of terminating the CRB unless Hoo-ver's terms were met, Hoover himself was lining up support in other direc-tions. On November 20 he informed his representative in Paris that he had now "recommended" to the Belgian government-in-exile that it "take over" the relief of the Belgian people itself and leave the care of northern France to the CRB (provided that the French government thereupon subsidized the commission directly). The situation inside Belgium was "redolent with poli-tics and . . . war-vanity," he told his French associate. Francqui "absolutely repudiates any obligation" to the British government.[5]

Hoover's proposal to the Belgians was less a "recommendation" than an ultimatum. He was proposing to the government-in-exile (he told some asso-ciates) that unless it accepted his terms it should "take over the Belgian side and release us from all connection therewith."[6] As the Belgians pondered their next move, so, too, did the French. In early December Hoover received word from Paris that the government there entirely supported the CRB and would adhere to the British position in the controversy. It would also accept a "separation of funds" if necessary. The French had only one caveat: they wished not to upset Belgian "susceptibilities" unduly.[7]

Hoover had little interest, however, in making concessions to Belgian pride. Gratified by the news from Paris, he nevertheless pressed hard for an imme-diate separation of his Belgian victualing from that in northern France, and for the funneling of French subsidies to the latter through sources other than the Belgian government-in-exile.[8] Such a plan of action, of course, would salvage a role for his commission should it be obliged to withdraw from Bel-gian territory. It would also tend to isolate the exiled government from its principal allies—precisely the specter that Hoover desired to invoke. No doubt he was gambling that the little nation's government would not dare to "go it alone."

Meanwhile he moved to solidify his own ranks. On November 20 he noti-fied his colleagues in New York of the crisis. The "root of the whole trouble," he asserted, was the Comité National's departure from "its original purpose of pure philanthropy into realms of ward politics," and its support in this from the exiled Belgian government. If the CRB is to continue to serve the Belgian people, he declared, it must do so "upon terms which protect the destitute and the dignity of the Americans as a whole."[9] Unfortunately, he

told the head of his New York office, there was now a "concerted programme" afoot in Belgium—a program abetted by its own government—to
"reduce" the CRB to "mere tools" in order to claim that the relief was a *native*
achievement and "American intervention" a mere "cloak" for Belgian political operations. If this scheme was unchecked, said Hoover, it would "totally
demoralise" aid to the destitute and "expose us to the severest criticism of all
time." The Comité National was inefficient, he charged; the "unceasing
intervention" of the CRB was a "complete necessity." Indeed, his commission had responsibilities to the American people and the world which it could
not "hand over to the Comité National." Hoover believed that his colleagues
would "unite with me" in this position.[10]

The CRB chairman had no need to worry. His New York office at once
concurred that the situation was intolerable and in need of immediate rem-
edy.[11] In the meantime Hoover kept up the drumfire in London and Brussels. On November 24 he sent Lord Percy a massive dossier of recent
correspondence between Vernon Kellogg and Francqui concerning the beleaguered Department of Inspection and Control. Hoover pointed out that as a
result of "recent changes" the control apparatus had reverted to the unsatisfactory condition of late 1915—news certain to disconcert the British.[12] Three
days later he sent some other materials to Brand Whitlock and asked for his
support. Pointing out that the French government was "entirely and absolutely with us in this matter," Hoover declared that success would come "if
all of us stand together on fundamental ideals in this work and the respect
which they must command." It was a not too subtle bid for the fastidious
Whitlock to line up unequivocally in Hoover's corner.[13]

Throughout these anxious days Hoover frequently denied that his differences with Francqui involved any element of "personal friction."[14] To an
outside observer, it might have appeared otherwise, and certain Belgians, in
fact, were assiduously cultivating just that impression: that the current troubles stemmed from Hoover's personal attitude.[15] If such a perception of the
controversy took hold, a simple solution might become attractive to the various governments: namely, Hoover's resignation and replacement by a more
congenial personality. The CRB chairman had no intention, however, of
becoming a solitary sacrificial lamb. He informed the Belgians that if he retired
from the relief, the entire commission would follow him.[16] Some days later,
no doubt with his knowledge, his number two man in London notified the
CRB's New York office that every word and deed of Hoover's expressed the
"unanimous judgment of [the] entire Commission." Hoover was acting, he
said, not as an individual but as the representative of every single member of
the CRB.[17]

As usual, Hoover did not stop there. In late November one of his trusted
publicity aides, George Barr Baker, was in London. On November 30, almost
certainly at Hoover's instigation, Baker wrote Ambassador Page a letter of
record extolling the CRB and decrying the "petty, but destructive, annoy-

ances" emanating from two unnamed Belgians—evidently Francqui and the
Belgian government's London liaison to the CRB, Chevalier Edmond Carton
de Wiart. Baker accused the Belgians of erroneously regarding the leaders of
the commission as "private individuals" instead of accepting it as "a body,
one and indivisible," organized to "express" American ideals to the Belgians.
If the two Belgian malefactors should "succeed in wearing down Mr. Hoover
to a point where he is obliged to quit," Baker warned, "the entire body will
go with him. . . ." The resulting "disruption of the machinery, with its
attendant scandal, would kill the Belgian cause in the United States beyond
the possibility of resurrection."[18]

While Hoover was bolstering his position in Paris, London, and New York,
his Belgian critics were also busy. Late in October his old antagonist van de
Vyvere complained to the British about Hoover's methods and objectives.
Hoover did not sufficiently consult with the Le Havre-based government,
the finance minister charged, nor did he render a full account for the Belgian
money advanced to him. Furthermore, he ignored the Belgian government's
political objectives in the relief work. Van de Vyvere's protest evoked a strong
rejoinder from the Foreign Office. The British denied that either they or
Hoover sought to keep the exiled government "in the dark" or that they and
Hoover had developed policies independently of Le Havre. The Foreign Office
also denied that Hoover disagreed with Belgian political goals or that he wished
to pursue other objectives with his grants to Belgian charities. The relief
project must be under neutral control, said the British, in order that Belgian
political aims might be attained without endangering the relief workers.[19]

The Belgians did not confine their anger to diplomatic channels. In mid-
November Chevalier Carton de Wiart asked the CRB's New York advisory
committee for assistance in protesting the Germans' campaign of deportations. In reply Alexander Hemphill of the New York committee promised
to help but added that he deplored the current "unsatisfactory attitude" of
the Comité National and Belgian government toward the commission.
Hemphill demanded that the situation be immediately "clarified."[20]

Hemphill's cable incensed Carton de Wiart. The Belgian government, he
charged, had been "unjustly incriminated." Moreover, the New York committee had unfairly taken sides in the controversy without even hearing the
Comité National's viewpoint. He called upon Hemphill to defer any judg-
ments until the Belgians inside Belgium had had an opportunity to make
their case. "I know," said Carton, that "they think they have . . . serious
reasons for complaining" about the commission. He noted, too, that "personal questions may have something to do with both sides."[21]

Hoover was not convinced by the chevalier's show of anger. It was mere
pretense, he declared—"an attempt to fasten a personal quarrel on myself,
which is all part of the general programme initiated by Francqui. . . ."[22] To
keep Carton de Wiart from creating a diplomatic "incident," Hoover had
Hemphill retract his initial reference to the Belgian government.[23] But when

Carton then told Hemphill that the CN had serious grievances against the CRB, Hoover reacted with vigor. He demanded that Carton produce the evidence for his claim and submit it to Ambassador Page for review.[24] He asked Page to make the same demand of the Belgian ambassador (and wrote a draft of what he thought Page should say).[25] Hoover was particularly indignant at what he construed as an attempt to drive a wedge between himself and his American backers, thereby perhaps laying the groundwork for his ouster (although he himself had attempted a similar maneuver against Francqui).[26] Carton's action, he asserted angrily, was "an entire misjudgment of the American character and of American ideals." It was "only another phase in the history of some men, all of which will in time be given to the world."[27]

Once again, he did not need to worry. The commission's New York committee bluntly informed Carton de Wiart that the CRB's position in America was "impregnable" and that if the Comité National's "belligerent attitude" became known it would create "a deplorable revulsion of sympathy." Hoover, said Hemphill, "has our complete confidence and will be supported to the end."[28]

With relations between Hoover and the Comité National deteriorating and the fate of the revictualing uncertain, Lord Eustace Percy of the British Foreign Office now took an extraordinary step. On the night of November 17, without the knowledge of his own government, he stopped at the American embassy in London. There he delivered a personal message for transmittal to Francqui. Percy told the Belgian magnate-turned-philanthropist that the war was about to enter a terrible and more desperate phase. If Belgium was to survive as a nation and not a "desert," its only chance lay in the power of American public opinion to restrain the Germans. Percy therefore begged Francqui to avoid all friction with Americans in Belgium in the critical coming weeks, lest the weapon of American public opinion be lost.[29]

A few days later Percy addressed a similar private appeal to Hoover. The young British diplomat pledged on his honor that his government would not ask the American CRB men to continue except on terms compatible with "your dignity as Americans and your sense of responsibility as the originators and guarantors of the work." Nevertheless, said Percy, "you have got to face . . . the fact that your position, which has been anomalous from the beginning, must, in a measure, become more and more anomalous as time goes on." No longer was Belgium in chaos, as it had been when Hoover began. The very fact that the Belgian people now claimed "independent status" and that the Belgium government showed "independent self-consciousness" constituted "the most striking possible testimony" to Hoover's success. Percy declared that neither his government nor the commission could continue "carrying things with a high hand as we have, in a sense, done for the last two years." Instead, they must "negotiate, compromise," and tolerate behavior that might seem ungrateful and absurd.

Then, in a remarkable passage, Percy appealed to Hoover's private sympathy for the Allies and pleaded with him not to let his affronted dignity get in the way of transcendent political considerations:

> If, by any action of yours, you make it more difficult at this eleventh hour for America to act a part in preventing the destruction which threatens to follow upon the growth of German despair, you will lessen, instead of save, the dignity of America. Every sign points to a new campaign of frightfulness on the part of Germany; a campaign which is going to bring upon Belgium sufferings all the more bitter and overwhelming because they come at the very moment of reviving hope; and I ask you all with confidence to make greater sacrifices than ever in order that you may not be drawn into the greatest sacrifice of all, namely the sacrifice of your position as the advance guard and symbol of the sense of responsibility of the American people towards Europe.

Percy acknowledged that the British government was responsible for many of the "sacrifices" and even "indignities" that Hoover had had to bear—an evident reference to the Admiralty's attempt to smear Hoover as pro-German early in 1916, and to the consequent investigation of Hoover by Justice Rowlatt. But the British diplomat pledged to put that episode and indeed "the whole history of America's share in saving Belgium" in a "true light before the world" at the end of the war.[30]

Hoover was moved by Lord Percy's earnest plea—moved but not much swayed. The CRB chairman agreed that his commission was "a light, daily illuminating America's obligations to Europe"—"a signal which should be kept burning not only for its incidence to-day but to light the way to the infinitely greater service which the United States must yet give." But if the CRB were to attain its ideals, it must, he insisted, have "respect" inside Belgium. Instead, the commission today was partially "paralyzed" thanks to the hostility of "the Comité National group in Brussels." If the CRB is to contribute to "the greater purposes which you and I have so often discussed," Hoover told Percy, it must have "a dignified participation in administration" *in Belgium*, especially in the care of the destitute. Otherwise it would be a "living lie" to the American people. Reviewing his previous offers to withdraw, Hoover once more proposed to do so and to confine his operations to northern France. Let the Belgian government, he said, take care of its own.[31]

Meanwhile, in Brussels, an unexpected turn of events was occurring. On November 23 Francqui responded to Percy's appeal with an astonishing announcement: he had just reached an understanding with Hoover's new bureau chief in Brussels, Warren Gregory—an agreement that completely fulfilled the requirements of the British government. (Francqui gave no details.)[32] Brand Whitlock was elated. Relations between the CN and CRB were now "perfectly satisfactory," he informed Walter Hines Page a few days later; Francqui had risen "generously and nobly to the occasion."[33] He and Gregory were "getting on famously now";[34] Lord Percy's "noble stroke" had "cut the gordian knot."[35]

Hoover, in London, was decidedly skeptical of this reported volte-face. If true, of course, it could imperil his plan to subdue Francqui or withdraw from Belgium entirely. But was it true? Had Francqui really and suddenly reformed? Or was this just another feint in their neverending duel? Hoover probably remembered the beguiling bonhomie that Francqui had at first showered on Joseph C. Green—until Green had refused to bend to his wishes. Was the crafty Belgian using the same technique with Gregory? Had the credulous Whitlock been duped yet again? When Hoover learned of Carton de Wiart's seeming attempt to undercut him in New York, he had his answer. Wiart's action, observed Hoover drily to Whitlock in a letter, "offers a curious comment on your recent love feasts in Belgium."[36]

If Francqui for the moment seemed to be retreating from confrontation, so, too, was his government-in-exile. On November 25 Hoover informed his New York colleagues that the latest word from Le Havre was encouraging and that his anxieties were "much relieved." He did not elaborate.[37] A few days later the Belgian foreign minister, Baron Beyens, addressed a long letter to the British ambassador. The Belgian proposed that the two governments intervene in the dispute and reconcile the two "remarkable personalities" at the head of the relief. Both the CN and the CRB, he said, should coexist and collaborate, with neither body dominant over the other. Beyens outlined a formula for an appropriate division of powers (including a new CRB-run "Bureau of Control") and suggested that the two committees settle their differences at a conference in Le Havre.[38]

In early December Beyens's letter reached London, where Lord Percy furnished a copy to Hoover. The CRB chairman was appalled by what he considered its vagueness and ignorance of the complexities of his work. Once more Percy attempted to pacify his American friend:

> . . . I wish you could realise the nature of Foreign Offices in general. If you are expecting any diplomat or F.O., English or Foreign, to have any grasp of the details of an organisation [or] any ability to lay down detailed rules for its conduct, you will be very much disappointed. The note [by Beyens] I sent you was like any other diplomatic document—a mere indication of an attitude. That is [as] far as diplomacy usually gets. I never expected anything else from the Belgian Government. The memorandum of agreement in which what we want has got to be summed up and laid down permanently by the Allied Governments [has] got to be drawn up here and rammed down the throats of our respective governments by our humble selves. They will swallow it all right when it gets down on paper. Beyens' note is satisfactory because it indicates that the Belgians are quite receptive.
>
> So let me have the memorandum, but for goodness' sake don't worry

yourself into a fever about the failure of Governments to understand anything about the organisation which you have built up during two years in
the sweat of your brow. They never will understand it and they will thank
you and gabble their gratitude in nice phrases and in complete ignorance
of what they are talking about. We have got to be content if there are a
dozen *understanding* grunts among all the hundred of swine before whom
we cast our life's pearls.[39]

If Hoover was appeased by Percy's humor, there was no sign of it in his
correspondence. The harried wartime bureaucracies of the Allied governments might have other things on their minds than Belgian relief, but Hoover
had only one. And he wanted more than a few "grunts" from "swine." On
December 6 Percy requested that he draw up a statement about the relief
apparatus for use by the British ambassador to Belgium. Clearly high-level
diplomacy was in full swing, and Percy suggested that it would be helpful
under the circumstances if Hoover omitted all references to "present controversies."[40] Instead the CRB's executive promptly delivered a blistering memorandum warning that unless the relief remained a neutral effort it would be
"dissolved by its own protecting Governments." The Commission for Relief
in Belgium, he said, must be "absolutely the sole and independent administrator" of all relief tasks *outside* the occupied territories, and it must have
"equal and joint" responsibility for administration *inside* the occupied territories. Hoover objected strenuously to Beyens's proposed new Department
of Control, a proposal that said nothing about supervising "equitable distribution" and confined the CRB to policing the German guarantees. This was
just a repetition of Francqui's scheme to reduce the functions of the present
control bureau, Hoover, charged, and it was utterly unacceptable. "No neutral gentleman," he asserted, "would be content to remain in Belgium twenty-
four hours if his occupation were confined to spying on the Germans." If
that were all the CRB was to become, the organization would "crumble within
a month."

Hoover appeared to forget that for the first year or more of its existence
the CRB in substantial measure had had precisely such a raison d'être: to
oversee and enforce the German guarantees. It was only in 1916 that it had
undertaken systematic scrutiny of "equitable distribution," including the
assignment of subsidies to private Belgian charitable agencies. It was this
augmented role that Hoover was determined not to lose. He told Percy that
the men of the CRB were volunteers whose "sole objective" was "the care of
the destitute" of Belgium. If these men, who had sacrificed "positions of
importance," should now lose their administrative role in providing such care,
their "inspiration" would flag, their "esprit de corps" would suffer, and the
commission would collapse within thirty days.[41]

It is not known whether Hoover really believed what he was saying. The
Yankee executive, in any case, was not known for understated discourse, and

when it came to doing battle he usually preferred blunt combativeness to what he once called the "innocent and mild manners" of "these smooth diplomatic folk."[42] As the days of December passed, his desire for total victory did not lessen. When, around December 12, he heard that Francqui was going to visit London, he was delighted. Francqui, he predicted, would "receive a series of educational lectures along a line which I think will astonish him."[43] If Francqui has really changed his tune, Hoover informed Whitlock, he will sign "the contract which has been prepared here at the Foreign Office." Otherwise, "we shall retire from the Relief, as I have neither the nervous energy nor the patience to expend, nor any desire to go on living a lie to the world over this business. . . ." "I am either going to put the C.R.B. into the position that the world considers it does maintain vis-à-vis the organisation in Belgium, or I am going to ask the President to withdraw the whole bag of tricks. . . ."[44]

By now Whitlock was thoroughly sick of the endless disputation between Hoover and Francqui. When a message from the CRB chairman reached him on December 20, the weary American minister took note in his diary:

> A letter from Hoover, in the usual lugubrious strain. He is more hostile to Francqui than ever; has prepared, he writes, an educational campaign for him on his arrival, vows he will no longer "live a lie to the world," by which he means that he will not be satisfied unless the CRB are as much recognized by Francqui as they are recognized outside. . . . As to that quarrel between Francqui and Hoover—I wash my hands of it.[45]

Whitlock's attitude would only have angered Hoover, had he known about it. But by this point—and, indeed, well before—Whitlock was largely irrelevant; the decisive battlefield was not Brussels but London. Even as Hoover threatened for nearly the dozenth time in two years to withdraw unless he got his way, events in London were moving in his direction. On December 12 he informed a friend that the CRB, the British Foreign Office, and the American and Spanish ambassadors to Great Britain had settled upon a "contract" between the Allied governments and his commission. This document had gone to the Belgian government-in-exile, which was now waiting for Francqui's response. Hoover seemed confident of success. The Allied governments, he said, "insist absolutely that the Relief comes to an end unless we continue and unless we are placed in a position to exert a sufficiency of control to assure our main objectives."[46]

Whatever happened now, Hoover was determined not to be "relegated" to a "mere facade behind which any course can be taken, good or bad, without our approval."[47] He had seen too much Belgian "intrigue" to permit that. The Comité National, he told a colleague, "by virtue of elbowing everybody out," had "fallen solely into the control of the old corrupt political financial group created by Leopold II"—the notorious "old Congo group" that had helped the Belgian monarch create a personal fiefdom in central Africa a quarter of a century before. All our difficulties, said Hoover, have emanated from three sources: the "personal ambition of this group of men," the anti-German "political design" of the government-in-exile, and, above all, "the desire to build a Tammany for post-war purposes and to use its power in the meantime to force the alignments to this end."

> So long as all of these things did not affect the daily work in Belgium we were prepared to ignore them, no matter what we might think of them personally, but when it comes to the issue that a certain committee in Belgium in charge of children is, owing to their political complexion, unable to secure sufficient support and are compelled to turn hundreds of children away from their doors daily, this got to a point where we could not stand it.[48]

Alarmed at the danger such practices posed to his reputation, Hoover made a sweeping new request of Lord Percy. If at the end of the war it should be disclosed or alleged that the commission had been a cover for Belgian political activities, its chairman could very properly be criticized. Hoover therefore asked that the new "contract" make "perfectly clear" that the CRB was "necessarily independent of all belligerent control, either governmental or by belligerent subjects."[49]

At this point another issue opened up which gave Hoover an opportunity to put additional pressure on the Belgians. In early November Francqui had asserted that his country no longer needed foreign charitable donations and that his government could now supply all necessary funds for the destitute. If true, it could undercut one of the CRB's rationales for staying inside Belgium. Hoover was dubious of Francqui's claim and asked Vernon Kellogg to evaluate it. Kellogg was also skeptical; every indication was that Belgium needed more charity, not less. In a letter to Hoover in late November, he declared that it was up to the CRB to determine "in common honesty" whether Francqui's judgment was correct.

This intimation that Francqui could not be trusted was extraordinary enough. But Kellogg, in all probability with Hoover's approval, went even further. Even if there were no need for additional outside financial support— even if the Belgians could now pay all their bills—the CRB, he said, must *still* remain in Belgium. For so long as the commission was perceived by the world to be "the sole channel of charity" into that country, "it must bear a great measure of the responsibility for the adequate care of the destitute." If the CRB were now to be reduced to "a simple importing agency" and mere "canal" to the Comité National, the American-led organization "would lose all stimulus for its existence."[50] Clearly it was not about to curb its activities abroad on the suspect pronouncements of Francqui. It was one more indication of how badly Hoover wished to continue the work that had made him an international hero.

Then, in early December, Francqui unexpectedly played into his hands. In a memorandum from Brussels the Belgian accepted with gratitude a newly inaugurated program of monthly contributions from the British National Committee for Relief in Belgium. The funds were specifically designated for Belgian children's charities. Francqui, however, rejected the British plan to send these sums to the Belgian agencies directly. Such a scheme, he said, would fragment the relief effort, create "discord," result in attacks on the CN's "authority," and make it "impossible to get instructions carried out." Administrative "cohesion" and "unity" would be lost. He therefore requested that all such money be funneled through the CRB to the Comité National, which would allocate it through its Children's Section.[51]

Francqui's renewed insistence on centralizing charitable disbursements in his hands could not conceal what Hoover instantly noticed: the head of the Comité National had willingly accepted foreign charity and had thereby tacitly admitted that he was not self-sufficient after all. Seeing his opening, Hoover speedily responded. The question of charity "needs further planing out," he informed Francqui. Inasmuch as Francqui had declared that his exiled government would provide, Hoover notified him that the CRB was no longer "allocating any further monies to charitable purposes in Belgium. . . ." We have "no right" to do so, he said, unless such an expenditure was "an absolute and urgent necessity."[52]

Hoover now used the charity weapon to force the Belgian government into submission. On December 18 he addressed a letter to the Belgian ambassador to Great Britain, Paul Hymans. Pointing to the conflicting signals that he had received from Hymans's government and from Francqui, Hoover requested an unequivocal answer to the question: was the Belgian government now able "to do away with the solicitation of public charity" in the outside world, or was it not? If the country did not require such funds, it would be "dishonest" of the CRB to appeal for them. Hoover then dropped a bombshell:

> . . . I think you will agree with me [he told Hymans] that we should not expend any moneys which we are now receiving until this matter is cleared up, lest we should all come in for severe and just criticism from its donors. I am therefore holding between £200,000 and £300,000 in abeyance until we can come to some conclusion on the broad question of principle, and upon the question of its expenditure in Belgium in the terms upon which it has been solicited.[53]

It is not clear whether Hoover actually had such a sum at his disposal.[54] Very possibly he did not; very possibly—in fact, probably—he was bluffing. But the threatened loss of more than £200,000 in charitable funding would surely make the Belgian government take notice. This was hardball diplomacy indeed, the kind of "rough stuff" from which Brand Whitlock recoiled but to which Hoover willingly resorted without embarrassment.

The Hoover–Francqui contest was approaching a climax. With the French and British governments controlling the purse strings, with Hoover—the almoner of Belgium—"impregnable" in the eyes of Ambassador Page and the American public, it was obvious that the Belgian government and Francqui would have to surrender.[55] But Hoover was leaving no stone unturned. For some weeks certain Belgians had been circulating tendentious arguments about the origins of the relief in 1914—arguments that minimized Hoover's role "at the creation." They pointed out that Belgium's initial self-help efforts had antedated the founding of the CRB by many weeks. In response Hoover had prepared a detailed chronology showing that the Comité National (as a national organization) had actually been founded a week *after* the CRB.[56]

To Brand Whitlock such jockeying was an indication that the Great War had "got on men's nerves." Men, he told Page, " have grown touchy about precedence, eager for credit and applause."[57] To Hoover and Page, however, the Belgians' arguments were one more example of the unceasing attempt by Francqui and his cohorts to derogate America's part in saving their nation. On December 22, in language so Hooverian in tone that Hoover himself may have written it, Page informed Whitlock of some "elementary facts":

> It is obvious that charitable committees may have existed, and probably did exist, in Belgium years or even centuries before the creation of the American Commission . . . but . . . it should not be forgotten that not one dollar or one pound of food was available for the relief of Belgium, nor were any food stuffs allowed to cross the frontier until after the creation of the Commission for Relief in Belgium; and the continuance of the work has depended on the Commission and not on the Belgians.[58]

Belatedly recognizing his vulnerability, Francqui now tried a final maneuver. On Christmas Eve he cabled Hoover from France, to which the Belgian had journeyed with German permission. Explaining that he was forbidden to visit London, Francqui instead asked Hoover to come to Le Havre, confer with him and the government-in-exile, and resolve all their "misunderstandings."[59] Hoover refused to swallow the bait. We tried for three weeks in Brussels to settle our differences, he cabled back. Now a "memorandum" had been prepared that would win the Belgian government's approval if Francqui supported it. All else could wait until this crucial issue was settled. Furthermore, said Hoover, he was too preoccupied with urgent relief business to get away to Le Havre. Could not Francqui come to London?[60]

On December 28 Emile Francqui came to London. Traveling incognito lest he be noticed, he stayed but a few hours at the Savoy Hotel.[61] There he met Hoover in person and accepted the memorandum of agreement between the CRB and the CN that the British government had proposed to his government-in-exile. Francqui asked for only a few minor alterations. Hoover at once accepted them.[62]

The new document declared that the Commission for Relief in Belgium was to be "entirely independent of control or participation of any of the belligerent governments, and of any organization of belligerent subjects." The CRB was also to have "the sole administration of all relief activities exterior" to Belgium. Inside Belgium, it was to enjoy the energetic role and "equal voice" in "general policy" that Hoover demanded. In every area of dispute—inspection and control, supervision of food distribution, administration of *secours*, allocating of charitable moneys, ownership of property, and labeling of documents and relief buildings—the CRB was to have the responsibilities and recognition for which Hoover had strenuously contended. If any "irreconcilable differences" arose between the two bodies, the British, French, and Belgian governments, along with the neutral patron-ambassadors, would comprise the court of appeal.[63]

Proclaiming himself in "perfect accord" with the new "contract," Francqui now declared that if it had been proposed at any point he would gladly have accepted it! There had been no need for all the turmoil of the past three months, he said. Hoover did not let this claim go unchallenged. He pointed out how, many weeks before, Francqui had asserted in writing that the Americans should limit themselves to supervising the guarantees, how he had thwarted the Americans on many fronts and reduced the CRB in Belgium to "mere spies on the Germans," and how he had flatly refused even to use the term *collaboration*. Hoover recalled further how he had told Francqui that his attitude put the Americans in "a wholly impossible position of purporting to have a voice and participation in distribution and control which it did not possess." Nevertheless, Hoover now stated, inasmuch as Francqui had just assented to the "old basis" of joint collaboration, there was no point in rehashing this "painful" episode.[64]

At this point Francqui unexpectedly announced that he had "irrevocably" decided to resign as head of the Comité National. Why? Hoover wondered; Francqui had just said that he accepted the new "contract." Because, replied the Belgian, Hoover was indispensable to the relief and he, Francqui, had been "out of tune" with him for three months. It could "jeopardise the relief" if he remained "in a position where there was such possibility of breakage."

Hoover refused to acquiesce. There is no longer any "point of friction" between you and me, he rejoined; in fact, no one considers you more indispensable to the Belgian people than I do. Furthermore, you have made my own position untenable. If you were to resign because of a difference on policy, that would be one thing. But to resign because you cannot get along with me is something else; it is "a reflection on me." I cannot accept this, Hoover declared bluntly. If you insist on resigning from the leadership of the Comité National, I shall leave the Commission for Relief in Belgium.

You use a sledge hammer to kill gnats! Francqui exclaimed. "[F]ailing any other implement I would use a pile-driver to kill a malarial mosquito!" Hoover shot back.

At this point, Hoover reported afterward, the two men "thereupon agreed to go on, both of us to continue as before as the heads of our respective organisations, and [agreed] that the entire matter would be considered as a bad dream and excised from our recollections."[65]

There now remained only the niceties of a formal reconciliation. Francqui asked Hoover not to exhibit the memorandum inside Belgium until the Comité National leader had had a chance to bring his colleagues into line. Hoover agreed. Francqui also worried that the new "contract" might incite the CRB men to behave arrogantly toward their Belgian colleagues. Hoover promised not to permit this and to limit the document's circulation.[66] The Belgian government-in-exile gave full support for the new arrangement.[67]

A day or two later Hoover sent a conciliatory message to Francqui.[68] Replying on January 1, 1917, the humbled Belgian declared himself "much touched" by Hoover's sentiments and then proceeded to heap praise on his erstwhile antagonist. "Like a veritable apostle for more than two years you have been making your voice of authority heard everywhere in the world in favour of my unhappy fellow-countrymen. Be quite sure that they are aware of your beneficent work and that they will keep for you an eternal gratitude."[69]

Hoover made similar professions of regard. My "admiration" for Francqui's "abilities and his devotion to the Belgian people is in no sense diminished," he told Brand Whitlock, "and I hope we shall be able to demonstrate to him that while we will not accept the position of servants, we are the most advantageous of partners." But the CRB chairman could not conceal his satisfaction that at long last he had bested Francqui. "If I were to let myself down into pettiness for a moment," Hoover wrote Whitlock, "I might point out that this contract is identical in all its contents with the dispatch of Lord Grey of October 20th. . . ."[70]

A few weeks later Hoover informed a friend that until Francqui "breaks loose again everything is lovely,"[71] In the months and years ahead, the two men occasionally clashed, but their relations were never again as turbulent as they became in 1916. In a curious way both leaders seemed to agree tacitly never to ventilate their differences in public. After the war the Comité National published an enormous, multivolume report on its activities. In its hundreds and hundreds of pages, there was not a word about the Comité's difficulties with Hoover.[72] After the war, too, Hoover decided not to publish a history of the CRB written for him by one of his volunteers, Tracy B. Kittredge— largely because of the book's candid account of the Hoover–Francqui feud. Still later, Hoover went so far as to order that every copy of Kittredge's unpublished volume be destroyed. (He did not succeed.)[73] In his *Memoirs* and other autobiographical writings Hoover barely hinted at the tempest that had nearly shipwrecked his relief venture.[74] Instead, he praised Francqui's ability, humor, courage, and exemplary "devotion to his countrymen."[75] Toward the end of his life he even publicly asserted that he and Francqui had "remained affectionate friends" until the Belgian's death in 1935.[76]

Francqui, for his part, seemed willing to bury the hatchet. Although at times privately critical of Hoover,[77] he, too, maintained public silence about their past altercations. During the 1920s and early 1930s the two men collaborated in developing a number of foundations for the promotion of cultural exchange and scientific research.[78] In 1928 Francqui congratulated Hoover on his nomination and election to the American presidency; in reply Hoover invited Francqui to visit him in the White House.[79] Three years later, as a powerful figure in Belgian politics, Francqui did just that, staying overnight as the guest of his old adversary.[80]

And when, during Hoover's presidency, certain hostile American "biographers" accused him of having personally profited from the relief, Francqui came forth, when asked, with a stout endorsement of Hoover's conduct.[81] And so the two titans, who probably never forgot their old grievances, managed to appear officially friendly, and even to accord each other respect.[82] Perhaps each was a better diplomat than he realized.

I I

Thus ended the year 1916 and the most acrimonious episode of Hoover's "Belgian" years.[83] Even institutions founded with the most altruistic of motives, it seemed, could be tweaked, wracked, and nearly rent asunder by less than inspiring passions. Perhaps Brand Whitlock was right: in this area, too, the war had gone on too long, and human nature appeared to be "a little more intensely human than it ever has been before."[84]

Hoover, of course, had little time for such reflections. By the end of 1916 he stood preeminent in the greatest humanitarian undertaking the world had ever seen. Even as he savored his triumph over Francqui, he was beginning to glance beyond the marvelous relief machinery that he and his colleagues had built. A wider sphere of public service was beckoning, and Hoover had more than Belgium on his mind.

11

Lost Horizons

I

T H E casualties of war are not only physical, and combatants are not its only victims. Even the neutral and innocent can be drawn into its vortex of sacrifice. So it was with Hoover as the conflict of 1914 turned into an endless catastrophe. The Great War brought him fame and the pleasures of useful service, but it also exacted its price.

The first casualty of the war for Hoover was his long-deferred plan to reestablish himself permanently in the land of his birth. For years he had dreamed of returning to the United States and entering American public life—had dreamed, in particular, of acquiring a newspaper in New York or Washington, D.C.[1] In the summer of 1914 an opportunity to consummate this ambition arose in California: through his friend Ben S. Allen he attempted to purchase the *Sacramento Union*. The lowering war clouds in Europe compelled him to abandon his negotiations in late July.[2]

As Hoover's hopes of becoming a newspaper magnate faded, so, too, did any chance for a more settled family life. During August and September he repeatedly postponed plans for a trip back to California with his wife and sons. When Lou and the boys finally sailed from England on October 3, her husband Bert was not with them. The demands of his teetering mining enterprises held him back.

The Hoovers did not anticipate a lengthy separation. As late as October 20, 1914, only two days before he founded the CRB, Hoover cabled to his wife from London that if nothing else intervened, he should be able to spend Christmas in California.[3] Instead, as Christmas approached and the relief of Belgium burgeoned, it was Lou who came alone back to him.[4] She did not see her children again for seven months.

Mrs. Hoover's separation from her sons had certain advantages: in California Allan and young Herbert would receive an American education and would be safely distant from the war. Still, the parting was not easy, for Lou was aware of the possibility that she might never see her two children again. Before leaving New York on a voyage across the submarine-infested north Atlantic, she designated a friend and fellow Stanford alumnus, Jackson E. Reynolds, class of 1896, as the legal guardian of her sons if she and her husband should die or become incapacitated.[5]

In a long letter to Reynolds, Lou poured out instructions for her sons' upbringing, advice that revealed much about her—and her husband's—philosophy of life:

> I think a few years as little boys in California,—where they have plenty of outdoors, and *village* life,—. . . might be very good. But I should like them to have a few years in the East,—at a big school as well. . . .
>
> I dont know now of course whether there will be a considerable fortune for them, or very little. However, unless the United States follows the example of Europe, there will be enough to educate them. . . .
>
> But I dont need to suggest to *you* in either case, not to let them get a money measure for all the affairs of life.
>
> The ambition to do, to accomplish, irrespective of its measure in money or fame, is what should be inculcated. The desire to make the things that are, better,—in a little way with what is at hand,—in a big way if the opportunity comes. And they are well on the road to that already,—altho' still so little.

Mrs. Hoover cautioned Reynolds against the harmful influence of various relatives and friends, several of whom she bluntly dismissed as "impractical." And while not averse to her sons' studying in Europe for some specialized purpose later on, she firmly opposed their having "an English or continental education." An *American* education, imbued with idealism, tempered by practicality, geared to accomplishment and to making the world a better place: that was what the Hoovers wanted for their children. On Lou, as on Bert, the Stanford ethos had left its mark.[6]

To her son Herbert, aged eleven, Lou addressed a separate letter filled with her thoughts about God, immortality, and prayer. God is the "great power beyond us, that controls and guides us and all the affairs about us," she told her son. Through prayer our souls can ask Him for the strength we need to succeed in our daily lives.

Now that soul we *know* does not die when our bodies die, or get buried in the ground, or lost in the sea, or burned up. . . . With some it just goes straight back to God, in the place they call Heaven, that we dont really know very much about. If it has been rather a lazy useless soul, it may just sort of go to sleep there. But sometimes they go about helping, and if another soul that is still in a body like yours is wanting some help and is praying for some force to come from God, this helping soul may take some along and help. Or even without being prayed to particularly, it may take some force along anyway and just wait about to help another soul that it loved very much before its body died. And that's what I want you to be perfectly sure about me. I *know* that if I should die, I can pray my soul to go over to my two dear little boys and to help and comfort their souls. Of course you cant see it or hear it. But sometimes you will know I am there, because your own little soul inside you will feel nice and comfy and cosy, because my bigger, older one is cuddling it. And when you are in trouble, and call for me to come to help you, and pray God to give you more force, why I can come right to you and bring along the new force he is sending to you. . . .

So you be sure to send out that strong wish for me to come to help you any time you are in trouble—or other times just to love me. And of course some times I wont be able to help you in the way you want,—but I'll just help and love and comfort you all I can. And I will ask God not to have me go up in that place he has called Heaven, until it is time for you to come too. I will just wait there and help and love you, until we can all go together.[7]

Despite her anxieties Mrs. Hoover reached London safely in early December 1914.[8] Soon afterward she joined her husband on a Christmas visit to Brussels, followed, a few weeks later, by a second trip to Belgium and one to wartime Berlin. Raised as a virtual tomboy by her father, trained as a geologist (hitherto a man's subject) at Stanford, Lou had long been accustomed to traveling fearlessly wherever her husband happened to wander, and she did so with gusto now. But for the most part she remained in London during the winter and spring of 1915.

She was not, however, unoccupied; idleness was something of which both Hoovers were incapable. Already, during her autumn sojourn in California, Lou had galvanized public support for her husband's Commission for Relief in Belgium.[9] She had also helped to organize a California chapter of the Committee of Mercy, founded to aid women and children made destitute by the war in the belligerent countries. In addition, she had become a member of the committee's national board.[10] Now, in England, she turned with zeal to similar endeavors.

As president for 1914–15 of the Society of American Women in London, she helped to organize numerous war-related philanthropic schemes, including a "knitting factory" for impoverished British women who had lost their jobs because of the conflict. By March 1915 the society's factory, a house located in one of London's poorest boroughs, employed more than forty such women full time, at minimum union wages. Contributions from Mrs. Hoover and other well-to-do women helped to finance the enterprise, as did sales of knitted garments to those who wished to distribute them to soldiers and the destitute. With a club room (furnished with newspapers, a gramophone, and a piano) open to the neighborhood, as well as an inexpensive daily hot lunch program, the "War Relief Knitting Factory" became a virtual settlement house in working-class London.[11]

All this did not exhaust Mrs. Hoover's energies and passion for good works. During these hectic months the American Women's War Relief Fund established a modern, fully staffed, two-hundred-bed surgical facility known as the American Women's Hospital in the town of Paignton. Here wounded soldiers and sailors came for treatment. Mrs. Hoover served with Lady Randolph Churchill, the Duchess of Marlborough, and others on the fund's executive committee.[12] Promoting and sustaining this remarkable venture became one of her principal activities for more than two years. Lou also acted as secretary-treasurer of the fund's economic relief committee and as chairman of the women's division of the American Committee.[13]

Thus even as Herbert Hoover administered relief to the people of Belgium, his wife helped hundreds of British and American women who had been victimized by the dislocations of war. Like Bert, Lou was efficiently practical. Displaying managerial ability reminiscent of her husband's, she took pleasure that during her tenure the Society of American Women in London evolved from a primarily social organization into a philanthropic one.[14] "The ambition to do, to accomplish. . . . The desire to make the things that are, better": such impulses impelled both halves of the Hoover "team."

On May 29, 1915 Hoover's home life, such as it was, underwent yet another disruption. On that day, scarcely three weeks after the sinking of the *Lusitania*, his wife set sail from England to rejoin their sons in California. As Lou boarded the ship at Liverpool, her husband sent her a terse telegram from London: "Goodbye. Love, Bert."[15] No wasted words; no cloying sentiment. He did not see his wife again for more than five months.

In mid-June Lou reached California, where she rejoined the boys for a relaxing summer, including camping trips to Yosemite.[16] But then, in August, as another season of schooling approached, the question arose: where should she and her sons spend the coming year? In California? New York? London? At first Hoover left the decision up to his wife and children.[17] A few weeks later, however, he changed his mind and cabled that he considered it safe for them to join him in England. The work of the CRB must continue another year, he reported. Under the circumstances it seemed best for them to return to Europe.[18]

Lou and the boys did not come over at once. Instead they stayed for several weeks in Palo Alto with the wife of a Stanford professor who was working in Belgium for the CRB.[19] Perhaps it was just as well; in September German Zeppelins staged an air raid on London in which they dropped a bomb that crashed through the CRB's own offices. Fortunately, the attack was at night, the target unintentional, and the bomb itself a dud.[20] Finally, in mid-October, Lou, young Herbert, and Allan boarded a train from California for New York, to which Hoover had come to resolve the muddle created by Lindon Bates. Early in November the Hoovers sailed back to England—reunited as a family at last.[21]

For the next fourteen months the CRB chairman and his family resided at their home in London. Even then they were not always together. Half a dozen times in 1916 Hoover took trips to the continent, sometimes for as long as two weeks.[22] Mrs. Hoover, too, was as busy as ever with her philanthropies; many times, no doubt, it was the household servants who looked after her boys. During this period young Herbert and Allan attended a nearby British private school, where, to the chagrin of their parents, they quickly developed Oxford accents. Absorbed in relief work, Bert and Lou evidently never visited the academy.[23]

As they had done in London since late 1907, the Hoovers lived in a two-story villa known as the Red House on Hornton Street in the borough of Kensington. Built in the 1830s and set in a spacious garden enclosed by a high brick wall, the building reflected the tastes of its prosperous upper-middle-class occupants. An oak-paneled library, a walnut-paneled dining room, a conservatory, a gymnasium, a drawing room, a wine cellar, even a billiard room with a cocktail mixer, were among its most interesting features. The house was stuffed with unusual furnishings: Persian rugs, Russian peasant ware, exquisite Chinese blue-and-white porcelain vases (a hobby of Lou's), and countless books, including nearly a thousand on the history of mining and metallurgy. In the garage were two much-used automobiles. (Before the war, driving in the country had been a favorite family diversion.)[24]

To manage this household the Hoovers employed a corps of servants: Atkinson, the butler; Gilbert, the chauffeur; a nurse-governess for the boys; and various maids and housekeepers.[25] Philosophically a democrat and a severe critic of the British class system, Hoover nevertheless lived in the ample manner of an English country squire. Still, he did not permit the disparity in income between himself and his staff to harden into a shell of indifference. When, for example, his butler was drafted into the British army and hospitalized with war wounds, Hoover permitted the man's wife to live rent- and fuel-free in their apartment over the Red House garage. Eventually Hoover sold his lease to the Red House, and Mrs. Atkinson had to find other quarters. Even then, he voluntarily paid her a weekly allowance for the duration of the war.[26]

Acts such as these—acts that he never publicized and often took pains to conceal—earned Hoover the loyalty of nearly every person who ever worked for him. One such man was Paul Potous, his private secretary since 1910. Late in the war, when Hoover terminated his London-based mining career, he provided Potous a sum of money sufficient to make him independent for the rest of his life.[27] Long before this, Potous expressed to Mrs. Hoover his feelings of devotion to his chief:

> I find it very difficult to say all I think of Mr. Hoover. He has stood by me in so many ways all these years. . . . I have never once heard anyone who knew him to say anything but the kindest things of him. They say if you wish to know a man's character you should watch how he treats his servants. I am his servant and I know.[28]

It was not just family servants who experienced Hoover's quiet generosity. Before 1914 he and Lou had become famous for their hospitality among American travelers and residents of London. By the outbreak of the war they had entertained literally thousands of dinner guests at their home: mining engineers, Stanford professors, journalists, businessmen, novelists, actors. It was as if neither Bert nor Lou could bear to be alone. Now, though the circumstances were less propitious, their beloved Red House remained a "mecca for Californians"[29] and other Americans, including the CRB volunteers. Hoover himself called the Red House "a general commissariat" for relief workers;[30] "Hoover Hotel" would have been an equally appropriate name. Sitting under the mulberry tree in the Hoovers' back yard on an August night and gazing at eucalyptus-like trees across the lawn, one guest suddenly felt homesick for California.[31] Many others long remembered charming evenings of conversation and good cheer—like Christmas Eve 1915, when the Hoovers invited in about twenty young CRB men for a celebration. On a huge Christmas tree were placed gifts for each guest. The dinner was magnificent. Even Hoover—so often aloof, preoccupied, and asocial—managed, if only briefly, to relax.[32]

In another way, too, the Hoovers persisted in their prewar pattern of living: formal religious observance was entirely absent from their lives. Although nominally a Quaker (he maintained a membership in the Salem, Oregon, meeting that he had joined as a teenager) Hoover had no contacts with Friends groups in London. So far as is known, he never attended church services of any kind during the early war years (except possibly, once or twice, in Brussels, on occasions of patriotic significance). In explaining and defending his humanitarian mission, he did not offer an explicitly Christian rationale. Nor did he give his boys any religious instruction; decades later, his surviving son recalled that the family never discussed religion at any time.[33]

Sometimes the war impinged less benignly on the rambling old home in Kensington. One night in 1916 the Hoovers awoke to the sound of a fearsome explosion nearby. It was a bomb; German Zeppelins were again raiding London, as they had since early in the war. Alarmed and anxious to take shelter, the Hoovers called out for their sons. There was no answer. Searching frantically, Bert and Lou finally found the boys on the Red House roof—contentedly observing the searchlights and the "show."

Suddenly, in the distance, a Zeppelin crashed from the sky, a flaming victim of British antiaircraft fire. Early the next morning Hoover drove with his sons to the site, where they collected some prized souvenirs.[34]

If war could be exciting for little boys, it was much less so for their parents. By the end of 1916 the Hoovers reluctantly realized that life at the Red House—life as they had known it before the war—could not continue much longer. Not when bomb-laden Zeppelins were appearing, however infrequently, in the skies of London. Not when young Herbert and Allan were talking like little British gentlemen and were missing the American way of life that their parents ardently desired for them.[35] Early in November Hoover's older brother Theodore, also a mining engineer, finally pulled up his stakes from London after a stay of almost ten years. With Theodore and his family now ensconced in California (on a ranch near Santa Cruz), Hoover's own yearning to return to his adopted state undoubtedly became stronger still.[36]

And so, at the beginning of 1917, as the chairman of the CRB prepared for a fund-raising mission to the United States, Lou and the boys got ready for a more permanent uprooting. On January 11 they sailed from England for America; two days later Hoover departed on a separate vessel.[37] As she left her Kensington home for the ocean journey back to the States, Lou sensed that she would never see her London residence again.[38] As far as is known, she never did. The Red House on Hornton Street, the Victorian country house in the city, the "mecca for Californians" in the heart of imperial London, had been the setting for the happiest years of the Hoovers' lives. Now it was part of a world that they were leaving behind forever.

I I

A N unsettled family life was not the only burden that Hoover had to carry in the early months of the Great War. Down in the City (London's financial district), distractions of a different sort assailed him daily.

In the summer of 1914 Hoover stood at the apex of his profession—a man regarded by some of his colleagues as the ablest mining engineer alive.[39] He was a director of eighteen mining and financial companies having a total authorized share capital of more than £11,000,000, or more than $55,000,000.[40] On every continent except Antarctica he had significant business interests. Entrenched in London, the mining and financial capital of the world, he had become what he had striven to be since his days as a young engineer on the make: a millionaire by the age of forty.

Among the farflung ventures whose destiny he in part controlled, three in particular stood out. In Australia: the Zinc Corporation, created by himself and others in 1905 to extract zinc from millions of tons of tailings that lay in gigantic dumps at the city of Broken Hill. By 1914 this once struggling company had become a giant, producing more than 80,000 tons of zinc concentrates a year—nearly 20% of the entire output of that continent.[41]

Far to the northwest, in the jungles of upper Burma, lay an enterprise more promising still. There, 600 miles by rail from Rangoon and only 50 miles from the Chinese border, a company called Burma Mines, Ltd. was exploring an abandoned Chinese silver mine known as Bawdwin. Hoover had launched this undertaking in 1906, but not until 1913 had workers at the site finally confirmed his conviction: that below the old surface workings was one of the richest silver-lead-zinc deposits on earth. Hailing the find as one of the "ten most notable mineral discoveries in the whole world" since 1900, Hoover had promptly reorganized the venture's finances and had made plans for development on a grand scale, including installation of an ore-producing capacity of 300,000 tons a year. With his engineers predicting £1,000,000 in profits for every hundred feet that the ore body extended in depth, such optimism had seemed fully justified.

By 1914, Hoover held at least a one-seventh interest in this multimillion-dollar enterprise, a portion second only to that of one other shareholder. As yet, the mine had yielded no dividend. Systematic exploitation and profits would have to await construction of a 7,400-foot-long horizontal tunnel into the side of the ore-bearing mountain: an audacious feat of engineering that would take over two years to complete. In the summer of 1914 excavation had barely begun. But as of August only time—time and laborious development work—stood between Hoover and a magnificent fortune.[42]

Meanwhile, thousands of miles from southeast Asia, a third jewel in his crown was gaining luster. In the years immediately before the war he had become increasingly prominent in a number of British-controlled mining ventures in the heart of tsarist Russia. By mid-1914 he was an influential director of three such companies embracing a mining empire of staggering potential. At Kyshtim, in the Ural Mountains, he and his associates had successfully converted a moribund, antiquated enterprise on a vast semifeudal estate into a sophisticated industrial complex, the second largest copper producer in Europe. Two hundred miles to the south a similar transformation was occurring in the vicinity of Tanalyk, an area rich in copper and manganese.[43]

Far to the east, in the vastness of Siberia, were the most glittering potential prizes of all. In 1912 Hoover had helped to found (and had then become a director of) an investment and exploration company called the Russo-Asiatic Corporation. During the next two years it had acquired three enormous mining concessions, two of them on property belonging to Tsar Nicholas II himself. One of these, the Ridder, alone encompassed 3,000 square miles. Located in the Altai Mountains near the Irtish River, not far from the Mongolian border, the Ridder concession contained a massive zinc-silver-lead deposit with rich admixtures of copper and gold. By the summer of 1914 American engineers under Hoover's command had determined that the undeveloped Ridder deposit was a stunning bonanza, with an assured profit in sight of more than $35,000,000. Not without reason did Hoover later describe it as "probably the greatest and richest single body of ore known in the world."[44] All in all, by mid-1914 the Anglo-American investing group of which Hoover was a leading member controlled mines, smelters, forests, exploration rights, and development rights on Russian territory more extensive than the entire country of Belgium.[45]

Australia, Burma, Russia: it was a mighty empire in the making. There was only one hindrance that Hoover and his associates had not foreseen: the assassination in Sarajevo of the heir to the Hapsburg throne.

The initial impact of the war on Hoover's mining network was devastating—or so it appeared in London in the summer and early autumn of 1914. "The whole clock-work machinery of financial and industrial affairs just stopped," Lou Henry Hoover remarked to a friend.[46] At the Kyshtim and Tanalyk mines in Russia military mobilization swept away nearly 40% of the work force and administrative staff.[47] More threatening still, Russia was now largely cut off by its enemies from contact with Great Britain and the West. Out in Burma construction of the Tiger Tunnel had begun in the spring and was continuing without interruption, but where the mine's product could ultimately be refined was a mystery. Before the war, samples had all gone to German smelters, but this outlet was now foreclosed.[48]

Hardest hit of all was the Zinc Corporation at Broken Hill. Before August 1914 it had sold its zinc concentrates to Germany, since existing British smelters were unable to treat its complex ores. Now, as a consequence of the war, the corporation had no market for its product. Late in September it was obliged to close its mine and zinc concentrating plant indefinitely.[49]

All this must have seemed maddeningly ironic to Hoover. The greatest war the world had ever seen was raging, an inferno that, if it lasted, would consume stupendous quantities of copper, lead, and zinc. A fortune awaited those who could supply these strategic metals to the munitions makers of the belligerent powers.[50] Yet thanks to the shape of the battle lines, the crippling contracts with German metallurgical companies, and Germany's monopoly of modern zinc smelting plants, his potential mining colossus was in disarray.

By early October Hoover's business interests were at their nadir; so, at least, he indicated to various acquaintances.[51] At one point during the month he even told an old friend that he was flat broke (although Lou Henry Hoover later stated that they had considerable assets at this point in gilt-edged securities).[52] It was not, he said, that he faced penury. He could always make an excellent living as "an adviser and expert"—as a member, in other words, of various boards of directors. It was his fortune, rather, that had been lost. And it hurt. "I wanted that pile," he confessed to a friend. ". . . I wanted that pile to play around with—to start a few things—not for myself—things in which I'm interested."[53]

"Let the fortune go to hell." Perhaps, in these dispiriting circumstances, Hoover found it easier to leap wholeheartedly into Belgian relief work. There was little else to do. His fortune—at least his prospective fortune—had already seemingly vanished from his grasp.

While in this mood of gloomy resignation, the American engineer apparently made a decision. Early in November 1914 he spoke with his brother Theodore at their office in No. 1, London Wall Buildings. According to Theodore's later recollection, Herbert told him that he would probably never enter his office again. He declared that his London business was to be closed down and that all his shareholdings were to be sold at their current low prices. The task of managing this withdrawal, he said, was to be Theodore's.[54]

Yet if Hoover really decided at this juncture to make his long-sought final break with London, he did not follow through immediately. Scarcely three weeks later the Russo-Asiatic Corporation formed a subsidiary called the Irtysh Corporation to develop the remarkable Ridder concession and the almost equally remarkable Ekibastus coal field nearby. Hoover at once became a director of the new £2,000,000 enterprise, which promptly unveiled plans to construct a large concentrating mill, a modern lead-zinc smelter, and a fifty-five-mile-long railway: all in a region remote from London and St. Petersburg. It was a daring venture to initiate in the midst of a European war. But Siberia was a long way from the fighting, and the coal, zinc, and other products of the nascent enterprise, it was said, could find a ready market in Russia itself.[55]

To obtain the necessary working capital, the Irtysh Corporation immediately issued £500,000 in debentures, underwritten by a recently formed entity called the Inter-Siberian Syndicate. Hoover was one of its four directors. As a large shareholder in this syndicate he indirectly guaranteed the debenture issue; in return he received an option to purchase up to 10,000 £1 Irtysh shares at par over the next several years.[56] If during this time the shares should rise in value, he could exercise his option, buy the shares at par, resell them *above* par, and make a handsome profit: his "engineering fee," as he liked to call it, for his services.

The Irtysh flotation of November 1914 was the kind of business arrangement at which Hoover had become adept in the years just preceding the war, when he had become known in London as an outstanding "engineer-financier."[57] It was not so much the technical aspects of mining that interested him now as it was the financial side of enterprise-building.

Hoover's successful launching of the Irtysh Corporation was not an isolated relapse into his prewar professional activities. Early in 1915, in furtherance of negotiations begun months before, he created and became a director of a British holding company known as the Natomas Land and Dredging Trust. This effort was part of a complicated scheme to reorganize Natomas Consolidated of California, an ailing land and mining company with large interests in the Sacramento Valley.[58] In addition, during 1915 he remained, at least nominally, on the boards of numerous British-based mining companies and was even chairman or managing director of six.[59] At mid-year, in fact, he actually sat on more boards than he had at the same point a year before.[60]

And on these boards he remained, being reelected, for instance, a director of Russo-Asiatic as late as December 1915.[61] According to Theodore, his brother retained certain directorships at the "earnest request" of his colleagues, who evidently did not want to lose the prestige value of the Hoover name.[62] In any case, the process of extricating himself from his business interests was turning out to be a protracted one.

In a way Hoover's continued (if fitful) involvement in mining was not surprising. Like most people at the start of the war, he anticipated that the conflict would be short.[63] Why, then, should he sell out precipitously? Moreover, with so many of his investments tied up in semi-developed properties, he probably welcomed the income provided by his director's fees. He had better hold onto what he could.

Nevertheless, the insistent demands of the Commission for Relief in Belgium prevented him from devoting himself systematically to anything else. I have no time for private interests, he told a friend in March 1915. "If anybody thinks this is a dilettante's job he ought to come over here and take a look at it."[64] Two months later he again lamented that his professional work had "simply gone all to pieces" and that it would take "a year or two of steady work" after the war to recoup completely.[65] In October he acknowledged to a Russian associate that he had given "comparatively little attention" to their "mutual interests" in the preceding year.[66]

Instead, as the months passed, Hoover increasingly relied on a trusted group of largely American associates to handle his engineering affairs. One was Edgar Rickard, publisher of the *Mining Magazine* and a colleague in the CRB, who became a kind of administrative assistant, office manager, and keeper of Hoover's personal accounts—a role he filled for years to come.[67] Another was John Agnew, whom Hoover had known since 1898 and who had risen through the ranks at Hoover's old firm of Bewick, Moreing & Co. Just before the war Hoover had hired Agnew to work for him full time and to serve, when asked, as his alternate on various boards of directors.[68] Eventually Agnew became his principal business agent in London.[69] Others in the group included his old friends Deane P. Mitchell (Stanford '96), R. Gilman Brown, and A. F. Kuehn—mining engineers all—who, with Agnew, dominated the supervisory "technical committees" at several Hoover-directed companies.[70] Still another was Theodore Hoover, who later wrote that he spent 90% of his time from late 1914 to late 1916 caring for his brother's business interests.[71]

Rickard, Agnew, Mitchell, Brown, Kuehn, brother Theodore, and the rest: it was a talented team. The capacity to select, and to inspire the loyalty of, able lieutenants was one of Hoover's principal abilities. It was, he knew, the foundation of his own success.[72]

As 1915 yielded to 1916, Hoover's mining career seemed to be in suspense. Unable actively to lead what he once described as a mining "army of 100,000 workpeople,"[73] he nevertheless gave little sign of retiring. As of mid-1916 he still remained on the boards of thirteen different companies.[74]

Meanwhile news from the field was proving surprisingly favorable. Contrary to his glum remarks of September and October 1914, the war did not immediately shatter his mining empire. By early 1916, in fact, most of his principal interests were flourishing. Out in Burma engineers at the Bawdwin site had verified the existence of more than 2,000,000 tons of high-grade ore, and the estimate was constantly rising.[75] One expert declared that the mine seemed certain to become "the largest single lead-zinc-silver producer in the world."[76] Slowly but steadily the Tiger Tunnel was approaching completion, and with it the day when the mine's riches could be exploited on a massive scale.

From Russia, too, came reports of progress and hope. At Kyshtim and Tanalyk the war-induced labor shortages and production losses of late 1914 had proved temporary. Despite soaring costs, transportation difficulties, and stringent currency restrictions that prevented the transfer of profits from Russia to Great Britain, the Kyshtim Corporation by 1916 was producing more than 8,000 tons of refined copper annually, as well as sulphur pyrites, iron castings, and other materials that the Russian government requested for the war effort.[77] To the east the Irtysh Corporation was rapidly erecting zinc and lead smelters, preparing mines for production, laying a railway through difficult terrain, and developing a phenomenal coal basin containing literally hundreds of millions of tons of reserves—all with the encouragement and assistance of the tsar's government.[78] "The Anglo-Russian mining companies are doing well, and there is great activity at all points," observed a London mining journal.[79] The success of the Irtysh Corporation "seems assured," said another.[80]

With the London mining press acclaiming Russia as "a great field for investment,"[81] Hoover decided to act. Between June and December 1916 he exercised his option on 6,202 Irtysh shares at par. A short time later, he disposed of nearly all of these shares at double their face value. His profit on this single transaction was nearly $25,000.[82]

Even the Zinc Corporation—so paralyzed in the early months of the war—was struggling back to health by early 1916. At the outset of hostilities the company had been encumbered by a long-term contract requiring it to sell its zinc concentrates exclusively to the German smelting firm of Aron Hirsch & Sohn. Obviously this contract was inoperative while England and Germany were enemies.[83] But was it inoperative permanently? When the Zinc Corporation asserted in the British courts that the war had completely voided the contract, the German firm rejoined that the war had merely suspended it and that it would regain its full legal force when the fighting ceased. If true, this would severely hamper the Zinc Corporation's ability to develop alternative markets in the meantime. It would also guarantee a resumption of German hegemony over the Australian base metals industry after the war.[84]

For more than a year the bitter legal battle dragged on in the British judicial system. Nearly all this time, the plaintiff's zinc mill at Broken Hill remained closed. It was not until May 1916 that the British government finally intervened and abrogated the contract, thereby freeing the corporation from its paralyzing incubus of uncertainty.[85]

Yet even if the Australian enterprise had won instant release from its smelting agreement, its prosperity would not have been assured. For Hoover and his business allies, the problem of 1914 went deeper: where would their zinc concentrates go if *not* to Germany or German-held Belgium and northern France? Existing zinc smelters in England were few, small, and technologically inferior. Hence Broken Hill's dependence on the Germans in the first place.[86]

To Hoover, surveying the scene that August, the solution was simple: the Zinc Corporation should immediately construct its own smelter in Great Britain. That very month he boldly asked the British government's Board of Trade for nothing less than a £1,000,000 loan for this purpose and made tentative plans to locate the facility in Wales.[87] At the same time he dispatched his brother to the United States to study American smelting operations and line up skilled labor for the project.[88] The Guggenheim-controlled American Smelting and Refining Company apparently agreed to assist.[89]

Alas for the energetic Yankee, the British government did nothing. The war was young, and the complacent "business-as-usual" attitude still prevailed in the corridors of Whitehall. Then, too, the status of the German contracts was still unclear, casting a pall of risk over the expensive scheme. As a result, Hoover's plan for a government-subsidized national zinc works was not implemented.[90]

Instead, the hobbled Zinc Corporation was consigned to a year of false starts and frustration. Early in 1915 it attempted to sell its zinc concentrates in America—only to be underbid by its desperate competitors at Broken Hill.[91] Later in the year, a syndicate headed by Hoover and a colleague acquired a small zinc smelter in Wales that had belonged before the war to Aron Hirsch & Sohn.[92] But when the Zinc Corporation attempted to persuade its competitors to cease their ruinous competition, market their concentrates together, and share the profits from smelting, it met indifference and even opposition.[93] To Hoover, a veteran corporate consolidator, it was imperative that the producers act together.[94] But his Australian rivals were not so easily convinced.[95]

Finally, in the spring of 1916, under pressure from the Australian government, the Zinc Corporation and its Broken Hill competitors combined to form the Zinc Producers Association as a marketing agency for their output for fifty years. The catalyst for the breakthrough was Australia's dynamic wartime premier, William Hughes. Where Hoover and his associates had initially labored in vain, Hughes, with the power of his office and patriotic sentiment behind him, succeeded in overcoming all resistance.[96] On a trip to London in 1916 he took the next decisive step by promulgating a sweeping "Imperial Scheme" to construct zinc-smelting works in England and Australia under government auspices, and to shelter these industries against German competition after the war. Never again, he argued, should Great Britain be dependent upon outside sources for such a critical war material. Nor should the Broken Hill companies go under because of their prewar thralldom to the German metals combine. As a result of his intervention the British government agreed to purchase at least 250,000 tons of zinc concentrates annually from the Zinc Producers Association throughout the war and for ten years thereafter. The great Broken Hill zinc industry was saved. Several months later the National Smelting Company was established in England under government sponsorship, including a £500,000 loan to build facilities at Avonmouth.[97] Thus nearly three years after Hoover first approached the Board of Trade, the foundation for a modern British zinc industry finally took shape along lines that he himself envisaged.

Hoover kept himself apprised of these developments as best he could and offered his opinions on occasion. At the time of Premier Hughes's visit to London, the American engineer advised a British business ally on how to set up a "metals selling business" that could overcome German dominance of the base metals field. The key, he argued, was financial: the entire "basis" of the "whole German combination" had been its ability to provide generous financial terms (particularly loans) to ore producers and smelters.[98] But aside from this letter, there is little evidence that Hoover paid much attention to the negotiations of Hughes, the zinc producers, and His Majesty's Government. One of Hoover's closest associates, Francis A. Govett (who did participate), later declared that the much-touted "Imperial Scheme" was "almost identical" with what he and Hoover had unsuccessfully urged upon the British government much earlier.[99] Perhaps Hoover took some consolation from the fact that others, belatedly, had come around to his way of thinking. But by the spring of 1916 he was no more than a supporting actor—if even that—in a drama being played out by others.[100]

With the advent of mid-1916 Hoover faced a dilemma. On the one hand his principal mining ventures were improving. All were far from the war zone. None had suffered damage. All, despite dislocation, showed signs of long-term profitability. Thanks to the British government's guaranteed purchases, thanks to the belated severance of what the *Financial Times* called the "tentacles" of the "Hun 'octopus,' "[101] and thanks to the high wartime price for its *lead* concentrates, the Zinc Corporation had escaped the abyss.[102] At the Burma mine, where Hoover had committed his own resources the most, the Tiger Tunnel—a monument to his daring and imagination—was nearing completion. It was finished in September 1916.[103]

On the other hand, for many months his personal involvement in these enterprises had been minimal. To be sure, competent subordinates were supervising them and guarding his interests in the process. But Hoover was not a man to delegate such matters indefinitely to others. As with the CRB, so with his mines: at bottom he liked to run things himself.

And so, as his Belgian relief labors persisted into the dim and ever-lengthening future, he found himself wondering whether he should abandon mining engineering altogether.[104] After all, had he not been planning on it for years? And yet, if he left now, he would be sacrificing "great connections for the future"[105] as well as leadership of remarkable undertakings at the dawn of his anticipated reward.

Nevertheless, for some months Hoover had been showing signs of wanting, or feeling obliged, to pull out. In September 1915 he received a six months' leave of absence from the Zinc Corporation's board of directors.[106] In June 1916 he resigned his directorship entirely.[107] Another clue to his intentions emerged that summer when the Guggenheim Brothers of New York asked him (through an intermediary) whether they could acquire a substantial—perhaps even a controlling—interest in the Burma and Irtysh corporations.[108] Hoover replied that while an outright takeover was infeasible, there were "certain interests in both Companies" that could be obtained at a price below the profit in sight.[109] It is likely that these unnamed "interests" were those of Hoover himself.

In the second half of 1916 the chairman of the CRB crossed the Rubicon at last. ". . . [O]nly one conclusion was possible," he later wrote in his *Memoirs*.[110] Accordingly, he resigned one company directorate after another—all, by January 1917, except one: the Burma Corporation, Ltd.[111] Here he retained not only his seat on the board but also a direct and indirect shareholding amounting to more than 100,000 shares.[112]

The official reason given for Hoover's departure was his labor at the Commission for Relief in Belgium.[113] It required "the whole of his time and attention," a colleague remarked when announcing Hoover's resignation from the Kyshtim board.[114] But if the importunities of his relief work and his long-standing desire to return to America fundamentally determined his decision, another factor affected its timing—a factor Hoover never mentioned in his *Memoirs*. On April 17, 1916 his former business partners, the firm of Bewick, Moreing & Company, brought suit against him in the British courts.

From late 1901 to mid-1908 Hoover had been a partner in this distinguished British firm of mining engineers. During these years, largely by dint of his expertise and acumen, the company's business had tripled and its worldwide reputation had soared. Behind the scenes, however, Hoover and his senior partner, C. Algernon Moreing, had clashed repeatedly over policy, had mingled little outside the office, and had conceived a hearty antipathy for each other. In 1908 Hoover (with his partners' consent) had formally severed his association, but his leaving had not been amicable. As a condition of dissolving the partnership, Moreing had insisted on Hoover's signing a restrictive covenant barring him from practicing his profession of mining engineering anywhere in Great Britain or the British empire for ten years without Bewick, Moreing's consent.

Almost immediately friction broke out between the American engineer and his erstwhile partners. Convinced by 1910 that Hoover was insolently engaging in competitive practices that his terms of withdrawal prohibited, Moreing and his associates sued in London for breach of contract. The lawsuit quickly achieved notoriety in British mining circles. After considerable behind-the-scenes negotiations, including apparent threats by Hoover to oust Moreing's firm from its management of numerous companies unless Moreing came to terms, the two parties settled out of court in early 1911. Their new agreement permitted Hoover to serve as a company director and mining financier anywhere in the world without further obligation to his former partners. But once again, and this time more explicitly, it prohibited Hoover (before 1918) from conducting business as a mining engineer, mine manager, or company manager in the British empire unless Bewick, Moreing gave its permission. Moreing's objective was clear. Whatever Hoover might do as a company director, promoter, or financier, he must not establish a competing group of mining engineers or mine managers, a firm that could threaten Moreing's livelihood.

The treaty of 1911 proved illusory. During the next four years relations between the firm and Hoover steadily worsened. In 1911 (according to the firm) Hoover, operating from his vantage point as a company director, deliberately orchestrated the breakup of Bewick, Moreing's cooperative stores purchase system in Australia, at a substantial loss (so the firm alleged) to itself. In 1913–14 he reorganized the Burma mines enterprise, became chairman of the parent Burma Corporation, stripped Bewick, Moreing of the management, and replaced it with a so-called technical committee consisting of Theodore Hoover and other close associates. To the outraged firm it was obvious that Hoover was the "controlling technical brain" of the Burma venture. Not only was he rendering it his professional knowledge, he was managing it in substance—all (claimed the firm) in clear defiance of his dissolution agreement.

Still another source of contention involved the firm's management contracts. During the years of Hoover's partnership, Bewick, Moreing had customarily arranged to manage mining companies for long periods of time with long periods of advance notice required for termination. It was a form of job protection for the firm's professional staff. But in the years after 1908, Hoover and his associate Govett, as directors of various Bewick, Moreing-managed companies, repeatedly demanded renewals for short periods only and with only short periods of notice. The result, according to the firm, was constant quarreling with Hoover.

Most alarmingly of all (in the firm's eyes), in 1911 Hoover created and became managing director of a London-based mining investment business called the Lake View and Oroya Exploration Company. By 1914 it had a "technical committee" and staff providing office space and other services to more than twenty mining companies—the very services that Bewick, Moreing offered *its* clients. To Moreing and his partners the pattern was painfully clear: through Lake View and its technical advisers (such as Theodore Hoover and John Agnew) Hoover was acting as a mining engineer and mine manager in blatant breach of his severance agreement. In the thriving Lake View and Oroya Exploration Company Moreing saw what he most feared: a Hoover-led mines management firm in direct competition with his own.

Moreing's apprehension was well founded. Between 1909 and 1914 a number of his ablest men quit his employ and went to work at once for Herbert Hoover. According to Moreing, Hoover interfered incessantly with the firm's technical staff and schemed to lure Moreing's best employees away. Probably not by coincidence, as a liberated Hoover climbed rapidly to new eminence in his profession, the prestige and success of his former associates began to wane.[115]

Long before August 1914, then, the Hoover–Moreing rivalry had taken on the character of a feud. Privately Moreing called Hoover "conceited" and his brother Theodore "an ill-mannered, ill-tempered cub."[116] Hoover, who later described Moreing as having been "a wholly impossible partner,"[117] no doubt reciprocated with equal asperity.

In the early months of the war, an event occurred that rekindled their smoldering animosity. On November 26, 1914 the Zinc Corporation (comanaged by Hoover and Govett) voted to terminate its general management contract with Bewick, Moreing & Company. The next day Govett gave the firm the required two years' notice.[118]

C. Algernon Moreing was furious. In a letter to Govett, he asserted that for some time it had been apparent that illegal and immoral steps were being taken to interfere with his business. Such measures, he added, were quite foreign to the usual methods of business conduct in London—an oblique reference, perhaps, to Hoover's American nationality.[119]

The Zinc Corporation's decision at once touched off a row. Moreing stated that he was insulted by Govett's letter of November 27. Govett stated that *he* was insulted by Moreing's reply. A few weeks later the corporation's directors resolved that because of Moreing's offensive letter they were no longer able to enter his office (where the corporation kept its records). Instead, the board decided to meet henceforth at Hoover's office.[120]

Meanwhile, in December, one of Moreing's longest-serving employees, F. C. Heley, suddenly announced his intention to resign. Heley was also secretary of the Zinc Corporation. Moreing quickly discovered (or so he later alleged) that Hoover and Govett were planning to remove the corporation's headquarters from Moreing's office and that Heley, at their instigation, was about to seize the corporation's files and take them to the Lake View and Oroya Exploration Company's offices. Furthermore, said Moreing, Hoover had promised to retain Heley as corporation secretary if he left his firm's employ. To thwart this "intrigue" (as Moreing labeled it), he summarily dismissed Heley and ejected him from his office. More contention with the Zinc Corporation directors ensued.[121]

Moreing now attempted to counterattack. He proposed that independent accountants examine the corporation's investment of its reserve capital.[122] At a board meeting in January 1915, Hoover moved, Theodore Hoover seconded, and the board unanimously resolved that this was ridiculous.[123] A month later Moreing proposed an audit of all emoluments given to the corporation's directors. It was an unsubtle hint that Hoover and his colleagues had feathered their nests at the stockholders' expense. Hoover promptly moved that no such audit be made; his fellow directors concurred.[124]

Although rebuffed by the board, Moreing did obtain a temporary consolation: Hoover and Govett apparently dropped their imputed plan to oust Bewick, Moreing immediately.[125] Instead, on January 21, 1915 the Zinc Corporation directors formally resolved that they had *not* dismissed Bewick, Moreing & Company in November but had only given notice to terminate its current contract, which still had nearly two years to run. In the opinion of the board, the existing arrangement (which allowed the firm a percentage of the corporation's profits) was quite liberal and needed revision.[126]

And there, for more than a year, the matter rested. Then, in April 1916, Moreing discovered (or so he later alleged) that the Zinc Corporation board did not intend to "revise" its agreement with him at all. Instead, it had decided to drop his firm completely and install as general manager the very man who was currently serving as his superintendent at the Broken Hill site. Thus still another of Moreing's lieutenants was about to abandon the firm. In addition, according to Moreing, Hoover was planning to turn the "technical control" of the Zinc Corporation over to the "technical committee" of Lake View and Oroya Exploration—a committee consisting largely of his friends. For Moreing and his partners this was the final straw. On April 17 they filed their second breach-of-contract suit against Hoover in six years.[127]

In its statement of claim and other documents, Bewick, Moreing & Company recited Hoover's alleged misdeeds: his coup at the Burma Corporation, his plot to evict the firm from the Zinc Corporation, his transforming of Lake View and Oroya Exploration into a rival management company, and more. In all these ways, the firm contended, Hoover—assisted particularly by his brother and by Govett—had willfully and systematically broken his promises not to practice as a mining engineer or mine manager in competition with Moreing in the British empire. But Hoover, the firm insisted, had done even more. From the beginning he had "persistently endeavoured . . . to covertly break down and deprive [the firm] of their business. . . ."[128] In short, Hoover had not simply defeated his former partners in honest competition. He had intrigued, both illegally and unethically, to destroy them.

So, in mid-1916, the firm bitterly asserted. Hoover's precise defense against these charges is unknown. The firm's version of the story is recorded in legal briefs, memoranda, and correspondence found in its surviving papers.[129] Hoover's own papers contain nothing about either lawsuit.

But while Hoover's records and reminiscences are curiously silent about this episode (in his *Memoirs* he actually claimed that he and Moreing were always "good friends"),[130] one thing is certain: Hoover's prewar association with Moreing initially caused him embarrassment in his Belgian relief work. Early in the war the governor-general of Australia secretly informed the British Colonial Office that many "responsible" people in Australia questioned Hoover's "reliability," since he was "connected with Bewick Moreing a firm not in good repute."[131] The British government quickly replied that Hoover was no longer associated with the firm and that his conduct at the CRB had been quite satisfactory.[132] Nevertheless, incidents like these, and the suspicion among British opponents of the relief that he was an untrustworthy corporate wheeler-dealer, probably led Hoover to complain to a friend in 1915 about "being set up in the world as a previous associate of C. A. Moreing."[133]

If Moreing portrayed Hoover as a ruthless conniver, it soon appeared—at least to some—that the British engineer was capable of playing a similar game. Within weeks of the filing of his firm's second lawsuit, the Zinc Corporation suddenly became the target of a hostile takeover bid. Shortly before the corporation's annual meeting in June 1916, a group of shareholders led by Finlay C. Auld unleashed a virulent assault on the company's board. The dissidents accused the directors (including the Hoover brothers) of numerous acts of mismanagement and malfeasance, including unwise investment of the company's surplus funds. The insurgents asked their fellow shareholders to send proxies to the office of Bewick, Moreing & Company.[134]

To an angry Francis Govett (and probably to Hoover as well), Auld's attack looked like an attempt by Moreing to force the board to retain his firm as general managers.[135] But if this was Moreing's design, he soon saw fit to retreat. In a letter to Govett, and in a speech at the annual meeting on June 26, Moreing disclaimed all connection with Auld's committee. Instead, he accused Auld of using his name without his consent. Auld had no authority to ask for proxies to be sent to my office, said Moreing, adding that he was throwing his own support to the board. Auld, for his part, now admitted that he had "blundered" in not seeking Moreing's prior approval, although he also contended that Moreing privately disapproved of the company's financial position.[136]

Bolstered by Moreing's statement, and backed by a majority of the shareholders, Govett easily routed his opposition. An attempt to compel an independent investigation of the company's affairs went down to defeat. Govett's defense of the board won resounding praise from the mining and financial press. Never have we "seen an agitation against the Board of a company collapse so ignominiously" as the one against the Zinc Corporation board, said the *Financial Times*.[137] Auld's case was "without foundation," said another journal.[138] The whole affair, said still another, was a "fiasco."[139] As for Hoover himself—one target of the assault—he himself was not present to judge. Shortly before the annual meeting, he resigned his seat on the board and did not offer himself for reelection.[140] But many years later he referred to the agitators as "shysters."[141]

Despite their defeat, Auld and his allies persisted with their campaign throughout the summer.[142] At an informal shareholders' meeting on September 5, they accused the board of investing more than $1,000,000 of the corporation's reserve funds in companies in which the Hoover brothers had large personal stockholdings. The implication was strong that Hoover and his colleagues had used corporation funds to promote their own personal gain. The dissidents demanded that a committee be appointed to investigate.[143]

While the directors were willing to establish such a committee if a significant number of stockholders desired it (very few, as it turned out, did),[144] the board's forbearance had now entirely dissipated. Early in September Hoover, his brother, and other Zinc Corporation directors took out writs for libel against Auld and his associates.[145] The case never went to trial. Instead, Govett announced some months later that Auld and his chief ally had withdrawn all their charges, had apologized, and had agreed to pay their own legal costs.[146]

Although Moreing disavowed any connection with the Auld affair, suspicions to the contrary lingered on. Had Moreing triggered the disagreeable uproar in an effort to get even with Hoover and Govett? Had Moreing secretly instigated the proxy fight, only to back off when he saw that it would fail? Or did he, behind the scenes, make a deal? When the furor of 1916 finally subsided, Bewick, Moreing & Company remained as the Zinc Corporation's managers—a role it went on to fill for many years. Had Moreing forced the embattled directors to rehire his firm as his price for deserting the rebellion? Or had the directors themselves bought him off with a contract renewal in order to scatter the opposition?

The interior history of the Zinc Corporation imbroglio will probably never be known. Govett later publicly absolved Auld of primary responsibility for the affair and asserted instead that a "hidden hand" had pulled the strings.[147] Govett did not identify the malefactor. But more than one person in London long suspected that the "hand" he referred to was that of C. Algernon More-ing.[148]

The outcome of the Zinc Corporation controversy was no doubt welcome news to Hoover; his integrity, too, had been impugned. But it did not ter-minate Bewick, Moreing's lawsuit against him. During the summer and autumn of 1916, preliminary legal maneuvers took their course. And as they did, Hoover resigned nearly all his mining company directorates. To his friends and the public he portrayed his decision as an act of duty: he simply no longer had time for private business.[149] His self-sacrificing, martyrlike pos-ture won the admiration of Ambassador Page.[150] But in a visit to the Foreign Office in October, Hoover's attorney disclosed another motive: a desire to remove one of Moreing's grievances out of court.[151] If Hoover were no longer serving on any mining company boards, much of Moreing's complaint would disappear. To Moreing, of course, the resignations were an admission of guilt.[152]

Not all the issues between the two antagonists, however, could be so easily resolved. In October Hoover tried another tactic: postponement of the trial on the ground that he could not take time from CRB work to defend himself. Through his British attorney he boldly asked the Foreign Office to intervene in the case and inform the British court that his relief tasks were too critical for him to be diverted from them by private litigation.[153] In other words, a trial at this time would be detrimental to the Belgian relief. At the same time Hoover solicited and received letters from the Belgian and French ambassa-dors to Great Britain. Both diplomats affirmed his importance to the relief and expressed hope that he could continue to give it his "undivided atten-tion," "without any hindrance," and with complete freedom of movement.[154]

The British Foreign Office declined to intervene directly in Hoover's behalf; such involvement in a private lawsuit it considered "most undesirable."[155] On the other hand, Hoover's chief contact at the Foreign Office, the youthful Lord Eustace Percy, considered it potentially "disastrous" to the relief if Hoover were in fact tied up in the courts. Furthermore, Percy had a low regard for Bewick, Moreing's reputation.[156] With the permission of Foreign Secretary Grey, Percy replied cautiously to Hoover's solicitor. If, said Percy, the *court* wished to learn the Foreign Office's opinion about the importance of Hoo-ver's work and freedom of movement, the foreign secretary would willingly reply to the *court*.[157]

The effect of the Foreign Office's response is unknown. In any event, the pending lawsuit never came to trial. Instead, at the beginning of January 1917 Hoover and Moreing settled their differences out of court. Moreing and his partners agreed to drop their lawsuit and to abrogate the restrictive clauses of the amended severance agreement of 1908—a covenant due to expire any-way in 1918. In return, Hoover agreed to pay the firm £5,000, or nearly $25,000.[158]

The terms of the settlement indenture made no mention of the points at issue between Hoover and the firm. Instead, the document recalled that back in 1902, when Moreing and Hoover were partners, *another* partner named Rowe had caused them massive financial losses and had been expelled from the firm. In the ensuing crisis Moreing had absorbed a disproportionate amount of the losses, since Hoover at the time had lacked the means to assume his fair share. The 1917 indenture now declared that in compensation to Moreing for this deed, Hoover agreed to pay the firm (or Moreing personally) the sum of £5,000.[159]

This denouement was a curious one. Nowhere were the particulars of the Hoover–Moreing feud mentioned. Instead Hoover promised to pay his former partner a substantial sum for a "service" rendered nearly fifteen years earlier—a "service" never at issue in their lawsuit. Why?

It appears that without ever explicitly admitting that he had violated his severance agreement or had done Moreing any deliberate wrong, Hoover had bought the firm off. Now he would not have to undergo an inconvenient and possibly embarrassing public airing of the firm's complaints. Nor would any documentary residue, such as a court order, be left behind: only a formal indenture basing the settlement on an irrelevancy. Five thousand pounds sterling was no trifling sum in 1917. But with the duties of the CRB and a trip to America on his mind, Hoover probably considered it a fair price to pay for ridding himself permanently of Moreing and his partners.

Years later Hoover was to find that it was not quite so easily accomplished as that. He could not know it in 1917, but barely a decade later, when he became a candidate for President of the United States, his political enemies were to scour London for evidence of past business misconduct. The possible reaction of Moreing—who was still alive in 1928—was to cause Hoover considerable anxiety.

All this, of course, lay far in the unforeseeable future. At the end of 1916 Hoover had more immediate matters to consider. At the height of the pretrial maneuvering in October, he had "resigned" his seat on the Burma Corporation board, only to be replaced by one of his closest prewar business associates, A. Chester Beatty.[160] In all likelihood this was a purely nominal gesture, the kind of end-run around his restrictive covenant that so infuriated Moreing. In any case, in early 1917, as soon as Moreing's lawsuit was settled, Beatty promptly resigned from the corporation's directorate, and Hoover returned to the board.[161]

Despite onerous humanitarian duties that would have driven many other men to exhaustion, Hoover now found time for one last feat of mining and financial engineering of the kind at which he had become expert before the war. For many months the head of the CRB's New York office had been William L. Honnold, an American mining engineer with extensive experience in South Africa. Hoover had known him for years. Early in 1917, at Honnold's instigation, Ernest Oppenheimer (of the distinguished South African mining family) approached Hoover with a plan. Oppenheimer disclosed that he and Honnold wished to establish a corporation to develop the alluring goldfields of the Far Eastern Rand. Unfortunately, with a gigantic European war in progress, neither South Africa nor Great Britain possessed the capital needed to launch the ambitious venture. Only one source of ready money was available: the United States. Would Hoover help open the door?

Impressed by Oppenheimer's proposal, Hoover agreed to try. With his assistance, and with the powerful aid of the Hoover name, the South African entrepreneur soon gained access to some of the most prestigious financial houses in America.[162] Later in the year he succeeded in founding the Anglo-American Corporation of South Africa with a share capital of £1,000,000.[163] J. P. Morgan & Company, Guaranty Trust Company of New York, and other American firms invested substantially.[164] The new corporation became an instant giant in its field and has remained so even to this day.[165]

For his role in securing the indispensable financial backing and thus assuring that the venture could be formed, Hoover received (with Honnold) a joint 10% interest in the initial American holding of 500,000 shares—that is, a joint holding of 50,000 shares (worth nearly $250,000)—along with a five-year option to purchase 50,000 additional shares at par.[166] A few years later, when he sold out, Hoover donated the money for expansion of the student union building at Stanford University.[167]

The Anglo-American flotation and Hoover's decision to retain his strategic post in the Burma Corporation ran counter to the prevailing thrust of his actions by the early months of 1917. During the preceding autumn he decided to open an office at 120 Broadway in New York; he dispatched Edgar Rickard from London to handle the arrangements.[168] Meanwhile he proceeded not only to resign his directorships but also—if his later recollection was correct—to sell off virtually all his shareholdings (except for Burma).[169] Just how much he made in these transactions is unknown. In many of these companies his direct shareholdings were apparently quite small. At the Kyshtim, Tanalyk, and Russo-Asiatic corporations, for instance, his sales of stock evidently approximated a mere £3,200.[170]

In one respect Hoover's long-delayed departure from the London mining world was puzzling. His CRB obligations, his desire to follow Theodore back to America, his unseemly contretemps with Moreing: all help to explain his decision to give up his mining company directorates in 1916. But they do not explain his decision to dispose of nearly all of his *investments* as well. Why did he make such a sweeping break? Why, in particular—again, if his later recollections are correct—did he choose this moment to abandon his mining interests in tsarist Russia? Certainly he was not obliged to. If he could retain his foothold in the Burma Corporation, why not do the same in the Russian empire? Despite the handicaps of war, every one of these enterprises was prospering in 1916, and their long-term prospects seemed spectacular. It is hard to believe that Hoover, or anyone in his position, would voluntarily surrender what he later claimed was a fabulous prospective fortune.

Yet this, so he later insisted,[171] was what he did, and one can only speculate why. Perhaps, as the war lengthened and mining conditions in Russia grew more uncertain, he reasoned that a profit, however modest, in the hand was worth more than a dividend in the bush. He had, after all, gotten in (as he usually did) on the ground floor, with little actual cash invested.[172] Perhaps he calculated that he should make what he could now and pour his remaining assets into his greatest love: Burma.[173]

Another factor may also have influenced his withdrawal. In 1916 a leading British newspaper denounced the "pushful American" mining engineers who were allegedly taking over England's metals industry. The editorial evoked a flood of pent-up anger from British engineers, some of whom seemed eager to exclude their American counterparts from working in the British empire.[174] If anyone was the epitome of the "pushful American," it was Hoover. Before the war he had been known as "Hail Columbia" Hoover in Australia, as the "star-spangled" Hoover in parts of London.[175] His fervent and sometimes abrasive Americanism had evoked resentment among some of his colleagues.[176] Perhaps, in the wake of the British newspaper's attack, he began to wonder whether his old business haunts would be congenial ones much longer. Perhaps this was what he meant when he wrote to Theodore in March 1917: "The wisest stroke ever made in our lives was when you cleared out from London. . . ."[177]

Whatever his motive, Hoover did not liquidate all his Russian interests in late 1916. He retained a few hundred Irtysh Corporation shares which he held until that company's liquidation three years later, when his holding was automatically converted into 1,082 shares in a successor Russian mining concern. He did not dispose of these shares until July 1921.[178] Perhaps more significantly, in late 1916 he arranged with his successor on the Russo-Asiatic board, Deane P. Mitchell, to receive a proportion of any additional remuneration accruing to the directors.[179] In this indirect way, perhaps, he kept a claim on what he later called his "deferred interest" in the Irtysh. In 1919 this private understanding enabled Hoover to share in the profits from the sale of 5,000 Irtysh shares that Mitchell acquired as a director's bonus.[180]

If Hoover severed most of his Russian mining connections at the end of 1916, he did so in the nick of time. Scarcely three months later the first phase of the Russian revolution erupted. Late in 1917 the Communists seized power and nationalized foreign-owned mining properties. At Kyshtim, Tanalyk, Ridder, and the rest, local Communist bands took control. Although resident American technical men were not physically molested, conditions at the sites quickly deteriorated as committees of radicalized workers vainly attempted to supplant trained managers. In the spring of 1918 anti-Bolshevik forces expelled the Communist "jackals" (as Hoover later called them), and the great mines temporarily returned to normal. But in 1919–20 the triumph of the Communists, and the ensuing waves of purges and repression, sealed the doom of the progressive technological edifice Hoover had helped to construct.[181] Every one of his Russian enterprises was confiscated—a total loss to their investors. Hoover's colleague Leslie Urquhart, on behalf of the Russo-Asiatic investors, instituted a claim of £56,000,000 in compensation. Years went by; they never received a farthing.[182] But even if they had, there is no evidence that Hoover would have received any of it—unless, perhaps, he had some understanding with Mitchell.[183]

In 1916, then, Hoover apparently disposed of virtually all his direct Russian shareholdings at a modest profit. The fate of his *indirect* holdings was harsher. Years later he declared that his "deferred interest" in the Irtysh venture had been worth a minimum of $15,000,000 "on the proved profits of the mine—ex war." All this, he said—and his "interest" in the Kyshtim Corporation, too—had disappeared. It had all been subject to bond issues that had defaulted and then been foreclosed upon because of the war.[184] "Had it not been for the Great War," he later wrote, "I should have gained a large fortune from these industries—probably more than is good for anybody."[185]

Hoover never specified the nature of his "deferred interest" nor the moment that the devastating default occurred. (There is no evidence that it took place before the overthrow of the tsar in early 1917 or the Bolshevik revolution led by Lenin later that year.) But if the extent of Hoover's stake in Russia and the date of its loss remain unclear, on one point there seems little doubt: had it not been for the Great War—or, more precisely, the Russian Revolution—he would eventually have obtained from his Russian enterprises what he called in his *Memoirs* "the largest engineering fees ever known to man."[186]

How much had he lost? Some years later he stated that at the outbreak of the war he was in a position to accumulate a fortune of at least $30,000,000 in the years ahead but that the war (including its taxation) "crushed this fortune down by 95%."[187] Such a figure may have been inexact, but it probably embodied a truth. Despite his apprehensions of 1914, he did not lose what he had in hand. Rather, much that he *might* have had, never materialized. In this sense, his losses were enormous.

In another sense, too, he sacrificed. "Hoover deliberately threw away a chance to make himself the richest man in the world," a British colleague observed some years later.[188] If the American engineer-turned-philanthropist had not devoted himself almost totally to Belgian relief, if instead he had concentrated on money-making alone, doubtless he could have profited immensely from the war. His prestige as a mining expert and financier, as an authority on copper, lead, and zinc, was unsurpassed in London in 1914. At the very least, if he had been able to focus his tenacity and energy on the zinc crisis, Great Britain might well have developed a modern zinc-smelting industry long before it did—and he himself might have been at the head of it.[189]

In any case, by early 1917 "Hail Columbia" Hoover was a well-to-do, even a wealthy man. His Burma shareholdings alone were worth a million dollars or more, a figure equivalent to several million dollars today.[190] But his head and his heart were now elsewhere. Like the Red House on Hornton Street, his office in London's financial district represented a world that he had finally forsaken.

I I I

H oo v e r' s family obligations and mining career were not the only aspects of his prewar life to suffer from the onslaught of world war. In 1912, at the age of thirty-eight, he had been elected a trustee of his alma mater, Stanford University. Almost instantly he had become the dominant member of the board. By 1914, under his de facto leadership, the trustees had implemented a revised faculty salary schedule, an ambitious construction program, and other much-needed reforms. Largely at his instigation, Stanford's president for more than twenty years, David Starr Jordan, had been deftly removed from office and appointed chancellor (a largely honorific position), while Hoover's old geology professor and patron, John C. Branner, had been installed in Jordan's place. Many suspected that when Branner's own planned retirement occurred in 1915, a youthful Herbert Hoover would succeed him.[191]

The coming of war enlarged the scope of Hoover's ambition. Still, on October 25, 1914, only three days after the formal launching of the Commission for Relief in Belgium, he took time to write a four-page letter to the chairman of Stanford's board of trustees. With President Branner's anticipated term of office more than half over, Hoover was anxious to find a proper successor. It was a matter, he said, "very near to my heart."

Hoover's opinion on this subject was emphatic. Stanford, he declared, was "essentially a Western institution, with ideals entirely different from those which obtain on the Atlantic seaboard. . . ." Its development policies of the past two years (policies largely conceived by himself, he might have added) were "practically unique." Indeed, the university's "whole internal academic structure" was "essentially different from that of any other institution." To Hoover it was therefore evident that Stanford's next president should be "a Western man," and "a man from the present University body." He should also be preeminently an administrator. "The old-line President who was able to preside at Sunday School Conventions and make choicely classical orations on public occasions is not the type of man that Stanford needs," he argued. "Nothing would be more disastrous than to choose some classical Professor from the East." For Hoover only one man fit his criteria: the current dean of Stanford's medical school, Ray Lyman Wilbur.[192]

Hoover's reasoning was extremely revealing of his educational philosophy and self-image. He wanted Stanford to be led by a Westerner, not an Easterner; an executive, not an orator; a man of practical education, not a classically trained academic. A man, in short, like himself. If Wilbur was "deficient on the side of flowered and classical oratory," he remarked crisply, that deficiency could be supplied by Chancellor Jordan. Hoover also admired Wilbur's aggressiveness. If Stanford had "another ten Wilburs" in its other departments, he argued, "they would have been much further forward than they are to-day."[193] Hoover's choice was significant for another reason: Ray Lyman Wilbur was one of his oldest and most intimate friends.

Having circulated his views to key trustees, Hoover now awaited developments. At the beginning of 1915 President Branner duly announced his intention to retire on August 1, and the search for his successor began in earnest.[194] It quickly developed that opposition to Hoover's candidate was strong. During 1914 Wilbur had been embroiled in a bitter battle over the future status of his San Francisco-based department. In response to a cost-cutting directive from the trustees, President Branner had boldly proposed that Stanford terminate all financial support for its young and expensive medical school and turn the facilities over to the University of California. An aroused board of trustees led by Hoover had rebuffed him.[195] Apparently embittered by this defeat, Branner seemed determined not to let Wilbur succeed him.[196] He was not alone in his opposition. The Stanford faculty had overwhelmingly supported Branner's crusade to eliminate the medical school. Many now feared that Wilbur, as president, would place its interests ahead of those of other departments.[197]

Well aware of these sentiments, Hoover tried to neutralize them by proposing to his fellow trustees that his friend be appointed acting president for a trial period of one year. Hoover was certain that Wilbur would introduce so much administrative "steam and push" to the campus that he would "galvanise the whole place within twelve months."[198] But if he should not meet expectations, he could then return "with dignity" to the medical school and another person could be chosen president.[199] Far better to handle matters in this way, Hoover thought, than to embark upon what he called the "experiment" of hiring an educator from the East.[200]

Hoover's suggestion went nowhere. It soon transpired that the faculty's apprehensions about Wilbur were shared by certain trustees, some of whom, including W. Mayo Newhall and J. Leroy Nickel, wished to look outside the faculty—to the East, in fact—for a successor.[201] Hoover, in London, was angry at this turn of events. "I am . . . appalled at the idea of Nickel and Newhall dominating the appointment of a President for Stanford University," he told a friend. "Neither of these men has the university instinct, nor have they the remotest idea as to what constitutes such an institution."[202]

Meanwhile Stanford's newest trustee, Ralph Arnold '98, was pursuing an idea of his own. A petroleum geologist and businessman (as well as Ray Lyman Wilbur's second cousin), Arnold had known the Hoover brothers for years. In January 1915 he asked Hoover whether *he* would accept an offer of the Stanford presidency. Arnold was convinced that the university would be "making no mistake" if it installed Hoover as president for a long enough term to "thoroughly organize the faculty" and establish "a definite policy of administration."[203]

Hoover's reply was swift and clear: Ray Lyman Wilbur, he said, should be chosen. But then he added:

If it was not for the intervention of all these international troubles, I would have been quite prepared to take on the job for a couple of years, simply as acting president or acting trustee in charge of the University, in order to hold the position open for Ray. I have no intention to become a University President as a permanent occupation.

Hoover pointed out he could not "desert the Belgians until peace has been signed" and that he would then need three or four months to arrange his "private affairs" before he could "take on the job." How soon he might be available was therefore impossible to determine. Nevertheless, he seemed willing, at least in principle, to accept the position if offered it.[204]

Arnold was extremely pleased. He immediately replied that if certain circumstances materialized, he would nominate Hoover as a compromise candidate for acting president or acting trustee in charge of the university.[205] Hoover, significantly, did not object.

Then, in the winter of 1915, an unexpected event threw the selection process into turmoil. David Starr Jordan, who as chancellor had been attending trustees' meetings, announced publicly that Wilbur would probably be selected as president. Not long afterward, Jordan, a strong advocate of Wilbur, compounded his indiscretion by practically demanding that the board come to a decision in April—a move interpreted by some as an attempt to stampede the board toward Wilbur. Jordan's behavior incensed the trustees, fortified the anti-Wilbur faction among them, and obliged the rest to defer a choice for some time. As a result, the spring of 1915 passed without result, and Branner was induced to remain as president for as much as another year.[206]

Reporting all this to London, Ralph Arnold again expressed his wish that Hoover could step in for two or three years as president and reorganize the entire university. Not only would the institution benefit, he argued, the interim period would enable Wilbur to solidify his credentials as Hoover's successor. How Arnold yearned for Hoover's presence at the showdown meeting of the trustees! At such a meeting, he knew, Hoover's influence would be "dominant."[207]

Far from the environs of Stanford, Hoover was disgusted at the course events were taking. He told Arnold that it was a source of "humour" to think that "a narrow-minded farmer like Newell [Newhall] or an extremely avricious, egotistical banker like [trustee Frank B.] Anderson are either one or the other at all capable in choosing a President for Stanford." As for Branner, who was about to head east on a search for candidates:

You and I have known for years that Branner is capable of the most violent and consistent prejudices and that with all his admirable qualities these prejudices absolutely blind him to the merits or demerits of individuals. I should consider that he above all men associated with Stanford University is the least qualified to nominate a new President; but when I think of Jordan's judgment I am equally appalled. As to myself, if it does not work out in the next six months that Ray is possible, until the above gentlemen have been completely removed from the scenery and their influence entirely excised, I might manage to take the job and hold it for two or three years, provided I had a clear six months to get prepared in. Much depends upon how long this War lasts and a hundred other contingencies, but rather than see some loud-mouthed Princetown [sic] professor put in the position, I would be willing to take three years out of my life and throw them away.[208]

Hoover's worries about a "loud-mouthed Princetown professor" proved apposite. After a trip east late in the spring to investigate presidential possibilities, Branner and Newhall returned with an enthusiastic endorsement of Edwin Capps, professor of classics at Princeton—the very epitome of all that Hoover found objectionable.[209] Thoroughly alarmed, Arnold cabled London that Wilbur's "only chance" depended on Hoover's attending the next trustees' meeting.[210] Only Hoover, he said, could win over trustee Anderson and sufficiently isolate the opposition to prevail. Once again Arnold held out the prospect of Hoover's becoming president if Wilbur's bid should fail, and he disclosed that two other trustees seemed amenable to this possibility.[211]

Hoover's reaction to the Capps candidacy was scorching. The Princeton professor, he cabled, was a "social fop" and "sycophant to [the] Wall Street bunch." He was the "absolute negation of [the] type required for president." But for all his vehemence, Hoover had to record that he had "no hope" of visiting California until the war was over. Millions of people were dependent on his venture in humanitarian relief. The CRB, he said, would collapse into "absolute chaos" without him.[212]

By now the Stanford board of trustees was deeply divided between the pro- and anti-Wilbur factions.[213] Chancellor Jordan agreed with Arnold that only Hoover, appearing in person, could persuade the board to select his nominee.[214] To Jordan, Leland Stanford would "turn over in his grave" if he knew that "a Professor of classics from the most reactionary university in America" were to become president.[215] Alas, the one man who seemed capable of resolving the impasse in Wilbur's favor was thousands of miles away.

At its August meeting the board of trustees decided to interview several candidates; clearly a decision was some time away. Arnold immediately informed Hoover that he might yet be "the victim of circumstances" if Wilbur were blocked and that "[trustees] Hopkins and Eells are strong for you in case Wilbur cannot get it."[216] Lou Henry Hoover, cabling to her husband from California, was more succinct. "Presidential campaign at deadlock," she said. "May insist on you."[217]

Immersed in Belgian relief problems six thousand miles away, Hoover could do little to influence the outcome. As it turned out, his personal presence was not required. During the autumn, a majority of the trustees voted for Wilbur, the minority acquiesced, and the board tendered its offer.[218] Wilbur accepted—in order that (he later wrote) "medicine would not be destroyed as a part of the University." To Wilbur the time had arrived for Stanford to fulfill its early promise and become in full measure a university, not simply a small college with a large endowment. The acquisition of the medical school, in his view, had been the first great step in this transition.[219] With all these aspirations Hoover emphatically agreed. Now, thanks in considerable part to Hoover's own "steam and push," Wilbur was to have his opportunity.

Shortly after the board made its decision, Hoover sent the president-elect a seven-page letter of advice and felicitation. For "the first time in its history," he predicted, Stanford University under Wilbur would "take absolutely first rank." Hoover urged his friend to reorganize Stanford's system of "faculty control" in order that "leaders of the University" might emerge instead of "secondary men." Specifically, he suggested that Wilbur bring related faculty departments together into "groups," administered by committees of department heads, who in turn would elect representatives to a small "legislative body" to be known as the University Executive Committee or University Senate. In this way, he argued, the "best brains" could prevail in university governance, and the influence of assistant professors and instructors could be reduced. With such a body drawn from the "pre-eminent professors," Wilbur might even be able to abolish "the well known Debating Society called the 'Academic Council.'" Returning to a theme he had expounded often before the war, Hoover also advocated that Stanford hire more "illustrious men." These select few were the key, he asserted, to the university's success and to its standing in the academic world.

Hoover offered his friend one other self-revealing suggestion:

> There is one bit of advice that I will hazard you on the whole question of the administration of any institution and that is never to be afraid of the ability of one's lieutenants but to bear in mind that the more able the men with whom one surrounds oneself the more certainty one has of ultimate success.[220]

With Wilbur's accession to the presidency in January 1916, Hoover believed that his "usefulness in the institution" was "more or less at an end," except insofar as he could "deliver the goods" on the board in behalf of his friend's policies.[221] This feeling of a service completed, combined with his recognition that the European war—and hence his absence from America—would probably last another year, led him on May 30, 1916 to submit his resignation from Stanford's board of trustees. It did not seem "fair," he wrote, to remain a trustee "as I am of no service in executive work."[222]

Hoover's action disturbed President Wilbur. "You must not get an attack of conscience," he wrote his patron. "We need you from time to time and we need you badly."[223] Hoover's colleagues on the board agreed. Instead of accepting his resignation, they merely laid his letter on the table, where the matter quietly died.[224] More than one of them stated that if Hoover insisted on withdrawing now, they would resign later, if necessary, to make way for his return.[225] Such was the esteem in which he was held by his associates. Still, it was now clear that Hoover's next contribution to his alma mater would have to await the end of the war.

Not long after Wilbur assumed the Stanford presidency, Brand Whitlock happened to write to Herbert Hoover. The American minister to Belgium had journeyed on leave to the United States in late 1915. Upon his return to Brussels, he told Hoover that everywhere in America people had expressed their regard for the CRB chairman. "[I]f you don't look out," Whitlock added, "they will try to run you for Vice President. . . ."[226]

A few days later Hoover responded:

As to your remark about Vice-Presidents, nothing could be more abhorrent to me in the wide world than to go into politics in any shape or form. The one chance which had been my life ambition has come and gone as Stanford University, which offered me its presidency, could not wait on my intangible arrival pending the completion of the Belgian job, and therefore they accepted my suggestion and elected Dr. Wilbur to that position, so that I shall go back to the lead mines with a sufficient amount of experience in public affairs to know that it is an evil connection if one values contentment or even constructive results.[227]

Hoover's reply was not quite accurate. Stanford University never formally or informally offered him its presidency. But during the long behind-the-scenes struggle to select a successor to John C. Branner, at least three of the university's fifteen trustees had been ready to support Hoover as a "compromise" candidate, and he almost certainly could have obtained the position had he sought it. Alas for his "life ambition," he had other, far larger commitments.

Hoover's tone of wistfulness in his letter to Whitlock was probably genuine. Yet despite his disclaimer of political yearnings and his professed expectation of returning to the "lead mines," by 1916 it was clear that neither Stanford University nor mining engineering encompassed his growing ambition. Long before the war he had evinced a desire to enter public service. The conduct of the CRB, the stormy machinations of diplomacy, the achievement of "constructive results" for the unfortunate, had refined and deepened his longings. The war had remorselessly shattered his once-settled world and aspirations. But it was now about to provide him with greater opportunities gained.

12

New Horizons

FROM 1914 to 1917 Herbert Hoover occupied an extraordinary niche in the cockpit of a Europe at war: he was probably the only American citizen permitted to travel freely through enemy lines, consulting with leaders of governments at every stop.[1] "I dealt constantly with civil officials and often with high military officers in Britain, France and Germany," he later wrote. "I talked incessantly with soldiers, civilians and newspaper men."[2] As familiar with the corridors of the British Foreign Office as with the headquarters of the German General Staff in northern France, personally acquainted with the presidents and prime ministers of at least four belligerent countries, Hoover was one of the best informed men in Europe on the social consequences of the war. Walter Hines Page, for one, marveled at his facility for "knowing what is going on."[3] But Hoover's experience went deeper still. "I saw that war in the raw," he later observed, ". . . probably more intimately than any other American."[4] It was to have a searing impact on his social philosophy and future career.

Hoover, of course, was no stranger to Europe. As a cosmopolitan, London-based mining engineer, he had visited the continent often before the war and had observed the seething rivalries beneath the placid surface of Old World civility. Although raised a Quaker, he was no advocate of fashionable prewar panaceas for international peace and disarmament. Deep-running "currents of nationalism," he believed, "undermined the whole hypothesis on which such propaganda was based." Well before the fateful assassination of Archduke Franz Ferdinand at Sarajevo, or so, at least, he said in 1915, Hoover had concluded that "the only safeguard of peace" was "preparedness for war."[5]

Despite his intuition of European instability, the American engineer, like most people, did not foresee the cataclysm of August 1914.[6] And despite his premonition, on that dismal August 4, that the world was about to undergo "seven years of considerable privation,"[7] he quickly adopted the prevailing view that the war would be a short one and that the Allies would win. After all, he reasoned, they possessed more manpower, controlled the seas, had the Central Powers engaged on two fronts, and enjoyed greater access to the world's resources.[8]

Hoover's first visit to wartime Germany (in February 1915) demolished this sanguine illusion.[9] All around him he saw an aroused and regimented nation—men and women alike—mobilizing for conflict with unprecedented thoroughness.[10] The Germans' superiority in organization, he concluded, combined with their military skill and interior lines of movement, would surely offset the advantages of the Allies. He returned to London convinced that the war would be a long one and that neither side would win.[11] "The more terrible forms of this struggle have not yet I believe been developed," he told a CRB associate in late February.[12] To an American friend he confessed in June, ". . . I had not expected when I entered upon this Belgian business that it would last so long." Now the war seemed likely to endure for another year.[13]

In a remarkable letter evidently written on June 3, 1915 he elaborated:

I have returned a few days ago from France, Germany and western Russia. I wish again to reiterate to you that the evidences of certain psychological currents amongst these people are of the strongest possible character; that in Germany especially, there is no doubt in my mind, that there is building up a revival of the old Roman sentiment which may be expressed in the old Roman phrase—"The Masters of the World." This does not apply to a few men at the top but is becoming the ambition of every German of even half intelligence. I do not believe that they have any faith of accomplishing this by the peaceful arts of commerce. Some of these days the civilised world has got to fight these people to a finish. The English people have already in their history gone through a mild case of this contagion, and are pleased to sit under the illusion that they are already the masters of the world, and the fire of their ambitions has largely died out, and I do not believe that they will again be on the offensive unless they are deeply stirred up.

For Hoover the implication of his analysis was plain:

To me this simply means preparedness. So long as the richest nation in the world is unable to defend itself for twenty minutes it is likely to become the victim of this ambition. I do not mean preparedness by way of putting two million men under arms, but I mean it by way of accumulation of arms, ammunition and defensive works to accomodate two million men. It is always possible with the high intelligence of the American to make a good soldier of him in three or four months if he can be properly armed and properly officered.[14]

In contrast to Germany's grim and Spartan efficiency was the behavior of its enemy across the Channel. While Hoover's private sympathies lay with the British,[15] he was appalled by their "fumbling," their "groping," and their "business-as-usual" attitude in the early months of the fighting.[16] In June 1915 he vented his disgust in a conversation with some friends in Brussels. The British "will muddle through," he declared. "The Englishman likes to muddle through." "They were to be ready in May," someone said. "Next May," Hoover replied.[17] He told Ambassador Page in July that the new British minister of munitions, Lloyd George, was as valuable as the rest of the Cabinet put together. "They'll have to make him Prime Minister before the war ends," Hoover remarked.[18]

All this seemed to reinforce the CRB chairman's conviction that the United States must be ready to defend itself if need be. ". . . I believe that there are ambitions inherent in races," he told a friend in mid-1915, "and that anything which tends to undermine the preparedness of a people for its own defence is rank folly to say the least of it."[19] Hoover had never been a pacifist. Fifteen years before, as an engineer working in China, he had lived through the terrible siege of Tientsin during the Boxer Rebellion. In its aftermath he had declared, "Diplomacy with an Asiatic is of no use. If you are going to do business with him you must begin your talk with a gun in your hand, and let him know that you will use it."[20] Now, fifteen years later, he viewed with deep skepticism the efforts of various American "peace" activists to promote neutral "mediation" of the war—a movement culminating in Henry Ford's pathetic "peace ship" that sailed to Europe in 1915 to "get the boys out of the trenches by Christmas."[21]

Yet if Hoover was pro-Ally and pro-preparedness, and instinctively combative by nature, by the late summer of 1915 he resolutely opposed intervention in the conflict by the United States. Such an action, he wrote to President Wilson in September, would result in an "infinite disaster to the American people."[22] It could only be the "last alternative to continued transgression" of American rights.[23] Hoover was too familiar (he later wrote) with "European power politics" to have much faith that his own country could alter these forces sufficiently to create a lasting peace. America, he believed, could best influence the eventual settlement if it stayed out of the war in the meantime and exerted its moral, economic, and military power at the peace conference.[24]

Hoover's antipathy to the British Admiralty, which tried to destroy the CRB and brand him as pro-German in 1916, may also have tempered his initial sentiments. Certainly this episode helped to instill in him what Lord Percy labeled a lifelong "personal dislike" of the Admiralty.[25] While the CRB chairman remained sympathetic to the Allied cause, the British leaders to whom he was personally closest were almost entirely Liberals like Foreign Secretary Grey, Sir Herbert Samuel, and Francis W. Hirst of the *Economist*—not the Tories, the military, or the advocates of all-out economic warfare against Germany. It was a Liberal government, after all, that had allowed his relief commission to be formed, and it was the Liberals within the government who had largely permitted him to continue. With this part of England he found rapport. The anti-CRB maneuvers of British "hawks," however, plus the presence in the Allied camp of the authoritarian tsarist regime in Russia, prevented him from viewing the European conflict as an unequivocal "holy war for democracy."[26] He remained opposed to American entry until March 1917.[27]

In truth, Hoover in many ways was a defensive-minded, nineteenth-century liberal and, in the British context, a Liberal, too. What, after all, was his Commission for Relief in Belgium but gentlemanly, humanitarian liberalism institutionalized? And like other liberal men of good will and moderation, he grew increasingly alarmed as the conflagration around him burned on. This war will leave Europe impoverished and burdened by unimaginable debt, he told Brank Whitlock in mid-1915.[28] A few months later he informed a friend, "The world is going to see a period of twenty years of economic demoralisation. . . . [I]f I do not misjudge the situation in Europe the aftermath of this war is going to be social revolution. . . ."[29] In mid-1916 he remarked that the world would feel the effects of the war for a quarter of a century to come.[30]

By early 1916 Hoover was haunted by the realization that he was witnessing a phenomenon hitherto unknown in world history. Once upon a time soldiers had fought primarily against soldiers; the harshness of war, he wrote, had been somewhat mitigated by "certain elements of chivalry." Now, for the first time, civilians themselves—entire societies—were the targets of enemy assault. On the Allied side, a blockade not just of weapons but of food "stretched hate into every [German] home three times a day." On the German side, submarine attacks on merchant shipping threatened food supplies for the Allies, while Zeppelin raids on British cities killed women and children indiscriminately. The result, on both sides, was mass privation and an unprecedented inflammation of popular psychology. "Total war," as Hoover put it, had produced "total hate."[31]

Trapped in this rising inferno, the leaders of the belligerent countries, Hoover believed, were no longer free to negotiate a compromise peace. They were "imprisoned by the emotions of their people." No outcome short of victory could justify the staggering sacrifices of blood and treasure. The war seemed destined to go on until one side or the other collapsed in exhaustion. European civilization, he thought, was "busy committing suicide."[32]

The awful reality of total war impressed Hoover further in the summer of 1916. On a visit to the German General Staff's headquarters in northern France he was invited to witness the ongoing battle of the Somme. He never forgot what he saw:

> We motored for several hours to a point near a hilltop observation post in the forest, a distance back from the forward trenches and a mile or two away from the main roads. During the last few miles an occasional shell cracked nearby but the ingenious camouflage of the road—to the extent of a false parallel—seemed to give protection to our route. At the post the constant rumble of artillery seemed to pulverize the air. Seen through powerful glasses, in the distant view lay the unending blur of trenches, of volcanic explosions of dust which filled the air where over a length of sixty miles a million and a half men were fighting and dying. Once in a while, like ants, the lines of men seemed to show through the clouds of dust. Here under the thunder and belching volcanoes of 10,000 guns, over the months of this battle, the lives of Germans and Englishmen were thrown away. On the nearby road unending lines of Germans plodded along the right side to the front, not with drums and bands, but in the silence of sodden resignation. Down the left side came the unending lines of wounded men, the "walking cases" staggering among cavalcades of ambulances. A quarter of a million men died and it was but one battle in that war.
>
> The horror of it all did not in the least affect the German officers in the post. To them it was pure mechanics. Not one of the Germans showed the slightest anxiety. They said that the British were losing two to one—butting their heads against a stone wall. And that was true. It was all a horrible, devastating reality, no romance, no glory.[33]

This awareness of being a privileged witness to events of epochal significance led Hoover in early 1915 to one of the most far-reaching decisions of his life. On a journey across the English Channel on CRB business in December 1914 or January 1915, he carried with him a copy of the autobiography of Andrew D. White, the distinguished historian, diplomat, and first president of Cornell University. In it White described how, as a student in France in the 1850s, and for years thereafter, he had assembled a vast collection of documents on the history of the French Revolution, including books, pamphlets, manuscripts, cartoons, reports, and other "fugitive publications." His library eventually helped a friend prepare one of the best accounts of the French Revolution written in the English language.[34]

Reading this passage, Hoover realized (he later remarked) that he was "in a unique position to collect fugitive literature" about another revolution: the titanic global conflict that he himself was witnessing. With the eagerness of a lifelong bibliophile, the decisiveness of an executive, and the assurance of a man of means, he resolved to undertake an audacious project similar to White's: the systematic collecting of contemporary documents on the Great War before they were lost to history.[35]

Hoover was therefore probably in a receptive mood, when, early in March 1915, he received a letter from Professor E. D. Adams of Stanford University. Between the two men were two deep bonds of interest: the course of modern history and the development of the university in Palo Alto. Less than a year before, Hoover had given his friend a gift of $400 to acquire transcripts of crucial British documents for a book that Adams was preparing on Great Britain and the American Civil War.[36] But it was not money that the historian was seeking now.

Instead, in his letter Adams called attention to the extraordinary historical importance of the records of the Commission for Relief in Belgium. The CRB, he wrote, was "an absolutely new thing in History" and would seem even more unique in fifty years than it did now. It was "the one great bright spot" in the war and would "reflect greatly upon Stanford such as nothing else has done" in the years to come. He therefore strongly urged Hoover to deposit the CRB's records someday at his alma mater.[37]

Hoover quickly replied that he found Adams's suggestion to be of "extreme value." He agreed that the CRB's files should be retained (as in fact was being done already), "if for no other purpose than to prove our innocence in the inevitable persecution which we are bound to receive from one quarter or another" after the war. "[E]very atom of material," he told Adams, would be preserved. It would be a "fine idea," he added, "to store them at Stanford University."[38] Curiously, though, he said nothing about his plan to collect "fugitive literature," a plan he later said antedated Adams's letter.

Adams was delighted by Hoover's response, and from time to time in the next three years he reminded Hoover of his promise.[39] President Wilson's adviser, Colonel Edward House, during a visit to London in the winter of 1915, also urged Hoover to preserve the CRB's files.[40] The commission's chairman needed little prodding. Convinced of his relief records' importance, he even supplemented them on one occasion by having his trusted friend Hugh Gibson provide him copies of certain documents at the U.S. embassy in London.[41] (Hoover's facilities for obtaining information were more extensive, perhaps, than Ambassador Page knew.) At the moment, as the battles and economic strife raged on, there was relatively little that Hoover could do to fulfill his ambition of assembling a personal archive on the Great War.[42] But in his reading of Andrew D. White's autobiography and his correspondence with E. D. Adams lay the germ of an enterprise that was to become the world's largest private repository of documents on twentieth-century political history: the research center known today as the Hoover Institution.[43]

I I

H E R B E R T Hoover was constitutionally incapable of extended repose. As the months of 1915 passed—and as if directing the relief of Belgium were not sufficient burden for any man—the chairman of the CRB moved beyond the role of passive observer to that of active (if marginal) player on the stage of wartime diplomacy.

In early February Colonel Edward House arrived in London on the first of his confidential peace missions for President Wilson. A week and a half later, at the American embassy, he met Hoover, just back from a trip to Berlin. During the next ten days the two men had several conversations.[44]

House was immediately impressed by his interlocutor. He is "a resourceful fellow and needs to be," House noted approvingly in his diary.[45] The colonel publicly lauded the CRB's efficiency.[46] Hoover, however, was far less impressed by his visitor. House, he later wrote, was "totally ignorant of European politics or the forces moving among the peoples at war." Both Wilson and House, he felt, seemed to be "living in a stratosphere far above the earthly ground on which the war was being fought." To Hoover the American president's dreams of mediating an end to the war on the basis of a compromise peace were "all unreal."

> The hard facts were that the leaders on both sides had no idea of a stalemate; they wanted victory; they wanted world power, new territorial possessions. The masses in each country believed that they were fighting for defense of their firesides against monstrous enemies and were going to get full compensation and vengeance upon them.

Wilson, Hoover thought, was "an eminent historian," but "he did not seem to grasp the fact that the forces in Europe were the distillation of the mores of these widely different peoples, their centuries of dangers, ambitions, wrongs, fears and hates. This war was not just a fortuitous incident apart from the inheritance of Europe."[47]

Nevertheless, during the next two years Hoover willingly served as an unofficial "outpost observer of war forces"[48] for Colonel House, who valued the impressions and "inside" information that Hoover alone could give.[49] From time to time Hoover conferred with House in person; occasionally he even gave House copies of important CRB correspondence.[50] In August 1915, for instance, after visiting German headquarters on the western front, Hoover, on his own initiative, sent House a detailed summary of his recent conversations with German officers and a confidential assessment of German attitudes toward Woodrow Wilson's diplomacy.[51] A few months later Hoover attempted to get the presidential adviser to intervene at the White House to make Hugh Gibson minister to Belgium.[52]

For his part the colonel became a steady ally of the CRB, particularly during the dangerous Lindon Bates affair of 1915. It was through House that Hoover first corresponded with President Wilson early that year—inaugurating a friendship that was to be critical to Hoover's career.[53] On at least one occasion the colonel used Hoover to convey messages to the Germans. Tell them, he urged Hoover (in November 1915), of the "futility of making Zeppelin raids on London."[54]

Hoover's contacts with the American government were not limited to Edward House, nor did he remain a mere "outpost observer." In the spring of 1915 the chairman of the CRB attempted audaciously to influence American foreign policy at the highest level. The occasion was the German sinking of the *Lusitania*.

Like millions of his countrymen, Hoover was aghast. But the head of the Belgian relief effort did not stop at expressing his outrage. On May 10, only three days after the *Lusitania* went down, he approached Ambassador Page in London with a plan to meet the crisis. Hoover proposed that the United States "instantly" call a convention of neutral nations in Washington, D.C., to vindicate "the rights of neutrals against all belligerents." At this gathering, he argued, the neutrals should resolve that "acts against life" (such as the *Lusitania* incident) were criminal deeds requiring "absolute punishment." The delegates should then demand that the perpetrators of such acts, including those who issued the orders from above, be turned over to the neutral powers for "trial and punishment." Furthermore, this alliance of neutrals should agree to employ its "whole military and naval strength" "as a unit" to carry out acts of punishment and enforce international law.

Hoover recognized the drastic implications of his proposal. Because the neutral country of Holland bordered on Germany and was thus vulnerable to its pressure, he declared that the American navy might have to be stationed in Dutch ports for her protection. And because the Allies, he believed, were unlikely to commit crimes requiring military retribution, he knew that the effect of his scheme would be that any further German misdeeds would inevitably force the neutrals into war on the side of the Allies. Nevertheless, Hoover was willing to take the risk. He was convinced that a "strong line" now would stop these heinous acts and arrest the "steady slide of the world into barbarism." Certainly mere gestures like the severance of diplomatic relations would be both "puerile and futile," while the acceptance of monetary compensation for the *Lusitania* disaster would "degrade the whole plane of American life."[55]

Meanwhile, around May 11, Hoover received an indirect feeler from the U.S. government: what effect might American action in the crisis have on the duties of the Commission for Relief in Belgium? Hoover believed that certain members of President Wilson's Cabinet were using fear of jeopardizing the relief as an excuse for "weak action" against Germany.[56] On May 12, therefore, he and his American colleagues in the CRB London headquarters cabled a message to President Wilson. Even if a diplomatic break came, they said, Americans in Belgium and northern France could be withdrawn, other neutrals could replace them, and the work of food relief could go on. This presumed, of course, that the Allies and Germans would permit it to continue and that the Germans would maintain their guarantees. Still, the cablers noted confidently that the Germans were eager for the food imports to Belgium to keep coming.[57]

The communication to Woodrow Wilson did not stop there. Hoover was convinced that unless the American people "put up a strong front" now, they "would, in the long run, seriously jeopardise the whole of our independence from encroachment from Europe."[58] In several hundred more words, therefore, he and his associates poured out a cascade of outspoken advice. The work of the CRB, they said, "pales . . . into insignificance" compared to the issues now confronting humanity:

> We are certain that unless America to-day takes a strong lead in the vindication of the rights of neutrals and the upholding and enforcement of international agreements, the world will have slipped back two hundred years towards barbarism. Since this war began one agreement after another has been set aside by one belligerent after another, and as the sanctity of international undertakings and the proof of their ability to stand is fundamental to the world's ultimate peace, any deviation from the insistence by neutrals of these undertakings undermines irretrievably the whole future of our civilisation. We believe that the hour has struck when America must stand on this issue.

Hoover and his associates did not believe that America should go to war over the episodes that had occurred thus far. But they did endorse a policy of "vigor" based upon a distinction between "violations against property" and "violations against life." Transgressions against property, they argued, could always be compensated for in money. But "transgressions against life" must be met by punishment. The U.S. government should therefore demand that henceforth "the actual perpetrators and those responsible for such violence should be handed over to them or some independent tribunal, for trial and execution, and that the whole of our resources [should] be pledged to secure this. . . ." If it did so, said Hoover and his friends, "it is our belief that these acts would be brought to an end."

The CRB men also confessed their "humiliation" at the way people in Great Britain were interpreting President Wilson's recent remark, "There is such a thing as a man being too proud to fight." Hoover and his colleagues could not believe that Wilson meant "that we are prepared to submit to the continued cold-blooded murder of our women and children and not fight. It is not upon this doctrine that the American Republic has been built up, maintained, and can endure." Instead, they insisted that the American government defend its traditional principles, including the doctrine that "no ships shall be sunk where the safety of the lives of our citizens is not provided for."

Lest the President be tempted to take a less militant course, Hoover and his associates denounced as "degrading" the idea of accepting monetary compensation for the lives lost on the *Lusitania* and dismissed as "puerile" "such diplomatic inventions as the withdrawal or dismissal of Ambassadors." Rather, the U.S. government should firmly support "the ideal that international agreements must from this day forward be upheld so far as they affect neutrals." If it did so, it would receive "unqualified support" from all neutrals, restore American prestige to its rightful level, and probably quell the heinous acts of belligerents. But if these acts recurred, then, concluded Hoover and his colleagues, "we shall have gone to war for an ideal which history will justify."[59]

As if this manifesto were not enough, Hoover dispatched a separate letter to the President. Only "a strong line of constructive character," he argued, could save America from being drawn into the European "holocaust" yet contribute also the Europe's "ultimate redemption." He urged Wilson to challenge the German government on the lofty plane of "ideals" and tell the Germans that America intended "to see such ideals lived up to" in her relations with the German state. Such a course would powerfully affect German public opinion, deter German "transgressions," and render further American action unnecessary.[60]

Hoover acknowledged to Ambassador Page that his bluntly worded cable to the President was "mighty long and possibly pretty crude." Certainly his indignant messages seemed closer in spirit to Theodore Roosevelt than to the Quaker faith of his childhood. But the Yankee humanitarian was not becoming famous for tact or timidity, and he added that it was "the inalienable right of every American to speak his mind."[61]

There now followed a period of anxious waiting, while the "diplomatic *pourparlers*" (as he put it) took their course.[62] The CRB chairman was not pleased by the Wilson administration's initial protest note of May 10. In it the President demanded that Germany end its unrestricted submarine warfare, disavow the *Lusitania* sinking, and make reparation for the lost American lives. But to Hoover the note "bore down too long on mere incident" and gave the Germans an opportunity to reply in kind. If I had drafted the document, he told a friend, I would have demanded concurrence on principles first; matters of "incident" could be settled later.[63] "I do believe," said Hoover, "that if the President had enunciated great ideals and high principles, he would have caught the support of German public opinion against their own military clique. . . ." He had not done so, and the crisis, in Hoover's view, was now "impossible of solution."[64]

Hoover was even more disturbed by the Wilson administration's aloofness toward the CRB during its own recent shipping difficulties with the Germans:

> . . . I take it that the American government is sticking closely to the formula that all the operations of this Commission are entirely disassociated from that Government; that all the Officials of the Government who lend us their kindly help do so entirely in unofficial capacities. . . . To put the matter plainly, we are an orphan and have to do the best we can without any rightful guardians.[65]

On June 9, after receiving an unsatisfactory reply from the Germans, Wilson dispatched a second, stronger *Lusitania* note, just as Hoover had predicted.[66] It was a missive so demanding that Secretary of State Bryan, fearing war, resigned rather than sign it.[67] A few weeks later the crisis finally subsided, with the United States warning in yet another note that any repetition of *Lusitania*-type incidents would be regarded as "deliberately unfriendly."[68]

By this time Hoover's belligerent mood had apparently vanished. If in the spring of 1915 he sharply criticized Wilsonian diplomacy and was willing to go to war, if necessary, to defend neutral rights, by the end of the summer he was—or professed to be—completely satisfied by Wilson's handling of the *Lusitania* affair. On September 3 he even congratulated the President by letter. Only your "firmness" and "extraordinary appeal . . . to justice and humanitarian sentiment in Germany," he wrote, had brought about success. In "any less capable hands," he added, the crisis would have "drifted" into "the appalling result of war."[69]

Never again, before April 1917, did Hoover advocate a tougher American policy toward the European belligerents. Never again, during this period, did he express disapproval of Woodrow Wilson's leadership.[70] In mid-1916 he declared himself pleased that Wilson had kept America out of the war.[71] He told a relief associate that even if Wilson should be defeated for reelection he would probably be elected again later on. Wilson, said Hoover, was a very great man.[72] A Bull Moose supporter of Theodore Roosevelt for the presidency in 1912, Hoover took no part in the election four years later.[73] But if he had done so, he probably would have voted for Wilson.

The *Lusitania* affair was but one element in a darkening configuration of events that perturbed Hoover throughout 1915: the intensifying British naval blockade of Germany and the mounting German submarine campaign against Allied shipping. Both measures were giant steps on the road to total war. Both jeopardized American maritime commerce, affronted American convictions about neutral rights and freedom of the seas, and subverted traditional canons of humane warfare. Struggling with these challenges to international law and morality, and especially with their implications for the relief, Hoover was led in mid-1915 to another (and more persistent) venture in unofficial diplomacy. This time his target was the British Cabinet.

Early that summer, in a conversation with certain members of the Foreign Office, he boldly asserted that the British naval blockade on food shipments into Germany was a mistake. Not only was it illegal and immoral, he argued, it was politically and economically foolish as well. Why not raise the blockade on food entirely? he asked. Without it Germany would lose a justification for her pernicious submarine warfare. Moreover, the German currency, artificially sustained by the embargo, might very well plummet. To Hoover's surprise the men at the Foreign Office agreed with him. But, they claimed, there was one (unnamed) member of the Cabinet who adamantly opposed such a step.[74]

Not long afterward, Hoover visited German army headquarters in northern France. He returned more convinced than ever that the British food embargo was at the heart of current diplomatic difficulties. The German army leadership, he told Colonel House, was "suffering from a form of mental fanaticism" on the subject and could see no "immorality in any kind of reprisals." Hoover was certain that the Germans would never alter their methods of submarine warfare—at least not in principle—so long as the hated British food blockade was in force.[75]

Back in London in early August, Hoover decided to act. After conferring with Ambassador Page, and at the request, he told a friend, of "certain ministers," he addressed a nine-page letter to Page on August 5. The Allied embargo on food supplies into Germany, he declared, had been a "gigantic mistake." Strictly from the perspective of "actual pressure" it had been "an absolute failure": Germany, with its "disciplined economy," had been able to produce adequate food supplies despite the blockade and was likely to do so in the future. Indeed, the embargo had actually been counterproductive. More than any other factor, it had created "an absolute solidarity amongst the whole of the Germans," right "down to the very children." Germany was a nation "with its back to the wall," said Hoover, "fighting as a people in a way the world has never seen before." The Allied food blockade was largely responsible. "The German people eat black bread three times a day," he noted, and hold the Allies responsible for their misery. As a result there was burning throughout that nation "a flame of enduring passion which has reached the elevation of religious martyrdom and while it exists no peace will ever be made with these people."

From an economic point of view also, said Hoover, the Allies' blockade had failed. Instead of harming the Germans, it had "induced an unprecedented national economy" of expenditure, "great discipline" ("pregnant with great after-war effects"), and relief from an unfavorable trade balance. If Germany had been allowed to import food, Hoover argued, "there would have

been an economic drain of securities or gold from the country" and a consequent "grave disturbance" in her economic equilibrium. Instead, the Allied
blockade had "stemmed the tide of depreciation" and sustained German self-
sufficiency. Remove the embargo, he argued, and Germany would be financially worse off than before.

Moreover, Hoover contended, the psychological effects of the blockade
had become a formidable obstacle to peace. In the opinion of the CRB chairman, the war could not be won militarily; "the power of modern arms in
defence" had made victory impossible for either side. No, the war must end
in a stalemate and a subsequent negotiated settlement. But before such a
peace could be attained, popular passions must abate and statesmen must
become free to be peacemakers. But, said Hoover, the "passion in Germany
cannot be lowered so long as the embargo on food continues. Similarly, it
cannot be accomplished in England as long a war on non combatants goes
on."

In short, Hoover believed that the time had come for the Allies to open
the "food-gates" to Germany. If they did, he believed that the Germans would
abandon their "measures of reprisals" and their "ruthless sacrifice of noncombatants." (He also believed that Germany's allies should lift *their* embargo
on neutral food ships passing through the Dardanelles.) If this happened,
Hoover predicted, it would substantially reduce "war passions" on both sides,
enhance the prospects for "enduring peace,"and facilitate the relief of Belgium, which would be free again to import food.

Hoover saved his moral arguments for last. He dismissed the contention
that since food in Germany technically belonged to the government, any
food imports were tantamount to supplies for the armed services. Instead, he
invoked the traditional distinction between combatants and noncombatants
(another casualty of the deepening conflict). Once more Hoover the liberal
confronted the phenomenon of total war."One can rest absolutely assured,"
he asserted, "that the German army will be fed and that the women and
children will starve with a fine sense of martyrdom in order that this may be
done." The army will *always* be fed, he insisted. Any successful food blockade was simply "pressure on the women and children."

And this, to Hoover, was revolting. Even as he observed the all-consuming
character of modern warfare, in which the distinction between soldiers and
civilians was breaking down, he reaffirmed the moral categories of the past.
". . . I believe it is wrong to even threaten to cut off the food-supply of
women and children and thus carry war on to non-combatants in a most
virulent form," he now wrote. "[N]o nation has the right of might" to make
war on noncombatants.[76]

Hoover's proposal contained an obvious element of self-interest. If the Allies
did relax their blockade, the people of occupied Belgium could then obtain
their food through seaborne commerce, and the burdens of his commission
would lift. At this very moment, in fact, the CRB and Comité National were

devising a scheme to permit Belgian industries to import and export goods through the blockade. But Hoover's plan seemed too heartfelt to be a mere ploy to lighten his own labors.

In a separate cover note the American relief executive asked Page to show his lengthy letter to Sir Edward Grey. But why, one might wonder, should Great Britain abandon its food embargo weapon unilaterally? Hoover suggested to Page a rationale: the British could do so as a concession to the United States, and the United States could then use this to secure reciprocal concessions on submarine warfare from the Germans.[77]

It is not known whether Page passed Hoover's letter along to the Foreign Office. But less than two weeks later, "at the request" (Hoover told Colonel House) "of a cabinet friend of mine here,"[78] the chairman of the CRB prepared a memorandum elaborating his arguments of August 5. Once again he asserted that the "Allied programme of starvation" was a failure and the prime source of the hatred of Britain now consuming the German people. Hoover stated that he was not offering any "peace proposals from either side."

> I have only one constructive suggestion to make, and that is that it is in the joint interest of both sides that the embargo should be taken off food-supplies the world over [including the North Sea and the Black Sea]. . . . The final and complete acknowledgment of foodstuffs as non-contraband and not subject to blockade and embargo in this war would be one of the most constructive steps towards civilisation and permanent peace that the world has yet taken.

If, he said, the embargo on food supplies were now lifted "in all quarters," if submarine warfare "in its present form" against merchant ships were abolished, and if "all other reprisals" were likewise abandoned, the prevailing "bitterness on both sides" would recede. If this happened, and if the Allies held their lines against the Germans on the western front in the next several weeks, "the pathway to peace" would open in the autumn.[79]

Hoover's suggested *quid pro quo* was not original. Back in February the German government had professed willingness to call off its submarine campaign against Allied merchant ships if the Allies would permit Germany to import foodstuffs for civilian use unmolested. The American secretary of state, William Jennings Bryan, had quickly made this the basis for a proposed modus vivendi, only to have the Germans increase their demands and the British reject the plan in favor of an unprecedented embargo of all shipping—including neutral shipping—into Germany.[80] It remained to be seen whether His Majesty's Government would respond any differently now.

Hoover promptly sent a copy of his memorandum to Colonel House. The CRB chairman confessed that he did not suppose it had any "practical value"— only, perhaps, some "academic interest."[81] But Hoover was not given to writing letters without a purpose. Barely three weeks later, he raised the issue again, this time in a letter to Woodrow Wilson. It was not so much the "original causes" of the war or even losses of life on the battlefield that were embittering the nations of Europe, he told the President. It was the acts of warfare "directed against civilians on all sides." Any measure that lessened "the amount of impact on civilians," he argued, would help to mitigate "public feeling to a point where a peace proposal might be possible of execution." He did not mention his own recent initiative toward this end.[82]

If Hoover hoped that by informing Page, House, and Wilson of his thinking he might elicit American government support for his plan, there is no evidence that he succeeded. Meanwhile his proposal was circulating at the highest levels of the British government. One of Hoover's London neighbors and closest British friends was the distinguished editor of the *Economist*, Francis W. Hirst, a man Hoover considered "one of the Economic leaders of the World both scholastically and practically."[83] Hirst was an ardent nineteenth-century liberal, a biographer of Adam Smith, and an arch-critic of British imperialism and militarism. As a disciple of Richard Cobden and John Morley, he strenuously opposed his government's blockade and other interventionist wartime policies, so offensive to traditional liberal doctrine. Hoover frequently conversed with this uncompromising Gladstonian journalist.[84] To Hirst (and perhaps to others) he submitted his memorandum in mid-August.[85]

Delighted by Hoover's document, Hirst evidently circulated it to his intimate friend, the Liberal home secretary, Sir John Simon. With Simon and a professor of economics at Oxford University, Hirst submitted a report to the British government advocating Hoover's proposal. Soon (according to Hoover) Sir Edward Grey, Lloyd George, and the Conservative leader Arthur Balfour endorsed the daring scheme. For a brief moment Hoover thought he had won.[86]

By early September, however, his plan was dead. On a trip to Brussels he informed Brand Whitlock that certain Tories—notably the attorney-general, Sir Edward Carson—had killed it. "Let the brutes starve," Carson apparently said. Unable to achieve consensus, the shaky coalition government dropped the idea.[87]

A few months later, in January 1916, Colonel House again visited London and renewed his personal contacts with the head of the CRB. Hoover, as usual, was gloomy. The "tempo of hate" was accelerating, he told the presidential envoy. What could be done to diminish it? House asked. Only one thing, Hoover replied: "[R]estore the old rules that food was non-contraband and that civilians were not to be attacked from the air or by submarines." It was only a "very very remote hope," he added. He had "no faith" that his suggestion could "prevail against the military minds."[88]

Nevertheless, Hoover told House that the belligerent powers were weary and would welcome an end to the war—a reference, apparently, to the leaders, not the masses. He invited House to dinner at the Red House in order to meet what House called "English pacifists," including Francis W. Hirst.[89]

It was apparently on this occasion that Hoover introduced House to a young antiwar Labour politician named Ramsay MacDonald, later the prime minister of Great Britain.[90]

Such actions, of course, yielded no results. By late January Hoover was convinced that the end of the war was at best months away. "All the belligerent and much of the military world is anxious for peace," he informed a CRB associate, but they seemed determined to "have a go" on the western front first.[91] Still, Hoover continued to object in principle to food embargoes—at least as applied to innocent civilians like the Belgians. "[T]he blockade of the foodstuffs of a combatting population" may be morally justifiable, he told an American diplomat that winter, "on the ground that the population has the option to deliver itself from pressure by making peace. But . . . the blockade of foodstuffs from the non-combatting population, who have no such option, can have no moral justification. . . ."[92]

Hoover's imaginative "deescalation" plan of 1915, then, came to nothing. He was rowing against the tide. "Tighten the blockade," was the cry on one side. "Unleash the submarine," on the other. In this fiery "furnace of hate," as Hoover called it,[93] the cause of "civilized" warfare was dying—and with it the world of gentleman-liberals, the world of Hoover and of Hirst.

Only once more before 1917 did the CRB's leader step outside the boundaries of humanitarian service and enter the diplomatic lists. On a trip to Belgium in September 1916 he learned from Emile Francqui of a recent German peace feeler toward Belgium. In mid-June a distinguished German physicist, Walter Nernst, had visited an old friend in Brussels: a prominent Belgian banker named Franz Philippson who was a member of the Comité National. Nernst was also a close friend of the imperial German chancellor, Bethmann Hollweg, and in fact had made the journey to Brussels at the chancellor's request. To the Belgian banker, Nernst had proposed that the British, French, German, and Belgian governments sponsor an unofficial peace conference in Rotterdam, with a Belgian delegate as presiding officer. The results of the confidential parley would be forwarded to the respective governments, which could then decide whether to convene a formal conference. Not content with this suggestion, Nernst had sketched out a set of peace terms. Among other things, Germany would evacuate Belgium and restore its independence. Nernst had urged Philippson to convey his proposal personally to Belgium's King Albert, who would then become a mediator between the Allies and the Central Powers. Despite the German scientist's subsequent assurance that his plan had his government's approval, and despite German promises of safe passage, Philippson had uneasily declined to go. He had, however, reported the demarche to his fellow relief leaders.[94]

At about this same time the German authorities had invited a leading French mine owner and relief worker to Berlin and had proposed that German and French iron interests organize a cartel that would send 5,000,000 tons of iron ore per year into Germany. After learning of the Philippson affair in Brussels, the French businessman had returned home and stayed silent, convinced that the offer was merely part of a German diplomatic "game."[95]

All this Hoover learned from his Belgian associates. Meanwhile he himself had become a target of the German peace offensive. On his September visit he was approached by Dannie Heineman, erstwhile director of the CRB's Brussels office. A close friend of the imperial German secretary of the treasury, Heineman had made a special trip from Berlin to Brussels in order to meet his former colleague. Heineman declared that the time had come to formulate peace proposals and that it would be good if businessmen on both sides did so before the diplomats did. Heineman acknowledged that he did not know what the German conditions might be but asked Hoover to ascertain British terms anyway. Hoover refused. He was "not in the peace business," he replied. If the British gave him a message he would transmit it, but he would not take any initiative himself.[96]

Hoover may not have been in the "peace business," but he wasted no time in passing along what he had just heard. On his return to London in late September, he disclosed the Philippson–French mine owner–Heineman stories to Lord Percy at the British Foreign Office. He informed the Belgian minister to Great Britain as well.[97] In this way the Allies learned all about the Germans' peace soundings without Philippson's ever having to leave Brussels. Perhaps the Germans intended their initiatives to leak. In any case, despite his posture of aloofness toward Heineman, Hoover, back in London, quickly offered to play the role of "informant" (that is, messenger) if the Belgian government-in-exile so desired.[98]

The Philippson episode provoked a crisis in the Belgian Cabinet. When word of the German *sondage* reached Paris, the French foreign minister demanded that Philippson be forbidden to see his king. The French were evidently afraid that Belgium might be lured into making a separate peace. The exiled Belgian government's discomfiture increased when it discovered that King Albert was not entirely averse to receiving such a caller. Racing to the king's headquarters at the front, the Belgian foreign minister obtained royal approval for Hoover to tell Philippson that a peace mission to the monarch at this time would have no chance of success and that it was better to await a "more favorable" moment.[99]

Alarmed at this hint that the king might entertain a German peace feeler at some other time, and no doubt feeling the brunt of French fury, the Belgian Cabinet furiously rejected this projected response. In the end, it decided simply to notify Philippson that his proposed mission was "inopportune." But when the Belgian prime minister suggested that Hoover convey this message, King Albert objected. A Belgian should be the courier, he thought, lest the government appear to be "in the tow of the foreigner." As a result, the Belgians chose another courier, and Philippson remained in Brussels.[100] Hoover's involvement in the abortive peace feeler was over.

Years later, in his *Memoirs* and other writings about World War I, Hoover never mentioned his militant response to the *Lusitania* crisis, his attempt to induce the British to lift their food embargo, or his role as "informant" in the Philippson affair.[101] Perhaps he did not find them worthy of notice. Perhaps he found them inconsistent with his public posture of disinterested humanitarianism. Few people, then or later, realized just how strenuously he had tried to influence British and American foreign policy in 1915. Perhaps Lindon Bates's charge that he had violated the Logan Act made Hoover reluctant, even long afterward, to disclose his behind-the-scenes lobbying.

The CRB chairman's forays into wartime diplomacy revealed, perhaps, something more. Hoover was correct: he was not in a conventional sense in the "peace business." His task was to feed people, not end wars. But each of these episodes thrust him further into the thick of things, into the world of statesmanship and maneuver where he loved—and had long yearned—to be. It is not too speculative to suggest that the excitement of the *Lusitania* affair, of his campaign to abolish the British food blockade, and of the German peace feelers of late 1916, enhanced Hoover's eagerness to make public affairs a permanent occupation.

I I I

T h e second half of 1916 was a period of impending transition for Herbert Hoover. His mining business was largely ending; the Stanford University presidency was gone. His own family life was unsettled; his brother Theodore was on his way home. In a moment of uncharacteristic optimism in midsummer, Hoover remarked to Brand Whitlock that there was reason to hope that the war would end in October.[102] If true, he would soon be looking for a new career.

From an early point in the war some of the men around him had envisaged a larger role for their chief. In June 1915 Hugh Gibson and another CRB associate, Gilchrist Stockton, established an informal, two-man, Hoover-for-President Club; they were not alone in thinking him "of presidential calibre."[103] In early 1916 *Harper's Weekly* suggested him for vice president.[104] Hoover, of course, vigorously disclaimed political ambition.[105] But that he harbored *some* public ambition, there was no doubt. "I don't want to be just a rich man," he remarked one time to a friend.[106] Even after the war began, he continued to hope to purchase someday a major newspaper in New York or Washington, D.C.[107]

Hoover seemed to covet the role of business statesman, of the man-of-affairs-turned-public-philosopher. Before the war he had even begun to make notes for a book along these lines and had given them to his novelist-friend Mary Austin, who suggested that he call his book *The New Nationalism*. Later, during the war, she proposed that they complete the manuscript together;

by then Hoover had no time.[108] In a conversation with Brand Whitlock and Vernon Kellogg in the autumn of 1916, Hoover discussed what he planned to do after the war. There were so many ideas that he wished the country to adopt, he said. But how are you going to bring these to the public? Whitlock asked. "Are you going to write them and publish them?" "Well," Hoover replied (thinking perhaps of his newspaper dream), "I am going to publish them, but I shan't bother to write them myself. I shall get somebody to write them for me. You can get a man to write anything for £5 a week."[109]

As the United States drifted into ever more fragile neutrality in late 1916, some Americans were becoming interested in what he might do even before the war was over. During the summer the U.S. Congress established a Council of National Defense to study ways of mobilizing the nation's resources in the event of war. Shortly after the bill was passed, a noted engineer told the secretary of the navy that Hoover was perhaps "the best man fitted in all the world" to direct the council's work on food, sanitation, and "problems of distribution to masses of people."[110] Some time later, on December 22, William Honnold of the CRB's New York office cabled Hoover that President Wilson would probably create a "National Relief organization" to coordinate and collect funds for existing agencies. Hannold reported the "feeling" in America that Hoover should be the "executive head."[111]

As it happened, Hoover needed little encouragement in this direction. In a letter to his friend Ray Lyman Wilbur on November 22, 1916, the head of the CRB declared more clearly than ever before his availability and eagerness for public office—specifically, in the Wilson administration.

> The fact of the case is that I feel I have worn out my usefulness on the present job and that someone else could quite well take it on now. We have built the thing up into practically a Government Department. It is practically almost wholly supported by Government funds, and unless we can see more support than we can see now on the charity side it will be scarcely worth while pursuing it.
>
> As a Government organ, I do not feel that it has any more right to call on me and all of these other Americans for volunteer service than Governments have a right to call for volunteer service in any other direction, and I feel that I can be more useful in my own country, not only to my own countrymen but to myself.
>
> Furthermore, in the upbuilding of this enterprise, which has run so much at cross-currents with political, military, and private ambitions from all quarters, I have had to quarrel with a goodly number of people and I feel that if the whole engine were placed simply on a governmental basis it would be actually safer than in the hands of a volunteer body because it is now established and fixed so long as the war continues.
>
> For all these reasons, and many others, I would like to get out of Europe and I would like to get out with dignity, and such an opportunity as you

mention would be exactly what I require. Moreover, I believe I could be of great service. The one thing which the American people need is preparedness, not only on the military side but also on the economic side. A great economic shock must follow the war, and unless there is preparation, the shock will be infinitely more disastrous to the American people. I am somewhat familiar with the punitive economic measures that are being prepared, particularly in Germany, and it is my belief that adequate organisation must be created to meet them.[112]

Wilbur speedily took his cue. On December 7 he urged President Wilson by letter to bring back Hoover to America for "immediate service to this country." Wilbur ventured his opinion that Hoover's "present work in Belgium" was "so organized that there is no pressing need for him to continue in it." No doubt, said Wilbur, the President could find a "sphere" for Hoover's "great powers of organization," perhaps in strengthening the army or navy or in "the economic and educational rehabilitation" of the revolution-ravaged nation of Mexico.[113]

At about the time that Wilbur appealed to Wilson by correspondence, another old friend of Hoover lobbied the President in person. On November 26 Will Irwin, now a war reporter, returned to the United States from London. Before his departure he was approached by Ambassador Page, who informed him that the Germans intended to initiate unrestricted submarine warfare soon and that America would be drawn into the conflict by spring. Page urged Irwin to visit President Wilson and present Hoover's qualifications for wartime service. He is "made to order for the job of directing our production of munitions," said the ambassador.

Early in December Irwin obtained an interview with the President and launched into a fulsome tribute to Herbert Hoover. In less than five minutes Wilson cut Irwin off. I am quite aware of Hoover's merits, the President said, and I certainly plan to use him "in case we're unhappily forced into the war"—although perhaps not, he added, in the field of munitions.[114]

A few weeks later Page became more direct. In a memorandum for the President on December 30, the ambassador declared that Hoover would "make a useful officer" in the State Department.

He is probably the only man living who has privately (i.e. without holding office) negotiated understandings with the British, French, German, Dutch, and Belgian Gov'ts. He personally knows & has had direct dealings with these Gov't's, and his transactions with them have involved several hundred million dollars. . . . I do not *know*, but I think he wd. be glad to turn his European experience to the patriotic use of our Gov't.

Page added that Hoover did not know about this memorandum.[115]

Then, late in December, an opportunity for government service opened up—from a totally unexpected direction. During the Lindon Bates imbroglio Hoover had become acquainted with Franklin K. Lane, a Canadian-born Californian who was Wilson's secretary of the interior. Lane was an avid supporter of the Commission for Relief in Belgium. It was he who had helped Hoover gain an audience with the President at that time and who had helped Irwin obtain a similar interview a year later. In an address at Brown University in June 1916, an address soon reprinted in *The Survey*, Lane had publicly acclaimed Hoover as "the incarnation of the spirit of American desire to help the world."[116] Now, just a few days before Christmas, he invited Hoover to become assistant secretary of the interior, with "administrative control" over the Bureau of Mines, Bureau of Indian Affairs, Reclamation Service, and Alaskan Engineering Commission.[117]

Lane's offer was unrelated to Hoover's relief work. For several years professional engineers in the United States had been arguing that the assistant secretary's post in a department comprising so many engineering-related bureaus should be filled by one of their own. The chance to consummate their long-sought goal was upon them, and some now pressed Hoover to accept, if only to establish a precedent. The facts that the vacancy need not be filled for several months, and that Lane said it would enable Hoover to do "great constructive work of national importance," were no doubt additional incentives.[118]

But could Hoover sever his connection to the enterprise that had brought him world renown? As soon as Lane's offer arrived by cable, the chairman of the CRB turned to one of his most trusted friends, Curtis H. Lindley. Hoover had known the eminent San Francisco lawyer since the age of twenty-two; the sixty-six-year-old man was a virtual father figure to him. Hoover now sought Lindley's "prayerful advice," on the assumption that the Belgian relief could be "carried on by someone else." ". . . I have only one desire," Hoover added, "and that is to be of the greatest service that I am capable of."[119]

Lindley's reply to Hoover's plea is not known.[120] But as it happened, the California attorney had already written a letter to Secretary Lane in Hoover's behalf—on December 7, the same day that Ray Lyman Wilbur wrote to President Wilson. Lindley apparently acted on his own initiative, and Lane did not read his communication until after he had cabled his own offer to Hoover.[121]

The CRB chairman also consulted Brand Whitlock:

I am much torn about as between the call of the two services. I have no ambitions from a political point of view, and therefore I am not attracted by that phase. I do not believe that any man on earth is irreplaceable in either of these jobs. I do believe, however, that men can give better service in some positions than others. If I thought that by virtue of making a change of this kind I should in any way jeopardise the Relief, I could of course not consider it for one moment. I am not at all convinced that this is the case, and I should be glad to have your whole-hearted consideration on the subject at any early date.[122]

Despite his growing ambivalence about Hoover's management style, Whitlock frankly admitted that he hated to see his colleague depart. Nevertheless he advised Hoover to accept Lane's offer—assuming, of course, that it would not imperil the relief—and despite the fact that the prospective position, in Whitlock's opinion, was "not big enough for you, for you are distinctly of Cabinet rank." He tendered this advice, Whitlock wrote Hoover,

because I think the movement of democracy in America, which is a part of liberalism in the larger world, has need of such men as you, and because I believe that in that movement you would find a satisfaction and perhaps a consolation that would mean much to you. I am not going to let any selfish consideration stand in the way of helping that big movement along.[123]

The American minister to Belgium went even further. Unaware as yet that Hoover had been trying for more than a year to dislodge him from his position, and willing still to overlook Hoover's perceived tactlessness and ill temper, Whitlock wrote to Secretary of War Newton D. Baker on January 17. The diplomat urged his old friend and the Wilson administration to get acquainted with the CRB's dynamic chairman. He is "precisely the man that the liberal movement in America . . . needs," Whitlock declared.

You will find him at first the type of the strong-willed, indomitable, American business man and executive, but his hardness is all on the surface. He is a gentleman of rather wide culture and an immense amount of certain kinds of information, distinguished in his own calling as engineer, of a most democratic nature and with great human sympathies; his work in the Commission of course is one of the modern wonders of the world, if there are any more wonders in this world.[124]

As it happened, Whitlock's letters reached their destinations long after Hoover's decision had been made. On January 4, 1917 the chairman of the CRB regretfully cabled Secretary Lane that "duty here demands that I decline your kind offer." I could not retire or even announce my retirement, he reported, "without seriously jeopardising the whole work." "Discordant elements" in the relief "at least for the present necessitate my remaining at the helm."[125]

Nine days later Hoover set sail for America in search of crucial new funding for the relief. Even as he did so, still another letter from still another American friend was making its way from London across the Atlantic. Earlier in the war Hoover had become acquainted with Norman Hapgood, an energetic American magazine editor, staunch Progressive, and leader of the Committee of Mercy. (It was Hapgood who as editor of *Harper's Weekly* had promoted Hoover for vice president in 1916.) While on a trip to London in early January 1917, Hapgood wrote to his friend Justice Louis D. Brandeis. Hoover, said Hapgood, was "one of the most interesting men I know" and was sailing for New York in a few days. The editor urged Brandeis to contact the CRB chairman. You will, he said, enjoy learning about his experiences.[126]

As he boarded the ship that would take him home for the first time in fourteen months, Hoover had no firm prospects for entry into the "big game" of American public life. Wilbur, Irwin, Page, Lindley, Whitlock, and Hapgood: all in recent weeks had taken steps in his behalf, yet nothing appropriate had materialized. But the forty-two-year-old American could take satisfaction from this fact: powerful men in Washington, including the President of the United States, were aware of his remarkable abilities. He could not realize that in just a few weeks an armada of German U-boats would create the chance for wider service that he craved.

13

"Come Out in Glory"

I

S H O R T L Y before sailing from Liverpool for New York in mid-January 1917, Hoover dispatched a farewell message to his Brussels office. All around them, he noted, were portents of deepening trouble. The warring nations of Europe were growing more desperate, the world's food reserves were diminishing, financial support for the relief was approaching exhaustion. "It is going to be an uphill fight to keep the work going until the finish," he acknowledged, "but I believe that we shall succeed. . . . I hope to return from America in four or five weeks. . . ."[1]

For three months Hoover had been endeavoring to set up a new mode of finance for the CRB: a vast, $150,000,000 "relief loan" issued in America. Now he was heading home (he said) to "boom" it.[2] If successful, he would garner enough money to fund his efforts for an entire year. $150,000,000: the equivalent of more than half a billion dollars today. Hoover was not thinking small.

He could not afford to. Ninety per cent of his income came from the governments of France and Great Britain, and now, more than ever, they were feeling the strain. Early in October 1916, in fact, the French had gravely warned him that because of worsening currency exchange problems they might not be able to support his work in northern France much longer.[3] Toward the end of that month Hoover had managed to win an increase in the Allied subsidy for his program inside Belgium—but only half the amount he had requested.[4] Scarcely two months later, thanks to the soaring price of foodstuffs around the world, his operating deficit was climbing toward £1,000,000 a month.[5]

Where was the needed money to come from? How could his relief commission avert collapse? For Hoover there was but one answer: America must come to the rescue. The device: a massive loan floated in the United States and promoted, as he put it, "on sentimental and national grounds."[6]

Despite his contemplated appeal to American "sentiment," Hoover had at first been unsentimentally adamant on one point: the projected loan should definitely *not* apply to Belgium. Its proceeds should be spent on northern France alone. To obtain proper security for the loan from Belgian municipalities, he argued, would entail "infinite difficulties" and "a vast alteration of our methods of relief." It would also require the approval of the Germans, who would surely try to get control of the ensuing expenditures—something he could never allow.[7] Hoover's third objection, however, was, one suspects, the crucial one. "[O]ur relations with Comité National and Belgian Government are very unsatisfactory," he told his New York office on November 20. As a result, "we are not prepared to pledge our good faith for them in present circumstances."[8]

Under pressure from his New York colleagues, Hoover agreed in late November to broaden the proposed loan to encompass Belgium as well as France.[9] But the CRB chairman immediately insisted on one condition. This loan, he declared, would be raised "on sentimental bases" by his own organization, which had "moral responsibilities" to the outside world and the U.S. government. Under these circumstances, the CRB must have "the entire control of the local organisations" inside Belgium. "There is no use in mincing matters in this connection," he told a colleague,

> although it may be sugar-coated to some extent. I simply will not allow my countrymen's sympathies to be played upon or their money to be administered by groups for whom neither I nor any other American would be prepared to vouch, unless such groups consent to such a measure of control as may afford substantial guarantees.[10]

In plain language, Hoover had no confidence in the efficiency or integrity of his Belgian associates.

By mid-December Hoover had arranged most of the preliminaries with leading American banks as well as the French and British governments.[11] As he desired, there would be no need to collect certificates of indebtedness from French and Belgian communes, nor to extract authority to do so from the Germans. Instead, the loan would be solicited—and guaranteed—by the British, French, and exiled Belgian governments, who would apportion the financial obligation among themselves. The money thus raised would become the CRB's sole source of financing for that year ahead. In one respect the plan bore the distinctive imprint of Hoover's idealism. Back in October he had boldly asserted that American bankers should handle the scheme free of charge as a gesture of support for "America's greatest philanthropic effort."[12] In late December the bankers agreed—as a "Christmas expression of appreciation" to Hoover.[13]

All parties were now aware of the ambitious scheme—all, that is, except the Belgians, whom Hoover and the two leading Allies had so far kept ignorant of the loan negotiations.[14] Hoover anticipated trouble as soon as London and Paris informed Le Havre of his plan. In fact, he predicted that the Belgians would protest strenuously, since "they are trying to save up their sentimental resources in the United States for post-war finance." Even worse, he expected that they would "want to introduce to themselves a voice in this matter" or "introduce the Comité National as their agents." To Hoover, any such Belgian involvement was "hopeless" from the standpoint both of "preserving our neutrality" and of maintaining sufficient control inside Belgium to protect the "helpless" (evidently from Emile Francqui). It was "absolutely necessary," said Hoover, that the Belgian government and Comité National be excluded from any role in administering the loan.[15]

The American relief magnate therefore took steps to ward off this prospective intrusion. He told Brand Whitlock that the American bankers had stipulated, as a condition of making the loan, that it be expended "entirely under the sole direction" of the commission.[16] Another "condition," he said, was that the CRB must direct the expenditure of all receipts from food sales inside Belgium.[17] The CRB—not the Comité National. In effect, under the proposed new financial arrangement one man—Herbert Hoover—would control the disbursement of $150,000,000. It was unlikely that the American bankers had invented these "conditions" by themselves.

At the beginning of 1917, and at Hoover's request, Francqui notified the exiled Belgian prime minister at Le Havre.[18] Several days later Hoover himself explained the plan in a letter to the Belgian finance minister, van de Vyvere. The terms were noncontroversial—except one. Because the loan would be endorsed by the CRB, subscribed to by Americans, and facilitated by American bankers without profit, there would have to be (said Hoover) a "formula" governing its expenditure. Never one to overlook an important detail, he at once spelled it out to van de Vyvere: the loan must be disbursed and administered by the CRB exclusively. Once again his keen sense of stewardship—and distrust of Francqui & Co.—shone through.

Claiming that his "colleagues" were anxious to "strike the iron [in America] while it is hot," Hoover asked for rapid Belgian action. To induce van de Vyvere (who detested him) to intervene, Hoover wielded both a carrot and a stick. The projected loan would be advantageous, he asserted. It would resolve the relief mission's financial troubles, guarantee its "continuity," and enable Belgium to appear before America as a borrower with "dignity" instead of a supplicant for "charity." The alternative, he said, was grim. The CRB was sliding toward financial disaster, and "unless we see some daylight I see no alternative but to reduce the food supply by the end of this month." The loan, then, on Hoover's terms, or starvation: it was an ultimatum likely to concentrate a finance minister's mind.[19]

Would the Belgians now consent to a plan that would make Americans their creditors in place of the British and the French? Would they willingly accept the CRB as the sole trustee and administrator of $150,000,000? Indeed, would the Spanish diplomats Merry del Val and Villalobar, as joint patrons of the relief enterprise, permit the control of such a sum to rest entirely in Yankee hands?

Herbert Hoover was none too sure—and determined to allow no other outcome. To the French, the British, and the bankers he immediately insisted that his "formula" must not be altered. The money to be raised, he declared, would be American money, "subscribed under humanitarian conditions" and designated for disbursement in German-occupied territory on the assumption that Americans would distribute it "with the protection of their own flag and countrymen." This responsibility, he asserted, could not be "shared with other parties nor in any way abrogated." Only Americans—and "no other Government or parties"—could command "the necessary confidence of the American people." Only on these terms could the loan issue succeed.[20]

To his New York office Hoover was more explicit still. If any attempt is made while I am on the high seas to inject the Comité National or the Spanish minister-patrons into the "formula," or to limit our control of disbursements, he cabled, "I trust you will absolutely refuse" to consider it.[21]

Hoover's concern that the loan campaign would fail, unless Americans were known to control its proceeds, may have been exaggerated—a convenient argument to keep the Belgians and Spanish at bay. But on one point his sincerity was certain: the CRB in his eyes was an *American* institution, responsible to the American people above all. He would not allow its reputation for probity to be tarnished as he knew it might be if certain governments and "parties" got their hands in the till. As he prepared to launch the greatest humanitarian fund drive in history, the fear of scandal seemed never far from his thoughts—scandal that could stain this epic in idealism and ruin his own good name.

On January 13, 1917 Hoover sailed at last for the United States—confident that the relief loan package would be ready for unveiling by his arrival. Eight days later he reached New York and cabled London: what was the status of the loan?[22] To his dismay the Allied governments still had not worked out all the details.[23] The British Treasury itself was openly stalling, evidently apprehensive that Hoover's loan might jeopardize another loan that *it* was about to place on the American market for war purposes.[24] Not until January 23 did the Treasury bother to contact the Belgians, who, it soon developed, had their own reasons for declining to board the Hoover express.[25]

Exasperated by the delay, the CRB chairman could only wait—and badger the stubborn British from another direction. He could hardly do less. Each day he was nearing the financial precipice. Because of soaring commodity prices in the wake of the poor harvest of 1916, his January food purchases were more than $2,000,000 over budget. On January 29 his London office director duly apprised the Foreign Office that the relief organization must either obtain an increased Allied subsidy of £1,000,000 per month *immediately* or reduce the value of its imports to Belgium by 40%.[26] Neither Hoover nor his man in London seemed to be bluffing.

Meanwhile, inside Belgium, a tragedy more visible than hunger was adding to the population's despair. By mid-January the German army of occupation had seized at least 60,000 Belgium men for forced labor, including a thousand or more relief personnel who were supposedly exempt.[27] Hoover was aghast. The "premeditation" and "dimensions" of this campaign, he told the State Department, made it "the greatest crime against human liberty which the world has witnessed since the world began."[28] Early in the month, while still in London, he had suggested that President Wilson appeal to Kaiser Wilhelm II and had asked the CRB's New York office to solicit a public condemnation of the German deportations from Samuel Gompers, president of the American Federation of Labor. Such a remonstrance, directed by American workers to German workers, might, Hoover reasoned, do some good.[29] Back in the States in late January, he pursued the matter with vigor.

On January 25, at Gompers's invitation, he addressed the AFL's executive council in Washington. Never had there been a council meeting such as this, Gompers said afterward. Never had the assembled union leaders been as deeply moved as they were by Hoover's plea. His delivery was rather monotonous, but, in Gompers's words, "The very bleakness of his presentation was convincing."[30] The executive council immediately authorized the protest he sought.[31] And Hoover soon found in Gompers a devoted friend—eager, like so many others, to promote him for higher public service.

The pending relief loan and the German roundups of Belgian civilians were not the only subjects on Hoover's mind in late January. For some months he had been contemplating a radical change in the status of his relief commission. In July 1916 he had asked Secretary of the Interior Lane whether the U.S. Congress could be persuaded to appropriate money to pay for the CRB's "incidental expenses." Hoover had put this figure at $1,000,000 since the CRB's inception and $500,000 for the year to come. He had pointed out that this sum represented only three-quarters of one percent of his commission's total expenditures—a record "without parallel in the administration of charity."[32]

Lane's reaction to this idea is not known. But within months Hoover had become more audacious. During December he wondered aloud whether Congress might constitute the CRB as an agency of the U.S. government. Such an act, he argued, would "enormously strengthen" his commission's effectiveness in dealing with the European belligerents. Thus fortified, the

CRB would be able to "survive the tightening and more desperate situation" now evident "on all sides." Moreover, he confided to a colleague, "the steady campaign which has been carried on for the last six months to minimise the American complexion of the work, and to demonstrate that America has really done nothing in Europe would be a great deal checked. . . ." Instead of being a "neutral" commission, composed of "heterogeneous nationalities," the CRB would become "cleanly American," and the "Spanish element" would be out.

> Practically the only thing that we have to get out of this labour is the impression which we had hoped to make on Europe that there are other ideals in American life than fishing in this pool of blood, and we stand in a very fair way [to be so vilified], in view of the dirty attitude of certain Belgians, egged on by other forces, to constantly depreciate the American participation in the Relief.

By "other forces" he probably meant Villalobar.[33]

Hoover apparently soon dropped his idea of converting the CRB into a U.S. government commission.[34] But the possibility of winning a congressional appropriation for its administrative costs was another matter. On January 12, 1917 his entire New York advisory committee asked Colonel House to obtain Woodrow Wilson's backing for the proposal.[35] Nine days later, upon landing in New York, Hoover himself informed House that such support was virtually imperative; House passed the word along to the President.[36] Only four days after that, Hoover was in Washington, lobbying Secretary of State Lansing for a $2,000,000 grant.[37]

All now depended on President Wilson. Would he ask Congress for the money, or would he shun such an official "entanglement" in the European war? Always ready to go to the top to plead his case, Hoover asked Secretary Lane to secure him an interview with the President. Through Lane and Lansing the CRB chairman quickly obtained an appointment to call at the White House on January 31.[38]

It was not the $2,000,000, of course, that Hoover mainly wanted;[39] it was the formal recognition from his government that it would connote. If he now obtained it, and if the imminent relief loan then succeeded, the future of the commission would be assured. And, perhaps not coincidentally, Hoover would then be free to leave it for other pursuits—like leadership of the growing movement to coordinate European war relief charities in the United States.

Hoover's visit to the United States in January 1917 was his first in more than a year. What a difference those months had made! Fifteen months before, he had arrived almost incognito to deal with the dangerous rebellion by Lindon Bates. Now he was almost a celebrity, interviewed upon arrival by the *New York Times.*[40] In the *Bellman* his friend William C. Edgar acclaimed him as "undoubtedly the greatest living American," a man of "marvelous business genius" who had "done more to help suffering humanity than all other Americans combined."[41]

Hoover was or professed to be embarrassed by such adulation. He told Edgar humorously that "the things you write about me in your infernal paper" deserved "cursing."[42] Nevertheless, he was an emerging national hero, and in his heart, one senses, he enjoyed the growing accolades.

Hoover's visit, in fact, was preceded and accompanied by a barrage of articles in the *New York Times, Literary Digest,* and other influential organs of opinion—all extolling the CRB and stressing its critical need for additional funds. The articles recounted the pitiful plight of Belgium's children and pointed out how relatively little the American people had contributed to the cause. In the nearly two and a half years since its founding, the commission had spent more than $200,000,000. Of this only about $9,000,000 had come from the United States.[43] Such verbal drumfire—orchestrated, at least in part, by the CRB's effective public relations apparatus—was no doubt an intended backdrop for the coming loan campaign.

Hoover threw himself into the preparations for the drive. Shortly after his arrival he lunched with former President Theodore Roosevelt, who at once pledged his all-out support.[44] "The one pre-eminently neutral and entirely useful organization is the Belgian Relief Commission," Roosevelt told a friend. The U.S. government ought to provide it "ample funds."[45] Before long, in an eloquent public letter, Roosevelt urged men and women of the American West to rescue Belgium's children from suffering, and war-profiteering America from "moral suicide."[46] Hoover also turned to his associates in the mining fraternity. He discovered that the Rocky Mountain Club of New York, a bastion of mining engineers, had collected $500,000 for a new clubhouse. Within twenty-four hours of his arrival in New York, the club's directors voted to donate the entire sum to the CRB.[47]

On the evening of January 29 the club held a huge dinner in Hoover's honor, at which the gift was announced. For Hoover public speaking was an ordeal, but his words that night touched hundreds of hearts:

> The feeling that the food supply of the community may cease at any moment; that your women and children are in jeopardy, and the feeling of every thinking man that a disturbance by the population only means blood in the streets; that there is no possible salvation or solution; a population that shivers at rumors; it goes beyond ability to describe. That has been the situation of Belgium and Northern France, with 10,000,000 people, for the last two years. . . .

He told how the people of Belgium "have come to look upon the Americans as their sole saviors: to look upon the American flag as the flag which is fighting to protect them." He told how, just a few weeks before, he had visited a Brussels relief station where 1,500 children received their daily food.

"The children were sitting down to their meal, and when they saw me they rose and feebly sang the first stanza of 'The Star Spangled Banner.' Now, knowing that the food supply was not American, I could feel nothing but shame."

To his fellow mining professionals Hoover pleaded for support. "This relief has come to be America's greatest exhibit in Europe," he said. "We want to give a demonstration of that great humanity which we know runs through our people." Introducing "the Chief" to the gathering, Alexander Hemphill declared: "The Belgian relief would never have been undertaken if Mr. Hoover had not been in London when the war started. . . . If it were not for Mr. Hoover's work in Belgium, the United States would not have a friend abroad."[48] Both of Hemphill's assertions were probably true.

Daily, now, the CRB chairman's uneasiness was mounting. What was happening in Europe? On February 1 he was scheduled to address the New York Chamber of Commerce—an ideal forum for unveiling the relief loan. Yet still he had no final authorization from the Allied governments. On January 31 he anxiously cabled his London office. What was happening? he demanded to know. "Are we to consider this business is on or is it off?"[49]

That same day he journeyed by train to Washington for an appointment with President Wilson. Presumably he appealed for the government to reimburse his commission's expenses; if he did, the President was evidently noncommittal. The CRB chairman also announced his plan for the loan. According to his later recollection, the President of the United States wished him well.[50]

Hoover's meeting with Wilson occurred at five o'clock in the afternoon.[51] As he left the White House in the twilight for the train trip back to New York, he did not yet know that at 4:10 p.m. the German ambassador had handed a stunning message to Secretary of State Lansing: after months of reluctant self-restraint in its use of its U-boat fleet, the German government was resuming unrestricted submarine warfare. Decreeing a total blockade of the French coast and the British Isles, the Germans announced that with only trivial exceptions any vessel entering this forbidden zone would be attacked and sunk without warning.[52] Any vessel: military or commercial, belligerent or neutral, armed or unarmed.

Gone was any lingering German respect for the pre-1914 conventions of naval warfare. Gone was any residual deference to the high Wilsonian principle of "freedom of the seas." War to the uttermost! Starve the Allies into submission!

The Commission for Relief in Belgium was entering its greatest ordeal.

I I

THE next day Hoover addressed the New York Chamber of Commerce. It was supposed to have been the occasion for launching his massive relief loan.[53]

Instead, with no loan ready to be "boomed," he could only exhort his audience to greater charitable exertions. "The justification of any rich man in the community is his trusteeship to the community for his wealth," he asserted. "The justification of America to the world-community today is her trusteeship to the world-community for the property which she holds." Undoubtedly aware of the interest of many of his listeners in international trade, he warned that "a note of bitterness" was developing in Europe because of America's profits from the war—a mood that he claimed was certain to affect U.S. relations with Europe for years to come. There was only one possible way to assuage this ill feeling, he contended: America must "properly . . . assume its burden toward the helpless in Europe."[54]

Hoover's speech was immediately hailed by the *New Republic* as one of the three or four most important utterances in America since the war began. The CRB, said the liberal journal, was not only a wonderfully efficient volunteer relief agency. It was an "American institution," "an outpost of the Republic" whose continued success was of the highest national priority. Hoover and his associates, the journal argued, had "created an American obligation in Europe." It would be a "national humiliation"—and worse—if the CRB should now collapse through lack of American financial support.[55]

The *New Republic's* approving editorial no doubt pleased Herbert Hoover. Its blended appeal to humane sentiment, national pride, and national self-interest was one that he himself invoked in the coming weeks. But far more than a dearth of dollars was vexing and harrying him now. At the very moment he spoke to the New York business elite, "wolf packs" of German U-boats, released from all constraint, were prowling the blockaded waters around Great Britain. Seventeen of his own relief ships were at sea, bound via the British port of Falmouth for Rotterdam.[56] Would the Germans allow them to cross the English Channel unmolested?

The next day Hoover got his answer: there would be no exceptions in the blockade zone. Henceforth CRB vessels must avoid Falmouth and the Channel entirely. Instead, they must follow a route north of Scotland and thence, down a narrow corridor of the North Sea, to Holland. German guarantees of safe passage would apply only to this restricted "northern route."[57]

To Hoover the German regulations were "absolutely infeasible." For one thing, his ships were obliged to call at Falmouth as a condition of obtaining insurance and charters; for another, most of them had to stop there to refuel.[58] Furthermore, the British required CRB vessels to visit England for inspection before proceeding on to Rotterdam.[59] And the so-called northern route was infested with minefields.[60] On February 3 he hurried to Washington for four days of consultations with U.S. government officials.[61] The day after his arrival, Secretary of State Lansing cabled Europe that the Germans' shipping policy was "wholly impracticable" and that "on their shoulders must rest squarely the entire responsibility of the starvation of the French and Belgian people unless they are ready to respect the Belgian Relief Commission's flag of mercy."[62] The cable was signed by Lansing, but the words were unmistakably Hoover's.[63]

On February 3 Hoover learned that the CRB ship *Euphrates*, plainly marked and carrying a German safe conduct pass, had been torpedoed without warning.[64] Two days later a second relief vessel, the *Lars Cruse*, was sunk off the Belgian coast.[65] In both cases most of the crewmen were drowned. With the Germans flatly refusing to respect the commission's flag unless its ships sailed the northern passage, and with the northern lane itself insecure, Hoover, on February 4, suspended all CRB shipping until further notice.[66] Of his cargoes already at sea, only two made it safely to Rotterdam. Two others were torpedoed, while the rest took hasty refuge in British ports.[67]

The Commission for Relief in Belgium's transportation service was now paralyzed. On the sea lanes its vessels dared not navigate, while inside Belgium itself the severest winter in twenty-five years had turned the canals into ribbons of ice two feet thick.[68] Hoover's men could do something about the ice: they persuaded the Germans to let them move food across Belgium by rail.[69] But the menace of the U-boat was far less amenable to reason.

Nearly three weeks of transatlantic cables and negotiations now ensued. On February 9 came the first break: the British agreed to drop their requirement that every CRB cargo touch at an English port—provided that the relief ships call at some *other* port (such as Halifax, Nova Scotia) for inspection. In return, the British asked the Germans to let the CRB use either the northern *or* southern route in safety.[70]

At once Hoover turned the heat on Berlin. We must secure a safe lane for our ships, he cabled. The Falmouth-to-Rotterdam route was the "only logical" one. The fate of the relief, he warned, lay solely with the Germans and their allies.[71]

In the past, such threats and remonstrances had achieved results. But this time the Germans did not yield. "We are not going to have the English putting the C.R.B. flag on their ships and thus passing through the danger zone," Baron von der Lancken declared in Brussels.[72] On February 18 the German foreign ministry reaffirmed that the commission vessels would receive safe conduct passes only if they took the northern route, outside the "war zone" around the British Isles.[73]

Hoover had little choice but to back down. On February 24 he resumed his food shipments in compliance with the Germans' policy. At least they had promised that his vessels on the northern route would be safe from the U-boats.[74]

By now virtually an entire month had elapsed in which practically no cargoes from the outside world had entered Belgium.[75] Fortunately, at the outset of the crisis Hoover's stocks on the continent were sufficient for perhaps sixty days.[76] But as the weeks passed, his margin of safety steadily diminished. Neutral carriers were becoming more and more difficult to charter. And the northern route added a thousand miles to the dangerous voyages his little fleet must make.

Meanwhile more than a dozen food-laden CRB vessels were languishing in British harbors, along with other accumulated supplies held in storage. For weeks Hoover and his colleagues struggled in vain to get the British and Germans to agree upon terms by which these stranded ships could proceed unhampered across the Channel. In the end, to avert spoilage the British government ordered the CRB to unload its cargoes and dispose of them in England. Nearly 100,000 tons of food thus never reached its destination. Hoover's only consolation was that the proceeds of the forced sales temporarily relieved his financial difficulties.[77]

The shipping emergency was not the only problem Hoover had to confront in the cruel month of February 1917. On February 3 the United States government severed diplomatic relations with the German empire. Instantly the position of every American relief worker in Belgium and northern France became fraught with peril. What would happen to these dedicated men—and the CRB itself—if the United States and Germany went to war? Would they become hostages—or worse?

Hoover was in Washington on the day the diplomatic breach was announced. That afternoon he ghostwrote a cable that the State Department promptly dispatched to its London embassy. In it the department expressed its "strong feeling" that the work of the CRB must continue no matter what.[78] In a separate message the department instructed Brand Whitlock to remain in Brussels if the Germans would let him and to obtain diplomatic protection for the American relief workers.[79] Hoover himself, in a communication to his lieutenants in Europe, deemed it "extremely desirable" for all CRB volunteers in Brussels to "remain at their posts." They should do so, he said, even after the U.S. legation staff departed—provided, of course, that the Germans promised them freedom to leave the country if necessary.[80] Both the "Government and myself," he said, were "very anxious" that CRB men in Belgium stay "until the last moment."[81]

On February 5 Baron von der Lancken assured the CRB's director in Brussels that the Americans could continue their duties for the time being with undiminished status.[82] The Germans did not desire a disruption of the victualing if they could help it. But the very next day von der Lancken and other senior officers hastened to Berlin for a conference on the future of the commission.[83] Clearly the eviction of the Yankees and the shattering of Hoover's organization could come at any time.

In London and Washington the CRB's leaders tried to prepare for the worst. Eighteen months earlier, during the *Lusitania* crisis, Hoover had decided that if Americans were compelled by diplomatic exigencies to withdraw from Belgium and northern France, he would simply recruit Dutch nationals as substitutes. The relief organization *outside* Belgium would continue unchanged.[84]

At the beginning of February 1917, William B. Poland of the CRB's London office quickly developed a course of action along these lines. If the Americans were forced to abandon their posts (he proposed), Dutch, Spanish, and

Danish neutrals could be hired to replace them. In addition, the Dutch chargé d'affaires in Brussels (van Vollenhoven) and the Spanish minister (Villalobar) would continue to serve as patron-protectors. Every other aspect of the far-flung relief apparatus would remain the same. Both Ambassador Walter Hines Page and Lord Percy of the British Foreign Office endorsed Poland's contingency plan.[85]

It soon transpired, however, that Herbert Hoover did not. On February 4 and 5 he informed London that if the Americans were expelled from Belgium, the entire enterprise—inside *and outside* Belgium—should be taken over officially by the Dutch government.[86] Such a move, he asserted with his usual force, was "absolutely critical."[87] No group of volunteers from "minor nationalities" could exert pressure on the Germans and safeguard the food supply as well as could Dutch government personnel, he asserted. No motley group of volunteers could maintain "proper control" over food distribution or engage in "proper communication." Nor could the CRB vouch for the loyalty and integrity of such a body. All these and other problems would be resolved, said Hoover, if the Dutch government itself stepped in. Furthermore, Dutch prestige in the United States was great—a factor that would enable him to continue fund raising for Belgium at home. Because of existing American sentiment, he stated, "no such support could be commanded for the Relief if it were conducted under [a] body of mixed neutrals, or under Spanish hands."[88] He did not mention the fact, but it was less than twenty years since the Spanish-American War, and in the eyes of many Americans, Spain was a land of corruption and incompetence.

But what, then, would happen to the CRB? According to Hoover, it would be "utterly impossible to hold the C.R.B. together abroad" if America went to war, since the entire staff would probably wish to serve their country. It was therefore "imperative," if the Americans left Belgium, to "liquidate the C.R.B. as an institution" and "secure its honourable discharge."[89] Such a radical step, of course, would free him, too, for other service.

If the Dutch would not take over, Hoover went on, then the Danish government should do so. And if not the Danish, then the Swiss.[90] Almost anyone, it seemed, but the Spanish. In short, instead of simply replacing the forty or so Americans in Belgium and northern France with other neutrals, and leaving the rest of his operation undisturbed, Hoover now proposed to abolish the CRB completely.

Hoover's desire to exclude the Spanish from relief administration derived from more than his recognition of anti-Spanish prejudice in the United States. Too much had happened since the *Lusitania* disaster for him to implement the measures contemplated then. For two exasperating years he had contended with the machinations of the Marquis de Villalobar. He had not forgotten how the troublemaking Spanish diplomat had conspired to depose him from the relief enterprise leadership a year before. Whatever happened now, Hoover was tenaciously determined that the Spanish "element"—and

Villalobar above all—should *not* get their hands on the relief.

Hoover's sweeping proposal immediately encountered obstacles in Europe. The Spanish, for one, were not about to be so easily shunted aside. In London Alfonso Merry del Val reminded the Foreign Office that he and Ambassador Page had *simultaneously* founded the CRB in 1914 and that it was both an American *and* Spanish organization. If the Americans retired, said he, "the interests of the Commission would automatically remain in Spanish hands." He thereupon announced that he was taking his *own* measures to prepare for this contingency.[91] Meanwhile (and without consulting Hoover) the Belgian government-in-exile asked the Dutch and Spanish governments to form a *joint* relief organization—a step that the British Foreign Office, for diplomatic reasons, seemed willing to accept. On February 8 Hoover's office in London had to inform him that it would simply not be possible to create an exclusively Dutch successor organ.[92]

By now Hoover was convinced that "the general crack-up" of the CRB was not far off.[93] Then, from Brussels, came further sensational news. On February 9 Baron von der Lancken, just back from Berlin, announced that the American CRB men could no longer serve in northern France or the Belgian provinces. They must be replaced by other neutrals and must give up their use of automobiles in the meantime. The baron said that his government *would* permit five or six Americans to reside in Brussels and work at the CRB's headquarters—where, presumably, they could be kept under surveillance. As for Brand Whitlock, he, too, could remain, as a kind of eminent patron of the relief, but with neither diplomatic status, nor transportation, nor means of communication with the outside world.[94] In a letter to the Marquis de Villalobar, the German official unctuously suggested that the Spanish diplomat select the replacements for Hoover's men.[95]

From a purely military point of view, von der Lancken's order made sense. Obviously the German army did not care to have potential enemy aliens circulating freely behind its lines on the eve of war. But could the Commission for Relief in Belgium permit such peremptory interference with its tasks? To Brand Whitlock it looked like the Germans were attempting "to put the onus on us if the revictualing ends."[96]

Certainly von der Lancken was acting as if he, and not the CRB, was in command. By February 12 he was trying to dictate the nationality of the Americans' successors. They will be Swiss, he announced. "The Swiss Government [has] offered delegates, and the German Government [has] accepted."[97]

By the morning of February 12 news of von der Lancken's order had reached London. Outraged at this challenge to the CRB's independence, Ambassador Page instantly counseled drastic action: *all* Americans in Belgium should leave, he declared, and should "close the commission's business [there] immediately." Let the British, French, and Germans decide how the *ravitaillement* would henceforth be conducted. The Americans, he argued, could now "retire with [a] clear record," "leaving the onus on the German Government." Any delay could lose "the present tactical advantage."[98]

William B. Poland agreed. Later that day, after conferring with Page and apparently without first consulting Hoover, he instructed the Brussels office to notify the Germans that the American members of the CRB were officially withdrawing from German-held territory. Poland made it plain that the relief itself was not ending—only the American involvement behind German lines.[99] All else, for the moment, was left unchanged.[100]

Poland now notified Hoover of his decision.[101] He also alerted the London office of the Associated Press, which evidently then cabled a dispatch to Hoover for clearance.[102] Once again, as so often before, Hoover's friend Ben S. Allen at the AP office was proving a cooperative ally.

When the AP's cable reached Hoover, he released it at once to the press.[103] "We absolutely agree your immediate withdrawal from Belgium all members," he telegraphed Poland.[104] Now that the Americans were coming out, he added, it was time for Brand Whitlock to come also. For him to stay on in Brussels under present conditions would be "undignified from a national point of view." Furthermore, Whitlock by himself could have no "independent information" or diplomatic influence over the Germans. The only way to reestablish "a proper neutral control in Belgium," Hoover asserted, was to "force the situation" by withdrawing *all* Americans, including Whitlock, immediately. Otherwise, we would be "playing the German game of trying to secure [inadequate] half measures with a neutral color."[105]

Hoover had another reason for wanting Whitlock out, a reason he promptly confided to Colonel House. For eighteen months, Hoover disclosed, he had battled the Belgians incessantly "to secure efficient, honest, and equitable distribution of the food-stuffs" to their own people. This experience had given him "the most profound distrust" of the Comité National's leadership, "both as to their political activities and as to the administration of this work. . . ." If Whitlock were now to remain in Brussels without American CRB men to apprise him of what was going on, he would "find himself standing sponsor for an organization of which he [would] have no inside knowledge whatever," an organization whose "whole tendency" was to minimize German "infractions" lest the Allied governments become alarmed.[106]

So Whitlock, who only a few days before had received orders from the State Department to stay, should now leave: so, on February 13, said Hoover, who speedily conveyed his views to the department as well as Colonel House.[107]

With his ships driven off the seas and his men on the brink of expulsion from Belgium, Hoover now had to confront yet another disaster: the vast relief loan scheme on which he had labored for four months was foundering. Day after day no signal to proceed came from London. Day after day the British Treasury procrastinated. Evidently it calculated that if the United States entered the war no special relief loan would be necessary, while if the United States did not enter, the private loan issue in America would probably fail.[108] The Belgian government-in-exile also hesitated to sanction the plan. Just as Hoover had foreseen, it did not much care for his "formula."[109]

By February 11 William B. Poland reported "continuous stalling all along the line" in London. The time had come, he suggested bluntly, for "shirt sleeve diplomacy."[110] But three days later a harassed and preoccupied Hoover was obliged to suspend the loan plan entirely until he could solve more pressing problems.[111] The project, in its original form, was dead.

Meanwhile Hoover's announcement of the impending American departure from Belgium had touched off a wave of repercussions. From the government of the Netherlands came an offer to form a Dutch committee to take over the commission's duties inside Belgium.[112] From the French and British came expressions of official regret mixed with lavish encomiums of the CRB.[113] In an interview with Ben S. Allen, Lord Robert Cecil of the British Foreign Office declared that the only thing which had made the relief effort possible had been the "absolute confidence" which Hoover and his colleagues had "inspired in all the Allied Governments." These Americans, he added, were leaving behind a reputation which America could consider a "national possession in future years."[114]

Not all the diplomatic reverberations, however, were so benign. In Washington a worried Belgian minister to the United States expressed alarm at the prospect of American withdrawal,[115] while in London Merry del Val promptly announced, as "founder and President" of the CRB, that the Spanish would now carry on its administration! The ambassador notified the Allied governments and the press that Hoover's successor would be a man named José Roura.[116]

Hoover, of course, had no intention of permitting his Spanish "colleagues" to take over. On February 13 he cabled his own plan for reorganization to London: the CRB would completely sever its ties with the Allies and become instead simply "a recruiting agency for benevolence and propaganda" in the United States. All its other functions outside Belgium would be assumed by the Allied governments, the Belgian government-in-exile, or a body selected by them. As for operations inside German-occupied territory, Hoover deemed it "hopeless to protect the food supplies" and "guarantee an efficiency of administration" unless a "forcible neutral body" took the commission's place. If such a body were to win American financial and diplomatic backing, he stated pointedly, it must be "of northern European complexion."[117]

As if this message were not explicit enough, Hoover followed up later that day with an even tougher cable to London. "I wish to make it absolutely clear," he thundered: the CRB "must be liquidated and disappear" except as "a purely benevolent soliciting agency" in the United States. "The whole of the files" must be transferred to New York, away (though he didn't openly say so) from the clutches of Villalobar. "[W]e have created" the "name and traditions" of the relief, he asserted. They "are a matter of pride and solicitude. In no other way can we draw a clear-cut line between the two eras of

Belgian Relief. . . ." Only by setting up a completely new organization in
Europe could the commission obtain "a discharge of our responsibilities."
There must be "a clean cut separation involving complete dissolution." The
CRB, he said, would "positively refuse" to surrender its money, its organi-
zation, or its ships "on any other terms than these."[118]

That evening Hoover attended a dinner in his honor at the Astor Hotel in
New York. Five hundred of the city's most prominent citizens attended.
Nicholas Murray Butler, president of Columbia University, acclaimed him
as a "brave and modest man" whose work would be remembered in history
as "the epic of this great war." It was not his past success that gripped Hoover's mind that night, however. It was what he called, in a voice hoarse with
emotion, the "tragedy of possible failure."

> If we must retire, as it appears today that we must, then other neutrals
> must take up this work. The world cannot stand by and witness the star-
> vation of the Belgian people and the Belgian children. God still reigns, and
> other people must carry on this work.

Only hours earlier he had threatened by cable not even to cooperate with a
successor relief agency unless his terms of dissolution were met. Now, in a
gentler mood, he exhorted his audience to remember that the American people's "obligation" toward Belgium—indeed, toward humanity itself—continued and must not falter.[119]

The cheers and applause at the Astor did not linger long in Hoover's ears.
The next morning he was back at his office, reading incoming cables, preparing replies, plotting strategy, struggling without letup to avert the debacle
he feared. Up to this point he had concurred with the Poland–Page response
to the Germans' assault on the CRB's status: flight, not fight; withdrawal,
not retaliation. He had even issued the press release in America announcing
this decision. Suddenly, on February 14, he changed his mind and issued
new instructions to his London office. Stop the liquidation, he ordered.[120]
Tell all our men in Belgium to stay "at their posts" as long as possible. Convinced that the Germans' "stultifying arrangements"[121] were an attempt "to
throw responsibility [for terminating the relief] on to us," Hoover characteristically counterattacked. He proposed that Brand Whitlock issue an ultimatum to the Germans: either permit all CRB men in Belgium to remain with
complete freedom of movement as before, and restore Whitlock his "full diplomatic privileges," or Whitlock and the entire relief staff would withdraw.
Hoover was quite candid about his motive. "The object of this" (he told
Poland) "is obviously that we shall throw responsibility on to [the] Germans. . . ."[122]

Why, however, this sudden reversal of tactics? Just before dispatching his
new directive, Hoover had received a cable from the Marquis de Villalobar
via Berlin. Villalobar informed him that the Germans had not actually ordered

the Americans out of Belgium. In fact, they were anxious for the CRB to continue until a new agency was established.[123] Hoover evidently concluded from this that the Germans were maneuvering to put the moral burden of a crackup on his shoulders. And this he would not countenance at all.

That night Hoover took a train down to Washington.[124] The next day the State Department—seemingly as pliable in his hands as was Walter Hines Page—duly sent new instructions to Whitlock. Your position as it stands is "untenable," it warned. Inform the Germans that the CRB and the U.S. government are willing to continue the relief but only if the CRB men and Whitlock retain their former privileges. Otherwise, get out of Belgium immediately, take the American relief workers with you, and tell the Germans that the "sole responsibility" for the consequences rests on them.[125]

Hoover's new directive reached his London headquarters on February 15—by coincidence, at almost the very moment as a startling message from Brussels.[126] William B. Poland's cable of the twelfth ordering the Americans out of Belgium had stunned German officialdom, particularly von der Lancken, who had no desire to take responsibility for causing a total American pullout.[127] At a meeting with Whitlock and others on the fourteenth, the embarrassed German officer capitulated: the CRB delegates in Belgium, he said, could remain and operate as before. Apparently when he had imposed his restrictions a few days earlier, he had thought war with America inevitable. Now, he claimed awkwardly, it seemed less so. Whatever his motive, the vital point had been conceded: for the CRB, at least, the status quo ante was restored.[128]

Scurrying for diplomatic cover, the German government in Berlin soon confirmed von der Lancken's assurances. We have "no intention" of forcing the CRB to suspend its work, Foreign Minister Arthur Zimmermann declared. Americans can "remain at their posts until further orders."[129] When the chips were down, it seemed, the Germans—like the British across the Channel—did not dare to destroy the relief outright.

Von der Lancken's abrupt retreat evoked joy and amusement in Brussels. Even Villalobar, who (like Whitlock) mistakenly thought that it was Hoover who had sent Poland's cable, was constrained to praise his old adversary. "Hoover," he exclaimed, "is the best diplomat of all of us!"[130]

Ironically, of course, the Germans' turnabout occurred before Hoover's and the State Department's cables reached Brussels.[131] Poland's cable alone had been sufficient to call the Germans' bluff (if it had been one). In any case, Poland now canceled his order to liquidate, and the press announced that the Americans would remain in Belgium after all.[132] After two frenzied weeks of cables, consultations, and more cables, the CRB was right back where it had started.

On February 18 Hoover informed his London office that political tensions between America and Germany were abating and that "[a]s matters stand today we may continue indefinitely."[133] The problems he faced, however, were hardly over. At any time a *casus belli* between Germany and the United States could erupt, and with it the enforced exodus of Americans from Belgium. If Hoover on the eighteenth seemed guardedly optimistic about the immediate future, only four days earlier he had been convinced that America was "surely drifting into war" and that the relief organization must be "rehabilitated on some new line." Not only for its own safety, he added, but so that "we may have our hands free for service to our own country" in event of war.[134] Once again his personal prospects were intersecting with those of the commission.

On precisely what terms, however, should this "rehabilitation" be effected? Throughout late February Hoover continued to insist that if and when his American associates were obliged to leave Belgium the CRB must totally withdraw from its mission "except as to benevolence in America."[135] Furthermore, Dutch government personnel and *only* Dutch government personnel should assume responsibility for food distribution behind German lines.[136] As for purchasing and shipping of food from abroad, why not (he proposed) let the Belgian government-in-exile take on these functions? It could thereby develop a "proper efficient organisation" that would be invaluable for relief purposes after the war.[137]

Hoover at once discovered that there were limits to what his formidable will could accomplish. In London Merry del Val strenuously insisted that if the Americans did pull out, the CRB would *not* disappear but would go right on under Spanish supervision.[138] According to William P. Poland, neither the Allied governments nor Ambassador Page were much inclined to "combat" him on this point. In fact, the British government seemed downright anxious to involve the Spanish further in such circumstances—apparently to propitiate the neutral king of Spain.[139] Even worse, Poland warned that if Hoover and his colleagues attempted to dissolve the CRB unilaterally they would arouse "great opposition" in London.[140]

To further complicate matters, the Belgian government quickly indicated that it did not wish to take over the external management of the relief at all. Instead, through its agent in London, Carton de Wiart, the exiled government implored the Americans to "remain in as many features of [the] Relief as possible" after their departure from the continent. Even van de Vyvere and Francqui joined in the chorus.[141] However much certain leading Belgians disliked Hoover personally, they did not wish to lose the diplomatic, charitable, and material support of the United States of America.[142]

Hoover's reaction to all this was predictable. Merry del Val's suggestions were "[the] worst dis-service he can do [the] Belgians and Allies," he exploded on February 17. The Spanish ambassador, he charged, was destroying the CRB's goodwill in America and impairing its ability to raise funds for its successor.[143] Hoover now declared that he would not surrender control of the commission to anyone until he had first obtained a $20,000,000 bank guarantee covering all the liabilities for which he and his American colleagues were personally responsible.[144] Still more infuriating to Hoover was the thought that he could not dissolve the CRB whenever he alone determined to do so. It "seems to me," he told Poland, "that in [a] final emergency it is within our powers without anybody's approval or consent to carry out" our plan for liquidation.[145]

As for the Belgians, Hoover's response was swift. To Carton de Wiart, who only two months before had tried behind the scenes to undercut him, Hoover now declared with perhaps contrived innocence:

> We have acted on the impression that it was the desire and the interest of Comité National and the Belgian Government that the Belgians should take over as many features of the Relief as possible and we considered that in the event of our leaving Belgium a favorable opportunity would be offered for such a transition.[146]

For the past year, Hoover told some friends privately, the Belgian government had been "so anxious" to augment its prestige and demonstrate its people's self-sufficiency that he was positive it would be eager to handle the purchase and shipping of supplies.[147] Now, when he thrust this opportunity upon them, the Belgian leaders protested, desirous to let him alone carry the ball. It is unlikely that the irony escaped him.

The CRB chairman and the Allied governments now struggled to devise an arrangement satisfactory to all parties. On February 16 Hoover proposed that the CRB transfer its assets and operations to a new committee to be formed at once under Dutch and Spanish patronage, with the identical staff of American volunteers who would "retire as fast as new neutrals are found." The CRB would then become a charitable agency in America.[148] But when Brand Whitlock proposed, a few days later, simply to infiltrate non-American neutrals into the commission's *existing* apparatus inside Belgium, Hoover pronounced the idea "hopeless." "I confess that I do not know any volunteer neutrals whom I could trust," he asserted, "and the gradual replacement of our members simply means that we will be taking the entire responsibility, both individually and nationally for a body over which we have no control and of which we would have practically no knowledge as to integrity, ability, or anything else." It was "obvious," he added, "that such a body as this would suit both the Belgians and the Germans. . . ."[149]

There was but one significant difference between the two plans: Whitlock proposed to leave the CRB intact; Hoover most emphatically did not. And that, for him, was the crux of the matter. We "initiated the whole Belgian Relief," he told two of his closest colleagues. "We made the C.R.B. into an institution of world-wide repute for integrity and efficiency and high ideals. For us to step out and allow some other administration to come in is a risk to these principles and the reputation of this institution to which we do not deserve to be exposed."[150]

By late February the Allied governments had sketched out a somewhat cumbersome contingency plan that (in the private words of a Foreign Office cable) would "to some extent protect us from having to accept Spanish business control in succession to Americans."[151] Under it an official "Inter-Allies Relief Committee" (with Belgian, French, and British members) based in London would handle external business functions, while a private "Spanish Dutch Ravitaillement Committee" based in Rotterdam would supervise operations in German-held territory.[152] Despite his continued insistence that the use of "mixed neutrals" in the occupied areas would mean "failure,"[153] and that the Dutch government alone should control food distribution, Hoover expressed pleasure at this outcome. The Commission for Relief in Belgium could now, if necessary, "retreat" into charitable work in the United States, he said—exactly what "I have been striving for ever since the German break. . . ." Now, he told the State Department on February 27, the Allies would *have* to finance the relief and support it "to the hilt."[154]

And then, without warning, less than forty-eight hours later, the CRB chairman reversed himself. On March 1 he dramatically cabled London that he was now prepared to "carry on the Commission" after all, even if his American volunteers were forced to retire from Belgium. Drop the inter-Allied relief committee proposal for the time being, he ordered. Abandon plans to liquidate the CRB. Despite this "apparent reversal of previous attitude" (as he delicately put it), he now declared that it was the commission's "duty" to continue its external operations if the Allied governments approved.[155]

What had happened? Why, after a month of vehement opposition to this course of action, had Hoover so suddenly changed his mind? In his cable he cited "Belgian protests"—presumably the pleas from Carton de Wiart and others that the Americans play the maximum possible role in the relief effort. He also alluded obliquely to "changed conditions" in the United States and to consultations with unnamed "important men." Hoover's principal impetus, however, was what he frankly called "national reasons": a desire to strengthen American "sentiment" for the "allied cause" and to maintain the CRB's "prestige . . . before [the] American charitable public."[156] Obviously his commission would have far less stature and influence if it became but one wartime charity among many in the United States.

Hoover's decision was almost certainly influenced by the staggering news of the day before. On February 28 President Wilson had released to the press an intercepted telegram from German Foreign Minister Zimmermann offering Mexico the states of Texas, New Mexico, and Arizona if she would ally herself with Germany in the event the United States and Germany went to war. Two days before this, Wilson, already aware of the Zimmermann note, had asked Congress for authority to arm American merchant ships. Clearly the United States government was approaching the point of no return.

As the danger of American intervention escalated, Hoover apparently concluded that the Commission for Relief in Belgium could better serve his country's interests by maintaining the highest possible international profile. Its very existence was for many Americans a standing rebuke to the Germans—proof of the superior morality of the Allies. He may also have been affected by the Belgian finance minister's plea, just a few days earlier, that the CRB cooperate in the "economic reconstruction of Belgium" after the war.[157] Under the circumstances Hoover probably reasoned that this was no time to dismantle his unique institution and sacrifice much of the influence that he himself had attained.

In any case, the CRB's chairman's startling switch evoked immediate satisfaction from the Allies. For them one more headache had been removed; Eustace Percy called it a "great relief."[158] Now they would not have to set up a new and perhaps inefficient relief apparatus and risk antagonizing the Spanish besides. Within a few days the Belgian, French, and British governments all enthusiastically endorsed Hoover's decision.[159] From Brussels came word that even the Comité National and the Germans favored continued American control of the relief.[160]

Hoover, nevertheless, was sensitive about his reversal, and, as usual, he went to considerable lengths to justify it. He asserted to friends in London that his previous position of total withdrawal ("except as to benevolence in America") had been "dominated" by a desire to let the Belgians take over the purchase and transport of food from abroad. After all, he said, this had been their "ambition" for the past eighteen months, an ambition arising out of their desire to show the world their self-sufficiency.[161] When the British ambassador in Washington rather pointedly called attention to Hoover's about-face,[162] the CRB chairman instantly expressed "regret" at the "confusion" that (he alleged) had arisen in London. Hoover himself took no responsibility for this "confusion." Instead, he again stressed his previous wish to let the Belgians assume the external functions of the relief—a responsibility, he noted, that they had just declined to undertake. It was after learning of this, he said, and after learning of the Allies' difficulties in trying to reorganize the relief, that he had concluded that "duty" required him to change his mind.[163]

Hoover's explanation was disingenuous. There is no evidence that a wish to have the Belgians take on more duties had "dominated"—or even influenced—his initial plan to withdraw from relief administration. In fact, when he first raised the possibility of pulling out (on February 4 and 5), he had explicitly proposed that in this contingency *all* aspects of the relief should be turned over to the *Dutch*. Not until February 15 did he suggest any role whatever for the Belgians. Nor did Allied problems in establishing a successor organization decisively affect his change of heart. The Allies, in fact, had already devised a rearrangement plan several days before Hoover's March 1 cable, and he himself (on February 27) had endorsed it. There was thus no need for him to let them off the hook just two days later.

Hoover's true motivation lay elsewhere. His initial decision to withdraw totally (if necessary) and liquidate the CRB had nothing to do with solicitude for the Belgians, many of whom he thoroughly distrusted. It sprang, rather, from his fierce resolve to preserve his commission's reputation, to prevent a Spanish takeover, and to free himself (and his colleagues) for wartime service if the United States entered the conflict. Similarly, his reversal of March 1 occurred not for the Allies' sake but for American political reasons—and very possibly personal considerations as well. Hoover's "official" explanation of his conduct was a convenient cover story for the Allies, but it concealed motives that he could scarcely divulge to the Europeans.

Hoover was more candid with William B. Poland and Vernon Kellogg. In a long confidential letter to them on March 5 he laid out the "principles" that he said had governed his behavior during the previous month. Among them:

1. Simple replacement of Americans in Belgium by "mixed volunteer neutrals" would be disastrous. It would inevitably lead to "internal friction," "intrigue with the Germans," inadequate control of distribution, and "ultimate breakdown."

2. Neutral governmental personnel would be preferable to volunteers, of whom there were simply not enough of "a high degree of idealism" in any eligible European country. In effect, Hoover asserted that he could not find three dozen satisfactory volunteers in all of Holland, Denmark, Switzerland, and Spain—an extraordinary testimony to his fervent Americanism.

3. Exclusive Spanish control would be ruinous. We "cannot disguise the fact," said Hoover, that American and British "racial prejudice against the Spanish people (based on tradition and not on merit) creates a lack of confidence in their ability to handle a large commercial organisation" and would "preclude the continuous moral and charitable support of the rest of the world" if the Spanish took charge. The Dutch, by contrast, enjoyed an excellent reputation for integrity and efficiency and had food resources available for export to Belgium.

4. The CRB must continue to exist in the United States, both to raise money and (even more) to mobilize public opinion in behalf of Belgium's needs.

5. The CRB must do nothing to create the impression that Hoover and his associates were "running away" from the relief.

6. If, however, the CRB were compelled to abandon its mission (except in America), then it must at that time "absolutely" be liquidated as a business enterprise and released from all financial obligations.

7. The commission's representatives in Belgium must meanwhile stay where they were "unless the Germans render our position intolerable, thus securing to themselves" the blame for any rupture. "There is a responsibility attaching to breaking down this work," said Hoover frankly, "which we do not wish ourselves to assume. . . ."

All in all, Hoover was now content with the status of the reorganization plans.[164]

By early March, then, Hoover had arranged that the great work of his relief commission would go on unaltered, even if America entered the war, except for the task of supervision inside Belgium. This would be assigned to a Dutch–Spanish committee, the precise composition of which was as yet undetermined. While Hoover still preferred to freeze out the Spanish completely, he had come to recognize that this objective was diplomatically unattainable.[165]

I I I

H o o v e r ' s seemingly erratic behavior—and his obvious influence over the State Department—brought him into conflict with the man who, only weeks before, had warmly recommended him for a high position in the Wilson administration: Brand Whitlock. The entire month of February, in fact, had been one unending ordeal for the American minister to Brussels, who felt at times like a shuttlecock in a long-range duel between Hoover and the Germans.

When Woodrow Wilson severed relations with Germany on February 3, Whitlock evidently expected that he would soon be obliged to leave Belgium. From a purely diplomatic perspective this was the logical course to follow. Since the United States no longer had direct contacts with Germany, why should Whitlock continue to represent the United States in a German-occupied country? "But nothing was ever simple in Belgium," the diplomat later wrote— not when the succor of a nation was at stake.[166]

Whitlock's tribulations began in a curious manner. The State Department's initial instruction to him—cable no. 248, dated February 3—was itself unorthodox. Instead of simply ordering him out (as diplomatic protocol dictated), the department advised him to remain in Brussels unless the Germans asked him to leave! If they did, he should then go to the Belgian government-in-exile at Le Havre.[167] Obviously Washington was cognizant of his role as patron of the relief.

The department's coded message, however, did not reach Whitlock in this integral form. When it finally arrived four days later, it simply stated (according to Whitlock) that he should turn over his legation's interests to the Spanish and proceed to Le Havre.[168] This seemingly plain instruction was accompanied by a *second* dispatch telling him to remain at his post unless the Germans objected.[169] The two messages, as received in Brussels, were contradictory.

What had happened? Whitlock immediately surmised that Hoover (who was then in Washington) had inspired the second command.[170] Already he had seen one cable from Washington written in Hooverian style and had sensed, correctly, that the CRB chairman's "tremendous will" was "at work."[171]

Then, on February 9, von der Lancken drastically curtailed the CRB's personnel in Belgium and invited Whitlock to remain merely as "honorary chairman" of the relief commission.[172] A few days after that came William B. Poland's blast from London ordering the CRB volunteers to leave Belgium immediately. Believing, incorrectly, that Hoover had prepared this cable, Whitlock noted wryly that it had "created the expected sensation."[173] Von der Lancken (who evidently had been trying to keep the relief work going but maneuver the Americans out) instantly backed down—in part. The CRB was restored its privileges. Brand Whitlock, however, was not. Deprived of his diplomatic pouch and cipher, no longer addressed officially by the Germans, he was now little more than a "distinguished personality," reduced to smuggling out messages through the Spanish legation's courier.[174]

The situation inside Brussels had now developed in a way that Hoover apparently had not foreseen. Instead of surrendering completely, the Germans had driven a wedge between the CRB and its resident American sponsor. On the subject of the prerogatives of the relief commission, the Germans had yielded with alacrity. On the subject of Whitlock's diplomatic status, however, they had not retreated in the least. Brand Whitlock's position was more anomalous than ever.

Exhausted by the strain, Whitlock was nonetheless willing to endure his embarrassing loss of standing if, by his continued presence in Brussels, he could safeguard the endangered relief work. That, in his mind, transcended all the indignities he had to suffer.[175] But would the State Department agree with his views? On February 17 he received a smuggled-in copy of the department's cable of February 15 ordering him to secure a full restoration of the CRB's status—*and his own*—or leave Belgium at once. The department's instructions (prepared after consulting Hoover) were by now half out of date: von der Lancken had already reinstated the CRB's privileges before the department sent its cable.

Privately Whitlock railed at what he perceived to be the sheer unrealism of the department's message and began to blame Hoover for his plight:

> Just why they think at Washington that they can break off diplomatic relations, and expect the Germans to continue to recognize our diplomats, is beyond me. Do you expect to be able to recall our Ambassador from Berlin, pack off the German Ambassador from Washington, and then have the Germans recognize a Minister in territory the Germans control? They let Hoover change their instructions—as in the famous telegram 248, in which there was no necessity for correction, but evidently a clumsily dovetailed second thought—Hoover's, of course.[176]

Still, the U.S. government had issued its orders, and when they arrived officially on February 21 via the Spanish legation,[177] Whitlock prepared to call on von der Lancken. The American minister had no hope that the Germans would bow before the State Department's ultimatum.[178] On February 23 he secretly cabled Washington that he had "waited as long as I should" for the relief work to be reorganized and would now notify the Germans that if his diplomatic status were not restored immediately, he would leave.[179]

By this time Hoover had learned of Whitlock's proposal of mid-February[180] that the CRB should gradually replace its American personnel inside Belgium with men from other neutral countries. To Hoover, of course, such a staffing policy would be disastrous if implemented under CRB auspices, although, he commented tartly, it would no doubt gratify "both the Belgians and the Germans."[181] On February 25 he accordingly drafted a cable for the State Department to send to Brussels conveying his objections to the idea and insisting that the Dutch alone take the Americans' place.[182] The next day the department dutifully dispatched a message along these lines.[183]

By this time, too, Hoover had reversed his position of ten days before that Whitlock and the CRB delegates inside Belgium should withdraw. Now that von der Lancken had retreated (vis-à-vis the commission), Hoover emphatically wanted his people to remain. To do otherwise would violate his "principle" of pinning the blame on the Germans if and when the Americans left. On February 25, therefore, he recommended to the State Department that Whitlock stay right where he was, provided that he was "treated with consideration" and given a respectful hearing on issues affecting the relief.[184] The next day the department concurred and so advised its stranded minister to Brussels.[185]

Determined to avoid the appearance of deserting his duty, Hoover now requested that if the State Department should eventually decide to recall Whitlock, it should order out the American CRB men simultaneously.[186] The CRB should receive the "moral backing of the American Government" in this fashion. Such an official action, he argued, would clearly establish "the fact that we have stayed on our job until the last moment."[187] To his colleagues in London Hoover reiterated that his men behind the lines were to "remain [there] until they are ordered out by the Germans." Whatever happened, he said, he was "extremely anxious that we shall leave Belgium" at the command of the Germans or of the U.S. government.[188]

Meanwhile, on February 24, unaware of Hoover's change of attitude and its rationale, Whitlock had visited von der Lancken. The German diplomat was all smiles and cordiality, full of compliments for the relief, eager for Whitlock and the Americans to remain, willing, in fact, to accommodate Whitlock in nearly every way—except one: the Germans would *not* accord him full diplomatic status. Two days later, the baron deliberately addressed Whitlock as a private citizen. The American diplomat resolved to withdraw from Belgium at once.[189]

The State Department immediately overruled him. We do not want to convey the impression, it said, that either our legation in Brussels or the CRB was "withdrawing voluntarily." Whitlock should stay put until notified otherwise.[190]

Whitlock's simmering anger now boiled over. On February 28 he received Hoover's proposal (via the State Department) that the Dutch government take charge of the relief. To Whitlock this suggestion plainly reflected Hoover's "hatred of Villalobar and Francqui."[191] Nevertheless, the next day he raised the subject with the feisty Spaniard, only to learn that the Dutch and Spanish had already devised a scheme to replace the Americans, if necessary.[192] Three days later Whitlock learned of the proposal (already discarded by the time the news of it got to him) for an inter-Allied relief committee.[193] Three days after that came Hoover's cable of March 1 repudiating the idea.[194]

Vexed and wearied by the unending confusion, the maddening delays in cabling, and the inconsistent dispatches from the world outside, Whitlock vented his frustration in his diary. Hoover "must be losing his head," he charged, "saying that the C.R.B. must not retire voluntarily from Belgium."[195] The diplomat was disgusted by what he considered Hoover's irresponsible, "romantic" posturing—the same trait he so disliked in his former deputy, Hugh Gibson.[196] Concerned for the personal safety of the American CRB men if war with Germany should come, Whitlock again urged—as he had for weeks—that they be withdrawn as quickly as possible and replaced by other neutrals.[197] Unfortunately for him, the CRB was listening only to Hoover.[198]

So, too, was the U.S. Department of State. "The Government has no ideas on the revictualing that Hoover doesn't give it," Whitlock complained to associates on March 7. Look at the long list of contradictory dispatches from Washington, he exclaimed: "[G]o, stay, don't go, don't stay, take our courier, keep the courier." Look at the department's cable referring to Whitlock's withdrawal plan as one that "would gratify the Germans and certain Belgians." "What did the Government know of our internal quarrels," he fumed, "of the significance of those words 'certain Belgians' which expressed Hoover's old, unchanging dislike and distrust of Francqui?" Whitlock's wife was even more cutting: "The voice is Jacob's voice," she said, "but the hands are the hands of Esau."[199]

Whitlock would have been even more perturbed if he had known that at this very moment Hugh Gibson, of all people, was at the State Department pending reassignment. Hoover, of course, could not have been happier;[200] now he had yet another friend in high places. In the days ahead the young diplomat collaborated closely with his "chief."

Whitlock was angry for still another reason. For all these weeks he had repeatedly recommended that Dutch and Spanish delegates supplant the Americans in Belgium and that the relief operation otherwise continue unchanged. Now, in his cable of March 1, Hoover had seemingly authorized precisely this course—without so much as acknowledging that it had been

Whitlock's all along. What Whitlock did not understand was that Hoover was *not* sanctioning a mere change of CRB personnel but rather the creation of a completely new supervisory organization for which the CRB would not be responsible. Failing to grasp this crucial distinction, the American diplomat seemed to feel that Hoover had not the courtesy to give credit where credit was due.[201]

Hoover, for his part, had not altered *his* opinion of Whitlock: the man was a weak and gullible dilettante whose impulse was to shrink from unpleasantness rather than face it. The CRB chairman had no intention of succumbing to Whitlock's nervous entreaties—a stance that appeared to require increasing effort to maintain. On March 5 Hoover confided to Gibson: "[W]e seem to be having some difficulty in exercising repression on Mr. Whitlock to keep him back in Belgium until the situation has developed to a point where we all come out in glory."[202]

Suddenly, in the first days of March, news from behind the German lines turned ominous. From its beleaguered minister in Brussels the State Department received a report that American CRB men were now being prevented from leaving Belgium. Moreover, the Germans had given only oral assurances that the Americans could depart when they desired.[203] The specter that had long haunted Whitlock was now in view: that if war did break out, the Germans might not permit the American relief workers to go home at all—might imprison them as enemies instead. The State Department immediately ordered Whitlock to obtain written assurances; independently, it requested clarification from the Germans.[204] If the Germans did not reply satisfactorily, the department intended to recall Whitlock and the CRB together.[205]

Upon hearing Whitlock's news Hoover was understandably indignant. He urged Washington to take "every necessary step" to obtain the "immediate release" of his men from this "monstrous situation." They were not "ordinary nationals," he declared, but persons "in a quasi diplomatic position, the agents of a great international work."[206]

Whitlock's report from Brussels may have been somewhat inaccurate. The Germans had indeed closed the Belgian–Dutch frontier for a time but had apparently done so for reasons unrelated to the relief. In any case, on March 8 they let Vernon Kellogg through the lines.[207] In addition, after several days of offering merely oral assurances that the Americans could leave Belgium whenever they chose, the Germans finally reduced their pledges to writing— with, however, an unwelcome proviso: any departing American could be "quarantined" for up to four weeks for military reasons. In practice, said the Germans, this would apply only to CRB men in the militarily sensitive region of northern France.[208]

Meanwhile, in northern France itself, the already tenuous supervision of the relief was breaking down. In early February the CRB's six delegates in the territory had journeyed to Brussels for their regular staff meeting. There they had learned that they would probably be interned for several weeks in Germany if war should come. Furthermore, they had discovered that they would no longer be permitted to go to Brussels once a week as before but instead just once a month (at most). Unwilling to accept these new restrictions—especially the threat of a prolonged "quarantine"—Hoover's Brussels director, Warren Gregory, had refused to permit his men to return to their posts. The result was that the Germans had promptly begun to administer the relief in northern France by themselves.[209]

When news of Gregory's decision finally reached London at the beginning of March, the effect was predictable. The British government requested that other neutrals be sent in immediately. William B. Poland and Ambassador Page agreed that the Americans must either return to their stations at once or "permanently withdraw from French control."[210]

Apprised of this deteriorating situation, Hoover demanded that the Germans allow his men to return to "full control" in northern France, with a written promise of safe conduct out of the country in case of withdrawal and not more than two weeks' "intermediate stoppage." Otherwise, he told London, "we must obviously secure other neutrals" for that region.[211] Poland immediately communicated this order to Brussels.[212] Crisscrossing the frontier, Vernon Kellogg reported that the Germans had promised safe conduct but continued to insist upon a three- or four-week "immunity bath." Rather than submit to this restraint, Kellogg reported that Gregory was arranging to rush Spanish and Dutch consuls to northern France.[213] Poland ordered him to take no definite action until advised from the United States.[214]

Hoover now confronted a crescendo of pressure to get his men out of Belgium without delay. On March 3 Whitlock urged that Dutch "understudies" be brought in to learn the procedures and then relieve the Americans; his cable reached Washington on March 7.[215] That same day Hoover's London office learned that Whitlock wished to withdraw the Americans "without waiting till war" but that Gregory wanted to hold out until the end.[216] Poland warned Hoover that the CRB was "traversing [the] gravest crisis in its history" and that the American position in both Belgium and northern France was becoming "impossible."[217]

On March 9 the CRB's London office openly proposed that the commission withdraw from Belgium and France at once on the grounds that it could not fulfill its obligations because of "diminished privileges" and German interruption of its services. "Otherwise [the] psychological moment . . . when we can retire as a body" was "likely to pass."[218] In a dispatch of his own, Walter Hines Page was even more emphatic. There was "hopeless conflict and confusion in Brussels," he said. If the CRB had departed from German-held territory when the diplomatic break had occurred in early February, he remarked sharply, the blame would have fallen squarely on Germany. Instead (contrary to Page's advice) it had stayed on and had become enmeshed in "controversies and entanglements" as the Germans maneuvered to force it out to its own discredit. Any further delay in withdrawing, Page contended, would "result in the humiliation of the Commission and its ejection."[219]

Hoover was unmoved by the barrage. "Our London Office seems to have the jumps," he told Hugh Gibson on the tenth. When the CRB "goes out of action," he wrote, it must do so "at the demand of some superior and very evident force." Otherwise "it is likely to bring us some national discredit." And "national discredit" he wished at all costs to avert. Hoover himself now expected that his men would have to "come out" in the next few weeks. But, he told Gibson candidly, "we want to throw the responsibility for it upon somebody else."[220] It was an objective that Whitlock, Page, and now his London office seemed not to comprehend.

As usual, the State Department and Hoover were in agreement. On March 10 the department informed Whitlock bluntly that relief operations inside Belgium should continue under American control exclusively and until the Americans were forced to desist. Take no steps toward withdrawal, it ordered, until you receive further instructions.[221] Whitlock's anxious hands were again tied. In a separate dispatch the department told Ambassador Page that the CRB had become "a national matter" and that "any action on its part to bring about a voluntary liquidation or cessation of its work would have a disastrous effect on public opinion."[222]

Not surprisingly, the department's cable to London had a Hooverian sound. It was, in fact, a lightly edited version of a draft that Hoover himself had prepared. He submitted it to the department through Gibson.[223]

With the State Department backing him to the hilt, Hoover now notified his London office of Whitlock's proposal to withdraw ("based," said Hoover caustically, "on his timidity as to German guarantees of safety"). He also told London of the department's firm reply—not mentioning, however, that he had largely written it. In the blunt, commanding tone that was his trademark, the CRB chairman ordered his lieutenants into line:

We are in absolute accord with our Government in this matter and trust our staff will act accordingly. We cannot agree with your proposals for any initiative or steps toward liquidation in any direction on our part and this idea should not be entertained for one moment. This Commission has now become a national trust and with an enormous attention and public opinion behind it and any voluntary withdrawal on our part would impress the American people as cowardly. . . .

Furthermore, whatever the difficulties that may arise because of "international conflict" concerning the CRB, we must, said Hoover,

continue absolutely at our posts until the Commission has been suppressed by some superior force or until we have been recalled by our own Government. I do trust that you will accept this as the absolute complete policy of the Commission and that no steps whatever will be taken varying from this steadfast intention to carry this task through if it is humanly possible. . . .

While certain Dutchmen were now to be sent into Belgium to learn the work under American guidance, the Americans (said Hoover) were to "remain in absolute control." Do not worry about the Spanish, he added. ". . . [S]o long as we stay at our posts we control the situation."[224]

Marooned in Brussels for the indefinite future, Whitlock chafed in helpless indignation. Here (in his eyes) was Hoover recklessly jeopardizing the safety of his men, and the Department of State going right along with him. "Very well," wrote Whitlock in his diary:

> I have done my duty, and the Department has again allowed itself to be dominated by Hoover, who despite all the vacillation he has shown in the last month, still clings obstinately to his stubborn purpose to have those men remain in here, exposed to dangers that, with the Germans in their present frame of mind, are easily imagined. I have again and again pointed out this danger, and urged decisive action. . . . But Hoover, though three thousand miles away, thinks he knows more than Gregory, or Kellogg, or I, or any one who is here, and seems able to impose his brutal will on the Department. If any horror occurs, I shall have only the melancholy satisfaction of being on record—and have to take the blame anyhow![225]

To Whitlock, Hoover was permitting his personal prejudices, especially his "inveterate hatred of Villalobar,"[226] to dictate the formulation of his policies. It seemed not to occur to Whitlock that Hoover might have grounds for his antipathies.

While the CRB hovered on the brink of possible dissolution, its tireless chairman appealed for financial support from the American public. On February 17 he addressed the National Geographic Society in Washington; three nights later he spoke to the American Institute of Mining Engineers in New York.[227] Every argument, every symbolic gesture, that he could think of to stir, even shame, his apathetic countrymen, he invoked. He had hoped, he confessed at one point, to write "a bright chapter of American history in this war—of American efficiency, of American humanity, of an institution devoted, not to destruction, but dedicated to self-sacrifice and the saving of life; but I fear tonight that this chapter will never be completed" and that America would not fulfill "the great task" he and his colleagues had set for it.[228] On February 28 he carried his campaign to a joint session of the New York State legislature. The luncheon that followed consisted of a slice of bread, a small piece of bacon, and a plate of soup—a typical daily ration in Belgium.[229]

Even as he targeted the political and business elites of the Eastern seaboard,[230] Hoover laid plans to launch his most ambitious fund-raising scheme yet: a national appeal for every American to donate a day's income to the Belgian relief cause.[231] Through Colonel House he sought a pledge from President Wilson and calculated that his drive could yield $30,000,000–40,000,000.[232]

By the beginning of March 1917 the CRB had received a total of more than $1,000,000 from American contributors during the preceding four months— a respectable sum indeed, but pitifully short of requirements.[233] Hoover told a British colleague that his campaign would have gained $20,000,000 had it not been for the "German break" and the resultant "impossibility of our bringing matters to fruition in face of constant expectation of war."[234] More than ever he seemed to pin his hopes on the "one day's income" campaign. On March 6 he formally requested a "five minute interview" with Woodrow Wilson—evidently to secure a presidential endorsement of his plan.[235]

The meeting with President Wilson never occurred.[236] Instead, on March 7 Hoover asked Edward House whether it seemed worthwhile to continue Belgian fund-raising efforts in the United States. No, the colonel replied, the time was not "opportune." "The people are engrossed with our entry into the war," he observed, "and cannot be brought to think of anything else."[237]

House's advice was apparently decisive. Stymied yet again by the currents of war, Hoover cabled London that he was returning to Europe.[238] The "one day's income" drive, like the Allied relief loan, had died aborning.

Popular sentiment may not have been the only obstacle in Hoover's path. Just a few days before, President Wilson had privately complained to Colonel House that Hoover was a man "obsessed with one idea."[239] Perhaps for this reason, the chairman of the CRB failed to obtain an appointment to call at the White House in early March.[240] The President of the United States had other matters on his mind.

I V

ON March 13, 1917 Hoover left New York for Europe on "an ancient Spanish cargo jalopy," the *Antonio Lopez*. With North Atlantic passenger service suspended because of the U-boat threat, it was the best accommodation he could get.[241] The forty-year-old vessel had no cold storage. Its supply of meat and poultry consisted of a pen full of live animals.[242] Hoover's wife and son Allan saw him off and then went on to California (where young Herbert was already staying), to await the Chief's return.[243]

Before departing, he issued a statement to the press. The Commission for Relief in Belgium, he said, was "the largest venture in the history of international benevolent economic service and charity." It was an "American institution" that had brought "lustre" to America's name. Its survival should be "a matter of first American pride." He announced that Dutchmen would now distribute the food in northern France and would replace the Americans in Belgium if war broke out between the United States and Germany.[244] That same day he authorized his London office to recruit six Dutchmen for the French districts and even to begin replacing Americans with Dutchmen inside Belgium "as soon as opportunity offers."[245]

The *Antonio Lopez* took twelve days to cross the Atlantic—finally arriving at the Spanish port of Cadiz on March 25.[246] While at sea Hoover learned by the ship's wireless that a revolution had occurred in Russia and that the tsar had been forced to abdicate. One of the last barriers to American entry into the war on the side of the Allies had fallen.[247] Other news was equally portentous: on a single day in mid-March German submarines had sunk three American merchant vessels.[248] Now, for certain, war could not be far off.

Meanwhile, in Europe, the CRB's impending retirement from northern France had touched off a diplomatic imbroglio. What should be the nationality of the six men who would replace the Americans in this region? Hoover and the French government wanted them to be all Dutch. The Dutch foreign minister suggested that four should be Dutch and two Spanish. The Marquis de Villalobar demanded four Spaniards and two Dutchmen.[249]

The struggle soon took on the features of a comic opera. Taking a leaf from Hoover's book of undiplomatic diplomacy, Villalobar attempted a fait accompli of his own. Without informing the CRB, he selected five Spaniards to take the Americans' place in northern France. The five showed up unheralded in Brussels in early March; the CRB promptly told them to wait until there were vacancies.[250]

Hoover's aides were furious at the Spanish diplomat's interference. "Villalobar has no executive function whatever towards [the] Commission," Poland exclaimed; the power of appointment of personnel rested solely with the commission.[251] With the backing of the British, French, and Dutch governments, Vernon Kellogg went to Rotterdam on March 14 and quickly chose six men—all Dutch—to relieve the Americans in northern France.[252]

Villalobar was not to be so swiftly outmaneuvered. His government, he declared, was insisting that four of the six delegates to northern France be Spanish, and he would not accept an all-Dutch contingent until Madrid so advised him.[253] Several days now passed, and still no instructions came. The Spanish diplomat, said one CRB man, was "no novice in the art of diplomatic obstruction."[254] Meanwhile, at Villalobar's instigation, the German authorities refused to grant passports to the Dutch volunteers to enter Belgium![255] Only vigorous French protests at Madrid broke the logjam. The stubborn Villalobar withdrew his objections, and the Dutch were finally allowed into Belgium in late March.[256]

The squabble over northern France was now subsumed in a larger controversy. In mid-March, while Hoover was crossing the Atlantic, three duly marked and certified CRB vessels were attacked by German submarines without warning off Norway. At least half a dozen crew members were killed.[257] For the U.S. State Department this was the final straw. On March

2 3 it took the step that humanitarian inhibitions had caused it to defer taking for several weeks: it instructed Brand Whitlock and the American members of the relief commission to withdraw from Belgium at last. In light of the assaults on CRB shipping in gross violation of German promises, the department considered that American CRB men could "no longer serve with advantage in Belgium."[258] The department did not say so, but three days earlier President Wilson had decided to seek a declaration of war against Germany.[259] It was Wilson, in fact, who on the afternoon of the twenty-third authorized the department's message to Whitlock.[260]

Out in the Atlantic, Hoover had gotten what he wanted: a "superior force" had compelled his men to depart. Now they, and he, could finally "come out in glory."

V

PERHAPS not fully aware of the diplomatic thicket into which it was wandering, the department innocently announced that it was accepting Holland's offer to have Dutch subjects assume the Americans' duties inside Belgium.[261] Nothing was said about a role for the Spanish.

On March 26 Hoover reached Madrid on his northward journey to London. In an interview with the Spanish foreign minister he attempted to outflank Villalobar. The selection of relief personnel for northern France, Hoover claimed, was a "purely practical question." The Allies, he said, wished to give the Dutch exclusive responsibility there in order to oblige them to export more foodstuffs to the relief.[262] The foreign minister, it turned out, was also practical. "What is your salary?" he asked Hoover. "What salary will our nationals receive if the situation develops to require them?" He seemed unwilling to believe that Hoover and his fellow Yankees were receiving no compensation for their labors.[263]

Hoover's reassuring "explanation" may have mollified the foreign minister, but his troubles with the Spanish were not over. On March 26 José Roura appeared at the CRB's London headquarters and announced that he and some Spanish associates were ready to replace the departing Americans. William B. Poland told him that Dutchmen had already been chosen for northern France. Furthermore, said Poland (adding insult to injury), it was not yet known whether any Spaniards would be needed in Belgium either.[264] Two days later Ambassador Merry del Val angrily complained to Poland that the Spanish were being deliberately excluded from involvement in the CRB's management. If this continued, he warned, the Spanish government might well withdraw its patronage of the relief enterprise.[265] Villalobar, too, was adamant, suggesting that his government might cease to sponsor the relief effort in northern France unless half the delegates to that region were Spanish subjects.[266] Meanwhile, in Brussels, Villalobar's hand-picked replacements lingered on, with nothing to do.[267]

By now the British, the French, and Ambassador Page had concluded that however desirable it might be to rely solely on Dutch personnel, it would be wise to make concessions to the Spanish if an impasse developed.[268] Clearly that moment had come. Hoover, in Paris, quickly came forward with a compromise: the new Dutch–Spanish committee must have a Dutch director in Brussels who would appoint and control his staff, some of whom would be Spanish, selected in accord with Villalobar. The choice of the director, Hoover said, was the key. If we can install a suitable Dutch chairman, he confided to London, "we can secure [the] main issue and give some sop to Spanish amour-propre."[269]

At this point the Dutch foreign minister unexpectedly announced that his government had already selected a Brussels director, who would travel to Belgium on March 31. The Spanish minister to Holland speedily objected. So, too, did the CRB's Rotterdam bureau chief, who informed the Dutch government that the CRB was "still a private organization," "responsible to Hoover alone," and that Hoover must approve all appointments. Under pressure from the commission and the British government, the Dutch foreign minister pulled back. His director-designate for Brussels canceled his trip and decided to wait for Hoover to act.[270]

With the Dutch and Spanish governments openly vying for control of the relief administration inside Belgium—and the prestige that went along with it—Hoover must have found it diverting to travel from Paris on March 30 to a district of northern France recently evacuated by the German army. Here, far from the parlors of feuding diplomats, he could see what his mission of mercy was accomplishing. At the war-ravaged town of Noyon, members of the French General Staff and the mayors of thirty liberated communes greeted him. The aged mayors reported that the bread of the CRB had saved their own, and their children's, lives. Many wept openly as a member of the French Senate expressed his heartfelt gratitude to America. Hoover himself never forgot the moving ceremony.[271]

From France he hastened to London on April 1—racing, racing against time.[272] Within hours most of his men would be out of Belgium, and still no successor organization was ready. Meanwhile the Marquis de Villalobar was threatening to quit as relief patron if only Dutchmen went to northern France. The Dutch chargé d'affaires in Brussels, for his part, did not want any Spaniards assigned to Belgium. The German army wanted Dutchmen and not Spanish in Flanders in a bid to win over Flemish-speaking Belgians.[273] And while they bickered and haggled, the Germans were shipping Belgian cattle to the Fatherland in flagrant disregard of their pledges.[274]

Desperate to find some way out of the impasse, Hoover now proposed another solution. He suggested that the new neutral committee have *two* chairmen in Brussels, one Dutch and one Spanish. It should have a Dutch director in Holland, a Spanish director in London, and a staff of both nationalities in Belgium and northern France. Hoover's CRB would handle all external administrative tasks, as before, while the Comité National and its French analogue would handle internal distribution. Inspection and supervision of the guarantees would devolve upon the Spanish and the Dutch.[275] The various interested governments quickly accepted Hoover's compromise, although wrangling over details persisted for several weeks.[276]

In one respect Hoover had failed. Despite two months of maneuvering against the idea, a team of "mixed neutrals" would take over behind German lines. But Hoover had succeeded in circumscribing its role, and the CRB— meaning himself—would control all external transactions. Villalobar and Merry del Val had proven impossible to dislodge, but their capacity for interference had been contained.

As Hoover strained over the transitional arrangements, an era in the relief drew to a close. On March 29 seven American CRB men left Brussels for Switzerland. On April 2 most of the rest, led by Brand Whitlock and his legation staff, followed suit. Ten Americans remained temporarily: Prentiss Gray and three accountants (to close the books and train their successors), and six others who had recently been in militarily sensitive areas. The Germans promised not to harm them and kept their word. All ten left Belgium in early May.[277]

As Whitlock's train left the Gare du Nord in the capital city, Belgian citizens by the thousands bade it farewell.[278] A few days earlier, the Comité National had expressed the conquered nation's sentiments in a letter to Warren Gregory. Emile Francqui had read it aloud:

As you leave us you and your fellow-workers may take with you the assurance that Belgians will never forget the great work that has been realised through you. Each day the bread they eat, the food they enjoy, will recall them to the colossal work still carried beyond our frontiers by our American friends, a work on which the feeding and existence of the country absolutely depend.

In the history of mankind there is no example of a generosity so noble, and the sorrowful history of Belgium will show that your action has resulted in helping us, not only to live, but also to preserve our faith in the greatness of humanity and in the possible beauty of the future.[279]

As the train of CRB volunteers rolled through the Belgium countryside on the night of April 2, Woodrow Wilson addressed the Congress of the United States. Denouncing Prussian autocracy with solemn eloquence, he asked his country's representatives to take the American people into war. Three thousand miles across the Atlantic, Herbert Hoover and his associates responded with a message to the commander-in-chief:

We wish to tell you that there is no word in your historic statement to congress but finds response in all our hearts. For two and a half years we have been obliged to remain silent witnesses to the character of the forces dominating this war, but we now are at liberty to say that although we break, with great regret, our association with many German individuals who have given sympathetic support to our work, yet, your message enunciates our conviction, born of our intimate experience and contact, that there is no hope for democracy or liberalism and consequently for real peace or the safety of our country unless the system which has brought the world into this unfathomable misery can be stamped out once and for all.[280]

On April 6, 1917 the United States of America formally entered the Great War against Germany. Hoover was in London that day but was ready, even eager, to come home. To Gibson at the State Department he cabled: "This business will have been so reorganized within ten days that if more important national work arises I could undertake same. Will you convey this to [Secretary of the Interior] Lane and any others to whom it might be helpful."[281] Gibson promptly notified Lane and Colonel House.[282]

14

Homeward Bound

I

H o o v e r's message to Gibson was no mere impulse of the moment. Behind it, in fact, lay a long campaign to win himself a place in the American war effort.

Back in January, when Hoover had come to the United States on his relief loan mission, he had immediately called upon Edward House. For two years the head of the CRB had provided President Wilson's confidant with "inside" information on the war, and he did not disappoint the colonel now. The military situation in Russia, he reported, was "critical." The French and British feared that the tsar's armies might not resume fighting in the spring.[1] When, the next day, President Wilson publicly urged the warring nations of Europe to accept "peace without victory," Hoover offered the President a suggestion through House:

> It is that the next move should be to ask each of the belligerent governments whether they agree to the principles laid down in your speech. If not, to what do they object. If they agree then it is well within your province to ask them to meet in conference.[2]

House, as always, was impressed. He told the President that Hoover "is a man of good sense and has unusual facilities for obtaining information."[3] It was not long before the colonel was envisaging a role for him in the Wilson administration, should the United States enter the war.[4]

Hoover himself remained opposed to American intervention in the European conflict. Even on February 2, two days after the Germans launched their indiscriminate submarine attacks on shipping, he expressed his hope to a friend that "even yet we may keep out of this war." Unlike the ardent interventionists so numerous along the Eastern seaboard, Hoover confessed that his mind was "clothed with great fears." For one thing, he was "much discouraged over the ability of our people to pull themselves together" if hostilities came. The whole question was not being confronted with sufficient realism, he lamented.

It is an infinitely more serious issue than is contemplated, except by the very few, in this country. It means that the country must discipline itself morally, financially, physically—not for six months, but for at least two years. It means practically that we should be like the English, who came into this war with a dilettante idea that they had a three-months job on the seas, and have found themselves obliged to take over more and more kilometres of the line in France until they will be carrying the greatest load of the war within the next three months. I have the feeling that if we came in we should gradually have to replace the Englishman in carrying this weight and that broadly the only difference that our entry would make would be the degree of stalemate which would result, for I have no confidence in modern arms being able to effect anything definitive from a military point of view. Above all, I have no confidence in the supposed uplifting qualities of war.

Nevertheless, Hoover, in his own words, was "no extreme pacifist," and he admitted that "there are eventualities in which a nation may find itself that are worse than all these possibilities. . . ."

What, then, should America do?

If we have got to go into this war, I am extremely anxious that we should not go into it in alliance with anybody, but that we should have our own individual go simply in co-operation so far as is necessary to accomplish the objects upon which we set out. I dread the horrible entanglement of this country with all of the objectives of certain of the Allies. . . .

America should be free, he said, "to take single and direct action on its own at any time, without the horrible drag the English people find upon themselves to-day."[5]

Despite his qualms and reservations, by early February Hoover realized that war with Germany was increasingly likely—and that it would afford him new opportunities to fulfill his long-held dream of entering American public life. Back in December, a number of American charity leaders had

proposed to consolidate all American fund raising for European relief purposes under a single national umbrella organization, to be headed (it was
widely assumed) by Hoover himself.[6] The CRB chairman had responded
instantly to their invitation to become involved. Upon arriving in New York
in January, he had plunged into the task of creating a coordinated national
network that could tap the American pocketbook as never before.[7] Such an
effort, of course, would mesh nicely with his own impending drive for a CRB
relief loan. And although he might not admit it, leadership of this movement
would make him, at age forty-two, the most prominent humanitarian in the
country.

On February 3 Hoover journeyed down to Washington, in part to obtain
Woodrow Wilson's endorsement of a national war relief campaign. Alas, the
German U-boat campaign had upset his calculations. Consulting with other
charity magnates, he swiftly shifted his focus. Instead of launching a drive
for war sufferers in Europe, he now proposed "as a matter of preparedness"
to form "a great national relief fund" to "meet the present crisis *at home*."[8]
The money thus raised would go primarily to the American Red Cross and
only "secondarily" to other agencies "at home and abroad." In a letter on
February 5, Hoover and his associates asked President Wilson officially to
appoint a small committee to get the consolidated effort underway.[9]

Hoover's revised plan for a "National Relief Organization"[10] was doomed.
Unable to gain an interview with the President, he was obliged to submit his
request in writing.[11] The White House did not acknowledge his letter.[12]
Wilson was evidently as reluctant as ever to sanction a scheme that might
appear unneutral or seem to concede that American belligerency was inevitable.[13] And the international situation was too volatile for Hoover and his
colleagues to settle upon a satisfactory strategy.[14] Discouraged by his failure
to receive any encouragement from the White House, Hoover returned to
New York on February 6.[15]

Days now went by, and Hoover's "relief fund" idea made not "a particle
of headway" in the nation's capital.[16] One of his associates commented sadly
that there seemed to be "no enthusiasm in Washington over our proposed
plan."[17] By late February the scheme was moribund, and Hoover was at
work on yet another: the "one day's income" appeal for the Commission for
Relief in Belgium.

His four-day trip to Washington, however, had not been a total loss. During his visit he had met Justice Louis Brandeis; the impression he made was
profound. "In one hour," the justice remarked long afterward, "I learned
more from Hoover than from all the persons I had seen in connection with
war matters heretofore." Convinced that the Wilson administration must find
a place for Hoover's services, Brandeis arranged for him to meet Secretary
of War Newton D. Baker and Secretary of the Treasury William McAdoo.[18]

Still another Wilsonian whom Hoover instantly impressed was a member
of the Federal Reserve Board, Adolph Miller; the two met at the home of

Secretary of the Interior Franklin K. Lane. One thing was on Hoover's mind that evening, and one thing only: the fate of the Commission for Relief in Belgium. Taking Miller suddenly by the arm after supper, Hoover steered him into an unoccupied parlor. "You are the only person here who seems to sense the vital importance of the subject under discussion," he said. "When can we have a good, long talk together?"

It was Saturday evening. Miller suggested that they meet the next day. Why not for lunch, he offered, or perhaps eleven o'clock? Hoover bluntly replied, "That is not early enough. I want plenty of time!" Finally Miller invited him to breakfast. The next morning the CRB chairman came for breakfast—and lunch—and stayed most of the day. Never had Miller met a person who spoke with such utter concentration on his purpose as did Hoover on that February Sunday. It was the start of a lifelong friendship.[19]

Stymied in his proposal for a national relief fund drive, Hoover soon turned his attention to matters of far greater import. On February 13 he conferred with Colonel House on immediate measures to be taken if the United States went to war with Germany. That very same day he codified his views for the colonel in a four-page letter. "I trust," wrote Hoover, that America "will enter into no political alliance" with the Allies but will instead "confine itself to naval and military cooperation." The United States should concentrate on supplying the Allies with foodstuffs and munitions, and it should help the Allies purchase such commodities in America itself.

Some of Hoover's suggestions were decidedly unsentimental. He declared that the United States should tighten the existing Allied food blockade against Germany—particularly by restricting American food exports to Scandinavia, thereby curbing "leakage" from this source to the Germans. Furthermore, the U.S. government should coerce these "northern neutrals" into making their surplus shipping available to the Allies. How? By refusing them coal for their vessels, for instance, unless they cooperated. The American people themselves, said Hoover, would have to reduce their own food consumption if the hard-pressed Allies were to be fed. But the CRB chairman opposed rationing or other "drastic measures" for his own countrymen. Instead, he advocated such "indirect methods" as "the suppression of the consumption of grain and sugar for brewing and distilling purposes."

Hoover did not confine himself to nonmilitary advice. He told House that the United States should not rely upon "large naval units" to protect its commercial shipping but should build "a mosquito surface fleet" for that purpose. Nor should America send an expeditionary force to Europe. It would take a long time to create, it would impinge on scarce transport, and it would entail "political difficulties in association" besides. Let the Allied armies recruit Americans over here, he counseled. Let American men be trained in Europe; they would be "ready for front-line work within four or five months," and there would be no need to transport the "impedimenta" of an expeditionary force.

On the other hand, Hoover considered it "absolutely necessary" that the

United States create "a large defensive force" for the dangerous postwar era. He felt it imperative that this force be in existence "when peace approaches." America's "terms of peace," he warned, would probably conflict with European proposals. Under the circumstances, "our weight in the accomplishment of our ideals will be greatly in proportion to the strength which we can throw into the scale." Hoover's boyhood religious upbringing was Quaker, but there was no hint of Quaker pacifism in his recommendations to Colonel House.

Indeed, on one issue Hoover's sentiments had hardened and metamorphosed remarkably. In 1915 and 1916 he had repeatedly denounced the Allied food blockade of Germany as a self-defeating and supremely immoral measure. Now, to Colonel House, he stated that although he still had "no sympathy" for it, the food blockade had nevertheless "proceeded to such a length that from a military point of view it is necessary that it should be now continued to the end." In fact, he now argued, it should even be reinforced "at every point."

Hoover's reversal of attitude was extraordinary, and he offered no further explanation for it. Why should the "military point of view," which he had so often disparaged in the past, now prevail so easily in his mind? Why should he now advocate tactics that he had once so fervently condemned? One can only speculate. Perhaps he considered the blockade so entrenched and politically unassailable that it was futile for him to oppose it. Perhaps he believed that the new, unbridled German campaign to starve the Allies into submission had altered the moral equation and now justified the most stringent reprisals. Perhaps he had concluded that there was no longer any plausible alternative to victory. Perhaps he even calculated that if he were to gain a high position in the Wilson administration, he must demonstrate that he was tough-minded and not averse to the harsh imperatives of total war.

That Hoover in fact coveted such a post was transparently obvious from his letter to House. All his proposals, he wrote in conclusion, would entail "a large amount of intimate military, naval, and economic cooperation with the Western Allies." Any attempt to effect it through the usual diplomatic channels would be "hopeless of practical and effective results." The "only proper solution," he declared (in recommendation no. 9), would be to create "a branch of the American Government in Europe, headed by a man of Cabinet rank," who would have "direct access" to "every official and department in Europe."[20]

Hoover suggested no candidate for this job. But his silence was deafening, and Colonel House immediately got the message. Forwarding Hoover's letter on to the President, House remarked: "If No. 9 is adopted, Hoover would undoubtedly be the best man for that place."[21]

In short, without explicitly saying so, Hoover had adroitly volunteered to be nothing less than the supreme coordinator of the American war effort in Europe!

Suddenly, from a new direction, opportunity beckoned. On February 12 the newly formed Council of National Defense invited Hoover to come to Washington and speak to it on the situation in Europe.[22] Two days later he obligingly journeyed down to the nation's capital for the fourth time in barely three weeks.

The next day Hoover addressed a joint meeting of the council and its Advisory Commission; the event was very nearly a disaster. The Council of National Defense consisted of six members of Woodrow Wilson's Cabinet: the secretaries of war, agriculture, commerce, labor, the interior, and the navy, while the Advisory Commission included several of the foremost industrialists in America. Apparently awed by this high-powered assemblage, Hoover acted nervous and embarrassed. One of those present remarked afterward, "We were not impressed with him as an orator." Finally Secretary of War Baker, attempting to put him at ease, invited him to sit down and answer questions informally. The meeting went much better after that.[23]

Hoover's shortcomings as a public speaker did not prove fatal. That same afternoon the Advisory Commission formally asked the council to engage his expert services on the subject of increasing domestic production of items "essential to the support of armies and of the people during the interruption of foreign commerce."[24] The next day Secretary Lane confided to a relative that the Council of National Defense was developing a plan for "the mobilization of all our national industries and resources." He added that he intended to "urge Hoover as the head of the work." In the view of the Cabinet secretary, Hoover's "Belgian experience has made him the most competent man in this country for such work. . . . He will correlate the industrial life of the nation against the day of danger and immediate need."[25]

Lane also disclosed that "Hoover has promised to come to me as one of my assistants. . . ." If so, Hoover had very recently changed his mind, for only a few weeks earlier he had declined Lane's offer of such a post.[26] By this time Lane had concluded that Hoover was too qualified to be a mere assistant secretary of the interior. The "other work is the larger," Lane now said, "and I can get on with a smaller man."[27]

Meanwhile, on February 17, Hoover, working at full steam, submitted three lengthy documents to the Council of National Defense and promptly supplied copies to Colonel House. One was a detailed analysis of various methods of food control. One (requested by Lane) was a series of recommendations for organizing an effective American munitions industry—suggestions made, said Hoover, after "observing the blunders of various European nations during the last two years." The third was an eleven-point memorandum entitled "America's Action In Case of War With Germany."[28]

In the latter document, Hoover elaborated upon his letter of February 13 to Colonel House. Once again Hoover opposed creation of an American expeditionary force[29] and urged instead that the French army simply recruit American volunteers. Once again he called for more "mosquito craft," a tighter food blockade, and stricter control of trade with the northern neutrals. He urged careful "advance organization" of the munitions industry, thereby avoiding the example of England, which had "floundered" in this area for the first eighteen months of the war. He advocated "every pressure conceivable" to curb "extravagance and waste" and cushion the "terrible expense" of modern war: by suppression of imported luxuries and fresh fruits, for example; by "repression" of food consumption through "heavy taxation of income, luxuries and luxurious expenditure" such as theater tickets; and above all, by comprehensive "propaganda of instruction in saving" under the aegis of a "national savings committee."

All this, of course, meant unprecedented intrusion by the State into the everyday life of the American people. But Hoover, the would-be war manager, did not flinch from this necessity. He declared flatly that to wage war "under modern conditions" involving the mass mobilization of civilian energies it would be "absolutely necessary to further strengthen the powers of centralization of the Federal Government, so as to give it the proper control of economic forces in the country."

Furthermore, he declared, it was "absolutely imperative" that the United States establish "a large and effective army," not only for the sake of having "a proper weight" at the peace settlement but for self-protection "from very imminent subsequent dangers." If, he said, "by our joining in this war we could secure the creation of such an adequately poised and equipped force, it would to my mind be worth the price for this purpose alone." Hoover had no utopian expectations for the aftermath of the Great War: "The economic pressure and lawless national spirit in Europe after this war is over, contrasted with the wealth, disintegration, and apathetic national spirit in the United States, especially in the face of so many points of possible friction, will produce the most dangerous period in American history." The Allies might meddle in Mexico, for example. An "impoverished" and "throttled" Germany might do the same in South America—unless she were convinced of the "military resolution" of the United States. "Universal disarmament would be our national salvation," Hoover acknowledged, and all Americans must strive to achieve it. But "a cry from us for disarmament because we are not armed will carry but little weight in world counsels."

What kind of army, then, should America have? Once again Hoover broke with the tradition of classical liberalism exemplified by his British friend Francis Hirst. Said Hoover now to the Council of National Defense:

> If we could draft all men from 19 to 22 we would provide a large force and evade the difficulty of drafting skilled or married men and would have laid the foundations of national training. The raising of a volunteer force is terrible in its selection of the best in character, intellect and patriotism and gains but little advantage in military efficiency.

Conscription, then, not an elite, all-volunteer army: that was what Hoover desired. Perhaps he was thinking of Great Britain's tortured experience with this issue during the past two years.

And as with Colonel House, so now with the Council of National Defense, Hoover vigorously urged that "a man of Cabinet rank" be ensconced in Europe as coordinator of the American war effort overseas. Such a branch of the American government, he argued, would not only cut governmental red tape. It could "accumulate the experience of Europe in this war" and apply it to America's own preparations.[30] He did not need to state who had more experience in this field than any other living American.

This same day, February 17, Hoover, through Lane's intercession, obtained another interview with Woodrow Wilson. One topic of conversation, Hoover later recalled, was the continuing plight of the Belgians and the CRB. Another was the growing prospect for American intervention in the war, an outcome that Wilson still seemed determined to avert. Hoover himself told the President that he did not believe the Germans wanted the United States in the war but that "in their madness anything could happen."

Then, just as their conference was ending, the President made a remark that must have set his visitor's heart aflutter. Referring to Hoover's recent letter to Colonel House (which House had immediately passed along),[31] Wilson suggested that it could be helpful if Hoover studied Allied wartime economic organization when he returned to Europe. It was the strongest signal yet that if America became a belligerent, Hoover would be called upon to assist the administration. Not without reason, he later declared that his letter of February 13 to Colonel House was the event that inaugurated his "connection" with "American Food Problems."[32]

In late February and early March Hoover worked to ready his Belgian relief enterprise for this contingency. If any intimations came from official circles during this period about his own prospective role in an American mobilization, the record today does not reveal it. In mid-March Secretary Lane told a correspondent that he and Hoover had "a pretty good understanding," evidently about the part Hoover might play, but the secretary did not say what it was.[33]

Hoover himself was willing, even eager, to plunge in. Just before returning to Europe in mid-March, he gave Colonel House the impression that he was going back for the express purpose of "closing out the American-Belgian Relief"[34]—a clear hint that he would soon be available for something else. Privately he told Hugh Gibson on March 10 that as soon as the CRB left Belgium its "centre of gravity" would be New York. "Consequently," Hoover declared, "I intend to come back to this country for good within a month or two, unless of course some superior job turns up in Europe which I must undertake."[35] Evidently he was still hoping to become supreme coordinator of the American war effort "over there."

Not long before he sailed on the *Antonio Lopez*, Hoover gave an interview to Will Irwin, who promptly wrote an account of it for the *Saturday Evening Post*. Clearly convinced that American entry into the European conflict was all but inevitable, Hoover enumerated ways in which his country must develop the "social machinery" needed for conducting a modern war. All the ideas that he had pressed upon Colonel House and the Council for National Defense were here: expert development of the munitions industry; a standing army for the postwar era; "national propaganda to limit extravagance in eating, in dress and display"; the banning of imports of precious items like diamonds ("a useless luxury"); conservation of the nation's food supply; "a man of cabinet rank" stationed in Europe; and more. America was a "wasteful" country, he said. Among other things, he would "stop brewing and distilling for beverage purposes, at once"; they consumed "enormous quantities of the grain that Europe needs so badly." Declaring himself "a pacifist, but not a peace-at-any-price pacifist," Hoover said:

> If we are to have war, with its hatreds, its disturbances, its check to all good causes—perhaps with its spilling of our strongest blood—we should at least have the compensations. So far as we can, we should check extravagance in living, dress, travel and amusement, and set the people to saving. It will be good not only for the conduct of the war but for our souls.

The humanitarian-turning-war-mobilizer was well aware that his appeal for centralized social control ran against the American tradition of states' rights and even (he noted several times) the Constitution. But to him there was no alternative:

> Democracy is a form of government born of peace, constructed for peace and maintainable only in peace. To carry on war successfully requires a dictatorship of some kind or another. A democracy must submerge itself temporarily in the hands of an able man or an able group of men. No other way has ever been found.

"Paradoxical as it may seem," he added, "we shall do best for democracy if we make our regulations of all kinds strict rather than easy—if we lean to the side of rigorous control while the emergency lasts." Why? Because when the war is over, "democracy wants to go back again to the fullest practical measure of personal liberty." If America adopts "half measures," said Hoover— measures "not noticed as especially galling in the general anxiety and discomfort of war"—the enemies of democracy from within, the would-be oligarchs "of blood or money or position," might succeed in keeping the restraints in place in peacetime. "Full measures, strong enough to hurt, produce a reaction," he declared; "when the war is over the people insist on abolishing them entirely."

But who would administer America's "social machinery" during the coming trial by fire? For Hoover, again, there was but one answer: "the best brains of the country—which means its industrial brains." The engineer-executive was certain that such talent would never be found in the regular government bureaucracy. A bureaucracy by its very nature, he said, "tends toward mediocrity. Industry does not." Industry "allows full play to the struggle for existence," he remarked. "Promotion, there, is not by seniority, but by the hard law of merit."

And this was not the only problem with bureaucracies as a possible source for leadership in wartime. Another, said Hoover, was that they contained too many lawyers. "Law produces a qualitative mind," he told Irwin. "War is a quantitative thing and requires a quantitative mind."

Hoover's comments were provocative and outspoken. Perhaps for this reason, Irwin did not identify his source in his article. Only later (after Hoover had entered the Wilson administration) did Irwin publicly reveal the name of his interviewee.[36]

By the time Hoover reached London on April 1, war between the United States and Germany was imminent. On April 3 he reminded Colonel House by cable that his relief work was nearly reorganized and that he would be "available for any appropriate service" within ten days.[37] On April 7 House replied: "I have repeatedly given the President my estimate of you and of the desirability of having you in some place commensurate with your great abilities, and I hope he will soon consider it wise to press you into service here."[38]

The first summons for Hoover, however, did not come from the White House.[39] Instead, on April 5 the Council of National Defense voted to invite him to assist in its work on food problems.[40] The next day, acting independently and without knowledge of this step, the Council's Advisory Commission went further. Convinced of the need for a strong administrative board to regulate food prices and conservation, the commissioners agreed that Herbert Hoover was the only man to head it. But Hoover is in England, someone said. At this point one of the commission members, Samuel Gompers, spoke up. As president of the American Federation of Labor he had seen Hoover address his executive council meeting on the subject of Belgium scarcely two months before. Persuaded then and there of Hoover's "sincerity and dependability," Gompers now made the decisive suggestion: that the commission recall Hoover by cable and "entrust him with the job of feeding the American people."

Out, then, went a cable to London while the commission was still in session that morning: would Hoover consider accepting such a post? Within hours he cabled his reply: yes, he would accept, if invited to do so in a properly authorized manner.[41]

The next day, April 7, the council and its Advisory Commission convened in joint session. The advisory body was eager to have the president create a price-fixing raw materials control board under Hoover's "absolute authority" as administrator. The council—especially the secretary of agriculture—was not prepared to go that far. In the end the two groups voted merely to request Hoover to become chairman of an advisory "committee on food supply and prices." This committee would report to the council on the experience of

European governments and would recommend ways of curbing price speculation and stimulating food production.[42]

Meanwhile several of Hoover's friends were exerting their influence in his
behalf. Late in March Hugh Gibson had confided to his mother that he was
"anxious to have Hoover free for work at home" when America entered the
war.[43] On April 6 he cheerfully notified various leading Wilsonians of Hoover's announced willingness to serve.[44] That same evening Hoover's intimate
friend Edgar Rickard came down from New York to Washington—ostensi-
bly to raise money for the CRB, but also, no doubt, to lobby for the Chief.
He conferred with Secretary Lane and discussed with Hugh Gibson a favorite topic: "the future of Hoover."[45] Out of Stanford University, President
Ray Lyman Wilbur was already arranging to travel to Washington to help
Hoover attain a proper position.[46] Such was the loyalty that Hoover engendered in his friends that they were thus willing to make themselves instruments of his ambition.

The Council of National Defense's invitation appeared in the press on
April 8.[47] There was little doubt what Hoover's answer would be. On April
11 he publicly accepted its call and announced that he would return shortly
to the United States.[48]

His dream of at least a decade was finally coming to fruition. Now he was
really in the "big game."[49]

II

Even as he prepared to move to Washington, Hoover made it clear that
he would continue to serve for the time being as chairman of the relief commission.[50] There was no reason, he said privately, why his new assignment
should interfere with his leadership of the CRB. In fact, he argued, "such a
combination" was "distinctly desirable," since there was "bound to be considerable overlapping" on questions of shipping and supply.[51] It was a typi-
cally Hooverian response. Others in his position might have relinquished one
of these burdens. Hoover chose instead to take on both.

Before he could get away, however, he had to navigate past a last set of
shoals that threatened to wreck the Belgian relief. Between late February and
late March, despite all the solemn German promises of safe conduct, the
CRB lost three more vessels to U-boat attacks. In the final days of American
neutrality, the pace of calamity accelerated. On March 31 the relief ship
Feistein sank in broad daylight off the Dutch coast; 4,650 tons of wheat were
lost. On April 2 the *Anna Fostenes* was hit; more than 3,000 tons of wheat
went down. On April 4, the *Trevier*. On April 8, the *Camilla*. All displayed
the proper CRB markings. All (said Hoover) were outside the "war" zone.
All carried German guarantees for their safety.[52]

The effect of these losses (and of the stranding of other CRB cargoes in

British ports) was staggering. During the entire month of February only 24,294 tons of CRB food reached Rotterdam. In March the figure fell to 10,116 tons.[53] By comparison, deliveries in 1916 had averaged over 105,000 tons per month.[54] Inside Belgium, stocks of wheat plummeted, already meager rations were reduced, and millions underwent a degree of privation that they had not experienced before.[55] In one Belgian town (and probably not an atypical one), a CRB worker discovered families whose cupboards were literally bare. The allotments meted out by the Comité National were their only daily sustenance. At times women fainted from hunger, while entire families skipped supper and went to bed early to avoid the pain. In some towns food riots broke out and hungry citizens plundered stores. The authorities thereupon decreed 6:30 p.m. curfews. In mid-April the Germans threatened to cut the individual Belgian flour ration further, from eight ounces to five ounces a day. The CRB's remaining director in Brussels only staved off tragedy by borrowing 10,000 tons of wheat from the Dutch government.[56]

Hoover responded with the only weapon at his command: pressure on the Germans to respect his shrinking fleet. On April 5 he asked the Marquis de Villalobar to intercede; on April 8 he made the same request of Merry del Val.[57] He told the State Department that German submarines had "failed to adhere to any of the undertakings guaranteeing safety to commission ships." He asked it to protest vigorously through the neutral Swiss.[58]

Privately Hoover believed that the German depredations were the work either of reckless submarine commanders or of a runaway German Admiralty and that the "storm we have raised will stop it." He was certain that the German army and civilian leadership were "genuinely supporting us" and that "we shall undoubtedly continue," unless it transpired that the Germans were sinking his ships as a matter of deliberate policy. The Allied governments themselves, he told associates, agreed "that relief must continue even at cost of some ships."[59]

Between April 6 and 15 eight loaded CRB vessels arrived safely in Rotterdam, a sign that the Germans wished its work to go on.[60] From Brussels came word that the German authorities in Belgium and Berlin were upset at the submarine attacks and that von der Lancken was trying to get the navy to stop them.[61] Not that the Germans were accepting any responsibility in the matter; von der Lancken insisted to Villalobar that none of the "accidents" had been the fault of the U-boats. Rather, the mishaps had all been caused by "fortuitous circumstances," "acts of imprudence" by CRB ship captains, or failure of the CRB adequately to instruct its skippers.[62] Von der Lancken pledged anew that the relief ships would not be molested if they stayed outside the "war" zone.[63]

Hoover put no credence in these "explanations," many of which contradicted the accounts of his crewmen.[64] Perhaps in disgust, perhaps as a tactic, he warned his Rotterdam office around April 20 that the Germans must respect the commission's flag everywhere. If not, they must take upon themselves the responsibility for feeding Belgium. His message quickly made its way to Brussels.[65]

The German assaults on Hoover's shipping now subsided—probably in consequence of his "storm" of diplomatic protests. But the CRB chairman was not yet in the clear. For now it was the British government's turn to rile the waters. Citing the German menace to CRB shipping, in mid-April it seized 90,000 tons of Hoover's relief supplies bottled up in British ports and ordered all his vessels coming from America to stop at the Faro Islands north of Scotland until further notice.[66] Several days later it held up CRB ships at Halifax pending clarification of German intent.[67] As if for good measure, the Foreign Office suggested that the Germans replace the relief ships and supplies that they had sunk.[68]

The CRB and its supporters now scrambled to recover from this bombshell. In a letter dated April 30 that Hoover later said he drafted, William B. Poland did his best to minimize the Germans' misdeeds. In the case of the *Feistein,* Hoover had told Merry del Val on April 8 that it had been torpedoed. Poland now told the British that it had probably struck a mine. The same for the *Anna Fostenes:* torpedoed, said Hoover on the eighth; mined, said Poland on the thirtieth. The *Trevier:* in the "safe" lane, according to Hoover; "just within the danger zone," according to Poland. The *Camilla:* Hoover had said it was in the "safe" zone; Poland now stated that the CRB had "no accurate report" of where it was when attacked. In short, by Hoover's account all four sinkings had occurred in the "safe" lane. By Poland's account three weeks later, every vessel that the Germans had destroyed had apparently been in the "war" zone after all.

Poland did not try to excuse the Germans' "dastardly record." But he insisted to the British that it did not add up to a deliberate intent to "break down the relief." The CRB was "amply justified" in proceeding with its tasks, he said. His Majesty's Government should release the vessels held at Halifax.[69]

In the end, after protests from the French, the Belgians, and the CRB, the British Admiralty very reluctantly lifted its embargo. But not before most of the month of May had been lost—and Belgium forced to new depths of near-starvation.[70]

The German and British navies were not the only sources of anxiety for Hoover during his final days in London. Despite agreement by all parties that a joint Dutch–Spanish committee should assume the CRB's duties inside Belgium, the transition from principle to practice soon bogged down. Hoover wanted the Dutch cochairman to supervise northern France (and the Belgian *etappen* zone) and the Spanish cochairman to supervise the Belgian "occupation zone." The Marquis de Villalobar wanted the two chairmen to oversee the entire area together.[71] The British and the Dutch governments supported Hoover; the French and Belgian governments backed Villalobar.[72] More seriously still, despite Hoover's entreaties[73] the Dutch and Spanish governments appeared to procrastinate. Each, it seemed, feared that the other would gain preeminence in the new committee.[74] As the deadlock continued, Villalobar began to advocate that Prentiss Gray remain in Brussels as director of the CRB. Gray, an American, had volunteered to stay on during the transition.[75]

By mid-April, two weeks after most of the Americans had left Belgium, no Spanish or Dutch directors had been chosen, and no neutral replacement committee had been formed. Hoover was dismayed. "The Belgian Relief will struggle on as best it may," he told Whitlock, "but the conflict between the Dutch and the Spanish as to who has the greatest prestige out of it will probably sooner or later wreck the business." The head of the CRB was also disgusted at the Belgians. It was their "supineness," he said, "and the seeming total inability to help themselves and disentangle their own affairs which make me despair of getting a proper administration set up in Belgium."[76]

Hoover now turned the heat on the Spanish. In letters to Merry del Val and Villalobar, he urged the Dutch and Spanish governments to "get the machine going in Belgium." Delay was dangerous, he warned. Freed from neutral oversight, the Germans were shipping "vast quantities of cattle" to the Fatherland. Their "encroachment" was causing the "greatest possible disturbance" among the Allies. Hoover insisted that the "total responsibility" for carrying on the relief organization inside Belgium now rested on Spain and Holland. As for Prentiss Gray, the CRB chairman announced that he could not remain in Brussels beyond May 1. Any negotiations between him and the Germans were "wholly irregular, and not countenanced by our Government."[77]

Shortly after firing these salvos, Hoover received some unwelcome news: buffeted by the diplomatic crosswinds, the Belgian government-in-exile was itself anxious for Gray to stay in Brussels. If this were done, the commission would still have a presence inside the occupied country—without, however, any personnel of its own choosing. In other words, it would have responsibility without power—precisely what Hoover had fought against for weeks. To make matters worse, he now discovered that Brand Whitlock—timid, softheaded Whitlock—was planning to urge the State Department to accede to the Belgians' wish.[78]

Furious at this turn of events, Hoover instantly brought matters to a head. On April 21 he ordered Gray to leave Belgium by the first of May.[79] He requested his New York office not to "countenance" Whitlock's recommendation.[80] To Whitlock himself he addressed a stinging cable: "Belgian Government states that you have undertaken at Washington to secure Gray in Belgium. I feel they are entirely wrong in their own interest and in this I am supported by English and French governments." Hoover then bluntly explained what was really behind the Belgians' maneuver:

This arises from representations of Dutch and Spanish and is simply attempt on their part load part of responsibility for guarantees onto Americans who have no influence in the matter. Since Commission left Belgium abstraction cattle has increased to thousand per day and there are other evidences of entire breaking down of guarantees. Only hope of saving guarantees and Relief is put entire responsibility squarely on shoulders of Dutch Spanish Governments with intervention their sovereigns and this can only be done by compelling them take entire and sole responsibility inside Belgium. Villalobar has childish idea he may save question of precedence and his own dominating position by having Gray retained and therefore reducing protective organisation to mere nonentity. Furthermore Gray not safe in Belgium and as long as he remains there we are absolutely tied from denouncing any German infraction of guarantees as he becomes a practical hostage for silence of every member of Commission because Villalobar's undertakings [have] no more value than those of Germans themselves.

Hoover then disclosed his decision:

I have directed Gray positively to leave Belgium first day May and he is loyal member of Commission and will obey my direction. I am protesting to Washington that under no circumstances should they interfere with Relief Commission this matter and I do trust that in interests of Relief and Belgians themselves you will not take course indicated by Belgian Government.

There was nothing ambiguous about his message.[81]

Hoover's actions abruptly ended the impasse. On April 21 Gray, Villalobar, Francqui, the Dutch foreign minister, and others gathered for a conference in Rotterdam. Faced with Hoover's announcement of Gray's impending departure, the Dutch and Spanish agreed to appoint their respective cochairman quickly.[82] In a cable to Hoover, Villalobar admitted that the Dutch and Spanish had not done so earlier out of a desire to "hold Gray in Brussels" as "the most efficient person to continue work."[83]

Whitlock, too, immediately deferred to Hoover's wishes, although he was not happy with what he privately called the "rough, positive tone" of Hoover's "characteristic" telegram.[84] Before I left Belgium (Whitlock informed Hoover) I told Gray that the U.S. government did not want him to stay in Brussels and that if he did so it would be on his own responsibility. "The Belgian Government," Whitlock remarked, "finds itself in a very difficult situation owing to conflicting pressures, and I feel that we should do everything in our power to save its sensibilities."[85]

Hoover evidently did not reply to this dispatch. But his opinion of such reasoning could easily be guessed: once again, instead of standing up for his fellow Americans, Whitlock was trying to soothe the Belgian government's "sensibilities." Once again he had been the dupe of Villalobar.

The final arrangements now moved forward with unwonted rapidity. By the first of May a dozen Dutch and Spanish "delegates" were in Belgium, and a new entity at last was at work: the Comité Hispano-Hollandais pour la Protection du Ravitaillement de la Belgique et du Nord de France.[86] Ever the diplomat, Villalobar pledged his support to Hoover but added that "nothing can be accomplished without you." Belgium, he said, "feels so indebted to your genius, your activity, your constant attention and interest."[87]

While all of these squalls blew around him, Hoover again turned to his most importunate need of all: money to buy the food to keep 9,000,000 people alive. During the desperate days of mid-February, as his loan scheme and other fund-raising ideas fell apart, it had occurred to him that perhaps the U.S. Treasury could be his financial salvation. On February 17 he had asked Woodrow Wilson outright for an appropriation for the CRB. The President had promised to recommend one to the Congress at a propitious time.[88] Perhaps not coincidentally, at the beginning of March, Colonel House had urged the President to set aside $150,000,000 for the relief out of any loan that the United States might make to the Allies. The President had tentatively given his approval.[89]

The Allies, too, were searching for assistance. In early March the British Foreign Office confidentially notified Hoover that it could not increase its relief subsidy to the level he needed. As an alternative, it suggested that the United States provide at least £500,000 a month "on more or less [the] same lines" as the Allied subsidies. In other words, the U.S. government should share the load from now on.[90] Hoover replied that the time was "not ripe for such an arrangement." The "public mind" in America was "unsettled" and the political situation "indefinite." But surely within two months, he added, his country's relation to the war would be clarified. Then he could return to the United States (after a trip first to Europe) and put American support for the relief on a "very much enlarged basis."[91] Obviously nothing could be done just yet.

By the end of March the CRB's subsidy from the Allies was running nearly $2,500,000 a month short of expenditures.[92] Balking at any increased contribution, the British War Cabinet finally agreed to grant one—if the French government agreed to pay half. The French, however, were in no mood to go along. Not only were they already funding half of the Belgian part of the subsidy, they were also footing the entire bill for their own people; in other words, about 70% of the total relief outlay. As hard pressed, if not more so, than the British, they were loath to increase their fiscal burden any further. They were also angry at the British Treasury for obstructing Hoover's relief loan project back in January—thus helping to bring about its demise.[93]

Suddenly the CRB's fortunes appeared to brighten. With American entry into the war clearly looming, the commission's New York office announced publicly on March 24 that if Congress decided to loan money to the Allies, at least $150,000,000 of it would undoubtedly be earmarked for Hoover's relief.[94] A few days later the CRB's New York advisory committee petitioned President Wilson to do just that. Perhaps emboldened by the mounting war fever, it asked him also to seek a congressional gift of $2,000,000 to cover the CRB's "working expenses" since its inception.[95]

On March 26 the New York office informed London of the earmarking scheme.[96] Surprisingly, Hoover was skeptical. All this talk about credits for the Allies, he said, was "absolute rumor" until Congress had actually declared war. There would be time enough to arrange relief financing after that.[97] Apparently the CRB chairman misconstrued the credit proposal as somehow entailing an outright American gift to France. Responding to his New York office, he warned "on highest authority" that such a "present . . . while it would not be refused would be considered indelicate and gauche on part of American people . . . one gentleman cannot present money to another and France is not a beggar in rags."

Instead, he proposed that the United States government absorb *all* CRB expenditures—past, present, and for the rest of the war—and repay through the commission all sums loaned thus far by the Allies. This approach, he claimed, would be "extremely acceptable" to the French. It would also be "consonant with American feeling and with the reputation which has already been unwarrantably given [to America] here" for the revictualing.[98] Although he did not say so, his plan, at one stroke, would make the United States the sole benefactor of the Franco-Belgian relief. And it would free him from having to negotiate with Europeans ever again.

Hoover's counterproposal was not popular in Washington. The CRB's New York office soon reported that it stood "no chance in Congress" and that, if pushed, it "might result in no support whatever."[99] War or no war, the Congress had no desire to assume Allied debts. A *loan*, however, was something else. In mid-April Hoover's bureau chief at New York reported that a massive credit to the Allies would shortly pass the Congress and that President Wilson was "anxious" to allot $150,000,000 of it for the CRB's use—provided that Hoover supplied assurances that the affected European governments actually wanted it.[100]

Hoover had no trouble lining up the British and the French. As now proposed, the American credit would be in the form of a loan to the French and Belgian governments for the CRB's feeding of their conquered populations. This arrangement, of course, would instantly release the British from any further relief expeditures. It would also permit France to stop subsidizing the Belgian portion of the vast revictualing program. Hoover swiftly pointed out these advantages to London and Paris.[101] He argued, too, that the new financial scheme would strengthen American public opinion "on the humane side of the war."[102] Within days the Quai d'Orsay and Whitehall assented.[103]

The Belgians, however, were another story. Already the government-in-exile at Le Havre had let it be known that it was "anxious to avoid falling too much into the hands" of Hoover's commission, especially after the war ended.[104] In fact, the Belgians strongly preferred the financial status quo, which made them debtors to the British and French only.[105] The government-in-exile evidently calculated that it would have more postwar leverage on its nearby allies than on a distant and powerful United States. Indeed, the exiled government apparently hoped to induce the French and British to cancel their relief loan completely after the war.[106] The Belgians did not, it seems, anticipate such consideration from Uncle Sam.

Hoover was not deterred by their reluctance. On April 15 he asked the Belgian government to approve the credit proposal. As always, he was resourceful in argument. A direct loan from the U.S. government would not only cement his countrymen's support for the Belgian cause, he said; it would strengthen the CRB's chances of obtaining needed food and ships.[107] This was the carrot. To the French ambassador in London he showed the stick: ". . . [I]t is of great importance," he wrote, "that the Belgian Government be compelled" to request this loan.[108]

On April 18 he took his case to the British War Cabinet, chaired by Prime Minister Lloyd George. It was an extraordinary, perhaps unprecedented occasion: an American citizen had been permitted to address the supreme war council of the British empire. There was perhaps no better measure of his standing among the men who ruled England. Hoover told the assembled officials that the U.S. government earnestly wanted to take over the finance of the relief "for sentimental and not belligerent reasons." After hearing his pleas, the War Cabinet decided to inform the Belgians that it preferred "the proposed new arrangements."[109]

That same day the Belgians agreed to accept the loan: so, at least, Hoover cabled to New York.[110] The drama, however, was not quite over. Increasingly it dawned upon the exiled government that someday it would have to *repay* its projected share of this credit,[111] a figure that might reach considerable magnitude. Not until May did the government authorize its minister to Washington to apply for the unwelcome loan.[112] Under its terms the U.S. government agreed now to appropriate $75,000,000: $7,500,000 per month for Belgium and $5,000,000 per month for northern France. Although credited to the French and Belgian governments, these sums would be expended, as before, by the CRB.[113] Seventy-five million dollars: it was only enough for six months. But as Hoover informed his London office, "We can always increase [the] amount and period at our will and upon justification."[114]

As usual, he was correct: from this point forward to the end of the war, the U.S. government was the CRB's sole source of funding.[115] On only one issue did Hoover fail to achieve his objective: because of the opposition of the chairman of the House Appropriations Committee,[116] the commission's request for a $2,000,000 gift from Congress to cover its past administrative expenses went nowhere. On May 19 Hoover withdrew his request for this appropriation.[117] He had sought it mostly for "political" reasons anyway, to buttress the CRB's standing in Europe.[118] Now it enjoyed more official recognition than had seemed possible just a few months before.

III

W HILE Hoover, in London, struggled to wrap up his commission's loose ends, he turned eagerly to his new assignment from Washington. Within twenty-four hours of the Council of National Defense's published invitation to him to chair its food committee, he initiated a survey of food conditions in the Allied countries, using idle CRB colleagues as his investigators.[119] He placed Vernon Kellogg in charge of the inquiry. Soon CRB men in London, Paris, and elsewhere were energetically collecting confidential governmental data on Allied food reserves, import requirements, and methods of food control.[120]

Ever mindful of the power of a cultivated and informed public opinion, Hoover promptly issued a hortatory press release to the American press. In it he adumbrated themes with which his countrymen would soon become familiar. "The foremost duty of America toward her allies in this war," he asserted, "is to see that they are supplied with food." Warning that the entire Allied population confronted a shortage of foodstuffs, he exhorted Americans to increase their own production and, beyond that, to "stop waste in every scrap of foodstuff." Eighty-five percent of America's food was consumed at home, he said; the homemakers of the United States therefore had a role to fill. "There is no body of women in the world so capable of rising to an emergency as American women."

Hoover made no promise of a speedy peace. The war would probably last another year, he said. The world's food reserve was so attenuated that every exertion would be required "to carry our allies through with their full fighting stamina." But the chairman of the CRB was confident that his fellow citizens, with their "high ideals of self-sacrifice," could master the challenge. Legislation and regulations, he concluded, "can accomplish far less than the voluntary self-denial and devotion of our people."[121]

Within days Hoover devised a plan for an international food board that would coordinate the policies of the United States and the Allies by rationalizing purchase and allocation of supplies. Such a scheme, he argued, would be far better than having the Allies compete with one another for American food, as they were now doing, thereby driving up the price. He presented a memorandum on his proposal to the British Foreign Office and was quickly invited to meet with the War Cabinet. On April 18, at the same session at which he successfully appealed for an American-financed CRB loan, the War Cabinet approved his inter-Allied food board in principle.[122] The French and Italians likewise assented.[123] When Hoover spoke, it seemed, statesmen listened.

At least European statesmen did. Would Americans, who knew him less well, do the same? The initial signals from Washington were none too promising. The Council of National Defense, after all, had only made him chairman of a fact-finding, advisory committee—hardly the powerful executive post that he sought. After taking soundings in Washington, Edgar Rickard warned him that "this food control business" did not seem likely to "carry the authority that it should."[124] Hugh Gibson had the same fear.[125]

Three thousand miles from the scene of the action, Hoover worried and chafed. He told Norman Hapgood that he did not wish to undertake the food control challenge unless he had enough independence to be successful. He certainly did *not* want to be "under any department." Hapgood promptly notified Colonel House and President Wilson.[126] To the President, Hapgood wrote delicately that Hoover was afraid he would not be able "to give as good an account of himself as he has given in the Belgian work, because of his functions not being sufficiently combined with free initiative."[127]

But Hoover had powerful supporters. Praising his appointment by the council, the *New York Times* observed that Hoover was universally recognized by the European belligerents "as one of the best executives brought to the fore by the war."[128] The *New Republic* extolled him as "incontestably better qualified than any other American" to direct the regulation of the nation's food supply.[129] On April 16 the head of the CRB's New York office, William Honnold, advised him not to worry: "You may take it that your position will be what you make it. . . . Press and country have already with remarkable unanimity accepted food control under you as a matter of course and Washington is impatient for you to arrive and tell them what to do."[130] Perhaps with these reassuring words in mind, Hoover wrote to Brand Whitlock that very day that he was returning to Washington at once "to go into the food business." It would be, he said, "an aggrandised Belgian relief extending to all the Allied countries."[131]

Honnold gave Hoover some other advice: before returning, give out an interview that will "confirm in the mind of the country" that America is in "a life and death struggle" and that "the overshadowing matter of food control can only be met by wholehearted sacrifice and conformity to regulation."[132] Hoover immediately adopted his suggestion. On April 20 he again appealed to the American people to reduce their food consumption:

> If we do not do it, we stand a grave chance of losing the war, because our allies cannot fight without food. . . .
> I feel it my duty to emphasize that the food situation is one of the utmost gravity, which, unless it is solved, may possibly result in the collapse of everything we hold dear in civilization.[133]

These were not mere propagandistic words. Across the North Atlantic, ship after Allied ship was going down. From the food survey conducted by his CRB volunteers, he had just learned that France, Italy, and England had only about eight weeks' reserves.[134]

The waning hours of his London sojourn passed quickly: days (and nights) spent preparing his coming campaign to mobilize America's food resources for victory.[135] Kellogg was with him; Poland was with him, and more than a dozen other CRB veterans. Near him also was Ben S. Allen, who had served the CRB so well at the Associated Press's office in London. Hoover now asked Allen to return to America with him as, in effect, his press agent and public relations adviser. Allen was ecstatic. The AP let him go.[136]

On April 21, 1917 Herbert Hoover left the Red House—and the happy prewar world it symbolized—for the last time. Later that year another party took over his lease.[137] At London's Euston Station he waited for the train that would take him to Liverpool, where the cruiser *Philadelphia* was about to embark across the Atlantic. It was not a voyage to look forward to; the German U-boat campaign was at its height. With gloomy humor Hoover confessed to a hunch that his ship was certain to be torpedoed.

At Euston Station a dozen or more of his devoted colleagues gathered to say farewell to their Chief. Inwardly touched, Hoover remarked afterward that it was the greatest sendoff he had ever received. But the CRB chairman was not a man to display effusive emotion or waste time on casual amenities. Having said goodbye, he boarded the train with his secretary, took a seat by the window in his compartment, and immediately set to work on his correspondence. The train began to move. The men on the platform waved. Absorbed in dictating a letter, he did not look out or look back.[138]

15

The Master
of Efficiency

I

A s he prepared to embark for America in April 1917, Herbert Hoover had reason to be proud. In the nearly two and half years since the CRB had been founded, he and his associates had handled more than $200,000,000 in charitable gifts and governmental subsidies, with not a whiff of scandal and an administrative overhead of well under 1%.[1] They had acquired and then transported more than 2,500,000 tons of foodstuffs across dangerous international waters to Rotterdam—and thence, by rail and canal, to more than 4,700 communes in Belgium and northern France: an area of nearly 20,000 square miles, thus rescuing more than 9,000,000 people from hunger. Around the world at least 130,000 volunteers continued to participate in one aspect or another of the effort—including approximately 40,000 on distributing committees in Belgium, another 15,000 in occupied France, and 50,000 on fund-raising bodies in the United States.[2] At the apex of this pyramid was the Commission for Relief in Belgium, averaging fifty-five members, including three dozen in Belgium itself and another six in the districts of northern France. Their numbers were few but their duties many, and their very presence a form of insurance that the mission of relief could go on.

The commission's functions were far more complicated than its charter of responsibility indicated. Writing to his parents in early 1917, one of the principal CRB delegates, Joseph C. Green, explained what assuring "equitable distribution" of food "exclusively to the civil population" actually entailed:

Take the one item of bread for example. First the [CRB] Provincial Representative has to figure out periodically the exact population of his Province, and the exact quantities of native wheat and rye and of imported wheat and maize on hand. From this he calculates the quantity of imported grain necessary to cover a certain period. This he reports to Brussels, and Brussels to London. London supplies the ships. New York purchases and sees to the loading. Rotterdam tranships into canal barges. In the meantime Brussels has decided upon the exact quantities to be shipped to each mill in the country, and Rotterdam ships accordingly. The provincial man must see to the unloading and the milling. The milling involves questions of percentages of bran and flour, of mixtures of native and foreign grains, of the disposal of byproducts and so on.

And this was just the start:

When the flour is finally milled, the real work of distribution begins. Sacks must be provided and kept in rotation. The exact quantity of flour required by a given Commune for a given period must be ascertained. Shipments by canal or rail or tram or wagon must be made to every Commune dependent upon the mill. Boats and cars and horses must be obtained and oil must be supplied for engines and fodder for horses. When the flour has reached the Local Committee it must be carefully distributed among the bakers in accordance with the needs of each. Baking involves yeast, and the maintenance of yeast factories, and the disposal of byproducts, and questions of hygiene and a dozen other minor matters. When the bread is baked it must be distributed to the population by any one of a dozen methods which guarantee an absolutely equitable distribution, each man, woman and child getting the varying ration to which he is entitled, paying for it if he can afford it, and getting it free if he can't. All this involves financial problems, and bookkeeping, and checking and inspection, all along the line; and the whole process to the tune of endless bickering with German authorities high and low, and endless discussions with a thousand Belgian committees.

Now, if you have digested that, you have some idea of what it means to supply a nation with bread. But that is only one item among many. Lard, rice, milk, clothing, etc., etc.: each involves its own special series of problems.[3]

But "relief in Belgium" meant even more than this. By the middle of April 1917 nearly 5,000,000 people in Belgium and northern France were destitute.[4] Using the CRB's gifts from abroad and the profits from its own food sales to the well-to-do, the Comité National financed a vast and growing web of benevolence, including more than 2,700 local charitable committees (one for every Belgian commune) as well as various other more specialized insti-

tutions. All in all, Hoover calculated that more than half the entire population was receiving some kind of assistance in the spring of 1917, including at
least 2,700,000 who were helped by the communal charitable committees.[5]

One object of special solicitude was the young. It was our task and the
Belgians', Hoover wrote later, "to maintain the laughter of the children, not
to dry their tears."[6] Thanks to the CRB's external fund raising and food
imports, and the dedicated zeal of Belgian volunteers, the challenge was
impressively met. By early 1917 (to cite but one example) three-fourths of
Belgium's children were receiving daily hot lunches at canteens established
especially for this purpose.[7]

Another particular concern to Hoover was the plight of Belgium's renowned
lace workers. Deprived of essential raw material by the invasion and subsequent blockade, a workforce of 40,000 women faced destitution, long-term
idleness, and possible attenuation of their skills until Hoover and his associates stepped in. The CRB arranged to import needed thread for the lacemak-
ers and to sell some of their finished products abroad. It also helped committees
make advances to the women for their unsold production, such money to be
recovered from the export of accumulated merchandise after the war. In these
ways an entire industry was kept alive and thousands of skilled women self-
supporting, thereby averting what Vernon Kellogg's wife Charlotte called
"the demoralization that follows unemployment."[8] The sale of the exquisite
lace in England and the United States also no doubt helped to sharpen "the
club of public opinion" in behalf of little Belgium's cause.

In an introduction to a book by Mrs. Kellogg in 1917, Hoover paid tribute
to the labors of a veritable army of Belgian women:

> To create a network of hundreds of cantines for expectant mothers,
> growing babies, for orphans and debilitated children; to provide the
> machinery for supplemental meals for the adolescent in the schools; to
> organize workrooms and to provide stations for the distribution of clothing
> to the poor; to see that all these reliefs cover the field, so that none fall by
> the wayside; to investigate and counsel each and every case that no waste
> or failure result; to search out and provide appropriate assistance to those
> who would rather die than confess poverty; to direct these stations, not
> from committee meetings after afternoon tea, but by actual executive labor
> from early morning till late at night—to go far beyond mere direction by
> giving themselves to the actual manual labor of serving the lowly and help-
> less; to do it with cheerfulness, sympathy and tenderness, not to hundreds
> but literally to millions. . . .

All this, wrote Hoover, the women of Belgium and northern France had
done.[9]

The men, also, had performed magnificently, he declared—buying, transporting, and distributing food supplies, creating the elaborate machinery of

soup kitchens and canteens, supervising wheat processing and breadmaking, inspecting the apparatus of control, protecting precious food from the German army, and more. Out of all this labor had grown an army of 55,000 volunteers "of a perfection and a patriotism without parallel in the existence of any country." And standing beside the people, as "an encouragement and protection" and "a shield to their despair," was the Commission for Relief in Belgium.[10]

Hoover was acutely aware of the unique, unprecedented character of the mission to which he had now devoted more than two years of his life without pay. Mindful of its remarkable niche in the unfolding tragedy of the Great War, in January 1917 he asked Joseph C. Green to prepare a comprehensive official history of the CRB. Later that year, after Green joined the U.S. army, another relief veteran, Tracy Kittredge, took over the assignment.[11]

Others, too, appreciated the commission's extraordinary character. "There never was anything like it in the world before," Ambassador Page told his staff in early 1917, "and it is all one man and that is Hoover."[12] To the *New York Times* Hoover's administration of the CRB ranked as "perhaps the most splendid American achievement of the last two years."[13] *The Independent* enthusiastically agreed: "If there was ever an efficient job done, it is that of carrying relief to the wretched millions of Belgium." Hoover, it said, had "established beyond a peradventure his right to the title of Master of Efficiency."[14]

In an autobiographical statement written sometime after the war, Hoover declared: "There is little importance to men's lives except the accomplishments they leave to posterity." It is in "the origination or administration of tangible institutions or constructive works," he wrote, that men's contributions can best be measured. "When all is said and done," he asserted, "accomplishment is all that counts."[15]

By this standard Hoover as of 1917 had already lived a life full of striking achievement. If he had died that spring—a victim, perhaps, of a U-boat attack in the North Atlantic—he would have been gratefully remembered by millions for the "institution" that he more than anyone had shaped: the Commission for Relief in Belgium.

But, of course, in 1917 his years of accomplishment still lay mostly ahead. As he sailed that April for America, he was not yet forty-three years old.

II

W H O was this man who in thirty turbulent months had leapt from seeming obscurity to worldwide acclaim as Belgium's savior? "In appearance he is astonishingly youthful, smooth-shaven, dark-haired, with cool, watchful eyes, clear brow, straight nose, and firm, even mouth. His chin is round and hard." So wrote an associate of Hoover in 1916.[16] Five feet eleven and one-half inches tall (according to his passport), with gray-green eyes, dark brown hair, and a medium complexion, he did not much stand out in a crowd.[17] "There is nothing theatrical or picturesque in his looks or bearing," a friend remarked.[18] At work he dressed invariably in blue serge suits.[19]

To those who observed him at close range, certain features of his physiognomy seemed pronounced. His face, said Will Irwin, was "full of curves," a mark (he asserted) of many men of ability.[20] Some noticed his high forehead; some his soft hands (he did not exercise).[21] Others noticed his peculiar habit of rarely looking a person in the eye and wondered what quirk of personality it exposed. Shiftiness, said his enemies; shyness, said his friends.[22] Still others noted his strong, determined jaws—jaws that (in the words of a Belgian diplomat) denoted both energy and will.[23]

Energy, will, determination: such words sprang frequently to mind among those who knew Hoover best by 1917. His will was "tremendous," declared Brand Whitlock; "indomitable," said William C. Edgar.[24] Edmond Carton de Wiart called it a "will of iron."[25] No obstacle, it seemed, was too formidable, no custom or bureaucratic regulation too sacred, to stymie the relentless chairman of the Commission for Relief in Belgium. Many times among friends he fretted and wondered how he would ever succeed. At least once he dreamed wistfully of returning to his lead mines. But when the going was roughest, said his colleague and admirer Hugh Gibson, Hoover would sometimes remark: "But we must remember that we are here to *feed the Belgians.*" Then he would grit his teeth and persevere.[26] And far more often than not, he would get his way.

Coupled with his singular drive was a seemingly boundless capacity for work. Laboring regularly at commission affairs well into the evening, and usually on weekends as well, Hoover appeared never to rest.[27] Always there was work to do: the toil of saving the Belgians. Sometimes he would sit abstractedly at his desk for hours, composing letters with a pencil, all the while oblivious to the hustle and bustle around him.[28] More often, and more characteristically, he would pace up and down the floor, deep in thought.[29] When conversing with colleagues or addressing a meeting, he would frequently jingle the coins in his pocket—a habit he had acquired in boyhood.[30] Behind his mask of reserve, some sensed, was a man of restless vitality.[31]

Hoover's energy was "prodigious," said a Belgian associate.[32] It exhausted Brand Whitlock just to watch him.[33] "Cold, keen, alert" in his prewar business dealings,[34] he behaved with similar intensity as a humanitarian. Only once did his body rebel, in early 1916, when an abscess in his ear forced him to stay in bed for a month. But during that year he lost a disturbing amount of weight, and at least one of his associates feared that he was on the verge of a breakdown.[35] Still, Hoover pressed ahead, though he often bore an appearance of weariness that betrayed his heavy expenditure of nervous energy. Will Irwin claimed that Hoover did not need to exercise to control his weight. At times, the journalist wrote, Hoover "fairly thinks himself thin. . . ."[36]

Of his executive ability, no one by 1917 evinced any doubt. Again and again associates marveled at his superlative organizational skill; "genius" was a word frequently used to describe it.[37] Hoover "is a perfect wonder," declared one colleague—"one of the most remarkable men I have ever met."[38] Dozens enthusiastically concurred.[39] Surveying Hoover's achievement as the helm of the CRB, the Belgium minister to Great Britain later wrote: "Il conduisit les opérations du ravitaillement avec une admirable sûreté de coup d'oeil, une rapidité de décision, une facilité de moyens qui assurerent, pendant plus de quatre ans, le fonctionnement de cet extraordinaire mécanisme."[40] Francis W. Hirst, his British editor-friend and neighbor, declared:

One may admire his skill in organising a staff of workers. One may envy the political gift of so handling men (some of whom were bent upon deceiving or thwarting him) that the various Governments and interests were all eventually brought into co-operation. But with all this in mind I can hardly believe, on looking back over the record, that my friend contrived to pull through and to win not a partial but a complete victory. It was a modern Pilgrim's Progress.

Hoover, said Hirst, had "won admiration from most and extorted respect from all."[41] Even Baron von der Lancken, in his memoirs after the war, acknowledged the American's "great capabilities."[42]

One such talent was a gift for pithy and effective expression. Hoover was not a good public speaker; in fact he dreaded such occasions like a curse.[43] His speech, said a friend, was "unornamented."[44] His gestures were few. His delivery (in Samuel Gompers's words) was "somewhat monotonous."[45] Sometimes he spoke so low that he could barely be heard at the end of a dinner table.[46]

But in a small group setting—among fellow relief workers, perhaps, an embassy staff, or a meeting of British Cabinet officials—Hoover's impact, when he chose to let go, was profound. Meeting him for the first time in 1915, the Kansas editor William Allen White felt "mesmerized by the strange low voltage of his magnetism."[47] Joseph C. Green never forgot the night in Brussels when Hoover gave his men an extemporaneous account of happenings in the outside world. It was, Green said later, "an extraordinary performance"—vivid, forthright, orderly, comprehensive.[48] Another CRB volunteer, Gilchrist Stockton, had a similar experience and promptly informed his parents:

Mr. Hoover let himself loose for once. He is a most reticent man, but when he does talk he beats anybody I have ever heard. I was thrilled to the marrow with the idealism and the practical efficiency of the man. I wish that I could picture him as he was that night. I have never known a man of such power.[49]

No, Hoover was not a conventional orator. But, said Green, he was "a really remarkable speaker. . . . His sentences have the habit of sticking in your memory."[50] A friend of Hoover's from his prewar mining days observed in 1917 that "he always got right to the heart of the matter under consideration by the shortest route. . . . He was eminently logical, and his ability for lucid expression was complete."[51] It was still true in his CRB days, as many a European statesman could attest.

Another quality that distinguished Hoover was an almost legendary power of concentration. According to Will Irwin, the CRB chairman had "a capacity for thinking at will," the way other men might walk or run or throw a ball at will.[52] When he did so, his absorption in the problem at hand became almost total. One day in late 1915 Joseph C. Green visited his bureau chief in Brussels:

> When I came into his office I found Mr. Hoover [who had arrived the day before] standing with his back to the wall, gazing fixedly at a spot on the floor five or six feet in front of us.
>
> I went over, said goodmorning, and was about to proffer my hand in the Belgian fashion when I became aware that he was absolutely unconscious of my presence. I stood about awkwardly for a few minutes till he came to with a start, and recognised me with a nod.[53]

On another occasion Hoover called upon Hugh Gibson at the American legation. Throughout their conversation the CRB chairman paced unceasingly, back and forth, back and forth, in a little upstairs room. Suddenly, without explanation, he walked out into the hall. Gibson surmised that his friend was going to resume his pacing there—until he heard rapid footsteps on the stairs. Gibson rushed out to find Hoover leaving the building, without concluding the conversation or pausing to say goodbye.[54]

Hoover's utter concentration on commission business—even, occasionally, to the point of absentmindedness—was reflected at times in indifference to his own personal attire. It was as if, with 9,000,000 hungry people on his mind, he could not be bothered by trivia. According to Brand Whitlock, Hoover's suits were rarely brushed, never pressed, and always had "scuffs" on the shoulders, while his shoe laces "were usually broken and tied in rough knots." The fastidious Whitlock was horrified when Hoover, on his first visit to wartime Belgium in late 1914, arrived for a formal dinner at Francqui's home with a stud missing from his shirt front. Even worse, the buttonhole was soiled—a sign that Hoover had been fingering it. In the hallway Whitlock informed Hoover that he had lost a stud. "No," Hoover replied (perhaps a bit defiantly), "I didn't lose it. I forgot to bring one. But it doesn't matter, does it?" No, Whitlock said, it didn't matter, except that the leading men of Brussels were coming to the dinner and might form the wrong impression of their guest. Hoover thereupon borrowed a stud from Francqui's valet.[55]

More crucial to the CRB chairman's success than his powers of exposition and capacity to concentrate was an acute ability to size up friends and foes and turn their strengths and frailties to his advantage. Hoover, wrote a colleague, "had an intuitive perception of where and how he could best exert his influence and pressure."[56] He had a knack for tailoring arguments to particular audiences—so much so that one could not always be certain which arguments he truly believed. He seemed to fathom quickly the inner character of his interlocutors and associates—a trait that he shared with Francqui.[57] In 1916, for instance, a New York society woman visited England and offered to help the commission. With a shrewdness honed by experience Hoover instructed his New York office how to handle her on her return:

She has most extraordinary abilities and would be of enormous use to you. . . . She is of an independent sort of character and wants to feel that she is the boss of something. Therefore in order to get the best of her—and there is a great deal to get—you need to sort of give her a departmental stunt and put the responsibility up to her. I am sure she would bring results. . . .[58]

Hoover did not always confine such opinions to himself or to intimate associates. He did not suffer fools or rogues gladly and, when sufficiently provoked, could unleash a burst of angry profanity.[59] An admiring friend observed, "He can express himself so accurately and indignantly that his victim will go off nursing a grudge for the rest of his natural life."[60] Such episodes seldom happened, however, with the men in his own ranks. It was not necessary. Of the 169 Americans who served the CRB in Belgium by April 1917, very few let him down.[61]

Once he judged a person fit for service, Hoover did not constrain him with detailed directives. He expected his men to show initiative and resourcefulness, just as he himself had done in his rise to eminence as a mining engineer. One day in 1916 he called one of his youngest relief workers, a twenty-six-year-old newcomer, into his Brussels office. Hoover came instantly to the point: "I'd like to know in a brief, succinct manner what ought to be known about the welfare agencies of this country. I'll be back in three weeks or four weeks. Bring me a report." And that was all. Commenting long afterward about this assignment, the CRB volunteer remarked: "He didn't give me any instructions because that wasn't his nature. He gave a man an assignment—a challenge to do this—and left it up to him to produce."[62]

On another occasion Hoover asked a fellow mining engineer, Walter Lyman Brown, to take charge of the CRB's office in Rotterdam. But I'm a mining man, Brown protested; I don't know anything about shipping. Hoover persuaded him anyway. Finally Brown inquired: "What are my orders?" "Just keep the food moving," Hoover replied. And said no more.[63]

Initiative and resourcefulness: what Hoover encouraged in others he himself displayed in profusion. He had a "contempt of precedent," one acquaintance wrote.[64] He was always "a diplomat in a hurry."[65] "If a thing was really necessary," Hoover once said of his first months as relief director, "we did it first and asked permission afterwards."[66] Impatient with "titled office boys," if he wanted some dispensation from governments he went, whenever possible, to the top.[67] He was no " 'gum shoe' diplomat," a friend observed. "He goes straight at a condition or a person, and if the person is compact of petty pride and self-importance, so much the worse for that person."[68] Negotiations for Hoover were a form of mental combat at which he was rarely outmaneuvered. He could not afford to be if the people of Belgium were to be fed.

The CRB chairman's unconventional administrative style had its critics. Years later Brand Whitlock complained bitterly that he had repeatedly seen Hoover "hesitate and vacillate about a question, then decide it impulsively, and act on it in a brutal manner. . . ."[69] Whitlock by then was quite hostile to Hoover, and his assessment was hardly a balanced one. Yet even the loyal and sympathetic Vernon Kellogg remarked in 1916 upon his chief's "impetuosity."[70] "For a man of his personal force and independence," Kellogg added, "he is sometimes easily influenced—for the moment at any rate—by casual suggestions or reports. . . ."[71] His approach to life, said a mining colleague, was "the principle of 'get there quick.' "[72]

To all these qualities of mind was linked a most unusual temperament. Hoover "rarely speaks," a young CRB volunteer recorded in his diary in 1916.[73] He was "very reserved," recalled another years later.[74] Aloof, laconic, taciturn, with neither talent nor inclination for small talk, Hoover often crossed the English Channel or conducted inspection trips in Belgium without saying a single word to his companions.[75] On one ninety-kilometer automobile journey with Gilchrist Stockton, the CRB's leader said virtually nothing until he boarded a train at the end. Then he said, "Goodbye, Stockton," and was off.[76] One CRB man joked that Hoover expressed himself in few words. One was "yes" and the other was "no."[77]

This extreme reticence did not conceal the forcefulness of personality underneath. Those with whom he parleyed soon sensed an assertive temperament that was not to be dissuaded or denied. Colonel House once called him "pugnatious"; Brand Whitlock called him "*fruste.*"[78] Hoover himself on one occasion spoke of "my naturally combative disposition."[79] A dozen times or more in 1915 and 1916 he threatened or "offered" to close down the commission entirely unless his antagonists—usually the Germans or the Belgians—came to terms. To Lord Eustace Percy at the Foreign Office, Hoover "was temperamentally a free lance, and his very soft heart and very hard head alike prompted an instinctive attitude to all governments which could best be summed up in the words: 'kindly get out of my way.' " There was "no government more calculated to arouse that instinct in such a man," Percy added, "than the British—except always the German."[80] And it was precisely the British and the Germans with whom Hoover most had to deal.

Not surprisingly, the CRB chairman dominated his organization. Hoover "did not like you to disagree with him," one CRB worker later recalled. "He *definitely* did not like you to disagree with him."[81] It was said that the office next to his "frequently changed its occupant.'"[82] While willing to foster initiative in the carrying out of assignments, he made it plain that the orders themselves could issue from only one source. The delicate, always besieged relief mechanism, he believed, could survive in no other way.[83]

The CRB chairman's aggressiveness helped him win many crucial battles. Who else but Hoover would have confronted Prime Minister Asquith to the point of impertinence in December 1914? Who else but Hoover would have dared to stand up to Lloyd George? Who but Hoover would have challenged the old Prussian von Bissing and gone over his head to Berlin? A man of lesser nerve—or less than total commitment to his mission—would have had his ships requisitioned by the Admiralty, his independence whittled away by the Germans, his prestige sapped and subverted by the connivings of Villalobar and Francqui. Not Hoover. Time and again the CRB's desperate circumstances required the intervention of a man of force. It is doubtful that the relief work would have lasted if a gentler, less assertive person had been at the CRB's helm.[84]

Hoover's strenuous tactics were not employed without cost—in strained and exacerbated relationships with Whitlock and numerous others. In 1916 Vernon Kellogg privately admitted that "there are a good many who are not friendly to him."[85] Hoover's "manners are far from 'finished,' " an American journalist wrote gently in 1917—a judgment with which some CRB men agreed.[86] The Belgian minister to London found his manner of speaking "*parfois impératif.*"[87] Whitlock later accused him of "sullen boorishness" and claimed that he rarely saw him in a good temper.[88] In certain British social circles he was known as "the rudest man in London."[89]

Hoover's "rudeness," however, did not generally appear to be deliberate.[90] In part it emanated from his habit of total concentration, a trait that often rendered him oblivious to his social environment. Belgians, with their elaborate manners, found it difficult to understand such a man.[91] In part, too, it stemmed from his constant preoccupation with the never-ending burdens that he bore.[92] Absorbed with the responsibility of feeding an entire nation, haunted by what he called "the tragedy of possible failure," Hoover seemed to regard good manners as an expendable, time-consuming frill.[93] "I can understand how some might have felt he was brusque," his niece observed many years later. "His mind was busy with important matters and he tended to brush off superficial conversation as one might brush away a buzzing fly."[94]

In some measure also Hoover's abrupt aloofness derived from his unusual temperamental makeup. Meeting him in London in 1916, Will Irwin's wife at first thought him "a little cold" but concluded that it was "only his characteristic pessimism."[95] To William Allen White he seemed "constitutionally gloomy," a man who "always saw the doleful side of any situation."[96] In truth, Hoover was an almost paradoxical combination: an intellectual and political idealist who was also a temperamental pessimist. Lou Henry Hoover herself once said of her husband: "If you want to get the gloomiest view of any subject on earth, ask Bert about it."[97]

In some men such a blend of traits might have engendered caution, even paralysis. Not, however, in Hoover. There was about him a drive and intensity that startled many who encountered him. Years later, after reading Brand Whitlock's published wartime diary, Newton D. Baker (President Wilson's secretary of war) remarked on its portrait of "the 'terrible Hoover' as he appeared at the head of the Belgian Relief Commission":

> Terrible to the Germans, terrible to the British and French, terrible to most of his American associates, terrible because of his relentless and unconquerable determination to keep the Belgians from starving, he scolded, threatened, and out-bullied every human obstacle; changed the policies of nations; and thwarted the most resolute determinations of cabinets, governments and military establishments. He squeezed money out of stones and gathered food from deserts.[98]

Baker did not raise the question, but he, too, might have asked: who else but Hoover could have accomplished this daunting task?

Yet Hoover was more than a singleminded, hard-driving executive with a "will of iron." No one who worked with him in those days, Lord Percy later recorded, could overlook his "emotional humanity" and "personal affectionateness."[99] Despite Hoover's constitutional gloominess, William Allen White found him in 1915 "a most intelligent person who smiled naively with a certain vinegary integrity"—a man whose "perverse acerbity" was mixed with "an adolescent sweetness."[100]

This son of Iowa Quakers—orphaned before he was ten, raised in Oregon for six years by an austere and strong-willed uncle—had long since learned to mask his emotions. Still, at times, they came through—as when he and Whitlock first visited a Brussels relief station in 1914.[101] The episode was apparently traumatic. According to Mrs. Hoover some months later, "My own husband will not visit a bread-line unless literally compelled to, and . . . has his eyes near full of tears before he leaves."[102] Whitlock, too, noticed that Hoover's eyes grew "soft and pitying" when he discussed the suffering of the Belgians.[103]

Particularly among children his unsentimental exterior dissolved.[104] He, too, had been a child once and had known, as an orphan, the loneliness of being an outsider. As a result he seemed to feel a special affinity for children anywhere who were in need. No wonder the *soupes scolaires* were such an affecting sight. "The pathos of the long lines of expectant, chattering mites" (as he called them), "each with a ticket of authority pinned to its chest or held in a grimy fist":[105] this was an image of the relief that he could not forget. For all his brusqueness and peremptoriness of manner, there was (said a Belgian diplomat) a look of kindness in the depths of his eyes.[106] The sufferings of the children of Belgium drove him on.

Hoover rarely smiled, one acquaintance noted.[107] Some even called him "morose."[108] But at least one business associate detected before the war what only intimates fully realized: that Hoover had "a keen sense of humor," although "when it bubbled up he got it off as soon as possible, and never let it interfere with the serious business of life."[109]

Now and then, during his "Belgian" days, Hoover's dry whimsicality asserted itself. In 1916, for instance, Brand Whitlock asked him to send over a pet dog. On July 5 Hoover replied to Mrs. Whitlock:

> I am . . . sending you by this courier one Pekinese pup. This transaction is one of a most confidential order which we have ever undertaken. As I can see enormous possibilities by way of American yellow journalism on the subject of import of dogs in[to] Belgium to divide the food supply already attenuated below human endurance, I shall be compelled in the event of such an exposure to state that this was merely an attempt to provide the Embassy with a further reserve of meat supply, that the embargo on the export of meat from England, together with the prohibition of imports from Holland into Belgium, has reduced the Embassy to the last resource! In this case, however, it will be necessary to insist that it was not a Pekinese pup but was a full-grown Newfoundland![110]

On another occasion during the war, Hoover called his older son, Herbert, into his study. Hoover's middle name was "Clark," his son's "Charles." Nevertheless, the boy was generally known as Herbert C. Hoover, Jr. With a twinkle in his eye Hoover informed his son that he was tired of writing the letter 'C" in the middle of his signature. He had to sign his name so frequently now that by dropping his middle initial he calculated that he could save several miles of writing a year. The father added, however, that he wished to consult his son before acting. He pointed out that if each dropped his middle name they would not only save ink but also evade confusion over whether young Herbert was really "Jr." The boy accepted his father's proposal. From that point on (so the son later said) Hoover always signed his name "Herbert Hoover." "H. C. Hoover"—his standard signature from the 1890s until World War I—disappeared. The son ever afterward signed *his* name "Herbert Hoover, Jr."[111]

Such glimpses of a relaxed, even playful personality were few indeed during these leaden wartime years. Before August 1914, it had been a different story. Before the war Hoover had motored all over Britain, had stopped at little streams and dammed them, had cooked food over campfires in the woods, had explored the beauties and curiosities of the English countryside. He had attended the London theater, had entertained endless guests at the Red House, had translated (with his wife) the monumental Latin mining text *De Re Metallica*. There was little opportunity for such diversions any more.

One of his pleasures, though, continued unabated: his bedtime habit of reading detective stories—not for their literary value, but, characteristically, as a game in which he tried to outwit the author and guess "whodunit" before the last page.[112] Even when at rest, he seemed to crave mental exercise.

To those who knew him best, there was still another trait that belied his cool public persona. There was the Hoover who quietly supported fellow mining engineers who had been thrown out of work by the war. There was the Hoover who secretly paid Vernon Kellogg's Stanford University salary while the professor was on leave to help the CRB. There was the Hoover who signed a personal note of indebtedness for $600,000 to keep the commission going early in the war. There was the Hoover who evidently took thousands of dollars out of his own pocket to cover the living expenses of his men. There was the Hoover who was prepared in 1916 to pledge his entire personal fortune—worth a million dollars or more—as security against any liability to his New York advisory committee. There was the Hoover who let his butler's wife live rent-free at the Red House while her husband recovered from a war wound.

The CRB chairman did not boast about these benefactions. He was apt in fact to be embarrassed by displays of gratitude. But to those who served him loyally—be they family servants, engineers, or relief associates—he responded with remarkable generosity. And they in turn admired and revered him all the more. John Agnew, his long-time mining associate (and, since 1914, his alter ego on certain company boards) was not alone in the sentiments he expressed to a friend in 1917:

> Long ago I put both Mr. and Mrs. Hoover on pedestals and if there is such a thing as hero-worship then I am an ardent devotee in their case. I should be sorry to say this to them personally, my only desire being to have the privilege of furthering their interests to the best of my ability, and without ostentation in every way possible.[113]

Agnew's unabashed "hero-worship" was no idiosyncrasy. If Hoover was wary and often prickly in his dealings with his equals, his relationship to his subordinates was very different. For the young men of the CRB especially, the man they called the Chief was a person of heroic stature who evoked almost boundless devotion. "Mr. Hoover is such a fine, quiet, kindly man," wrote Gilchrist Stockton in 1915, "that everybody votes for him on sight— and no second choice! He is a personified combination of idealism and power. . . . If you want to start a wave of enthusiasm among the younger members of the C.R.B., simply say 'Mr. Hoover.' . . . he has no idea of our absolute loyalty."[114]

"Hoover is the soul of the C.R.B.," Stockton declared on another occasion. "Though he never notices any of us very much we all idolize him."[115] Not surprisingly, the *esprit de corps* of the commission was superb.[116] "I have learned to value organizations and individuals by the atmosphere they create around them," one relief worker wrote during the war. "Of all the significances of the C.R.B. its atmosphere of love and devotion is pronounced. To me it is becoming an obsession. . . . It is to my appreciation a training ground for the millenium."[117]

What was it about Hoover that (in William Allen White's phrase) "drew to him in a steel-bound loyalty the men whom he touched"?[118] What qualities of character and leadership filled the CRB volunteers with such awe that some hardly dared to approach him?[119] Part of his appeal lay in his sheer devotion to his work—work of self-denying humanitarianism.[120] Part lay in his tremendous idealism and in what one colleague called his "complete personal disinterestedness."[121] Hoover also showed faith in his lieutenants and backed them to the hilt in crises. When, for instance, in 1915 the Germans tried to expel Joseph C. Green from Belgium as a "spy," Hoover bluntly threatened to withdraw the entire CRB in three days rather than have Green's and his comrades' reputations falsely impugned. Up to that point Green, a newcomer, had been skeptical of his younger co-workers' "wild enthusiasm for Mr. Hoover." Nobody could be *that* great, he thought. But after this episode, in which the Chief instantly accepted his denial of wrongdoing and then defended him before Baron von der Lancken, Green "saw what the other men saw" in Herbert Hoover.[122]

Despite his reserve and preoccupation with burdens far heavier than theirs, Hoover nevertheless conveyed a feeling of solicitude for the men in his ranks. On trips to Brussels he would call in his delegates from the field and inquire how things were in their "bailiwicks."[123] He encouraged them to disclose their problems and share their daily frustrations. "You felt you had a willing listener," one CRB veteran remarked.[124] In London he invited his associates to the Red House for events like Christmas Eve dinner.[125]

One of Hoover's London customs in England was a daily staff luncheon held in a room in his offices at No. 3, London Wall Buildings. Twelve to fifteen of his colleagues would attend these gatherings, at which meals were brought in from a nearby restaurant and cocktails invariably served. The lunch period provided an opportunity for the staff to make reports, resolve difficulties, and share their expertise. Intentionally or not, it also augmented morale and brought the men closer to their leader. Hoover seldom spoke at these functions; instead he preferred to listen. But if incapable of bonhomie, he was not too proud to learn from his lieutenants. One of his "chief characteristics," said a CRB man in 1917, "is his willingness to listen to the ideas of his subordinates; he seizes upon information and ideas with remarkable rapidity and often puts them to immediate use."[126] The CRB's staff lunches were a significant means to this end.[127]

Hoover in fact seemed to depend on the intellectual ferment generated by the able men around him, although it was not always easy for them to transcend the barrier they perceived between themselves and the Chief. One time several CRB men heard a rumor that he was about to appoint one of their colleagues to a position for which they all considered him unqualified. No one, however, wished to be the man to carry such a message to the top. At a dinner with Hoover one evening, the young relief workers squirmed until one of them finally ventured to call their leader aside.

What would happen? the others wondered. Would Hoover explode in wrath? The tête-à-tête was over in half a minute. "Why the devil didn't you tell me that before?" Hoover replied. "That's the kind of thing I want to know." The Big Chief said nothing further; the projected appointment was quashed.[128]

The chairman of the CRB appeared not to realize the veneration with which his men regarded him. Certainly he did little in any conventional way to elicit or cultivate such feeling. Hoover "didn't pat us on the back very much," said one relief worker long afterward; "he just expected us to do our duty and that was all."[129] When a young CRB volunteer completed a task for him, Hoover would thank him briefly and say no more.[130] Yet somehow his very lack of effusiveness inspired and motivated his men. "His least word meant everything," one of them later recalled. "He just charged us like a dynamo with enthusiasm and devotion and willingness to go through any experience to please him as well as do our job."[131] To him they responded with a loyalty of almost fanatical proportions. "He was the Chief, we were his boys, and we would have done anything in the world for him."[132]

Long before 1917 more than a few men in the commission began to hope that the Chief might someday become chief executive of the United States government.[133] The topic arose frequently among them.[134] As the director of the Rotterdam office put it in the summer of 1915, "it is the private opinion of most of the Americans who are working on this job under him that nothing is too good for him."[135] Such sentiments were not confined to relief personnel. In the spring of 1917 Hoover's intimate associate in mining affairs, the British stockbroker Francis A. Govett, publicly asserted that Hoover's "progress is not yet complete" and that his friend would eventually occupy "the highest office in the United States—the Presidential Chair."[136]

Did Hoover himself desire the presidency as early as 1917? Certain of his acquaintances suspected so. Emile Francqui and Brand Whitlock—not the most objective of witnesses—came to believe that Hoover deliberately "tried to build himself up politically by using the young men of the C.R.B., who were constantly flattering him." According to Francqui, it was "evidence of Hoover's lack of greatness."[137] What Francqui and Whitlock did not seem to realize was that the CRB men's "hero-worship" was both spontaneous and unsolicited.

Hoover himself denied having political aspirations. He told Govett in the spring of 1917 that his acceptance of governmental food control duties was (in Govett's words) "death to all political ambition."[138] Yet Hoover, undeniably, was attracted to public life. How he had yearned for years to "get into the big game somewhere" in America—through ownership of a newspaper, or the presidency of Stanford University, or the authorship of a book. How he had maneuvered in early 1917 to find a niche for himself in the impending American war mobilization. And not just *any* niche but nothing less than the role of supreme coordinator of the American war effort in Europe! Had this post been created, Hoover would have been second only to President Wilson in the conduct of wartime administration.

Hoover's political tendencies belonged to the "progressive center." When asked in England to label himself he chose the term *Liberal*, although (Will Irwin stressed) Hoover's was "an advanced liberalism, looking forward to a better organization of free society, not backward to an unsystematic freedom."[139] A Republican by heritage, a Bull Moose Progressive in 1912, Hoover was a member of the Republican Club of the City of New York, which he had joined in 1909.[140] Yet in 1916 Hoover apparently approved Woodrow Wilson's reelection, and his political contacts were with the Wilson administration. He had no similar ties to the Republicans. It is interesting to speculate what Hoover's career might have been if Charles Evans Hughes had won the presidency in 1916.

For a man about to enter American public life, however, Hoover in 1917 faced some significant hurdles. He disliked and was not adept at public speaking. As a friend once put it, "After the crowd passed fifty, the influence of his charm began to weaken."[141] He was indifferent to governmental decorations: "toys," he called them—"not the kind of reward which I am searching for in this world."[142] He concealed his benefactions. He hated to be photographed for publication.[143] He strenuously objected—or at least professed to object—when his admirers showered effusive tributes on him in the press. It was the *institution* that mattered, he insisted, not the personalities who happened to administer it.

Yet Hoover was fascinated by the press and by its power to affect the body politic. Many of his best friends in this period—Will Irwin, Ben S. Allen, William Goode, Frederick Palmer—were newspapermen. He never forgot that his masterful cultivation of American public opinion had been critical to the CRB's success. If averse to unseemly *personal* publicity, he nevertheless loved to orchestrate publicity—for a cause, of course, but, inevitably, a cause with which he was identified. Ambitious for success and recognition, he often seemed uncomfortable when he got them. It was a pattern of behavior common among orphans.[144]

There is no conclusive evidence that Hoover wanted to be President as early as 1917. It would have been uncharacteristic, in fact, for him openly to express such a motive. But among the men around him the thought was already in the air, and he could not have been oblivious to the possibility.[145]

On one subject, however, there was no doubt: his unashamed ardor for his native land. "Hail Columbia" Hoover had been his epithet among mining friends before 1914; some even called him "the star-spangled Hoover." The trauma of a European war only deepened his patriotic sentiments. He "didn't like foreigners very much," one CRB veteran later recalled. "He never went native."[146] By the spring of 1917 he had developed, from bitter experience, a lifelong animosity toward the British Admiralty.[147] Add to that his encounters with Prussian bureaucrats, Spanish diplomats, and certain French and Belgian politicians, and America looked better and better by contrast.

And not just America but his beloved adopted state of California. Hoover rhapsodized about California, his friend Francis Hirst reported, the way the poet Virgil wrote about Italy. For most of the twenty years since 1897, the peripatetic mining engineer and businessman had lived outside his country. But for all his incomparable exposure to faraway peoples and places, his feelings remained essentially as he had expressed them in a letter home from the outback of Australia in August 1897: San Francisco was the center of civilization, and Stanford "the best place in the world."[148]

III

AND now, in early middle age, the Yankee engineer turned-humanitarian was finally heading home to stay. Arriving in Liverpool on April 21, he, Vernon Kellogg, and Ben S. Allen boarded the S.S. Philadelphia, newly repainted and equipped with guns for defense against German submarines.

Then, unaccountably, the homeward voyage stalled. For three and a half days the vessel waited in vain for clearance to leave Liverpool harbor. Rumors of danger abounded. Hoover and his colleagues paced the decks in frustration.

Finally, early on the morning of April 25, 1917, the British navy escorted the Philadelphia out to sea. At noon the last boat departed; the old ship was now on its own. Early that evening it veered suddenly and hard. Then it continued on its way. Hoover learned afterward that it had missed two huge mines by less than fifty feet.

Having barely averted disaster, the ship sailed westward across the Atlantic.[149]

Bibliographical Note

THE period covered in this volume encompasses just under three years—an epoch in which Herbert Hoover devoted himself almost exclusively to a single mission. Although the time span is comparatively short and the topic unusually focused, the resources available for understanding it are both widely scattered and immense, including more than eighty manuscript collections and archival groups in the United States and abroad.

Hoover's principal activity during these years, of course, was his leadership of the Commission for Relief in Belgium (CRB). Since the early 1920s, the Hoover Institution on War, Revolution and Peace, at Stanford University, has been the repository for the CRB's extensive files, comprising 265 linear feet of correspondence, shipping records, account books, photographs, and memorabilia. Fortunately for a biographer, not all of this enormous assemblage of material is equally valuable or germane. At the heart of the collection are thirty-three boxes of correspondence to and/or from the leading personalities of the relief. This series includes twelve indispensable boxes of Hoover's own outgoing letters and cables, chronologically arranged. The CRB collection also contains 125 dossiers prepared by the commission's London office during World War I. Each consists of typewritten copies of commission correspondence and memoranda pertaining to a particular topic; in each, the documents are presented in chronological order. By examining these sometimes bulky compilations, a researcher can trace many complex episodes with clarity.

Also particularly useful at the Hoover Institution are the Herbert Hoover Collection and the papers of several individuals who were closely associated with him in the relief of Belgium and northern France, notably Ben S. Allen, Hugh Gibson, Joseph C. Green, Tracy B. Kittredge, and Gilchrist Stockton. In addition, the Institution possesses a small assortment of papers of the American Committee, a group of American residents of London (led by Hoover) who helped thousands of their countrymen traveling in Europe find their way back to the United States in the confused early weeks of World War I.

The Herbert Hoover Presidential Library in West Branch, Iowa, is a second crucial source of documentation on Hoover's "Belgian" years. The key collection is the Herbert Hoover Papers, divided into several series, of which the Pre-Commerce (that is, pre-1921) portion is most relevant for this volume. The Pre-Commerce Papers comprise not only Hoover's correspondence with numerous individuals during the war but also many of the original cable files of the Commission for Relief in Belgium: twenty-three boxes storing literally thousands of such messages. The Pre-Commerce Papers additionally include the minutes of the CRB's New York advisory committee, established in 1915. Also of note at the presidential library are 140 bound volumes of relief-related news clippings assembled by the CRB's staff, as well as the papers of Maurice Pate (a CRB volunteer) and the Belgian American Educational Foundation (founded by Hoover and others in 1920). Another excellent source is the recently opened papers of Lou Henry Hoover; these shed light on the Hoovers' family life during this period.

A third essential locale for a study of Hoover in the early years of World War I is Washington, D.C. At the Manuscript Division of the Library of Congress the papers of Oscar T. Crosby, Gifford Pinchot, Theodore Roosevelt, Woodrow Wilson, and especially Brand Whitlock proved useful. At the National Archives a few blocks away, the General Records of the Department of State (RG 59) for 1914–1917 were exceptionally rewarding. Among these holdings are several thousand pertinent documents in the department's records relating to the internal affairs of Belgium, 1910–1929 (especially, file 855.48). Another treasure trove is RG 84: Records of the Foreign Service Posts of the Department of State. The Belgian relief files of two such posts— the American embassy in London and the American legation in Brussels— turned out to be massive and indispensable. In these thick and dusty volumes I discovered much that illumined the often labyrinthine story of Hoover's humanitarian efforts.

The Commission for Relief in Belgium was an international undertaking, and to comprehend it fully I have drawn upon non-American sources. In Great Britain the Andrew Bonar Law and Sir Herbert Samuel collections at the House of Lords Record Office include a few items of interest. The papers of Sir Edward Grey (later Viscount Grey of Fallodon) and of Viscount Cecil of Chelwood—both at the Public Record Office in Kew—contain more. Alas, the papers of Prime Minister H. H. Asquith (Oxford University) and Reginald McKenna (Cambridge University) turned out to include no directly Hoover-related documents. Another disappointment is the complete absence of personal papers for Lord Eustace Percy, Hoover's principal contact at the Foreign Office. Fortunately, at the Public Record Office the extensive files of the British Foreign Office pertaining to Belgian relief are of considerable value, in part because many senior officials wrote internal memoranda about the correspondence flowing in. From these I was better able to discern the context surrounding the sometimes misleading paper trail.

Also at the Public Record Office (and now available on microfilm) are the reports of Prime Minister Asquith to King George V on the proceedings of Cabinet meetings (Cab. 41), various wartime Cabinet memoranda (Cab. 37), and the minutes of the War Cabinet for December 1916 to November 1919 (Cab. 23). From them one can glean much about British attitudes and policy toward Hoover's unprecedented relief program.

Certain Belgian sources also deserve mention. Although the papers of the CRB's Belgian counterpart, the Comité National, have evidently disappeared, its elaborate, multivolume *Rapport général sur le fonctionnement et les opérations du Comité National de Secours et d'Alimentation* (1919–1921) contains copies of scores of documents, including printed transcripts of the CN's general meetings between 1914 and 1917. At the Ministry of Foreign Affairs in Brussels, the papers of the Belgian foreign minister during part of World War I, Eugène Napoléon Beyens, contain a number of Hoover-related items that help to clarify the exiled government's posture toward the relief. So also do certain other personal collections in various Belgian archives; for a convenient list, see Liane Ranieri, *Emile Francqui, on l'intelligence créatrice* (Paris, 1985), a recent biography of the executive head of the Comité National. For a thorough understanding of the "inner history" of Hoover's work in Belgium, however, including his often stormy relationship with the Comité National, the best—indeed, virtually the only—extant source materials are in British and American archives. (On this point, see Ranieri, *Emile Francqui*, p. 364.)

I shall not enumerate separately every other manuscript collection that I found to hold material, however fragmentary, on Hoover's humanitarian work between 1914 and 1917. But several of these are sufficiently significant to merit individual citation: the William C. Edgar and Family Papers (Minnesota Historical Society), the Edward M. House Papers and Frederic C. Walcott Papers (Yale University Library), the Allan Nevins Papers (Rare Book and Manuscript Library, Columbia University), the Walter Hines Page Papers and William Phillips diary (Harvard University), and the archives of the Rockefeller Foundation (Rockefeller Archive Center). Other sources are cited, where appropriate, in the footnotes.

Not surprisingly, the spectacular experience of rescuing more than 9,000,000 people from the ravages of war and starvation generated a substantial array of memoirs and histories by participants. Among the most important are the following: Herbert Hoover, *The Memoirs of Herbert Hoover*, vol. I: *Years of Adventure* (New York, 1951); Hoover, *An American Epic*, vol. I (Chicago, 1959); Hugh Gibson, *A Journal from Our Legation in Belgium* (New York, 1917); Vernon Kellogg, *Fighting Starvation in Belgium* (New York, 1918); Eustace Percy, *Some Memories* (London, 1958); Brand Whitlock, *Belgium: A Personal Narrative*, 2 vols. (New York, 1919); Allan Nevins, ed., *The Letters and Journal of Brand Whitlock*, 2 vols. (New York, 1936). For one Belgian diplomat's perspective, see Paul Hymans, *Mémoires*, 2 vols. (Brussels, 1958). For a German perspective, see Oscar Freiherr von der Lancken-Wakenitz, *Meine Dreissig Dienstjahre, 1888–1918* (Berlin, 1931). The oral history memoir of one CRB volunteer, Perrin C. Galpin, is in the Columbia University Oral History Collection. Similar typescript reminiscences by other CRB veterans are held at the Herbert Hoover Presidential Library and the Hoover Institution.

Also of special note is George I. Gay and H. H. Fisher, *Public Relations of the Commission for Relief in Belgium*, 2 vols. (Stanford, Calif., 1929), a compendium of nearly 700 documents drawn from the CRB's files. An exceptionally helpful and never-published monograph is Tracy B. Kittredge, "The History of the Commission for Relief in Belgium, 1914–1917," copies of which are in the Hoover Institution and the Herbert Hoover Presidential Library.

Finally, although Hoover from 1914 to 1917 was increasingly absorbed in his new role as a professional humanitarian, he still pursued two other compelling interests: his slowly diminishing career as a mining engineer and his campaign to improve his alma mater, Stanford University. The detailed sources for his mining activities are given in the footnotes for chapter 11; for additional background information, see George H. Nash, *The Life of Herbert Hoover: The Engineer, 1874–1914* (New York: Norton, 1983). For the study of his profound Stanford ties and benefactions, the Hoover Institution Records, the Pre-Commerce Papers at his presidential library in Iowa, the E. D. Adams, John C. Branner, and Ray Lyman Wilbur papers at the Stanford University Archives, and the Ralph Arnold Collection at the Huntington Library are all vital, as the footnotes suggest. For more on this central theme in Hoover's long life, see my monograph *Herbert Hoover and Stanford University* (Stanford, Calif.: Hoover Institution Press, 1988).

It is tempting at this point to launch into a commentary on the various secondary sources that in one way or another proved worthwhile, but I shall forbear. The interested reader will find them cited in the footnotes that follow.

ABBREVIATIONS

CRB   Commission for Relief in Belgium
HHPL   Herbert Hoover Presidential Library, West Branch, Iowa
HI   Hoover Institution on War, Revolution and Peace, Stanford University
LC   Library of Congress, Washington, D.C.
NARA   National Archives and Records Administration, Washington, D.C.
PRO   Public Record Office, Kew, Surrey, United Kingdom
RG 59 Record Group 59: General Records of the Department of State
RG 84 Record Group 84: Records of the Foreign Service Posts of the Department of State

All quotations in the text appear as originally written. In general, I have not inserted the distracting word *sic* to indicate misspellings or other anomalies.

Notes

CHAPTER 1

1. Herbert Hoover to E. D. Adams, July 21, 1914, Hoover Institution Records, Series F-01, HI.
2. See: New York *World*, August 3, 1914, p. 3, and August 4, 1914, p. 3; *New York Tribune*, August 4, 1914, p. 3; Walter Hines Page cable to Secretary of State Bryan, August 4, 1914, Walter Hines Page Papers, Harvard University; Page to Woodrow Wilson, August 9, 1914, Woodrow Wilson Papers, LC; Franklin H. Martin, *Digest of the Proceedings of the Council of National Defense During the World War*, 73rd Congress, Senate Document 193 (Washington, D.C., 1934), pp. 6–8.
3. New York Times, August 4, 1914, p. 4.
4. Ibid., p. 5; New York *World*, August 4, 1914, p. 3; Ernest Hamlin Abbott, "The Experiences of an American Refugee from Paris," *Outlook* 107 (August 29, 1914): 1027; Martin, *Digest*, pp. 7–9; Fred I. Kent to Joseph Chapman, September 10, 1914, Fred I. Kent Papers, Box 9, Princeton University; Fred I. Kent to Edwin V. Krick, December 19, 1950, Carol Green Wilson Papers, Box 3, HI; Oscar S. Straus, *Under Four Administrations* (Boston, 1922), pp. 371–72.
5. Page cable to Bryan, August 4, 1914; *New York Tribune*, August 5, 1914, p. 3; Kent to Krick, December 19, 1950. See also *New York Times*, August 5, 1914, p. 3.
6. Page cable to Bryan, August 5, 1914, file 341.11/6, RG 59, NARA.
7. Page cable to Bryan, August 4, 1914; *New York Times*, August 5, 1914, p. 3; New York *World*, August 6, 1914, p. 3; Fred I. Kent to a Mr. Bartlett, October 2, 1914, Kent Papers, Box 9.
8. *New York Times*, August 5, 1914, p. 3; New York World, August 6, 1914, p. 3.
9. Lou Henry Hoover to her parents, August 22, 1914 (date of mailing from London). Original in the possession of Mr. and Mrs. Delano Large, Palo Alto, California. Copy in the author's possession.

10. Hoover, *The Memoirs of Herbert Hoover*, vol. 1: *Years of Adventure* (New York, 1951), p. 141. Hoover, incidentally, incorrectly recalled the date of the telephone call as August 3, not August 4. See the text below.

11. Robert Skinner, "President Hoover" (typescript, n.d.), enclosed with Skinner to Hoover, October 26, 1957, Post-Presidential Individual File, Herbert Hoover Papers, HHPL.

12. Ibid.; New York *World*, August 5, 1914, p. 3; *New York Tribune*, August 5, 1914, p. 3; Lou Henry Hoover to her parents, August 22, 1914; Herbert Hoover to Walter Hines Page, September 23, 1914, "American Citizens Committee—London," Pre-Commerce Papers, Hoover Papers. The New York *World* and *New York Tribune* both mentioned Hoover by name. According to their accounts, Hoover announced that he would continue to aid American travelers as long as his currency lasted.

13. New York *World*, August 6, 1914, p. 3.

14. Ibid.; *New York Times*, August 6, 1914, p. 3.

15. Secretary of State William Jennings Bryan to Walter Hines Page, August 5, 1914 (received in London, August 6), Page Papers; New York *World*, August 6, 1914, p. 3, and August 7, 1914, p. 3; Henry Breckinridge, *Report on Operations of United States Relief Commission in Europe* (Washington, D.C., 1914), pp. 1–2, copy in Reprint File, HHPL; Henry Breckinridge oral history interview, 1953, p. 138, Columbia University Oral History Collection.

16. *New York Tribune*, August 6, 1914, p. 5.

17. *New York Times*, August 7, 1914, p. 3; New York *World*, August 7, 1914, p. 6.

18. *New York Tribune*, August 6, 1914, p. 3, and August 7, 1914, p. 3; New York *World*, August 7, 1914, p. 6.

19. *New York Times*, August 6, 1914, p. 3; typescript report of the Resident American Women's Relief Committee, August 15, 1914, "American Women's War Relief Fund—Reports of Activities and Finances," Subject File, Lou Henry Hoover Papers, HHPL; Lou Henry Hoover to her parents, August 22, 1914; Lou Henry Hoover, "Report of Chairman of Resident American Women's Relief Committee of London," in Breckinridge, *Report*, pp. 49–50. A typescript copy of Mrs. Hoover's report is in the American Committee Papers, HI.

20. Lou Henry Hoover to her parents, August 22, 1914. For a published photograph of the Citizens' Committee (including Mrs. Hoover), see *Outlook* 108 (September 9, 1914): 82.

21. Hoover cable to Lindon W. Bates, August 5, 1914, CRB Miscellaneous Files, HI.

22. Hoover to Page, September 23, 1914, in Breckinridge, *Report*, pp. 38–44; Breckinridge, *Report*, pp. 46, 58; Hoover cable (night letter) to Lindon W. Bates, August 6, 1914, CRB Miscellaneous Files, HI. In his cable to Bates, Hoover said: ". . . I was today elected President Relief Committee established in London by American Residents to look after the forty thousand stranded Americans. . . ."

23. Among the committee's members listed on the masthead of its stationery were several mining engineers who were close friends of Hoover: A. Chester Beatty, R. Gilman Brown, A. F. Kuehn, and Edgar Rickard. See Clarence Graff, the committee's treasurer, to Harold A. Titcomb, August 7, 1914, in Harold A. Titcomb Collection, Western History Research Center, University of Wyoming.

24. Breckinridge, *Report*, pp. 37–38.

25. Ibid., pp. 39, 46–47.

26. Hoover to Clarence L. Graff (plus enclosure), August 10, 1914, CRB Miscellaneous Files.

27. See ibid. According to this source, two other Americans—H. Gordon Selfridge and Clarence Graff—contributed the same amounts as Hoover.

28. See Graff to Titcomb, August 7, 1914.

29. Hoover to Frederick C. van Duzer, August 8, 1914, CRB Miscellaneous Files; Hoover to Page, September 23, 1914, in Breckinridge, *Report*, p. 39.

30. New York *World*, August 8, 1914, p. 4. See also *New York Times*, August 8, 1914, p. 3. The dispatch in both newspapers was dated August 7. Both stated that "an authoritative com-

mittee of Americans resident in London" had been formed in London "under official auspices" today (August 7). In fact, Hoover's Residents' Committee had already been formed on August 6 and was soliciting contributions that very day. (See Harold A. Titcomb to Clarence Graff, August 6, 1914, Titcomb Collection.) What probably occurred on August 7 was simply the announcement of the committee's formation under Ambassador Page's patronage.

31. New York *World*, August 8, 1914, p. 4.
32. Ibid.; *New York Times*, August 8, 1914, p. 3.
33. Hoover to Walter Hines Page, August 7, 1914, CRB Miscellaneous Files.
34. Hoover to van Duzer, August 8, 1914.
35. Hoover to Page, September 23, 1914, in Breckinridge, *Report*, p. 39; Kent to Joseph Chapman, September 10, 1914; Kent to a Mr. Bartlett, October 2, 1914. The New York *World*, August 23, 1914, p. 4, reported that the Committee of American Residents in London "had charge" of "financial relief" "from the beginning." This was not quite accurate; the American Citizens' Committee also distributed some relief, but only about £700. See Lou Henry Hoover's report in Breckinridge, *Report*, p. 57. The great bulk of "relief"—that is, loans and outright charity—emanated from the two committees headed by Hoover and his wife.
36. Lou Henry Hoover to her parents, August 22, 1914; Breckinridge, *Report*, pp. 30, 40, 47.
37. *New York Times*, August 9, 1914, p. 4.
38. New York *World*, August 19, 1914, p. 4; Breckinridge, *Report*, pp. 31, 41.
39. Breckinridge, *Report*, p. 51.
40. Ibid., p. 54. By mid-August large numbers of Americans were leaving Britain on ocean liners again available for Atlantic service.
41. New York *World*, August 10, 1914, p. 6, and August 29, 1914, p. 4; Breckinridge, *Report*, pp. 42, 44–46.
42. Hoover to W.A.M. Goode, August 31, 1914, CRB Miscellaneous Files.
43. Page to Wilson, August 9, 1914; *New York Tribune*, August 10, 1914, p. 3; Kent to Bartlett, October 2, 1914. At this point Ambassador Page seemed to be working most closely with Kent and the American Citizens' Committee.
44. *New York Tribune*, August 20, 1914, p. 4; Hoover to Page, September 23, 1914, in Breckinridge, *Report*, p. 40.
45. Hoover to Clarence L. Graff, August 14, 1914, CRB Miscellaneous Files. See also Hoover to Josephine Bates, December 10, 1914, ibid.
46. Breckinridge, *Report*, pp. 2–3.
47. Ibid., p. 3; Hoover to Clarence L. Graff, August 18, 1914, CRB Miscellaneous Files.
48. Breckinridge oral history, p. 149.
49. Hoover to Graff, August 18, 1914. In this letter Hoover said that he had met with Ambassador Page and the assistant secretary of the treasury. Hoover almost certainly meant Assistant Secretary of War Breckinridge.
50. *New York Times*, August 20, 1914, p. 4; *New York Tribune*, August 20, 1914, p. 4; New York *World*, August 20, 1914, p. 4. See also New York *World*. August 19, 1914, p. 4. On August 23 the *World* reported that Hoover's committee "has now taken complete charge, under direction of the Embassy, of looking after the American tourists in London" (p. 4).
51. Page to Hoover, August 20, 1914, in "Page, Walter Hines," Pre-Commerce Papers. Copy in CRB Miscellaneous Files.
52. Hoover to Page, September 23, 1914, printed in Breckinridge, *Report*, p. 40.
53. New York *World*, August 21, 1914, p. 4.
54. Ibid., August 20, 1914, p. 4; Breckinridge, *Report*, p. 41.
55. Breckinridge, *Report*, p. 48.
56. Ibid., pp. 28, 31, 32, 44, 48, 54, 55; New York *World*, August 20, 1914, p. 4; "American Relief Committee" (typescript, n.d.), in CRB Correspondence, Box 1, HI.
57. *New York Times*, September 15, 1914, p. 4; Breckinridge, *Report*, pp. 36, 41–42, 50.

58. Secretary of State Bryan to Page, August 6, 1914, Page Papers; Page cable to Bryan, September 22, 1914, file 840.48/667, RG 59, NARA; Breckinridge, *Report*, pp. 36–37, 58–59.
59. Report by Hoover's associate F. C. van Duzer, September 29, 1914, in Breckinridge, *Report*, p. 59.
60. Ambassador Page to the Secretary of State (plus enclosures), September 16, 1914, file 840.48/719, RG 59, NARA; C. H. van Tyne to Hoover, September 27, 1914, American Committee Papers; H. B. Hutchins to Hoover, October 2, 1914, ibid.; van Tyne to Hoover, October 2, 1914, ibid.; Hutchins to Hoover, October 20, 1914, ibid.; Page to the Secretary of State (plus enclosures), October 23, 1914, file 840.48/888, RG 59, NARA.
61. Hoover to Lindon W. Bates, October 2, 1914, CRB Correspondence, Box 32.
62. Breckinridge, *Report*, pp. 37, 53–54.
63. Hoover to Bates, October 2, 1914. In this letter Hoover mistakenly identified Breckinridge as "Bainbridge." Mrs. Hoover also seemed annoyed by the paperwork and rigid rules of the government commission. See her report, in Breckinridge, *Report*, pp. 53–54.
64. *New York Times*, September 15, 1914, p. 4; New York *World*, September 15, 1914, copy in American Relief Committee News Cuttings, HHPL.
65. Hoover, *Years of Adventure*, p. 147; Will Irwin, *Herbert Hoover: A Reminiscent Biography* (New York, 1928), p. 128.
66. New York *World*, August 29, 1914, p. 4, and August 30, 1914, p. 5; *New York Times*, September 6, 1914, p. 4, September 10, 1914, p. 4, and September 12, 1914, p. 4; Hoover to Page, September 23, 1914, in Breckinridge, *Report*, pp. 39–40, 42; Mrs. Hoover's report, ibid., p. 52.
67. "The American Committee" (printed leaflet, October 10, 1914), in Ben S. Allen Papers, Box 2, HI; "American Relief Committee" (typescript, n.d.; see note 56). See also Breckinridge, *Report*, pp. 37, 41.
68. Hoover to Timothy Hopkins, October 7, 1914, CRB Correspondence, Box 1.
69. Breckinridge, *Report*, pp. 28–29, 43; "The American Committee" (leaflet).
70. Breckinridge, *Report*, p. 38.
71. Hoover to Page, September 23, 1914, in ibid., pp. 38–39; Hoover, *Years of Adventure*, pp. 141–43. Mrs. Hoover also made the same mistake, asserting in her report (printed in Breckinridge, *Report*, p. 49) that *both* the American Citizens' Committee and Hoover's Residents' Committee had begun *simultaneously*, on August 3, and that both were "in vigorous operation" by Tuesday, August 4. In fact, Mrs. Hoover's letter to her parents on August 22, as well as newspaper reports printed on August 5 and 6, clearly indicate that the Hoovers' involvement began on August 4 and that the Hoovers' two relief committees were formally organized after the Kent/Hetzler/Straus group met at the Waldorf Hotel. This chronology is consistent with Consul-General Robert Skinner's recollection that Hoover "set up shop" at the American consulate on August 4.

    Both Hoovers' reports, written in September 1914, noticeably minimized the work of the American Citizens' Committee. Some weeks later Hoover privately charged that "the Tourists Committee" had "quietly folded its tent and walked away" after "carefully providing itself with transportation." The "real work," he asserted, had been done by the Residents' Committee. See Hoover to Josephine Bates, December 10, 1914.
72. Hoover, *An American Epic*, vol. 1 (Chicago, 1959), p. 1. In his *Memoirs* (*Years of Adventure*, p. 143) Hoover stated that his associates "insisted" that he "direct the refugee work"—again implying reluctance on his part to do so. I have found no evidence of such hesitation in the contemporary documents.
73. Hoover, *Years of Adventure*, pp. 142–43. According to Hoover the Citizens' Committee agreed and disbanded "a few days later." The committee did not, of course, dissolve until the latter part of August.
74. Certainly the extensive press reports failed to mention it.
75. Page to Wilson, August 9, 1914.

76. Page to Bryan, September 16, 1914; Page to Edward M. House, September 22, 1914, Edward M. House Papers, Yale University Library.
77. Page to Hoover, August 20, 1914.
78. F. Hessenberg to [Hoover?], September 23, 1914, "American Citizens' Relief Committee," Subject File, Lou Henry Hoover Papers; Lou Henry Hoover to a Miss McLeod, September 28, 1914, "American Women's War Relief Fund, 1914–15," Subject File, ibid.; *The American Committee: Report Embracing the Work of Committee from Its Inception on August 4th [sic] 1914, to September 25th, 1915* (booklet, 1915), especially p. 18, in CRB Miscellaneous Files.
79. *The American Committee: Report*, p. 9.
80. *New York Tribune*, October 10, 1914, p. 3.
81. Hoover, *Years of Adventure*, p. 140. Hoover added: "The substance and bottom seemed to go out of everything."
82. Ibid., p. 148.

CHAPTER 2

1. The Hoovers' reports are printed in Henry Breckinridge, *Report on Operations of United States Relief Commission in Europe* (Washington, D. C., 1914), pp. 38–44, 49–58, copy in Reprint File, HHPL.
2. Hoover Calendar, HHPL; Hoover to Lindon W. Bates, October 2, 1914, CRB Correspondence, Box 32, HI.
3. Hoover to Ray Lyman Wilbur, August 4, 1914, Ray Lyman Wilbur Personal Papers, Box 31, Stanford University Archives.
4. Hoover to Bates, October 2, 1914.
5. Hoover to William J. Cox, September 15, 1914, "AIMME—Personal Correspondence," Pre-Commerce Papers, Herbert Hoover Papers, HHPL.
6. Hoover to Timothy Hopkins, October 7, 1914, CRB Correspondence, Box 1.
7. Hoover to Cox, September 15, 1914; Hoover to Bates, October 2, 1914.
8. Hoover to Henry W. Hill, October 1, 1914, "Hill, C.-J. S.," Pre-Commerce Papers.
9. Hoover to Hopkins, October 7, 1914.
10. Hoover to Bates, October 2, 1914. He told another correspondent that "about all we can do is to nurse our pinched fingers." Hoover to A. H. Ackerman, October 7, 1914, "Mining—Correspondence: Ackerman, A. H.," Pre-Commerce Papers.
11. Hoover to L. W. Mayer, September 9, 1914, Sir A. Chester Beatty Papers, Selection Trust, Ltd., London, U.K.
12. Mayer to Hoover, October 13, 1914, ibid.
13. For the effect of the outbreak of World War I upon Belgium, see: Vernon Kellogg, "The Authentic Story of Belgian Relief," *World's Work* 34 (June 1917): 169–71; Tracy B. Kittredge, "The History of the Commission for Relief in Belgium, 1914–1917" (unpublished bound page proof version, ca. 1918), pp. 6–9, copy at HHPL; Arthur Marwick, *The Deluge: British Society and the First World War* (Boston, 1966), p. 43; E. H. Kossman, *The Low Countries, 1780–1940* (Oxford, 1978), pp. 522–23. An especially dramatic account by a witness is Brand Whitlock, *Belgium: A Personal Narrative* (New York, 1919).
14. Hugh Gibson to his mother, September 1, 1914, Hugh Gibson Papers, Box 32, HI.
15. *Rapport général sur le fonctionnement et les opérations du Comité National de Secours et d'Alimentation*, part 1: *Le Comité National: Sa fondation, son statut, son fonctionnement* (Brussels, 1919), pp. 22–23, 351–52; Fernand Vanlangenhove, "Dannie Heineman: La vocation internationale d'un grand ingénieur au siècle de l'électricité,"[Belgium, Académie Royale des Sciences, des Lettres, et des Beaux-Arts] *Bulletin de la classe des lettres et des sciences morales et politiques*, 5th ser., 63(1977): 17–18 (full article: 13–56); Kittredge, "History," pp. 11–14; Millard Shaler, "Mr. Shaler's Notes Regarding the Beginning of the Provisioning of Belgium" (typescript, ca.

November 1, 1914), CRB Correspondence, Box 31; Millard Shaler et al., "Development of the Relief Movement: Organisation of the Commission for Relief in Belgium" (typescript, ca. November 17, 1916), and particularly enclosures nos. 17–20, in American Embassy, London, Correspondence, 1914, vol. 47, file 848—Belgium, RG 84, NARA. The latter source is a succinct narrative buttressed with copies of more than two dozen original documents pertaining to the origins of the relief. It is thus a minidocumentary history of considerable usefulness. For the probable identity of Shaler's coauthors, see note 26.

16. The sources cited in the previous footnote tell this story in detail. See also Hugh Gibson to his mother, September 22, 1914, Gibson Papers, Box 32. A convenient summary is Kittredge, "History," pp. 14–16, 33–35. See also Kellogg, "Authentic Story of Belgian Relief," pp. 171–73. The German-speaking Heineman was a key figure in obtaining the Germans' promise of nonrequisition.

17. Millard Shaler to Brand Whitlock, September 29, 1914, in American Legation, Brussels, Correspondence, 1914, file 848, RG 84, NARA; Walter Hines Page to Whitlock, October 2, 1914, ibid.; *New York Tribune*, September 30, 1914, p. 3, and October 13, 1914, p. 2; Shaler et al., "Development of the Relief Movement," including enclosures nos. 2 and 3.

18. Kittredge, "History," pp. 35–36; Shaler, "Mr. Shaler's Notes"; Shaler et al., "Development of the Relief Movement"; Gibson to his mother, October 5 and 11, 1914, Gibson Papers, Box 32.

19. E. W. Smith (of the Board of Trade), memorandum, October 23, 1914, FO 371/1911/63254, PRO.

20. Ibid. Smith recorded that "there was never any idea that the permit was issued on condition that this particular procedure should be adopted."

21. Walter Hines Page to Secretary of State William Jennings Bryan, October 6, 1914, file 855.48/1, RG 59, NARA.

22. Secretary of State Bryan to Ambassador James Gerard (in Berlin), October 7, 1914, ibid.

23. Kittredge, "History," p. 16.

24. Hugh Gibson memorandum to Belgian legation, October 1, 1914; Gibson to American Consul-General, Antwerp, October 1, 1914. Included as enclosures nos. 2 and 3 of Shaler et al., "Development of the Relief Movement."

25. *The Times* (London), October 13, 1914, p. 11.

26. Shaler et al., "Development of the Relief Movement." The names of Shaler's coauthors of this important account are not entirely clear on the original document, but they appear to be Hoover's and Gibson's. This is a very logical—and likely—possibility, and accordingly I shall consider Hoover and Gibson as coauthors along with Shaler.

27. The precise date of Hoover's first involvement in Belgian relief—a matter of more than ordinary biographical interest—is uncertain. Years later, in his *Memoirs* and elsewhere, Hoover recalled that Shaler came to him shortly after reaching London in late September and that he, Hoover, soon introduced him to Ambassador Page—*before* Page's cable to Washington on October 6. Hoover's memory was at least partially in error; Shaler in fact never met Page before October 16. See Hoover, *The Memoirs of Herbert Hoover*, vol. 1: *Years of Adventure, 1874–1920* (New York, 1951), p. 152; Hoover, *An American Epic*, vol. 1 (Chicago, 1959), pp. 1–2; Shaler to Hugh Gibson, October 16, 1914, in American Legation, Brussels, Correspondence, 1914, file 848, RG 84, NARA. In this letter Shaler stated that he had not yet met Ambassador Page.

In 1916 Edgar Rickard stated that Hoover conferred with Ambassador Page about Belgian relief as early as October 4, 1914 (see Rickard to Hoover, May 10, 1916, CRB Correspondence, Box 6). I find no evidence for this assertion; the Shaler–Hoover–Gibson narrative written in November 1916 ("Development of the Relief Movement") makes no mention of such an early meeting. Rickard's letter was written at a time when he and Hoover were anxious to assert their precedence over the relief organization established inside Belgium by the Belgians, and it contains a number of inaccurate and dubious claims.

One other source ascribes to Hoover an active interest in Belgian relief prior to October 6, 1914: the published journal of the diplomat Hugh Gibson. Gibson's published entry for October 5, 1914 records that Shaler had already discussed Belgian relief with Hoover, "who has given some very helpful ideas and may do more still." This is certainly possible, but there is a difficulty with the source: Gibson's "journal" in reality consisted of excerpts of letters written to his mother at the time, and the reference to Hoover quoted here is not found in the original letter. It was added later. When Gibson published his *Journal* in 1917, in fact, he included many key passages that do not exist in his original correspondence home. A number of these passages contain flattering references to Herbert Hoover, by then a world-famous figure and a close personal friend. Just when Gibson composed these additional passages—and why—is uncertain. Gibson later denied that he "touched up" his account of Hoover's role in the founding of Belgian relief, but he did admit to discussing the origins of the relief with Hoover prior to publishing the *Journal* and to then correcting one "mistake." See Hugh Gibson, *A Journal from Our Legation in Belgium* (New York, 1917), p. 261; Gibson to his mother, September 19, 1917, Gibson Papers, Box 34. In preparing my own account of Hoover's role in the founding of the Belgian relief, I have relied on Gibson's original letters to his mother, not the altered versions published in his *Journal*.

In short, there is no conclusive evidence that Hoover had any active association with Belgian relief matters prior to October 6, 1914. The earliest unimpeachable evidence of his interest is his letter of October 8 cited in note 28. The circumstantial evidence suggests a date of approximately October 6.

28. Hoover to Herbert Satterlee, October 8, 1914, CRB Correspondence, Box 1.
29. Page, address to the National Committee for Relief in Belgium, June 15, 1917, quoted in *The Morning Post* (London), June 16, 1917, p. 6. In his speech Page did not give the date of Hoover's visit. But the Shaler–Hoover–Gibson account written in November 1916, cited above, states that Hoover, after studying the Belgian refugee problem, "finally broached the matter" to Page on October 10 and informed him that the crisis in Belgium itself seemed "much more critical." Kittredge, "History," pp. 37–38, evidently following this source, stated that Hoover's interview with Page occurred on October 10. This seems correct; it was evidently Hoover's first conference with Page about Belgium's plight. As noted above (note 27), Edgar Rickard stated that Hoover first met Page on October 4 (thereby asserting a role for Hoover prior to Page's cable of October 6), but I have found no corroboration anywhere of this assertion.

In 1916 Page wrote to Hoover that the Belgian relief endeavor "came into being around you and *at your suggestion* [emphasis added] and in response to your impulse to do this work of philanthropy." Page's letter was probably written at Hoover's instigation. Nevertheless, he signed it, and it provides further confirmation of the point made in the text: that it was Hoover who first approached Page (not vice versa) with the idea of providing humanitarian assistance for Belgium. Years later Hoover understated his initiatives at this point, but in 1916 he was anxious to establish the fact; hence Page's letter. See Page to Hoover, February 25, 1916, photostat copy in George I. Gay and H. H. Fisher, *Public Relations of the Commission for Relief in Belgium* (Stanford, Calif., 1929), I, opposite p. 18; hereinafter cited as *PR-CRB*.

For the context of Page's letter of February 25, 1916, see chapter 7.
30. Shaler et al., "Development of the Relief Movement."
31. Ibid.
32. *New York Herald*, October 15, 1914, p. 12. This interview took place on October 14 and was reported in America the next day.
33. Shaler et al., "Development of the Relief Movement."
34. *New York Herald*, October 15, 1914, p. 12.
35. The State Department was still waiting for a reply from Germany.
36. See my volume, *The Life of Herbert Hoover: The Engineer, 1874–1914* (New York, 1983), especially pp. 541–59.

37. Ibid., pp. 558–59, 574; Kittredge, "History," pp. 39–40.

38. *New York Tribune,* October 7, 1914, p. 2, and October 11, 1914, p. 3; Kittredge, "History," pp. 38–39.

39. *New York Times,* October 13, 1914, p. 2; *New York Tribune,* October 13, 1914, p. 2; *PR-CRB,* I, p. 9, n. 10.

40. Shaler admitted, "We have . . . been getting at State Dept. through Patchin. . . ." Shaler to his wife, October 14, 1914, Tracy B. Kittredge Papers, HI.

41. *New York Times,* October 18, 1914, p. 2; *New York Tribune,* October 18, 1914, p. 3; Shaler et al., "Development of the Relief Movement"; Shaler, "Mr. Shaler's Notes."

42. Shaler et al., "Development of the Relief Movement."

43. Ambassador Gerard to the Secretary of State, October 17, 1914, file 855.48/5, RG 59, NARA.

44. Acting Secretary of State Robert Lansing to Page, October 19, 1914, ibid.

45. *New York Tribune,* October 19, 1914, p. 1.

46. Kittredge, "History," pp. 19, 21, 25–26, 42–43.

47. Ibid., pp. 43–46; minutes of the meeting of the Comité Central de Secours et d'Alimentation, October 15, 1914, in Shaler et al., "Development of the Relief Movement," enclosure no. 25, and in *Rapport général . . . du Comité National,* part 1, pp. 352–58; Vanlangenhove, "Dannie Heineman," p. 20.

48. Brand Whitlock to the Secretary of State, October 22, 1914 (plus twelve enclosed documents), file 855.48/33, RG 59, NARA; Allan Nevins, ed., *The Journal of Brand Whitlock* (New York, 1936), pp. 50, 53–57; Hugh Gibson to his mother, October 19 [18], 1914, Gibson Papers, Box 32; Kittredge, *History,* p. 46.

49. Gibson to his mother, October 19 [18], 1914; *Journal of Brand Whitlock,* p. 54.

50. Gibson to his mother, October 19 [18], 1914; Whitlock to Page, October 16, 1914, in American Embassy, London, Correspondence, 1914, vol. 47, file 848—Belgium, RG 84, NARA; minutes of the meeting of the Comité Central, October 15, 1914.

51. Whitlock to Woodrow Wilson, October 16, 1914, printed in *Journal of Brand Whitlock,* p. 56, and in United States, Department of State, *Papers Relating to the Foreign Relations of the United States, 1914, Supplement* (Washington, D.C., 1928), p. 811.

52. Whitlock to the Secretary of State, October 16, 1914, file 855.48/7, RG 59, NARA.

53. Whitlock to Page, October 16, 1914.

54. According to Gibson, Francqui and Lambert "croaked failure from the first." Gibson to his mother, October 23, 1914, Gibson Papers, Box 32.

55. *New York Tribune,* October 19, 1914, p. 1; Shaler, "Mr. Shaler's Notes"; Gibson to his mother, October 20, 1914, Gibson Papers, Box 32.

56. Kittredge, "History," pp. 41, 47.

57. Gibson to his mother, October 20, 1914; Shaler, "Mr. Shaler's Notes."

58. Brand Whitlock, *Belgium: A Personal Narrative* (New York, 1919), p. 399.

59. Nash, *Life of Herbert Hoover: The Engineer,* pp. 179–80, 210–11.

60. Ibid., pp. 161, 165; *Journal of Brand Whitlock,* p. 55; Whitlock, *Belgium: A Personal Narrative,* pp. 346–47; *New York Times,* November 17, 1935, section 2, p. 11; *The Times* (London), November 18, 1935, p. 19; entry for Francqui in Académie Royale des Sciences Coloniales, *Biographie coloniale belge,* vol. 4 (Brussels, 1955), pp. 311–19; Liane Ranieri, *Emile Francqui, ou l'intelligence créatrice, 1863–1935* (Paris, 1985), chaps. 1–4.

61. Whitlock, *Belgium: A Personal Narrative,* p. 400.

62. Ibid., p. 398.

63. Joseph C. Green, "Some Portraits: Emile Francqui" (typescript, February 15, 1917), Joseph C. Green Papers, Box 20, HI. Green was not present at this conversation, and his anecdote is accordingly derivative. But to this author it has the ring of verisimilitude.

64. Dannie Heineman to Firmin van Brée, March 25, 1955, "Van Brée, Firmin," Name File, Belgian American Educational Foundation Papers, HHPL.

65. Hoover, *Years of Adventure*, pp. 153–54.

66. According to one of Hoover's recollections, Francqui and Lambert stated at this meeting that Belgium had food left for only thirty-six hours! This seems unlikely; Francqui had just told the Comité Central pn October 15 that Brussels, at least, had enough flour available for four to six weeks. Brand Whitlock gave Belgium two weeks (not thirty-six hours) before starvation would set in. Notes of Burton J. Hendrick's interview with Hoover, n.d. (early 1920s), Walter Hines Page Papers, Harvard University; Kittredge, "History," p. 44; Whitlock to President Wilson, October 16, 1914.

67. Kittredge, "History," p. 48; Hoover–Hendrick interview notes, Page Papers. According to Hoover, when the conversation at the October 19 meeting turned to the question of a director of the relief effort, Ambassador Page instantly turned to him and said, "Hoover, you're it!" Hendrick used this anecdote in his *Life and Letters of Walter Hines Page* (Garden City, N.Y., 1922), II, p. 311.

68. Hoover, *Years of Adventure*, p. 155. Hoover recalled here that he gave this response a day later, after thinking the matter over.

69. Hoover to Whitlock, October 20, 1914, in *PR-CRB*, I, p. 16.

70. Hoover memorandum for Page, October 20, 1914, printed in *PR-CRB*, I, pp. 13–16.

71. Shaler, "Mr. Shaler's Notes"; Hoover to Page, October 20, 1914, CRB Correspondence, Box 1; *New York Times*, October 21, 1914, p. 2. In his letter to Page, Hoover said: "I am making the necessary applications to the Board of Trade for permits to export these various materials. . . ." He did not state, however, precisely when (or whether) he had done so.

72. Shaler, "Mr. Shaler's Notes"; Hoover statement to the American press, October 22, 1914, printed in *PR-CRB*, I, p. 18. See also Hoover to Messrs. William H. Pim, Jr. & Co., October 21, 1914, CRB Correspondence, Box 1.

73. Hoover memorandum to Page, October 20, 1914; Shaler et al., "Development of the Relief Movement"; *New York Tribune*, October 24, 1914, p. 2; *Rapport général . . . du Comité National*, part 1, pp. 54, 359.

74. *New York Times*, October 21, 1914, p. 2; *New York Tribune*, October 21, 1914, p. 3.

75. Lansing to Page, October 20, 1914, file 855.48/7, RG 59, NARA.

76. Hugh Gibson to his mother, October 20, 1914; *New York Times*, October 21, 1914, p. 2; A. Nicolson (of the British Foreign Office) to Page, October 20, 1914, in American Embassy, London, Correspondence, 1914, vol. 47, file 848—Belgium, RG 84, NARA.

77. Prime Minister H. H. Asquith to Venetia Stanley, October 21, 1914, in Michael and Eleanor Brock, eds., *H. H. Asquith: Letters to Venetia Stanley* (New York, 1982), p. 281.

78. *New York Times*, October 21, 1914, p. 2.

79. Nicolson to Page, October 20, 1914.

80. Hugh Gibson to his mother, October 23, 1914; Hoover to Oscar Crosby, June 30, 1915, CRB Correspondence, Box 14. Hoover told Crosby that Asquith and Grey promised the subsidy "subject to Cabinet" approval.

81. *New York Times*, October 22, 1914, p. 2; *New York Tribune*, October 22, 1914, p. 2.

82. Gibson to his mother, October 22, 1914, p. 2.

83. Asquith to Venetia Stanley, October 21, 1914; Asquith to Sir Edward Grey, October 21, 1914, FO 800 / 100 / 322-23, PRO; Edward David, ed., *Inside Asquith's Cabinet: From the Diaries of Charles Hobhouse* (New York, 1977), pp. 201–2.

84. Specifically, the British government decided "not to interfere with any food supplies going from neutral countries to Rotterdam to be distributed to the civil population of Belgium" and controlled by the American and Spanish ministers in Brussels. Sir Edward Grey to the Belgian Minister of the Interior, October 22, 1914, copy in American Embassy, London, Correspondence, 1914, vol. 47, file 848—Belgium, RG 84, NARA.

85. Ibid.; Asquith to King George V, October 22, 1914, Cab. 41 / 35 / 54, PRO; Hoover to Crosby, June 30, 1915. For the Asquith government's public explanation of this decision,

see Great Britain, Parliament, House of Commons, *Parliamentary Debates*, 5th ser., 68(1914): 416–17.

86. Gibson to his mother, October 23, 1914.

87. Ibid.; *New York Times*, October 25, 1914, p. 3; Page to Walter Runciman (president of the Board of Trade), October 26, 1914, in *PR-CRB*, I, p. 19; memorandum by Sir Edward Grey, October 25, 1914, ibid., pp. 120–21; *New York Times*, October 27, 1914, p. 3; Runciman to Page, October 27, 1914, in American Embassy, London, Correspondence, 1914, vol. 47, file 848—Belgium, RG 84, NARA; Page to Henry van Dyke, October 31, 1914, ibid.; Hoover to E. Wildbore Smith, October 28, 1914, CRB Correspondence, Box 1; *New York Times*, October 31, 1914, p. 4. The first food shipment from England did not leave until October 30.

88. Rickard's later account of this episode is printed in *Canadian Mining Institute Bulletin* (May 1917): 421. This same anecdote is recounted in Lewis R. Freeman, "Hoover and the Belgians," *Outlook* 111 (September 8, 1915): 82. Neither Richard nor Freeman identified the British Cabinet official, but he appears to have been the president of the Board of Trade, Walter Runciman, or possibly his associate, E. Wildbore Smith.

89. Hoover to Harold Fowler, October 22, 1914, in American Embassy, London, Correspondence, 1914, vol. 47, file 848—Belgium, RG 84, NARA. In this letter Hoover said that the Belgian legation had applied for permission to export "three days ago"—meaning October 19 or (if he was counting the day of his letter) October 20.

90. Ibid. He told Fowler in this letter that "we cannot begin loading until we get" the requisite export license, something that he did not yet have.

91. Page to Runciman, October 26, 1914; Hoover to E. Wildbore Smith, October 28, 1914.

92. Hoover, undated typewritten draft of an essay or speech on the role of American engineers in the American Committee and the early Belgian relief movement, in American Committee Papers, HI. Although this draft is undated, internal evidence suggests that Hoover composed it in the autumn of 1914, within a few weeks (at most) of the founding of the Commission for Relief in Belgium.

93. Ibid.

94. Rickard's account, cited in note 88.

95. Minutes of the founding meeting of the Commission for Relief in Belgium, October 22, 1914, as published in *PR-CRB*, I, pp. 16–17. See also Millard Shaler's cable to Thomas F. Ryan, October 22, 1914, Rockefeller Foundation archives, RG 1.1, Series 100, Box 66, Folder 653, Rockefeller Archive Center, North Tarrytown, New York. Hugh Gibson's letter to his mother on October 23, 1914 alludes briefly to this meeting.

96. Hoover, *Years of Adventure*, p. 157; Hoover, *An American Epic*, I, p. 4. The published minutes (in *PR-CRB*, I, pp. 16–17) of the October 22, 1914 meeting of Hoover's relief commission do not mention any decision to hire an accounting firm. In early 1916, however, Hoover had occasion to submit to Ambassador Page what he said was a copy of "the shorthand note" of this founding meeting. This version of the minutes includes an item recording the decision to retain Deloitte, Plender, Griffiths & Co. See Hoover to Walter Hines Page, February 21, 1916 (plus enclosure), in American Embassy, London, Correspondence, 1916, vol. 109, file 848—Belgian Relief, RG 84, NARA.

Thus there exist two versions—one published, one not—of the proceedings of the founding session of the Commission for Relief in Belgium. Curiously, the two documents differ considerably in appearance. The printed version is little more than a list of decisions taken; the version sent to Ambassador Page contains not only a list but a lengthy summary of Hoover's remarks to his colleagues. Furthermore, the lists of the actions taken at the meeting are not identical. While the documents do not contradict each other, each contains entries not included in the other version.

It has not been possible to resolve these puzzling discrepancies. Conceivably two different people kept notes at the meeting. Perhaps someone prepared the summaries afterward at different times. Whatever the explanation, at its initial meeting (or soon afterward) Hoover's commission did select a distinguished accounting firm to audit its books. In mid-November Hoover so informed Emile Francqui. See Hoover to Francqui, November 14, 1914, in *PR-CRB*, I, p. 35.

97. Hoover statement to the American press, October 22, 1914; Kittredge, "History," pp. 50–51; Whitlock to Hoover, October 25, 1914, in *PR-CRB*, I, p. 19; Hoover to Sr. Merry del Val, October 25, 1914, CRB Correspondence, Box 1; Kellogg, "Authentic Story of the Belgian Relief," p. 175.

98. Woodrow Wilson, remarks at his press conference of October 22, 1914, printed in Arthur S. Link et al., eds., *The Papers of Woodrow Wilson*, vol. 31 (Princeton, N.J., 1979), p. 206; *New York Times*, October 23, 1914, p. 3.

99. Hoover to Page, October 22, 1914, in American Embassy, London, Correspondence, 1914, vol. 47, file 848—Belgium, RG 84, NARA.

100. Hoover statement to the American press, October 22, 1914. One version, already cited, is printed in *PR-CRB*, I, pp. 17–18; in this form it appeared in the *New York Sun*, October 23, 1914. The original text of the press release, which differs slightly and is the one quoted here, is in Shaler et al., "Development of the Relief Movement," enclosure no. 15.

101. Hoover to Page, October 22, 1914.

102. Hoover to Fowler, October 22, 1914.

103. Hoover statement to the American press, October 22, 1914; Kittredge, "History," p. 50.

104. Gibson to his mother, October 23, 1914; Kittredge, "History," pp. 51, 76–77; Kellogg, "Authentic Story of the Belgian Relief," p. 175.

105. Whitlock, *Belgium: A Personal Narrative*, p. 399

106. Hoover, *Years of Adventure*, p. 156; Hoover–Hendrick interview notes. Hoover told Hendrick that everyone thought the war would end in three or four months.

107. Will Irwin, *Herbert Hoover: A Reminiscent Biography* (New York, 1928), p. 134.

108. *The Times* (London), October 24, 1914, p. 8; Hoover statement to the American press, October 22, 1914.

109. Hoover, *Years of Adventure*, pp. 152–55; Hoover, *An American Epic*, I, pp. 2–3; Hoover–Hendrick interview notes. Hoover erroneously indicated in the first two sources cited that his conference with Francqui et al. occurred on October 18. The meeting took place a day later.

110. Shaler to Gibson, October 16, 1914.

111. I have found no corroboration for Hoover's later assertion that he drafted the cable that Page dispatched to the secretary of state on October 6. This claim is also made in *PR-CRB*, I, p. 3. Significantly, however, the elaborate Shaler–Hoover–Gibson narrative of November 1916 ("Development of the Relief Movement") does not mention this point at all and in fact states that Hoover first approached Page about Belgian relief on October 10. This source is probably the most accurate one.

112. In his *Memoirs* (*Years of Adventure*, p. 155), Hoover stated that he had even booked passage to sail back to America on October 25. Then (October 18) came the telephone call from Ambassador Page. Hoover apparently did not recall the press dispatch of October 17 announcing that he would be "one of the leading members" of the prospective American relief organization.

113. Nash, *Life of Herbert Hoover: The Engineer*, pp. 509–13.

114. Irwin, *Herbert Hoover*, p. 135.

115. I shall examine Hoover's mining activities during World War I in chapter 11.

116. Lindon W. Bates to Hoover, October 19, 1914, quoted in Kittredge, "History," p. 62.

C H A P T E R   3

1. Hoover to Don Alfonso Merry del Val, October 25, 1914, CRB Correspondence, Box 1, HI.
2. Hoover to William C. Edgar, November 15, 1914, William C. Edgar and Family Papers, Box 1, Minnesota Historical Society; Hoover cable to Lindon W. Bates, November 13, 1914, CRB cable files, Pre-Commerce Papers, Herbert Hoover Papers, HHPL.
3. Hoover to Merry del Val, October 25, 1914; Hoover speech at American Luncheon Club, London, December 18, 1914, in Herbert Hoover Collection, Box 149, HI. Much of the text of this speech can also be found in the *New York Times*, December 19, 1914, p. 3.
4. Hoover speech, December 18, 1914.
5. Hoover, *An American Epic*, vol. 1 (Chicago, 1959), pp. 33, 455. According to Hoover a few members of the CRB did receive compensation after the war. During the early days of the relief Hoover often cited the voluntary service of himself and his associates as a "selling point" for his organization. See, for example, his memorandum (plus enclosures) for Sir Edward Grey, November 5, 1914, in FO 371 / 1912 / 67903, PRO; copy in CRB Miscellaneous Files, HI.
6. Hoover cable to his wife, October 26, 1914, "Hoover, Lou Henry," Pre-Commerce Papers.
7. Emile Francqui to Hoover, October 26, 1914, printed in George I. Gay and H. H. Fisher, *Public Relations of the Commission for Relief in Belgium* (Stanford, Calif., 1929), I, pp. 31–34; hereinafter cited as *PR-CRB*.
8. Janssens Wadeleux to American Commission for Relief in Belgium—Rotterdam, October 31, 1914, copy enclosed with Hoover's memorandum for Sir Edward Grey, November 5, 1914, cited in note 5.
9. Emile Devreux and Emile Buisset to Hoover, October 24, 1914, enclosed with Hoover's memorandum for Sir Edward Grey, November 5, 1914.
10. J. F. Lucey to Hoover, October 29, 1914, printed in *PR-CRB*, I, pp. 29–31; Lucey cable to Hoover, October 29, 1914, quoted in *New York Times*, October 30, 1914, p. 3.
11. Hoover cable to his wife, October 26, 1914.
12. Francqui cable to Hoover, October 26, 1914, printed in *PR-CRB*, I, p. 119.
13. Statement by the Marquis of Villalobar and Brand Whitlock, November 2, 1914, enclosed with Hoover's memorandum for Sir Edward Grey, November 5, 1914.
14. Hoover memorandum for Sir Edward Grey, November 5, 1914 (plus enclosures); Francqui cable to Hoover, October 26, 1914; Hoover cable to Mrs. Lindon Bates, October 31, 1914, in *PR-CRB*, I, p. 251; Hoover press release of October 31, 1914, printed in *New York Times*, November 1, 1914, section II, p. 6.
15. *The Times* (London), October 24, 1914, p. 8.
16. Hoover cable to Thomas F. Ryan, October 29, 1914, CRB cable files; Hoover cable to Lindon W. Bates, October 30, 1914, CRB Correspondence, Box 1; *New York Times*, November 1, 1914, section II, p. 6.
17. Hoover cable to Ryan, October 29, 1914. See also Hoover to the patron-ambassadors (honorary chairmen) of the Commission for Relief in Belgium, November 3, 1914, in American Embassy, London, Correspondence, 1914, vol. 47, file 848—Belgium, RG 84, NARA; printed in *PR-CRB*, I, pp. 20–23.
18. Hoover to Chevalier Edmond Carton de Wiart, November 4, 1914, CRB Correspondence, Box 1.
19. Hoover cable to his wife, October 26, 1914.
20. Hoover cable to various state governors, November 2, 1914, printed in *PR-CRB*, II, p. 252.
21. Hoover cable to Governor Francis McGovern, November 2, 1914, Francis McGovern Papers, Box 18, State Historical Society of Wisconsin.
22. *PR-CRB*, II, p. 252. Many such "state" ships were organized; for a list, see ibid., p. 244.
23. Hoover cable to W. J. Chambers, October 27, 1914, printed in ibid., pp. 247–48.

24. For the text of King Albert's appeal, see *New York Times*, November 1, 1914, section II, p. 6. For background on this episode, see: Hugh Gibson to his mother, October 29 and November 2, 1914, Hugh Gibson Papers, Box 32, HI; Hugh Gibson, *A Journal from Our Legation in Belgium* (New York, 1917), p. 294; *PR-CRB*, II, p. 246n.
25. *New York Times*, November 1, 1914, section II, p. 6.
26. Hoover, *An American Epic*, I, p. 30; *PR-CRB*, II, p. 240n; Hoover to Brand Whitlock, November 10, 1914, in American Legation, Brussels, Correspondence, 1914: Commission for Relief in Belgium, Part I, RG 84, NARA. The AP even transmitted direct appeals for the CRB throughout the American press—something Hoover said it had never done before.
27. *PR-CRB*, II, p. 240n.
28. Hoover cable to Lindon W. Bates, November 20, 1914, CRB Correspondence, Box 1.
29. Hoover cable to Lindon W. Bates, November 11, 1914, CRB cable files, printed in *PR-CRB*, II, pp. 255–56.
30. Ibid.; Hoover to Whitlock, November 10, 1914; Hoover to Wickliffe Rose, November 21, 1914, Rockefeller Foundation archives, RG 1.1, Series 100, Box 66, Folder 653, Rockefeller Archive Center, North Tarrytown, New York; Will Irwin, *The Making of a Reporter* (New York, 1942), pp. 254, 256. Irwin remained with the CRB's New York office until the end of January 1915.
31. Hoover to Emile Francqui, November 14, 1914, in American Legation, Brussels, Correspondence, 1914: Commission for Relief in Belgium, Part II, RG 84, NARA; mostly printed in *PR-CRB*, I, pp. 34–38.
32. Hoover to Whitlock, November 10, 1914. See also Hoover to Rose, November 21, 1914.
33. *PR-CRB*, II, p. 246n. For Goode's prewar association with Hoover, see my volume, *The Life of Herbert Hoover: The Engineer, 1874–1914* (New York, 1983), pp. 547–58.
34. *PR-CRB*, II, p. 245.
35. Ibid., p. 245n; Suzanne Tassier, *La Belgique et l'entrée en guerre des Etats-Unis, 1914–1917* (Brussels, 1951), pp. 79–80.
36. Hoover cable to Lindon W. Bates, November 20, 1914, CRB cable files.
37. Will Irwin cable to Hoover, November 16, 1914, ibid.
38. *PR-CRB*, II, p. 246.
39. Hoover to Brand Whitlock, November 4, 1914, in American Legation, Brussels, Correspondence, 1914, file 848—Belgium, RG 84, NARA.
40. William Goode to Melville Stone, December 7, 1914, CRB cable files.
41. *New York Times*, November 25, 1914, p. 3; Hoover to Sir Edward Grey, November 25, 1914, Cab. 37 / 122 / 201, PRO, printed in *PR-CRB*, I, pp. 221–22.
42. Will Irwin cables to Hoover, November 16, 17, and 20, 1914, CRB cable files.
43. Hoover to Whitlock, November 10, 1914.
44. Ibid.
45. Hoover, quoted in Victoria French Allen, "The Outside Man" (typescript, n.d.), p. 166, HHPL.
46. Hoover to Lindon W. Bates, August 31, 1915, printed in *PR-CRB*, II, pp. 268–70.
47. Hoover cable to Ryan, October 29, 1914; Hoover cable to Mrs. Lindon Bates, October 31, 1914; Hoover press release of October 31, 1914, printed in *New York Times*, November 1, 1914, section II, p. 6.
48. Hoover cable to Ryan, October 29, 1914; Hoover press release of October 31, 1914. Hoover personally wrote this press release. Allen, "The Outside Man," pp. 146–48.
49. Walter Hines Page cable to the Secretary of State, October 26, 1914, file 855.48 / 10, RG 59, NARA.
50. Allen, "The Outside Man," p. 146.
51. Hoover cable to Lindon W. Bates, November 11, 1914, CRB cable files; printed in *PR-CRB*, II, pp. 255–56.
52. Hoover to Brand Whitlock (plus enclosures), December 14, 1914, in American Legation,

Brussels, Correspondence, 1914, file 848—Belgium, RG 84, NARA.

53. Allen, "The Outside Man," pp. 146–49.

54. Ibid., p. 149.

55. William Goode, letter to the editor, in *The Times* (London), October 2, 1928, p. 17. Eventually Hoover went to a photographer, but he forbade the circulation of photographs of himself unless specific requests were made for one. Allen, "The Outside Man," p. 149.

56. *New York Tribune*, January 10, 1915, section V, p. 3.

57. Hoover cable to Lindon W. Bates, January 23, 1915, CRB cable files.

58. *New York Times*, October 28, 1914, p. 3; J. F. Lucey report on his activities, ca. December 10, 1914, printed in United States, Department of State, *Papers Relating to the Foreign Relations of the United States, 1914, Supplement* (Washington, D.C., 1928), pp. 821–22; Tracy B. Kittredge, "The History of the Commission for Relief in Belgium, 1914–1917" (unpublished bound page proof version, ca. 1918), pp. 67–74, copy at HHPL.
    One of Lucey's assignments was to prepare daily reports suitable for release to the press.

59. Kittredge, "History," p. 172; Lucey report, ca. December 10, 1914; Emile Francqui to Hoover, November 18, 1914, CRB Correspondence, Box 15; *New York Times Magazine*, February 28, 1915, pp. 7–8.

60. Kittredge, "History," pp. 76–78, 84; *PR-CRB*, I, p. 34; Brand Whitlock diary, November 24, 1914, in Allan Nevins, ed., *The Journal of Brand Whitlock* (New York, 1936), p. 68; Ernest Mahaim, *Le Secours de chômage en Belgique pendant l'occupation allemande* (Paris, 1926), pp. 16–17; Henri Pirenne, *La Belgique et la guerre mondiale* (Paris, 1928), pp. 142–45; Liane Ranieri, *Emile Francqui, ou l'intelligence créatrice* (Paris, 1985), pp. 135–36. For a comprehensive account of the Comité National's activities and policies, see its massive *Rapport général* (1919–21), cited in chapter 2, note 15. Copies of this report are at HI and the Library of Congress.

61. Hoover cable to J. F. Lucey, October 29, 1914, in American Legation, Brussels, Correspondence, 1914: Commission for Relief in Belgium, Part I, RG 84, NARA; *New York Times*, October 31, 1914, p. 4; Hoover to Emile Francqui, October 31, 1914; CRB Correspondence, Box 1; Lucey report, ca. December 10, 1914.

62. Hoover to the CRB's patron-ambassadors, November 24, 1914, in American Legation, Brussels, Correspondence, 1914: Commission for Relief in Belgium, Part I, RG 84, NARA; Rockefeller Foundation, *Annual Report: 1913–14* (New York, 1915), p. 214.

63. Hoover cable to Ryan, October 29, 1914; Hoover memorandum for Grey, November 5, 1914.

64. Ranieri, *Emile Francqui*, pp. 122–23.

65. *New York Tribune*, October 24, 1914, p. 2; Hoover to Merry del Val, October 25, 1914; Hoover cable to Ryan, October 29, 1914.

66. Hoover to Francqui, October 31, 1914; Hoover to the CRB's patron-ambassadors, November 3, 1914, in American Embassy, London, Correspondence, 1914, vol. 47, file 848—Belgium, RG 84, NARA; printed in *PR-CRB*, I, pp. 20–23.

67. Hoover memorandum for Grey, November 5, 1914; Hoover to Carton de Wiart, November 4, 1914.

68. Hoover to Francqui, November 14, 1914; Hoover cable to Lindon W. Bates, November 15, 1914, CRB cable files; Hoover to the CRB's patron-ambassadors, November 17, 1914, in American Legation, Brussels, Correspondence, 1914: Commission for Relief in Belgium, Part I, RG 84, NARA.

69. Lindon W. Bates cables to Hoover, November 16, 18, 19, 1914, CRB cable files; *New York Times*, November 30, 1914, p. 4; Hoover to Emile Francqui, December 12, 1914, in American Legation, Brussels, Correspondence, 1914: Commission for Relief in Belgium, Part II, RG 84, NARA; *PR-CRB*, II, p. 245n.

70. Kittredge, "History," p. 72.

71. *PR-CRB*, II, pp. 182, 236–37, 469. The CRB's overhead was 0.43% of its total expenditures.

72. Hoover to Walter Hines Page, October 30, 1914, in American Embassy, London, Correspondence, 1914, vol. 47, file 848—Belgium, RG 84, NARA.
73. Hoover to Francqui, October 31, 1914.
74. Ibid.
75. Hoover to the CRB's patron-ambassadors, November 9, 1914, in American Legation, Brussels, Correspondence, 1914: Commission for Relief in Belgium, Part I, RG 84, NARA.
76. Hoover, quoted in Lewis R. Freeman, "Hoover and the Belgians," *Outlook* 111 (September 8, 1915): 82.
77. Hoover to Francqui, October 31, 1914; Hoover to the CRB's patron-ambassadors, November 3, 1914; Hoover to Carton de Wiart, November 4, 1914.
78. Hoover to the CRB's patron-ambassadors, November 3, 1914.
79. Ibid.; Hoover cable to J. F. Lucey, October 29, 1914, in American Legation, Brussels, Correspondence, 1914: Commission for Relief in Belgium, Part I, RG 84, NARA; Hoover to Francqui, October 31, 1914; Hoover to Carton de Wiart, November 4, 1914; Belgian Minister of the Interior Berryer to Belgian Minister Havenith in Washington, D.C., November 18, 1914, copy in CRB cable files; Hoover to Rose, November 21, 1914.
80. Hoover cable to Lucey, October 29, 1914.
81. Hoover to Francqui, October 31, 1914.
82. Hoover to Carton de Wiart, November 4, 1914.
83. *New York Times*, October 27, 1914, p. 1.
84. Hoover cable to Lucey, October 29, 1914.
85. Hoover memorandum for Grey, November 5, 1914 (cited in note 5); Hoover memorandum of meeting with Grey on November 5, 1914, printed in *PR-CRB*, I, pp. 217–18; Grey memorandum of this same meeting, FO 800 / 94 / 592-94, PRO. A copy of Hoover's memorandum presented to Grey (but not the supporting documents) is in *PR-CRB*, I, pp. 218–21.
86. Emile Francqui to Hoover, November 6 and 7, 1914, CRB Correspondence, Box 15; Hoover cable to Lindon W. Bates, November 15, 1914, CRB cable files; *Rapport général . . . du Comité National*, part 1, pp. 56, 369.
87. Hoover to Francqui, November 12, 1914, CRB Correspondence, Box 1. Hoover promptly released the news to the press; see *New York Times*, November 13, 1914, p. 4.
88. Hoover to Francqui, November 12, 1914; Francqui to Hoover, November 18, 1914, CRB Correspondence, Box 15; Hoover to Rose, November 21, 1914; Kittredge, "History," pp. 59–60; *PR-CRB*, II, pp. 227–28; *Rapport général . . . du Comité National*, part 1, p. 369.
89. Hoover cable to Bates, November 11, 1914.
90. *New York Times*, November 13, 1914, p. 4.
91. Hoover to Lord Eustace Percy, November 20, 1914, FO 371 / 1911 / 73581, PRO.
92. Hoover to Sir Edward Grey, November 25, 1914, FO 371 / 1911 / 75425, PRO; also in Cab. 37 / 122 / 20, PRO.
93. Percy, internal memo, November 21, 1914, FO 371 / 1911 / 73581, PRO.
94. Lou Henry Hoover (in London) to certain friends, December 14/15, 1914, copy in General Accessions—A. T. and Florence Stewart, HHPL, and printed in *San Francisco Examiner*, January 1, 1915, p. 20; Hoover to Brand Whitlock, December 16, 1914, in American Legation, Brussels, Correspondence, 1914: Commission for Relief in Belgium, Part II, RG 84, NARA.
95. Ibid,; Hoover to L. A. Jouques, November 16, 1914, "Mining—Correspondence: Jouques, L. A.," Pre-Commerce Papers.
96. *Mining News* 40 (December 3, 1914): 205.
97. *PR-CRB*, II, pp. 235–36.
98. Hoover to Rose, November 21, 1914.
99. Hoover to Francqui, November 14, 1914; Lou Henry Hoover to Mary Austin, n.d. (ca.

November 24, 1914), Mary Austin Collection, Box 11, the Huntington Library, San Marino, Calif.

100. *PR-CRB*, II, p. 238.

101. Ibid.

102. Rockefeller Foundation press release, October 30, 1914, Rockefeller Foundation archives, RG 1.1, Series 100, Box 60, Folder 587; Rockefeller Foundation, *Annual Report: 1913–14*, pp. 24–26.

103. *PR-CRB*, II, p. 237; Kittredge, "History," p. 61; Lindon W. Bates cables to Hoover, October 30 and November 8, 1914, CRB cable files: Starr Murphy memorandum re Belgian Relief Committee, November 11, 1914, Rockefeller Foundation archives, RG 1.1, Series 100, Box 66, Folder 650; *Belgian Relief Bulletin*, no. 1, November 25, 1914, copy in Rockefeller Foundation archives, RG 1.1, Series 100, Box 60, Folder 587; entry for Robert de Forest in *Dictionary of American Biography: Supplement One* (New York, 1944), pp. 236–37.

104. Millard Shaler cable to Brand Whitlock, September 29, 1914, in American Legation, Brussels, Correspondence, 1914, file 848, RG 84, NARA; Hoover cable to Lindon W. Bates, October 28, 1914, CRB Correspondence, Box 1, HI; Hoover to Bates, January 17, 1915, ibid., Box 2; Kittredge, "History," p. 61; entry for Thomas Fortune Ryan in *Dictionary of American Biography*, vol. 16 (New York, 1935), pp. 265–68.

105. *New York Times*, October 21, 1914, p. 2.

106. Millard Shaler cable to Thomas Fortune Ryan, October 22, 1914, Rockefeller Foundation archives, RG 1.1, Series 100, Box 66, Folder 653.

107. Hoover cable to Lindon W. Bates, October 28, 1914, CRB cable files; Nash, *Life of Herbert Hoover: The Engineer*, pp. 448–52, 462–65; Lindon W. Bates to the Secretary of State, November 19, 1914, file 855.48/50, RG 59, NARA. In the latter document Bates declared that he had been Hoover's "most intimate friend and business associate for many years."

108. Bates cable to Hoover, October 29, 1914, CRB cable files. See also Hoover cable to Mrs. Lindon W. Bates, October 31, 1914; Mrs. Bates cable to Hoover, November 1, 1914, CRB cable files.

109. Sydney Ball and Lindon W. Bates cable to Hoover, October 28, 1914; Hoover cable to Ryan, October 29, 1914; both in CRB cable files. Hoover evidently did not learn of Ryan's acceptance until after Hoover had invited Bates to assist him.

110. Ryan cables to Hoover, October 30, 1914, CRB cable files.

111. *New York Times*, October 31, 1914, p. 11, and November 3, 1914, p. 5; Ryan cable to Hoover, November 2, 1914, CRB cable files.

112. *New York Times*, November 3, 1914, p. 5.

113. Robert de Forest to Hoover, October 30, 1914, in American Embassy, London, Correspondence, 1914, vol. 47, file 848—Belgium, RG 84, NARA.

114. Hoover cable to Bates, October 30, 1914, CRB cable files.

115. Ibid.; Ryan cables to Hoover, October 30, 1914, ibid.

116. Hoover to Francqui, October 31, 1914; Hoover cable to Bates, October 30, 1914.

117. Hoover cable to Ryan, November 2, 1914, CRB cable files; Hoover cable to Bates, November 2, 1914, copy in Rockefeller Foundation archives, RG 1.1, Series 100, Box 67, Folder 658.

118. Hoover cable to Robert de Forest, November 3, 1914, CRB cable files.

119. Hoover, separate cables to Ryan and Bates, November 3, 1914, ibid.

120. Ryan cable to Hoover, November 2, 1914, ibid.

121. Hoover to Walter Hines Page, November 4, 1914, in American Embassy, London, Correspondence, 1914, vol. 47, file 848—Belgium, RG 84, NARA.

122. Hoover to Carton de Wiart, November 4, 1914. See also Hoover cable to J. F. Lucey, November 4, 1914, CRB Correspondence, Box 1.

123. Hoover memorandum for Grey, November 5, 1914. It was at this meeting, of course, as

related earlier in the text, that Hoover tried unsuccessfully to obtain a transportation subsidy on the spot. Such a subvention would have eliminated any need to rely on Ryan and
de Forest. Hoover did not reveal to Grey this motive for his haste.

124. Hoover cable to Lucey, November 4, 1914.
125. Rockefeller Foundation press release dated October 31, 1914, Rockefeller Foundation
archives, RG 1.1, Series 100, Box 60, Folder 587; issued on November 1 and printed in
New York Times, November 2, 1914, pp. 1, 6.
126. Hoover cable to John D. Rockefeller, Jr., November 2, 1914, CRB cable files.
127. Walter Hines Page cable to Starr Murphy, November 2, 1914, Rockefeller Foundation
archives, RG 1.1, Series 100, Box 67, Folder 657.
128. Robert de Forest and Starr Murphy cable to Ambassador Page, November 5, 1914. Copies in Rockefeller Foundation archives, RG 1.1, Series 100, Box 67, Folder 657, and in
American Embassy, London, Correspondence, 1914, vol. 47, file 848—Belgium, RG 84,
NARA.
129. *New York Times*, November 9, 1914, pp. 1, 4.
130. See Page's notation on the incoming cable in the embassy correspondence file (cited in note
128).
131. Francqui to Hoover, November 7, 1914, mentions that the cable was sent "yesterday."
132. See Hoover to Francqui, November 12, 1914, cited in note 87.
133. Page cable to Starr Murphy (via the State Department), November 7, 1914, file 855.48/
32, RG 59, NARA; copy also in American Embassy, London, Correspondence, 1914, vol.
47, file 848—Belgium, RG 84, NARA.
134. Hoover cable to Robert de Forest, November 7, 1914, CRB cable files.
135. Millard Shaler cable to Thomas Fortune Ryan, November 7, 1914, ibid.
136. *New York Times*, November 9, 1914, p. 2.
137. Ibid., November 13, 1914, p. 4.
138. Hoover cables to Emanuel Havenith, Robert de Forest, and Lindon W. Bates, November
13, 1914, all in CRB cable files; Hoover to the CRB's patron-ambassadors, November 17,
1914.
139. Hoover cable to de Forest, November 13, 1914.
140. Hoover to Lindon W. Bates, November 13, 1914, CRB Correspondence, Box 1.
141. Hoover cable to Bates, November 15, 1914.
142. Francqui to Hoover, November 7, 1914. The Rockefeller–de Forest cable reached Hoover
sometime on the sixth.
143. Ibid. To obtain the loan, Francqui had to give two assurances: that food imported by the
CRB must not be sold in Belgium below cost, and that such food must be fully covered
against fire, war risks, and other hazards. The food itself was the only security Francqui
could offer for the £600,000 loan.
144. Ibid. Francqui's letters to Hoover said nothing about restricting the loan to transportation
expenses. In fact, his letter of November 7 clearly implied that the money would be used
by Hoover to purchase food.
145. Hoover to Francqui, November 12, 1914.
146. Hoover to Francqui, November 14, 1914.
147. Ibid.
148. Hoover cable to Lindon W. Bates, November 13, 1914, CRB cable files.
149. Hoover cable to Bates, November 11, 1914.
150. Hoover to Whitlock, November 10, 1914.
151. Bates cable to Hoover, November 1, 1914.
152. Bates cable to Hoover, November 5, 1914, CRB Correspondence, Box 13.
153. Hoover cable to his wife, November 9, 1914, CRB cable files.
154. Hoover to Bates, November 13, 1914.
155. *New York Times*, November 9, 1914, p. 4.

156. Hoover to Brand Whitlock, November 14, 1914, in American Legation, Brussels, Correspondence, 1914: Commission for Relief in Belgium, Part I, RG 84, NARA.

157. Ibid.

158. Hoover to Whitlock, November 10, 1914.

159. *New York Times*, November 9, 1914, p. 4.

160. Rockefeller Foundation, *Annual Report: 1913–14*, p. 28.

161. As it happened, Page's cable of November 7 did not reach the Rockefeller Foundation until November 9, and its reply of November 9 did not reach Hoover until November 11. To Hoover this delay was deliberate. See Hoover to Bates, November 13, 1914.

162. *New York Times*, November 10, 1914, p. 2. In all likelihood this story was generated by Hoover and transmitted to America via Ben S. Allen at the AP's office in London.

163. Starr Murphy cable to Ambassador Page, November 10, 1914. Copies in Rockefeller Foundation archives, RG 1.1, Series 100, Box 67, Folder 657; the CRB cable files at HHPL; and American Embassy, London, Correspondence, 1914, vol. 47, file 848—Belgium, RG 84, NARA.

164. Hoover cable to Starr Murphy, November 12, 1914, copies in CRB cable files and Rockefeller Foundation archives, RG 1.1, Series 100, Box 67, Folder 657.

165. Starr Murphy to John D. Rockefeller, Jr., November 20, 1914, Rockefeller Foundation archives, RG 1.1, Series 100, Box 67, Folder 657.

166. Hoover cable to Murphy, November 12, 1914.

167. Ibid.; Hoover to Bates, November 13, 1914.

168. Hoover cable to Bates, November 11, 1914; Hoover to Bates, November 13, 1914.

169. Hoover cable to Bates, November 11, 1914; Hoover cable to de Forest, November 13, 1914.

170. Hoover cable to Bates, November 13, 1914; Hoover cable to Bates, November 15, 1914, CRB Correspondence, Box 1.

171. Hoover to Bates, November 13, 1914.

172. *New York Times*, November 13, 1914, p. 4.

173. Hoover to Bates, November 13, 1914.

174. Hoover to Whitlock, November 14, 1914.

175. Hoover to Walter Hines Page, November 14, 1914, in American Embassy, London, Correspondence, 1914, vol. 47, file 848—Belgium, RG 84, NARA; Hoover cable to Bates, November 15, 1914, CRB cable files.

176. Hoover cable to Bates, November 13, 1914, CRB cable files.

177. Hoover cables to Bates, November 15, 1914; Starr Murphy to Bates, November 16, 1914, Rockefeller Foundation archives, RG 1.1, Series 100, Box 67, Folder 657.

178. Hoover cables to de Forest and Bates, November 13, 1914; Hoover cable to Emanuel Havenith, November 13, 1914, CRB cable files; Hoover to Walter Hines Page, November 13, 1914, CRB Correspondence, Box 1.

179. Hoover cable to Bates, November 15, 1914 (for transmission to the Rockefeller Foundation).

180. Bates to the Secretary of State, November 19, 1914; *New York Times*, November 20, 1914, p. 12.

181. Hoover cable to Ryan, October 29, 1914; Hoover cable to his wife, October 30, 1914, CRB cable files.

182. Hoover cable to Lucey, October 29, 1914; Hoover to Francqui, October 31, 1914; Hoover cable to Lucey, October 30, 1914, CRB Correspondence, Box 1.

183. Belgian Foreign Minister to Minister Havenith in Washington, D.C., November 3, 1914, copy in American Embassy, London, Correspondence, 1914, vol. 47, file 848—Belgium, RG 84, NARA.

184. Hoover cable to Havenith, November 3, 1914, CRB cable files; printed in *PR-CRB*, II, pp. 253–54.

185. *New York Times*, November 3, 1914, p. 5, and November 9, 1914, pp. 1, 4; Murphy–de Forest cable to Page, November 5, 1914.

186. Robert de Forest cable to Hoover, November 3, 1914, CRB cable files.

187. Hoover to Carton de Wiart, November 4, 1914.

188. Hoover cable to Lucey, November 4, 1914.

189. Lindon W. Bates cable 4 to Hoover, November 17, 1914; Bates cables 20 and 23 to Hoover, November 21, 1914; all in CRB cable files.

190. Starr Murphy memo on Belgian Relief Committee, November 11, 1914; Bates cable 4 to Hoover, November 17, 1914; Mrs. Lindon W. Bates to Hoover, November 28, 1914, "Belgian Relief," Subject File, Lou Henry Hoover Papers, HHPL. According to de Forest, Havenith was demanding the entire country for his sphere of operations and was trying to confine de Forest to the New York City area.

191. Bates and Robert McCarter cable 3 to Hoover, November 16, 1914, CRB cable files. According to Bates, Havenith was attempting to make the Washington-Baltimore branch of his relief fund the "dominant U.S. body." Bates to Mrs. Hoover, November 11, 1914, "Belgian Relief," Subject File, Lou Henry Hoover Papers.

192. Belgian Minister of the Interior Berryer to Minister Havenith in Washington, D.C., November 18, 1914 (cited in note 79); printed (under the erroneous date of November 19) in *PR-CRB*, II, p. 254.

193. Hoover cable 10 to Bates, November 18, 1914, CRB cable files.

194. Bates cable 25 to Hoover, November 22, 1914, CRB cable files.

195. Bates cable 28 to Hoover, November 23, 1914; Bates cable 30 to Hoover, November 24, 1914; both in CRB cable files.

196. Bates cable 28 to Hoover, November 23, 1914.

197. Berryer cable to Havenith, November 25, 1914, copy in CRB cable files; Hoover cable 32 to Bates, November 25, 1914, ibid.

198. Hoover cable to James Whitely, November 25, 1914, ibid.; Carton de Wiart cable to Whitely, November 25, 1914, ibid.

199. Brand Whitlock to the Secretary of State, November 29, 1914, file 855.48/68, RG 59, NARA. Whitlock's cable was sent out on the very day he met Hoover for the first time. Whitlock, *Journal*, pp. 69–70.

200. Havenith cable to Bates, November 25, 1914, quoted in Bates cable 34 to Hoover, November 25, 1914, CRB cable files.

201. Bates cable to Hoover, January 2, 1915, ibid.; Hoover to Ambassador Page, March 4, 1915, CRB Correspondence, Box 3.

202. *New York Times*, November 30, 1914, p. 4.

203. Page to Norman Hapgood, October 23, 1914, printed in *New York Times*, November 11, 1914, p. 5.

204. Page to Secretary of State Bryan and Colonel Edward M. House, November 3, 1914, file 840.48/890, RG 59, NARA.

205. Edward M. House diary, November 9, 1914, Edward M. House Papers, Yale University Library; House to Walter Hines Page, November 11, 1914, ibid., Box 86.

206. Bates cable to Hoover, November 1, 1914, CRB cable files.

207. Hoover to Bates, October 30, 1914, CRB cable files; Bates cable to Hoover, October 31, 1914, CRB Correspondence, Box 13; S. R. Bertron to Woodrow Wilson, October 31, 1914, Woodrow Wilson Papers, LC.

208. House to Page, November 11, 1914.

209. House to Woodrow Wilson, November 10, 1914, House Papers, Box 120.

210. De Forest to S. R. Bertron, November 11, 1914, ibid., Box 13.

211. *New York Times*, November 12, 1914, p. 5.

212. Bertron to House, November 13, 1914, House Papers, Box 13.

213. *Washington Post*, November 12, 1914, p. 1.

214. William C. Edgar telegram to Woodrow Wilson, November 12, 1914, Wilson Papers.
215. Woodrow Wilson, draft press release (not issued), November 14, 1914, House Papers, Box 120.
216. Hoover to William C. Edgar, November 23, 1914, CRB Correspondence, Box 1.
217. Hoover to Rose, November 21, 1914.
218. Edgar telegram to Wilson, November 12, 1914. I have not found any direct indication that Hoover inspired Edgar's telegram, but it is at least possible that he did so.
219. Will Irwin to Ben S. Allen, November 14, 1914, in a miscellaneous assortment of Ben S. Allen papers in the possession of William H. Allen of Arlington, Virginia, hereinafter cited as Allen Collection.
220. House's notation on Wilson's draft press release of November 14, 1914; Secretary of State William Jennings Bryan to Joseph Tumulty, November 14, 1914, Wilson Papers. On November 15 Irwin cabled London that the "national commission proposition" had been "killed." Irwin cable to Ben S. Allen, November 15, 1914, Allen Collection.
221. Page cable to President Wilson and the Secretary of State, November 22, 1914, file 855.48/48, RG 59, NARA.
222. Acting Secretary of State Robert Lansing cable to Page, November 23, 1914, ibid.
223. Bryan cable to Page, November 14, 1914, in American Embassy, London, Correspondence, 1914, vol. 47, file 848—Belgium, RG 84, NARA.
224. Hoover to Page (two letters), November 18, 1914, ibid.; Curtis H. Lindley to Hoover, November 18 and 23, 1914, CRB Miscellaneous Files, HI.
225. Hoover to Page, November 18, 1914 (two letters).
226. Hoover to Curtis H. Lindley, November 22, 1914, CRB Miscellaneous Files.
227. Page cable to Bryan, November 19, 1914, ibid.
228. Ben S. Allen to William Phillips, November 19, 1914, file 840.48/966, RG 59, NARA.
229. Clarence Graff to William G. McAdoo, November 18, 1914, file 855.48/59, ibid.
230. Curtis H. Lindley memo for Franklin K. Lane, n.d. (ca. November 18, 1914), in Arthur S. Link et al., eds., *The Papers of Woodrow Wilson*, vol. 31 (Princeton, N.J., 1979), pp. 331–32.
231. Franklin K. Lane to Secretary of State Bryan, November 17, 1914, file 855.48/103, RG 59, NARA.
232. Curtis H. Lindley cable to Hoover, November 21, 1914, American Committee Papers, HI; Lindley to Hoover, November 23, 1914.
233. Hoover to Curtis H. Lindley, December 7, 1914, CRB Correspondence, Box 1.
234. Bates cables to Hoover, November 13, 1914; de Forest cable to Hoover, November 15, 1914; all in CRB cable files.
235. Murphy to Bates, November 16, 1914; Bates cable 6 to Hoover, November 17, 1914, CRB cable files.
236. Hoover cable 8 to Bates (for transmittal to Rockefeller Foundation), November 18, 1914, CRB cable files.
237. Starr Murphy to John D. Rockefeller, Jr., November 20, 1914; Rockefeller Foundation's War Relief Commission memoranda, November 20 and 21, 1914, Rockefeller Foundation archives, RG 1.1, Series 100, Box 63, Folder 623; Jerome Greene cable to Wickliffe Rose, November 22, 1914, ibid., Box 67, Folder 657.
238. Nash, *Life of Herbert Hoover: The Engineer*, pp. 462–65.
239. Murphy to Rockefeller, November 20, 1914; Bates cable 19 to Hoover, November 20, 1914, CRB cable files.
240. War Relief Commission memoranda, November 20 and 21, 1914; Wickliffe Rose to Starr Murphy, November 23, 1914, Rockefeller Foundation archives, RG 1.1, Series 100, Box 66, Folder 653.
241. Rose to Murphy, November 23, 1914.
242. War Relief Commission memorandum, November 21, 1914.

243. Ibid.
244. Rose to Murphy, November 23, 1914. See also *New York Times*, November 22, 1914, section II, p. 5.
245. Hoover cable 23 to Bates, November 23, 1914, CRB cable files; Hoover to the CRB's patron-ambassadors, November 24, 1914.
246. Hoover to Alfonso Merry del Val, November 24, 1914, in American Embassy, London, Correspondence, 1914, vol. 48, file 848—Belgium, RG 84, NARA; Hoover to Grey, November 25, 1914.
247. *New York Times*, November 25, 1914, p. 3, and November 30, 1914, p. 3; Jerome Greene to Acting Secretary of State Lansing, December 1, 1914, file 855.48/61, RG 59, NARA; *New York Times*, December 2, 1914, p. 4.
248. Rockefeller Foundation, *Annual Report: 1913–14*, p. 27; *New York Times*, February 1, 1915, p. 3.
249. Rockefeller Foundation, *Annual Report: 1913–14*, pp. 26, 214.
250. Hoover to Mrs. Lindon W. Bates, December 10, 1914, CRB Correspondence, Box 1. The rivalries affected the women's division of the CRB as well. See Bates to Hoover, November 11, 1914, and Mrs. Bates to Hoover, November 28, 1914.
251. Lindon W. Bates cable 101 to Hoover, December 14, 1914, CRB Correspondence, Box 32; *New York Times*, December 17, 1914, p. 3, and December 19, 1914, p. 20.
252. Bates cable 142 to Hoover, December 26, 1914, CRB cable files; Will Irwin, confidential report on Herrick, enclosed with Hoover to Ambassador Page, January 13, 1915, in American Embassy, London, Correspondence, 1915, vol. 95, file 848—Belgium, RG 84, NARA.
253. Hoover cable 94 to Bates, December 14, 1914, CRB cable files.
254. Hoover cable to Bates, December 15, 1914, ibid.
255. Hoover cable 93 to Bates (for transmittal to Myron T. Herrick), December 14, 1914, ibid.
256. Hoover cable 103 to Bates, December 18, 1914, ibid.
257. For an account of its wartime achievements, see Percy Mitchell, *The American Relief Clearing House: Its Work in the Great War* (Paris, 1922).
258. Hoover to Bates, January 13, 1915, CRB Correspondence, Box 2.
259. Bates cable to Hoover, December 18, 1914, ibid., Box 13.
260. Bates cable to Hoover, January 2, 1915; Edward M. House to Woodrow Wilson, March 1, 1915, House Papers, Box 120.
261. Hoover to Bates, January 17, 1915, CRB Correspondence, Box 2.
262. Hoover to Bates, February 19, 1915, ibid.
263. Ibid.
264. Hoover cable 93 to Bates (for Herrick), December 14, 1914.

CHAPTER 4

1. Report by J. F. Lucey, ca. December 10, 1914, printed in United States, Department of State, *Papers Relating to the Foreign Relations of the United States, 1914, Supplement* (Washington, D.C., 1928), pp. 821–22; Tracy B. Kittredge, "The History of the Commission for Relief in Belgium, 1914–1917" (unpublished bound page proof version, ca. 1918), pp. 67–74, copy at HHPL.
2. Kittredge, "History," pp. 69–70, 73; Emile Francqui to Hoover, November 18, 1914, CRB Correspondence, Box 15, HI.
3. Francqui to Hoover, November 18, 1914.
4. Kittredge, "History," p. 87.
5. Brand Whitlock, *Belgium: A Personal Narrative* New York, 1919), I, p. 298; Whitlock to

Walter Hines Page, December 19, 1914, in American Legation, Brussels, Correspondence, 1914: Commission for Relief in Belgium, Part II, RG 84, NARA.

6. Kittredge, "History," pp. 70, 73, 78–79.

7. Brand Whitlock diary, November 7, 1914, in Allan Nevins, ed., *The Journal of Brand Whitlock* (New York, 1936), p. 65.

8. Whitlock to J. F. Lucey, November 23, 1914, and Francqui to Hoover, November 23, 1914, both quoted in Kittredge, "History," p. 89.

9. Hoover cable to Lindon W. Bates, November 10, 1914, CRB cable files, Pre-Commerce Papers, Herbert Hoover Papers, HHPL; Hoover to Francqui, November 14, 1914, in American Legation, Brussels, Correspondence, 1914: Commission for Relief in Belgium, Part II, RG 84, NARA, and mostly printed in George I. Gay and H. H. Fisher, *Public Relations of the Commission for Relief in Belgium* (Stanford, Calif., 1929), I, pp. 31–34, hereinafter cited as *PR-CRB*.

10. Rockefeller Foundation's War Relief Commission memorandum, November 20, 1914, of its visit to London, in Rockefeller Foundation archives, RG 1.1, Series 100, Box 63, Folder 623, Rockefeller Archive Center, North Tarrytown, New York; Brand Whitlock diary, November 4, 1914, in his *Journal*, p. 63.

11. "War Relief Report No. 1: Belgian Relief: Report of the War Relief Commission to the Rockefeller Foundation" (typescript: Rotterdam, January 1, 1915), pp. 16, 24, 44–45, copy in Rockefeller Foundation archives, RG 1.1, Series 100, Box 62, Folder 616. Hereinafter cited as "Report of the War Relief Commission."

12. Kittredge, "History," pp. 89–90.

13. Ibid., p. 90; Perrin C. Galpin to Hoover, November 23, 1914, CRB Correspondence, Box 17; Hoover to Galpin, November 24, 1914, ibid., Box 1; Hoover telegram to Galpin, November 26, 1914, ibid.; Perrin C. Galpin oral history interview, 1956, pp. 1–2, Columbia University Oral History Collection.

14. Hoover cable 62 to J. F. Lucey, December 4, 1914, CRB cable files; [?] to J. F. Lucey, December 4, 1914, CRB Correspondence, Box 1; *New York Times*, December 5, 1914, p. 3; Kittredge, "History," p. 90.

15. Hoover to the CRB's patron-ambassadors, December 8, 1914, in American Embassy, London, Correspondence, 1914, vol. 48, file 848—Belgium, RG 84, NARA.

16. *New York Times*, December 5, 1914, p. 3.

17. Hoover left London on November 26 and arrived in Brussels (via Rotterdam) on November 29. Hoover cable to Galpin, November 26, 1914; *New York Times*, November 26, 1914, p. 2; Hugh Gibson to his mother, November 29, 1914, Hugh Gibson Papers, Box 32, HI; Brand Whitlock diary, November 29, 1914, in his *Journal*, pp. 69–70.

18. Hoover, *The Memoirs of Herbert Hoover*, vol. 1: *Years of Adventure* (New York, 1951), p. 159; Hoover, *An American Epic*, vol. 1 (New York, 1959), pp. 12–13.

19. Whitlock diary, November 29, 1914.

20. Ibid., November 29–30, December 1, 7, 1914, in his *Journal*, pp. 69–73, 74–76; Whitlock, *Belgium*, I, pp. 401–8; Wickliffe Rose to Starr Murphy, December 7, 1914, Rockefeller Foundation archives, RG 1.1, Series 100, Box 66, Folder 653.

21. Whitlock diary, November 29, 1914, Brand Whitlock Papers, Box 1, LC. In the published version of this entry (cited above), the word *brutal* was omitted and the word *says* substituted for *tells*. In a number of places Whitlock's posthumously published journal deviated from the more pungent wording of the original document. Some of the excisions were made by the editor at the request of Whitlock's widow. See Allan Nevins to Mrs. Brand Whitlock, August 22, 1936, Allan Nevins Papers, Rare Book and Manuscript Library, Columbia University.

22. Hoover reached Rotterdam on his return trip on December 2. Marshall Langhorne to the Secretary of State (plus enclosures), December 7, 1914, file 855.48/115, RG 59, NARA.

23. Whitlock to Walter Hines Page (plus enclosure), December 1, 1914, file 855.48/109, ibid.;

Whitlock, *Belgium*, I, pp. 405–8; Kittredge, "History," p. 91; minutes of the meeting of the Comité National, December 1, 1914, in its *Rapport général*, part 1, pp. 373–74, cited in chapter 2, note 15.

24. Hoover, *Years of Adventure*, p. 159; Hoover, *An American Epic*, I, p. 13.
25. *New York Times*, December 5, 1914, p. 3.
26. Whitlock diary, December 1, 1914; Whitlock, *Belgium*, I, pp. 402–4.
27. Hoover interview in *New York Times*, December 5, 1914, p. 3.
28. Hoover to the CRB's patron-ambassadors, December 8, 1914; Emile Francqui to Hoover, December 8, 1914, printed in *PR-CRB*, I, p. 43.
29. Langhorne to the Secretary of State (plus enclosures), December 7, 1914; Hoover to the CRB's patron-ambassadors, December 8, 1914.
30. Hoover memorandum, n.d., of his negotiations with the British government, December 4–7, 1914, CRB Correspondence, Box 1; Lou Henry Hoover to certain friends, December 14/15, 1914, copy in General Accessions—A. T. and Florence Stewart, HHPL, and printed in *San Francisco Examiner*, January 1, 1915, p. 20. Mrs. Hoover sailed from New York for England on the *Adriatic* on November 25, 1914, and arrived on December 3. Lindon W. Bates cable 45 to Hoover, November 29, 1914, CRB cable files; *The Times* (London), December 4, 1914, p. 15.
31. Hoover Calendar, HHPL.
32. Hoover to the CRB's patron-ambassadors, December 8, 1914; Hoover memorandum, n.d., of his negotiations with the British government, December 4–7, 1914. Hoover's interview with Asquith occurred on December 4.
33. Whitlock, *Journal*, pp. 77–78.
34. Hoover memorandum, n.d.
35. Ibid.
36. Hoover report, printed in *New York Times*, December 5, 1914, p. 3, and in *Stanford Alumnus* 16 (December 1914): 143–46.
37. Hoover memorandum, n.d.; Hoover to Whitlock, December 7, 1914, in American Legation, Brussels, Correspondence, 1914: Commission for Relief in Belgium, Part II, RG 84, NARA; Hoover to the CRB's patron-ambassadors, December 8, 1914.
38. Hoover to Sir Herbert Samuel, December 8, 1914, A155/4/38, Samuel Papers, House of Lords Record Office, London.
39. Hoover to Ambassador James Gerard (in Berlin), December 5, 1914, in American Embassy, London, Correspondence, 1914, vol. 48, file 848—Belgium, RG 84, NARA; in *PR-CRB*, I, pp. 513–15.
40. Sir Edward Grey memorandum for the British Cabinet, December 3, 1914, FO 371/1911/75425, PRO; copy in Cab. 37/122/179, PRO. See also Prime Minister H. H. Asquith to King George V, December 4, 1914, Cab. 41/35/62, PRO.
41. Hoover to Gerard, December 5, 1914.
42. Ibid.; Grey memorandum, December 3, 1914; Asquith to King George V, December 4, 1914.
43. Whitlock, *Journal*, p. 77.
44. Hoover to Walter Hines Page, December 5, 1914, in American Embassy, London, Correspondence, 1914, vol. 48, file 848—Belgium, RG 84, NARA; Hoover to Lord Eustace Percy (plus enclosures), December 5, 1914, FO 371/1911/80099, PRO; Hoover to Earl Grey, December 15, 1914, CRB Correspondence, Box 2; Hoover speech at American Luncheon Club, London, December 18, 1914, in Herbert Hoover Collection, Box 149, HI, and partially printed in *New York Times*, December 19, 1914, p. 3. A summary also appeared in *The Times* (London), December 19, 1914, p. 5.
45. Hoover speech, December 18, 1914.
46. Hoover interview, *New York Times*, December 5, 1914, p. 3.
47. Hoover to Earl Grey, December 15, 1914.

48. Ibid.; Hoover interview, *New York Times*, December 5, 1914, p. 3; Hoover speech, December 18, 1914; Frederick Palmer statement in *New York Times*, November 25, 1914, p. 3; Hoover memorandum enclosed in Hoover to Page, January 6, 1915, in American Embassy, London, Correspondence, 1915, vol. 95, file 848—Belgium, RG 84, NARA.
49. Hoover to Earl Grey, December 15, 1914.
50. *New York Times*, December 5, 1914, p. 3; Hoover speech, December 18, 1914.
51. Hoover speech, December 18, 1914.
52. *New York Times*, December 5, 1914, p. 3; *The Times* (London), December 7, 1914, p. 7.
53. Hoover speech, December 18, 1914 (see note 44).
54. Hoover to Earl Grey, December 15, 1914.
55. Hoover to Gerard, December 5, 1914.
56. Hoover cable to Gerard, November 27, 1914, in *PR-CRB*, I, p. 223.
57. Hoover to Gerard, December 5, 1914.
58. Hoover speech, December 18, 1914; Kittredge, "History," p. 56.
59. Hoover memorandum for Sir Edward Grey, November 5, 1914, in FO 371 / 1912 / 69903, PRO, and CRB Correspondence, Box 1, and in *PR-CRB*, I, pp. 218–21; Grey memorandum of conversation with Hoover et al., November 5, 1914, FO 800 / 94 / 592-94, and copy in Cab. 37 / 122 / 156, PRO; Hoover memorandum, November 10, 1914, in *PR-CRB*, I, pp. 306–7.
60. German Foreign Office note verbale, November 23, 1914, printed in *PR-CRB*, I, p. 307.
61. Kittredge, "History," p. 57. See also *PR-CRB*, I, p. 313.
62. Hoover cable 29 to Lindon W. Bates, November 24, 1914, CRB cable files; Hoover to Page, January 6, 1915.
63. British Admiralty circular letter to British War Risk Clubs, December 2, 1914, in *PR-CRB*, I, p. 308.
64. Hoover to Lord Eustace Percy, December 5, 1914, CRB Correspondence, Box 1; Lord Eustace Percy to Hoover, December 6, 1914, in *PR-CRB*, I, pp. 308–9; Hoover, *An American Epic*, I, p. 122.
65. Richard Webb to Hoover (plus enclosure), December 7, 1914, in *PR-CRB*, I, pp. 309–10.
66. Hoover to Whitlock, December 7, 1914; Hoover to the CRB's patron-ambassadors, December 8, 1914; Hoover to Walter Runciman, December 10, 1914, copy enclosed with Hoover's letter to Brand Whitlock, December 10, 1914, in American Legation, Brussels, Correspondence, 1914: Commission for Relief in Belgium, Part II, RG 84, NARA. Portions of the letter to Runciman are in *PR-CRB*, I, pp. 310–11.
67. Hoover to Chevalier Edmond Carton de Wiart, December 8, 1914, enclosed with Hoover to Whitlock, December 10, 1914.
68. Hoover to Runciman, December 10, 1914.
69. Hoover had raised this issue with the Belgian government in his letter to its London liaison, Carton de Wiart, on December 8. Just two days later, as noted in the text, Hoover told the British that the Belgians had agreed to make the desired guarantee. I have found no confirmatory evidence that the Belgians acted that quickly. It is possible, of course, that Carton de Wiart assured Hoover orally that the exiled government would accede to the request. It is at least as possible that Hoover did not wait for a Belgian reply and sought to create a fait accompli.
70. Hoover to Runciman, December 21, 1914, in *PR-CRB*, I, pp. 311–12; Hoover to Page, January 6, 1915; Hoover, *An American Epic*, I, p. 125.
71. Hoover to Page, January 6, 1915.
72. Asquith to King George V, December 4, 1914; Sir Edward Grey, internal note, December 2, 1914, on Hoover's letter to Lord Eustace Percy, November 20, 1914, FO 371 / 1911 / 73581, PRO.
73. Hoover to Whitlock, December 10, 1914.

74. Hoover to Page, November 25, 1914, in *PR-CRB*, I, pp. 222–23; Francqui to Hoover, December 8, 1914; *PR-CRB*, I, p. 228; "Report of the War Relief Commission," pp. 71–73; Comité National, *Rapport général*, part 1, pp. 56–57.

75. Hoover to Whitlock, December 1, 1914; Whitlock to Page, December 1, 1914; in *PR-CRB*, I, pp. 224–25. The Germans promised not to seize the money thus earmarked.

76. Hoover to Whitlock, December 7 and 10, 1914.

77. Aloys van de Vyvere (Belgian finance minister) to Hoover, January 9, 1915, in *PR-CRB*, I, p. 227; Comité National, *Rapport général*, part 1, p. 57. In *PR-CRB*, I, pp. 227–28, it is stated that the Belgian government's payment of £1,000,000 in January 1915 to the CRB was its second such advance and that the government had turned over another £1,000,000 the month before. I have found no corroboration for this statement, although Hoover did tell Whitlock on December 10, 1914 that the Belgian government had "found the resources" to make a £600,000 advance "and intends to make the advance monthly for the present." It appears, however, that this "intention" did not become a reality until January 1915, by which time the commitment had grown to £1,000,000. The Comité National's *Rapport général* states that the Belgian government made its first payment (£1,000,000) in January 1915.

78. "Report of the War Relief Commission," pp. 73, 76. According to this source, the Belgian government allocated this money from its budget, which was already financed by the British, and the British had vetoed the Belgians' doing this after February 1915.

79. Sir Edward Grey had made this clear to Hoover. Grey memorandum of conversation with Hoover et al., November 5, 1914.

80. Hoover to Whitlock, December 14, 1914, in American Legation, Brussels, Correspondence, 1914: Commission for Relief in Belgium, Part II, RG 84, NARA.

81. Whitlock to Hoover, December 8, 1914, ibid.

82. *New York Times Magazine*, February 28, 1915, p. 8.

83. Hoover to Whitlock, December 7, 1914; Hoover to the CRB's patron-ambassadors, December 8, 1914.

84. Whitlock to Hoover, December 8, 1914.

85. Hoover to Whitlock, December 16, 1914, in American Legation, Brussels, Correspondence, 1914: Commission for Relief in Belgium, Part II, RG 84, NARA.

86. Hoover to Whitlock, December 14, 1914.

87. Whitlock to Hoover, December 8, 1914; Whitlock to Page, December 19, 1914; Whitlock diary, December 6, 7, 8, 1914, in his *Journal*, pp. 74–76.

88. Whitlock to Page, December 19, 1914.

89. Kittredge, "History," pp. 91–94.

90. Whitlock to Hoover, December 17, 1914, in American Legation, Brussels, Correspondence, 1914, file 848, RG 84, NARA.

91. Whitlock to Page, December 19, 1914.

92. Whitlock to Hoover, December 17, 1914.

93. Hugh Gibson to Millard K. Shaler, December 19, 1914, in American Legation, Correspondence, 1914: Commission for Relief in Belgium, Part II, RG 84, NARA.

94. Ibid.

95. Kittredge, "History," p. 94.

96. Quoted in ibid., p. 97.

97. Hoover to Page, December 20, 1914, "Page, Walter Hines," Pre-Commerce Papers.

98. Hugh Gibson to his mother, December 25, 1914, Box 32, Gibson Papers.

99. Brand Whitlock diary, December 24, 1914, in his *Journal*, p. 79.

100. Whitlock diary, December 26, 1914, in ibid., p. 81.

101. Hoover to Will Irwin, January 18, 1915, CRB Correspondence, Box 1.

102. Ibid.; Kittredge, "History," p. 97; George H. Nash, *The Life of Herbert Hoover: The Engineer, 1874–1914* (New York, 1983), pp. 145–48, 152–70, 176–82.

103. Hoover's "general scheme" of organization is in *PR-CRB*, I, pp. 39–42. According to the editors of *PR-CRB* (I, p. 39), Hoover wrote this document during his first trip to Belgium. Kittredge, "History," p. 95, however, says that it was "drawn up toward the end of December." The latter is probably correct.

104. Hoover to Irwin, January 18, 1915.

105. Ibid.; Hoover to Henry James, Jr., January 11, 1915, Rockefeller Foundation archives, RG 1.1, Series 100, Box 66, Folder 653.

106. He left in January. Whitlock, *Belgium*, II, p. 814.

107. Whitlock diary, December 30, 1914, in his *Journal*, pp. 82–83.

108. Hoover to Lindon W. Bates, January 17, 1915, CRB Correspondence, Box 2.

109. Whitlock diary, December 30, 1914.

110. Hoover, *Years of Adventure*, p. 206; Robert M. Crunden, *A Hero in Spite of Himself: Brand Whitlock in Art, Politics, and War* (New York, 1969), pp. 244–45.

111. Hoover to Wickliffe Rose, November 21, 1914, Rockefeller Foundation archives, RG 1.1, Series 100, Box 66, Folder 653.

112. Whitlock diary, December 23 and 24, 1914, in his *Journal*, pp. 76–80. As printed, the earlier diary entry is dated December 10, but internal evidence (and other information) indicates December 23 as the true date.

113. Hoover cable to Bates, January 18, 1915, CRB Correspondence, Box 2.

114. Hoover to Irwin, January 18, 1915.

115. In his *Memoirs* Hoover praised the Rhodes scholars highly and omitted all mention of his troubles with them. Hoover, *Years of Adventure*, pp. 158–59.

116. Whitlock to Hoover, January 13, 1915, in American Legation, Brussels, Correspondence, 1915, file 848—Belgium, RG 84, NARA.

117. Hoover to Bates, February 21, 1915, CRB Correspondence, Box 32, HI.

118. He reached London on January 6. *New York Times*, January 7, 1915, p. 4.

119. James Gerard cable to the Secretary of State, December 26, 1914, file 855.48/126, RG 59, NARA; Gerard to Arthur Zimmermann (at the German Foreign Office), December 28, 1914, in *PR-CRB*, I, p. 516; *New York Times*, January 2, 1915, p. 11; Hoover, *An American Epic*, I, pp. 90–91.

120. Whitlock to Page, December 30, 1914, in American Embassy, London, Correspondence, 1915, vol. 95, file 848—Belgium, RG 84, NARA; Whitlock cable to the Secretary of State, December 30, 1914, in American Legation, Brussels, Correspondence, 1914, file 848, ibid., and in file 855.48/131, RG 59, NARA.

121. Hoover statement, January 6, 1915, printed in *New York Times*, January 7, 1915, p. 4; Commission for Relief in Belgium printed report, January 19, 1915, copies in Gifford Pinchot Papers, Box 439, LC, and Woodrow Wilson Papers, microfilm edition, reel 68, LC.

122. Lord Eustace Percy memorandum of a conversation with Hoover, January 6, 1915, Cab. 37/123/11, PRO.

123. Hoover to Ray Lyman Wilbur, January 10, 1915, Ray Lyman Wilbur Personal Papers, Box 31, Stanford University Archives.

124. Hoover cable to Henry James, Jr., January 15, 1915, CRB cable files; Hoover to Starr Murphy, January 19, 1915, Rockefeller Foundation archives, RG 1.1, Series 100, Box 67, Folder 657; Hoover to Bates, January 17, 1915.

125. In November 1914 Hoover had estimated the cost of importations at £1,000,000 per month. In its report of January 19, 1915, the CRB reported its food and transportation costs as £1,250,000 per month. See also Lord Percy's memorandum, January 6, 1915.

126. Hoover to Page, January 6, 1915; Percy memorandum, January 6, 1915; Henry James, Jr., to Starr Murphy, January 18, 1915, Rockefeller Foundation archives, RG 1.1, Series 100, Box 67, Folder 657; Page to Woodrow Wilson, January 12, 1915, Wilson Papers.

127. Hoover cable to Henry James, Jr., January 15, 1915; Hoover to Starr Murphy, January

19, 1915, Rockefeller Foundation archives, RG 1.1, Series 100, Box 67, Folder 657.
128. James to Murphy, January 18, 1915.
129. James cable to Murphy, January 18, 1915, enclosed with ibid.
130. Van de Vyvere to Hoover, January 9, 1915.
131. Hoover to Bates, January 17, 1915.
132. Ibid.; Hoover to Wilbur, January 10, 1915.
133. Hoover to Wilbur, January 10, 1915.
134. Hoover to Bates, January 17, 1915.
135. That is, contributors would send money to a New York or London bank, which would turn it over to the CRB for food purchases. The corresponding sum would then be delivered to designated recipients from food ration receipts available in Brussels. Hoover to Lord Eustace Percy, January 9, 1915, FO 371 / 2284 / file 609, PRO; Hoover to Sir Edward Grey, January 13, 1915, ibid., also in *PR-CRB*, I, pp. 230–31; Hoover memorandum of a conversation with Grey, January 13, 1915, in *PR-CRB*, I, pp. 228–29; Hoover, *An American Epic*, I, p. 61.
136. The word *agitation* was Hoover's. Hoover memorandum of his conversation with Grey, January 13, 1915.
137. Percy memorandum, January 6, 1915.
138. *New York Times*, January 8, 1915, p. 2. Palmer was present at Brand Whitlock's Christmas Eve dinner with the Hoovers. Whitlock diary, December 24, 1914.
139. Commission for Relief in Belgium printed report, January 19, 1915.
140. Hoover to Henry James, Jr., January 21, 1915, Rockefeller Foundation archives, RG 1.1, Series 100, Box 67, Folder 657.
141. Hoover to Murphy, January 19, 1915; Hoover to Bates, January 17, 1915; Commission for Relief in Belgium printed report, January 19, 1915.
142. Hoover to Bates, January 24, 1915, CRB Correspondence, Box 2.
143. *PR-CRB*, I, p. 228n; Hoover, *An American Epic*, I, p. 60; Kittredge, "History," p. 110.
144. Prime Minister H. H. Asquith to King George V, January 13, 1915, Cab. 41 / 36 / 1, PRO.
145. Hoover memorandum of his conversation with Grey, January 13, 1915.
146. Ibid.; Hoover cable to James Gerard, January 3, 1915, in *PR-CRB*, I, pp. 231–32. Hoover made this suggestion with the knowledge of Foreign Secretary Grey.
147. Whitlock diary, January 8, 1915, in his *Journal*, p. 85.
148. Hoover memorandum of his meeting with David Lloyd George (and others), January 21, 1915, in *PR-CRB*, I, pp. 232–35. For the details of the commercial exchange scheme, see *PR-CRB*, I, p. 235. The plan proved to be a modest success. Hoover, *An American Epic*, I, p. 65.
149. Kittredge, "History," p. 112.
150. Lewis R. Freeman, "Hoover and the Belgians," *Outlook* 111 (September 8, 1915): 82.
151. Kittredge, "History," p. 112; Hoover, *An American Epic*, I, p. 62.
152. Quoted in Page to Wilson, January 12, 1915.
153. Hoover memorandum, January 26, 1915, in *PR-CRB*, I, p. 236; Hoover memorandum, January 28, 1915, CRB Correspondence, Box 2.
154. Hoover cable to Secretary of State Bryan, January 27, 1915, file 855.48 / 161, RG 59, NARA; printed in *PR-CRB*, I, pp. 236–37. On January 30 Acting Secretary of State Lansing authorized Ambassador Gerard in Berlin to suggest "unofficially" to the German government that successful American fund raising for Belgian relief depended on abandonment of the indemnity.
155. Hoover memorandum, January 28, 1915; Kittredge, "History," p. 114.
156. Hoover press statement, January 30, 1915, in *PR-CRB*, I, pp. 237–40; Kittredge, "History," p. 114.
157. Hoover, *Years of Adventure*, p. 165.

158. *PR-CRB*, I, pp. 240–41; Kittredge, "History," p. 115.

159. Hoover, *Years of Adventure*, pp. 166–67.

160. This account is based upon Hoover's memoranda in *PR-CRB*, I, pp. 240–58. See also Hugh Gibson to his mother, February 3, 4, 9, and 11, 1915, Gibson Papers, Box 32.

161. *PR-CRB*, I, pp. 241–60; Kittredge, "History," pp. 117–18; Hoover, *An American Epic*, I, p. 72.

162. Kittredge, "History," p. 118.

163. *PR-CRB*, I, p. 254.

164. Ibid., p. 255.

165. Kittredge, "History," pp. 118–19.

166. Hoover, *An American Epic*, I, p. 73.

167. Hoover memorandum of conversation with Lloyd George, February 17, 1915, in *PR-CRB*, I, pp. 262–63.

168. Hoover to Lloyd George, February 17, 1915, in *PR-CRB*, I, pp. 263–66.

169. Hoover memorandum of conversation with Lloyd George, February 18, 1915, in ibid., p. 266; Hoover, *An American Epic*, I, p. 78.

170. The Franco–British subvention was part of a £20,000,000 Allied loan to Belgium approved by the British Cabinet on February 18. See Prime Minister Asquith to King George V, February 19, 1915, Cab. 41 / 36 / 6, PRO.

171. *PR-CRB*, I, p. 314.

172. Frederick Palmer, *With My Own Eyes* (Indianapolis, 1932), p. 309.

173. Hoover, *An American Epic*, I, p. 78. As it happened, the Belgians never repaid the relief loan. According to Hoover, Lloyd George never expected them to. The designation "loan" was just a ruse to avoid an unwanted recourse to Parliament.

174. Hoover to Bates, February 28, 1915, CRB Correspondence, Box 2.

175. *New York Times*, February 24, 1915, p. 3.

176. Grey to Hoover, February 22, 1915, in ibid., and in *PR-CRB*, I, pp. 260–62. Enclosed also with Hoover to Woodrow Wilson, February 26, 1915, Wilson Papers.

177. Hoover to Grey, February 24, 1915, in *New York Times*, February 24, 1915, p. 3, and enclosed with Hoover to Wilson, February 26, 1915.

178. Hoover to Chevalier Carton de Wiart (plus enclosure), February 17, 1915, CRB Correspondence, Box 2; copy in a dossier entitled "De Sadeleer Correspondence," in CRB Miscellaneous Files, HI.

179. Ibid.; Hoover cable 260 to Bates, February 17, 1915, "De Sadeleer Correspondence"; Hoover to Bates, February 18, 1915, ibid. See also Bates cable 349 to Hoover, ibid., copy in CRB Correspondence, Box 13.

180. Edmond Carton de Wiart to Hoover, February 17, 1915, "De Sadeleer Correspondence"; Hoover to Bates, February 18, 1915.

181. Hoover to Bates, February 18, 1915.

182. Hoover to Bates, February 18, 1915 (second letter), "De Sadeleer Correspondence." See also other correspondence in this dossier.

183. Hoover to Ambassador Page, March 4, 1915, in American Embassy, London, Correspondence, 1915, vol. 94, file 848—Belgium, RG 84, NARA.

184. Hoover to the Reverend J. F. Stillemans, March 3, 1915, copy enclosed with ibid.

185. *New York Times*, February 25, 1915, p. 4.

186. Bates cable 365 to Hoover, February 25, 1915, CRB cable files.

187. Hoover cable to Henry van Dyke (American minister to the Netherlands), February 25, 1915, CRB Correspondence, Box 2; Hoover memorandum of an interview with Colonel Hunsiker and Colonel House, February 27, 1915, ibid.

188. Hoover memorandum of his interview with Colonels Hunsiker and House, February 27, 1915.

189. Hoover cable 279 to Bates, February 27 , 1915, CRB cable files.

190. Hoover cable to Bates, February 28, 1915, copy enclosed with Hoover to Bates, February 28, 1915. See also Hoover to Bates, February 28, 1915 (second letter), CRB Correspondence, Box 32. In this latter missive, Hoover declared: "As to that plauged [sic] New York Committee, you need have no anxiety about them as I will proceed to dash their brains out within the next week."

191. Hoover memorandum of his interview with Colonels Hunsiker and House, February 27, 1915.

192. Ibid.; *New York Times*, March 1, 1915, p. 3; Edward M. House to Woodrow Wilson, March 1, 1915, Edward M. House Papers, Box 120, Yale University Library.

193. Hoover cable to van Dyke, February 28, 1915.

194. Hoover to Bates, February 28, 1915 (first letter); Hoover memorandum of an interview with Ambassador Page and Colonel House, February 27, 1915, CRB Miscellaneous Files.

195. *PR-CRB*, II, p. 1.

196. Page to Hoover, March 1, 1915, in American Embassy, London, Correspondence, 1915, vol. 96, file 848—Belgium, RG 84, NARA. The text is also included in Hoover cable 289 to Bates, March 2, 1915, CRB cable files. According to Hoover's memorandum of his interview with Page on February 27, the draft that he submitted did not seem strong enough to Page and House, and Page agreed to write the letter himself. However, Page's letter shows unmistakable signs of Hoover's influence.

197. Hoover to Stillemans, March 3, 1915.

198. Hoover address, December 18, 1914.

199. George I. Gay, *The Commission for Relief in Belgium: Statistical Review of Relief Operations* (Stanford, Calif., 1925), p. 2, copy at HHPL.

200. Hoover to Stillemans, March 3, 1915.

201. *New York Times*, February 28, 1915, section II, p. 3.

202. Ibid., February 12, 1915, p. 4; *New York Times Magazine*, February 28, 1915, pp. 7–8. See also Rose to Murphy, December 7, 1914.

203. *New York Times*, February 28, 1915, section II, p. 3.

204. Whitlock diary, February 22, 1915, in his *Journal*, p. 103.

205. *New York Times*, February 12, 1915, p. 4.

206. *PR-CRB*, I, p. v. One journalist declared that the CRB had attained "almost the standing of a distinct neutral Power." Ben S. Allen, "Feeding Seven Million Belgians," *World's Work* [London], April 1915, copy in Reprint File, HHPL.

207. Hoover to Bates, January 24, 1915.

208. Hoover to Lindon W. Bates, March 7, 1915, CRB Correspondence, Box 32.

209. Belgian Senator François in a speech in the Belgian parliament in February 1932, quoted in a memorandum from Perrin C. Galpin to Edgar Rickard, June 6, 1932, "Foreign Affairs: Countries—Belgium—1932," Presidential Papers, Hoover Papers.

210. Gilchrist B. Stockton to his parents, November 30, 1915, "Stockton, Gilchrist B.," Pre-Commerce Papers; Francis C. Wickes oral history (1970), p. 7, HHPL. The appellation *the Chief* was first applied to Hoover in World War I. I have found no evidence for the assertion that he acquired this nickname in his prewar mining days when (as the story goes) he was "chief engineer" at various mines.

   During the war Hoover was sometimes referred to as the Big Chief. Vernon Kellogg, *Fighting Starvation in Belgium* (New York, 1918), p. 157; Joseph C. Green, "Some Portraits: Mr. Hoover" (typescript, February 9, 1917), Joseph C. Green Papers, Box 20, HI.

211. Hoover memorandum, February 11–12, 1915, portion photostated and reproduced in *PR-CRB*, I, between pp. 242 and 243.

212. Brand Whitlock diary, February 12, 1915, in his *Journal*, p. 99.

213. Hoover speech, December 18, 1914.

214. Hoover to Gerard, December 5, 1914.

215. Hoover, quoted in Victoria French Allen, "The Outside Man" (typescript, n.d.), pp. 143–44, copy at HHPL.
216. Hoover to Bates, March 7, 1915. Hoover told his wife that the CRB's effort was "the greatest work to which we could be devoted." Hoover cable to his wife Lou, n.d. (ca. November 5, 1914), CRB cable files.
217. Hoover to Stillemans, March 3, 1915.
218. Hoover to Bates, January 17, 1915.
219. British Foreign Office memorandum to the French ambassador, January 2, 1915, FO 371 / 2284 / 609, PRO.
220. House to Wilson, February 26, 1915, printed in Arthur S. Link et al., eds., *The Papers of Woodrow Wilson*, vol. 32 (Princeton, N.J., 1980), pp. 293–94.
221. Page to Wilson, January 12, 1915.

C H A P T E R   5

1. Tracy B. Kittredge, "The History of the Commission for Relief in Belgium, 1914–1917" (unpublished bound page proof version, ca. 1918), pp. 138–39, copy at HHPL; George I. Gay and H. H. Fisher, *Public Relations of the Commission for Relief in Belgium* (Stanford, Calif., 1929), I, pp. 391–93, hereinafter cited as *PR-CRB*.
2. James W. Gerard to Hoover, January 2, 1915, in *PR-CRB*, I, p. 395.
3. Kittredge, "History," pp. 136–38.
4. Ibid., p. 139.
5. Ibid.
6. *New York Times*, January 7, 1915, p. 4.
7. Lord Eustace Percy memorandum, January 6, 1915, Cab. 37 / 123 / 11, PRO.
8. Kittredge, "History," p. 138.
9. Hoover to James W. Gerard, January 6, 1915, in *PR-CRB*, I, pp. 395–96.
10. Hoover to President Raymond Poincaré of France, February 17, 1915, in *PR-CRB*, I, pp. 397–99.
11. Hoover to Walter Hines Page, January 26, 1915, in *PR-CRB*, I, pp. 396–97.
12. Hoover to Louis Chevrillon, March 10, 1915, quoted in Kittredge, "History," pp. 140–41.
13. Hoover to Page, January 26, 1915.
14. For Hoover's press release, see *PR-CRB*, I, pp. 237–40. The number of French citizens living behind German lines was approximately 2,150,000. Kittredge, "History," p. 138.
15. Kittredge, "History," p. 141.
16. Henry James, Jr., to Starr J. Murphy, January 18, 1915, Rockefeller Foundation archives, RG 1.1, Series 100, Box 67, Folder 657, Rockefeller Archive Center, North Tarrytown, New York.
17. Hoover to Gifford Pinchot, February 16, 1915, Gifford Pinchot Papers, Box 439, LC; Hoover to James W. Gerard, February 25, 1915, ibid.; Hoover to William G. Sharp, February 23, 1915, CRB Correspondence, Box 1, HI; M. Nelson McGeary, *Gifford Pinchot: Forester-Politician* (Princeton, N.J., 1960), pp. 19–22.
18. Hoover to Poincaré, February 17, 1915.
19. Pinchot memorandum, February 27, 1915, CRB Miscellaneous Files, HI; in *PR-CRB*, I, pp. 400–401.
20. Hoover cable to Pinchot, February 25, 1915, CRB cable files, Pre-Commerce Papers, Herbert Hoover Papers, HHPL; in *PR-CRB*, I, pp. 399–400. See also Hoover to Pinchot, February 25, 1915, Pinchot Papers, Box 439.
21. Pinchot memorandum, February 27, 1915; Francis Bertie to Sir Edward Grey, March 25,

1915, FO 371 / 2362 / file 30051, PRO; Hoover to Lindon W. Bates, March 28, 1915, CRB Correspondence, Box 3.
22. Pinchot memorandum, February 27, 1915.
23. Ibid.
24. Kittredge, "History," p. 145.
25. Hoover to Gerard (through Rotterdam), March 9, 1915, cited in ibid.
26. Hoover to Louis Chevrillon, March 10, 1915, in *PR-CRB*, I, p. 401.
27. Chevrillon to Hoover, March 9, 1915; Hoover cable to Chevrillon, March 9, 1915; both in *PR-CRB,* I, pp. 402–3.
28. Hoover cable to Pinchot, February 25, 1915.
29. Hoover to Pinchot, February 25, 1915.
30. Hoover cable to Chevrillon, March 11, 1915.
31. Ibid.
32. Kittredge, "History," p. 146.
33. Ibid., pp. 143, 145; Hoover, *An American Epic*, vol. 1 (Chicago, 1959), pp. 47, 83.
34. Chevrillon to Hoover, March 9, 1915.
35. Kittredge, "History," p. 144.
36. Hoover cable to Pinchot, March 15, 1915, in *PR-CRB*, I, p. 123.
37. Hoover to Aloys van de Vyvere, March 18[16?], 1915, in *PR-CRB*, I, pp. 405–6; Kittredge, "History," p. 146.
38. Hoover to Lindon W. Bates, March 14, 1915, CRB Correspondence, Box 32.
39. Stamp on Hoover's French visa issued in London ("Annexe du Passeport No. 1022"), March 1915, HHPL. According to another stamp on this document, Hoover returned to England on March 24. See also "Memorandum of Mr. Hoover's Trip to Havre and Paris, March 1915," in CRB—London office dossier 73: "Negotiations for a Subsidy from the Belgian Government," HI.
40. Sir Edward Grey to Sir Francis Bertie, March 20, 1915; Bertie to Grey, March 25, 1915; both in FO 371 / 2362 / file 30051, PRO.
41. Kittredge, "History," pp. 146–47.
42. Memorandum by Edgar Sengier, March 22, 1915, in *PR-CRB*, I, pp. 406–7; Emile Francqui to Aloys van de Vyvere, March 23, 1915, printed in ibid., pp. 407–8; Bertie to Grey, March 25, 1915; Hoover to Bates, March 28, 1915.
43. Sengier memorandum, March 22, 1915; Francqui to van de Vyvere, March 23, 1915; Sengier memorandum, March 26, 1915, in *PR-CRB*, I, p. 408; van de Vyvere to Hoover, March 26, 1915, in ibid., pp. 408–9; Kittredge, "History," p. 147; Hoover, *An American Epic*, I, p. 86.
44. *New York Times*, March 26, 1915, p. 5.
45. George I. Gay, *The Commission for Relief in Belgium: Statistical Review of Relief Operations* (Stanford, Calif., 1925), p. 2.
46. *New York Times*, March 26, 1915, p. 5; *PR-CRB*, I, p. 411.
47. *PR-CRB*, I, pp. 414–17; Kittredge, "History," pp. 150–52.
48. Hoover, *An American Epic*, I, p. 20.
49. Kittredge, "History," p. 149; Brand Whitlock diary, March 31, 1915, in Allan Nevins, ed., *The Journal of Brand Whitlock* (New York, 1936), pp. 116–17; Walter Hines Page cable to the Secretary of State, April 6, 1915, in American Embassy, London, cables sent to the State Department, 1915, RG 84, NARA.
50. Hoover to Brand Whitlock, April 5, 1915, CRB Correspondence, Box 3.
51. Hoover, *An American Epic*, I, p. 20; Kittredge, "History," p. 206.
52. Kittredge, "History," pp. 152–53.
53. Hugh Gibson to his mother, February 9 and 11, 1915, Hugh Gibson Papers, Box 32, HI.
54. Kittredge, "History," p. 129.
55. Ibid., pp. 128–29.
56. Ibid., p. 132.

57. Brand Whitlock diary, May 13, 1915, in his *Journal*, pp. 143–44; Hoover, *An American Epic*, I, p. 50; obituary for von Bissing in *New York Times*, April 19, 1917, p. 15; entry for von Bissing in *Neue Deutsche Biographie*, vol. 2 (Berlin, 1955), pp. 278–79.

58. Hoover, *An American Epic*, I, pp. 50–51; Hoover, *The Memoirs of Herbert Hoover*, vol. 1: *Years of Adventure* (New York, 1951), p. 190.

59. Hoover memorandum of conversation with Governor-General von Bissing, February 11, 915, photostat copy in *PR-CRB*, I, between pp. 242 and 243 and between pp. 274 and 275. A typescript copy is in CRB Miscellaneous Files.

60. Whitlock diary, February 12, 1915, in his *Journal*, p. 98.

61. Hoover to Governor-General von Bissing, February 12, 1915, in *PR-CRB*, I, pp. 47–49.

62. Hoover memorandum of conversations with Baron von der Lancken and Dr. Schacht, February 12, 1915, photostat copy in *PR-CRB*, I, between pp. 274 and 275. A typescript copy is in CRB Miscellaneous Files.

63. Von Bissing to Dannie Heineman, February 20, 1915, in *PR-CRB*, I, pp. 50–51.

64. Hoover to Whitlock, March 6, 1915, in *PR-CRB*, I, pp. 52–53.

65. Hoover cable to Ambassador James W. Gerard (via Rotterdam), March 9, 1915, in *PR-CRB*, I, pp. 53–54.

66. Whitlock diary, March 11, 1915, in his *Journal*, p. 107; Emile Francqui to Hoover, May 7, 1915, CRB Correspondence, Box 32.

67. Hoover to Whitlock, March 18, 1915, in *PR-CRB*, I, pp. 54–55.

68. Von Bissing to the German Foreign Office, March 21, 1915, quoted in Kittredge, "History," pp. 131–32.

69. Hoover to Whitlock, April 6, 1915, CRB Correspondence, Box 3.

70. Whitlock diary, May 13, 1915.

71. *PR-CRB*, I, p. 314; E. Von Haniel to Lindon W. Bates, February 15, 1915, in ibid., pp. 315–16.

72. Hoover cable to CRB—New York office, February 17, 1915; CRB—Rotterdam office to Hoover, February 25, 1915; both in *PR-CRB*, I, pp. 316–17.

73. Hoover to Emile Francqui, March 11, 1915, CRB Correspondence, Box 3.

74. Hoover cable to CRB—New York office, February 17, 1915; Hoover cable to CRB—Rotterdam office, February 26, 1915, in *PR-CRB*, I, p. 317.

75. Gottlieb von Jagow to James W. Gerard, March 5, 1915, in *PR-CRB*, I, pp. 317–18.

76. Hoover to Francqui, March 11, 1915.

77. Whitlock diary, March 11, 1915, in his *Journal*, pp. 107–8; Whitlock to Walter Hines Page, March 22, 1915, in American Embassy, London, Correspondence, 1915, vol. 96, file 848—Belgium, RG 84, NARA.

78. Hoover to Whitlock, March 29, 1915, copy in American Embassy, London, Correspondence, 1915, vol. 96, file 848—Belgium, RG 84, NARA.

79. *New York Times*, March 23, 1915, p. 3.

80. Walter Hines Page cable to the Secretary of State, April 13, 1915, in American Embassy, London, Correspondence, 1915, vol. 96, file 848—Belgium, RG 84, NARA; Hoover to Page, April 16, 1915, ibid.

81. Hoover to Page, April 16, 1915.

82. Hoover to Lindon W. Bates, April 18, 1915, CRB Correspondence, Box 3.

83. Ibid.

84. CRB—Rotterdam office to Hoover, April 16, 1915; Hoover to John Beaver White, April 16, 1915; both in *PR-CRB*, I, pp. 320–21.

85. Hoover to Whitlock, April 20, 1915, CRB Correspondence, Box 3.

86. Whitlock diary, April 16, 1915, in his *Journal*, p. 126.

87. Quoted in *PR-CRB*, I, pp. 320–21.

88. Page cable to Gerard, April 18, 1915, copy in CRB cable files; also in *PR-CRB*, I, pp. 318–

19. This cable has—to this biographer—a distinctly Hooverian sound. In all likelihood Hoover ghostwrote this cable and Page signed it. It was a familiar pattern.

89. Ibid.

90. Hoover to Whitlock, April 16, 1915, CRB Correspondence, Box 3.

91. Von Jagow to Gerard, April 18, 1915, in *PR-CRB*, I, pp. 321–22.

92. Hoover to Page, May 7, 1915, in American Embassy, London, Correspondence, 1915, vol. 96, file 848—Belgium, RG 84, NARA.

93. Hoover, *An American Epic*, I, p. 133.

94. Hoover to Gerard, May 1, 1915, in *PR-CRB*, I, p. 528.

95. Whitlock diary, May 4, 1915, in his *Journal*, p. 135; Whitlock diary, May 10, 1915, copy in Brand Whitlock Papers, Box 2, LC.

96. Whitlock diary, May 8 and 9, 1915, in his *Journal*, pp. 139–40.

97. Hoover to Gerard, May 1, 1915.

98. Hoover to C. A. Young, May 13, 1915, printed in *PR-CRB*, II, pp. 128–30; Hoover to Bates, May 14, 1915, quoted in CRB—London office dossier 45: "The Episode of Mr. Lindon Bates," p. 48, HI.

99. Hoover to Young, May 13, 1915.

100. Hoover to William C. Edgar, May 17, 1915, in William C. Edgar and Family Papers, Minnesota Historical Society.

101. *PR-CRB*, I, pp. 516–19. The nonexempt food sources included oats, hay, potatoes, and fresh vegetables.

102. Von Bissing to the Comité National, March 12, 1915, in ibid., p. 520.

103. Lord Eustace Percy to Hoover, April 6, 1915, in ibid., pp. 543 46.

104. Hoover to Gerard, March 27, 1915, in ibid., pp. 522–25.

105. Hoover, *An American Epic*, I, p. 94; Lord Eustace Percy, handwritten memorandum, May 1, 1915, in FO 371 / 2362 / file 30051, PRO.

106. Percy memorandum, May 1, 1915.

107. Hoover to Gerard, May 1, 1915, in *PR-CRB*, I, pp. 527–28.

108. Gerard to von Jagow, May 5, 1915, in *PR-CRB*, I, pp. 530–31.

109. Percy to Hoover, May 4, 1915, in FO 371 / 2362 / file 30051, PRO, printed in *PR-CRB*, I, p. 529; [Sir Edward Grey] to Sir Francis Bertie, May 4, 1915, in FO 371 / 2362 / file 30051, PRO. In the latter communication Grey, referring to Lord Percy's letter (actually two letters) to Hoover, said: "These two letters have been written to Mr. Hoover at his own request, in order to strengthen his negotiations with the German authorities. . . ."

110. [Grey] to Bertie, May 4, 1915.

111. Governor-General of Australia to the Secretary of State for the Colonies, ca. March 18, 1915, copy in FO 371 / 2285 / file 609, PRO; [Lord Eustace Percy] to the Undersecretary of State for the Colonies, March 23, 1915, ibid. According to the governor-general, "responsible quarters" in Australia were concerned about Hoover's connection with the mining engineering firm of Bewick, Moreing & Co., "a firm not in good repute." In fact, Hoover had severed his ties with the firm in 1908.

112. Whitlock diary, June 10, 1915, in his *Journal*, p. 159; Walter Hines Page to Woodrow Wilson, July 2, 1915, printed in Arthur S. Link et al., eds., *The Papers of Woodrow Wilson*, vol. 33 (Princeton, N.J., 1980), pp. 549–55. In 1916 Page retold this story in much more dramatic form. According to Page, when the British government approached Hoover with its offer of an "important executive post" (if he became a British subject), Hoover replied: "I'll do what I can for you with pleasure, but I'll be damned if I'll give up my American citizenship—not on your life!" Page memorandum, December 30, 1916, printed in Arthur S. Link et al., eds., *The Papers of Woodrow Wilson*, vol. 40 (Princeton, N.J., 1982), p. 369. One suspects that Page's later version was somewhat embellished.

113. Whitlock diary, June 10, 1915.

114. Page to Wilson, July 2, 1915.

115. Francqui to Hoover, May 7, 1915 (printed in part in *PR-CRB*, I, pp. 531–32); Kittredge, "History," p. 161.
116. Percy to Hoover, May 26, 1915, in *PR-CRB*, I, pp. 532–33.
117. Ibid.
118. Hoover to Percy, May 27, 1915, CRB Correspondence, Box 3; Percy memorandum, June 6, 1915, in FO 371 / 2291 / file 70828, PRO.
119. Hoover to Whitlock, May 26, 1915, in *PR-CRB*, I, p. 533.
120. Hoover cable to Bates, June 1, 1915, in ibid., p. 534.
121. Hoover to Oscar T. Crosby, June 1, 1915, CRB Correspondence, Box 4.
122. Hoover to Bates, June 6, 1915, quoted in CRB—London office dossier 45, p. 51.
123. Percy memorandum, June 6, 1915.
124. Ibid.
125. [Percy] to the Undersecretary of State for the Colonies, March 23, 1915.
126. Whitlock diary, June 9, 1915, in his *Journal*, p. 157.
127. Whitlock diary, June 14, 1915, in ibid., pp. 161–62.
128. Whitlock diary, June 16 and 17, 1915, in ibid., pp. 165–69.
129. Whitlock diary, June 14, 1915.
130. Whitlock diary, June 15, 1915, in his *Journal*, pp. 162–65.
131. Hoover to Sr. Don Jose Congosto, March 18, 1915, CRB Correspondence, Box 3.
132. Hoover, *Years of Adventure*, p. 206. Hoover added, however, that Villalobar was "devoted to the Belgian Relief."
133. Hoover to Bates, April 5, 1915, quoted in CRB—London office dossier 45, p. 59.
134. Hugh Gibson to his mother, June 25, 1915 (part of his letter to her dated June 21, 1915), Gibson Papers, Box 33.
135. Hoover, *An American Epic*, I, pp. 40–41.
136. Gibson to his mother, June 25, 1915.
137. Ibid.
138. Whitlock diary, June 16, 1915.
139. Ibid, June 16 and 17, 1915.
140. Ibid. According to Whitlock's diary, Hoover played no direct part in the negotiations of June 16–17. Hoover did not attend the diplomats' meetings with the Germans. Instead his CRB deputy in Belgium, Oscar T. Crosby, participated.
141. Whitlock diary, June 17, 1915; "Memorandum for Baron von der Lancken," June 18 [actually June 17 or earlier], 1915, in *PR-CRB*, I, p. 535.
142. Whitlock diary, June 17, 1915.
143. Whitlock diary, June 23, 1915, in his *Journal*, pp. 170–71.
144. Hoover memorandum for Baron von der Lancken (sent via Whitlock), June 22, 1915, in *PR-CRB*, I, pp. 535–36.
145. See chapter 6.
146. The London cable and Hoover's reply are quoted in Whitlock's diary, June 18, 1915, in his *Journal*, p. 169. One cannot prove that the London cable was inspired by Hoover, but this is a possibility. Why would the British wish to jeopardize the harvest negotiations at this point? If the negotiations collapsed the Germans would then be free to seize the entire Belgian harvest—and leave the British in a dilemma: either allow the Germans to get away with it or take on the moral burden of terminating the relief entirely. It was not in the British interest that Hoover should fail.
147. Whitlock diary, June 24, 1915, in his *Journal*, pp. 171–72; Comité National, *Rapport général*, part 1, p. 385 (cited in chapter 2, note 15).
148. Von Bissing to Whitlock, July 4, 1915, in *PR-CRB*, I, pp. 538–39. See also Whitlock to Hoover, June 25, 1915, ibid., pp. 536–37, and von Bissing's decree of June 30, 1915, ibid., pp. 542–43.
149. *New York Times*, June 29, 1915, p. 4.

150. Hoover to Walter Hines Page, June 28, 1915, enclosed with Page to Lord Crewe, June 30, 1915, in FO 371 / 2291 / file 70828, PRO.
151. Kittredge, "History," pp. 191, 344–45; Ernest Mahaim, *Le Secours de chômage en Belgique pendant l'occupation allemande* (Paris and New Haven, 1926), pp. 49, 52–53, 59; Henri Pirenne, *La Belgique et la guerre mondiale* (Paris and New Haven, 1928), p. 142; Oscar Freiherr von der Lancken-Wakenitz, *Meine Dreissig Dientsjahre* (Berlin, 1931), pp. 200–201.
152. Whitlock diary, April 15, 16, 20, and 22, 1915, in his *Journal*, pp. 124–31. In April the Germans boldly took control of another relief agency, the Belgian Red Cross. Belgian charities thereupon refused to cooperate with it. Pirenne, *La Belgique*, p. 156.
153. Whitlock diary, April 22 and May 4, 1915, in his *Journal*, pp. 130–31, 135; Kittredge, "History," pp. 191–92.
154. Whitlock diary, April 15 and 22, 1915.
155. Hoover to Page, July 5, 1915, in *PR-CRB*, I, pp. 58–60.
156. Whitlock diary, May 13, 1915, in his *Journal*, p. 145.
157. Von Bissing to Whitlock, June 26, 1915, in *PR-CRB*, I, pp. 56–58.
158. Whitlock diary, June 28 and 29, 1915, in his *Journal*, pp. 172–74.
159. Hoover to Page, July 5, 1915.
160. Hoover to Aloys van de Vyvere, June 29, 1915, CRB—London office dossier 25: "The Question of Forced Labour in Belgium," HI.
161. Kittredge, "History," p. 191.
162. Hoover, *An American Epic*, I, pp. 77–78; "Memorandum on Mr. Hoover's Trip to Havre and Paris (March 1915)."
163. Hoover to Page, July 5, 1915.
164. Ibid.; Hoover to Gifford Pinchot, July 7, 1915, Pinchot Papers, Box 189.
165. Hoover to Lord Percy, June 30, 1915, in *PR-CRB*, I, pp. 537–38.
166. Lord Crewe to Page, July 7, 1915, in ibid., pp. 539–42. Portions of Crewe's letter were identical to Hoover's letter of June 30 to Lord Percy.
167. Whitlock diary, July 8, 1915, in his *Journal*, p. 176.
168. Ibid., July 8 and 9, 1915, in Whitlock's *Journal*, pp. 176–78; Brand Whitlock, *Belgium: A Personal Narrative* (New York, 1919), pp. 657–61; Kittredge, "History," pp. 194–95.
169. Whitlock diary, July 8, 1915.
170. Whitlock diary, July 15 and 16, 1915, in his *Journal*, pp. 178–79.
171. Ibid., July 16, 1915; Whitlock diary, July 26, 1915, in his *Journal*, pp. 201–3; Whitlock to Baron von der Lancken, July 16, 1915, in *PR-CRB*, I, pp. 546–47. Compare the tone of the latter document with Lord Crewe's letter (cited in note 166).
172. Whitlock diary, July 19, 1915, in his *Journal*, pp. 179–80; Whitlock to Page, July 19, 1915, in *PR-CRB*, I, pp. 62–63.
173. Stamp on Hoover passport (no. 17,655), General Accessions, HHPL.
174. Grey to Page, July 17, 1915, in *PR-CRB*, I, pp. 61–62.
175. Whitlock diary, July 19 and 20, 1915, in his *Journal*, pp. 179–80.
176. Whitlock diary, July 26, 1915.
177. Ibid.
178. Von der Lancken to Whitlock, July 29, 1915, in *PR-CRB*, I, pp. 63–65.
179. Lord Percy memorandum, August 3, 1915, in FO 371 / 2285 / file 609, PRO; Hoover, *An American Epic*, I, p. 148.
180. Whitlock diary, July 15, 16, 19, 26, 1915.
181. *PR-CRB*, I, pp. 267, 549. Many complicated details of crop administration remained to be worked out. See Kittredge, "History," pp. 166–68; *PR-CRB*, I, pp. 549–55; Hoover to William C. Edgar, August 1, 1915, Edgar and Family Papers, Box 1.
182. Hoover to Edgar, August 1, 1915; Kittredge, "History," p. 169.
183. For details of Hoover's arrangements for acquiring a portion of the harvest in northern France and the "étappen" region of Belgium, see: *PR-CRB*, I, pp. 267, 403n, 417–31, 560–

.77; Kittredge, "History," pp. 168–73; Hoover, *An American Epic*, I, pp. 113–18; Hoover to Edgar, August 1, 1915; Hoover to Colonel Edward M. House, August 16, 1915, Edward M. House Papers, Box 61, Yale University Library.

184. Hoover approved. Hoover to Edgar, August 1, 1915.
185. Kittredge, "History," pp. 166–68; von Bissing decree of June 30, 1915; *PR-CRB*, I, pp. 549–50; von Bissing decree of July 23, 1915, in ibid., pp. 544–45.
186. Kittredge, "History," p. 167; *PR-CRB*, I, p. 554.
187. Whitlock diary, June 20, 1915, in his *Journal*, p. 170.
188. Hoover to Lord Percy, October 11, 1915, in FO 371 / 2291 / file 70828, PRO.
189. Kittredge, "History," p. 168; *PR-CRB*, I, p. 549.

C H A P T E R 6

1. John L. Simpson, "Activities in a Troubled World: War Relief, Banking, and Business," typescript of an oral history conducted 1978 by Suzanne Riess, Regional Oral History Office, the Bancroft Library, University of California, Berkeley, 1978, 263 pp. Courtesy, the Bancroft Library. (The reference here is to p. 32.)
2. Tracy B. Kittredge, "The History of the Commission for Relief in Belgium, 1914–1917" (unpublished bound page proof version, ca. 1918), p. 90, copy at HHPL; George F. Spaulding, "The 'Commission for Relief in Belgium' and the Chateau de Mariemont," *Cahiers de Mariemont* (April 1973): 5–21, copy at HHPL.
3. Brand Whitlock diary, February 14 and 22, 1915, printed in Allan Nevins, ed., *The Journal of Brand Whitlock* (New York, 1936), pp. 99–100, 103.
4. Hundreds of these embroidered flour sacks are preserved at the Herbert Hoover Presidential Library today. They are one of the most popular exhibits.
5. Whitlock diary, February 14, 1915; *New York Times*, February 28, 1915, section II, p. 3.
6. Kittredge, "History," pp. 86, 196–97; George I. Gay and H. H. Fisher, *Public Relations of the Commission for Relief in Belgium* (Stanford, Calif., 1929), I, p. 478, hereinafter cited as *PR-CRB*; Comité National, *Rapport général*, part 1, p. 72 (cited in chapter 2, note 15).
7. Hoover to Brand Whitlock, March 13, 1915, CRB Correspondence, Box 3, HI.
8. Ibid.
9. Hoover to Whitlock, March 6, 1915, in *PR-CRB*, I, pp. 52–53.
10. Hoover to Whitlock, March 13, 1915.
11. Ibid.
12. Ibid.
13. Hoover cable 289 to the CRB's New York office, March 2, 1915, CRB cable files, Pre-Commerce Papers, Herbert Hoover Papers, HHPL.
14. Hoover to the Reverend J. J. Stillemans, March 3, 1915, enclosed in Hoover to Walter Hines Page, March 4, 1915, in American Embassy, London, Correspondence, 1915, vol. 94, file 848—Belgium, RG 84, NARA.
15. *PR-CRB*, I, p. 41. See also Hoover's memorandum of a conversation with Lord Eustace Percy, February 27, 1915, CRB Miscellaneous Files, HI.
16. Hoover to Whitlock, March 13, 1915.
17. Kittredge, "History," pp. 175–76; A. N. Connett to the CRB's provincial delegates in Belgium, February 5, 1915, in *PR-CRB*, I, pp. 45–46.
18. Hoover cable to his Rotterdam office (for transmittal to A. N. Connett), March 11, 1915, CRB Correspondence, Box 3.
19. Kittredge, "History," p. 176.
20. Quoted in ibid., p. 176.
21. Hoover cable to his Rotterdam office, March 11, 1915.
22. Hoover to Lindon W. Bates, March 14, 1915, CRB Correspondence, Box 32.

23. Hoover to Whitlock, April 5, 1915, CRB Correspondence, Box 3.
24. Kittredge, "History," p. 177.
25. Hoover to Whitlock, March 13, 1915.
26. Hoover cable to his Rotterdam office, March 11, 1915; Hoover to Whitlock, March 13, 1915.
27. Connett to the CRB's provincial delegates, February 5, 1915; Kittredge, "History," p. 177. This was done with Brand Whitlock's approval.
28. Whitlock diary, March 11, 1915, in his *Journal*, p. 108; Kittredge, "History," p. 197.
29. Kittredge, "History," pp. 197–98.
30. Ibid., pp. 198–99; Lord Eustace Percy memorandum, June 6, 1915, in FO 371 / 2291 / file 70828, PRO.
31. Emile Francqui to Hoover, May 7, 1915, CRB Correspondence, Box 15.
32. Hoover to Whitlock, June 24, 1915, CRB Correspondence, Box 4.
33. Kittredge, "History," pp. 199–200.
34. Whitlock diary, July 20, 1915, in his *Journal*, p. 180.
35. Hoover cable to his wife Lou, July 12, 1915, "Hoover, Herbert, 1915," Personal Correspondence, 1874–1920, Lou Henry Hoover Papers, HHPL; Lou Henry Hoover telegram to Ralph Arnold, July 16, 1915, Ralph Arnold Collection, Box 38, the Huntington Library, San Marino, California.
36. [Hoover], *procès-verbal* of a meeting of CRB and Comité National representatives, Brussels, July 20, 1915, printed in *PR-CRB*, I, pp. 66–69. Although Hoover is not identified as the author of this document, it has a Hooverian ring and was, in all likelihood, drawn up by Hoover himself.
37. Whitlock diary, July 22, 1915, in his *Journal*, pp. 198–99.
38. Kittredge, "History," pp. 204–6.
39. Ibid., p. 204.
40. These volumes are preserved at the Herbert Hoover Presidential Library.
41. For example, Mabel Hyde Kittredge, "Taking Care of Belgium," *New Republic* 3 (July 31, 1915): part II, pp. 1–8.
42. *PR-CRB*, II, p. 264.
43. Frank Marshall White, "No Dividends: Big Business Works for Charity," *Saturday Evening Post* 188 (August 28, 1915): 17 (full article: 16–18, 33–34); Hoover to CRB—New York office, August 31, 1915, CRB Correspondence, Box 4; Lindon W. Bates cable 166 to Hoover, September 13, 1915, CRB cable files.
44. Commission for Relief in Belgium, *Report covering the period of about eight months from the inception to June 30th, 1915* (August 1915), copies in Woodrow Wilson Papers, microfilm edition, reel 302, LC, and in FO 371 / 2286 / file 609, PRO. For a sample of the press coverage, see *New York Times*, September 20, 1915, p. 3, and the clippings collected in the scrapbooks cited in note 40.
45. Woodrow Wilson to Hoover, September 20, 1915, Wilson Papers.
46. "The Relief of Belgium," *Economist* 81 (September 4, 1915): 360–61.
47. Hoover to Emile Francqui, June 24, 1915, CRB Correspondence, Box 4.
48. Hoover, quoted in *New York Times*, September 20, 1915, p. 3.
49. Hoover to Lindon W. Bates, February 22, 1915; Hoover cable to Bates, March 2, 1915; Hoover to Bates, August 31, 1915; all in CRB—London office dossier 45: "The Episode of Mr. Lindon Bates," pp. 18–19, 26–29, HI. Hoover's letter of August 31 to Bates is also in *PR-CRB*, II, pp. 268–70.
50. Hoover to CRB—New York office, August 31, 1915.
51. Hoover to Bates, February 22, 1915. See also Hoover to CRB—New York office, October 13, 1915, CRB Correspondence, Box 4.
52. For a provocative examination of the influence of orphanhood (and, more broadly, of deprivation of love in childhood) on personality development, see Lucille Iremonger, *The Fiery*

Chariot: A Study of British Prime Ministers and the Search for Love (London, 1970). See also Craig Lloyd, *Aggressive Introvert: Herbert Hoover and Public Relations Management, 1912–1932* (Columbus, Ohio, 1972).

53. William C. Edgar, "Two American Heroes," *Bellman* 19 (July 3, 1915): 9–13. The other "hero" was Brand Whitlock.

54. Hoover to William C. Edgar, August 1, 1915, William C. Edgar and Family Papers, Minnesota Historical Society.

55. When further sensational stories about him appeared in the American press in the fall of 1915, Hoover instructed his wife to repudiate them: "Lou wish you would send out emphatic general denial and express my profound distaste King and other fantastic stories and simply represent me as an engineer of varied experience. . . . All this absurd untrue personal publicity by our zealous friends is doing our work infinite harm." Hoover cable to his wife, October 2, 1915, "Hoover, Lou Henry," Pre-Commerce Papers.

56. Starr J. Murphy to John D. Rockefeller, Jr., November 20, 1914, Rockefeller Foundation archives, RG 1.1, Series 100, Box 67, Folder 657, Rockefeller Archive Center, North Tarrytown, New York; Rockefeller Foundation's War Relief Commission memorandum of its London interviews, November 21, 1914, ibid., Box 63, Folder 623; Jerome Greene cable to Wickliffe Rose, November 20, 1914, ibid., Box 67, Folder 657; Greene to F. T. Gates, November 29, 1915, ibid.; Edward M. House diary, February 27, 1915, Edward M. House Papers, Yale University Library; House to Woodrow Wilson, March 1, 1915, ibid. Box 120.

57. Hoover memorandum (16 pages) included at the beginning of CRB—London office dossier 45; documents in CRB—London office dossier 45, pp. 17–22.

58. CRB's European directors cable to Hoover, October 23, 1915, CRB Correspondence, Box 20; CRB—London office cable 331 to CRB—New York office, November 23, 1915, in CRB—London office dossier 45, pp. 174–76.

59. *New York Times*, May 12, 1915, p. 5; ibid., May 16, 1915, section II, p. 5.

60. Hoover draft of cable to Mr. and Mrs. Lindon W. Bates, n.d. (ca. May 8, 1915), CRB Correspondence, Box 32.

61. *New York Times*, September 15, 1915, p. 4.

62. Ibid., May 12, 1915, p. 5, and May 16, 1915, section II, p. 5.

63. Hoover memorandum in CRB—London office dossier 45; Hoover to Alexander Hemphill, October 27, 1915, CRB Correspondence, Box 4. In this letter Hoover said that he had noticed "the occasional strangeness of Mr. Bates's conduct" since the *Lusitania* disaster.

64. White, "No Dividends," pp. 16–18, 33–34 (cited in note 43); Hoover memorandum in CRB—London office dossier 45; Bates cable 166 to Hoover, September 13, 1915.

65. Hoover to CRB—New York office (plus enclosed memorandum), August 31, 1915, CRB Correspondence, Box 4. Copies of this letter (and enclosure) are in the Edgar and Family Papers, Box 1, and in CRB—London office dossier 45, pp. 32–35.

66. Ibid.; Hoover to Bates, August 31, 1915 (cited in note 49).

67. Hoover to CRB—New York office, August 31, 1915.

68. Hoover to Bates (plus enclosure), September 1, 1915, CRB Correspondence, Box 13.

69. Hoover memorandum in CRB—London office dossier 45.

70. Hoover to Bates (plus enclosure), September 1, 1915.

71. Hoover to William C. Edgar, September 10, 1915, Edgar and Family Papers.

72. Hoover to John Beaver White, January 27, 1916, CRB Correspondence, Box 5.

73. Hoover to Edgar, September 10, 1915; [William C. Edgar], "Small Work by Small Men," *Bellman*, September 25, 1915, copy in Clippings File, HHPL.

74. Hoover to Hemphill, October 27, 1915.

75. Hoover memorandum in CRB—London office dossier 45; Bates cable 166 to Hoover, September 13, 1915.

76. Hoover memorandum in CRB—London office dossier 45; Hoover to William C. Edgar, October 12, 1915, Edgar and Family Papers, Box 1.
77. Hoover cable 210 to Bates, September 22, 1915, CRB cable files.
78. Hoover cable 212 to Bates, September 22, 1915, ibid.
79. CRB—New York office cable 198 to Hoover, October 1, 1915, ibid.
80. Edgar Rickard cable to John Beaver White, September 27, 1915, ibid.
81. *New York Times*, September 15, 1915, p. 4; Hoover memorandum in CRB—London office dossier 45.
82. Hoover to CRB—New York office, October 13, 1915, CRB Correspondence, Box 4.
83. Hoover to Emile Francqui, October 14, 1915; Hoover to Millard Hunsiker, October 14, 1915. Both in CRB Correspondence, Box 4.
84. Hoover to CRB—New York office, October 13, 1915.
85. Hoover cable 251 to Bates, October 15, 1915, CRB Correspondence, Box 4.
86. CRB—London office cable to William C. Edgar, October 16, 1915, CRB cable files.
87. CRB's European directors cable to Hoover, October 23, 1915.
88. Hoover memorandum in CRB—London office dossier 45; Hoover Calendar, HHPL.
89. Hoover Calendar, HHPL.
90. Lou Henry Hoover had sailed from England on May 29, had addressed a memorial service for Lindon Bates, Jr., in June, and had spent most of the summer and fall in California, including a trip to Yosemite. In late October she and her sons left for the East Coast to meet Hoover. Ibid.; *New York Times*, June 11, 1915, p. 15; various clippings in Hoover Family Clippings, 1915 folder, HHPL.
91. Hoover memorandum in CRB—London office dossier 45.
92. For further information on Hoover's effort to revive Belgian industry, see *PR-CRB*, II, pp. 1–30, and Kittredge, "History," pp. 216–24.
93. Lindon W. Bates dossier submitted to the State Department, October 1915, in CRB—London office dossier 45, pp. 42–89.
94. Hoover memorandum in CRB—London office dossier 45.
95. Ibid.; Edward M. House diary, October 25, 26, 28, 29, 31, November 2, 6, 1915, House Papers; Gordon Auchincloss diary, October 31, 1915, Yale University Library; House to Walter Hines Page, October 29, 1915, Walter Hines Page Papers, Harvard University.
96. House diary, October 25, 1915.
97. Hoover memorandum in CRB—London office dossier 45.
98. Hoover to Hemphill, October 27, 1915.
99. Ibid.; Hoover to CRB—London office, November 2, 1915, CRB Correspondence, Box 4; Hoover cable to Brand Whitlock, ca. November 15, 1915, ibid. Hoover told Whitlock that he thought Bates's mind had been "partially unhinged since his son's death."
100. Hoover memorandum in CRB—London office dossier 45. The State Department officials whom he met were the third assistant secretary, William Phillips, and the assistant counsellor, Frank Polk.
101. Hoover, *An American Epic*, vol. 1 (Chicago, 1959), p. 162.
102. Secretary of State Robert Lansing cable to American Embassy, London, October 16, 1915, file 855.48/322a, RG 59, NARA; Walter Hines Page cable to Lansing, October 18, 1915, file 855.48 / 323, ibid.
103. Henry Cabot Lodge to William Phillips, October 22, 1915, file 855.48 / 389, ibid.
104. Hoover to Hemphill, October 27, 1915.
105. Notes of interview with Tracy B. Kittredge, June 2, 1951, Carol Green Wilson Papers, HI. Kittredge erroneously dated this episode as occurring in 1916.
106. Hoover to William Phillips, October 30, 1915 (three letters), file 855.48 / 395, RG 59, NARA; copies in CRB Correspondence, Box 4, and in House Papers, Box 89.
107. Hoover memorandum in CRB—London office dossier 45.
108. Ibid.

109. Hoover to Edward M. House, August 16, 1915 (plus enclosed memorandum), House Papers, Box 61. A copy of these documents is in CRB—London office dossier 45.
110. Lindon W. Bates to William Phillips, October 29, 1915, file 855.48 / 394, RG 59, NARA.
111. Hoover to William Phillips, October 31, 1915, file 855.48 / 398, ibid.; copy in House Papers, Box 89. See also Hoover to Phillips, November 1, 1915, file 855.48 / 399, RG 59, NARA, and Hoover to House, November 1, 1915, House Papers, Box 61. In his letter to House, Hoover labeled Bates's assertion that the August memorandum was prepared for a *British* Cabinet friend "an unwarranted assumption" since Hoover did not "enjoy the acquaintance [to] the degree of friendship of any gentleman holding such a position."
112. Sir Edward Grey to Hoover, June 9, 1914, "Grey, Sir Edward, 1914–1916," Pre-Commerce Papers.
113. Whitlock diary, September 13, 1915, in his *Journal*, p. 210. For more on this episode see chapter 12.
114. Hoover memorandum in CRB—London office dossier 45.
115. Hoover to Bates, October 31, 1915, CRB Correspondence, Box 4.
116. Hoover to Alexander Hemphill, November 2, 1915, ibid.
117. Ibid.
118. Hoover memorandum in CRB—London office dossier 45; Hoover to Bates, October 31, 1915; Bates to Hoover, November 3, 1915, CRB Correspondence, Box 32, copy in file 855.48 / 400, RG 59, NARA.
119. Hoover to CRB—London office, November 2, 1915.
120. Hoover memorandum in CRB—London office dossier 45.
121. Ibid. Hoover probably wrote this memorandum in early November.
122. William Goode cable to Walter Hines Page, received in London, November 1, 1915, in American Embassy, London, Correspondence, 1915, vol. 95, file 848—Belgium, RG 84, NARA.
123. Some of Goode's phraseology ("whole work," for instance) had a Hooverian sound.
    It is unclear whether there was in fact any effort underway in Washington to induce Hoover to resign as chairman of the CRB. No corroborating evidence has been found. This suggestion may have been a ploy by Goode (and Hoover?) to elicit a strong supporting cable from the reliable Ambassador Page.
124. Walter Hines Page cable to Secretary of State Lansing, November 2, 1915, file 855.48 / 326, RG 59, NARA.
125. Hoover, *An American Epic*, I, p. 39.
126. Hoover memorandum in CRB—London office dossier 45; Franklin K. Lane to Hoover, November 4, 1915, ibid., p. 155; Hoover to Lane, November 6, 1915, ibid., p. 156.
127. House diary, November 2, 1915.
128. Hoover memorandum in CRB—London office dossier 45.
129. Ibid.; Hoover cable to CRB—London office, November 7, 1915, CRB Correspondence, Box 4; Wilson to Joseph P. Tumulty, November 3, 1915, printed in Arthur S. Link et al., eds., *The Papers of Woodrow Wilson*, vol. 37 (Princeton, N.J., 1981), pp. 541–42. Wilson, in the latter document, called Bates a "mischief-maker." See also William Phillips to Henry Cabot Lodge, November 4, 1915, file 855.48 / 396, RG 59, NARA. In this letter Phillips said that he and his colleague Frank Polk had "about come to the conclusion that there is no necessity for taking any drastic action which would curtail the Commission's actions."
130. Wilson to Edith Bolling Galt, November 3, 1915, in Arthur S. Link et al., eds., *The Papers of Woodrow Wilson*, vol. 35 (Princeton, N.J., 1980), p. 165.
131. Hoover memorandum in CRB—London office dossier 45. Hoover's complete account (in this document) of his meeting with President Wilson is as follows:

We saw the President at the White House at 10:30 on Wednesday morning [November

3, 1915] and he stated that these matters had been brought to his attention, and that he was desirous of saying how much he and all of the Administration appreciated the work of the Commission and thoroughly supported it in all its actions. I mentioned to him my difficulty and my belief that Mr. Bates' mind was upset by virtue of the great blow he had had whilst in the midst of nervous overstrain and my fear that Mr. Bates' passion for personal publicity might lead him to endeavour to create a public scandal; that I had asked and had in view the asking of a number of gentlemen in New York to join our Executive Committee, but that they were a little loath to come into a quarrel and suggested it would be of the greatest possible service to us if he would add his personal request to my own urging. This he agreed to do and asked the nature of the letter which I would like written. He also stated that it might be useful for the Administration to make a public statement as to their unqualified approval of all the work of the Commission and of its actions, and said he would like our suggestion as to whether he should do it at once or wait until we were attacked. I immediately replied that I believed it would be desirable to do it at once as it would probably head off any attack. He said he would do so some time during the day. He spoke again in the warmest possible terms of all the members of the Commission and the appreciation in which they were and should be held in the minds of the American people.

132. Woodrow Wilson press statement, November 3, 1915, in *Papers of Woodrow Wilson*, vol. 37, p. 542. This source states erroneously that the President's statement was not actually issued to the press. In fact, the text was printed at once in many American newspapers, including the *Boston Herald* and *New York Herald*. For a sample of the coverage, see: CRB News Cuttings (New York office), vol. 10, p. 42, HHPL. See also CRB—London office dossier 45, p. 152.

133. Hoover memorandum in CRB—London office dossier 45; Woodrow Wilson to Herbert S. Eldridge, November 3, 1915, in CRB dossier 45, p. 154; Wilson to Hoover, November 3, 1915, ibid., p. 155; Hoover cable to CRB—London office, November 7, 1915. The seven men to whom Wilson wrote were: Otto Bannard, S. R. Bertron, Herbert S. Eldridge, Alexander Hemphill, Melville Stone, Oscar Straus, and John Beaver White.

134. Hoover memorandum in CRB—London office dossier 45; Henry Cabot Lodge to William Phillips, November 4, 1915, file 855.48 / 336, RG 59, NARA. Many years later, in his *Memoirs* and elsewhere, Hoover recalled his interview with Senator Lodge as "chilly" and "not very satisfactory." This was not how he or Senator Lodge portrayed it at the time; according to Hoover's memorandum (prepared just a few days after the interview), the senator had been "very sympathetic." See Hoover, *The Memoirs of Herbert Hoover*, vol. 1: *Years of Adventure* (New York, 1951), p. 201; Hoover, *An American Epic*, I, p. 162. Hoover's accounts of the Bates episode in these two later sources contain many inaccuracies; see note 173.

135. Hoover to CRB—London office, November 5, 1915, CRB Correspondence, Box 4; Hoover memorandum in CRB—London office dossier 45. Hoover did not, however, see a copy of Senator Lodge's letter to Bates. This letter has not been found, but an extract is quoted in Lindon W. Bates to Hoover, November 6, 1915, file 855.48 / 332, RG 59, NARA; copy in CRB Correspondence, Box 13. Bates tried to portray Lodge's letter as supportive, but the quoted extract seems to be a polite suggestion to Bates to drop his fight against Hoover and the CRB.

136. Hoover memorandum in CRB—London office dossier 45. According to Hoover's recollection many years later, he thereupon paid a visit to former President Theodore Roosevelt at his home in Oyster Bay, Long Island. According to Hoover, Roosevelt enthusiastically commended the commission and offered his support if needed. Hoover, *Years of Adventure*, pp. 201–2; Hoover, *An American Epic*, p. 162. I can find no other evidence, however, that this meeting occurred at that time. Hoover's contemporary, day-by-day memorandum of

the Bates episode did not record such a meeting, nor did he mention it in any of his known cables and letters to his associates. In contrast, he referred freely to his interview with President Wilson, and there seems to be no reason why he would have concealed a similar appointment with Roosevelt. Weighing the evidence, one wonders whether Hoover's memory misplaced the date of his rendezvous with Roosevelt. In early 1917 he did meet the former President about Belgian relief matters. One suspects it was *this* meeting that he later mistakenly recalled as occurring in November 1915.

137. See Alexander Hemphill to Woodrow Wilson, November 4, 1915; Oscar Straus to Wilson, November 5, 1915; Melville Stone to Wilson, November 9, 1915; John Beaver White to Wilson, November 16, 1915; S. R. Bertron to Wilson, November 17, 1915; all in Wilson Papers. See also Hoover to Oscar T. Bannard, November 3, 1915, CRB—London office dossier 45, p. 158; Hoover to Melville Stone, November 3, 1915, ibid., p. 159. Of the original seven men contacted by President Wilson, two—Bannard and Stone—declined to serve, while a third (Eldridge) died shortly afterward on a trip to Peru. CRB—London office dossier 45, p. 171.

138. Hemphill to Wilson, November 4, 1915.

139. Straus to Wilson, November 5, 1915.

140. Stone to Wilson, November 9, 1915. Stone, incidentally, had also lost a son on the *Lusitania*.

141. Minutes of a meeting of the New York committee of the Commission for Relief in Belgium, November 5, 1915, in CRB—New York committee minutes, Pre-Commerce Papers. Copy in CRB—London office dossier 45, pp. 160–60b.

142. Ibid. In his memorandum in CRB—London office dossier 45, Hoover recorded that he asked the president on November 3 for help in persuading the business leaders to "join our Executive Committee." Join, not replace. But in his letter of November 5 to his associates in London, Hoover said he told the President that he had asked "certain gentlemen of importance in New York to join a *newly constituted* New York Committee . . ." (emphasis added). It is not known whether President Wilson was aware of this subtle but significant change.

143. CRB—New York committee minutes, November 5, 1915.

144. Edward M. House to James W. Gerard, November 3, 1915, House Papers, Box 48.

145. Hoover to CRB—London office, November 5, 1915.

146. Hoover to Bates, November 4, 1915, CRB Correspondence, Box 4.

147. Bates to Hemphill, November 5, 1915, file 855.48 / 329, RG 59, NARA.

148. CRB—New York committee minutes, November 6, 1915, Pre-Commerce Papers. Copy in CRB—London office dossier 45, pp. 161–61a.

149. Bates to Hoover, November 6, 1915.

150. CRB—New York committee minutes, November 6, 1915; Hoover memorandum in CRB—London office dossier 45; Bates to the Secretary of State (plus enclosure), November 6, 1915, file 855.48 / 329, RG 59, NARA; William Goode cable to CRB—London office, November 22, 1915, in CRB—London office dossier 45, p. 173.

151. Hoover cable to CRB—London office, November 7, 1915.

152. Lou Henry Hoover to Laurine A. Small, November 26, 1915, "Small, Laurine A.," Personal Correspondence, 1874–1920, Lou Henry Hoover Papers.

153. Hoover memorandum in CRB—London office dossier 45; House diary, November 6, 1915.

154. Hoover memorandum in CRB—London office dossier 45; Hoover cable to CRB—London office, November 7, 1915.

155. CRB—London directors' cable to Hoover, November 8, 1915, in CRB—London office dossier 45, p. 166, and in American Embassy, London, Correspondence, 1915, vol. 95, file 848—Belgium, RG 84, NARA.

156. Walter Hines Page to William Honnold, November 8, 1915, in American Embassy, Lon-

don, Correspondence, 1915, vol. 95, file 848—Belgium, RG 84, NARA; Comité National (Brussels) cable to Hoover, November 8, 1915, in CRB—London office dossier 45, p. 167.

157. Hoover memorandum in CRB—London office dossier 45.

158. Hoover cable 325 to CRB—New York office, November 20, 1915, in CRB—London office dossier 45, p. 169.

159. Bates to Hemphill, November 19, 1915, enclosed with Bates to William Phillips, November 22, 1915, file 855.48/401, RG 59, NARA.

160. Bates to Phillips, November 22, 1915.

161. CRB—New York office cable 272 to CRB—London office, November 22, 1915, in CRB cable files and CRB—London office dossier 45, p. 172; Goode cable to CRB—London office, November 22, 1915.

162. Hoover cable 332 to CRB—New York office, November 23, 1915, in CRB—London office dossier 45, p. 177.

163. CRB—London office cable 321 to CRB—New York office, November 23, 1915, in CRB—London office dossier 45, pp. 174–76.

164. CRB—New York office cable 279 to CRB—London office, November 24, 1915, in CRB cable files and CRB—London office dossier 45, p. 179; CRB—New York committee minutes, November 29, 1915, Pre-Commerce Papers.

165. *New York Herald*, December 7, 1915, p. 11.

166. Hoover to CRB—London office, November 5, 1915.

167. Lou Henry Hoover to Laurine A. Small, November 26, 1915.

168. Even Senator Lodge declared himself willing to "sustain [the CRB] to the limit." Lodge to Phillips, November 4, 1915.

169. Hoover was also obliged to dissolve the CRB—New York office's women's section, headed by Lindon Bates's wife. CRB—New York committee minutes, November 29, 1915; *New York Herald*, December 7, 1915, p. 11; CRB—London office dossier 45, pp. 181–84. Mrs. Bates, like her husband, was embittered at Hoover.

170. The New York committee soon comprised Hemphill, White, Bertron, Straus, C. A. Coffin, R. Fulton Cutting, Elbert H. Gary, Henry L. Stimson, Frank Trumbull, and Frank A. Vanderlip. Kittredge, "History," p. 212.

171. Bates to the Secretary of State, November 19, 1914, file 855.48/50, RG 59, NARA.

172. H. B. Brougham, "Why Mr. Hoover Reorganized His New York Commission for Relief in Belgium" (typescript, ca. 1920), in Raymond Robins Papers, Box 45, State Historical Society of Wisconsin. One such individual with whom Bates came in contact was Senator James A. Reed of Missouri, Hoover's fiercest critic in Congress in the the years 1917–20.

173. *New York Times*, April 23, 1924, p. 21. In his *Memoirs* (*Years of Adventure*, pp. 199–202) and his *An American Epic*, I, pp. 161–62, Hoover gave brief accounts of the Bates affair. Unfortunately, these reminiscences contain a number of serious errors. In his *Memoirs*, for example, Hoover placed the date of the controversy as May 1915 (not October–November) and made Senator Lodge appear to be the villain of the piece, when in fact there is no evidence that Lodge was then unfriendly to him or desirous of attacking him publicly. Furthermore, Hoover stated that the complaint against him at the State Department was initiated by "a discharged and consequently aggrieved member of the Commission." In fact, Bates had *not* been "discharged" when he first contacted the department. Hoover's ascription of a motive to Bates was quite incorrect. Other inaccuracies of detail follow, including the doubtful account of Hoover's meeting with Theodore Roosevelt. The animus against Senator Lodge appears also in the account given in *An American Epic*, along with other inaccurate recollections, including the assertion that Bates "was persuaded to retire peaceably." In fact, of course, Bates withdrew on his own volition and in anger. In constructing my own account of this episode, I have relied whenever possible on contemporary records and not on Hoover's imperfect published recollections.

174. *New York Times*, November 10, 1915, p. 22.

175. *PR-CRB*, II, pp. 1–30; Kittredge, "History," pp. 216–24.
176. Hoover, *An American Epic*, I, pp. 135–40; *PR-CRB*, I, pp. 322–31.
177. Hoover to Bates, September 1, 1915.
178. *PR-CRB*, I, pp. 126, 213; ibid., II, p. 476; Kittredge, "History," p. 73.
179. Kittredge, "Taking Care of Belgium," p. 2.
180. George I. Gay, *Commission for Relief in Belgium: Statistical Review of Relief Operations* (Stanford, Calif., 1925), p. 2; *PR-CRB*, II, pp. 469, 478.
181. *PR-CRB*, II, pp. 310–47, 482; Ernest Mahaim, *Le Secours de chômage en Belgique pendant l'occupation allemande* (Paris and New Haven, 1926), pp. 21–24.
182. *PR-CRB*, II, pp. 331–34; Hoover, *Years of Adventure*, p. 176.
183. *PR-CRB*, II, pp. 333–34.
184. Ben S. Allen, "Feeding Seven Million Belgians," *World's Work* [London], April 1915, copy in Reprint File, HHPL; *PR-CRB*, II, pp. 479–80; Kittredge, "History," p. 182.
185. Kittredge, "History," p. 182. The subject of milling ratios frequently arose in Hoover's correspondence with William C. Edgar, editor of the *Northwestern Miller* and somewhat of a fanatic on the desirability of using white flour for making bread. See Hoover's letters to Edgar, May 25, June 29, August 1, August 3, and September 2, 1915, all in Edgar and Family Papers. See also Hoover to Brand Whitlock, April 5, 1915, CRB Correspondence, Box 3.
186. Allen, "Feeding Seven Million Belgians."
187. Edgar Rickard to Andrew C. Lawson, April 17, 1915, Andrew C. Lawson Papers, the Bancroft Library, University of California at Berkeley; Kittredge, "History," p. 236; *PR-CRB*, II, p. 469n.
188. *Outlook* 110 (June 9, 1915): 295; *PR-CRB*, II, p. 480.
189. Hoover, *Years of Adventure*, p. 176.
190. Hoover to Lord Eustace Percy (plus enclosure), August 24, 1915, in FO 368 / 1211 / file 2402, PRO, and in *PR-CRB*, II, pp. 6–9; British Cabinet memorandum circulated August 31, 1915, in Cab. 37 / 133 / 25, PRO.
    Ultimately the number of Belgians dependent at least to some degree on charity reached more than 75% of the population. *PR-CRB*, II, p. 310.
191. "Foreword" to Kittredge, "Taking Care of Belgium," p. 2.
192. Lord Curzon at a meeting, October 12, 1915, in support of the Lord Mayor's City of London committee of the National Committee for Relief in Belgium. Quoted in *Manchester Guardian*, October 13, 1915, in CRB News Cuttings (New York office), vol. 10, p. 4, HHPL.
193. Goode cable to Page, received in London, November 1, 1915; Page cable to Secretary of State Lansing, November 2, 1915.

CHAPTER 7

1. Lou Henry Hoover to Ray Lyman Wilbur, December 1, 1915, Ray Lyman Wilbur Personal Papers, Box 31, Stanford University Archives.
2. *New York Times*, November 10, 1915, p. 22; Hoover to New York committee of Commission for Relief in Belgium, November 6, 1915, printed in George I. Gay and H. H. Fisher, *Public Relations of the Commission for Relief in Belgium* (Stanford, Calif., 1929), II, pp. 274–76, hereinafter cited as *PR-CRB*; Hoover to William C. Edgar, December 13, 1915, William C. Edgar and Family Papers, Minnesota Historical Society.
3. Close study of the primary sources indicates that Hoover made at least eight visits to Belgium between November 1914 and December 31, 1915. His last trip of 1915 brought him to Brussels on November 27. See Hugh Gibson to Brand Whitlock, December 1, 1915, Hugh Gibson Papers, Box 65, HI.

4. Gilchrist B. Stockton to his parents, November 30, 1915, extract in "Stockton, Gilchrist B.," Pre-Commerce Papers, Herbert Hoover Papers, HHPL; Hugh Gibson to his mother, December 1, 1915, Gibson Papers, Box 33.

5. Gibson to his mother, December 1, 1915; Gibson to Whitlock, December 1, 1915; Gibson to an unknown correspondent, December 6, 1915, Gibson Papers, Box 45; Gibson to his mother, December 9, 1915, ibid., Box 33.

6. The phrase was Gibson's in his letter to an unknown correspondent, December 6, 1915.

7. Tracy B. Kittredge, "The History of the Commission for Relief in Belgium, 1914–1917" (unpublished bound page proof version, ca. 1918), pp. 224–27, copy at HHPL; CRB—London office dossier 22: "The German Espionage Charges," HI; Hugh Gibson to Secretary of State Robert Lansing, January 7, 1916, in American Legation, Brussels, Correspondence, 1916, vol. 71, file 848, RG 84, NARA.

8. Kittredge, "History," pp. 227–28; Hugh Gibson memorandum of conversation with von der Lancken, November 30, 1915, printed in *PR-CRB*, I, pp. 73–75; Gibson to Lansing, January 7, 1916.

9. Kittredge, "History," pp. 227–28.

10. Ibid., p. 231; Hugh Gibson memorandum, December 1, 1915, in CRB—London office dossier 22.

11. Hoover memorandum, n.d., in CRB—London office dossier 22; Vernon Kellogg memorandum, December 2, 1915, printed in *PR-CRB*, I, pp. 75–77; Kittredge, "History," pp. 229, 232–33; Gibson to an unknown correspondent, December 6, 1915; Gibson to Lansing, January 7, 1916.

12. Gibson to an unknown correspondent, December 6, 1915.

13. Kellogg memorandum, December 2, 1915; Kittredge, "History," pp. 230–32; Hugh Gibson to Secretary of State Robert Lansing, January 3, 1916, in American Legation, Brussels, Correspondence, 1916, vol. 71, file 848, RG 84, NARA.

14. Kellogg memorandum, December 2, 1915.

15. Gibson to Lansing, January 3, 1916.

16. Kittredge, "History," p. 233; Gibson to Lansing, January 7, 1916; Hoover to Lord Eustace Percy, February 18, 1916, CRB Correspondence, Box 5, HI; Hoover to John Beaver White, April 17, 1916, ibid., Box 6; Joseph C. Green to his parents, January 14, 1917, Joseph C. Green Papers, Box 1, HI.

17. Hoover to Percy, February 18, 1916.

18. Ibid.; Gibson to Lansing, January 3, 1916; Hoover to White, April 17, 1916; Kittredge, "History," pp. 233–34; CRB—London office dossier 22.

19. Kellogg memorandum, December 2, 1915; Hoover to Percy, February 18, 1916; Hoover to White, April 17, 1916; Wallace Winchell and George Taggart, *A Yankee Major Invades Belgium* (New York, 1916), pp. 48–53. Winchell eventually was permitted to enter Belgium and conduct relief work for the Salvation Army.

20. Hoover to Percy, February 18, 1916; Hoover to White, April 17, 1916.

21. Hoover to Percy, February 18, 1916. See also Hoover to White, April 17, 1916.

22. Hoover memorandum, December 8, 1915, in CRB—London office dossier 22; Hoover to Percy, February 18, 1916; Kittredge, "History," pp. 233–34.

23. Kittredge, "History," pp. 234–35, 287.

24. Victoria French Allen, "A Member of the Fourth Estate" (typescript, n.d.), pp. 93–94, in Allen Collection (cited in chapter 3, note 219).

25. Kittredge, "History," p. 238.

26. Ibid., p. 239; Lord Robert Cecil, memorandum for the War Cabinet, December 22, 1916, in Cab. 23 / 1 / 87, PRO.

27. Kittredge, "History," pp. 239–40.

28. Ibid., p. 240; Secretary of the Admiralty to Undersecretary of State at the Foreign Office, December 10, 1915, in FO 371 / 2286 / file 609, PRO; Maurice de Bunsen (of the Foreign

Office) to Secretary of the Admiralty, December 13, 1915, ibid.

29. Eustace Percy to Hoover, December 16, 1915 (two letters); Eustace Percy memorandum, December 16, 1915; internal Foreign Office memorandum on meeting of War Trade Advisory Committee, December 16, 1915. All in FO 371 / 2286 / file 609, PRO. See also Kittredge, "History," pp. 240–41, and *PR-CRB*, I, pp. 128–29 (wherein one of Percy's letters of December 16 is printed).

30. Percy to Hoover, December 16, 1915.

31. Hoover to Percy, December 16, 1915, in FO 371 / 2286 / file 609, PRO; copy in CRB Correspondence, Box 5.

32. Ibid.

33. Hoover to William Goode (Secretary, National Committee for Relief in Belgium), December 16, 1915, CRB Correspondence, Box 5.

34. Hoover to Percy, December 16, 1915.

35. Some, at least, sold their rations, and the aggregate was not insignificant. Kittredge, "History," p. 238. Hoover acknowledged that it was possible for Belgians to take their individual rations and sell them to the German army. But he insisted that the Belgians themselves were "most zealous" about protecting the distribution of imported supplies. Hoover to Percy, December 16, 1915.

36. Hoover to Percy, December 21, 1915, in *PR-CRB*, I, pp. 129–34; Maurice de Bunsen to Secretary, Commission Internationale de Ravitaillement, December 24, 1915, in FO 371 / 2286 / file 609, PRO; Eustace Percy to a Mr. Wills, December 27, 1915, ibid.; de Bunsen to Secretary of the Admiralty, December 29, 1915, ibid.; Kittredge, "History," pp. 241, 246. Kittredge and *PR-CRB*, I, p. 136, both state that Hoover appeared before the War Trade Advisory Committee's subcommittee on December 23. But the Foreign Office memo of December 16 cited in note 29 indicates that the meeting was to occur on December 22, the date I have given in the text. It is possible, of course, that the meeting was postponed for a day.

37. Sir Edward Grey to Walter Hines Page, December 31, 1915, in *PR-CRB*, I, pp. 136–38.

38. Kittredge, "History," pp. 247–48.

39. Percy memorandum, December 16, 1915.

40. Secretary of the Admiralty to Undersecretary of State at the Foreign Office, December 10, 1915.

41. De Bunsen to Secretary of the Admiralty, December 13, 1915.

42. Hoover to Percy, December 20, 1915, in FO 371 / 2286 / file 609, PRO; Hoover to Walter Runciman, December 30, 1915, copy in American Embassy, London, Correspondence, 1916, vol. 112, file 848—Serbia, RG 84, NARA.

43. Hoover to Runciman, December 30, 1915.

44. Percy to Hoover, December 28, 1915, printed in *PR-CRB*, I, pp. 134–35; internal Foreign Office notes on condensed milk tins, January 2 and 3, 1916, in FO 371 / 2286 / file 609, PRO.

45. Hoover to Percy, December 29, 1915, in FO 371 / 2286 / file 609, PRO.

46. Foreign Office to William Honnold, January 11, 1916, ibid.

47. Hoover, *An American Epic*, vol. 1 (Chicago, 1959), pp. 174–75.

48. Kittredge, "History," p. 253.

49. Hoover to William B. Poland, January 13, 1916, in American Legation, Brussels, Correspondence, 1916, vol. 71, file 848, RG 84, NARA; Hoover to Brand Whitlock, January 18, 1916, ibid.; Hoover to Alexander J. Hemphill, January 27, 1916, CRB Correspondence, Box 5.

50. Hoover to Walter Hines Page, January 7, 1916, in American Embassy, London, Correspondence, 1916, vol. 112, file 848—Serbia, RG 84, NARA.

51. Hoover to John Beaver White, January 27, 1916, CRB Correspondence, Box 5; Hoover to

Brand Whitlock, January 28, 1916, in American Legation, Brussels, Correspondence, 1916, vol. 72, file 848, RG 84, NARA.

52. Hoover to Hemphill, January 27, 1916.

53. Hoover to John Beaver White, January 29, 1916, "C.R.B.—New York Committee: Minutes and Agenda," Pre-Commerce Papers; Henry L. Stimson to Alexander J. Hemphill, February 4, 1916, ibid.

54. Hoover to Edmund Speyer, February 17, 1916, CRB Correspondence, Box 5.

55. CRB—New York committee, minutes of January 21, 1916 meeting, Pre-Commerce Papers.

56. Lou Henry Hoover cable to Hoover, September 8, 1915, Herbert Hoover Collection, Box 317, HI; Hoover cable to his San Francisco office, December 24, 1915, ibid.; Hoover to Ray Lyman Wilbur, August 12, 1916, CRB cable files, Pre-Commerce Papers. Hoover funneled his gift to Kellogg through an old friend, Ray Lyman Wilbur, who became president of Stanford University in 1916.

57. Brand Whitlock diary, February 24, 1916, printed in Allan Nevins, ed., *The Journal of Brand Whitlock* (New York, 1936), p. 240.

58. Hoover cable to his San Francisco office, December 24, 1915; Hoover to Wilbur, August 12, 1916; Hoover to Wilbur, September 27, 1916, Wilbur Personal Papers, Box 31.

59. Hoover to Hugh Gibson, January 11, 1916, in American Legation, Brussels, Correspondence, 1916, vol. 71, file 848, RG 84, NARA; Hoover to Louis Chevrillon, January 12, 1916, CRB cable files; Hoover to Brand Whitlock, January 18, 1916; Lou Henry Hoover to the Ray Lyman Wilbur family, January 18, 1916, Wilbur Personal Papers, Box 31.

60. Hoover to Gibson, January 11, 1916.

61. Hoover to David P. Barrows, January 21, 1916, David P. Barrows Papers, the Bancroft Library, University of California, Berkeley.

62. Hugh Gibson to his mother, January 20, 1916, Gibson Papers, Box 33.

63. *New York Times*, February 8, 1916, p. 2; *PR-CRB*, I, p. 333; Hoover cable to Brand Whitlock, February 8, 1916, in ibid., pp. 340–41.

64. Hoover cable to Louis Chevrillon, February 3, 1916, in *PR-CRB*, I, p. 337; Hoover cable to Whitlock, February 8, 1916.

65. Hoover to James Gerard, February 7, 1916, CRB Correspondence, Box 5.

66. Hoover to Hugh Gibson, January 25, 1916, in American Legation, Brussels, Correspondence, 1916, vol. 71, file 848, RG 84, NARA.

67. Hoover to Whitlock, February 8, 1916.

68. Ibid.

69. *PR-CRB*, I, p. 333.

70. Hoover to Gibson, January 25, 1916.

71. Eustace Percy to Hoover, January 21, 1916, copy enclosed in Hoover to Brand Whitlock, January 24, 1916, in American Legation, Brussels, Correspondence, 1916, vol. 72, file 848, RG 84, NARA.

72. Hoover to William B. Poland, January 24, 1916, CRB Correspondence, Box 5; copy enclosed in Hoover to Whitlock, January 24, 1916.

73. Hoover to Whitlock, January 24, 1916.

74. Hoover to Comité National, January 24, 1916, enclosed in ibid.

75. Hoover to Gibson, January 25, 1916.

76. Hoover to Gibson, January 11, 1916; Hoover to Poland, January 24, 1916. See also Poland to Gibson, January 3 and 17, 1916, both in American Legation, Brussels, Correspondence, 1916, vol. 71, file 848, RG 84, NARA.

77. Hoover to Gibson, January 11, 1916.

78. Kittredge, "History," p. 271.

79. Henri Pirenne, *La Belgique et la guerre mondiale* (Paris and New Haven, 1928), p. 150.

80. Emile Francqui to Hoover, January 31 and February 4, 1916, CRB Correspondence, Box 15. Francqui claimed that Hoover's letter had displayed "excitement by no means justified by the incident itself."
81. Kittredge, "History," pp. 269, 361.
82. Poland to Gibson, January 17, 1916.
83. Kittredge, "History," pp. 237–39, 262, 264; Joseph C. Green memorandum, May 21, 1917, Green Papers, Box 20.
84. Kittredge, "History," p. 262; Hoover to Eustace Percy, November 24, 1916, CRB Correspondence, Box 7.
85. Hoover to Gibson, January 25, 1916.
86. Hoover memorandum on Belgian foodstuff leakages, February 8, 1916, in American Legation, Brussels, Correspondence, 1916, vol. 72, file 848, RG 84, NARA.
87. Ibid.
88. Hoover to Eustace Percy, February 8, 1916, in *PR-CRB*, I, pp. 80–81.
89. Hoover to Poland, January 24, 1916; Hoover to Gibson, January 25, 1916.
90. Brand Whitlock to Walter Hines Page, January 17, 1916 (two letters), January 24, 1916, and February 7, 1916, all in American Embassy, London, Correspondence, 1916, vol. 109, file 848—Belgian Relief, RG 84, NARA; Whitlock to Hoover, January 24, 1916, in American Legation, Brussels, Correspondence, 1916, vol. 71, file 848, RG 84, NARA; Whitlock diary, January 21, 23, 24, and 31, 1916, in his *Journal*, pp. 229–33.
91. Hoover to Gerard, February 7, 1916.
92. Hoover arrived in Paris on February 10, 1916. Kittredge, "History," p. 311; Hoover memorandum of visit to France, dated February 18, 1916, in *PR-CRB*, I, pp. 435–38.
93. Hoover memorandum, February 18, 1916.
94. For a good account of Hoover's trip to Paris and its results, see Kittredge, "History," pp. 308–14.
95. Hoover to Eustace Percy, February 18, 1916, CRB Correspondence, Box 5.
96. Kittredge, "History," pp. 310–14.
97. See *PR-CRB*, I, pp. 129–34, 432–34, and Hoover, *An American Epic*, I, p. 179.
98. Hoover to Eustace Percy, February 16, 1916.
99. W. Langley (for Sir Edward Grey) to Walter Hines Page, February 23, 1916, in American Embassy, London, Correspondence, 1916, vol. 109, file 848—Belgian Relief, RG 84, NARA.
100. Eustace Percy to Hoover, February 23, 1916, in *PR-CRB*, I, pp. 140–41; Hoover, *An American Epic*, I, pp. 181–82, 186.
101. CRB–CN statement of organization of Department of Inspection and Control, February 23, 1916, in *PR-CRB*, I, pp. 86–89; Kittredge, "History," pp. 269–73, 361.
102. Hoover to Percy, February 8, 1916.
103. Hoover to Eustace Percy, April 5, 1916, in *PR-CRB*, I, pp. 82–84.
104. Hoover to Percy, November 24, 1916.
105. Kittredge, "History," pp. 361–62; Joseph C. Green memorandum, May 21, 1917.
106. Kittredge, "History," p. 270.
107. Joseph C. Green memorandum, May 21, 1917.
108. Kittredge, "History," pp. 253–54; Hoover memorandum on the Marquis de Villalobar, n.d. (probably March 1916), in CRB—London office dossier 77: "Villalobar," HI; Baron von der Lancken to Brand Whitlock, February 16, 1916, printed in *PR-CRB*, II, pp. 402–4.
109. Hoover memorandum on Villalobar.
110. Walter Hines Page diary, February 25, 1916, Walter Hines Page Papers, Harvard University.
111. Ibid.
112. Hoover to Walter Hines Page, February 24, 1916, in American Embassy, London, Correspondence, 1916, vol. 109, file 848—Belgian Relief, RG 84, NARA; printed in *PR-CRB*, I, pp. 90–92.

113. Sir Edward Grey to Lord Crewe, February 21, 1916, FO 800 / 100 / 480, PRO.
114. Whitlock diary, February 24, 1916, in his *Journal*, p. 240.
115. Whitlock diary, March 22, 1916, in his *Journal*, pp. 244–45.
116. Ibid.
117. Hoover memorandum, October 24, 1916, in CRB—London office dossier 77.
118. Hoover memorandum on Villalobar.
119. Ibid.; Hoover to Villalobar, February 25, 1916, in CRB—London office dossier 77.
120. Hoover memorandum on Villalobar; Whitlock diary, March 22, 1916.
121. Ibid.; Page diary, February 25, 1916; Hoover to Brand Whitlock, March 1, 1916, in American Legation, Brussels, Correspondence, 1916, vol. 72, file 848, RG 84, NARA; Sir Edward Grey to Page, March 13, 1916, in American Embassy, London, Correspondence, 1916, vol. 109, file 848—Belgian Relief, RG 84, NARA (in *PR-CRB*, I, pp. 94–95).
122. Sir Edward Grey to the Marquis de Villalobar, February 28, 1916, copy in American Embassy, London, Correspondence, 1916, vol. 109, file 848—Belgian Relief, RG 84, NARA.
123. Emile Francqui to Walter Hines Page, February 26, 1916, copy in American Embassy, London, Correspondence, 1916, vol. 109, file 848—Belgian Relief, RG 84, NARA. Printed in a slightly different translation in *PR-CRB*, I, pp. 92–93.
124. Hoover memorandum on Villalobar.
125. Ibid.; Whitlock diary, March 22, 1916.
126. Page diary, February 25, 1916; Hugh Gibson to his mother, February 26, 1916, Gibson Papers, Box 33; Whitlock diary, March 22, 1916. In reconstructing this episode I have relied on contemporary sources only. Hoover's later account of the affair, given in his *An American Epic*, I, pp. 196–205, contains several inaccuracies, including the claim that he actually welcomed the plan to have the Comité National supplant the CRB! In his letter of "resignation" to Ambassador Page on February 24, Hoover of course made it appear that he was willing to step aside. But he hardly approved the idea, as his memorandum written soon after the event abundantly indicated. Contrary to his account in *An American Epic*, he emphatically did *not* welcome the Francqui–Lambert–Villalobar plot to oust the CRB.
127. Hoover to Whitlock, March 1, 1916.
128. Hoover to Frederic C. Walcott, February 28, 1916, Frederic C. Walcott Papers, Box 6, Yale University Library; Walcott to Jerome D. Greene, February 29, 1916, ibid.
129. A typescript copy of Walcott's press release is in his papers, Box 5. It was printed in the *New York Times*, February 28, 1916, p. 3, as well as in the British press.
130. Grey to Page, March 13, 1916.
131. Hoover to Walter Hines Page, March 18, 1916, in American Embassy, London, Correspondence, 1916, vol. 109, file 848—Belgian Relief, RG 84, NARA; copy in CRB Correspondence, Box 5.
132. Sir Edward Grey to Walter Hines Page, May 16, 1916, in American Embassy, London, Correspondence, 1916, vol. 109, file 848—Belgian Relief, RG 84, NARA; also in *PR-CRB*, I, p. 75.
133. Hoover to Eustace Percy, April 5, 1916, in *PR-CRB*, I, pp. 82–84; Whitlock diary, March 29 and 31, 1916, in his *Journal*, pp. 249–50, 252.
134. Green memorandum, May 21, 1917.
135. Ibid.; Whitlock diary, March 31, 1916; Kittredge, "History," pp. 271–81.
136. Kittredge, "History," pp. 253–57, 279, 332; Whitlock diary, April 14, 1916, in his *Journal*, p. 255; Baron Oscar von der Lancken to Brand Whitlock, April 14, 1916, in *PR-CRB*, I, pp. 154–57; Maurice de Bunsen to Walter Hines Page, May 6, 1916, in ibid., I, pp. 157–59.
137. Whitlock diary, March 22, 1916, in his *Journal*, p. 244.
138. Whitlock diary, March 24, 1916, in his *Journal*, p. 246.
139. Ibid.

140. Whitlock diary, March 22, 1916, in his *Journal*, p. 245.
141. Hoover memorandum of his visit to northern France, March 28, 1916, reproduced in *PR-CRB*, I, between pp. 438 and 439.
142. Hoover to Eustace Percy, April 5, 1916, in *PR-CRB*, I, pp. 150–53.
143. Whitlock recorded in his diary on March 30 that Hoover was "sick over his visit to Lille" (*Journal*, p. 251).
144. Hoover to Percy, April 5, 1916 (cited in note 142).
145. Hoover to Percy, April 5, 1916 (two letters, both previously cited).
146. Eyre A. Crowe to Walter Hines Page, April 11, 1916, in American Embassy, London, Correspondence, 1916, vol. 109, file 848—Belgian Relief, RG 84, NARA (in *PR-CRB*, I, p. 154 as a letter addressed to Hoover); Hoover to Crowe, April 12, 1916, in American Legation, Brussels, Correspondence, 1916, vol. 67, file 848, RG 84, NARA; Kittredge, "History," pp. 316–17.
147. De Bunsen to Page, May 6, 1916; de Bunsen to Hoover, May 10, 1916, in *PR-CRB*, I, p. 159; *The Times* (London), June 2, 1916, p. 10.
148. Hoover, *An American Epic*, I, p. 199.
149. Ibid., pp. 199–200; Hoover to Walter Hines Page, April 12, 1916, in American Embassy, London, Correspondence, 1916, vol. 109, file 848—Belgian Relief, RG 84, NARA (copy in CRB Correspondence, Box 6).
150. Eustace Percy, *Some Memories* (London, 1958), pp. 45, 47; Justice Sir Sydney A. T. Rowlatt, report to Sir Edward Grey, April 13, 1916, FO 800 / 195 / 46-52, PRO. A slightly condensed version of Rowlatt's report is in the Rickard files, Misrepresentations File, HHPL.
151. Rowlatt report, April 13, 1916; Admiral Edmond P. Slade to Sir Eyre Crowe, February 12, 1916, FO 368 / 1664 / file 2962, PRO. According to Slade, Hoover had been "in the German Zinc Combine before the war" and was "still very intimate" with the Mertons of Frankfurt, a prominent German mining family.
152. Hoover to Page, April 12, 1916.
153. Hoover to Justice Sir Sydney A. T. Rowlatt, April 12, 1916, CRB Correspondence, Box 6.
154. For an account of Hoover's career in China and the lawsuit that resulted from it, see my volume, *The Life of Herbert Hoover: The Engineer, 1874–1914* (New York, 1983), pp. 96–222. As noted above in chapter 2, this was the trial at which Hoover had blamed Emile Francqui for the breach of contract eventuating in the lawsuit.
155. Hoover to Justice Rowlatt, April 7, 1916, CRB Correspondence, Box 6; Hoover to Page, April 12, 1916.
156. Rowlatt to Hoover, April 7, 1916, copy enclosed in Hoover to Walter Hines Page, April 14, 1916, in American Embassy, London, Correspondence, 1916, vol. 109, file 848—Belgian Relief, RG 84, NARA; Rowlatt report, April 13, 1916.
157. Hoover to Page, April 12, 1916. See also Hoover to Page, April 14, 1916.
158. Hoover to Percy, February 18, 1916; Hoover to White, April 17, 1916; Karl Eilers to Hoover, April 25, 1916, in CRB—London office dossier 22; Charles F. Rand to Hoover, April 27, 1916, ibid. Hoover, of course, withdrew his recommendation of Erdlets.
159. Hoover to White, April 17, 1916.
160. Rowlatt report, April 13, 1916; Percy, *Some Memories*, p. 47.
161. Internal Foreign Office memorandum on Rowlatt report, in FO 382 / 1165 / file 142, PRO.
162. Lord Islington to Lord Robert Cecil, April 28, 1916, Cecil of Chelwood Papers, FO 800 / 195 / 34-36, PRO; Cecil to Islington, May 2, 1916, ibid., pp. 40–41.
163. Hoover, *An American Epic*, I, pp. 206–14; Percy, *Some Memories*, p. 47. Hoover's dossier on the Rowlatt investigation was entitled "The English Inquisition." CRB—London office dossier 21, HI.
164. [?] to Sir Edward Grey, April 15, 1916; Grey's reply, April 16, 1916; both in Cecil of Chelwood Papers, FO 800 / 195 / 24-25. See also Foreign Office internal memoranda on

Rowlatt report, April 18 and other dates, 1916, FO 382 / 1165 / file 142.

165. Transcript of proceedings of the annual meeting of the National Committee for Relief in Belgium, London, May 4, 1916, in CRB News Cuttings, vol. 14, between pp. 14 and 15, HHPL. For various press accounts of the meeting see *The Times* (London), May 5, 1916, p. 7, and CRB News Cuttings, vol. 14, p. 14, HHPL.

166. Grey to Page, May 16, 1916.

167. Hoover to Brand Whitlock, March 13, 1916, in American Legation, Brussels, Correspondence, 1916, vol. 72, file 848, RG 84, NARA.

168. Kittredge, "History," pp. 280–81; Whitlock diary, May 22, June 2, 8, July 6, 1916, in his *Journal*, pp. 263, 268, 271, 279; Vernon Kellogg to Whitlock, July 15, 1916, in American Legation, Brussels, Correspondence, 1916, vol. 70, file 848, RG 84, NARA.

169. Whitlock diary, May 17, 1916, in his *Journal*, p. 262; Kittredge, "History," pp. 286–88, 291–92, 323–26, 331–32.

170. Hoover to Louis Chevrillon, August 12, 1916, in *PR-CRB*, I, pp. 592–93.

171. Hoover, *An American Epic*, I, pp. 251–52.

172. Gibson to Whitlock, December 1, 1915.

173. Kittredge, "History," pp. 318–20.

174. Hoover to Brand Whitlock, April 17, 1916, in American Legation, Brussels, Correspondence, 1916, vol. 73, file 848, RG 84, NARA; Hoover, memorandum no. 13, April 20, 1916, ibid., vol. 67, file 848; Hoover to Edgar, May 4, 1916, Edgar and Family Papers.

175. Sir Edward Grey to Walter Hines Page, June 14, 1916, in *PR-CRB*, I, pp. 160–61.

176. Kittredge, "History," pp. 289–91.

177. Decree by Governor-General von Bissing, July 8, 1916, in *PR-CRB*, I, pp. 557–59; Hoover, *An American Epic*, I, p. 220.

178. Kittredge, "History," pp. 332, 334–35; Louis Chevrillon to Consul-General Kammerer, June 13, 1916, in *PR-CRB*, I, pp. 583–84.

179. Kittredge, "History," pp. 332–35; Hoover to Louis Chevrillon, March 18, 1916, in *PR-CRB*, I, pp. 579–80; Hoover to James Gerard, July 11, 1916, in ibid., pp. 587–88.

180. Robert Cecil to Walter Hines Page, July 7, 1916, in American Embassy, London, Correspondence, 1916, vol. 109, file 848—Belgian Relief, RG 84, NARA.

181. Eustace Percy to Hoover (plus enclosure), July 8, 1916, in *PR-CRB*, I, pp. 585–86; Hoover, *An American Epic*, I, pp. 235–36.

182. Hoover to Gerard, July 11, 1916; Hoover to Page, July 11, 1916, in American Embassy, London, Correspondence, 1916, vol. 109, file 848—Belgian Relief, RG 84, NARA; Gerard to Dr. Helfferich, July 18, 1916, printed in *PR-CRB*, I, pp. 588–89; Helfferich to Gerard, July 25, 1916, ibid., p. 589; Hoover, *An American Epic*, I, pp. 236–38.

183. Maurice Pate diary, July 27, 1916, HHPL; Whitlock diary, July 28, August 2, 1916, in his *Journal*, pp. 282, 284; Kittredge, "History," pp. 335–36; Vernon Kellogg, *Fighting Starvation in Belgium* (Garden City, N.Y., 1918), p. 58.

184. Pate diary, July 27, 1916.

185. Brand Whitlock, *Belgium: A Personal Narrative*, vol. 2 (New York, 1919), p. 374.

186. *New York Times*, July 28, 1916, p. 2.

187. Ibid., July 31, 1916, p. 7; Whitlock diary, August 6, 1916, in his *Journal*, p. 284.

188. *New York Times*, August 6, 1916, p. 1.

189. Kittredge, "History," pp. 336–37.

190. *New York Times*, July 31, 1916, p. 7; clippings in CRB News Cuttings, vol. 14, p. 119, and vol. 15, p. 1.

191. Kellogg, *Fighting Starvation*, pp. 58–59; Kittredge, "History," p. 337; Hoover, *The Memoirs of Herbert Hoover*, vol. 1: *Years of Adventure* (New York, 1951), pp. 193–94.

192. Whitlock, *Belgium*, II, p. 380; Kellogg, *Fighting Starvation*, pp. 60–67; Hoover, *Years of Adventure*, pp. 194–95.

193. Hoover, *Years of Adventure*, p. 195.
194. Kellogg, *Fighting Starvation*, p. 64; Percy, *Some Memories*, p. 48.
195. Hoover, *An American Epic*, I, p. 243; Hoover, *Years of Adventure*, p. 196.
196. Kellogg, *Fighting Starvation*, p. 64; Kellogg–von Kessler memorandum, August 26, 1916, printed in *PR-CRB*, I, p. 594; Hoover to Percy, September 4, 1916, in ibid., I, p. 595; Hoover, *An American Epic*, I, pp. 243–45.
197. Kittredge, "History," p. 341.
198. Hoover to Chevrillon, September 4, 1916, in *PR-CRB*, I, p. 596; Whitlock diary, August 26, 1916, in his *Journal*, p. 288.
199. Kittredge, "History," p. 340.
200. Hoover to Chevrillon, September 4, 1916.
201. Percy, *Some Memories*, p. 48.
202. Kittredge, "History," p. 333.
203. Hoover to Chevrillon, August 12, 1916.
204. Hoover memorandum, August 28, 1916, of conferences in Paris, in *PR-CRB*, I, pp. 442–44.
205. Ibid.; Hoover–Chevrillon memorandum, ca. August 28, 1916, enclosed with ibid., pp. 444–48; *PR-CRB*, I, p. 449n; Kittredge, "History," p. 339.
206. Kittredge, "History," pp. 342–43.
207. Chairman of Lille district committee to Hoover, November 18, 1916, in *PR-CRB*, I, pp. 452–53.

CHAPTER 8

1. Hugh Gibson to his mother, February 6, 1915, Hugh Gibson Papers, Box 32, HI; Herbert Hoover memorandum, May 26, 1915, CRB Correspondence, Box 3, HI; Rockefeller Foundation, *Annual Report: 1915* (New York, 1916), pp. 284–86; George I. Gay and H. H. Fisher, *Public Relations of the Commission for Relief in Belgium* (Stanford, Calif., 1929), II, pp. 83–84, hereinafter cited as *PR-CRB*.
2. *PR-CRB*, II, p. 84; Rockefeller Foundation, *Annual Report: 1915*, pp. 286–87. For more on the Rockefeller Foundation's Polish relief efforts, see Ernest P. Bicknell, "The Battlefield of Poland," *Survey* 37 (December 2, 1916): 231–36, and Bicknell, "Begging Bread for Poland," *Survey* 37 (January 6, 1917): 398–402.
3. Hoover memorandum, May 26, 1915. Hoover was still disgusted weeks later with the Rockefeller Foundation's handling of the Polish relief question. See Brand Whitlock diary, June 21, 1915, in Allan Nevins, ed., *The Journal of Brand Whitlock* (New York, 1936), p. 170. Hoover told Emile Francqui on June 24 that food "would be flowing into Poland to-day" if a systematic worldwide publicity campaign had been conducted in behalf of Poland, as he had done for Belgium. Hoover to Emile Francqui, June 24, 1915, CRB Correspondence, Box 4.
4. Rockefeller Foundation, *Annual Report: 1915*, p. 287.
5. Bicknell, "Begging Bread for Poland," p. 402; Vernon Kellogg report on conditions in Poland, November 1915, in *PR-CRB*, II, pp. 86–91. A copy of Kellogg's report is in the Edward M. House Papers, Box 61, Yale University Library.
6. CRB—London office to CRB—New York office, October 27, 1915, in *PR-CRB*, II, p. 86.
7. Hoover to CRB—London office, October 28, 1915, in *PR-CRB*, II, p. 86; *New York Times*, November 4, 1915, p. 5.
8. Kellogg report on conditions in Poland, November 1915.
9. Petition by citizens of Warsaw to CRB, December 3, 1915, in *PR-CRB*, II, pp. 93–96.
10. Hoover memorandum of meeting with Major von Kessler et al., December 2, 1915, in *PR-CRB*, II, pp. 91–93.

11. Hoover to CRB—New York office, December 15, 1915, CRB Correspondence, Box 5.
12. Hoover to William C. Edgar, December 13, 1915, William C. Edgar and Family Papers, Minnesota Historical Society.
13. Hoover to CRB—New York office, December 15, 1915.
14. Hoover to Sir Edward Grey, December 22, 1915, in *PR-CRB*, II, pp. 97–98. Copy in House Papers, Box 61.
15. Hoover to Walter Hines Page, January 7, 1916, in American Embassy, London, Correspondence, 1916, vol. 112, file 848—Serbia, RG 84, NARA; American Embassy, London, to State Department, January 11, 1916, in ibid., file 848—Poland, RG 84, NARA.
16. *Mining Journal* 112 (January 8, 1916): vii.
17. Lou Henry Hoover to Ray Lyman Wilbur, December 1, 1915, Ray Lyman Wilbur Personal Papers, Box 31, Stanford University Archives.
18. *New York Times*, January 22, 1915, p. 3; Hoover to Edward M. House, February 23, 1916, House Papers, Box 61.
19. *New York Times*, February 5, 1916, p. 3.
20. Rockefeller Foundation, *Annual Report: 1915*, p. 323.
21. H. O. Beatty cable to CRB—London office, November 25, 1915, CRB cable files, Pre-Commerce Papers, Herbert Hoover Papers, HHPL; Hoover to CRB—New York office, December 29, 1915, CRB Correspondence, Box 5; Hoover to Page, January 7, 1916.
22. CRB—London office cable to H. O. Beatty, November 29, 1915, CRB cable files; Hoover to CRB—New York office, December 29, 1915. Hoover told his New York office that he did not consider the situation inside Serbia to be "one of very extremely pressing order."
23. CRB—London office to Beatty, November 29, 1915.
24. Hoover to CRB—New York office, December 29, 1915.
25. Hoover to H. O. Beatty, December 23, 1915, copy enclosed in Hoover to CRB—New York office, January 12, 1916, CRB Correspondence, Box 5. Copy also in Frederic C. Walcott Papers, Box 5, Yale University Library.
26. Ibid.
27. Hoover to CRB—New York office, December 29, 1915; Hoover cable to American Relief Clearing House, January 16, 1916, CRB cable files; Hoover to CRB—New York office, January 12, 1916 (plus enclosures). On January 7, 1916 Hoover told Page that the situation in Serbia was "not absolutely critical as yet." Hoover to Page, January 7, 1916.
28. Hoover to N. Boshkovitch, December 28, 1915, in CRB—London office dossier 71: "Preliminary Negotiations for the Relief of Serbia," HI; Hoover to American Relief Clearing House, January 12, 1916; Hoover to Hugh Gibson, January 25, 1916, in American Legation, Brussels, Correspondence, 1916, vol. 71, file 848, RG 84, NARA; Hoover memorandum on Serbian relief, February 8, 1916, ibid., vol. 72, file 848, RG 84, NARA.
29. Hoover cable to American Relief Clearing House, January 12, 1916.
30. Hoover to H. O. Beatty, January 12, 1916, enclosed in Hoover to CRB—New York office, January 12, 1916.
31. J. F. Lucey cable to Hoover, January 8, 1916; Hoover cable to Lucey, January 10, 1916. Both in CRB cable files.
32. Hoover to Beatty, January 12, 1916.
33. H. O. Beatty to Hoover, January 18, 1916, in CRB—London office dossier 71.
34. See various documents in CRB—London office dossier 71.
35. Hoover to H. O. Beatty, January 24, 1916, in CRB—London office dossier 71.
36. Ibid.
37. Hoover cable 106 to CRB—New York office, February 16, 1916; Hoover to the Serbian minister to Great Britain, February 18, 1916. Both in CRB—London office dossier 71.
38. See various documents in CRB—London office dossier 71, particularly H. O. Beatty to Hoover, April 12, 1916.

39. Hoover to A. E. Naville, January 27, 1916; Hoover to Louis Chevrillon, March 18, 1916. Both in CRB—London office dossier 71.

40. Hoover to H. O. Beatty, April 26, 1916, in CRB—London office dossier 71.

41. Sir Edward Grey to Hoover, February 5, 1916, in *PR-CRB*, II, p. 102 (copy in House Papers, Box 61). For more on the British attitude, see *PR-CRB*, II, pp. 98–101, and *New York Times*, January 16, 1916, section II, p. 4.

42. Hoover memorandum on Polish relief, February 8, 1916, in American Legation, Brussels, Correspondence, 1916, vol. 72, file 848, RG 84, NARA.

43. Ibid.; Hoover to Gerard, February 7, 1916, in *PR-CRB*, II, pp. 103–4.

44. Hoover to Gerard, February 7, 1916.

45. German government at Warsaw, memorandum of agreement on relief principles, February 11, 1916, in *PR-CRB*, II, pp. 104–5.

46. Hoover–Walcott memorandum, February 21, 1916, in *PR-CRB*, II, pp. 107–8; Hoover to House, February 23, 1916.

47. Walter Hines Page to State Department, March 6, 1916, in American Embassy, London, Correspondence, 1916, vol. 112, file 848—Poland, RG 84, NARA; *PR-CRB*, II, p. 107n.

48. Page to State Department, March 6, 1916.

49. Frederic C. Walcott to H. O. Beatty, February 23, 1916, Walcott Papers, Box 6.

50. Hoover to Gerard, February 24, 1916, in *PR-CRB*, II, p. 109.

51. Ibid.

52. Ibid.; Walcott to Jerome D. Greene, Walcott Papers, Box 6.

53. Hoover to Walcott, February 28, 1916, Walcott Papers, Box 6. See also an interview of Walcott in *New York Times*, February 28, 1916, p. 3.

54. Page to State Department, March 6, 1916; William Phillips to House, March 18, 1916, House Papers, Box 89. See also Secretary of State Lansing to Page, February 26, 1916, in *PR-CRB*, II, pp. 108–9. In his letter of February 24, 1916 to Ambassador Gerard, Hoover stated that his "friends in America" were "agitating" the Polish relief question and that "the pressure of American opinion" might possibly influence the British government.

55. Hoover to House, February 23, 1916. See also Hoover to Page, February 28, 1916, in American Embassy, London, Correspondence, 1916, vol. 112, file 848—Belgium, RG 84, NARA.

56. Hoover to House, February 23, 1916; Walcott to Beatty, February 29, 1916, Walcott Papers, Box 6.

57. Louis Chevrillon to Hoover, March 15, 1916, in CRB—London office dossier 71.

58. Hoover to House, February 23, 1916. See also Walcott to Beatty, February 29, 1916.

59. Walter Hines Page to State Department, February 28, 1916, in American Embassy, London, Correspondence, 1916, vol. 112, file 848—Poland, RG 84, NARA.

60. Edward M. House diary, February 22, 1916, Yale University Library.

61. Hoover to Gerard, February 24, 1916.

62. Walcott to Greene, February 29 and March 21, 1916, and to Mrs. F. S. Kellogg, March 4, 1916. All in Walcott Papers, Box 6.

63. *PR-CRB*, II, p. 111; British Foreign Office to Page, May 10, 1916, in *PR-CRB*, II, pp. 111–13.

64. Warwick Greene to Jerome D. Greene, May 16, 1916, Rockefeller Foundation archives, RG 1.1, Series 100, Box 72, Folder 688, Rockefeller Archive Center, North Tarrytown, New York; John F. Smultski cable to Hoover, May 16, 1916, CRB cable files; Warwick Greene cable to Rockefeller Foundation, May 17, 1916, copy in Walcott Papers, Box 7.

65. Hoover cable to Warwick Greene, May 17, 1916, CRB cable files.

66. Gerard to Page, May 30, 1916, in American Embassy, London, Correspondence, 1916, vol. 112, file 848—Poland, RG 84, NARA. Copy (misdated June 1) in *PR-CRB*, II, pp. 115–16.

67. Grey to Page, June 15, 1916, in *PR-CRB*, II, pp. 116–17.

68. Page to Jerome D. Greene, June 8, 1916, in American Embassy, London, Correspondence, 1916, file 848—Poland, RG 84, NARA.
69. Page to Grey, July 8, 1916, in *PR-CRB*, II, p. 119.
70. Wilson to various European heads of state, July 20, 1916, in Arthur S. Link et al., eds., *The Papers of Woodrow Wilson*, vol. 37 (Princeton, N.J., 1981), p. 445; *New York Times*, July 22, 1916, p. 9.
71. *New York Times*, October 18, 1916, p. 3; Arthur S. Link et al., eds., *The Papers of Woodrow Wilson*, vol. 38 (Princeton, N.J., 1982), pp. 29–30, 62, 64–66, 79–81.
72. Hugh Gibson to William B. Poland, August 10, 1916, in *PR-CRB*, II, pp. 120–21.
73. Page to Secretary of State, July 22, 1916, in American Embassy, London, Correspondence, 1916, vol. 112, file 848—Poland, RG 84, NARA.
74. W. Langley to Page, July 26, 1916, in *PR-CRB*, II, pp. 119–20; *New York Times*, July 27, 1916, p. 4; ibid., July 28, 1916, p. 2.
75. As Lord Percy later acknowledged, it appeared for a time that he and his colleagues had "overplayed our hand." Eustace Percy, *Some Memories* (London, 1958), pp. 47–48.
76. *PR-CRB*, II, pp. 123–24.
77. Maurice de Bunsen to Walter Hines Page, July 20, 1916, in American Embassy, London, Correspondence, 1916, vol. 112, file 848—Serbia, RG 84, NARA.
78. *PR-CRB*, II, p. 111n; Rockefeller Foundation, *Annual Report: 1916* (New York, 1917), pp. 323–26.
79. Tracy B. Kittredge, "The History of the Commission for Relief in Belgium, 1914–1917" (unpublished bound page proof version, ca. 1918), p. 2, copy at HHPL.
80. Eustace Percy to the Undersecretary of State for the Colonial Office, March 23, 1915, FO 371 / 2285 / file 609, PRO; Lord Robert Cecil to Maurice Hankey, May 17, 1916, Cecil of Chelwood Papers, FO 800 / 195 / 59-62, PRO.
81. Cecil to Hankey, May 17, 1916.
82. Lord Robert Cecil memorandum for the Cabinet, December 22, 1916, Cab. 23 / 1 / 87-88, PRO.
83. Whitlock diary, May 18, 1916, in his *Journal*, p. 262.
84. Kittredge, "History," p. 304; Hoover, *An American Epic*, I, p. 266.
85. *PR-CRB*, I, p. 343n, and II, p. 476.
86. Ibid., II, p. 472.
87. Walcott to S. W. Childs, March 8, 1916, Walcott Papers, Box 6.
88. Walcott to Frank Hitchcock, May 9, 1916, ibid., Box 7.
89. David Barrows, quoted in *San Francisco Examiner*, September 15, 1915, copy in CRB News Cuttings, vol. 15, p. 26, HHPL.

CHAPTER 9

1. *New York Times*, September 25, 1916, p. 1; numerous newspaper clippings in CRB News Cuttings, vol. 15, pp. 4, 5, 34, HHPL; Hoover, *The Memoirs of Herbert Hoover*, vol. 1: *Years of Adventure* (New York, 1951), pp. 187–88.
2. See the newspaper clippings cited in note 1.
3. Hoover to Brand Whitlock and the Marquis de Villalobar, September 15, 1916, in George I. Gay and H. H. Fisher, *Public Relations of the Commission for Relief in Belgium* (Stanford, Calif., 1929), I, pp. 164–65, hereinafter cited as *PR-CRB; New York Times*, September 18, 1916, p. 11; Hoover to Lord Eustace Percy, October 7, 1916, in *PR-CRB*, I, pp. 165–71; Tracy B. Kittredge, "The History of the Commission for Relief in Belgium, 1914–1917" (unpublished bound page proof version, ca. 1918), pp. 293–94, copy at HHPL.
4. *New York Times*, October 12, 1916, p. 1.
5. Ibid., December 21, 1916, p. 8.

6. Hoover to Brand Whitlock, August 19, 1916, in American Legation, Brussels, Correspondence, 1916, vol. 73, file 848, RG 84, NARA.

7. Hoover to Percy, October 7, 1916.

8. Kittredge, "History," p. 295; Edgar Rickard to Charles Janin, November 17, 1916, Charles Janin Papers, Box 3, the Huntington Library, San Marino, California.

9. *New York Times*, September 18, 1916, p. 11, and October 12, 1916, p. 1.

10. Ibid., December 21, 1916, p. 8.

11. George Barr Baker cable to CRB—London office, October 18, 1916, CRB cable files, Pre-Commerce Papers, Herbert Hoover Papers, HHPL; *New York Times*, December 6, 1916, pp. 1, 4, and December 21, 1916, p. 8.

12. *Engineering and Mining Journal* 102 (December 9, 1916): 1034; *PR-CRB*, II, pp. 281, 283.

13. Hoover cable to CRB—New York office, December 28, 1916, CRB cable files.

14. Hoover continued to regard private charity as "erratic and uncertain." Hoover to Paul Hymans, August 24, 1916, in *PR-CRB*, I, pp. 268–70.

15. Hoover to Percy, October 7, 1916; Eustace Percy, memorandum regarding CRB's financial request, October 1916, copy in Bonar Law Papers, Box 72, House of Lords Record Office, London. See also Hoover to Hymans, August 24, 1916.

16. A. W. Lidderdale to Hoover, October 27, 1916, in *PR-CRB*, I, p. 270; Maurice de Bunsen to Walter Hines Page, October 30, 1916, in American Embassy, London, Correspondence, 1916, vol. 110, file 848—Belgium, RG 84, NARA; Herbert Hoover, *An American Epic*, vol. 1 (Chicago, 1959), p. 263.

17. Kittredge, "History," pp. 344–48; *PR-CRB*, II, p. 31.

18. Kittredge, "History," p. 345.

19. It was the commission's Brussels director, William B. Poland, who put a check to German ambitions. Shortly after the Lille deportations began, the U.S. ambassador to Germany, James Gerard, visited the Kaiser at the German General Staff's headquarters in northern France. Anxious to impress the ambassador, the German military hosted a tea party in his honor and invited Poland and other CRB men to attend. Throwing diplomatic etiquette to the winds, Poland personally denounced the deportations to Ambassador Gerard and a German general—right at the party. The effect was stunning. The general promised to investigate; the deportations immediately ceased.

   Poland's intervention proved decisive; it also evidently antagonized some Germans. Not long afterward Hoover replaced him at the Brussels office with Vernon Kellogg. Kittredge, "History," pp. 317–20, 348; *PR-CRB*, II, pp. 72–75; Brand Whitlock diary, July 5, 1917, in Allan Nevins, ed., *The Journal of Brand Whitlock* (New York, 1936), p. 428.

20. Kittredge, "History," pp. 350–53; Brand Whitlock diary, November 17, 1916, in his *Journal*, pp. 323–24.

21. *New York Times*, December 9, 1916, p. 1; *PR-CRB*, II, pp. 45, 51, 63.

22. *PR-CRB*, II, p. 45. See also Baron Moritz von Bissing (the German governor-general of Belgium) to Belgian burgomasters, October 28, 1916, in Ernest Mahaim, *Le Secours de chômage en Belgique pendant l'occupation allemande* (Paris and New Haven, 1926), pp. 227–28. Von Bissing personally opposed the deportation policy but was overruled.

23. Hoover to Brand Whitlock, November 8, 1916, Allan Nevins Papers, Rare Book and Manuscript Library, Columbia University; printed (as quoted here) in *PR-CRB*, II, p. 49.

24. Brand Whitlock diary, November 9, 1916, in his *Journal*, pp. 318–19.

25. Hoover to Walter Hines Page, October 11, 1916, in American Embassy, London, Correspondence, 1916, vol. 110, file 848—Belgium, RG 84, NARA; Hoover to Secretary of State Robert Lansing, October 10, 1916, in *PR-CRB*, II, 81–82.

26. Hoover cable 829 to CRB—New York office, November 24, 1916, copy enclosed in Hoover to Page, November 25, 1916, in American Embassy, London, Correspondence, 1916, vol. 110, file 848—Belgium, RG 84, NARA; Page cable to Secretary of State Lansing, November 24, 1916, ibid.

27. Hoover cable to CRB—New York office, November 20, 1916, in *PR-CRB*, II, p. 59.
28. *New York Times*, November 21, 1916, p. 2.
29. Hoover cable to CRB—New York office, November 20, 1916.
30. *New York Times*, December 9, 1916, p. 1 (quoting the U.S. protest to the German government on November 29).
31. *New York Times*, December 5, 1916, p. 1, and December 6, 1916, p. 4; Kittredge, "History," pp. 356–58.
32. Hoover to State Department, January 2, 1917, in *PR-CRB*, II, pp. 67–68.
33. Ibid.
34. Hoover memorandum 24G to Warren Gregory of the CRB's Brussels office, December 12, 1916, in American Legation, Brussels, Correspondence, 1916, vol. 64, file 848, RG 84, NARA; Hoover to Brand Whitlock, December 13, 1916, ibid.; Hoover to William Honnold (of the CRB's New York office), December 15, 1916, CRB Correspondence, Box 7, HI.
35. Ibid.
36. Hoover memorandum 24G, December 12, 1916.
37. William B. Poland memorandum, May 9, 1916 (plus enclosures), copy in CRB—London office dossier 15: "Differences with the Comité National," HI.
38. Ibid. For the minutes of this meeting, see the Comité National's *Rapport général*, part 1, pp. 396–405 (cited in chapter 2, note 15).
39. Poland memorandum, May 9, 1915.
40. See, for example, Whitlock's diary entries of May 1, October 1, and October 4, 1916, in his *Journal*, pp. 258, 299, 301.
41. Whitlock diary, May 22, 1916, in his *Journal*, p. 263.
42. Whitlock diary, April 19, 1916, ibid., p. 256.
43. Hoover, *An American Epic*, I, pp. 41, 198–99; Hoover to Hugh Gibson, February 19, 1937, "Gibson, Hugh," Post-Presidential Individual File, Hoover Papers.
44. Whitlock diary, June 16, 1915, in his *Journal*, p. 165. See also his diary comment of May 25, 1916 (in his *Journal*, p. 264): "I'm tired and sick of the whole miserable business."
45. Whitlock diary, February 10, 1916, in his *Journal*, pp. 235–36.
46. Ronald Swerczek, "The Diplomatic Career of Hugh Gibson, 1908–1938" (Ph.D. dissertation, University of Iowa, 1972), p. 69.
47. Ibid., p. 73; Whitlock diary, February 10, 1916.
48. Swerczek, "Gibson," pp. 74–75.
49. Hoover, *An American Epic*, I, pp. 41, 199.
50. Hugh Gibson to Hoover, December 20, 1915, Hugh Gibson Papers, Box 45, HI; Hoover to Gibson, December 28, 1915, ibid.; Hoover to Gibson, January 11, 1916, ibid.; Hoover cable to Colonel Edward M. House, May 12, 1916, Edward M. House Papers, Box 61, Yale University Library. At least twice Hoover interceded for Gibson with President Wilson's confidant, Colonel House.
51. Hugh Gibson to his mother, February 27, March 9, April 9, and May 26, 1916, Gibson Papers, Box 33.
52. Edward M. House diary, February 20, 1916, House Papers.
53. House diary, February 23, 1916.
54. House diary, February 20, 1916.
55. Ibid.; House cable to Secretary of State, February 20, 1916, file 123G35 / 179, RG 59, NARA.
56. Hoover to House, February 22, 1916, House Papers, Box 61.
57. See p. 194.
58. House cable to Secretary of State, February 20, 1916, file 123G35 / 178, RG 59, NARA.
59. House diary, February 25, 1916; Whitlock diary, February 10, 1916.
60. Whitlock cable to Secretary of State, March 13, 1916, file 123G35 / 95, RG 59, NARA.
61. Whitlock diary, March 26, 1916, in his *Journal*, p. 248.

62. Whitlock diary, March 31, 1916, in his *Journal*, p. 252.
63. Whitlock diary, November 23 and 30, 1917, Nevins Papers; printed (with both Colonel House's name and the Belgian informant's name omitted) in Whitlock's *Journal*, pp. 459, 461; Whitlock diary, December 9, 1917, printed in his *Journal*, p. 463; House diary, December 3, 1917. Said House on this occasion: "There seems to be a cabal against Whitlock of which Hoover is the head, Hugh Gibson the most active member and Walter Hines Page a sympathizer." At this point Hoover was evidently making another attempt to maneuver Whitlock out of his post in Belgium. Such at least was House's interpretation of Hoover's actions at that particular juncture.
64. See, for example, Whitlock's diary, May 6, 1918 (unedited version), Nevins Papers; printed (with a significant omission) in his *Journal*, p. 480. See also his diary entry of September 24, 1918, in his *Journal*, p. 505, and, much later, his long diary entry of November 3, 1932, in Brand Whitlock Papers, Box 7, LC.
    Hoover, of course, was equally critical of Whitlock. His published comments on the American diplomat have already been cited. An even harsher private appraisal is Hoover's letter to Hugh Gibson, February 19, 1937 (cited in note 43).
65. Poland memorandum, May 9, 1916.
66. Whitlock diary, May 17 and 22, 1916, in his *Journal*, pp. 261–62, 263.
67. Ibid.; Whitlock diary, May 25, 1916, in his *Journal*, p. 264; memorandum no. 15, May 9, 1916, copy in CRB—London office dossier 15; William B. Poland to Emmanuel Janssen, May 18, 1916, ibid.; Poland to Milton Brown, May 18, 1916, ibid.; Whitlock to Hoover, May 29, 1916, ibid.; Janssen to Hoover, June 4, 1916, ibid.; Eustace Percy to Hoover, March 14, 1916, printed in *PR-CRB*, I, p. 147; Sir Edward Grey to Walter Hines Page, June 14, 1916, ibid., I, pp. 160–61; Kittredge, "History," p. 369.
68. Hoover to Aloys van de Vyvere, April 17, 1916, in CRB—London office dossier 16; "Van de Vyvere Correspondence," HI. Hoover sent his letter after showing a draft (dated March 29) to Emile Francqui, who suggested certain changes. See Francqui to Hoover (plus enclosure), March 29, 1916, CRB Correspondence, Box 15.
69. Van de Vyvere to Hoover, April 27, 1916, in CRB—London office dossier 16.
70. Van de Vyvere to Hoover, April 27, 1916 (second letter), ibid.
71. Hoover memorandum drafted for Walter Hines Page, May 3, 1916, CRB Correspondence, Box 6.
72. Hoover to van de Vyvere, May 9, 1916, ibid. Copies also in CRB—London office dossier 16, and in American Legation, Brussels, Correspondence, 1916, vol. 67, file 848, RG 84, NARA.
73. [Hoover] memorandum 5F to Francqui, June 28, 1916, in American Legation, Brussels, Correspondence, 1916, vol. 67, file 848, RG 84, NARA; Hoover to van de Vyvere, July 18, 1916, in CRB—London office dossier 16; Hoover memorandum presented to van de Vyvere, July 15, 1916, enclosed with ibid. and printed in *PR-CRB*, II, pp. 185–86. I have found no evidence that van de Vyvere accepted Hoover's points as contained in his memorandum of July 15, 1916.
74. Whitlock diary, August 1, 21, 26, 1916, in his *Journal*, pp. 282–83, 287, 288. See also E. H. Kossman, *The Low Countries, 1780–1940* (Oxford, 1978), pp. 531–32, and Liane Ranieri, *Emile Francqui, ou l'intelligence créatrice* (Paris, 1985), pp. 137, 165–66.
75. Hoover to van de Vyvere, July 18, 1916.
76. See Liane Ranieri, "La Lente Gestation de la Fondation Universitaire, vue à travers les archives américaines," *Annales de la société royale d'archéologie de Bruxelles* 58(1981): 105–6 (full article: 103–120).
77. Ibid., pp. 107–11.
78. Paul Hymans, *Mémoires*, vol 1 (Brussels, 1958), p. 793.
79. See, for example, Francqui to Hoover, March 29, 1916, and Francqui to Paul Segers (Belgian minister of railways), April 28, 1916, CRB Correspondence, Box 15, HI. See also

Ranieri, "La Lente Gestation," pp. 106–11.
80. Francqui to Hoover, March 29, 1916.
81. Ibid.
82. Ibid. In this letter Francqui noted that he had informed the king of Belgium "of the intentions you [Hoover] and I entertained with regard to the employment of the money belonging to this fund which should be in our hands after the war." In his correspondence with Hoover, Francqui treated his American colleague as a knowing and willing co-venturer in the drive for some kind of benevolent postwar enterprise funded by relief profits. In at least two instances Hoover served as an intermediary on the subject between Francqui and the exiled Belgian government. See Francqui to Baron Napoléon Eugène Beyens, August 2, 1916, and Francqui memorandum 77 to Hoover, August 4, 1916; both in CRB Correspondence, Box 15. See also Hoover to van de Vyvere, August 15, 1916, in CRB—London office dossier 16.
83. Whitlock diary, August 1, 1916.
84. Ibid.
85. Hoover to van de Vyvere, July 18, 1916.
86. Hoover memorandum submitted to van de Vyvere, July 15, 1916, in CRB—London office dossier 16.
87. Francqui memorandum 77 to Hoover, August 4, 1916. Quoted also in Hoover to van de Vyvere, August 15, 1916.
88. Hoover took note of this silence in his letter to van de Vyvere of August 15, 1916.
89. Whitlock diary, August 1, 1916.
90. Hoover to van de Vyvere, September 28, 1916, in CRB—London office dossier 16.
91. Carton de Wiart (in behalf of van de Vyvere) to Hoover, November 2, 1916, ibid.
92. Francqui to Hoover, May 6, 1916.
93. Kittredge, "History," p. 364.
94. [Hoover] memorandum 5F, June 28, 1916.
95. Milton Brown, for example, was instructed to compile data distinguishing the amount of clothing work generated by the Comité National from that "resulting from importations under the auspices of the C.R.B." Memorandum 15, May 9, 1916, cited in note 67.
96. Francqui memorandum 36 to Hoover, June 16, 1916, CRB Correspondence, Box 15; Kittredge, "History," pp. 364–65; [Hoover] memorandum 5F, June 28, 1916. See also Francqui memoranda 52 and 55 to Hoover, July 11, 1916, CRB Correspondence, Box 15.
97. Edgar Rickard to Hoover, May 10, 1916, CRB Correspondence, Box 6.
98. [Hoover] memorandum 5F to Francqui, June 28, 1916.
99. [Hoover] memorandum 3F to Francqui, June 27, 1916, in American Legation, Brussels, Correspondence, 1916, vol. 67, file 848, RG 84, NARA.
100. Hoover to Eustace Percy, June 30, 1916, in *PR-CRB*, I, pp. 103–6.
101. Eustace Percy to Hoover, July 15, 1916, in ibid., I, pp. 96–99.
102. Ibid.
103. Hoover to Whitlock, August 3, 1916, Nevins Papers; Whitlock diary, July 28, 1916, in his *Journal*, p. 282.
104. Whitlock to Hoover, July 19, 1916, in Allan Nevins, ed., *The Letters of Brand Whitlock* (New York, 1936), pp. 195–96; Whitlock diary, August 1, 1916, in his *Journal*, pp. 282–83.
105. Whitlock diary, July 28 and August 1, 1916, in his *Journal*, pp. 282–83.
106. See also Hoover memorandum 19F to Francqui, July 25, 1916, CRB—London office records, July–August 1916 folder, HI. In this memorandum Hoover told Francqui that "we won't quarrel over anything internal."
107. Joseph C. Green memorandum on Emile Francqui, February 15, 1917, Joseph C. Green Papers, Box 20, HI.

108. Green to his parents, January 14, 1917, Green Papers, Box 1; Green memorandum on Department of Inspection and Control, May 21, 1917, ibid., Box 20.
109. Kittredge, "History," p. 277.
110. Green to his parents, January 14, 1917; Green memorandum, May 21, 1917.
111. Joseph C. Green memorandum, September 1, 1916, in CRB—London office dossier 15; Kittredge, "History," p. 371. See also Joseph C. Green, "Report on the Organization and Activities of the Department of Inspection and Control of the Commission for Relief in Belgium" (CRB—London office dossier 82, May 1917), p. 93, HI.
112. Green memorandum on Francqui, February 15, 1917.
113. Whitlock diary, September 13 and 20, 1916, in his *Journal*, pp. 292, 296.
114. See Vernon Kellogg to Francqui, October 9, 1916; Francqui to Kellogg, October 10, 14, 18, and 25, 1916. Copies in CRB—London office dossier 80: "Differences with the Comité National. Correspondence with Dr. Kellogg and Mr. Francqui," HI. See also Joseph C. Green memorandum, October 28, 1916, in CRB—London office dossier 79: "Documents concerning the organisation of the Department of Inspection and Control. . . ," HI.
115. Kellogg to Francqui, October 9 and 24, 1916, CRB—London office dossier 80. See also Kellogg to Whitlock, October 3, 1916, in American Legation, Brussels, Correspondence, 1916, vol. 64, file 848, RG 84, NARA.
116. Francqui to Kellogg, October 10, 1916.
117. Francqui to Kellogg, October 25, 1916.
118. Hoover to Walter Hines Page, October 16, 1916, in American Embassy, London, Correspondence, 1916, vol. 110, file 848—Belgium, RG 84, NARA. Copy in CRB—London office dossier 15.
119. Whitlock diary, October 26, 1916, in his *Journal*, p. 308.
120. Ibid.; Whitlock diary, October 30, 1916, in his *Journal*, p. 311, Page to Whitlock, October 18, 1916, in American Legation, Brussels, Correspondence, 1916, vol. 64, file 848, RG 84, NARA (copy in CRB—London office dossier 15).
121. Page to Whitlock, October 18, 1916; Page and Alfonso Merry del Val (the Spanish ambassador to Great Britain) to Lord Grey (the former Sir Edward Grey), October 18, 1916, in American Embassy, London, Correspondence, 1916, vol. 110, file 848—Belgium, RG 84, NARA; Merry del Val to Hoover, October 18, 1916, copy in CRB—London office dossier 15.
122. Hoover to Page, October 18, 1916, in American Embassy, London, Correspondence, 1916, vol. 110, file 848—Belgium, RG 84, NARA; Hoover to Percy, October 18, 1916, copy enclosed with ibid. Copies of both letters are in CRB—London office dossier 15. See also Hoover to William Honnold, October 26, 1916, CRB Correspondence, Box 7.
123. Page to Whitlock, October 18, 1916.
124. Lord Grey to Page, October 20, 1916, in American Embassy, London, Correspondence, 1916, vol. 110, file 848—Belgium, RG 84, NARA. Copies in CRB—London office dossier 15, and *PR-CRB*, I, pp. 99–103.
125. Robert Cecil (for Lord Grey) to Page, October 20, 1916, in *PR-CRB*, I, pp. 108–9.
126. Eustace Percy to Hoover, October 20, 1916, copy in American Legation, Brussels, Correspondence, 1916, vol. 67, file 848, RG 84, NARA.
127. Page to Whitlock, October 23, 1916, in *PR-CRB*, I, pp. 106–8 (copy in CRB—London office dossier 15). Page's remark that the Comité National was not the "pivot on which the relief revolves in Belgium" is reminiscent of Hoover's remark to Louis Chevrillon that the CRB should be considered "the absolute pivot on which the whole ravitaillement hangs" (Hoover to Chevrillon, August 12, 1916, in *PR-CRB*, I, pp. 592–93). I suspect that both passages had the same author.
128. Whitlock diary, October 26, 1916.
129. Whitlock diary, October 29, 1916, in his *Journal*, p. 311.
130. Hoover to Honnold, October 26, 1916.

131. Whitlock diary, October 29 and 30, 1916.
132. Ibid., October 30, 1916.
133. Ibid., November 6, 1916, in his *Journal*, pp. 312–16.
134. Hoover to Francqui, October 31, 1916, CRB Correspondence, Box 7.
135. Joseph C. Green report to the director of the CRB's Brussels office on activities of the Department of Inspection and Control for the week ending November 4, 1916, in American Legation, Brussels, Correspondence, 1916, vol. 67, file 848, RG 84, NARA.
136. Whitlock diary, November 6, 1916.
137. Hoover to Percy, June 30, 1916.
138. Francqui to Hoover, November 11, 1916, copy in CRB—London office dossier 15, and in Whitlock Papers, Box 61.
139. Whitlock diary, November 6, 1916.
140. Whitlock diary, June 12, 1916, in his *Journal*, p. 272.
141. Quoted in Joseph C. Green oral history (1967), p. 9, HHPL.
142. George H. Nash, *The Life of Herbert Hoover: The Engineer, 1874–1914* (New York, 1983), pp. 165, 641, n. 41.
143. Green to his parents, January 14, 1917; Green memorandum on Francqui, February 15, 1917.
144. Whitlock diary, November 6, 1916.
145. Ibid.
146. Ibid.; Hoover to Francqui (regarding charitable payments), October 31, 1916, copy in CRB—London office dossier 15.
147. Hoover to Francqui, November 4, 1916, copy in CRB—London office dossier 15.
148. Francqui to Hoover, November 5, 1916; Hoover to Francqui, November 8, 1916; Francqui to Hoover, November 11, 1916. Copies in CRB—London office dossier 15.
149. Hoover to Francqui, November 10, 1916, copy in CRB—London office dossier 15.
150. Hoover to Francqui, November 4, 8, and 10, 1916; Francqui to Hoover, November 5 and 9, 1916. Copies in CRB—London office dossier 15.
151. Whitlock diary, November 7, 1916, in his *Journal*, p. 316.
152. Whitlock diary, November 6, 1916.
153. Ibid.; Whitlock diary, November 8, 1916, in his *Journal*, pp. 317–18.
154. Whitlock diary, November 7, 1916. See also Whitlock to Page, November 20, 1916, in American Embassy, London, Correspondence, 1916, vol. 110, file 848—Belgium, RG 84, NARA; printed in part in Nevins, ed., *The Letters of Brand Whitlock*, pp. 204–5.
155. Hoover to Honnold, October 26, 1916; Whitlock diary, November 6, 1916.
156. Green memorandum on Francqui, February 15, 1917.
157. Whitlock diary, November 6, 1916.
158. Hoover to Whitlock, n.d. (ca. November 7, 1916), in American Legation, Brussels, Correspondence, 1916, vol. 64, file 848, RG 84, NARA.
159. Lord Grey to Page, November 7, 1916, in *PR-CRB*, I, pp. 270–71.
160. See Francqui to Hoover, November 11, 1916, in which Francqui mentioned Hoover's denial.
161. Hoover to Whitlock, November 10, 1916, in American Legation, Brussels, Correspondence, 1916, vol. 65, file 848, RG 84, NARA; copies in CRB Correspondence, Box 7, and CRB—London office dossier 15.
162. Whitlock diary, October 27 and 30, 1916.
163. See, for example, Nash, *Life of Herbert Hoover: The Engineer*, pp. 551–52, 555.
164. Hoover to Francqui, November 8 and 10, 1916; Francqui to Hoover, November 9, 1916.
165. Whitlock diary, November 13, 1916, in his *Journal*, pp. 321–22.
166. Francqui to Hoover, November 11, 1916.
167. Whitlock diary, November 13, 1916.
168. Ibid.

169. Ibid.
170. The term *paper history* was Kellogg's, and he applied it to Francqui's correspondence with him. See Kellogg to Hoover, November 24, 1916, CRB Correspondence, Box 20; copy in CRB—London office dossier 80.
171. Hoover to Francqui, November 12, 1916, copies in CRB—London office dossier 15, and CRB Correspondence, Box 7.
172. Hugh Gibson to his mother, November 16, 1916, Gibson Papers, Box 34.
173. Joseph C. Green report to Warren Gregory (CRB—Brussels office) for the week ending November 11, 1916, in American Legation, Brussels, Correspondence, 1916, vol. 67, file 848, RG 84, NARA.
174. Hugh Gibson to his mother, November 17, 1916, Gibson Papers, Box 34.

CHAPTER 10

1. Hugh Gibson to his mother, November 16, 1916, Hugh Gibson Papers, Box 34, HI.
2. Hoover to Walter Hines Page, November 17, 1916, in American Embassy, London, Correspondence, 1916, vol. 110, file 848—Belgium, RG 84, NARA.
3. Page to Lord Grey (formerly Sir Edward Grey), November 20, 1916, ibid.
4. Page cable 5209 to the Secretary of State, November 24, 1916, ibid.
5. Hoover to Louis Chevrillon, November 20, 1916, copy in CRB—London office dossier 15: "Differences with the Comité National," HI.
6. Hoover cable 814 to CRB—New York office, November 20, 1916, copies in CRB—London office dossier 15, and CRB Correspondence, Box 7, HI.
7. Chevrillon cables to CRB—London office, December 2 and 5, 1916, copies in CRB—London office dossier 15.
8. Hoover cables to Vernon Kellogg (via Chevrillon), December 4 and 6, 1916, ibid.
9. Hoover cable to CRB—New York office, November 20, 1916.
10. Hoover to William Honnold, November 24, 1916, copy in CRB—London office dossier 15.
11. CRB—New York office cable 694 to Hoover, November 24, 1916, ibid.
12. Hoover to Lord Eustace Percy, November 24, 1916, copy in CRB—London office dossier 80: "Differences with the Comité National," HI. Hoover sent this entire dossier to Percy.
13. Hoover to Brand Whitlock (plus enclosures), November 27, 1916, in American Legation, Brussels, Correspondence, 1916, vol. 64, file 848, RG 84, NARA; copy in Brand Whitlock Papers, Box 61, LC.
14. See, for example, his letter to Page, November 17, 1916, and his cable to the CRB's New York office, November 20, 1916.
15. William B. Poland cable to William Honnold, November 30, 1916, copy in CRB—London office dossier 15; Hoover cable to A. J. Hemphill, November 25, 1916, copy in CRB—London office dossier 9: "Chevalier Carton de Wiart Correspondence," HI. See also the other documents in the latter dossier.
16. Hoover to Honnold, November 24, 1916.
17. Poland cable to Honnold, November 30, 1916.
18. George Barr Baker to Page, November 30, 1916, in American Embassy, London, Correspondence, 1916, vol. 110, file 848—Belgium, RG 84, NARA. There is no direct evidence that Hoover wrote or "inspired" this letter. But it is highly unlikely that Baker did so on his own initiative. Hoover's lieutenants did not do things like that. As Ambassador Page had said long ago, Hoover was the CRB, and the CRB was Hoover.
19. Eyre A. Crowe or Eustace Percy to Sir Francis Villiers (the British ambassador to Belgium), November 11, 1916, in FO 382 / 1169 / file 142, PRO.
20. See CRB—London office dossier 9, particularly Alexander J. Hemphill cable to Chevalier

Edmond Carton de Wiart, November 21, 1916.

21. See Carton de Wiart to Hoover, November 23, 1916; Carton de Wiart cable to Hemphill, November 28, 1916. Copies of both documents in CRB—London office dossier 9. See also Carton de Wiart to Paul Hymans, December 6, 1916, ibid.

22. Hoover memorandum at beginning of CRB—London office dossier 9; Hoover to Hemphill, November 25, 1916, ibid.

23. Hoover cable to William Honnold, November 25, 1916; Hoover to Hemphill, November 25, 1916. Copies of both documents in CRB—London office dossier 9.

24. Hoover to Carton de Wiart, November 30, 1916, CRB—London office dossier 9.

25. Hoover to Page, November 30, 1916, ibid.

26. See p. 221.

27. Hoover to Whitlock, November 6, 1916, in American Legation, Brussels, Correspondence, 1916, vol. 64, file 848, RG 84, NARA; copy in CRB—London office dossier 9.

28. Alexander J. Hemphill (for the CRB's advisory committee in New York) cable to Chevalier Carton de Wiart, December 1, 1916, CRB cable files, Pre-Commerce Papers, Herbert Hoover Papers, HHPL. Interestingly, a copy of this cable is in the Edward M. House Papers, Box 61, Yale University Library.

29. Percy to Emile Francqui, November 17, 1916, copy (annotated by Hugh Gibson) in American Embassy, London, Correspondence, 1916, vol. 110, file 848—Belgium, RG 84, NARA. Ambassador Page authorized the transmission of Percy's message through American embassy channels.

30. Percy to Hoover, November 25, 1916, CRB Correspondence, Box 7.

31. Hoover to Percy, November 27 [first page dated 28], 1916, ibid.; copy enclosed with Hoover to Page, November 27, 1916, in American Embassy, London, Correspondence, 1916, vol. 110, file 848—Belgium, RG 84, NARA.

32. Emile Francqui to Percy, n.d. (November 23, 1916), copy in American Embassy, London, Correspondence, 1916, vol. 110, file 848—Belgium, RG 84, NARA. See also Whitlock diary, November 23, 1916, printed in Allan Nevins, ed., *The Journal of Brand Whitlock* (New York, 1936), p. 326, and Whitlock to Page, November 29, 1916, in American Embassy, London, Correspondence, 1916, vol. 110, file 848—Belgium, RG 84, NARA. The latter two documents help to establish the date of Francqui's letter as November 23. Incidentally, although Whitlock's letter to Page was marked "personal and confidential," it was nevertheless shown to Hoover in London on December 16, 1916. This was one more indication of the closeness between Hoover and Page.

33. Whitlock to Page, November 29, 1916.

34. Whitlock diary, November 23, 1916.

35. Whitlock to Hoover, November 29, 1916, in American Legation, Brussels, Correspondence, 1916, vol. 64, file 848, RG 84, NARA.

36. Hoover to Whitlock, December 6, 1916.

37. Hoover cable 833 to CRB—New York office, November 25, 1916, CRB—London office dossier 15. In a separate dispatch to his Brussels office director on the same day, Hoover remarked: "The pot regarding relations is boiling pretty fiercely and the matter is up squarely to the various Governments concerned." Hoover memorandum 10G to Warren Gregory, November 25, 1916, in American Legation, Brussels, Correspondence, 1916, vol. 67, file 848, RG 84, NARA.

38. Baron Napoléon Eugène Beyens to Sir Francis Villiers, November 30, 1916, copy in CRB—London office dossier 15.

39. Percy to Hoover, December 6, 1916, ibid.

40. Ibid.

41. Hoover memorandum, "Organisation of Relief to the Civil Population in the Occupied Area of Belgium and Northern France," enclosed with Hoover to Percy, December 9, 1916. Copies in CRB—London office dossier 15.

42. Quoted in George H. Nash, *The Life of Herbert Hoover: The Engineer, 1874–1914* (New York, 1983), p. 552.
43. Hoover memorandum 24G to Warren Gregory, December 12, 1916, in American Legation, Brussels, Correspondence, 1916, vol. 64, file 848, RG 84, NARA.
44. Hoover to Whitlock, December 13, 1916, ibid.
45. Whitlock diary, December 20, 1916, in his *Journal*, p. 335.
46. Hoover memorandum 24G to Gregory, December 12, 1916. The day before, Hoover had sent a draft "contract" to the American embassy. Hoover to Page, December 11, 1916, in American Embassy, London, Correspondence, 1916, vol. 110, file 848—Belgium, RG 84, NARA.
47. Hoover memorandum 24G to Gregory, December 12, 1916.
48. Hoover to William Honnold, December 15, 1916, CRB Correspondence, Box 7.
49. Hoover to Percy, December 9, 1916.
50. Kellogg to Hoover, November 28, 1916, copy in CRB—London office dossier 15.
51. Francqui memorandum 109, dated October 21, 1916 but actually written much later and received by Hoover on December 6, 1916; copy in CRB—London office dossier 15.
52. Hoover to Francqui, December 6, 1916, copy in CRB—London office dossier 15.
53. Hoover to Paul Hymans, December 18, 1916, copy enclosed with Hoover to Page, December 19, 1916, in American Embassy, London, Correspondence, 1916, vol. 110, file 848—Belgium, RG 84, NARA.
54. Only four days after his letter to Hymans, Hoover told Belgium Finance Minister van de Vyvere that unless the CRB received the balance of its increased Allied subsidy for November and December, it would have a deficit by early January of more than £1,000,000! Hoover cable to van de Vyvere, December 22, 1916, CRB cable files.
55. According to a recent biographer of Francqui, the British government demanded Francqui's capitulation as its price for supporting the flotation of a planned Belgian relief loan in the United States. The Belgian government-in-exile reluctantly yielded to this pressure, and Francqui had no choice but to go along. See Liane Ranieri, *Emile Francqui, ou l'intelligence créatrice* (Paris, 1985), p. 166.
     For an account of this relief loan, see chapter 13 of my text.
56. See Hoover's six-page chronology enclosed with his letter to Page, December 11, 1916 (cited in note 46). See also Lawrence Wellington to Millard K. Shaler, November 21, 1916, in American Embassy, London, Correspondence, 1916, vol. 110, file 848—Belgium, RG 84, NARA, and [Hoover, Hugh Gibson, and Shaler], "Development of the Relief Movement Organisation of the Commission for Relief in Belgium," ca. November 17, 1916, in American Embassy, London, Correspondence, 1914, vol. 47, file 848—Belgium, RG 84, NARA. Earlier in the year Hoover's close associate, Edgar Rickard, had written Hoover a long letter setting out the CRB's version of the origins of the relief. This letter was almost certainly solicited—and even drafted, at least in part—by Hoover himself. It was intended as a refutation of Francqui's claims. See Edgar Rickard to Hoover, May 10, 1916, CRB Correspondence, Box 6.
57. Whitlock to Page, November 20, 1916, in American Embassy, London, Correspondence, 1916, vol. 110, file 848—Belgium, RG 84, NARA.
58. Page to Whitlock, December 22, 1916, in American Embassy, London, Correspondence, 1916, vol. 110, file 848—Belgium, RG 84, NARA.
59. Francqui cable to Hoover, December 24, 1916, copy in CRB—London office dossier 15; Whitlock diary, January 7, 1917, in his *Journal*, p. 341.
60. Hoover cable to Francqui, December 25, 1916, copy in CRB—London office dossier 15.
61. Francqui telegram to Hoover, December 28, 1916, CRB Correspondence, Box 16; Whitlock diary, January 7, 1917.
62. Hoover to Whitlock, December 29, 1916, in American Legation, Brussels, Correspondence, 1917, vol. 90, file 848, RG 84, NARA. Copy in CRB Correspondence, Box 7.

63. "Memorandum of Agreement between the 'Commission for Relief in Belgium' and the 'Comité National de Secours et d'Alimentation' Approved by the British & Belgian Governments," dated London, December 30, 1916, copy in CRB—London office dossier 15. Printed in George I. Gay and H. H. Fisher, *Public Relations of the Commission for Relief in Belgium* (Stanford, Calif., 1929), I, pp. 109–115.
64. Hoover to Whitlock, December 29, 1916.
65. Ibid.
66. Ibid.
67. Paul Hymans to Page, January 10, 1917, in American Embassy, London, Correspondence, 1917, vol. 86, file 848—Belgium, RG 84, NARA; copy in CRB—London office dossier 9. At least one prominent Belgian, however—the finance minister—was far from happy. In a letter to a Cabinet colleague, van de Vyvere noted that the accord freed the CRB from all responsibility toward his government and turned the CRB into an independent organism "sans contrôle et sans participation." Van de Vyvere wanted his government to accept this change only "avec regret" and at the explicit request of the British government. Aloys van de Vyvere to Baron Beyens, January 22, 1917, Fonds du Havre 618, Cabinet du Roi, Brussels.
68. This message has not been found. But in a cable to Paris on December 29, Hoover asked his French representative to convey to Francqui (when he saw him) Hoover's "great feeling of devotion to and admiration of his abilities and services to the Belgian people, and our united desire of entirely smooth co-operation in the whole organisation." Hoover cable to Louis Chevrillon, December 29, 1916, copy in CRB—London office dossier 15.
69. Francqui to Hoover, January 1, 1917, copy in CRB—London office dossier 15.
70. Hoover to Whitlock, December 29, 1916. For another account of the Hoover–Francqui controversy—an account more sympathetic to Whitlock than the one presented here—see John Wells Davidson, "Brand Whitlock and the Diplomacy of Belgian Relief," *Prologue* 2 (Winter 1970): 145–60.
71. Hoover telegram to Charlotte Kellogg, January 22, 1917, CRB Correspondence, Box 7.
72. The Comité National did, however, insist that the work of *secours* and *alimentation* was "une institution essentiellement belge" (an essentially Belgian institution). By founding the Comité National, it said, the Belgian people had given to the entire world "une exemple merveilleux de self-help" (a marvellous example of self-help). See the Comité National's *Rapport général*, part 1, p. 72 (cited in chapter 2, note 15).
73. See: Perrin C. Galpin to Joseph C. Green, April 4, 1921, Joseph C. Green Papers, Box 1, HI; Tracy B. Kittredge to Green, April 19, 1921, ibid., Box 2; Galpin to Pitman B. Potter, March 25, 1942, "C.R.B. History by Kittredge," Belgian American Educational Foundation Papers, HHPL; Galpin to Suda L. Bane, August 26, 1948, ibid.; Galpin to Jacques van der Belen, March 15, 1957, ibid.; Joseph C. Green oral history, HHPL; Raymond Henle memorandum, December 4, 1968, in appendix of Green's oral history.

    Hoover himself claimed in 1942 that Kittredge's volume was "inaccurate" and "unreliable" and "could not be shown to anyone without going to enormous effort to point out its inaccuracies." He did not cite any inaccuracies but stated that Kittredge had prepared his book "when all of the material was not available." Hoover to Ralph Lutz, February 13, 1942, "C.R.B. History by Kittredge," Belgian American Educational Foundation Papers.

    At some point—probably in the 1940s—Hoover ordered his associate Perrin C. Galpin to collect and destroy all copies of Kittredge's unpublished book, which had long ago been set, in part, in bound page proofs. Galpin dutifully gathered the volumes but, in disobedience of Hoover's wishes, did not destroy all of them. One is now on the bookshelf at HHPL. A few others are at HI. It is a comprehensive and orderly institutional history based on the CRB's internal records, notably its dozens of dossiers of documents relating to key episodes and controversies. Kittredge's volume is of considerable value for understanding Hoover's career between 1914 and 1917.

A principal reason, no doubt, for Hoover's desire to suppress accounts of his troubles with Francqui was that in the 1920s and later he collaborated with Francqui and other Belgians in postwar reconstruction projects and various educational-cultural exchanges. Under these circumstances it would have been highly embarrassing to publicize the story of his past differences with prominent Belgians—particularly in an official history of the CRB. Hence Kittredge's carefully prepared volume was never published.

74. In his *Memoirs* Hoover alluded only briefly and obliquely to his difficulties with Francqui: "He was a gruff, rather unsympathetic personality. He had a quickness and adroitness of mind equal to any sort of intellectual battle. He was at times difficult to co-operate with. Our men in Belgium often came to grips with him and at times his temperament put a good deal of strain upon me as he usually demanded the removal of men who did not wholly agree with him."

And that was all. Hoover's other comments about Francqui were completely positive. See Hoover, *The Memoirs of Herbert Hoover*, vol. 1: *Years of Adventure* (New York, 1951), p. 207.

75. Ibid.; Hoover, *An American Epic*, vol. 1 (Chicago, 1959), p. 43.

76. Hoover, *An American Epic*, I, p. 43. In World War II Hoover arranged for Francqui's widow to receive food parcels in German-occupied Belgium. After liberation in 1944, Madame Francqui thanked Hoover for his assistance. See Randolph C. Wilson to Hoover, June 12, 1941, in Emile Francqui folder, Herbert Hoover Collection, Box 315, HI, and Madame Francqui to Hoover, October 1944, "Francqui, Emile and Mrs.," Post-Presidential Individual File, Hoover Papers.

77. See Brand Whitlock's diary, September 21, 1921, in his *Journal*, p. 709.

78. Clare M. Torrey, *The Seven Belgian American Foundations; An International Epic* (n.p., n.d.); Liane Isgour-Ranieri, "La Lente Gestation de la Fondation Universitaire, vue à travers les archives américaines," *Annales de la société royale d'archéologie de Bruxelles* 58(1981):103–20.

79. Francqui cable to Hoover, June 15, 1928; Hoover to Francqui, June 16, 1928. Both in "Congratulations on Nomination, Fr-Ft," Campaign and Transition Papers, Hoover Papers. Also: Francqui to Hoover, November 9, 1928; Hoover to Francqui, November 11, 1928. Both in "Congratulations on Election, Fra-Frd," ibid.

80. Hoover Calendar, October 27 and 28, 1931, HHPL.

81. Francqui to Perrin C. Galpin, October 30, 1931, in Galpin files, Misrepresentations File, HHPL. Francqui's letter was obviously prearranged, and it was dated only days after his overnight visit to the White House. It is very possible that President Hoover asked him to write a letter (or, more correctly, to sign a letter which had probably been prepared for him). In any case, Francqui signed the letter.

82. In the words of Francqui's biographer, Hoover and Francqui "ressentaient manifestement l'un pour l'autre l'estime que l'on porte à un rival coriace après avoir butté dans un même combat." See Ranieri, *Emile Francqui*, p. 169.

83. According to Joseph C. Green, the "constant and active hostility" of Francqui toward CRB participation in inspection work, and the complex negotiations that his attitude rendered necessary, comprised "one of the most unfortunate and one of the most unpleasant chapters in the history of the Commission." Joseph C. Green, "Report on the Organization and Activities of the Department of Inspection and Control of the Commission for Relief in Belgium" (CRB—London office dossier 82, May 1917), p. II, HI.

84. Whitlock to Page, November 20, 1916.

C H A P T E R 11

1. George H. Nash, *The Life of Herbert Hoover: The Engineer, 1874–1914* (New York, 1983), pp. 509–13; Hoover to E. D. Adams, June 6, 1915, E. D. Adams Papers, Stanford University Archives.
2. Nash, *Life of Herbert Hoover: The Engineer,* pp. 558–59, 574.
3. Hoover cable to his wife, October 20, 1914, "Hoover, Herbert," Personal Correspondence: 1874–1920, Lou Henry Hoover Papers, HHPL.
4. See various letters, 1914–15, in "Henry, Charles D. and Florence, 1914–20," Personal Correspondence: 1874–1920, Lou Henry Hoover Papers; Lou Henry Hoover telegram to Laurine Anderson, November 24, 1914, "Hoover, Herbert, 1914," ibid. The Stanford professor with whom Herbert Hoover's son Herbert stayed was A. B. Clark.
5. Lou Henry Hoover to "whomsoever it may concern," November 24, 1914, "Reynolds, Jackson E.," Personal Correspondence: 1874–1920, Lou Henry Hoover Papers.
6. Lou Henry Hoover to Jackson E. Reynolds, November 24, 1914, ibid.
7. Lou Henry Hoover to her son Herbert, November 25, 1914, ibid.
8. Lou Henry Hoover to certain friends, December 14/15, 1914, copy in General Accessions—A. T. and Florence Stewart, HHPL.
9. The Lou Henry Hoover Papers contain much on her fund-raising activities in California for the CRB in late 1914.
10. See documents in "Committee of Mercy," Subject File, Lou Henry Hoover Papers.
11. See: "The War Relief Knitting Factory of the Society of American Women in London" (brochure, January 1915), in "American Women's War Relief Fund—Economic Relief Committee, Reports and Miscellany," Subject File, Lou Henry Hoover Papers; Lou Henry Hoover speech typescript, March 1, 1915, in "American Women's War Relief Fund—Reports of Activities and Finances, 1915," ibid.
12. Victoria French Allen, "A Member of the Fourth Estate" (typescript, n.d.), pp. 64–65, Ben S. Allen Collection (see chapter 3, note 219); documents in "American Women's War Relief Fund" folders, Subject File, Lou Henry Hoover Papers.
13. Clipping from *American Bulletin,* September 19, 1914, in "American Women's War Relief Fund," Subject File, Lou Henry Hoover Papers; "American Women's War Relief Fund" (brochure, October 1914), in "American Women's War Relief Fund—Fundraising, 1914–18 and undated," ibid.; Lou Henry Hoover to Duchess of Marlborough, May 26, 1915, in "American Women's War Relief Fund—Economic Committee Correspondence, 1915," ibid.; Society of American Women in London, statement of receipts and expenditure for 1915, in "American Women in London, Society of, 1915–19 and undated," ibid.; Herbert Hoover, *The Memoirs of Herbert Hoover,* vol. 1: *Years of Adventure* (New York, 1951), p. 210.
14. Lou Henry Hoover to a Mrs. Griffiths, January 29, 1915, in "American Women's War Relief Fund—Correspondence, 1915," Subject File, Lou Henry Hoover Papers; Lou Henry Hoover speech typescript, March 1, 1915.
    Still another philanthropic interest of Mrs. Hoover's was California House, a club in London for severely wounded Belgian soldiers. Allen, "A Member of the Fourth Estate," p. 93; Lou Henry Hoover wartime service sheet, in "Hoover, Lou Henry, Biographical Data," Subject File, Lou Henry Hoover Papers.
15. Hoover telegram to his wife, May 29, 1915, "Hoover, Herbert, 1915," Personal Correspondence: 1874–1920, Lou Henry Hoover Papers.
16. Lou Henry Hoover cable to her husband, June 20, 1915, ibid.; Hoover, *Years of Adventure,* p. 210.
17. Lou Henry Hoover cable to her husband, August 8, 1915, and Hoover cable to his wife, August 9, 1915, both in "Hoover, Herbert, 1915," Personal Correspondence: 1874–1920, Lou Henry Hoover Papers.
18. Hoover cable to his wife, September 2, 1915, ibid.

19. Lou Henry Hoover cable to her husband, September 11, 1915, ibid.
20. Theodore J. Hoover, "Memoranda: Being a Statement by an Engineer" (typescript: Stanford University, 1939), p. 174, copy at HHPL; Brand Whitlock diary, September 13, 1915, in Allan Nevins, ed., *The Journal of Brand Whitlock* (New York, 1936), pp. 209–10.
21. Hoover Calendar, HHPL; *New York Times*, November 10, 1915, p. 22.
22. In his *Memoirs (Years of Adventure*, p. 212) Hoover stated that he was on the continent about two-thirds of the time. However, scrutiny of Hoover's passports and other contemporary documents indicates that in 1916 he made six or seven trips to the continent totaling approximately nine weeks, or about one-fifth of his time.
23. Ibid., p. 212; telephone interview with Allan Hoover, August 12, 1985. The school was the Gibbs School; the Hoover boys were the only American students.
24. Nash, *Life of Herbert Hoover: The Engineer*, pp. 383, 500–501; various correspondence, 1917–18, from Alice M. Dickson to Lou Henry Hoover et al., in "Dickson, Alice M.," Personal Correspondence: 1874–1920, Lou Henry Hoover Papers.
25. Details about the Hoovers' Red House staff can be gleaned from the Alice M. Dickson file cited in the preceding footnote.
26. Alice M. Dickson to Lou Henry Hoover, February 2, 1918, in the file cited in note 24.
27. [?] to D. C. D'Eath, August 10, 1934, in "Potous, Paul Alec," Post-Presidential General File, Herbert Hoover Papers, HHPL.
28. Paul Potous to Lou Henry Hoover, May 17, 1915, "Hoover, Herbert: Treatment of Workers," Subject File, Lou Henry Hoover Papers.
29. Nash, *Life of Herbert Hoover: The Engineer*, p. 501.
30. Hoover, *Years of Adventure*, p. 210.
31. Inez Irwin war diary, August 2, 1916, Inez Irwin Papers, Box 4, Schlesinger Library, Radcliffe College.
32. Allen, "A Member of the Fourth Estate," p. 93–94.
33. Telephone interview with Allan Hoover, June 26, 1986.
34. Hoover, *Years of Adventure*, p. 212.
35. Ibid.
36. Theodore Hoover, "Memoranda," pp. 174–75, 227; Edgar Rickard to Charles H. Janin, November 11, 1916, Charles H. Janin Papers, Box 20, the Huntington Library, San Marino, California.
37. Hoover Calendar, HHPL.
38. Hoover, *Years of Adventure*, p. 212.
39. *New York Tribune*, January 10, 1915, section V, p. 3.
40. Nash, *Life of Herbert Hoover: The Engineer*, p. 568.
41. Ibid., chapter 17; *Mining Magazine* 11(July 1914): 72, and 11(September 1914): 165–68.
42. Nash, *Life of Herbert Hoover: The Engineer*, chapter 20.
43. Ibid., chapter 21.
44. Ibid.; Hoover, *Years of Adventure*, p. 108.
45. Belgium contains nearly 11,800 square miles. In mid-1914 the Russian mines and concessions in which Hoover was interested comprised more than 15,200 square miles. (The largest of these, the Nerchinsk concession, with about 8,000 square miles, was abandoned as unpromising early in the war.)
46. Lou Henry Hoover to Everett Smith, November 23, 1914, in "Hoover, Herbert, Correspondence, 1914–20," Subject File, Lou Henry Hoover Papers.
47. *Mining Magazine* 11 (September 1914): 157; *Mining World and Engineering Record* 88 (January 30, 1915): 118.
48. *Mining World and Engineering Record* 89 (November 13, 1915): 518.
49. *Mining Magazine* 11 (September 1914): 165–68; *Mining Journal* 106 (September 19, 1914): 844; *Mining and Engineering Review* 7 (October 5, 1914): 24, and 7 (November 5, 1914): 39.
50. Lou Henry Hoover to her sons, July 1932, General Accessions—Allan Hoover, HHPL.

51. Ibid.; Hoover to William J. Cox, September 15, 1914, "AIME—Personal," Pre-Commerce Papers, Hoover Papers; Hoover to Henry W. Hill, October 1, 1914, "Hill, C.—J.S.," Pre-Commerce Papers.
52. Will Irwin, *The Making of a Reporter* (New York, 1942), p. 251; Lou Henry Hoover to her sons, July 1932.
53. Irwin, *Making of a Reporter*, p. 251.
54. Theodore Hoover, "Memoranda," p. 173.
55. *Mining Magazine* 11 (December 1914): 348–50; *Mining News* 40 (December 3, 1914): 205; *Mining Journal* 107 (December 12, 1914): 1038; Walter R. Skinner, *The Mining Manual and Mining Year Book for 1915* (London, 1915), pp. 317–19.
56. Ibid.; Inter-Siberian Syndicate file, BT 31 / 22364 / 36453, Public Record Office (PRO), Kew, Surrey, U.K. Hoover held 20,000 shares (4% of the nominal capital) in the Inter-Siberian Syndicate, which, as the underwriter for the Irtysh debenture issue, received an option to purchase 250,000 Irtysh Corporation shares at par. Thus Hoover, through his interest in the syndicate, obtained an option on some Irtysh shares.
57. See Nash, *Life of Herbert Hoover: The Engineer*, particularly chapter 19: "The Engineer-Financier."
58. Nash, *Life of Herbert Hoover: The Engineer*, pp. 560–63; Natomas Land and Dredging Trust file, BT 31 / 22712 / 139343, PRO; Skinner, *Mining Manual . . . 1915*, pp. 440–42.
59. Skinner, *Mining Manual . . . 1915*, p. 813.
60. Ibid.; compare Skinner's *Mining Manual and Mining Year Book, 1914* (London, 1914), p. 1028.
61. *Mining Journal* 111 (December 18, 1915): 879.
62. Theodore Hoover, "Memoranda," p. 173.
63. Herbert Hoover, *Memoirs*, paperbound page proof version, vol. 2, p. 280, Hoover Book Manuscript Material, HHPL.
64. Hoover to Ralph Arnold, March 25, 1915, Ralph Arnold Collection, Box 38, the Huntington Library, San Marino, California.
65. Hoover to Oscar T. Crosby, June 1, 1915, CRB Correspondence, Box 4, HI.
66. Hoover to Philip Ivanoff, October 13, 1915, ibid.
67. Rickard to Charles H. Janin, November 11, 1916.
68. Nash, *Life of Herbert Hoover: The Engineer*, pp. 573–74.
69. Edgar Rickard to John Agnew, February 8, 1918, U.S. Food Administration Papers, Box 231, HI.
70. Nash, *Life of Herbert Hoover: The Engineer*, pp. 391–92.
71. Theodore Hoover, "Memoranda," p. 173. Theodore Hoover also served on several boards and technical committees of companies directed by his brother.
72. Nash, *Life of Herbert Hoover: The Engineer*, p. 571.
73. Hoover to Ray Lyman Wilbur, August 4, 1914, Ray Lyman Wilbur Personal Papers, Box 31, Stanford University Archives.
74. Walter R. Skinner, *Mining Manual and Mining Year Book, 1916* (London, 1916), p. 795.
75. *Mining World and Engineering Record* 89 (November 13, 1915): 519; *Mining and Scientific Press* 111 (December 11, 1915): 912.
76. J. D. Hoffmann, "The Bawdwin Mines," *Mining Magazine* 13 (March 1916): 146.
77. *Mining and Scientific Press* 110 (January 16, 1915): 94; *Mining Magazine* 13 (October 1915): 186–87; *Mining Journal* 111 (October 16, 1915): 735; *Mining and Scientific Press* 111 (November 6, 1915): 694–95; *Mining World and Engineering Record* 90 (April 1, 1916): 336–38; *Mining Magazine* 14 (June 1916): 312–14.
78. *Mining and Scientific Press* 111 (December 4, 1915): 864–65; *Mining Journal* 111 (December 11, 1915): 854, and 111 (December 18, 1915): 878–79; Skinner, *Mining Manual . . . 1916*, p. 311; *Mining World and Engineering Record* 90 (April 8, 1916): 363–64; ibid., 91 (December 16, 1916): 630–31; ibid., 91 (December 23, 1916): 661–62.

79. *Mining and Scientific Press* 111 (December 4, 1915): 865.

80. *Mining World and Engineering Record* 90 (April 8, 1916): 364.

81. Ibid., 90 (April 1, 1916): 336.

82. Notes (compiled ca. April 1932) in Leslie Urquhart Papers, in the possession of Mr. W. R. B. Foster, Lexham Hall, King's Lynn, Norfolk, U.K. A microfilm edition of the Urquhart Papers is in the possession of MIM Holdings, Ltd., Brisbane, Australia.

83. The contract contained a clause suspending its operation for the duration of the war. See L. F. Fitzhardinge, *William Morris Hughes: A Political Biography*, vol. 2: *The Little Digger, 1914–1952* (Sydney, 1979), pp. 20, 43.

84. Ibid., p. 43.

85. *Mining World and Engineering Record* 88 (June 19, 1915): 674; ibid., 89 (September 11, 1915): 286; ibid., 89 (December 25, 1915): 704; *Financial Times*, September 9, 1915, p. 2; ibid., December 22, 1915, p. 5; ibid., June 27, 1916, p. 5; Skinner, *Mining Manual . . . 1916*, p. 732; Walter R. Skinner, *Mining Manual and Mining Year Book, 1917* (London, 1917), pp. 731–32.

86. *Mining and Engineering Review* 7 (November 5, 1914): 39; *Financial Times*, June 27, 1916, p. 5.

87. *Mining Magazine* 11 (September 1914): 167; Hoover to a Colonel Wright, September 2, 1914, "Wright, Colonel," Pre-Commerce Papers; Hoover to Lindon W. Bates, October 2, 1914, CRB Correspondence, Box 32. See also *Financial Times*, September 18, 1914, p. 2; ibid., June 26, 1917, p. 5; *Mining Magazine* 18 (June 1918), supplement, p. 37.

88. *Mining Magazine* 11 (September 1914): 167.

89. *Engineering and Mining Journal* 99 (January 9, 1915): 63.

90. Ibid.; *Financial Times*, June 27, 1916, p. 5.

91. *Financial Times*, June 27, 1916, p. 5.

92. *Mining and Scientific Press* 112 (June 17, 1916): 887.

93. *Financial Times*, June 27, 1916, p. 5; Fitzhardinge, *Little Digger*, pp. 21–22.

94. W. L. Baillieu to Hoover, October 20, 1915, "Mining Correspondence: Baillieu, E. L. and W. L.," Pre-Commerce Papers.

95. Ibid.

96. *Financial Times*, June 27, 1916, p. 5; Skinner, *Mining Manual . . . 1917*, p. 733; Fitzhardinge, *Little Digger*, pp. 21–26, 108–10.

97. *Financial Times*, June 27, 1916, p. 5; ibid., June 26, 1917, p. 5; *The Times* (London), April 27, 1917, p. 12; ibid., August 1, 1929, p. 19; Walter R. Skinner, *Mining Manual and Mining Year Book, 1920* (London, 1920), pp. 656–57; W. S. Robinson to R. Pitman Hooper, February 8, 1955, W. S. Robinson Papers, University of Melbourne Archives, Melbourne, Australia; E. J. Cocks and B. Walters, *A History of the Zinc Smelting Industry in Britain* (London, 1968), chapters 3 and 4; Fitzhardinge, *Little Digger*, pp. 75–76, 108–11.

98. Hoover to C. F. H. Leslie, April 20, 1916, "Hoover, Herbert—Metals Selling Business," Laurine Small Papers, HHPL.

99. Govett, quoted in *Financial Times*, June 27, 1916, p. 5.

100. Premier Hughes's aide on his 1916 journey, W. S. Robinson (a friend of Hoover), helped to negotiate the "Imperial Scheme," of which Hughes was the foremost advocate. There is no evidence in the Robinson Papers or elsewhere that Hoover helped to formulate this plan.

101. *Financial Times*, June 27, 1917, p. 2.

102. During 1916 the Zinc Corporation actually distributed four dividends. Skinner, *Mining Manual . . . 1917*, p. 732. Sales of lead concentrates had kept the corporation afloat.

103. Nash, *Life of Herbert Hoover: The Engineer*, p. 424.

104. Hoover, *Years of Adventure*, p. 211.

105. Ibid.

106. Minutes of meeting of board of directors of Zinc Corporation, September 16, 1915, Zinc

Corporation (1911) Minute Book No. 2, Rio Tinto-Zinc Corporation, Ltd., London.
107. *Financial Times,* June 27, 1916, p. 5.
108. Pope Yeatman to Hoover, August 1, 1916, "Yeatman, Pope," Pre-Commerce Papers.
109. Hoover to Yeatman, August 17, 1916, ibid.
110. Hoover, *Years of Adventure,* p. 211.
111. Skinner, *Mining Manual . . . 1917,* p. 792; Hoover Calendar, HHPL.
112. Nash, *Life of Herbert Hoover: The Engineer,* pp. 424, 710.
113. See, for example, *Financial Times,* June 27, 1916, p. 6.
114. *Mining World and Engineering Record* 91 (November 18, 1916): 495.
115. Nash, *Life of Herbert Hoover: The Engineer,* pp. 380–81, 453–62.
116. Moreing to C. C. Klug, December 7, 1911, Bewick, Moreing & Co. Collection, HHPL.
117. Hoover, "Information for Biographers" (typescript, n.d.; probably ca. 1914), p. 16, in Ben S. Allen Papers, Box 1, HI, and Pre-Commerce Papers.
118. Minutes of meetings of board of directors of Zinc Corporation, November 26, December 10 and 11, 1914, Zinc Corporation (1911) Minute Book No. 1, Rio Tinto-Zinc Corporation, Ltd., London; minutes of meeting of board of directors of Zinc Corporation, January 21, 1915, Zinc Corporation (1911) Minute Book No. 2.
119. Moreing to Francis A. Govett, December 1, 1914, quoted in minutes of the Zinc Corporation directors' December 11, 1914 meeting.
120. Minutes of Zinc Corporation directors' meeting of December 11, 1914 and January 21, 1915.
121. Bewick, Moreing & Co. statement regarding Herbert Hoover (n.d., but ca. 1916), Bewick, Moreing & Co. Collection; "Notes of Interview with Hoay," January 1, 1915, ibid.
122. Minutes of meeting of Zinc Corporation board of directors, January 7, 1915, Zinc Corporation (1911) Minute Book No. 1.
123. Minutes of Zinc Corporation directors' meeting of January 21, 1915.
124. Minutes of meeting of Zinc Corporation board of directors, February 18, 1915, Zinc Corporation (1911) Minute Book No. 2.
125. Bewick, Moreing & Co. statement regarding Hoover (1916).
126. Minutes of Zinc Corporation directors' meeting of January 21, 1915.
127. Bewick, Moreing & Co. statement regarding Hoover (1916); Bewick, Moreing & Co. Statement of Claim, May 31, 1916, in the lawsuit *Bewick, Moreing & Co.* v. *Herbert Clark Hoover,* Case No. 1916 B 1071, High Court of Justice, King's Bench Division, London; "Elaboration of allegations of Breach of Contract requested by Counsel" in the same case (typescript, 1916). All these documents are in the Bewick, Moreing & Co. Collection, HHPL.
   The writ in the case was issued on April 17, 1916.
128. "Elaboration of allegations. . . ." See also the other documents just cited and various related documents in the Bewick, Moreing & Co. Collection.
129. See the Bewick, Moreing & Co. Collection, HHPL.
130. Hoover, *Years of Adventure,* p. 98n.
131. Cable from the Governor-General of Australia to the Secretary of State for the Colonies (London), received in London, March 18, 1915, copy in FO 371 / 2285 / file 609, PRO.
132. [Eustace Percy] to the Undersecretary of State for the Colonies, March 23, 1915, ibid.
133. Hoover to Lindon W. Bates, probably early 1915, quoted in David Burner, *Herbert Hoover: A Public Life* (New York, 1979), p. 90.
134. *Financial Times,* June 22, 1916, p. 4; ibid., June 27, 1916, pp. 5–6.
135. Ibid., June 27, 1916, p. 5.
136. Ibid., pp. 5–6.
137. Editorial in *Financial Times,* June 27, 1916, p. 2.
138. *Mining World and Engineering Record* 91(July 1, 1916): 14–15.
139. *Mining News* 43 (June 29, 1916): 223–24. See also: *Financial News,* June 27, 1916, p. 2;

Mining Magazine 15 (July 1916): 8–9; *Mining and Scientific Press* 113 (July 22, 1916): 112.

140. *The Zinc Corporation, Limited, Directors' Report . . . for the Year ended 31st December 1915* [June 12, 1916], p. 10, copy in "Mining—Printed Material," Pre-Commerce Papers; *Financial Times,* June 27, 1916, p. 6.

141. Hoover, draft statement about Zinc Corporation (ca. 1931–32), in "Richey-Hoover Files: Statements and Refutations," Misrepresentations File, HHPL.

142. *Mining News* 44 (August 10, 1916): 45, and 44 (August 17, 1916): 54.

143. Ibid., 44 (September 7, 1916): 77; Walter W. Liggett, *The Rise of Herbert Hoover* (New York, 1932), pp. 214–20. Liggett, a vehemently anti-Hoover biographer, relied on Auld's account of this meeting.

144. *Financial News,* September 14, 1916, p. 2; *Mining News* 44 (September 21, 1916): 94; ibid., 44 (October 5, 1916): 109; *Mining World and Engineering Record* 91 (October 7, 1916): 362.

145. *Financial News,* September 19, 1916, p. 3; *Mining News* 44 (September 21, 1916): 94.

146. *Financial Times,* June 26, 1917, p. 5.

147. Ibid.

148. John Agnew to Edgar Rickard, February 13, 1930, Rickard Files, Misrepresentations File, HHPL.

149. See, for instance, the Zinc Corporation directors' report (June 12, 1916) cited in note 140.

150. Walter Hines Page to Brand Whitlock, October 23, 1916, in American Legation, Brussels, Correspondence, 1916, file 848, RG 84, NARA; copy in George I. Gay and H. H. Fisher, *Public Relations of the Commission for Relief in Belgium* (Stanford, Calif., 1929), I, pp. 106–8.

151. Eustace Percy memorandum of a visit by Hoover's solicitor, October 11, 1916, in FO 382 / 1176 / file 207318, PRO.

152. "Elaboration of allegations. . . ," p. 15.

153. Percy memorandum, October 11, 1916.

154. Ambassador Paul Cambon (France) to Hoover, October 12, 1916, "CRB—Correspondence, 1914–1918," Pre-Commerce Papers; Minister Paul Hymans (Belgium) to Hoover, October 17, 1916, ibid.

155. Internal Foreign Office comments on Percy's memorandum, FO 382 / 1176 / file 207318, PRO.

156. Percy memorandum, October 11, 1916.

157. Percy to Messrs. Broad & Son (Hoover's solicitors), October 13, 1916, FO 372 / 1176 / file 207318, PRO.

158. "Terms of Stay," January 4, 1917, between Hoover and Bewick, Moreing & Co., in Bewick, Moreing & Co. Collection; indenture dated January 4, 1917 between Hoover and C. Algernon Moreing, ibid.

159. January 4, 1917 indenture. At the end of 1902 Rowe absconded after forging stock certificates. The ensuing scandal cost Hoover and his remaining partners (who were entirely innocent) several hundred thousand dollars in their effort to make restitution to the victims of Rowe's frauds. See Nash, *Life of Herbert Hoover: The Engineer,* pp. 245–76.

160. Hoover resigned from the Burma Corporation board of directors (and was replaced by Beatty) on or shortly before October 11, 1916. Burma Corporation file, BT 31 / 21753 / 131501, PRO.

161. Hoover was listed as a Burma Corporation director again (in place of Beatty) on January 26, 1917. Ibid. Thus Hoover was nominally off the board for approximately four months.

162. Emily Hahn, "Diamond: VII—The Oppenheimers," *New Yorker* 32 (September 29, 1956): 57, 59; Theodore Gregory, *Ernest Oppenheimer and the Economic Development of Southern Africa* (Cape Town, 1962), pp. 81–90; Anthony Hocking, *Oppenheimer and Son* (Johannesburg, 1973), pp. 74–79.

163. Gregory, *Ernest Oppenheimer,* p. 89; Walter R. Skinner, *Mining Manual and Mining Year Book, 1923* (London, 1923), pp. 24–25.

164. Gregory, *Ernest Oppenheimer,* p. 89n; Hocking, *Oppenheimer and Son,* p. 79; Duncan Innes,

Anglo American and the Rise of Modern South Africa (London, 1984), p. 91.

165. "Anglo American's Golden Windfall," *Business Week* (March 17, 1980): 134–40.
166. Edgar Rickard to R. B. Burton, March 13, 1918, U.S. Food Administration Papers, Box 231.
167. Hoover to Ray Lyman Wilbur, February 28, 1920, Wilbur Personal Papers, Box 36; Wilbur to Hoover, February 23, 1921 (and later letters), Ray Lyman Wilbur Papers, Box 119, HI.
168. Rickard to Janin, November 11, 1916.
169. Hoover, *Years of Adventure*, p. 211.
170. Ibid., p. 108n.; Nash, *Life of Herbert Hoover: The Engineer*, p. 445; notes in Leslie Urquhart Papers (cited in note 82).
171. Hoover, *Years of Adventure*, p. 108n; Hoover, telegram to *New York Times*, September 11, 1922, Public Statements File, HHPL; Hoover to Senator Joseph I. France, February 10, 1923, "France, Joseph I.-Frand," Commerce Papers, Hoover Papers.
172. Nash, *Life of Herbert Hoover: The Engineer*, p. 393.
173. There is one factor that did not motivate Hoover's apparent decision to withdraw from Russia. Although he later stated in his *Memoirs (Years of Adventure*, p. 105) that he long felt that tsarist Russia would someday "blow up," there is no evidence that he foresaw, or bailed out in anticipation of, the revolution of 1917.
174. *Engineering and Mining Journal* 101 (May 13, 1916): 870.
175. Nash, *Life of Herbert Hoover: The Engineer*, p. 502.
176. Ibid., p. 570.
177. Hoover to his brother Theodore, March 3, 1917, Hulda Hoover McLean Papers, HI.
178. Leslie Urquhart affidavit, March 27, 1924, "Urquhart, Leslie," Commerce Papers; notes (previously cited) in Urquhart Papers.
179. Lewis L. Strauss to Edgar Rickard, April 8, 1919, in Frederic Walcott folder, U.S. Food Administration Papers, Box 177.
180. Ibid.; Strauss to Rickard, July 2, 1919, "A.R.A.—Rickard, Edgar, 1919," Lewis L. Strauss Papers, HHPL.
181. *Engineering and Mining Journal* 105 (January 23, 1918): 388; *Mining Magazine* 18 (February 1918): 65; Roland W. Boyden to Kate Boyden, May 20, 1918, copy in Herbert Hoover Collection, Box 313, HI; *Mining Magazine* 19 (September 1918): 123; *Mining World and Engineering Record* 95 (November 23, 1918): 409; *Mining and Scientific Press* 118 (February 1, 1919): 139–40; ibid., 119 (October 11, 1919): 497–98; R. G. Knickerbocker, "A Russian Copper Refinery Under Bolshevik Control," ibid., 120 (May 8, 1920): 677–82; Hoover, *Years of Adventure*, pp. 105n–106n, 108n.
182. Walter R. Skinner, *Mining Manual . . . 1923*, p. 504; Leslie Urquhart, "Attacks on President Hoover," *Truth* 111 (May 25, 1932): 832–33.
183. In 1919 the Kyshtim, Tanalyk, Irtysh, and Russo-Asiatic corporations were amalgamated into a new company, Russo-Asiatic Consolidated. Deane P. Mitchell became a director of this company and remained so until its dissolution in 1929. Walter R. Skinner, *Mining Year Book, 1930* (London, 1930), pp. 526–27.
184. Hoover, *Years of Adventure*, p. 108n; Hoover, undated handwritten autobiographical fragment. The latter source was once at HHPL but has not recently been located. I have relied upon a partial verbatim transcript of this document courteously provided to me by Professor Craig Lloyd, a researcher who did see the document and made notes upon it several years ago.
185. Hoover, *Memoirs*, paperbound page proof version, vol. 1, pp. 137–38, Hoover Book Manuscript Material.
186. Hoover, *Years of Adventure*, p. 108. In his *Memoirs* and elsewhere Hoover later strenuously denied that he lost his Russian mining interests because of the Bolshevik revolution. Instead, he insisted that he had sold out his direct Russian holdings *before* the revolution and that

his larger prospective fortune was a casualty of the war (specifically, bond foreclosures), *not* of the revolutionary upheaval of 1917. In short, he said, his stake in Russian mining—both actual and potential—disappeared before the Bolshevik seizure of power.

The available evidence does not entirely support Hoover's claims. First, he did not completely dispose of his Russian shareholdings before the revolution of 1917. As indicated in the text, he retained a few hundred Irtysh shares until 1919 and 1,082 other shares until 1921, as well as a private agreement with Deane P. Mitchell for a share in directors' bonuses in the Russo-Asiatic Corporation. The extent and duration of this profit-sharing arrangement is not known. Secondly, as shown in the text, Hoover's Russian enterprises were *not* destroyed by the war. At the time he resigned his directorates (late 1916), every one of these concerns had excellent economic prospects.

The question then becomes: if Hoover did have a vast fortune-in-the-making in Russia, precisely when and how did he lose it? When did the bond foreclosures that he alluded to occur? Unfortunately, the record on these questions is silent. In the unpublished version of his *Memoirs* (paperbound page proof edition, vol. 1, p. 138), Hoover stated that the British and French creditors foreclosed "during the last stages of the Russian collapse," but he did not date the event further—except to indicate, without quite saying so explicitly, that the foreclosures occurred before the revolution.

There is no evidence, however, that these foreclosures (presumably on behalf of the debenture holders) occurred before March 1917—the date of the outbreak of the Russian Revolution. Conceivably they occurred before the Communist (Bolshevik) revolution in the autumn of that year. If so, it could then be said (as Hoover afterward insisted) that his large prospective fortune in Russia vanished before Lenin and his cohorts seized power and issued their edicts of confiscation.

Again, however, there is no direct evidence to confirm this hypothesis.

In 1917 an event occurred that may have had a bearing on this puzzle. In Montreal, Canada, an entity known as the Russo-Canadian Development Corporation was established as a holding company for the property of the British-registered Irtysh, Kyshtim, and Tanalyk corporations. This property consisted of shares in their Russian subsidiaries. As part of a reorganization scheme, the Russo-Canadian Development Corporation acquired these shares. In return, the British companies' debenture-holders (who had held the shares as security on loans) received new security in the form of Russo-Canadian first debentures.

It is possible that in the course of this transaction (which lasted until late 1918) Hoover somehow lost his "deferred interest." But once more the record is inconclusive. For more on the Russo-Canadian debenture scheme, see: *The Times* (London), March 30, 1918, p. 9, April 10, 1918, p. 13, and September 28, 1918, p. 11. See also Walter R. Skinner, *Mining Manual and Mining Year Book, 1919* (London, 1919), p. 467.

Hoover's involvement in Russian mining before 1917 has long been a controversial question. For more details, see my *Life of Herbert Hoover: The Engineer*, pp. 426–46, 716–19. His Russian interests are also examined in a recent biography of one of his closest collaborators, Leslie Urquhart. See K. H. Kennedy, *Mining Tsar: The Life and Times of Leslie Urquhart* (Sydney, 1986).

187. Hoover, undated autobiographical fragment (cited in note 184). In 1917 a friend of Hoover reported that "by devoting himself to Belgian relief" he "sacrificed the chance" to make $30,000,000 in mining during the war. Edward Eyre Hunt, "Hoover of the C.R.B.," *World's Work* 34 (June 1917): 167.

188. Quoted in Irwin, *Making of a Reporter*, p. 252.

189. Hoover's close friend Ray Lyman Wilbur stated in 1920 that Hoover "was offered the opportunity to take over the control of the metals industries of the British Empire during the war." Ray Lyman Wilbur to L. Ward Bannister, May 31, 1920, Wilbur Personal Papers, Box 5. I have found no confirmation of this alleged offer. But in 1915 Hoover was

evidently offered the position of assistant to the new British minister of munitions (see p. 121).

190. Hoover held at least a 14% holding (more than 100,000 shares) in the Burma Corporation. During 1916 these shares ranged in market value from 31s. 3d. to 91s. 3d. per share. In early 1917 the market price reached £3 3/16 (or more than $18) per share. Skinner, *Mining Manual . . . 1917*, p. 101.

191. See Nash, *Life of Herbert Hoover: The Engineer*, chapter 25, especially pp. 527–40.

192. Hoover to W. Mayo Newhall, October 25, 1914, "Stanford, re Presidency," Pre-Commerce Papers. See also Hoover to W. Mayo Newhall and Timothy Hopkins, December 7, 1914 (separate letters), ibid.

193. Ibid.

194. Timothy Hopkins to Hoover, January 29, 1915, "Stanford, re Presidency," Pre-Commerce Papers.

195. Nash, *Life of Herbert Hoover: The Engineer*, pp. 534–40.

196. Ralph Arnold to Hoover, May 13 and June 28, 1915, Arnold Collection, Box 38; E. D. dams to Hoover, May 19, 1915, Adams Papers.

197. Hoover to Newhall, October 25, 1914; Timothy Hopkins to Hoover, November 12, 1914 and January 8, 1915, "Stanford, re Presidency," Pre-Commerce Papers.

198. Hoover to Newhall, October 25, 1914.

199. Ibid.; Hoover to Newhall and Hopkins, December 7, 1914 (separate letters).

200. Hoover to Newhall, December 7, 1914.

201. Arnold to Hoover, March 3 and 18, 1915, Arnold Collection, Box 38.

202. Hoover to Arnold, March 25, 1915, ibid.

203. Arnold to Hoover, January 18, 1915, ibid.

204. Hoover to Arnold, February 21, 1915, ibid.

205. Arnold to Hoover, March 18, 1915.

206. Arnold to Hoover, March 13, 18, and May 31, 1915, Arnold Collection, Box 38; Adams to Hoover, May 19, 1915.

207. Arnold to Hoover, May 13, 1915.

208. Hoover to Arnold, June 6, 1915, Arnold Collection, Box 38.

209. Arnold to Hoover, June 28, 1915, ibid.

210. Arnold cable to Hoover, June 28, 1915, ibid.

211. Arnold to Hoover, June 28, 1915.

212. Hoover cable to his wife, July 12, 1915, "Hoover, Herbert, 1915," Personal Correspondence: 1874–1920, Lou Henry Hoover Papers; slightly edited copy, dated July 16, 1915, addressed from Mrs. Hoover to Arnold, in Arnold Collection, Box 38.

213. Charles P. Eells to Arnold, July 21, 1915; Arnold to Hoover, July 23, 1915; both in Arnold Collection, Box 38.

214. David Starr Jordan to Hoover, July 29, 1915, "Stanford—Jordan, Dr. David S.," Pre-Commerce Papers.

215. Ibid.

216. Arnold to Hoover, August 9, 1915, Arnold Collection, Box 38. He added that two other trustees—Eells and Hopkins—now strongly supported Hoover if Wilbur could not be elected.

217. Lou Henry Hoover cable to her husband, August 8, 1915, "Hoover, Herbert, 1915," Personal Correspondence: 1874–1920, Lou Henry Hoover Papers.

218. Arnold to Hoover, September 30, 1915, Arnold Collection, Box 38; Joseph D. Grant to Hoover, October 7, 1915, "Grant, Joseph D.," Pre-Commerce Papers.

219. Ray Lyman Wilbur, *The Memoirs of Ray Lyman Wilbur* (Stanford, Calif., 1960), pp. 178–79.

220. Hoover to Ray Lyman Wilbur, November 11, 1915, copy in Adams Papers.

221. Ibid.

222. Hoover to W. Mayo Newhall, May 30, 1916, Board of Trustees Supporting Documents, August 1, 1916 folder, Stanford University Archives.
223. Wilbur to Hoover, June 29, 1916, "Stanford University, 1914–1921," Pre-Commerce Papers.
224. Stanford University Trustees minutes, August 1, 1916, Stanford University Archives; W. Mayo Newhall to Hoover, August 10, 1916, Board of Trustees Supporting Documents, August 1, 1916 folder; Joseph D. Grant to Hoover, August 16, 1916, "Grant, Joseph D.," Pre-Commerce Papers.
225. Newhall to Hoover, August 10, 1916.
226. Brand Whitlock to Hoover, January 24, 1916, in American Legation, Brussels, Correspondence, 1916, vol. 71, file 848, RG 84, NARA.
227. Hoover to Whitlock, January 28, 1916, in ibid., vol. 72.

CHAPTER 12

1. Herbert Hoover, *The Memoirs of Herbert Hoover*, vol. 1: *Years of Adventure* (New York, 1951), p. 212.
2. Herbert Hoover, *Memoirs*, paperbound page proof version, vol. 2: "The World War, 1914–1917," p. 279, Hoover Book Manuscript Material, HHPL.
3. Walter Hines Page to Woodrow Wilson, July 2, 1915, in Arthur S. Link et al., eds., *The Papers of Woodrow Wilson*, vol. 33 (Princeton, N.J., 1980), pp. 549–55.
4. Hoover, *Years of Adventure*, p. vi.
5. Hoover to Professor E. D. Adams, June 6, 1915, E. D. Adams Papers, HI.
6. Hoover, *Years of Adventure*, p. 137.
7. Hoover to Ray Lyman Wilbur, August 4, 1914, Ray Lyman Wilbur Personal Papers, Box 31, Stanford University Archives.
8. Hoover, "The World War, 1914–1917," p. 280.
9. Ibid.
10. Hoover, *Years of Adventure*, pp. 166–67.
11. Hoover, "The World War, 1914–1917," p. 280; Walter Hines Page to Woodrow Wilson, February 10, 1915, in Arthur S. Link et al., eds., *The Papers of Woodrow Wilson*, vol. 32 (Princeton, N.J., 1980), pp. 211–15.
12. Hoover to Lindon W. Bates, February 28, 1915, CRB Correspondence, Box 2, HI.
13. Hoover to Adams, June 6, 1915.
14. Hoover to an unknown person, June 3, [1915?], as quoted in his letter to E. D. Adams of June 6, 1915 (cited in note 5). The precise date of this passage is something of a puzzle. In his letter to Adams, Hoover stated that the quoted passage was "from a letter addressed to a friend in Washington on the 3rd of June." Presumably he meant June 3, 1915, just three days prior to his letter to Adams. However, I have been unable to find any evidence that Hoover, in June 1915, had just returned from a visit to France, Germany, and western Russia (as he stated in this quoted extract). Furthermore, Hoover cited this passage to Adams as proof that his views on preparedness (which he said he had formed before the war) were not an "afterthought." This phraseology suggests the quoted passage had actually been written *before* the war: in other words on June 3 of some other year.
    Whatever the explanation of this ambiguity, the long passage that I have quoted certainly reflected Hoover's views in June 1915, when he sent the extract along to Professor Adams.
15. Page to Wilson, February 16, 1915.
16. Hoover, *Years of Adventure*, pp. 167–68.
17. Brand Whitlock diary, June 12, 1915, in Allan Nevins, ed., *The Journal of Brand Whitlock* (New York, 1936), pp. 160–61.
18. Quoted in Page to Wilson, July 2, 1915.

19. Hoover to Adams, June 6, 1915.
20. Hoover interview in *New York Times*, November 19, 1900, p. 7.
21. Hoover, *Years of Adventure*, p. 214.
22. Hoover to Woodrow Wilson, September 3, 1915, in Arthur S. Link et al., eds., *The Papers of Woodrow Wilson*, vol. 34 (Princeton, N.J., 1980), pp. 409–10.
23. Ibid.
24. Hoover, *Years of Adventure*, p. 219; Hoover, "The World War, 1914–1917," p. 289.
25. Eustace Percy, *Some Memories* (London, 1958), p. 47.
26. Hoover, "The World War, 1914–1917," p. 291; Hoover, *Years of Adventure*, p. 220. In the autumn of 1915, while on a trip to New York, Hoover shocked some American friends who were pro-Allies by his criticisms of British treatment of the Commission for Relief in Belgium. William Allen White, *The Autobiography of William Allen White* (New York, 1946), p. 515.
27. Hoover *Years of Adventure*, pp. 220–22.
28. Whitlock diary, June 12, 1915.
29. Hoover to Ray Lyman Wilbur, November 11, 1915, copy in E. D. Adams Papers, Stanford University Archives.
30. Inez Irwin war diary, August 13, 1916, Inez Irwin Papers, Box 4, Schlesinger Library, Radcliffe College.
31. Hoover, *Years of Adventure*, pp. 214–15.
32. Ibid., pp. 218–19.
33. Ibid., p. 193. The precise date of Hoover's visit to the front is uncertain, but it seems to have occurred at the end of July 1916.
34. Andrew D. White, *The Autobiography of Andrew Dickson White*, vol. 2 (New York, 1905), pp. 489–90.
35. Hoover, *Years of Adventure*, pp. 184–85; Hoover, *An American Epic*, vol. 2 (Chicago, 1960), p. 389; typescript interviews of Herbert Hoover, June 13 and 29, 1961, in "Hoover Institution Book: Source Materials—Interviews with Herbert Hoover," Kenneth Colegrove Papers, HHPL; Colegrove, draft of chapter 1 of a proposed book about the Hoover Institution on War, Revolution and Peace, in "Hoover Institution Book—Drafts," Colegrove Papers.
36. E. D. Adams to Hoover, July 10, 1914; Hoover cable to Adams, July 21, 1914; Adams to Hoover, July 23, 1914; all in E. D. Adams Papers, HI. For more on the two men's friendship, see Adams, "Snap Shots of Herbert Hoover" (typescript, 1929), Adams Papers, Stanford University Archives.
37. Adams to Hoover, February 16, 1915, Adams Papers, HI.
38. Hoover to Adams, March 7, 1915, ibid.
39. Adams to Hoover, May 19 and September 3, 1915, and February 27, 1918, Adams Papers, Stanford University Archives; Adams to Hoover, August 14, 1916, copy in "Hoover Institution Book—Source Materials—Documents, 1914–16," Colegrove Papers.
40. Edward M. House diary, February 16, 1915, Edward M. House Papers, Yale University Library.
41. Hoover to Hugh Gibson, December 22, 1916, CRB Correspondence, Box 7, HI.
42. Years later, on various occasions, Hoover declared that he actively pursued his quest for "contemporary literature and fugitive documents" during the war, even as he directed the Belgian relief. He stated that he personally entered bookstores in Berlin, London, and Paris and requested dealers to collect and hold all appropriate books, newspapers, and other materials, for which he promised to pay after the war. He recalled also that he recruited university professors as collectors and encouraged his CRB colleagues to acquire relevant materials. According to Hoover, his men "plunged into the project with zeal." On one occasion Hoover later stated that he "established centers for such collections" in every belligerent country that he visited (perhaps an allusion to the bookdealers he said he contacted). According to Hoover, the materials thus reserved and assembled amounted to millions of

items "soon after the Armistice" of November 11, 1918. For some of Hoover's recollections of these activities, see the sources cited in note 35 and his "Foreword" to Nina Almond and H. H. Fisher, *Special Collections in the Hoover Library on War, Revolution, and Peace* (Stanford, Calif., 1940).

Hoover's later statements about his wartime collecting efforts provide an interesting sidelight on his conduct of the great relief effort. Unfortunately, despite considerable research in many archives I have found no contemporary documentation (such as letters, invoices, or receipts from booksellers) of these pursuits. The CRB's correspondence files, for example, appear to contain no references either by himself or his associates to his (or their) wartime collecting. The diaries of various relief associates are similarly silent. Nor have I found any evidence that Hoover's arrangements yielded a vast trove of millions of documents by the time of (or shortly after) the Armistice.

Certainly Hoover kept the CRB's files intact and may have instructed his subordinates to do the same. But there is no confirmatory evidence that his document hunting went beyond this while the war was on. Instead, the available evidence suggests that his systematic campaign of acquisitions really commenced after the war, in mid-1919, when he assembled a team of historians, led by Professor E. D. Adams, to conduct a search in his behalf all over Europe.

For more on this aspect of Hoover's life, see my monograph *Herbert Hoover and Stanford University* (Stanford, Calif., 1988).

43. Joseph C. Kiger, ed., *Research Institutions and Learned Societies* (Westport, Conn., 1982), p. 271.
44. House diary, February 16, 20, 24, 26, 1915.
45. House diary, February 20, 1915.
46. *New York Times*, March 1, 1915, p. 3.
47. Hoover, *Years of Adventure*, p. 213.
48. Ibid., p. 212.
49. See, for example, House diary, October 31 and November 2, 1915.
50. See, for example, Hoover to House (plus enclosures), February 23, 1916, House Papers, Box 61.
51. Hoover to House, August 16, 1915, ibid.
52. Hoover to House, February 22, 1916, ibid.
53. Hoover to House, February 26, 1915; Hoover to Woodrow Wilson, February 26, 1915; both in Link et al., eds., *The Papers of Woodrow Wilson*, vol. 32, pp. 293–94.
54. House diary, November 9, 1915. It is not known whether Hoover conveyed the message. Hoover was then on his way back to Europe from New York.
55. Hoover to Walter Hines Page, May 10, 1915, CRB Correspondence, Box 5.
56. Hoover to Adams, June 6, 1915, discusses this feeler.
57. Hoover et al., cable to Woodrow Wilson, May [12], 1915, enclosed with Hoover to Wilson, May 13, 1915, Woodrow Wilson Papers, LC.
58. Hoover to Adams, June 6, 1915.
59. Hoover et al., cable to Wilson, May [12], 1915.
60. Hoover to Wilson, May 13, 1915.
61. Hoover to Page, May 12, 1915, in American Embassy, London, Correspondence, 1915, vol. 95, file 848—Belgium, RG 84, NARA.
62. Hoover to C. A. Young, May 13, 1915, in George I. Gay and H. H. Fisher, *Public Relations of the Commission for Relief in Belgium*, vol. 2 (Stanford, Calif., 1929), pp. 128–30.
63. Hoover to Adams, June 6, 1915.
64. Hoover to Lindon W. Bates, May 14, 1915, Herbert Hoover Collection, Box 6, HI.
65. Hoover to Page, May 17, 1915, in American Embassy, London, Correspondence, 1915, vol. 96, file 848—Belgium, RG 84, NARA.
66. Hoover to Adams, June 6, 1915.

67. Hoover's letter of May 13 to Wilson was received at the White House on May 25. But there is no evidence that it influenced the President's course of action.
68. For an extensive account of Wilsonian diplomacy during the *Lusitania* crisis, see Arthur S. Link, *Wilson: The Struggle for Neutrality, 1914–1915* (Princeton, N.J., 1960), pp. 368–455.
69. Hoover to Wilson, September 3, 1915. In his letter to Colonel House on August 16, 1915, Hoover praised President Wilson's "boldly human" *Lusitania* notes to the German government and declared that Wilson's handling of the matter had "in effect been a complete American diplomatic victory." This sentiment was far indeed from Hoover's initial reaction as confided to Professor E. D. Adams.
70. I have found no evidence in Hoover's papers or elsewhere that Hoover expressed any criticisms, even privately, of Wilson's leadership after June 1915.
71. Inez Irwin diary, August 13, 1916. In this entry Mrs. Irwin, the wife of Hoover's old friend Will Irwin, recorded an account of her evening with the Hoovers at the Red House in London.
72. John L. Simpson oral history (1967), p. 13, HHPL.
73. Hoover evidently did not vote in any American presidential election before 1920—at least not between 1906 and 1920. George Barr Baker memorandum, May 21, 1920, "Citizenship," Pre-Commerce Papers, Herbert Hoover Papers, HHPL. In his *Memoirs (Years of Adventure,* p. 120), Hoover recorded that he contributed to Theodore Roosevelt's presidential campaign in 1912.
74. Whitlock diary, July 23, 1915, in his *Journal,* p. 200.
75. Hoover to House, August 16, 1915.
76. Hoover to Walter Hines Page, August 5, 1915, copy enclosed with Hoover to E. D. Adams, August 5, 1915, Adams Papers, Stanford University Archives.
77. Hoover, handwritten cover note to Page, August 5, 1915 (enclosing the letter cited in the previous footnote), Walter Hines Page Papers, Harvard University.
78. Hoover to House, August 16, 1915. Hoover did not name his "cabinet friend" and, as mentioned in the text on p. 148, he later denied that it was a *British* Cabinet member. However, as I have indicated on p. 148, Hoover's denial is not persuasive.
79. Hoover memorandum (n.d., but August 16, 1915, or shortly before), House Papers, Box 61. This document is quoted at length in Hoover, "The World War, 1914–1917," pp. 285–86, but is incorrectly recorded there as having been written in the summer of 1916. The memorandum is similar in phraseology to Hoover's letter to Ambassador Page on August 5, 1915.
80. Link, *Wilson: The Struggle for Neutrality,* pp. 325–26, 332–48; Ernest R. May, *The World War and American Isolation, 1914–1917* (Cambridge, Mass., 1963), pp. 127–28.
81. Hoover to House, August 16, 1915.
82. Hoover to Wilson, September 3, 1915.
83. Hoover to Wilbur, November 11, 1915.
84. For more on Hirst—who became a lifelong friend of Hoover—see: *New York Times,* February 27, 1953, p. 20; *Dictionary of National Biography, 1951–1960* (Oxford, 1971), pp. 481–83; *F. W. Hirst: By His Friends* (London, 1958). Hoover contributed a brief appreciative essay to the latter volume. The Hoover Papers at HHPL contain a number of letters from Hirst, particularly during the 1930s and 1940s.
85. Whitlock diary, September 13, 1915, in his *Journal,* pp. 209–11.
86. Ibid.
87. Ibid.
88. Hoover, "The World War, 1914–1917," p. 284; Hoover, *Years of Adventure,* pp. 214–15.
89. House diary, January 8, 1916.
90. Hoover, *Years of Adventure,* p. 215. Hoover had met MacDonald at the home of a leading British pacifist, Lord Courtney. Hoover, "The World War, 1914–1917," p. 258.

91. Hoover to Alexander Hemphill, January 27, 1916, CRB Correspondence, Box 5.

92. Hoover to James Gerard, February 7, 1916, ibid.

93. Hoover, *Years of Adventure*, p. 218.

94. Henri Haag, "Les Sondages de paix de W. Nernst auprès de F. Philippson (1915–1917)," [Académie royale des sciences, des lettres, et des beaux-arts, Commission royale d'histoire], *Bulletin* 150 (1984): 328–56, especially pp. 332–37, 350–52; Lord Eustace Percy memorandum, September 26, 1916, in FO 371/2803/file 2930, PRO (copy also in Cab. 37/155/38, PRO); Baron Beyens, *Un Diplomate belge au service de son pays* (Brussels, 1981), p. 136.

95. Percy memorandum, September 26, 1916.

96. Ibid.; Walter Hines Page cable to Woodrow Wilson and Robert Lansing, October 11, 1916, in Arthur S. Link et al., eds., *The Papers of Woodrow Wilson*, vol. 38 (Princeton, N.J., 1982), pp. 392–93; Leland Harrison to Robert Lansing, January 3, 1917, in Arthur S. Link et al., eds., *The Papers of Woodrow Wilson*, vol. 40 (Princeton, N.J., 1982), p. 388.

97. Percy memorandum, September 26, 1916; Beyens, *Un Diplomate belge*, p. 136.

98. Baron Beyens (the Belgian foreign minister) to Paul Hymans (the Belgian minister to Great Britain), October 12, 1916, in Beyens, *Un Diplomate belge*, pp. 251–52.

99. Haag, "Les Sondages," pp. 337–38; Beyens, *Un Diplomate belge*, pp. 137–38, 251–52; R. van Overstraeten, *The War Diaries of Albert I* (London, 1954), pp. 126–27.

100. Haag, "Les Sondages," p. 338; Beyens, *Un Diplomate belge*, p. 138; van Overstraeten, *War Diaries of Albert I*, pp. 127–28.

101. He did quote his 1915 memorandum on lifting the British naval embargo in the unpublished page proof version of his *Memoirs*. But he did not disclose its full context and claimed without explanation that he had prepared it at the request of Ambassador Page. The passage did not appear in the published version of his *Memoirs*.

102. Whitlock diary, July 28 and August 1, 1916, in his *Journal*, pp. 282–83.

103. Hugh Gibson notebook, June 20, 1915, quoted in Perrin C. Galpin, ed., *Hugh Gibson, 1883–1954: Extracts from His Letters and Anecdotes from His Friends* (New York, 1956), p. 42, copy at HHPL; Hugh Gibson to his mother, June 21, 1915, Hugh Gibson Papers, Box 33, HI; Gilchrist Stockton to his parents, June 26, 1915, "Stockton, Gilchrist," Pre-Commerce Papers.

104. *Harper's Weekly* 62 (January 8, 1916): 25.

105. David Starr Jordan to Lou Henry Hoover, December 30, 1915, "Jordan, David Starr," Personal Correspondence, 1874–1920, Lou Henry Hoover Papers, HHPL; Lou Henry Hoover to Jordan, February 15, 1916, ibid.; Hoover to Brand Whitlock, January 28, 1916, quoted on p. 280.

106. Mary Austin, *Earth Horizon* (Boston and New York, 1932), p. 323.

107. Hoover to Adams, June 6, 1915.

108. Mary Austin to Hoover, July 18, 1917, "Austin, Mary," Pre-Commerce Papers.

109. Brand Whitlock diary, November 3, 1932, Whitlock Papers, LC.

110. Howard Coffin to Josephus Daniels, September 16, 1916, File 21A-A4, Box 1502, Records of the War Industries Board, RG 61, NARA.

111. William Honnold cable to Hoover, December 22, 1916, CRB cable files, Pre-Commerce Papers; copy in Frederic C. Walcott Papers, Box 7, Yale University Library.

112. Hoover to Ray Lyman Wilbur, November 22, 1916, Ray Lyman Wilbur Papers, Box 21, HI.

113. Ray Lyman Wilbur to Woodrow Wilson, December 7, 1916, Ray Lyman Wilbur Personal Papers, Box 31.

114. Will Irwin, *The Making of a Reporter* (New York, 1942), pp. 324–25; Robert V. Hudson, *The Writing Game: A Biography of Will Irwin* (Ames, Ia., 1982), p. 102; White House appointments book, entry for December 11, 1916, Wilson Papers.

115. Walter Hines Page memorandum on Hoover, December 30, 1916, in Link et al., eds., *Papers of Woodrow Wilson*, vol. 40, p. 369.
116. Franklin K. Lane, "The American Spirit," *Survey* 36 (July 15, 1916): 411–12.
117. Franklin K. Lane cable to Hoover, December 19, 1916, "Lane, Franklin K.," Pre-Commerce Papers.
118. Ibid.; Hoover to Brand Whitlock, December 29, 1916, in American Legation, Brussels, Correspondence, 1917, file 848, RG 84, NARA.
119. Hoover cable to Curtis H. Lindley, December 20, 1916, "Lindley, Curtis H.," Pre-Commerce Papers.
120. Unless it is the letter cited in the next footnote.
121. Curtis H. Lindley to Hoover, January 16, 1917, "Lindley, Curtis H.," Pre-Commerce Papers.
122. Hoover to Whitlock, December 29, 1916.
123. Whitlock to Hoover, January 17, 1917, in Allan Nevins, ed., *The Letters of Brand Whitlock* (New York, 1936), pp. 212–13.
124. Whitlock to Newton D. Baker, January 17, 1917, Newton D. Baker Papers, Box 5, LC.
125. Hoover cable to Lane, January 4, 1917, "Lane, Franklin K.," Pre-Commerce Papers; copy, dated January 6, 1917, in American Embassy, London, Cables to State Department: January 2–April 30, 1917, RG 84, NARA. See also Hoover to Curtis H. Lindley, January 22, 1917, CRB Miscellaneous Files, HI.
126. Norman Hapgood to Louis D. Brandeis, January 10, 1917, Louis D. Brandeis Papers, University of Louisville.

CHAPTER 13

1. Hoover memorandum 76G to CRB—Brussels office, January 12, 1917, in American Legation, Brussels, Correspondence, 1916, vol. 67, file 848, RG 84, NARA.
2. Hoover to Louis Chevrillon, November 29, 1916, copy in CRB—London office dossier 46: "Correspondence in Regard to Negotiations for a Loan in America," HI.
3. Hoover to William L. Honnold, October 10, 1916, copy in CRB—London office dossier 46.
4. See page 197.
5. Tracy B. Kittredge, "The History of the Commission for Relief in Belgium, 1914–1917" (unpublished bound page proof version, ca. 1918), pp. 380–82, copy at HHPL.
6. Hoover cable 720 to CRB—New York office, October 16, 1916, copy in CRB—London office dossier 46.
7. Hoover letter (marked "confidential") to William L. Honnold, October 17, 1916; Hoover cable 812 to CRB—New York office, November 20, 1916. Copies in CRB—London office dossier 46.
8. Hoover cable 812 to CRB—New York office, November 20, 1916.
9. CRB—New York office cable 691 to Hoover, November 21 (?), 1916; Hoover cable 832 to CRB—New York office, November 25, 1916. Copies in CRB—London office dossier 46.
10. Hoover to Louis Chevrillon, November 29, 1916, copy in CRB—London office dossier 46.
11. Hoover memorandum 24G to Warren Gregory (CRB—Brussels office), December 12, 1916, in American Legation, Brussels, Correspondence, 1916, vol. 64, file 848, NARA; Hoover to Brand Whitlock, December 13, 1916, ibid. Also: British Foreign Office to [the French ambassador to Great Britain?], December 19, 1916; Hoover cable 912 to CRB—New York office, December 26, 1916; copies in CRB—London office dossier 46. See also: Hoover memorandum 42G to Warren Gregory, December 27, 1916, in American Legation, Brussels, Correspondence, 1916, vol. 67, file 848, RG 84, NARA. The French gov-

ernment, at Hoover's instigation, had formally proposed the loan to the British government on December 9.

12. Hoover cable 720 to CRB—New York office, October 10, 1916, copy in CRB—London office dossier 46.

13. CRB—New York office cable 763 to Hoover, December 22, 1916, copy in CRB—London office dossier 46.

14. Hoover and the British (and probably the French as well) were anxious not to disclose anything to the Belgians until the terms of the loan proposal were already formulated— another case of an attempted fait accompli. Hoover cables to Louis Chevrillon, December 5 and 14, 1916; British Foreign Office to [the French ambassador?], December 19, 1916. Copies in CRB—London office dossier 46.

15. Hoover to William L. Honnold, December 15, 1916, CRB Correspondence, Box 7, HI.

16. Hoover to Whitlock, December 13, 1916.

17. Hoover to Honnold, December 15, 1916.

18. Edgar Sengier memorandum for Hoover on the relief loan, January 3, 1917, copy in CRB— London office dossier 46.

19. Hoover to the Belgian finance minister, Aloys van de Vyvere, January 9, 1917, copy in CRB—London office dossier 46, in George I. Gay and H. H. Fisher, *Public Relations of the Commission for Relief in Belgium* (Stanford, Calif., 1929), I, pp. 278–80, hereinafter cited as *PR-CRB*.

20. Hoover to A. de Fleuriau, January 10, 1917; Hoover to Lord Eustace Percy, January 11 and 12, 1917; Hoover to E. C. Grenfell, January 12, 1917; Hoover cable 39 to CRB—New York office, January 12, 1917. Copies in CRB—London office dossier 46.

21. Hoover cable 39 to CRB—New York office, January 12, 1917.

22. *New York Times*, January 22, 1917, p. 2; Hoover cable to CRB—London office, January 21, 1917.

23. Louis Chevrillon and William B. Poland cable 59 (from London) to CRB—New York office, January 20, 1917; Hoover cable 41 to CRB—London office, January 22, 1917. Copies in CRB—London office dossier 46.

24. Memoranda, January 16, 18, and 19, 1917, copies in CRB—London office dossier 46.

25. CRB—London office cable 64 to CRB—New York office, January 23, 1917, copy in CRB— London office dossier 46.

26. William B. Poland to Lord Eustace Percy (plus enclosure), January 29, 1917, in *PR-CRB*, I, pp. 272–74.

27. Brand Whitlock to the Secretary of State, January 2, 1917, printed in United States, Department of State, *Papers Relating to the Foreign Relations of the United States, 1917*, Supplement I: *The World War* (Washington, D.C., 1931), pp. 666–68, hereinafter cited as *FRUS, 1917*, Supplement I; Hoover cable to CRB—New York office, January 12, 1917, copy (dated January 13, 1917) in American Federation of Labor Papers, Series 11, File 11-A, Box 20, State Historical Society of Wisconsin.

28. Hoover to Secretary of State Robert Lansing, January 27, 1917, CRB Correspondence, Box 7.

29. Hoover statement for Ambassador Page, January 2, 1917, in Arthur S. Link et al., eds., *The Papers of Woodrow Wilson*, vol. 40 (Princeton, N.J., 1982), pp. 409–11. Also: Hoover cable to CRB—New York office, January 4, 1917; Oscar Strauss to Samuel Gompers, January 5, 1917; William L. Honnold cable to Hoover, January 11, 1917; Honnold to Gompers, January 18, 1917. All in American Federation of Labor Papers, Series 11, File 11-A, Box 20.

30. Samuel Gompers to Herbert Hoover, January 24, 1917; Gompers to Honnold, February 6, 1917. Both in American Federation of Labor Papers, Series 11, File 11-A, Box 20. See also Samuel Gompers, *Seventy Years of Life and Labor*, vol. 2 (New York, 1925), p. 353.

31. Gompers to Honnold, February 6, 1917. The AFL's protest was never issued because of

the United States' diplomatic break with Germany a few days after the executive council meeting. As it turned out, the deportations ceased in February 1917 after the intervention of the Kaiser. Most of the Belgian victims were repatriated. See also E. H. Kossman, *The Low Countries, 1780–1940* (Oxford, 1978), p. 533.

32. Hoover to Franklin K. Lane, July 16, 1916, CRB Correspondence, Box 8.

33. Hoover to Honnold, December 15, 1916. In this letter Hoover referred to Villalobar's "intrigue" against the CRB.

34. I have found no other allusions to this proposal anywhere.

35. Alexander J. Hemphill et al. to Colonel Edward M. House, January 12, 1917, Edward M. House Papers, Box 11, Yale University Library.

36. Edward M. House to Woodrow Wilson, January 22, 1917, ibid., Box 121; printed in Link et al., eds., *Papers of Woodrow Wilson*, vol. 40, p. 540.

37. Hoover to Franklin K. Lane, January 26, 1917, enclosed with Lane to Robert Lansing, January 26, 1917, in Robert Lansing Papers, vol. 24, LC.

38. Ibid.; Lansing to Joseph Tumulty, January 27, 1917, Lansing Papers, vol. 24. Years later Hoover stated that Ambassador Page arranged this appointment. I have found no evidence of this; Hoover's recollection is probably erroneous. See Hoover, *The Ordeal of Woodrow Wilson* (New York, 1958), p. 4.

39. The CRB had been paying its administrative costs out of its charitable receipts and the Allied loan allotments all along. In dollar terms these "incidental expenses" were relatively insignificant.

40. *New York Times*, January 22, 1917, p. 2.

41. "Herbert Hoover," *Bellman* 22 (January 27, 1917): 89–90.

42. Hoover to William C. Edgar, February 2, 1917, CRB Correspondence, Box 8.

43. See, for example: *New York Times*, January 2, 1917, p. 5; "The Cry of the Belgian Children," *Literary Digest* 54 (January 6, 1917): 22–23; "Where the United States Has Fallen Short: Its Record in Belgium," *Outlook* 115 (January 10, 1917): 61–62; William L. Honnold, "The Commission for Relief in Belgium," *Engineering and Mining Journal* 103 (January 20, 1917): 136–39.

44. Hoover to Theodore Roosevelt, February 6 [1917], Theodore Roosevelt Papers, microfilm edition, reel 312, LC; Hoover address to Rocky Mountain Club, October 27, 1919, printed in *Addresses Given at the Rocky Mountain Club Dinner on the Anniversary of Theodore Roosevelt's Birthday, Monday, October 27, 1919*, copy in Reprint File, HHPL.

45. Theodore Roosevelt to Gilson Gardner, January 31, 1917, Roosevelt Papers, reel 415.

46. *New York Times*, March 16, 1917, p. 9.

47. Ibid., January 30, 1917, p. 1.

48. Ibid., pp. 1, 3.

49. Hoover cable 59 to CRB—London office, January 31, 1917, copy in CRB—London office dossier 46.

50. No contemporary account of this meeting has been found. For Hoover's recollection long afterward, see his book *An American Epic*, vol. 1 (Chicago, 1959), p. 285.

51. Appointments Book, 1917, Woodrow Wilson Papers, microfilm edition, reel 3, LC.

52. Kittredge, "History," p. 383; Arthur S. Link et al., eds., *The Papers of Woodrow Wilson*, vol. 41 (Princeton, N.J., 1983), pp. 74–79. Hoover left Washington for New York before news of the German blockade became public. *New York Times*, February 1, 1917, p. 2.

53. Hoover, *An American Epic*, I, p. 285. It should perhaps be mentioned that my account of the relief loan effort is largely based on contemporary sources and differs in some details from Hoover's recollection in *An American Epic*.

54. *New York Times*, February 2, 1917, p. 5; *Current History*, 6 (April 1917): 133–34.

55. "The American Revival," *New Republic* 10 (February 3, 1917): 3–5.

56. *PR-CRB*, I, p. 344.

57. Ibid., pp. 346–47; Kittredge, "History," pp. 385–86; Hoover, *An American Epic*, I, p. 286.

58. Hoover cable to CRB—London office (State Department cable 4391), February 4, 1917, in American Embassy, London, Correspondence, 1917, vol. 86, file 848—Belgium, RG 84, NARA. See also Secretary of State Robert Lansing's cable 4386 to Ambassador Walter Hines Page, February 3, 1917, copy in FO 382/1641/file 864, PRO, and in FRUS, 1917, Supplement I, p. 630.

59. Hoover, An American Epic, I, p. 287; New York Times, February 7, 1917, p. 13.

60. Hoover cable to CRB—London office, February 4, 1917.

61. Hoover Calendar, HHPL.

62. Secretary of State Lansing cable 4390 to Ambassador Page, February 4, 1917, in American Embassy, London, Correspondence, 1917, vol. 86, file 848—Belgium, RG 84, NARA.

63. In all likelihood Hoover drafted this cable.

64. PR-CRB, I, p. 361; Hoover, An American Epic, I, pp. 288, 322.

65. New York Times, February 6, 1917, p. 2.

66. Ibid., February 5, 1917, p. 7.

67. PR-CRB, I, p. 344.

68. Maurice Pate, "The Withdrawal of the American Commission from Belgium" (typescript, 1917), in Maurice Pate Papers, Box 2, HHPL.

69. Ibid.

70. CRB—London office cable to Hoover, February 9, 1917, in PR-CRB, I, pp. 348–49; Hoover, An American Epic, I, pp. 292–93.

71. Hoover cable 97 to CRB—London office, February 14, 1917, in PR-CRB, I, pp. 349–50; copy in CRB—London office dossier 85: "1917: Diplomatic Rupture between Germany & America," HI.

72. Brand Whitlock, Belgium: A Personal Narrative (New York, 1919), II, p. 722.

73. Arthur Zimmermann (the German foreign minister) to Luis Polo de Bernabé (the Spanish ambassador to Germany), February 18, 1917, in PR-CRB, I, pp. 350–51.

74. New York Times, February 25, 1917, section I, p. 2; Hoover, An American Epic, I, p. 295.

75. PR-CRB, I, p. 361.

76. Hoover, An American Epic, I, p. 288.

77. Ibid., pp. 295–96; PR-CRB, I, pp. 345, 353–57.

78. William Phillips diary, February 3, 1917, Houghton Library, Harvard University; Secretary of State Lansing, cable 4386 to Ambassador Page, February 3, 1917.

79. Lansing cable 248 to Brand Whitlock, February 3, 1917, in FRUS, 1917, Supplement I, pp. 630–31.

80. Hoover to William B. Poland and Vernon Kellogg, transmitted in Lansing cable 4386 to Page, February 3, 1917.

81. Hoover cable "Washington 1" to CRB—London office, February 4, 1917, copy in CRB—London office dossier 85.

82. Kittredge, "History," p. 388; New York Times, February 7, 1917, p. 13.

83. Kittredge, "History," p. 388; CRB—Rotterdam office cable 122 to CRB—London office, February 6, 1917, copy in CRB—London office dossier 85; memorandum dated February 6, 1917, copy in ibid.

84. Hoover to C. A. Young, May 13, 1915, in PR-CRB, II, pp. 128–30.

85. William B. Poland to Warren Gregory and W. L. Brown, February 2, 1917; Poland cable to Hoover, February 3, 1917. Copies in CRB—London office dossier 85.

86. Hoover cable to CRB—London office (State Department cable 4391), February 4, 1917; Hoover cable "Washington 4" to CRB—London office, February 5, 1917. Copies in CRB—London office dossier 85. See also Lansing cable 4386 to Page, February 3, 1917.

87. Hoover cable "Washington 6" to CRB—London office, February 6, 1917, copy in CRB—London office dossier 85.

88. Ibid.

89. Ibid.

90. Ibid.
91. Alfonso Merry del Val to Arthur Balfour, February 6, 1917, copy in American Embassy, London, Correspondence, 1917, vol. 86, file 848—Belgium, RG 84, NARA.
92. CRB—London office cable to Hoover, February 8, 1917, copy in CRB—London office dossier 85; Walter Hines Page cable 5649 to Secretary of State Lansing, February 9, 1917, in American Embassy, London, Correspondence, 1917, vol. 86, file 848—Belgium, RG 84, NARA; Page cable 5652 to Lansing, February 9, 1917, in *FRUS, 1917*, Supplement I, pp. 634–35.
93. Hoover to Ray Lyman Wilbur, February 8, 1917, CRB Correspondence, Box 8.
94. Brand Whitlock diary, February 9, 1917, in Allan Nevins, ed., *The Journal of Brand Whitlock* (New York, 1936), p. 353; CRB—Rotterdam office cables 150 and 151 to CRB—London office, February 11, 1917, copies in CRB—London office dossier 85; Marshall Langhorne cable to Page, February 11, 1917, copy in CRB—London office dossier 85; Christian Herter cable (via American legation in Switzerland) to Secretary of State Lansing, February 13, 1917, in *FRUS, 1917*, Supplement I, pp. 638–39; Whitlock, *Belgium: A Personal Narrative*, II, p. 713.
95. Baron Oscar von der Lancken to the Marquis de Villalobar, February 10, 1917, copy in CRB—London office dossier 85.
96. Whitlock diary, February 11, 1917, in his *Journal*, p. 354.
97. Whitlock diary, February 12, 1917, in ibid., p. 355; Whitlock, *Belgium: A Personal Narrative*, II, pp. 724–25.
98. Page cable 5673 to Lansing, February 12, 1917, in *FRUS, 1917*, Supplement I, pp. 636–37.
99. William B. Poland (CRB—London office) cable 135 to CRB—Rotterdam (for transmittal to Brussels), February 12, 1917; copy in CRB—London office dossier 85.
100. William B. Poland to Paul Hymans, February 13, 1917, copy in CRB—London office dossier 85.
101. CRB—London office cable to Hoover, February 12, 1917, copy in CRB—London office dossier 85.
102. *New York Times*, February 13, 1917, pp. 1, 7; Hoover cable 90 to CRB—London office, February 13, 1917, copy in CRB—London office dossier 85, and in CRB cable files, Pre-Commerce Papers, Herbert Hoover Papers, HHPL. In his cable to Hoover cited in note 101, Poland stated that he was making "no public announcement" in London about his withdrawal order, "thinking you would prefer to do so yourself from America."
103. Hoover cable 90 to CRB—London office, February 13, 1917.
104. Ibid. Hoover's account of this episode in his *An American Epic* (I, pp. 302–10) is inconsistent at points with the contemporary sources. Hoover states (p. 306) that he had wanted no publicity about Poland's withdrawal order but that it leaked anyhow to the press. He implies that he was surprised when the order reached the newspapers. In fact, Hoover himself released it, as he acknowledged in his cable 90 to his London office. See also Kittredge, "History," p. 392.
105. Hoover cable 90 to CRB—London office, February 13, 1917.
106. Hoover to Colonel Edward M. House, February 13, 1917, CRB Correspondence, Box 8.
107. Phillips diary, February 14, 1917. Phillips was a senior official in the State Department.
108. Poland to Louis Chevrillon, February 13, 1917, copy in CRB—London office dossier 46.
109. Poland to Hoover, February 1, 1917, copy in CRB—London office dossier 46.
110. Poland to Hoover, February 11, 1917, copy in CRB—London office dossier 46.
111. Hoover cable 94 to CRB—London office, February 14, 1917, copy in CRB—London office dossier 46.
112. Dutch minister van Rappard to Secretary of State Lansing, February 14, 1917, in *FRUS, 1917*, Supplement I, pp. 637–38.
113. Aristide Briand statement, ca. February 14, 1917, enclosed with Paul Cambon to William

B. Poland, February 14, 1917, copies in CRB—London office dossier 85; Lord Robert Cecil statement, February 14, 1917, in *New York Times*, February 15, 1917, p. 7.

114. Cecil statement, February 14, 1917.

115. Phillips diary, February 13, 1917.

116. Merry del Val to Paul Cambon, February 15, 1917; Merry del Val to Paul Hymans, February 15, 1917; Vernon Kellogg to Hoover, February 16, 1917. Copies in CRB—London office dossier 85.

117. Hoover cable 90 to CRB—London office, February 13, 1917.

118. Hoover cable 93 to CRB—London office, February 13, 1917. Copies in CRB—London office dossier 85, CRB cable files, and CRB Correspondence, Box 8.

119. *New York Times*, February 14, 1917, p. 7.

120. Hoover cable to CRB—London office (from Hotel Gotham in New York), February 14, 1917, CRB cable files.

121. Hoover's term. Hoover cable "Washington 8" to CRB—London office, February 15, 1917, copy in CRB—London office dossier 85.

122. Hoover cable 98 to CRB—London office, prepared on February 14 but dispatched on February 15, 1917; copy in CRB—London office dossier 85.

123. Hoover cable 97 to CRB—London office, prepared Wednesday, February 14, but dispatched on Thursday, February 15, 1917; copy in CRB—London office dossier 85. Villalobar's message is summarized in Kittredge, "History," p. 400, which, however, erroneously states that Hoover received the cable on February 15. He received it on or by February 14, as indicated in his cable 97, which was dated "Wednesday" (February 14) and prepared before cable 98, in which he reversed himself.

Hoover may have been sensitive about this startling volte-face, which Brand Whitlock, for one, considered a sign of vacillation. Hoover made no mention of it in his *American Epic*.

124. "I shall be in Washington Thursday [February 15]. . . ." Hoover cable (from Hotel Gotham) to CRB—London office, February 14, 1917 (Wednesday).

125. Lansing cable 253 to Whitlock, February 15, 1917, in *FRUS, 1917*, Supplement I, pp. 639–40; Phillips diary, February 15, 1917. See also Hoover cable "Washington 8" to CRB—London office, February 15, 1917.

126. CRB—London office cable 149 to Hoover, February 15, 1917, copy in CRB—London office dossier 85.

127. Whitlock diary, February 14, 1917, in his *Journal*, pp. 356–58; Kittredge, "History," pp. 395–96.

128. Whitlock diary, February 14, 1917; Whitlock, *Belgium: A Personal Narrative*, II, p. 730; CRB—Rotterdam office cable 166 to CRB—London office, February 15, 1917, copy in CRB—London office dossier 85.

129. Zimmermann to Polo de Bernabé, February 18, 1917.

130. Whitlock diary, February 14, 1917.

131. CRB—London office cable 149 to Hoover, February 15, 1917; Whitlock cable 43 to Lansing, February 21, 1917, in *FRUS, 1917*, Supplement I, pp. 642–43. The department's cable of February 15 did not reach Whitlock until February 21.

132. CRB—London office cables to: Louis Chevrillon, CRB—Rotterdam office (cable 147), and Hoover (cable 149), all on February 15, 1917, copies in CRB—London office dossier 85; *New York Times*, February 16, 1917, pp. 1, 2, and February 17, 1917, p. 2.

133. Hoover cable to CRB—London office, February 18, 1917, copy in CRB—London office dossier 85.

134. Hoover to Poland, February 14, 1917, CRB Correspondence, Box 8.

135. Hoover cable "Washington 8" to CRB—London office, February 15, 1917; Hoover cable "Washington 10" to CRB—London office, February 16, 1917, copy in CRB—London office dossier 85; Hoover to William Phillips, February 27, 1917, CRB Correspondence,

Box 8; Hoover cable "Gotham 1" to CRB—London office, March 4, 1917, in CRB—London office dossier 85.

136. Hoover cable "Washington 8" to CRB—London office, February 15, 1917; Hoover cable 129 to CRB—London office, February 27, 1917, copy in CRB—London office dossier 85.

137. Hoover cable "Washington 8" to CRB—London office, February 15, 1917; Hoover to William B. Poland and Vernon Kellogg, March 5, 1917, CRB Correspondence, Box 8.

138. CRB—London office cable 147 to Hoover, February 14, 1917; CRB—London office cable 156 to Hoover, February 16, 1917; copies in CRB—London office dossier 85.

139. Ibid.

140. Ibid.

141. Carton de Wiart cables to Hoover, February 17 and 23, 1917, copies in CRB—London office dossier 85; Hoover, *An American Epic,* I, p. 301.

142. Van de Vyvere, despite his intense dislike of Hoover, now said he wanted the CRB's cooperation in the "economic reconstruction" of Belgium after the war!

143. Hoover cable "Washington 11" to CRB—London office, February 17, 1917, copy in CRB—London office dossier 85.

144. Ibid.; Hoover cable "Washington 8" to CRB—London office, February 15, 1917,

145. Hoover cable "Washington 11" to CRB—London office, February 17, 1917.

146. Hoover cable to Carton de Wiart, February 18, 1917, CRB cable files.

147. Hoover to Poland and Kellogg, March 5, 1917.

148. Hoover cable "Washington 10" to CRB—London office, February 16, 1917.

149. Hoover to William Phillips, February 25, 1917, CRB Correspondence, Box 8.

150. Hoover to Poland and Kellogg, March 5, 1917.

151. British Foreign Office cable to Sir Cecil Spring Rice, March 6, 1917, in FO 382/1642/file 864, PRO.

152. CRB—London office cable to Hoover, February 25, 1917, copy in CRB—London office dossier 85.

153. Hoover cable to William Goode, February 27, 1917, CRB Correspondence, Box 8.

154. Hoover to Phillips, February 27, 1917; Hoover cable 129 to CRB—London office, February 27, 1917, copy in CRB—London office dossier 85.

155. Hoover cable 135 to CRB—London office, March 1, 1917, copy in CRB—London office dossier 85.

156. Ibid.

157. Carton de Wiart cable to Hoover, February 23, 1917.

158. Eustace Percy, memorandum ("minute"), March 5, 1917, in FO 382/1642/file 864.

159. CRB—London office cable 194 to Hoover, March 3, 1917; Paul Cambon to Hoover, March 5, 1917; Paul Hymans to Poland, March 7, 1917; Cecil Spring Rice to Hoover, March 8, 1917. Copies in CRB—London office dossier 85. See also British Foreign Office to Spring Rice, March 6, 1917, and [Robert Cecil] to Cambon, March 7, 1917, both in FO 368/1642/file 864.

160. Kellogg cable to CRB—London office (via Rotterdam), March 7, 1917, copy in CRB—London office dossier 85.

161. Hoover cable "Gotham 1" to CRB—London office, March 4, 1917.

162. Spring Rice to Hoover, March 8, 1917.

163. Hoover to Spring Rice, March 9, 1917, copy in CRB—London office dossier 85.

164. Hoover to Poland and Kellogg, March 5, 1917.

165. Ibid.

166. Whitlock, *Belgium: A Personal Narrative,* II, p. 715.

167. Lansing cable 248 to Whitlock, February 3, 1917, in *FRUS, 1917,* Supplement I, pp. 630–31.

168. Whitlock diary, February 7, 1917, in his *Journal,* p. 352; Whitlock cable 40 to Lansing, February 16, 1917, in *FRUS, 1917,* Supplement I, pp. 640–42. The department's cable

472

248, as received and deciphered in Brussels, is in Allan Nevins, ed., *The Letters of Brand Whitlock* (New York, 1936), p. 214. It should be compared with the department's own version, cited in the preceding footnote.

169. In Whitlock's *Letters*, p. 215.
170. Whitlock diary, February 7, 1917.
171. Whitlock diary, February 6, 1917, in his *Journal*, p. 351.
172. Whitlock diary, February 9, 1917, in ibid., p. 353; Herter cable to Lansing, February 13, 1917.
173. Whitlock cable 40 to Lansing, February 16, 1917, as printed in his *Letters*, pp. 216–18 (also in somewhat variant form in *FRUS, 1917*, Supplement I, pp. 640–42); Whitlock, *Belgium: A Personal Narrative*, II, p. 730.
174. Herter cable to Lansing, February 13, 1917; Whitlock cable 40 to Lansing, February 16, 1917; Whitlock diary, February 24, 1917, in his *Journal*, pp. 361–62.
175. Whitlock diary, February 11, 1917, in his *Journal*, pp. 354–55; Whitlock cable 40 to Lansing, February 16, 1917.
176. Whitlock diary, February 17, 1917, printed in his *Journal*, pp. 358–59.
177. Whitlock cable 43 to Lansing, February 21, 1917, in *FRUS, 1917*, Supplement I, pp. 642–43; Whitlock diary, February 23, 1917, in his *Journal*, p. 360.
178. Whitlock cable 43 to Lansing, February 21, 1917.
179. Whitlock diary, February 23, 1917, in his *Journal*, pp. 360–61; Whitlock to Lansing, enclosed in Marshall Langhorne cable 732 to Lansing, February 25, 1917, in *FRUS, 1917*, Supplement I, p. 644.
180. Contained in Whitlock's cable 40 of February 16, which did not reach Washington until February 21. *FRUS, 1917*, Supplement I, p. 640.
181. Hoover to Phillips, February 25, 1917.
182. Enclosed with ibid.
183. Lansing cable 256 to Whitlock, February 26, 1917, in *FRUS, 1917*, Supplement I, pp. 644–45.
184. Hoover draft cable for Whitlock, cited in note 182.
185. Lansing cable 256 (cited in note 183) and cable 257, February 26, 1917, in *FRUS, 1917*, Supplement I, p. 645.
186. Phillips diary, February 27, 1917; Hoover to Phillips, February 27, 1917.
187. Hoover to Phillips, February 27, 1917.
188. Hoover cable 129 to CRB—London office, February 27, 1917.
189. Whitlock diary, February 24, 1917, in his *Journal*, pp. 361–62; Whitlock cable 44 to Lansing, February 22, 1917, in *FRUS, 1917*, Supplement I, pp. 646–47.
190. Lansing cable 261 to Whitlock, March 1, 1917, in *FRUS, 1917*, Supplement I, p. 647; Phillips diary, March 1, 1917.
191. Whitlock diary, February 28, 1917, in his *Journal*, pp. 362–63.
192. Whitlock diary, March 1, 1917, in his *Journal*, pp. 363–64.
193. Whitlock diary, March 4, 1917, in his *Journal*, pp. 364–66.
194. Whitlock diary, March 7, 1917, in his *Journal*, pp. 366–67.
195. Whitlock diary, March 4, 1917.
196. Whitlock diary, March 7, 1917.
197. Whitlock diary, March 1 and 4, 1917; Whitlock cable 40 to Lansing, February 16, 1917; Whitlock cable 46 to Lansing, March 3, 1917, in *FRUS, 1917*, Supplement I, pp. 649–50; Whitlock, *Belgium: A Personal Narrative*, II, pp. 736, 790.
198. Whitlock, *Belgium: A Personal Narrative*, II, pp. 790–92; Whitlock diary, March 4, 1917.
199. Whitlock diary, March 7, 1917.
200. Hoover to Hugh Gibson, March 5, 1917, CRB Correspondence, Box 8.
201. Whitlock diary, March 7, 1917.
202. Hoover to Gibson, March 5, 1917.

203. Whitlock cable 45 to Lansing, March 1, 1917, in *FRUS, 1917*, Supplement I, p. 647; Phillips diary, March 2, 1917.
204. Phillips diary, March 2, 1917; Phillips telegram to Hoover, March 4, 1917, copy in Henry Stimson Papers, Box 61, Yale University Library.
205. Phillips diary, March 2, 1917; Hoover telegram to Phillips, March 2, 1917, copy in Stimson Papers, Box 61.
206. Hoover telegram to Phillips, March 2, 1917.
207. Whitlock diary, March 9, 1917, in his *Journal*, pp. 367–68.
208. Von der Lancken to Villalobar, March 12, 1917, in *PR-CRB*, II, pp. 157–58; Whitlock diary, March 13, 1917, printed in his *Journal*, p. 368; Whitlock cable 48 to Lansing, March 14, 1917, in *FRUS, 1917*, Supplement I, p. 654; Kittredge, "History," pp. 416–17.
209. Kellogg cable to Poland (via Rotterdam), March 2, 1917; Poland to Hoover, March 2, 1917; CRB—London office cable 202 to Hoover, March 7, 1917. Copies in CRB—London office dossier 85. See also Kittredge, "History," pp. 396, 414.
210. CRB—London office cable 202 to Hoover, March 7, 1917.
211. Hoover cable "Gotham 2" to CRB—London office, March 8, 1917, copy in CRB—London office dossier 85.
212. CRB—London office cable 211 to CRB—Rotterdam office, March 8, 1917; CRB—London office cable 212 to Hoover, March 9, 1917. Copies in CRB—London office dossier 85.
213. Kellogg cable to CRB—London office (via CRB—Rotterdam office cable 239 to CRB—London office), March 10, 1917; CRB—Rotterdam office cable 242 to CRB—London office, March 10, 1917. Copies in CRB—London office dossier 85.
214. CRB—London office cable 219 to CRB—Rotterdam office, March 10, 1917, copy in CRB—London office dossier 85.
215. Whitlock cable 46 to Lansing, March 3, 1917, in *FRUS, 1917*, Supplement I, pp. 649–50.
216. Kellogg cable to CRB—London office, March 6, 1917, transmitted in Marshall Langhorne cable to Page, March 7, 1917, copy in CRB—London office dossier 85.
217. CRB—London office cable 202 to Hoover, March 7, 1917.
218. CRB—London cable 209 to Hoover, March 9, 1917, copy in CRB—London office dossier 85; also in *FRUS, 1917*, Supplement I, p. 651.
219. Page cable to Lansing and Hoover, March 9, 1917, copy in CRB—London office dossier 85. Also (in slightly variant form) in *FRUS, 1917*, Supplement I, p. 650.
220. Hoover to Gibson, March 10, 1917, CRB Correspondence, Box 8.
221. Lansing cable 265 to Whitlock, March 10, 1917, in *FRUS, 1917*, Supplement I, p. 651.
222. Lansing cable 222 to Page, March 10, 1917, in *FRUS, 1917*, Supplement I, pp. 651–52.
223. Hoover telegram and letter (two items) to Gibson, March 10, 1917, CRB Correspondence, Box 8.
224. Hoover cable 162 to CRB—London office, March 10, 1917, CRB cable files; copy, dated March 11, 1917, in CRB—London office dossier 85.
225. Whitlock diary, March 13, 1917.
226. Whitlock diary, March 16, 1917, in his *Journal*, pp. 369–70.
227. *New York Times*, February 18, 1917, p. 3, and February 21, 1917, p. 9.
228. Ibid., February 18, 1917, p. 3.
229. Ibid., March 1, 1917, p. 22.
230. On February 9, 1917 he addressed the City Club of Philadelphia. *New York Times*, February 10, 1917, p. 3.
231. Edward M. House diary, February 20, 1917, House Papers; Hoover to William A. Law, March 5, 1917, CRB Correspondence, Box 8.
232. House diary, February 20, 1917; Hoover to House, February 23, 1917, House Papers, Box 61; Hoover to David Barrows, March 6, 1917, CRB Correspondence, Box 8.
233. *New York Times*, March 4, 1917, section II, p. 6.
234. Hoover cable to Goode, February 27, 1917.

235. Hoover to Law, March 5, 1917; Hoover to Barrows, March 6, 1917; Hoover to Joseph P. Tumulty (President Wilson's secretary), March 6, 1917, in Francis William O'Brien, ed., *The Hoover-Wilson Wartime Correspondence* (Ames, Ia., 1974), p. 19.
236. Hoover to Tumulty, March 10, 1917, in O'Brien, ed., *Hoover-Wilson Wartime Correspondence*, p. 20.
237. House diary, March 7, 1917.
238. Hoover cable "Gotham 2" to CRB—London office, March 8, 1917.
239. House diary, March 7, 1917.
240. Hoover to Tumulty, March 10, 1917.
241. Hoover, *An American Epic*, I, p. 314.
242. Hoover, *The Memoirs of Herbert Hoover*, vol. 1: *Years of Adventure* (New York, 1951), pp. 220–21.
243. Herbert Hoover, Jr., telegram to his father, March 11, 1917, "Hoover, Lou Henry," Pre-Commerce Papers; Hugh Gibson to his mother, March 19, 1917, Hugh Gibson Papers, Box 34, HI.
244. *New York Times*, March 14, 1917, p. 3.
245. Hoover cable "Gotham 4" to CRB—London office, March 13, 1917; CRB—New York office cable 172 to CRB—London office, March 13, 1917. Copies in CRB—London office dossier 85.
246. Hoover, *An American Epic*, I, p. 314.
247. Hoover, *Years of Adventure*, pp. 221–22.
248. Ibid.; Link et al., eds., *Papers of Woodrow Wilson*, vol. 41, p. viii.
249. CRB—Rotterdam office cable 242 to CRB—London office, March 10, 1917; CRB—London office cable 214 to CRB—New York office, March 10, 1917; William B. Poland to Lord Eustace Percy, March 12, 1917; Kellogg cable to CRB—London office, March 12, 1917, transmitted in Marshall Langhorne cable to Page, March 12, 1917; Louis Chevrillon cable to Poland, March 13, 1917. Copies in CRB—London office dossier 85. See also Kittredge, "History," p. 415.
250. Kittredge, "History," p. 415.
251. CRB—London office cable 238 to CRB—Rotterdam office, March 15, 1917, copy in CRB—London office dossier 85 and in American Embassy, London, Correspondence, 1917, vol. 86, file 848—Belgium, RG 84, NARA.
252. CRB—Rotterdam office cable 265 to CRB—London office, March 14, 1917; Roger Cambon to Poland, March 16, 1917; CRB—Rotterdam office cable 272 to CRB—London office, transmitted in Langhorne cable to Page, March 16, 1917; CRB—Rotterdam office cable 277 to CRB—London office, March 17, 1917; CRB—London office cable 241 to CRB—New York office, March 18, 1917. Copies in CRB—London office dossier 85. See also Kittredge, "History," p. 417.
253. Warren Gregory to CRB—Rotterdam office, March 19, 1917, copy in CRB—London office dossier 85.
254. Kittredge, "History," p. 418.
255. Ibid.; "Memorandum [probably by Poland and Kellogg] of discussions March 24th [1917], concerning other neutrals to replace Americans in Belgium and France," copy in CRB—London office dossier 85.
256. Kittredge, "History," p. 418. See also: CRB—London office cable 260 to CRB—Rotterdam office, March 21, 1917; CRB—London office cable 249 to CRB—New York office, March 21, 1917; CRB—Rotterdam office cable to CRB—London office, March 22, 1917, transmitted in Langhorne to Page, same date; CRB—Rotterdam office cable 308 to CRB—London office, March 24, 1917. Copies in CRB—London office dossier 85.
257. *New York Times*, March 21, 1917, p. 5; Hoover, *An American Epic*, I, p. 323.
258. Phillips diary, March 23, 1917; Lansing cable 268 to Whitlock, March 23, 1917, in *FRUS, 1917*, Supplement I, p. 655; State Department press release, March 24, 1917, printed in

New York Times, March 25, 1917, section I, p. 1, and in *FRUS, 1917*, Supplement I, p. 656. See also William L. Honnold cable 198 to CRB—London office, March 23, 1917, copy in CRB—London office dossier 85.

259. Link et al., eds., *Papers of Woodrow Wilson*, vol. 41, p. ix.

260. Hugh Gibson to his mother, March 23, 1917, Gibson Papers, Box 34.

261. State Department press release, March 24, 1917; Lansing to Dutch Minister van Rappard, March 23, 1917, in *FRUS, 1917*, Supplement I, p. 655.

262. Hoover cable (from Paris) to CRB—London office, March 28, 1917, copy in CRB—London office dossier 85.

263. Hoover, *Years of Adventure*, p. 222.

264. Memorandum of meeting between William B. Poland and José Roura, March 26, 1917, copy in CRB—London office dossier 85.

265. Memorandum of interview between William B. Poland and Ambassador Merry del Val, March 28, 1917, copy in CRB—London office dossier 85.

266. CRB—London office cable to Louis Chevrillon for Hoover (in Paris), March 28, 1917, copy in CRB—London office dossier 85.

267. Warren Gregory (CRB—Brussels office) cable 325 to CRB—London (via Rotterdam), March 27, 1917, copy in CRB—London office dossier 85.

268. "Memorandum of discussions March 24th."

269. Hoover cable (from Paris) to CRB—London office, March 28, 1917.

270. CRB—Rotterdam office cable to CRB—London office, transmitted in Langhorne cable to Page, March 29, 1917, copy in CRB—London office dossier 85.

271. *New York Times*, April 1, 1917, section I, p. 5; Hoover, *Years of Adventure*, pp. 223–24.

272. Kittredge, "History," p. 431.

273. Ibid., pp. 430–31.

274. CRB—Rotterdam office to CRB—London office (c/o American Embassy, London), April 3, 1917, copy in American Embassy, London, Correspondence, 1917, vol. 87, file 848—Belgium, RG 84, NARA. See also Whitlock diary, March 16, 1917.

275. Kittredge, "History," pp. 431–32; Hoover cable to CRB—London office, April 4, 1917, in *PR-CRB*, II, pp. 159–60.

276. Kittredge, "History," pp. 432–33; Hoover, *An American Epic*, I, pp. 319–20.

277. Kittredge, "History," pp. 422–24.

278. Ibid., p. 423; Whitlock, *Belgium: A Personal Narrative*, II, pp. 811–13.

279. Quoted in Kittredge, "History," p. 422.

280. Hoover et al., cable to Woodrow Wilson, April 4, 1917, printed in Link et al., eds., *Papers of Woodrow Wilson*, vol. 41, p. 543.

281. Hoover cable to Gibson, April 6, 1917, "Lane, Franklin K.," Pre-Commerce Papers.

282. Gibson to House, April 6, 1917, House Papers, Box 49; Gibson to Lou Henry Hoover, April 6, 1917, "Gibson, Hugh, 1915–20," Personal Correspondence: 1874–1920, Lou Henry Hoover Papers, HHPL.

CHAPTER 14

1. Edward M. House to Woodrow Wilson, January 22, 1917, Edward M. House Papers, Box 121, Yale University Library; printed in Arthur S. Link et al., eds., *The Papers of Woodrow Wilson*, vol. 40 (Princeton, N.J., 1982), p. 540.

2. House to Wilson, January 23, 1917, House Papers, Box 121; in Link et al., eds., *Papers of Woodrow Wilson*, vol. 40, p. 558.

3. Ibid.

4. Edward M. House diary, March 7, 1917, House Papers.

5. Hoover to William C. Edgar, February 2, 1917, CRB Correspondence, Box 8, HI.

6. William Honnold cable to Hoover, December 22, 1916, CRB cable files, Pre-Commerce Papers, Herbert Hoover Papers, HHPL; Edward M. House diary, January 5, 1917; Frederic C. Walcott to Vance McCormick, February 6, 1917, Frederic C. Walcott Papers, Yale University Library.

7. Walcott to McCormick, February 6, 1917.

8. Hoover and Eliot Wadsworth to Woodrow Wilson, February 5, 1917, copy in Walcott Papers, Box 8, and in Francis William O'Brien, ed., *The Hoover-Wilson Wartime Correspondence* (Ames, Ia., 1974), pp. 17–18. Emphasis added.

9. Hoover and Wadsworth to Wilson, February 5, 1917; Walcott to McCormick, February 6, 1917.

10. See Hoover, John R. Mott, et al. to Woodrow Wilson, February 2, 1917, "Wilson, Woodrow," Pre-Commerce Papers.

11. Frederic C. Walcott to William L. Honnold, February 5, 1917, CRB Miscellaneous Files, HI; Walcott to E. W. Rankin, February 9, 1917, Walcott Papers, Box 8.

12. Walcott to John R. Mott, February 9, 1917, Walcott Papers, Box 8.

13. Even before the Germans launched their all-out submarine attacks, President Wilson had been unwilling to take the initiative in the coordination of war relief charities. House diary, January 5, 1917.

14. Walcott to Eliot Wadsworth, February 5, 1917, Walcott Papers, Box 8.

15. Hoover Calendar, HHPL; Walcott to Mott, February 9, 1917.

16. Walcott to Charles V. Vickrey, February 9, 1917, Walcott Papers, Box 8.

17. Walcott to Rankin, February 9, 1917.

18. Alpheus Thomas Mason, *Brandeis: A Free Man's Life* (New York, 1956), p. 519; Hoover to Louis D. Brandeis, February 9, 1917, Louis D. Brandeis Papers, University of Louisville.

19. Carol Green Wilson notes of interview with Adolph Miller, June 3, 1951, Carol Green Wilson Papers, HI.

20. Hoover to House, February 13, 1917, in Arthur S. Link et al., eds., *The Papers of Woodrow Wilson*, vol. 41 (Princeton, N.J., 1983), pp. 227–29.

21. House to Woodrow Wilson, February 14, 1917, printed in ibid., p. 226. See also Josephus Daniels, *The Wilson Era: Years of War and After* (Chapel Hill, N.C., 1946), pp. 319–20.

22. Franklin H. Martin, *Digest of the Proceedings of the Council of National Defense During the World War*, 73rd Congress, 2nd Session, Senate Document No. 193 (Washington, D.C., 1934), p. 84.

23. Ibid., p. 89.

24. Ibid., p. 90.

25. Franklin K. Lane to George W. Lane, February 16, 1917, in Anne Wintermute Lane and Louise Herrick Wall, eds., *The Letters of Franklin K. Lane* (Boston and New York, 1922), pp. 236–37.

26. Hoover to Lane, January 4, 1917, "Lane, Franklin K.," Pre-Commerce Papers. Lane's offer is discussed in chapter 12.

27. Lane to George W. Lane, February 16, 1917.

28. Hoover to Walter S. Gifford (Director of the Council of National Defense) plus three enclosures, February 17, 1917, in Director's Office Correspondence, File 2A1, Box 38, Records of the Council of National Defense, RG 62, NARA; Hoover to House, February 17, 1917, House Papers, Box 61. A copy of one of the enclosures—Hoover's letter of February 16, 1917 to Lane—is in CRB Correspondence, Box 8.

29. Hoover asserted in this memorandum: "The creation of an expeditionary force of any consequential value would require at least 18 months and would involve an amount of shipping and transportation which they could ill spare from the supply of the present armies."

30. Hoover, "America's Action in Case of War with Germany."

31. Link et al., eds., *Papers of Woodrow Wilson*, vol. 41, p. 226 and p. 226, note 1.

32. There appears to be no record of this Hoover–Wilson meeting in the Wilson Papers. The

date of the interview—February 17, 1917—was ascertained from a later notation by Hoover on some calendar materials now at HHPL. For Hoover's recollection of this meeting, see: Herbert Hoover, *An American Epic*, vol. 1 (Chicago, 1959), p. 313; Hoover, draft of *An American Epic*, vol. 2, part I, "B" version, p. 8, in Hoover Book Manuscript Material, HHPL.

In his *Memoirs*, published in 1951, Hoover gave a detailed account of a meeting with President Wilson which he dated as having occurred in early March 1917. I can find no corroborating evidence of such a meeting at that time; in fact, as mentioned in chapter 13, Hoover was actually unsuccessful in obtaining an interview with Wilson at one point in early March. In all likelihood Hoover's recollection in his *Memoirs* is incorrect as to the date. The account given is probably one of the February 17 meeting. See Hoover, *The Memoirs of Herbert Hoover*, vol. 1: *Years of Adventure* (New York, 1951), p. 220.

33. Franklin K. Lane to William C. Edgar, March 15, 1917, William C. Edgar and Family Papers, Box 1, Minnesota Historical Society.

34. House diary, March 11, 1917.

35. Hoover to Hugh Gibson, March 10, 1917, CRB Correspondence, Box 8.

36. Will Irwin, "First Aid for America," *Saturday Evening Post* 189 (March 24, 1917): 6–7, 109–10, 113–14. Irwin eventually identified Hoover as his interviewee in an article in the *Saturday Evening Post* for June 23, 1917.

37. Hoover cable to Edward M. House, April 3, 1917, House Papers, Box 61.

38. House to Hoover, April 7, 1917, House Papers, Box 61.

39. In his *Memoirs* (*Years of Adventure*, p. 225) Hoover stated that on April 6, 1917 he received a message from Colonel House reporting that President Wilson wanted him to return to the United States "to take charge of food control." This recollection is almost certainly incorrect. I have found no such document in my research. Moreover, House's letter of April 7, quoted in the text, conveyed no such news. In fact, it plainly indicated that Wilson had *not* yet made any decision about Hoover—at least one which he shared with House. On April 7 House was still *hoping* that Wilson would take Hoover into his war administration. At least as far as House was concerned, Hoover's prospects were as yet undetermined.

40. Martin, *Digest*, p. 127.

41. Ibid., pp. 128–31; Lewis Strauss to Felix Frankfurter, April 26, 1920, "Campaign of 1920: Frankfurter, Felix," Lewis Strauss Papers, HHPL; Samuel Gompers, *Seventy Years of Life and Labor* (New York, 1925), II, p. 354.

42. Martin, *Digest*, pp. 130–31.

43. Hugh Gibson to his mother, March 23, 1917, Hugh Gibson Papers, Box 34, HI.

44. Gibson to his mother, April 6, 1917, Gibson Papers, Box 34.

45. Gibson to his mother, April 7, 1917, Gibson Papers, Box 34; Edgar Rickard to Lou Henry Hoover, April 21, 1917, "Rickard, Edgar," Personal Correspondence: 1874–1920, Lou Henry Hoover Papers, HHPL.

46. Alvin Johnson, *Pioneer's Progress* (New York, 1952), pp. 246–47.

47. *New York Times*, April 8, 1917, p. 5.

48. Ibid., April 12, 1917, pp. 1, 2.

49. Before the war Hoover had told friends that he wanted to retire from mining and "get into the big game somewhere" in America. "Just making money," he said, "isn't enough." See George H. Nash, *The Life of Herbert Hoover: The Engineer, 1874–1914* (New York, 1983), pp. 509–13.

50. *New York Times*, April 12, 1917, p. 1.

51. Hoover cable 319 to CRB—New York office, April 11, 1917, copy in Frank A. Vanderlip Papers, Rare Book and Manuscript Library, Columbia University.

52. Hoover to Alfonso Merry del Val (plus enclosure), April 8, 1917, printed in George I. Gay and H. H. Fisher, *Public Relations of the Commission for Relief in Belgium* (Stanford, Calif., 1929), I, pp. 360–62 (hereinafter cited as *PR-CRB*). See also Hoover's protest to the State Department enclosed in Walter Hines Page's cable to Secretary of State Robert Lansing,

April 13, 1917, printed in United States, Department of State, *Papers Relating to the Foreign Relations of the United States, 1917*, Supplement I: *The World War* (Washington, D.C., 1931), pp. 660–61 (hereinafter cited as *FRUS, 1917*, Supplement I). By April 9 the CRB had lost seven vessels since the Germans resumed unrestricted submarine warfare on February 1. *New York Times*, April 10, 1917, p. 6.

53. Hoover, *An American Epic*, I, p. 344.
54. Ibid., pp. 266, 344.
55. Maurice Pate diary, March 23 and April 17, 1917, HHPL. Pate was a CRB volunteer in Belgium at this time.
56. Pate diary, April 17 and 23, 1917; Pate, "The Withdrawal of the American Commission from Belgium" (typescript, 1917), pp. 7–9, 13, 16, Maurice Pate Papers, Box 2, HHPL.
57. Hoover to Marquis de Villalobar, April 5, 1917; Hoover to Merry del Val, April 8, 1917; both in *PR-CRB*, I, pp. 359–60.
58. Hoover protest enclosed in Page cable to Lansing, April 13, 1917.
59. Hoover cable 319 to CRB—New York office, April 11, 1917.
60. *Current History* 6 (May 1917): 238.
61. Merry del Val to Hoover, April 16, 1917, quoted in Hoover, *An American Epic*, I, p. 325.
62. Baron Oscar von der Lancken to Villalobar, April 13, 1917, quoted in Hoover, *An American Epic*, I, p. 325.
63. William B. Poland to Sir Hugh Daly, April 30, 1917, in *PR-CRB*, I, pp. 363–66.
64. Hoover, *An American Epic*, I, pp. 324–25.
65. Pate diary, April 23, 1917.
66. Ibid., April 17, 1917; Pate, "Withdrawal," p. 16.
67. Poland to Daly, April 30, 1917. See also British Embassy, Washington, to State Department, May 2, 1917, in *FRUS, 1917*, Supplement I, p. 661.
68. Eyre A. Crowe to CRB—London office, April 23, 1917, in *PR-CRB*, I, p. 363.
69. Poland to Daly, April 30, 1917. In his *An American Epic* (pp. 326–27), Hoover stated that he drafted Poland's letter of April 30. This seems unlikely inasmuch as Hoover left London on April 21 for Liverpool and a voyage to the United States. His ship did not sail immediately, however, and it is conceivable that he ghostwrote a portion of the letter while in Liverpool and sent it back to his office in London. If so, he presented an account of the CRB ship sinkings that markedly differed on points of fact from his memorandum to Merry del Val just three weeks earlier.
70. Walter Hines Page cable to Secretary of State Lansing, May 19, 1917, in *FRUS, 1917*, Supplement I, pp. 663–64. During the month of May 1917, the CRB managed to deliver only 19,742 tons of food at Rotterdam for transshipment into Belgium and northern France. Hoover, *An American Epic*, I, p. 344. For descriptions of Belgium's suffering in the terrible spring of 1917, see Pate, "Withdrawal," p. 13, and Emile Francqui to Hoover, May 8, 1917, quoted in Hoover, *An American Epic*, I, pp. 348–49.
71. Hoover cable to CRB—Rotterdam, April 4, 1917, in *PR-CRB*, II, pp. 159–60; Tracy B. Kittredge, "The History of the Commission for Relief in Belgium, 1914–1917" (unpublished bound page proof version, ca. 1918), p. 433, copy at HHPL.
72. Arthur Balfour to Merry del Val, April 6, 1917, in *PR-CRB*, II, pp. 160–62; French Embassy, London, to William B. Poland, April 13, 1917, in *PR-CRB*, II, pp. 162–63; Kittredge, "History," pp. 433, 435.
73. Kittredge, "History," pp. 433–34.
74. Ibid., p. 436.
75. Ibid., pp. 433, 436; Lord Eustace Percy to William B. Poland, April 14, 1917, in *PR-CRB*, II, p. 164.
76. Hoover to Brand Whitlock, April 16, 1917, CRB Correspondence, Box 8.
77. Hoover to Villalobar, April 17, 1917; Hoover to Merry del Val, April 19, 1917; both in *PR-CRB*, II, pp. 165–66.

78. Hoover cable to Brand Whitlock, April 21, 1917, CRB cable files; Whitlock cable to Hoover, April 22, 1917, copy in American Embassy, London, Correspondence, 1917, vol. 86, file 848—Belgium, RG 84, NARA.
79. Kittredge, "History," p. 436.
80. Hoover cable to CRB—New York office, April 21, 1917, quoted in ibid.
81. Hoover cable to Whitlock, April 21, 1917.
82. Kittredge, "History," p. 436.
83. Villalobar cable to Hoover, April 23, 1917, in *PR-CRB*, II, pp. 166–67.
84. Whitlock cable to Hoover, April 22, 1917; Whitlock diary, April 21, 1917, in Allan Nevins, ed., *The Journal of Brand Whitlock* (New York, 1936), p. 395.
85. Whitlock cable to Hoover, April 22, 1917.
86. Kittredge, "History," pp. 437, 441; *New York Times*, May 1, 1917, p. 4. A few minor irritants remained and were not smoothed out until summer. See Kittredge, "History," pp. 438–39, and Hoover, *An American Epic*, I, p. 320.
87. Villalobar cable to Hoover, April 23, 1917.
88. Hoover, *An American Epic*, I, p. 313.
89. House diary, March 29, 1917.
90. British Foreign Office to Sir Cecil Spring Rice, March 6, 1917, in FO 382/1642/file 864, PRO; Spring Rice to Hoover, March 8, 1917, copy in CRB—London office dossier 85: "1917: Diplomatic Rupture between Germany & America," HI.
91. Hoover to Spring Rice, March 9, 1917, copy in CRB—London office dossier 85; Spring Rice to the Foreign Office, March 10, 1917, in FO 382/1642/file 864, PRO.
92. Robert Cecil memorandum G.T.-238, n.d., printed as appendix to minutes of [British] War Cabinet meeting 109, March 30, 1917, Cab. 23/2, PRO. The British and French were supplying the CRB (through the Belgian government) a sum of £1,500,000 (or nearly $7,500,000) per month. But the CRB's food purchases had risen to about £2,000,000 per month, leaving a shortfall of £500,000 (or nearly $2,500,000) *each month.* This was the amount that the British had hoped the American government could provide—a suggestion Hoover was forced to decline as inopportune. (See the previous footnote.)
93. Minutes of War Cabinet meeting 109 (plus Appendix I: memorandum G.T.-238), March 30, 1917; Hoover cable 300 to CRB—New York office, April 5, 1917, copy in CRB—London office dossier 46: "Correspondence in Regard to Negotiations for a Loan in America," HI.
94. *New York Times*, March 25, 1917, section I, p. 2.
95. New York advisory committee of CRB to Woodrow Wilson, March 29, 1917, in *PR-CRB*, I, pp. 283–84. See also: minutes of New York advisory committee of CRB, March 27, 1917, Pre-Commerce Papers; S. R. Bertron to Edward House, March 28, 1917, House Papers.
96. CRB—New York office cable 204 to Hoover, March 26, 1917, CRB cable files; copy in CRB—London office dossier 46.
97. Hoover and Louis Chevrillon, cable to CRB—London office, March 28, 1917, CRB cable files.
98. Hoover cable 300 to CRB—New York office, April 5, 1917, copy in CRB—London office dossier 46.
99. William Honnold cable 245 to Hoover, April 7, 1917, copy in CRB—London office dossier 46.
100. Honnold cable to Hoover, April 15, 1917, copy in CRB—London office dossier 46.
101. Hoover to Alwyn Parker, April 15, 1917; Hoover to A. de Fleuriau, April 15, 1917. Copies in CRB—London office dossier 46.
102. Hoover to Parker, April 15, 1917.
103. A. de Fleuriau to Hoover, April 16, 1917, copy in CRB—London office dossier 46; minutes of [British] War Cabinet meeting 122, April 18, 1917, Cab. 23/2, PRO.

104. Minutes of War Cabinet meeting 109, March 30, 1917.
105. Minutes of War Cabinet meeting 122, April 18, 1917.
106. William B. Poland to Sir Hugh Daly, April 24, 1917, copy in CRB—London office dossier 46.
107. Hoover to Paul Hymans, April 15, 1917, copy in CRB—London office dossier 46.
108. Hoover to de Fleuriau, April 15, 1917.
109. Minutes of War Cabinet meeting 122, April 18, 1917.
110. Hoover cable 345 to CRB—New York office, April 18, 1917; Paul Hymans to Hoover, April 19, 1917. Copies in CRB—London office dossier 46.
111. Poland to Daly, April 24, 1917.
112. Only on May 11, 1917 did the Belgian minister in Washington receive specific authorization from his government to apply for the loan. William Honnold telegram to Hoover, May 12, 1917, copy in CRB—London office dossier 46.
113. *New York Times*, May 10, 1917, p. 5, and May 18, 1917, p. 8; *Engineering and Mining Journal* 103 (May 19, 1917): 899–900; "Belgian Relief," *Bellman* 22 (May 26, 1917): 567.
114. Hoover cable to CRB—London office, May 13, 1917, copy in CRB—London office dossier 46.
115. Except, of course, for private charitable contributions. But as part of the new arrangement the CRB suspended its charitable appeals as of June 1, 1917.
116. Honnold cable to Hoover, April 21, 1917, copy in CRB—London office dossier 46.
117. Hoover to Rep. Henry Flood, May 19, 1917, in *PR-CRB*, I, p. 286.
118. ibid.
119. Hoover cable to Louis Chevrillon, April 9, 1917, CRB cable files.
120. Ibid.; *New York Times*, April 12, 1917, pp. 1, 2; William G. Sharp cable to Secretary of State Lansing, April 14, 1917, file 811.50/1, RG 59, NARA.
121. Hoover press release in *New York Times*, April 12, 1917, pp. 1, 2.
122. Minutes of War Cabinet meeting 122, April 18, 1917; David Lloyd George, *War Memoirs of David Lloyd George*, vol. 3 (London, 1934), pp. 260–62. Hoover's plan for an inter-Allied food board was outlined in Walter Hines Page cable to Secretary of State Lansing, April 19, 1917, file 811.50/5, RG 59, NARA.
123. Norman Hapgood to Woodrow Wilson, April 18, 1917, Woodrow Wilson Papers, microfilm edition, reel 87, LC.
124. See Edgar Rickard to Lou Henry Hoover, April 21, 1917, "Rickard, Edgar," Personal Correspondence: 1874–1920, Lou Henry Hoover Papers.
125. Hugh Gibson to his mother, April 9, 1917, Gibson Papers.
126. Norman Hapgood to Edward House, April 18, 1917, House Papers, Box 55; Hapgood to Wilson, April 18, 1917.
127. Hapgood to Wilson, April 18, 1917.
128. *New York Times*, April 13, 1917, p. 12.
129. *New Republic* 10 (April 14, 1917): 306.
130. Honnold cable 264 to Hoover, April 16, 1917, CRB cable files.
131. Hoover to Whitlock, April 16, 1917.
132. Honnold cable 264 to Hoover, April 16, 1917.
133. Hoover interview of April 21, reported in *New York Times*, April 22, 1917, section I, p. 17.
134. Walter Hines Page cable to Secretary of State Lansing, April 19, 1917, in Arthur S. Link et al., eds., *The Papers of Woodrow Wilson*, vol. 42 (Princeton, N.J., 1983), p. 109.
135. Mary Austin to Lou Henry Hoover, May 13 [1917], "Austin, Mary," Personal Correspondence: 1874–1920, Lou Henry Hoover Papers.
136. Victoria French Allen oral history (1967), pp. 13–14, HHPL; Victoria French Allen, "A Member of the Fourth Estate" (typescript, n.d.), pp. 135–36, Ben S. Allen Collection (see chapter 3, note 219).
137. Alice M. Dickson to Lou Henry Hoover, December 4 and 13, 1917, "Dickson, Alice M.,"

Personal Correspondence: 1874–1920, Lou Henry Hoover Papers.
138. *Mining Magazine* 16 (May 1917): 260; Rickard to Lou Henry Hoover, April 21, 1917; Allen, "A Member of the Fourth Estate," p. 137; Joseph C. Green oral history (1967), pp. 11–12, HHPL.

CHAPTER 15

1. "Where the United States Has Fallen Short: Its Record in Belgium," *Outlook* 115 (January 10, 1917): 61–62; *New York Times*, March 27, 1917, p. 10.
2. For these and other statistics, see: George I. Gay, *The Commission for Relief in Belgium: Statistical Review of Relief Operations* (Stanford, Calif., 1925), and Herbert Hoover, *An American Epic*, vol. 1 (Chicago, 1959), especially pp. 163, 266, 344, 412–16.
3. Joseph C. Green to his parents, January 14, 1917, Joseph C. Green Papers, Box 1, HI.
4. Interview of Herbert Hoover in *Pall Mall Gazette*, April 19, 1917, copy in Clippings File, HHPL.
5. Hoover report, April 1917, on the work of the CRB's Benevolent Department in Belgium and northern France, in *Commission for Relief in Belgium, Special Departmental Reports covering the period of American service in Belgium and Northern France, November 1, 1914–March 31, 1917*, pp. 11–59, HI. Printed in part in George I. Gay and H. H. Fisher, *Public Relations of the Commission for Relief in Belgium* (Stanford, Calif., 1929), II, pp. 315–50 (hereinafter cited as *PR-CRB*).
6. Hoover, "Introduction," to Charlotte Kellogg, *Women of Belgium* (New York, 1917), p. xvii.
7. *Manual of the Commission for Relief in Belgium* (n.d. but 1917), p. 17, copy in Maurice Pate Papers, Box 1, HHPL.
8. Hoover report, April 1917, in *PR-CRB*, II, p. 335; *New York Times*, January 14, 1917, section V, p. 9.
9. Hoover, "Introduction," to Kellogg, *Women of Belgium*, pp. xiv–xv.
10. Ibid., pp. xii–xiv.
11. Joseph C. Green oral history (1967), pp. 13–14, HHPL; Tracy B. Kittredge, "The History of the Commission for Relief in Belgium" (unpublished bound page proof version, ca. 1918), p. 442, copy at HHPL.
12. Gilchrist B. Stockton diary, February 20, 1917, Gilchrist B. Stockton Papers, Box 7, HI; copy in "Page, Walter Hines," Pre-Commerce Papers, Herbert Hoover Papers, HHPL.
13. *New York Times*, January 31, 1917, p. 10.
14. "Herbert Hoover, Master of Efficiency," *Independent* 89 (March 19, 1917): 477.
15. Hoover, undated autobiographical fragment (see chapter 11, note 184).
16. Edward Eyre Hunt, *War Bread* (New York, 1916), p. 193.
17. Herbert Hoover passport, January 10 (?), 1916, General Accessions, HHPL.
18. Hunt, *War Bread*, p. 193.
19. Brand Whitlock diary, November 3, 1932, Brand Whitlock Papers, Box 7, LC.
20. Will Irwin, quoted in his wife Inez's war diary, August 13, 1916, Inez Irwin Papers, Box 4, Schlesinger Library, Radcliffe College.
21. William J. Donovan to his wife, April 5, 1916, quoted in Anthony Cave Brown, *The Last Hero: Wild Bill Donovan* (New York, 1982), p. 32. Brand Whitlock thought Hoover had a "bulging" forehead. Whitlock diary, November 3, 1932.
22. Whitlock diary, November 3, 1932. According to Whitlock, Hoover had a "shifty glance" and "never could look one in the eye."
23. Paul Hymans, *Mémoires* (Brussels, 1958), I, p. 140. In 1917 an American journalist noticed "a determined look to his jaws." Ernest Poole, "Hoover of Belgium," *Saturday Evening Post*

189 (May 26, 1917): 14 (full article: 14, 58, 61). Emile Francqui, it will be recalled, referred to Hoover as a *mâchoire* (jaw).

24. Brand Whitlock diary, February 6, 1917, in Allan Nevins, ed., *The Journal of Brand Whitlock* (New York, 1936), p. 351; [William C. Edgar], "Herbert Hoover," *Bellman* 22 (January 27, 1917): 89–90.
25. *New York Times*, March 12, 1916, section VI, p. 5.
26. Hugh Gibson, "Herbert C. Hoover," *Century* 94 (August 1917): 517 (full article: 508–17).
27. Brand Whitlock, *Belgium: A Personal Narrative* (New York, 1919), II, p. 374.
28. Joseph C. Green, "Some Portraits: Mr. Hoover" (typescript, February 9, 1917), Green Papers, Box 20.
29. Ibid.
30. Hunt, *War Bread*, p. 193; Will Irwin, "The Autocrat of the Dinner Table," *Saturday Evening Post* 189 (June 23, 1917): 26 (full article: 26, 54, 56–58, 61).
31. W. L. Baillieu, quoted in "Hoover's History," *The Herald* (Melbourne, Australia), November 24, 1917, copy in Clippings File, HHPL.
32. Chevalier Edmond Carton de Wiart, quoted in *New York Times*, March 12, 1916, section VI, p. 5.
33. Newton D. Baker, "Introduction" to Allan Nevins, ed., *The Letters of Brand Whitlock* (New York, 1936), p. xvii.
34. W. L. Baillieu in "Hoover's History."
35. Maurice Pate diary, July 27, 1916, Maurice Pate Papers, HHPL; Irwin, "Autocrat," p. 57.
36. Irwin, "Autocrat," p. 58.
37. [Edgar], "Herbert Hoover," p. 89; Carton de Wiart, quoted in *New York Times*, March 12, 1916, section VI, p. 5; Hymans, *Mémoires*, I, p. 140; Frederic C. Walcott to Frank Hitchcock, May 9, 1916, Frederic C. Walcott Papers, Box 7, Yale University Library.
38. Walcott to S. W. Childs, March 8, 1916, Walcott Papers, Box 6.
39. See, for example, Gilchrist B. Stockton to his parents, July 27, 1915, "Stockton, Gilchrist B.," Pre-Commerce Papers.
40. Hymans, *Mémoires*, I, p. 140.
41. [Francis W. Hirst], "Herbert C. Hoover," *Common Sense* 2 (May 12, 1917): 289–90.
42. Oscar Freiherr von der Lancken-Wakenitz, *Meine Dreissig Dienstjahre* (Berlin, 1931), p. 199.
43. Irwin, "Autocrat," p. 57.
44. Green oral history (1967), p. 8.
45. Samuel Gompers, *Seventy Years of Life and Labor* (New York, 1925), II, p. 353.
46. Green oral history, p. 8.
47. William Allen White, *The Autobiography of William Allen White* (New York, 1946), p. 515.
48. Green oral history (1967), p. 8.
49. Gilchrist B. Stockton to his parents, June 26, 1915, "Stockton, Gilchrist B.," Pre-Commerce Papers.
50. Green, "Some Portraits: Mr. Hoover."
51. W. L. Baillieu, quoted in "Hoover's History." A prominent CRB volunteer, Perrin C. Galpin, later said: "I have hardly known any man who could devote himself so to the solution of a problem—pick up all the different aspects of it, listen to all the sides, and then come up with a reasonable agreement." Perrin C. Galpin oral history (1956), p. 9, Columbia University Oral History Collection.
52. Irwin, "Autocrat," p. 58.
53. Green, "Some Portraits: Mr. Hoover."
54. Ibid.
55. Whitlock diary, November 3, 1932.
56. Kittredge, "History," p. 97.
57. Hymans, *Mémoires*, II, p. 795.
58. Hoover to William L. Honnold, December 15, 1916, CRB Correspondence, Box 8, HI.

59. Edward Eyre Hunt, "Hoover of the 'C.R.B.,' " *World's Work* 34 (June 1917): 167 (full article: 165–68).
60. Ibid.
61. Roy Temple House, "The School-Master in Belgium," *School and Society* 6 (December 22, 1917): 739–40; John Lowrey Simpson, "Activities in a Troubled World: War Relief, Banking, and Business," typescript of an oral history conducted 1978 by Suzanne Riess, Regional Oral History Office, The Bancroft Library, University of California, Berkeley, 1978, 263 pp. (The reference here is to pp. 30–31.) Said Simpson of the caliber of men selected for CRB work: "There were very few casualties."
62. Philip S. Platt oral history (1970), p. 12, HHPL. See also Galpin oral history, pp. 10–11.
63. Carol Green Wilson notes of interview of Walter Lyman Brown, July 25, 1950, Carol Green Wilson Papers, Box 5, HI.
64. Lewis R. Freeman, "Hoover and the Belgians," *Outlook* 111 (September 8, 1915): 82 (full article: 81–82, 91).
65. "Hoover and His Way of Bringing Things to Pass," *Current Opinion* 62 (January 1917): 21 (full article: 21–22).
66. Hoover, quoted in Freeman, "Hoover and the Belgians," p. 82.
67. Hunt, *War Bread*, pp. 196–97.
68. Hunt, "Hoover of the 'C.R.B.,' " p. 167.
69. Whitlock diary, November 3, 1917.
70. Vernon Kellogg to Oscar T. Crosby, January 17, 1916, Oscar T. Crosby Papers, Box 2, LC.
71. Kellogg to Crosby, January 19, 1916, ibid.
72. W. L. Baillieu, quoted in "Hoover's History."
73. Pate diary, September 14, 1916. See also his entry for July 27, 1916.
74. Simpson, "Activities in a Troubled World," p. 33.
75. Pate diary, September 14, 1916.
76. Gilchrist B. Stockton to his parents, September 20, 1915, "Stockton, Gilchrist B.," Pre-Commerce Papers.
77. John L. Simpson, *Random Notes: Recollections of My Early Life* (privately printed, 1969), p. 7, copy in Stanford University Library.
78. Edward M. House diary, February 22, 1916, Edward M. House Papers, Yale University Library; Brand Whitlock diary, November 29, 1914, in his *Journal*, p. 70.
79. Hoover to Walter Hines Page, April 12, 1916, in American Embassy, London, Correspondence, 1916, vol. 109, file 848—Belgian Relief, RG 84, NARA.
80. Eustace Percy, *Some Memories* (London, 1958), p. 46.
81. Simpson, "Activities in a Troubled World," p. 35.
82. Ibid., p. 34.
83. See, for example, his letter to Lindon W. Bates, February 21, 1915, CRB Correspondence, Box 32.
84. "Very soberly and sincerely I believe that no one else could have done what he has done for Belgium." Hunt, "Hoover of the 'C.R.B.,' " p. 168.
85. Kellogg to Crosby, January 7, 1916.
86. Poole, "Hoover of Belgium," p. 14; Green oral history (1967), pp. 11–12.
87. Hymans, *Mémoires*, I, p. 140.
88. Whitlock diary, November 3, 1932.
89. *Times-Republican* (Marshalltown, Iowa), August 4, 1917, copy in Clippings File, HHPL.
90. "I think Mr. Hoover was rude sometimes, but I don't think it was a calculated rudeness. I think it was preoccupation and being much more interested in his own matters." Simpson, "Activities in a Troubled World," p. 44.
91. Green, "Some Portraits: Mr. Hoover."
92. Simpson, "Activities in a Troubled World," p. 44.

93. Acccording to Joseph C. Green, one of Hoover's marked traits in his younger days was "his apparent contempt for the little things—small talk—good manners which weren't absolutely necessary, and so on." Green oral history (1967), p. 11.
94. Mildred Hoover Willis oral history (1971), p. 9, HHPL.
95. Inez Irwin war diary, August 13, 1916.
96. White, *Autobiography*, p. 515. White called Hoover a "congenital pessimist."
97. Lou Henry Hoover, quoted in *Literary Digest* 55 (September 8, 1917): 50.
98. Newton D. Baker, "Introduction" to Nevins, ed., *Letters of Brand Whitlock*, p. xvii.
99. Percy, *Some Memories*, p. 46.
100. White, *Autobiography*, p. 515.
101. See p. 68 for my account of this visit.
102. Lou Henry Hoover, "Belgium's Need" (speech, October 1915), pp. 13–14, "C.R.B.— Speech by Lou Henry Hoover," Pre-Commerce Papers.
103. Whitlock, *Belgium: A Personal Narrative*, I, pp. 400–401.
104. Eustace Percy stated that Hoover's "love of children" was one of his most notable traits. Percy, *Some Memories*, p. 46.
105. Hoover, "Introduction," to Charlotte Kellogg, *Women of Belgium*, p. xvii.
106. Hymans, *Mémoires*, I, p. 140.
107. Ibid.
108. W. L. Baillieu noted this in his newspaper interview, "Hoover's History."
109. Ibid.
110. Hoover to Mrs. Brand Whitlock, July 5, 1916, Allan Nevins Papers, Rare Book and Manuscript Library, Columbia University; Brand Whitlock to Hoover, July 19, 1916, printed in Whitlock's *Letters*, pp. 195–96.
111. Herbert Hoover, Jr., to Rita R. Campbell, August 22, 1967, Hulda Hoover McLean Papers, HI. Hoover's son stated that the father–son conference and change of signatures occurred in 1917. It may have occurred earlier. In 1914 and 1915 Herbert Hoover generally signed his CRB correspondence "H. C. Hoover," as he had in all his correspondence for years. But beginning in December 1915 or slightly earlier, Hoover switched to "Herbert Hoover," the form that he generally retained ever after (although occasionally, in 1916, he reverted to "H. C. Hoover"). His conference with his son may therefore have occurred in late 1915, perhaps just after Hoover's sons returned with him to England in November. It is also possible that Hoover changed his mode of signature to a more American form even before his talk with his older son.
112. Poole, "Hoover of Belgium," p. 14; Irwin, "Autocrat," p. 58.
113. John Agnew to Alice M. Dickson, quoted in Alice M. Dickson to Lou Henry Hoover, December 13, 1917, "Dickson, Alice M.," Personal Correspondence: 1874–1920, Lou Henry Hoover Papers, HHPL.
114. Stockton to his parents, July 27, 1915. See also his letter of November 30, 1915, "Stockton, Gilchrist B.," Pre-Commerce Papers. A visitor to London in 1916 thought Hoover "surprisingly lacking in a capable appearance—but he has a power—and the loyalty of his men." William J. Donovan to his wife, April 5, 1916, quoted in Brown, *The Last Hero*, p. 32. Donovan, incidentally, became a good friend and adviser to Hoover in the presidential campaign of 1928.
115. Stockton to his parents, June 26, 1915. "We were devoted to him" (Simpson, *Random Notes*, p. 7); "we adored him" (Simpson, "Activities in a Troubled World," p. 31).
116. Simpson, "Activities in a Troubled World," p. 31.
117. An unnamed CRB volunteer, quoted in Victoria French Allen, "A Member of the Fourth Estate" (typescript, n.d.), p. 93, Ben S. Allen Collection (see chapter 3, note 219).
118. White, *Autobiography*, p. 515.
119. Stockton letters to his parents, July 25 and September 20, 1915; Green, "Some Portraits: Mr. Hoover."

120. Pate diary, September 14, 1916.
121. Francis C. Wickes oral history (1970), p. 7, HHPL.
122. Green oral history (1967), pp. 4–6.
123. Simpson, *Random Notes*, p. 7; Simpson, "Activities in a Troubled World," p. 33.
124. Galpin oral history (1956), p. 10.
125. Gilchrist Stockton to his mother, December 28, 1916, Stockton Papers, Box 1.
126. Green, "Some Portraits: Mr. Hoover."
127. For descriptions of the Hoover staff lunches, see: Galpin oral history (1956), p. 10; Green oral history (1967), pp. 9–10; Wickes oral history (1970), p. 6.
128. Green, "Some Portraits: Mr. Hoover."
129. Gilchrist Stockton oral history (1969), p. 8, HHPL.
130. Platt oral history (1970), p. 14.
131. Ibid., p. 15.
132. Ibid. One Frenchman exclaimed, after talking with some CRB volunteers in 1917, "Why, those boys would die for him!" Irwin, "Autocrat," p. 61.
133. Recall, for example, the two-man Hoover-for-President Club that Hugh Gibson and Gilchrist Stockton created in 1915.
134. Green oral history (1967), p. 22.
135. C. A. Young to William C. Edgar, July 27, 1915, William C. Edgar and Family Papers, Box 1, Minnesota Historical Society.
136. Francis A. Govett speech at Zinc Corporation shareholders' meeting, London, June 25, 1917; quoted in *Financial Times* (London), June 26, 1917, p. 5.
137. Whitlock diary, September 24, 1921, printed in his *Journal*, p. 709.
138. Govett speech at Zinc Corporation shareholders' meeting, June 25, 1917.
139. Irwin, "Autocrat," p. 56.
140. George H. Nash, *The Life of Herbert Hoover: The Engineer, 1874–1914* (New York, 1983), pp. 503, 511.
141. White, *Autobiography*, p. 515.
142. Hoover to Brand Whitlock, November (?) 1917, quoted in Hoover, *The Memoirs of Herbert Hoover*, vol. 1: *Years of Adventure* (New York, 1951), p. 232; Hoover to Whitlock, February 23, 1915, CRB Correspondence, Box 2.
143. "Mr. Hoover is in fact quite averse to having his picture taken. At the time last year [1914] when he was presented with the gold medal of the Mining and Metallurgy Society of America, we were extremely desirous of publishing his picture, but no photograph was to be obtained, notwithstanding the considerable influence that we were able to exert in quarters near at home." "Herbert Clark Hoover," *Engineering and Mining Journal* 99 (January 30, 1915): 243.
144. For a provocative study of orphans who became successful British statesmen, see Lucille Iremonger, *The Fiery Chariot: A Study of British Prime Ministers and the Search for Love* (London, 1970).
145. Recall, for example, Francis Govett's *public* prediction in 1917 that Hoover would someday be President. Hoover obviously had to be aware of what at least a few of his friends were saying.
146. Simpson, "Activities in a Troubled World," p. 43.
147. Percy, *Some Memories*, p. 47.
148. Hoover to Harriette Miles, August 5, 1897, extract in "Mining—Australia, Herbert Hoover's Accounts of Western Australia," Pre-Commerce Papers.
149. Allen, "A Member of the Fourth Estate," pp. 137–38.

Index